Lecture Notes in Computer Science 2945
Edited by G. Goos, J. Hartmanis, and J. van Leeuwen

Springer
Berlin
Heidelberg
New York
Hong Kong
London
Milan
Paris
Tokyo

Alexander Gelbukh (Ed.)

Computational Linguistics and Intelligent Text Processing

5th International Conference, CICLing 2004
Seoul, Korea, February 15-21, 2004
Proceedings

 Springer

Series Editors

Gerhard Goos, Karlsruhe University, Germany
Juris Hartmanis, Cornell University, NY, USA
Jan van Leeuwen, Utrecht University, The Netherlands

Volume Editor

Alexander Gelbukh
Instituto Politécnico Nacional (IPN)
Centro de Investigación en Computación (CIC)
Col. Zacatenco, CP 07738, Mexico D.F., Mexico
E-mail: gelbukh@cic.ipn.mx

Cataloging-in-Publication Data applied for

A catalog record for this book is available from the Library of Congress.

Bibliographic information published by Die Deutsche Bibliothek
Die Deutsche Bibliothek lists this publication in the Deutsche Nationalbibliografie;
detailed bibliographic data is available in the Internet at <http://dnb.ddb.de>.

CR Subject Classification (1998): H.3, I.2.7, I.7, I.2, F.4.3

ISSN 0302-9743
ISBN 3-540-21006-7 Springer-Verlag Berlin Heidelberg New York

This work is subject to copyright. All rights are reserved, whether the whole or part of the material is
concerned, specifically the rights of translation, reprinting, re-use of illustrations, recitation, broadcasting,
reproduction on microfilms or in any other way, and storage in data banks. Duplication of this publication
or parts thereof is permitted only under the provisions of the German Copyright Law of September 9, 1965,
in its current version, and permission for use must always be obtained from Springer-Verlag. Violations are
liable for prosecution under the German Copyright Law.

Springer-Verlag is a part of Springer Science+Business Media

springeronline.com

© Springer-Verlag Berlin Heidelberg 2004
Printed in Germany

Typesetting: Camera-ready by author, data conversion by PTP-Berlin, Protago-TeX-Production GmbH
Printed on acid-free paper   SPIN: 10986073   06/3142   5 4 3 2 1 0

Preface

CICLing 2004 was the 5th Annual Conference on Intelligent Text Processing and Computational Linguistics; see www.CICLing.org. CICLing conferences are intended to provide a balanced view of the cutting-edge developments in both theoretical foundations of computational linguistics and the practice of natural language text processing with its numerous applications. A feature of CICLing conferences is their wide scope that covers nearly all areas of computational linguistics and all aspects of natural language processing applications. These conferences are a forum for dialogue between the specialists working in the two areas.

This year we were honored by the presence of our invited speakers Martin Kay of Stanford University, Philip Resnik of the University of Maryland, Ricardo Baeza-Yates of the University of Chile, and Nick Campbell of the ATR Spoken Language Translation Research Laboratories. They delivered excellent extended lectures and organized vivid discussions.

Of 129 submissions received (74 full papers and 44 short papers), after careful international reviewing 74 papers were selected for presentation (40 full papers and 35 short papers), written by 176 authors from 21 countries: Korea (37), Spain (34), Japan (22), Mexico (15), China (11), Germany (10), Ireland (10), UK (10), Singapore (6), Canada (3), Czech Rep. (3), France (3), Brazil (2), Sweden (2), Taiwan (2), Turkey (2), USA (2), Chile (1), Romania (1), Thailand (1), and The Netherlands (1); the figures in parentheses stand for the number of authors from the corresponding country.

In addition to a high scientific level, one of the success factors of CICLing conferences is their excellent cultural programs. CICLing 2004 was held in Korea, the beautiful and wonderful Country of the Morning Calm, as Korean people call their land. The participants enjoyed three full-day excursions to the most important natural and historical attractions around Seoul city; see photos at www.CICLing.org. Full-day excursions allowed for friendly personal interaction between participants and gave them a chance to make friends with the most famous experts in the field, people who are not easily accessible at larger conferences.

A conference is the result of the work of many people. First of all I would like to thank the members of the Program Committee for the time and effort they devoted to the reviewing of the submitted articles and to the selection process. Especially helpful were Manuel Vilares, John Tait, Alma Kharrat, Karin Verspoor, Viktor Pekar, and many others – a complete list would be too long.

Obviously I thank the authors for their patience in the preparation of the papers, not to mention the very development of their scientific results that form this book. I also express my most cordial thanks to the members of the local Organizing Committee for their considerable contribution to making this conference a reality. Last but not least, I thank our host – the ITRI of the Chung-Ang University. I would like to also thank RITOS-2 of CYTED for their support of the CICLing conferences.

December 2003   Alexander Gelbukh

Conference Chair

Alexander Gelbukh (CIC-IPN, Mexico, and Chung-Ang University, Korea)

Program Committee

Boitet, Christian (CLIPS-IMAG, France)
Bolshakov, Igor (CIC-IPN, Mexico)
Bontcheva, Kalina (U. Sheffield, UK)
Calzolari, Nicoletta (ILC-CNR, Italy)
Carroll, John (U. Sussex, UK)
Cristea, Dan (U. Iasi, Romania)
Gelbukh, Alexander (Chair, CIC-IPN, Mexico, and Chung-Ang U., Korea)
Hallett, Cătălina (U. Brighton, UK)
Han, Sang Yong (Chung-Ang U., Korea)
Harada, Yasunari (Waseda U, Japan)
Hasida, Kôiti (Electrotechnical Laboratory, AIST, Japan)
Hirst, Graeme (U. Toronto, Canada)
Hovy, Eduard (ISI, U. Southern California, USA)
Johnson, Frances (Manchester Metropolitan U., UK)
Kharrat, Alma (Microsoft Research, USA)
Kilgarriff, Adam (U. Brighton, UK)
Kittredge, Richard (CoGenTex Inc., USA/Canada)
Kübler, Sandra (U. Tübingen, Germany)
López López, Aurelio (INAOE, Mexico)
Loukanova, Roussanka (U. Uppsala, Sweden)
Lüdeling, Anke (Humboldt U., Germany)
Maegard, Bente (Centre for Language Technology, Denmark)
Martín-Vide, Carlos (U. Rovira i Virgili, Spain)
Mel'čuk, Igor (U. Montreal, Canada)
Metais, Elisabeth (U. Versailles, France)
Mihalcea, Rada (U. North Texas, USA)
Mitkov, Ruslan (U. Wolverhampton, UK)
Murata, Masaki (KARC-CRL, Japan)
Narin'yani, Alexander (Russian Institute of Artificial Intelligence, Russia)
Nirenburg, Sergei (U. Maryland, USA)
Palomar, Manuel (U. Alicante, Spain)
Pedersen, Ted (U. Minnesota, Duluth, USA)
Pekar, Viktor (U. Wolverhampton, UK)
Pineda Cortes, Luis Alberto (UNAM, Mexico)
Piperidis, Stelios (Institute for Language and Speech Processing, Greece)
Pustejovsky, James (Brandeis U., USA)
Ren, Fuji (U. Tokushima, Japan)
Riloff, Ellen (U. Utah, USA)
Sag, Ivan (Stanford U., USA)

Sharoff, Serge (U. Leeds, UK)
Sidorov, Grigori (CIC-IPN, Mexico)
Sun, Maosong (Tsinghua U., China)
Tait, John (U. Sunderland, UK)
Trujillo, Arturo (Canon Research Centre Europe, UK)
T'sou Ka-yin, Benjamin (City U. Hong Kong, Hong Kong)
Van Guilder, Linda (MITRE Corp., USA)
Verspoor, Karin (Los Alamos National Laboratory, USA)
Vilares Ferro, Manuel (U. Vigo, Spain)
Wilks, Yorick (U. Sheffield, UK)

Additional Reviewers

Babych, Bogdan (U. Leeds, Centre for Translation, UK)
Campbell, Nick (ATR Human Information Science Labs, Japan)
Liang, Shao-Fen (U. Sunderland, UK)
Llopis, Fernando (U. Alicante, Spain)
Martínez-Barco, Patricio (U. Alicante, Spain)
Montoyo, Andrés (U. Alicante, Spain)
Oakes, Michael (U. Sunderland, UK)
Saiz Noeda, Maximiliano (U. Alicante, Spain)
Stokoe, Christopher (U. Sunderland, UK)
Vicedo, José L. (U. Alicante, Spain)

Organizing Committee

Han, Sang Yong (Chair)
Gelbukh, Alexander (Co-chair)
Chang, Tae Gyu
Shim, Duk Sun
Kim, Jun Sung
Park, Ho Hyun
Kim, Hyung Suk
Moon, Suk Whan
Choi, Ok Kyung
Kang, Nam Oh
Shin, Kwang Chul

Organization, Website and Contact

The conference was organized by the Electronic Commerce and Internet Applications Laboratory of Chung-Ang University, Seoul, Korea, and the Natural

Language Laboratory of the Center for Computing Research of the National Polytechnic Institute, Mexico City, Mexico. The conference was hosted by the ITRI of Chung-Ang University.

The Website of the CICLing conferences is www.CICLing.org (mirrored at www.cic.ipn.mx/cicling). Contact: gelbukh@CICLing.org, gelbukh@cic.ipn.mx; see also www.gelbukh.com.

Table of Contents

Lexical Analysis

Named Entity Recognition

Word Sense Disambiguation

Anaphora Resolution

Lexicon and Corpus

Bilingual Resources

Machine Translation

Natural Language Generation

Human-Computer Interaction Applications

Speech Recognition and Synthesis

Intelligent Text Processing

Indexing

Information Retrieval

Question Answering and Sentence Retrieval

Browsing

Filtering

Information Extraction

Text Categorization

Document Clustering

Summarization

Language Identification

Towards an LFG Syntax-Semantics Interface for Frame Semantics Annotation

Anette Frank[1] and Katrin Erk[2]

[1] DFKI GmbH, Language Technology Lab, Stuhlsatzenhausweg 3,
66123 Saarbrücken, Germany,
Anette.Frank@dfki.de,
http://www.dfki.de/~frank
[2] Universität des Saarlandes, Computational Linguistics Department,
66123 Saarbrücken, Germany
erk@coli.uni-sb.de,
http://www.coli.uni-sb.de/~erk

Abstract. We present an LFG syntax-semantics interface for the semi-automatic annotation of frame semantic roles for German in the SALSA project. The architecture is intended to support a bootstrapping cycle for the acquisition of stochastic models for frame semantic role assignment, starting from manual annotations on the basis of the syntactically annotated TIGER treebank, with smooth transition to automatic syntactic analysis and (semi-)automatic semantic annotation of a much larger corpus, on top of a free-running LFG grammar of German. Our study investigates the applicability of the LFG formalism for modeling frame semantic role annotation, and designs a flexible and extensible syntax-semantics architecture that supports the induction of stochastic models for automatic frame assignment. We propose a method familiar from example-based Machine Translation to translate between the TIGER and LFG annotation formats, thus enabling the transition from treebank annotation to large-scale corpus processing.

1 Introduction

This paper is a first study of an LFG syntax-semantics interface for frame semantic role assignment. The architecture is intended to support semi-automatic semantic annotation for German in SALSA – the Saarbrücken Semantics Annotation and Analysis project[1] – which is based on Frame Semantics and is conducted in cooperation with the Berkeley FrameNet project [1,15].

The aim of SALSA is to create a large lexical semantics resource for German based on Frame Semantics, and to develop methods for automated assignment of corpora with frame semantic representations.

In the first (and current) phase of the SALSA project, semantic annotation is fully manual, and takes as its base the syntactically annotated TIGER treebank

---

[1] See [8] and the SALSA project homepage http://www.coli.uni-sb.de/lexicon

A. Gelbukh (Ed.): CICLing 2004, LNCS 2945, pp. 1–13, 2004.
© Springer-Verlag Berlin Heidelberg 2004

[2].[2] Due to the inherently sparser data seeds for semantic frames (as opposed to syntactic structures), it will be of utmost importance for the acquisition of high-performing stochastic models to process and collect data from larger corpora. In the second project phase we will thus proceed to semi-automatic semantic annotation of a much bigger, unparsed corpus. Here, a reliable and informative syntactic parse is essential: first, as a basis for semantic annotation, and second, since part of the information to be acquired is in itself syntactic.

Similar to the approach taken for syntactic annotation of the NEGRA corpus in [3,4], SALSA aims at a bootstrapping approach for semantic annotation. Stochastic models for frame annotation are learned from a seed set of manual annotations, thus speeding up the manual annotation process and yielding more data for learning. Ultimately, we will learn increasingly refined models for frame assignment, by automatic annotation and re-training on larger corpora.

In the remainder of this paper, we discuss diverse architectures to implement a bootstrapping cycle for frame annotation that bridges the gap between treebank-based and large-scale free text processing. We investigate the applicability of the LFG formalism for the frame annotation task, and design an LFG syntax-semantics interface for frame assignment. We discuss alternative models for the interface, in terms of co-description and description by analysis and discuss their implications in terms of disambiguation effects and the integration of additional knowledge sources. Finally, we present a method for learning the required mappings between LFG and TIGER-SALSA representations.

2   Annotating TIGER with Frame Semantic Roles

The TIGER Corpus [2] is a large syntactically annotated corpus of German. The annotation scheme is surface oriented and comparably theory-neutral. The dependency-oriented constituent structures provide information about *grammatical functions* (on edge labels) and *syntactic categories* (on constituent node labels). An example is given in the shaded tree of Fig. 1.

The FrameNet Project [1,15] is based on Fillmore's Frame Semantics. A *frame* is a conceptual structure describing a situation. It is introduced by a *target* or *frame-evoking element* (*FEE*). Roles, called *frame elements* (FEs), are local to particular frames and identify the participants and props of the described situations. The aim of FrameNet is to provide a comprehensive frame-semantic description of the core lexicon of English. The current on-line version of the frame database consists of about 400 frames, covering about 6,900 lexical entries.

The SALSA Project [8] annotates frames on top of the TIGER treebank. Frames are represented as flat, independent trees, as shown in the white-labeled trees with curved edges in Fig. 1. The root is labeled with the frame name. Edges are labeled by frame elements or by 'FEE' and point to syntactic constituents.

---

[2] With 80.000 sentences, TIGER is comparable, in size, to the Penn Treebank. From our current gold corpus we estimate an average of about 3 frames per sentence, thus approx. 240.000 frame annotations for the entire TIGER corpus. This number is comparable to the English FrameNet resource used in [13,10].

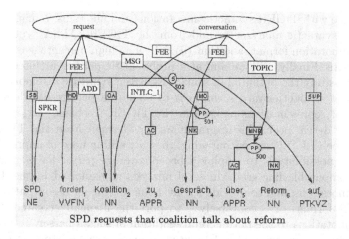

SPD requests that coalition talk about reform

Fig. 1. TIGER-SALSA graphical annotation

Fig. 1 contains two FEEs: *fordert... auf* (*auffordern*) and *Gespräch. auffordern* evokes the frame REQUEST. As the FEE does not form a single syntactic constituent, the label FEE is assigned to two edges. The SPEAKER is the subject (SB) NP *SPD*, the ADDRESSEE is the direct object (OA) NP *Koalition*, and the MESSAGE is the modifier (MO) PP *zu Gespräch über Reform*. The second FEE, the noun *Gespräch*, introduces the frame CONVERSATION, in which two groups talk to one another. The only NP-internal frame element is the TOPIC ("what the message is about") *über Reform*, whereas the INTERLOCUTOR-1 ("the prominent participant in the conversation") is realized by the direct object of *auffordern*.

Both the syntactic annotation of the TIGER corpus and the frames and frame elements that SALSA is adding are encoded in a modular XML format.

3   A Bootstrapping Architecture for Frame Annotation

The bootstrapping cycle for automatic frame and frame element assignment that we envision is similar to the process applied for NEGRA in [4]: First, stochastic models for frame and frame element annotation are learned from a seed set of manual annotations of the TIGER corpus. These models are applied to support interactive semi-automatic annotation of new portions of TIGER, with human annotators accepting or correcting assignments proposed by the system. New stochastic models derived from this larger set of TIGER data are applied for (semi-)automatic annotation of a larger, automatically parsed corpus, which again yields more training data, and continuously refined stochastic models.

3.1   From Treebank Annotation to Free Text Processing

To implement this bootstrapping cycle, we need a syntactic analyzer for free German text processing that (i) provides fine-grained syntactic information that is compatible with TIGER syntactic annotations and allows us to map the analyses of the syntactic analyzer to and from the TIGER-SALSA syntactic and semantic annotation format, and that (ii) delivers a high percentage of correctly analyzed data. Finally, (iii) we aim at a probabilistic parsing architecture that allows us to study the potential of semantics-driven syntactic disambiguation.

The most straightforward scenario is to employ a parser that delivers the same type of representations as used in the TIGER treebank. Yet, while first attempts to derive probabilistic grammars for German from the TIGER (or NEGRA) treebank [7,6] are encouraging, they are still in need of improvement.[3]

Another possibility is to employ a broad-coverage parser for German that provides comparable fine-grainedness of analysis as exploited in the TIGER-SALSA annotations, and to provide a conversion routine for its output to match the TIGER format, or – conversely – to port the manually created TIGER-SALSA annotations to the output representation of such a parser.

In the first case, with TIGER syntax as main format, stochastic models would be derived from a combination of TIGER syntax and frame annotation. Transfer from the parser's output to the TIGER format would be needed in all phases of the cycle. In particular, the parser output for any corpus would have to be transformed to TIGER syntax. In the second case, with the parser's output as main format, stochastic models would be derived from a combination of the parser's format and frame annotation, which means that a semantic frame projection for the parser output is needed. Transfer between TIGER-SALSA and parser output representation would be needed only in the first phases of the cycle, while processing data of the TIGER corpus.[4] Moreover, this scenario lends itself to an integrated semantic disambiguation model in the sense of (iii).

3.2   German LFG for Corpus Processing and Frame Annotation

We propose to use a German LFG grammar to support the bootstrapping cycle for frame annotation. The TIGER annotation process was supported by semi-automatic processing with a German LFG grammar [2,20].[5] In addition to the LFG-to-TIGER transfer module developed there, [11] has recently built a mapping from TIGER to LFG f-structures. These automatic conversions ensure that LFG representations are rich enough to match the syntactic TIGER representations. [2] report a coverage of 50% for the LFG grammar, with 70% precision. Newer figures are not yet available, but we expect the German grammar to soon reach the performance of the English LFG grammar described in [18].

We further opt for the second scenario of the previous paragraph: using LFG f-structures as the primary basis for building stochastic models. This scenario

---

[3] [7] do not assign functional labels, whereas [6] produce LFG (proto) f-structures. Though not fully comparable, [6] could be used for our purposes in similar ways, and possibly in tandem with the manually developed LFG grammar described below.

[4] Manual annotation is aided by an annotation tool based on the TIGER-SALSA format [9]. Also, the TIGER-SALSA corpus is intended as a theory-neutral reference corpus, and must include sentences that are out-of-coverage for the chosen parser.

[5] The grammar is being developed at the IMS, University of Stuttgart.

requires the design of an LFG semantics projection for frame assignment, and a mapping between TIGER-SALSA and LFG syntax-semantics representations to implement the bootstrapping cycle. However, it restricts transformations between syntactic formats to the learning phase, and lends itself to an exploration of semantic features for syntactic disambiguation. A further advantage of this model is that it allows for the extension of existing probabilistic methods for syntactic disambiguation in [18] to online semantic classification and disambiguation. The stochastic tools employed in [18,17] – provided with the LFG processing platform XLE – support training and online application of loglinear models. We can thus explore the disambiguation effects of semantic annotation in combination with, or independent from syntactic disambiguation.

4 LFG for Frame Annotation: Chances and Challenges

In the following sections we investigate the applicability of LFG for the frame annotation task, and design a syntax-semantics interface for Frame Semantics.

Lexical Functional Grammar [5] assumes multiple levels of representation for linguistic description. Most prominent are the syntactic representations of c(onstituent)- and f(unctional)-structure. The correspondence between c- and f-structure is defined by functional annotations of CFG rules and lexical entries. This architecture can be extended to semantic (and other) projection levels [14].

The f-structure representation abstracts away from surface-syntactic properties, and allows for uniform reference to syntactic dependents in diverse syntactic configurations. This is important for the task of frame annotation, as it abstracts away from aspects of syntax that are irrelevant to frame (element) assignment.

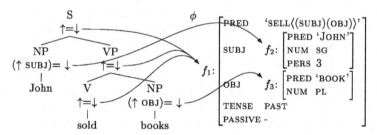

Fig. 2. LFG projection architecture with c– and and f–structure representation

The LFG syntactic analysis of word order, control and raising constructions, long-distance dependencies and coordination provides f-structure representations where non-local or implicit arguments are localized and thus allow for uniform association of local grammatical functions with frame semantic roles.

In (1), the SELLER role can be uniformly associated with the local SUBJect of *sell*, even though it is realized as a relative pronoun of *come* that controls the SUBJect of *sell*, (b.) an implicit second person SUBJ, (c.) a non-overt SUBJ controlled by the OBLique object of *hard*, and (d.) a SUBJ (*we*) in VP coordination.

(1) a. .. *the woman who* had come in to *sell flowers* to the customers overheard
     their conversation .. (from [15])
  b. Don't *sell the factory* to another company.
  c. It would be hard for *him* to *sell newmont shares* quickly. (from [15])
  d. .. *we* decided to sink some of our capital, buy a car, and *sell it* again
     before leaving. (from [15])

More challenging are phenomena as in (2.a,b), where the SUBJ of *sell* is
not syntactically represented as identical to (a.) the passive SUBJ of the matrix
clause, or (b.) the matrix SUBJ of an embedded adjunct clause containing *sell*.
Here the SELLER semantic role has to be assigned nonlocally (unless coreference
information is made available).

(2) a. .. the old adage about *most people* simply refusing to move rather than
     sell their house ..
  b. .. *we*'d do the maintenance and watering instead of just *selling* the
     plants .. (both from [15])

There are cases where a frame-evoking element and one of its FEs are both
parts of a single compound, e.g. in (3) the noun modifier *Auto* fills the GOODS
role in the COMMERCE frame evoked by the head noun *Verkäufer*. The LFG f-
structure analysis of nominal compounds provides a (flat) decomposition into a
nominal head and a set NMOD of noun modifiers. The NMOD modifier *Auto* can
thus be represented to fill the GOODS role in the frame evoked by the head noun.

(3) *Autoverkäufer* geben zur Zeit bis zu 10% Rabatt.
  Car dealers offer nowadays up to 10% reduction.

Formal Devices. The LFG formalism provides powerful descriptional devices that are essential for the design of a flexible syntax-semantics interface.

The regular expression-based specification of uncertain embedding paths
within f-structures – both outside-in and inside-out [16] – makes it possible
to refer to any piece of f-structure from anywhere within the f-structure.

The restriction operator [19] permits reference to partial f-structures. It can
be used to link semantic roles to partial f-structures, such as grammatical functions to the exclusion of embedded material (e.g. sentential adjuncts).

Examples that use these devices will be discussed in Section 5.1.

5   LFG Syntax-Semantics Interface for Frame Semantics

5.1   A Frame Semantics Projection

As a direct transposition of the SALSA annotation format we can define a Frame
Semantics projection σ_f from the level of f-structure (compare Figs. 1 and 3).

While in the traditional LFG projection architecture (as in [14]) f-structure
predicates are related to predicate-argument structures in s-structure, we define the σ_f–projection to introduce elementary frame structures, with attributes

FRAME, FEE (frame-evoking element), and frame-specific role attributes. Fig. 3 displays the σ_f–projection for the sentence in Fig. 1.[6]

Fig. 4 states the lexical constraints that define this mapping. σ_f is defined as a function of f-structure. Thus, the verb *auffordern* introduces a node $\sigma_f(\uparrow)$ in the frame semantics projection of $\uparrow$, its local f-structure, and defines its attributes FRAME and FEE. The frame elements are defined as σ_f–projections of the verb's SUBJ, OBJ, and OBL OBJ functions. For example, the SPKR role, referred to as $(\sigma_f(\uparrow)$ SPKR), the SPKR attribute in the frame projection $\sigma_f(\uparrow)$ of $\uparrow$, is defined as identical to the σ_f–projection of the verb's SUBJ function, $\sigma_f(\uparrow$ SUBJ).[7]

The noun *Gespräch*, which evokes the CONVERSATION frame, illustrates the use of inside-out functional equations to refer to material outside the local f-structure of a frame evoking predicate. The INTERLOCUTOR1 (INTLC_1) role corresponds to the OBJ of *auffordern*. This function is accessible from the noun's f-structure via the inside-out equation ((OBL OBJ $\uparrow$) OBJ): starting from $\uparrow$ (the f-structure of *Gespräch*), the path leads inside-out to the f-structure (OBL OBJ $\uparrow$) of the verb, from which it descends to the verb's OBJ: ((OBL OBJ $\uparrow$) OBJ).

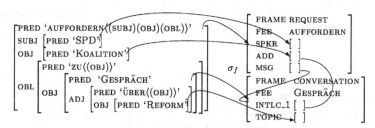

Fig. 3. LFG projection architecture for Frame Annotation

fordert V,   Gespräch N,

$(\uparrow\text{PRED})=\text{`AUFFORDERN}\langle(\uparrow\text{SBJ})(\uparrow\text{OBJ})(\uparrow\text{OBL})\rangle\text{'}$     $(\uparrow\text{PRED})=\text{`GESPRÄCH'}$

...   ...

$(\sigma_f(\uparrow)\text{ FRAME}) = \text{REQUEST}$ $(\sigma_f(\uparrow)\text{ FRAME})= \text{CONVERSATION}$

$(\sigma_f(\uparrow)\text{ FEE}) = (\uparrow\text{ PRED FN})$ $(\sigma_f(\uparrow)\text{ FEE})= (\uparrow\text{ PRED FN})$

$(\sigma_f(\uparrow)\text{ SPKR}) = \sigma_f(\uparrow\text{ SUBJ})$ $(\sigma_f(\uparrow)\text{ INTLC1})=\sigma_f((\text{OBL OBJ}\uparrow)\text{ OBJ})$

$(\sigma_f(\uparrow)\text{ ADD}) = \sigma_f(\uparrow\text{ OBJ})$ $(\sigma_f(\uparrow)\text{ TOPIC})= \sigma_f(\uparrow\text{ ADJ OBJ})$

$(\sigma_f(\uparrow)\text{ MSG}) = \sigma_f(\uparrow\text{ OBL OBJ})$

Fig. 4. Frame projection by co-description

Frames in Context. The projection of frames in context can yield partially connected frame structures. In Fig. 3, *Gespräch* maps to the MSG of REQUEST and also introduces a frame of its own, CONVERSATION. Due to the syntactic relation $(f_1\text{ OBL OBJ})=f_2$, (with f_1 and f_2 the f-structures of *auffordern* and *Gespräch*, respectively), the equations $(\sigma_f(f_1)\text{ MSG})$, $\sigma_f(f_1\text{ OBL OBJ})$ and $(\sigma_f(f_2))$ all refer

---

[6] In this paper we omit details involving set-based representations for ADJuncts.

[7] The MSG is coindexed with the lower frame, a projection of the noun *Gespräch*.

to a single node in the σ_f–projection. The CONVERSATION frame is thus defined as an instantiation, in context, of the MSG role of a REQUEST frame.

(4) a. Haft für Blutpanschen gefordert
        [NP_SB Haft] [PP_MO für Blutpanschen] [VV_HD gefordert]
        'Prison sentence demanded for unsanitary blood collection'

  b. *fordert:* $(\sigma_f(\uparrow)\ \text{MSG}) = \sigma_f(\uparrow\ \text{SUBJ})$
      $(\sigma_f(\uparrow)\ \text{MSG}) = \sigma_f(\uparrow\ \text{ADJ OBJ})$

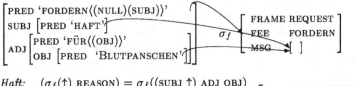

  c. *Haft:* $(\sigma_f(\uparrow)\ \text{REASON}) = \sigma_f((\text{SUBJ}\ \uparrow)\ \text{ADJ OBJ})$

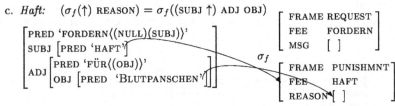

Special Configurations. Potentially problematic are configurations where multiple syntactic constituents are mapped to a single semantic role, as they may lead to an inconsistency in the σ_f–projection.[8]

An example is shown in (4). The SUBJect *Haft* and the modifier PP *für Blutpanschen* have jointly been annotated as the MSG role in the REQUEST frame of *fordern*. The projection of the MSG role from two constituents can be modeled by the equations in (4.b). Yet this simple model will lead to an inconsistency if the involved predicates introduce individual frames, at the same level of embedding.

In (4), the SUBJ *Haft* evokes a frame PUNISHMENT, in which the modifier *für Blutpanschen* fills the REASON role, as defined in (4.c). Due to this embedding asymmetry of SUBJ and modifier at the semantic level, the joint equations in (4.b,c) do not lead to inconsistency, but a circular semantic structure: By (4.b), ADJ OBJ and SUBJ are mapped to the same σ_f value both in (4.b) and (4.c), so in (4.c) the REASON of PUNISHMENT and the PUNISHMENT frame itself have to be equal – which is not a correct representation of the meaning of the sentence.

We found that in the SALSA annotations asymmetric embedding at the semantic level is the typical pattern for constituents that jointly constitute a single frame element. We therefore propose to make use of **functional uncertainty** equations to accommodate for embedded frames within either one of the otherwise re-entrant constituents. In (4.b), we thus relax the equation mapping the PP to MSG to $(\sigma_f(\uparrow)\ \text{MSG ROLE}*)=\sigma_f(\uparrow\ \text{ADJ OBJ})$, with ROLE instantiating to

---

[8] In the existing annotations, 909 (or 1.2%) of the frame elements match this pattern.

(5) der von der SPD geforderte Einstieg in eine Ökosteuerreform
    the by the SPD demanded start   of an ecological tax reform
    'the start of an ecological tax reform, demanded by the SPD'

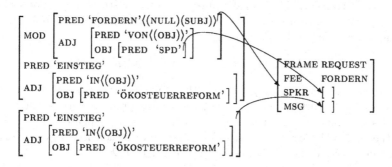

REASON in (4). In this way, the functional uncertainty over possible semantic roles accommodates for (possibly unassigned) asymmetrically embedded frames.

Another typical configuration where discontinuous constituents correspond to a single semantic role is illustrated in (5): *der* and *Einstieg in eine Öko-steuerreform* correspond to the MSG of a REQUEST, which is introduced by the adjectival head *geforderte* within the modifier of the phrase. Its *by-phrase* adjunct fills the SPKR role. This case differs from the one above in that the discontinuous constituents jointly form a headed phrase (with a local PRED in f-structure).

This configuration is similar to the well-known head-switching phenomena, and can be represented by use of the **restriction** operator [19]. The equation $(\uparrow\backslash\{\text{MOD}\})$ refers to the partial f-structure (displayed as a copy in (5)) consisting of $\uparrow$ *without* the function MOD. This unit can be defined to fill the MSG role of REQUEST. Since the frame evoking head is embedded within MOD itself, this involves an inside-out functional equation: $(\sigma_f(\uparrow) \text{ MSG}) = \sigma_f((\text{MOD }\uparrow)\backslash\{\text{MOD}\})$.

5.2 Co-description vs. Description by Analysis

Co-description. In the projection architecture we just presented, f- and s-structure equations jointly determine the valid analyses of a sentence. This method of defining and evaluating projection levels is called co-description.

With co-description, syntactic and semantic analysis interact, leading to semantics-driven syntactic disambiguation. Our example sentence in Fig. 1 is syntactically four-ways ambiguous. *SPD* and *Koalition*, being unmarked for case, can both be SUBJ or OBJ; the PP *über Reform* can be attached to *Gespräch* (as displayed), or be an adjunct of *auffordern*. However, the semantic constraints for *Gespräch* in Fig. 4 define its role TOPIC as a PP adjunct (ADJ OBJ) of the local head. This eliminates the readings where *Reform* is adjoined to the verb.

Description by Analysis (DBA). An alternative to the co-descriptive model is semantics construction via description by analysis [14]. Here, semantics is built on top of fully resolved (disjunctive) f-structure analyses. Analyses that are consistent with syntax-semantics mapping constraints are semantically enriched – while remaining solutions are left untouched.

Technically, this architecture can be realized by use of a term rewriting system as employed in transfer.[9] In a transfer approach, feature structures are described by sets of predicates. Non-prefixed predicates are constraints on the applicability of a rule, to be used e.g. for describing the shape of the f-structure:

$$\text{pred(A,auffordern), subj(A,B), obj(A,C), obl(A,D), obj(D,E)}$$

Here, features are encoded by predicates that take as arguments atomic values or variables for feature structure nodes. Predicates prefixed with $+$ introduce new nodes and values: Encoding the σ_f–projection by a predicate sem_f, we can enrich the matched f-structure with the frame information for *auffordern* and link the SPKR role to the σ_f–projection of the SUBJ *SPD*:

$$+\text{sem}_f(\text{A,SemA}), +\text{frame(SemA,request)}, +\text{fee(SemA,auffordern)},$$
$$+\text{sem}_f(\text{B,SemB}), +\text{spkr(SemA,SemB)}$$

Implications. Both models are equally powerful in terms of expressiveness.[10] While co-description integrates the frame semantics projection into the grammar and parsing process, DBA keeps it as a separate module. This means that DBA is more suited for the development phase of LFG-based frame assignment, while co-description, which is particularly interesting for studying joint syntactic and semantic disambiguation, may be used in later stages. With DBA, semantics does not interfere with grammar design and can be developed separately. Subsequently the transfer rule sets can be automatically converted to equivalent co-description constraints. Due to its greater modularity, the DBA approach also facilitates extensions of the projection architecture to include external semantic knowledge sources, such as word sense, named entity typing, and coreference.

6   Learning Translations between Representations

In the previous section, we investigated representational aspects of an LFG syntax-semantics interface for frame assignment. To implement the full bootstrapping cycle for (semi-)automatic frame assignment (cf. Sec. 3), we finally need a mapping to translate between TIGER-SALSA representations and LFG representations with frame semantics projection. With such a mapping, we can (i) port TIGER-SALSA annotations to the LFG format, to build a seed corpus for stochastic modeling, and (ii) extract transfer-based frame assignment rules from the seed annotations, to disjunctively apply them to new sentences. In the reverse direction, we can (iii) convert automatically assigned frames to the TIGER-SALSA format, to be corrected or confirmed by human annotators.

Transfer-based conversions between the LFG and TIGER formats have been built in [20,11]. But the transfer rules need to be updated with every change

---

[9] The XLE includes a transfer component that operates on packed f-structures [12].
[10] Except for functional uncertainty, which in transfer can only be of bounded length.

of the grammar. Instead, we propose to learn translations between LFG and TIGER formats using a method inspired by Example-based MT. We use the aligned LFG-TIGER treebank of [11] as a "parallel corpus". Starting out with pairs of TIGER and LFG structures, we want to obtain parallel path descriptions that – within the respective syntactic structures – identify the relevant frame (evoking) elements. Since we are operating on identical sentences, we can use the surface strings to establish the corresponding path descriptions.[11]

For example, the paths that identify the SPKR in our running example can be described by the correlated TIGER and LFG path expressions (cf. Figs. 1,3):

	TIGER path	string	LFG f-struct. path	LFG c-struct. path
SPKR	[S,SB,NE]	*SPD*	[SUBJ]	[S,NP]

Paths are given from the root down. For TIGER, we use paths with alternating categorial (node) and functional (edge) labels. In the LFG path descriptions functional and categorial descriptions are separated. To avoid spurious ambiguities in case of non-branching structures, we choose the shortest path (highest constituent) that yields the exact target string. For frame (evoking) elements that correspond to multiple or discontinuous elements (such as *fordert auf*) we generate a list of paths for the individual constituents:

	TIGER path	string	LFG f-struct. path	LFG c-struct. path
REQUEST	[S,HD,VVFIN]	*fordert*	[PRED]	[S,VP,V]
	[S,SVP,PTKVZ]	*auf*		[S,SVP,PTKVZ]

With these correspondences we can port frame annotations from the TIGER-SALSA corpus to the parallel LFG corpus, and freely translate between these formats. They can further be used to extract generalized transfer frame annotation rules, for application to new LFG-parsed sentences.

This method depends on a sufficiently rich set of seed annotations as training data, and for refinement of the rule extraction algorithm. This is ensured by the first bootstrapping cycles, with annotations being checked by human annotators.

7 Conclusions and Perspectives

This study investigates a general architecture for (semi-)automatic frame assignment that supports the transition from treebank-based annotation to large-scale corpus processing in a bootstrapping architecture, using LFG as the underlying syntactic formalism. Besides linguistic considerations, this choice is motivated by the availability of a large-scale German LFG grammar and a powerful processing platform that includes a translation component and tools for stochastic modeling. This combination will allow us to study the (combined and individual) effects of syntactic and semantic disambiguation.

We designed an LFG syntax-semantics interface for frame semantics and showed how to address potentially problematic configurations. To our knowledge,

---

[11] Hence the relation to EBMT, where translation rules are learned from examples. Here, we learn correspondences between syntactic structures for 'identical' languages.

this is the first study to investigate frame semantics as a target representation for semantics construction from syntax. We discussed two architectures for this syntax-semantics interface: the co-descriptive model, where semantic construction is integrated into the grammar, and description by analysis, which works as a separate module and is more robust. Rules for frame semantics projection can be derived from the annotated TIGER-SALSA corpus, given a mapping between the TIGER and LFG syntax formats. We propose to learn this mapping from the 'aligned' TIGER and LFG annotations of the TIGER corpus, to alleviate the maintenance problem of hand-coded transfer rules for corpus conversion.

References

1. C.F. Baker, C.J. Fillmore, and J.B. Lowe. 1998. The Berkeley FrameNet project. In *Proceedings of COLING-ACL 1998*, Montréal, Canada.
2. S. Brants, S. Dipper, S. Hansen, W. Lezius, and G. Smith. 2002. The TIGER Treebank. In *Proc. of the Workshop on Treebanks and Linguistic Theories*, Bulgaria.
3. T. Brants, W. Skut, and B. Krenn. 1997. Tagging Grammatical Functions. In *Proceedings of EMNLP*, Providence, RI, USA.
4. T. Brants, W. Skut, and H. Uszkoreit. 1999. Syntactic Annotation of a German newspaper corpus. In *Proceedings of the ATALA Treebank Workshop*, Paris, France.
5. J. Bresnan. 2001. *Lexical-Functional Syntax*. Blackwell Publishers, Oxford.
6. A. Cahill, M. Forst, M. McCarthy, R. O'Donovan, C. Rohrer, J. van Genabith, and A. Way. 2003. Treebank-Based Multilingual Unification-Grammar Development. in: *Proceedings of ESSLII'03 – Workshop on Ideas and Strategies in Multilingual Grammar Development*, Vienna, Austria.
7. A. Dubai and F. Keller. 2003. Probabilistic Parsing for German using Sister-Head Dependencies. In *Proceedings of the ACL 2003*, Sapporo, Japan.
8. K. Erk, A. Kowalski, S. Padó, and M. Pinkal. 2003. Towards a Resource for Lexical Semantics: A Large German Corpus with Extensive Semantic Annotation. In *Proceedings of the ACL 2003*, Sapporo, Japan.
9. K. Erk, A. Kowalski and S. Padó. 2003. The SALSA Annotation Tool. In *Proceedings of the Workshop on Prospects and Advances in the Syntax/Semantics Interface*, Nancy, France.
10. M. Fleischmann, N. Kwon and E. Hovy. 2003. Maximum Entropy Models for FrameNet Classification. In *Proceedings of EMNLP 2003*, Sapporo, Japan.
11. M. Forst. 2003. Treebank Conversion – Establishing a testsuite for a broad-coverage LFG from the TIGER treebank. In *Proceedings of the 4th International Workshop on Linguistically Interpreted Corpora (LINC '03)*, Budapest, Hungary.
12. A. Frank. 1999. From Parallel Grammar Development towards Machine Translation. In *Proceedings of Machine Translation Summit VII*, Singapore.
13. D. Gildea and D. Jurafsky. 2002. Automatic Labeling of Semantic Roles. In *Computational Linguistics 28.3*.
14. P.-K. Halvorsen and R.M. Kaplan. 1995. Projections and Semantic Description in Lexical-Functional Grammar. In M. Dalrymple, R.M. Kaplan, J.T. Maxwell, and A. Zaenen, eds, *Formal Issues in Lexical-Functional Grammar*, CSLI Lecture Notes.

15. C.R. Johnson, C.J. Fillmore, M.R.L. Petruck, C.F. Baker, M. Ellsworth, J. Rup-penhofer, and E.J. Wood. FrameNet: Theory and Practice. http://www.icsi.berkeley.edu/~framenet/book/book.html.

16. R.M. Kaplan and J.T. III. Maxwell. 1995. An Algorithm for Functional Uncertainty. In M. Dalrymple, R.M. Kaplan, J.T. Maxwell, and A. Zaenen, eds, *Formal Issues in Lexical-Functional Grammar*, CSLI Lecture Notes.

17. S. Riezler, T.H. King, R. Crouch, and A. Zaenen. 2003. Statistical sentence condensation using ambiguity packing and stochastic disambiguation methods for Lexical-Functional Grammar. In *Proceedings of HLT-NAACL'03*, Canada.

18. S. Riezler, T.H. King, R.M. Kaplan, R. Crouch, J.T. III Maxwell, and M. Johnson. 2002. Parsing the Wall Street Journal using a Lexical-Functional Grammar and Discriminative Estimation Techniques. In *Proceedings of ACL'02*, Philadelphia, PA.

19. J. Wedekind and R.M. Kaplan. 1993. Restriction and correspondence-based translation. In *Proceedings of EACL*, Utrecht.

20. H. Zinsmeister, J. Kuhn, and S. Dipper. 2002. Utilizing LFG Parses for Treebank Annotation. In *Proceedings of the LFG 2002 Conference*, Athens, Greece.

Projections from Morphology to Syntax in the Korean Resource Grammar: Implementing Typed Feature Structures

Jong-Bok Kim[1] and Jaehyung Yang[2]

[1] School of English, Kyung Hee University, Seoul, Korea 130-701
[2] School of Computer Engineering, Kangnam University, Kyunggi, Korea, 449-702

Abstract. Korean has a complex inflectional system, showing agglutinative morphology and using affixation as the major mechanism for word formation. A prerequisite to the successful development of any syntactic/semantic parsers for the language thus hinges on the efficient lexicon that can syntactically expand its lexical entries and map into syntax and semantics with robust parsing performance. This paper reports the system of the Korean Resource Grammar developed as an extension of HPSG (Head-driven Phrase Structure Grammar) and the results of implementing it into the Linguistic Knowledge Building (LKB) system (cf. Copestake 2002). The paper shows that the present grammar proves to be theoretically as well as computationally efficient enough in parsing Korean sentences.

1 Korean Resource Grammar

The Korean Resource Grammar (KRG) is a computational grammar for Korean currently under development since October 2002 (cf. Kim and Yang 2003). Its aim is to develop an open source grammar of Korean. The grammatical framework for the KRG is the constraint-based grammar, HPSG (cf. Sag, Wasow, and Bender 2003). HPSG (Head-driven Phrase Structure Grammar) is built upon a non-derivational, constraint-based, and surface-oriented grammatical architecture. HPSG seeks to model human languages as systems of constraints on typed feature structures. In particular, the grammar adopts the mechanism of type hierarchy in which every linguistic sign is typed with appropriate constraints and hierarchically organized. The characteristic of such typed feature structure formalisms facilitates the extension of grammar in a systematic and efficient way, resulting in linguistically precise and theoretically motivated descriptions of languages including Korean. The concept of hierarchical classification is essentially assigning linguistic entities such as phrases and words to specific types, and an assignment of those types to superordinate types. Each type is declared to obey certain constraints corresponding to properties shared by all members of that type. This system then allows us to express cross-classifying generalizations about phrases and words, while accommodating the idiosyncrasies of individual types on particular subtypes of phrases or words.

A. Gelbukh (Ed.): CICLing 2004, LNCS 2945, pp. 14–25, 2004.
© Springer-Verlag Berlin Heidelberg 2004

As the basic tool for writing, testing, and processing the Korean Resource Grammar, we adopt the LKB (Linguistic Knowledge Building) system (Copestake 2002). The LKB system is a grammar and lexicon development environment for use with constraint-based linguistic formalisms such as HPSG.[1]

The Korean Resource Grammar consists of grammar rules, inflection rules, lexical rules, type definitions, and lexicon. All the linguistic information is represented in terms of signs. These signs are classified into subtypes as represented in a simple hierarchy in (1):

(1)

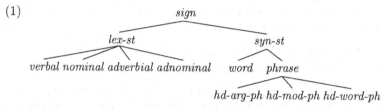

The elements in *lex-st* (*lexical-structure*) type, forming the basic components of the lexicon, are built up from lexical processes such as lexical rules. Parts of these elements will be realized as *word* to function as a syntactic element, as an element of *syn-st* (*syntactic-structure*). Phrases projected from *word* form basic Korean well-formed phrases such as *hd-arg-ph* (head-argument-ph) and *hd-mod-ph* (head-modifier-ph). In what follows, we will discuss how such projections are possible within a type-featured system, KRG.

2   Building the Lexicon through a Templatic Approach

The verb in Korean cannot be an independent word without inflectional suffixes. The suffixes cannot be attached arbitrarily to a stem or word, but need to observe a regular fixed order. Reflecting this, the verbal morphology has traditionally been assumed to be templatic. The template in (1) is a simplified one for the verbal suffixes in Korean, assumed in Cho and Sells (1994), among others.[2]

(2) V-base + (Passive/Caussative) + (Hon) + (Tense) + Mood + (Comp)

As can be seen from the above template, verb suffixes, attaching to the preceding verb stem or word, mark honorific, tense, and mood functions. Morphologically, the inflectional suffixes preceding Mood are optional, but a Mood suffix obligatorily needs to be attached to a verb stem in simple independent sentences. Thus the verbal stem and the mood suffix are mutually bound in the sense that the bare verb stem cannot be used uninflected in any syntactic context and it should be inflected at least with the mood suffix, as seen in (3).

---

[1] The LKB is freely available with open source (http://ling.stanford.edu).

[2] Abbreviations adopted in this paper are follows: Acc (Accusative), Comp (Complementizer), Conj (Conjunction), Decl (Declarative), Del (Delimiter), Gen (Genitive), Hon (Honorific), Imper (Imperative), Loc (Locative), Nom (Nominative), Nmlz (Nomilizer), Pl (Plural), Postp (Postposition), Prop (Propostive), tns (tense), Sug (Suggestive).

(3) a. ilk-(ess)-ta 'read-(Past)-Decl'
    b. *ilk-ess 'read-Past'

Also, as expected from the template, the verbal suffixes observe the rigid ordering restrictions: the template ordering cannot be violated.

(4) a. *cap-ass-si-ta 'catch-Past-Hon-Decl'
    b. *cap-ta-ass 'catch-Decl-Past'

The template given in (2) appears to capture the ordering generalizations as well as combinatory possibilities of verbal suffixes. However, the template alone could generate some ill-formed combinations, as given in (5).

(5) a. ka-(*si)-(*ess)-ca 'go-Hon-Past-Prop (Let's go!)'
    b. ka-(*si)-(*ess)-la 'go-Hon-Past-Imper (Go!)'

If we simply assume the template in (2) with the given suffixes in each slot, we would allow the ill-formed combinations here. The propositive mood suffix -*ca* and imperative mood suffix -*la* cannot combine either with the honorific suffix or with the tense suffix. They can combine only with a verb root as in *ka-ca* 'go-Prop' and *ka-la* 'go-Imper'. This means that verbal suffixes like -*ca* and -*la* have their own selectional or co-occurrence restrictions in addition to their being positioned into the Mood slot. The template alone thus fails to describe all the combinatory possibilities, demanding additional mechanisms. In addition, taking into consideration other types of verbal elements such as complementizer words or subordinator words, more templates are called upon. Leaving aside the issue of empty elements when optional suffixes are not realized, a templatic approach appears not to properly reflect the morphological structure of Korean inflections (cf. Kim 1998).

3   A Type-Hierarchy Approach

3.1   Verbal Morphology

The starting point of structuring the lexicon in the KRG is parts of speech in the language. Like the traditional literature, the KRG assumes *verbal, nominal, adverbial,* and *adnominal* as the language's basic categories. These are further subclassified into subtypes. For example, the type *verbal* is taken to have the hierarchy given in (6):

(6)

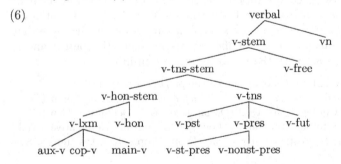

Such a classification aims to capture the basic verbal morphology of Korean. In turn, it means a verbal element will be built up step by step, starting from *v-lxm (v-lexeme)* to *v-free*:

(7) a. [[[[cap + hi]+si] +ess]+ ta] + ko] 'catch-Caus-Hon-Past-Decl-Comp'

b. v-lxm → v-hon (v-hon-stem) → v-tns (v-tns-stem) → v-free (v-stem) → v-comp

Such building processes are constrained by the type declarations, some of which are given in (8):[3]

(8)

a. v-hon:
$$\begin{bmatrix} \text{ORTH } \boxed{1} + \text{si} \\ \text{STEM} \begin{bmatrix} v\text{-}base \\ \text{ORTH } \boxed{1} \end{bmatrix} \\ \text{SYN.HEAD.HON } + \end{bmatrix}$$

b. v-tns-stem:
$$\begin{bmatrix} \text{STEM} \begin{bmatrix} v\text{-}hon\text{-}stem \\ \text{SYN } \boxed{1} \\ \text{SEM.RELS } \boxed{A} \end{bmatrix} \\ \text{SYN } \boxed{1} \\ \text{SEM.RELS } \boxed{A} \oplus \boxed{B} \end{bmatrix}$$

c. v-free:
$$\begin{bmatrix} \text{STEM } v\text{-}tns\text{-}stem \\ \text{SYN.HEAD.IC } bool \end{bmatrix}$$

The constraints in (8)a mean that the type *v-hon* will take *v-base* as its stem; those in (8b) mean that the type *v-tns-stem* will take an instance of *v-hon-stem* as its stem. One thing to note here is that any subtypes of *v-hon-stem* can serve as the stem of *v-tns-stem* in accordance with the type hierarchy system. The grammar makes only the instances of *v-free* serve as an input to syntax.

These constraints restrict the possible word internal structures in Korean word formation. The system could provide a clean account for the ill-formed combinations without employing mechanisms such as templates. Observe the following:

(9) a. *$_{v-hon-stem}$[$_{v-tns-stem}$[cap-ass]-si]-ta 'catch-Past-Hon-Decl'

b. *$_{v-free}$[$_{v-hon-stem}$[cap-usi]-ta]-ess 'catch-Hon-Decl-Past'

c. *[$_{v-hon-stem}$[$_{v-hon-stem}$[cap-usi]-usi]-ess]-ta 'catch-Hon-Hon-Past-Decl'

(9a) is ruled out because the honorific suffix co-occurs with the *v-tns-stem*, violating (8a); (9b) is ill-formed since the passive suffix *-ess* is attached to the *v-free* stem. This violates the constraint (8b) which requires its stem value be *v-hon-stem* or any of its subtypes. In the same vein, (9c) is not generated because the second honorific suffix occurs not with a *v-base*, but with a *v-hon* stem.

One important question arises: why do we need the notions of types in the morphological theory? The reason is simply that any morphological theory for Korean needs certain notions similar to types. We can find cases where we should have some notions referring to a specific group of morphological objects, so as to predict that a certain morphological phenomena applies only to this group. As noted, only instances of *v-free* can be pumped up to *v-word* occurring in syntax.[4]

---

[3] The implemented feature descriptions in the LKB system are slightly different from those represented here.

[4] The type *v-free* is further subtyped into *v-ind(ependent)*, *v-dep(endent)*, and *v-ger(undive)*. Each of these functions as an independent syntactic element. *v-ind* functions as a predicate in the independent clause, *v-dep* words are used as dependent verbs such as complementizer or subordinator predicates.

Being its subtype, *v-sug-infm* (v-suggestive-informal) requires its STEM value to be *v-base* as represented in the following:

(10)   a. $*_{v-hon-stem}$[ilk-usi]-ca 'read-Hon-Sug'
  b. $_{v-base}$[ilk]-ca 'read-Sug'

In a template analysis like (2), this would mean the honorific and tense slots should be empty. This would surely make the grammar much complicated. However, the present type-based system can efficiently avoid such an issue by simply referring to the type *v-base* as the STEM value of the type *v-sug-infm*.

3.2   Nominal Morphology

Nominal inflection is basically different from verbal inflection. Even though like verbal inflections, nominal suffixes are also under tight ordering restrictions, all the nominal suffixes are optional as represented in the following template and a true example:

(11)   N-base – (Hon) – (Pl) – (Postp) – (Conj) – (X-Delim) – (Z-Delim)

(12)   sensayng + (nim) + (tul) + (eykey) + (man) + (un)
  teacher + Hon + Pl + Postp + X-Delim + Z-Delim
  'to the (honorable) teachers only'

All the suffixes (often called particles) here, decoding various grammatical functions, need not be realized. Traditionally particles are treated as independent words even though they act more like verbal suffixes in terms of strict ordering restrictions, no intervention by any word element, and so forth. Our grammar, following lexicalist perspectives (cf. Cho and Sells 1994, Kim 1996), takes a quite different approach: we take particles not to exist as independent words but to function as optional inflectional suffixes. As a starting point, the KRG sets up different types of nominals corresponding to meaningful classes as represented in the hierarchy: (13):

(13)

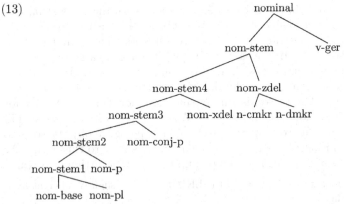

The building process of nominal elements starts from the type *nom-base* that includes subtypes such as *vn, n-bn, n-cn, n-cl, n-prop* (verbal nouns, bound nouns, common nouns, classifiers, proper nouns). Just like the process of building verbal elements, nominal word formation observes this hierarchical process:

(14) nom-base → nom-stem1 → nom-stem2 → nom-stem3 → nom-stem4 → nom-stem

One crucial difference from the forming process of verbal elements is that any of these processes can directly be realized as (pumped up to) a *word* element in syntax.[5] The constraints on each type place restrictions on the ordering relationship among nominal suffixes:

(15)

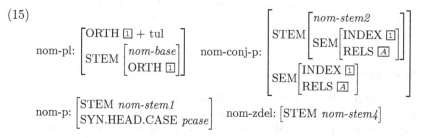

These constraints on the nominal types can place ordering restrictions among nominal particles:

(16) a. *[$_{nom-stem}$[sensayngnim-tul-un]-eykey] 'teacher-Pl-Del-Postp'
      b. *[$_{nom-stem3}$[sensayngnim-tul-kwa]-eykey] 'teacher-Pl-Conj-Postp'
      c. *[$_{nom-stem}$[sensayngnim-tul-un]-i] 'teacher-Pl-Del-Nom'

The so-called postposition *eykey* requires its STEM value to be an instance of *nom-stem*. This explains why (16a) and (16b) are not generated in the system. The nominative marker can combine only with *nom-stem4* or its subtypes. This explains why the system generates cases like (16c). However, it correctly generates cases like the following:

(17) a. $_{nom-base}$[sensayngnim]-i 'teacher-Nom'
      b. $_{nom-stem1}$[$_{nom-base}$[sensayngnim]-tul]-kwa 'teacher-Conj'

As noted, the type hierarchy system allows the STEM value to be any subtypes of the originally required one. For example, even though the case marked nominal (nom-cmkr) element would have its STEM value *nom-stem4*, *nom-base* can also satisfy this satisfaction since it is a subtype of *nom-stem4*.

In sum, the morphological system we have shown makes the Korean morphology much simpler and can capture the ordering restrictions as well as cooccurrence restrictions. Other welcoming consequences of adopting the typed feature system come from the treatment of well-known mixed constructions such as sentential nominal and light verb constructions. Both of these have received much attention because of their mixed properties.

---

[5] The grammar specifies only *v-free* to be realized as *v-word* whereas for nouns it permits all the instances of type *nominal* to be realized as *n-word*. This in turn means any subtype of *nominal* can serve as a syntactic element in accordance of the type hierarchy in (13).

4   Multiple Inheritance Hierarchy: Advantages

One main property of the typed feature system we developed here is that it allows us to adopt multiple inheritance hierarchies, commonly used in the object-oriented programming paradigm to organize multiple dimensions of information about objects in particular knowledge domains. In particular, this multiple inheritance system provides a straightforward and efficient method of capturing the mixed properties of phenomena such as light verb and nominalizations constructions, both of which are most common phenomena and notorious for their syntactic complexities.

4.1   Nominalization

One of the main puzzles in the treatment of Korean sentential nominalizations or verbal gerundive phrases (VGP) is that they display verbal properties internally and nominal properties externally. Internal verbal properties are prevalent. One telling piece of evidence comes from the inheritance of arguments from the lexeme verb from which the gerundive verb is derived. As shown in (18), the gerundive verb takes the same arguments, the nominative subject and accusative object:

(18) [John-i   ecey   ku chayk-ul/*uy
       John-NOM yesterday that book-ACC/*GEN
       ilk-ess-um]-i   myonghwak-hata
       read-PAST-Nmlz-Nom clear-do
       'John's having read the book yesterday is clear'

Various other phenomena also show that such gerundive phrases are internally similar to VPs. They can include a sentential adverb as in (19a); an adverbial element can modify the gerundive verb as in (19b); the phrase can include the sentential negation marker *an* as in (19c); it also can contain the full range of auxiliaries as in (19d), the phrase allows free scrambling of its elements as in (19e):

(19) a. John-i   **papokathi** ku chayk-ul   ilk-ess-um (Sent. Adv)
          John-Nom foolish   that book-Acc read-Past-Nmlz
          'John's having read the book foolish'
      b. John-i   chayk-ul **ppalli/*ppalun**   ilk-um (Adv Mod)
          John-Nom book-Acc fast(adv)/*fast(adj) read-Nmlz
          'John's reading books fast.'
      c. John-i   chayk-ul **an** ilk-um (Sentential Neg)
          John-Nom book-Acc Neg read-Nmlz
          'John's not reading books.'
      d. John-i   chayk-ul ilk-ko   **siph-um** (Aux verb)
          John-Nom book-Acc read-Comp want-Nmlz
          'John's wanting to read books'
      e. **ku chayk-ul** John-i   __ ilk-ess-um-(i   nollapta) (Scrambling)
          book-Acc   John-Nom __ read-Past-Nmlz-Nom surprising
          'It is surprising that John read the book.'

Meanwhile, its external structure is more like that of NPs. VGPs can appear in the canonical NP positions such as subject or object as in (20a) or as a postpositional object in (20b).

(20) a. [ai-ka   chayk-ul ilk-um]-i   nollapta
         child-Nom book-Acc read-Nmlz-Nom surprising
         'That child's reading a book is surprising'

     b. [John-i   enehak-ul   kongpwuha-m]-**eytayhay** mollassta
        John-Nom linguistics-Acc study-Nmlz-about   not.know
        '(We) didn't know about John's studying linguistics.'

These mixed properties of Korean sentential nominalization have provided a challenge to syntactic analyses with a strict version of X-bar theory. Various approaches (see Malouf 1998 and references cited therein) have been proposed to solve this puzzle, but they all have ended up abandoning or modifying fundamental theoretical conditions such as endocentricity, lexicalism, and null licensing.

In the KRG with the multiple inheritance mechanism, the type *v-ger* is classified as the subtype of both *v-free* and *n-stem1* as represented in the following hierarchy:[6]

(21)

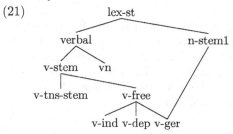

Such a cross-classification, allowing multiple inheritance, is also reflected in the feature descriptions in the LKB. The following represents a sample source code:

```
v-ger := v-free & n-stem1 &
[ SYN #syn & [ HEAD.MOD <> ],
  SEM #sem,
  ARGS < v-tns-stem & [ SYN #syn, SEM #sem ] > ].
```

As observed here, being a subtype of *v-free* and *n-stem1* implies that *v-ger* will inherit their properties. Since it is a subtype of *v-free*, *v-ger* will act just like as a verb: selecting arguments and assigning case values to them. In addition, *v-ger* can undergo the same nominal suffixation process since it is a subtype of *n-stem1*. For example, the gerundive verb *ilk-ess-um* will be generated through the following informally represented structure in the KRG.

---

[6] In capturing the mixed properties, the KRG system adopts the binary-valued features VERBAL and NOMINAL. Nominalized verbs are assigned to have [VERBAL +] and [NOMINAL +] with the HEAD value *verb*. Meanwhile, the verbal nouns are different form nominalized verbs with respect to the HEAD value: They are *noun*.

(22)

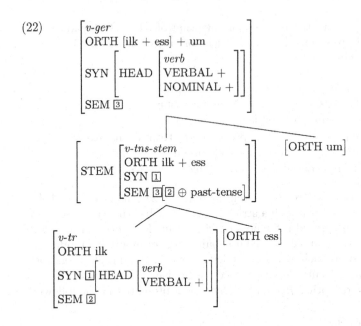

The gerundive verb starts from a transitive lexeme *ilk* 'read' and forms a *v-tns-stem* after the attachment of the past tense suffix *ess*. When this *v-tns-stem* is attached with the nominalizer suffix, it inherits [NOMINAL +] feature. As such, various verbal properties are inherited from *v-tran-lxm* whereas the nominal properties coming when it attaches to the nominalizer. This is a reflection of how information flow occurs in sentential nominalization:

(23)

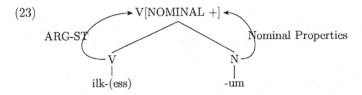

As can be seen in (20), the ARG-ST information is coming from the left element since the nominalized N still needs to combine with the complement(s) of the verb, while the categorial information comes from the righthand nominalizer.

Such a treatment is a clear advantage over previous theoretical or computational approaches in which nominalized verbs are simply taken to be either verbs or nouns. If they are taken to be verbs, ad hoc mechanisms are required to generate nominal suffixed nominalized verbs, causing heavy parsing loads. If they are simply taken to be nouns, we could not account for why gerundive verbs can be also inflected with tense and honorific and function just like verbs. The multiple inheritance system, designed with fine-grained feature declarations, can avoid such an issue.

4.2   Light Verb Constructions

As the name implies, VNs (verbal nouns) in Korean also display both nominal and verbal properties. The case markings on the VNs and the genitive case marking on its argument indicate that they have nominal properties:

(24) John-i   mullihak-uy yonkwu-lul hayessta
     John-Nom physics-Gen study-Acc did
     'John studied physics.'

They also have verbal properties in the sense that they select arguments and assign case markings on its arguments independently.

(25) a. John-i   mwullihak-ul yonkwu (cwung)
        John-Nom physics-Acc   study   (while)
        'John is in the middle of studying physics.'
     b. John-i   ku ceyphwum-ul mikwuk-eye yelshimhi swuchwul-ul hayessta
        John-Nom the item-Acc   US-Loc   diligently export-Acc did
        'John diligently exported the item to US.'

Just like the treatment of gerundive verbs, the multiple inheritance mechanism plays an important role in capturing the mixed properties. In the KRG, verbal nouns are also cross-classified as a subtype of both *n-base* and *verbal*.

```
vn := n-base & verbal &
 [ SYN.HEAD.TYPE t-none,
   SEM [ MODE statement,
         INDEX event ] ].
```

This feature description implies that *vn*, being a subtype of *n-base* and *verbal*, will inherit their properties. For example, the structure of the VN *swuchwul* 'export' would be something like the following:

(26)
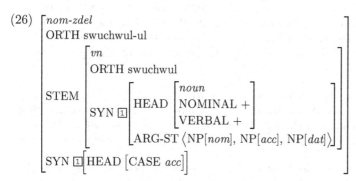

As a subtype of *n-base*, the HEAD feature of the VN will be *noun* and [NOMINAL +], and as a subtype of *verbal*, it will also inherit [VERBAL +] feature and ARG-ST value. This then would allow the VN to appear in any nominal position while internally acting like a verbal element.

5   Testing the Feasibility of the System

The grammar we have built within the typed-feature structure system here, eventually aiming at working with real-world data, has been first implemented into the LKB.[7] In testing its performance and feasibility, we used the SERI Test Suites '97 after the successful parsing of the self-designed 250 sentences. The SERI Test Suites (Sung and Jang 1997), carefully designed to evaluate the performance of Korean syntactic parsers, consists of total 472 sentences (292 test sentences representing the core phenomena of the language and 180 sentences representing different types of predicate). In terms of lexical entries, it has total 440 lexemes (269 nouns, 125 predicates, 35 adverbs, and 11 determiners) and total 1937 word occurrences. As represented in the following table, the testing results of the KRG prove quite robust:

(27)

	# of Lexemes	# of Words	# of Sentences
SERI	440	1937	472
KRG Parsing Results	440	1937	423
Coverage (%)	100	100	89.5

As the table shows, the system correctly generated all the lexemes in the test suites and inflected words. In terms of parsing sentences, the grammar parsed 423 sentences out of total 472. Failed 49 sentences are related to the grammar that the current system has not yet written. For example, the SERI Test Suites include examples representing phenomena such as honorification, coordination, and left dislocation of subject. It is believed that once we have a finer-grained grammar for these phenomena, the KRG will resolve these remaining sentences. Another promising indication of the test is that its mean parse (average number of parsed trees) for the 423 parsed sentences marks 1.67, controlling spurious ambiguity at a minimum level.

As noted here, the test results provide clear evidence that the KRG, built upon typed feature structure system, offers high performance and can be extended to large scale of data. Since the test suites here include most of the main issues in analyzing the Korean language, we believe that further tests for designated corpus will surely achieve nearly the same result of high performance too.

---

[7] The space does not allow us to explicate the morphological and semantic system of the KRG in Korean. As for morphology, we integrated MACH (Morphological Analyzer for Contemporary Hangul) developed by Shim and Yang (2002). This system segments words into sequences of morphemes with POS tags and morphological information.

As for semantics, we adopted the Minimal Recursion Semantics developed by Copestake et al. (2001). In the multilingual context in which this grammar has been developed, a high premium is placed on parallel and consistent semantic representations between grammars for different languages. Ensuring this parallelism enables the reuse of the same downstream technology, no matter which langauge is used as input. The MRS well suits for this purpose.

6 Conclusion

It is hard to deny the fact that in building up an efficient grammar, expressive accuracy has often been scarified in order to achieve computational tractability (Oepen et al. 2002). However, putting linguistic generalizations aside has brought difficulties expanding the coverage and eventually building a large scale of grammar. To build up any efficient parsing system for languages like Korean which displays an intriguing morphological properties, a prerequisite is a system that can build up morphological elements in a systematic way and project them into syntax and semantics to achieve proper grammatical compatibility. Conventional forms of standard morphological representations have proved problematic, neither being able to capture linguistic generalizations nor pinning down descriptive adequacy. In contrast, the morphological and syntactic system we have developed here with typed feature structures solve such preexisting problems while keeping linguistic insights, thus making the Korean morphology much simpler (e.g., in capturing the ordering restrictions as well as co-occurrence restrictions). Other welcoming consequences of the present system come from the treatment of well-known mixed constructions such as sentential nominal and light verb constructions. Both of these have received much attention because their mixed properties and even have been impediments to theoretical as well as computational linguistics. We have seen that once we have a rigorously defined type feature structure system of grammar, all these fall out naturally with high efficient parsing performance.

References

Cho, Young-Mee Yu, and Peter Sells. 1995. A lexical account of inflectional suffixes in Korean. *Journal of East Asian Linguistics* 4, 119–174.

Copestake, Ann, Dan Flickinger, Ivan Sag and Carl Pollard. 2001. Minimal Recursion Semantics: An introduction. Ms. Stanford University.

Copestake, Ann. 2002. *Implementing Typed Feature Structure Grammars*. CSLI Publications.

Kim, Jong-Bok. 1998. Interface between Morphology and Syntax: A Constraint-Based and Lexicalist Approach. *Language and Information* 2: 177–233.

Kim, Jong-Bok and Jahyung Yang. 2003. Korean Phrase Structure Grammar and Implementing it into the LKB (Linguistic Knowledge Building) System (In Korean). *Korean Linguistics* 21: 1–41.

Malouf, Robert. 1998. *Mixed Categories in the Hierarchical Lexicon*. Stanford: CSLI Publications.

Oepen, Stephan, Dan Flickinger, Jun-ichi Tusujii, and Hans Uszkoreit. 2002. *Collaborative Language Engineering*. Stanford: CSLI Publications.

Sag, Ivan, Tom Wasow, and Emily Bender. 2003. *Syntactic Theory: A Formal Approach*. Stanford: CSLI Publications.

Shim, Kwangseob and Yang Jaehyung. 2002. MACH: A Supersonic Korean Morphological Analyzer. In *Proceedings of Coling-2002 International Conference*, pp. 939–45, Taipei.

Sung, Won-Kyung and Myung-Gil Jang. 1997. SERI Test Suites '95. In *Proceedings of the Conference on Hanguel and Korean Language Information Processing*.

A Systemic-Functional Approach to
Japanese Text Understanding

Noriko Ito, Toru Sugimoto, and Michio Sugeno

RIKEN Brain Science Institute, 2-1 Hirosawa, Wako, Saitama 351-0198 Japan
{itoh,sugimoto,msgn}@brain.riken.jp
http://www.brain.riken.jp/labs/lbis/

Abstract. We have implemented a Japanese text processing system, combining the existing parser and dictionary with the linguistic resources that we developed based on systemic functional linguistics. In this paper, we explain the text understanding algorithm of our system that utilizes the various linguistic resources in the Semiotic Base suggested by Halliday. First, we describe the structure of the SB and the linguistic resources stored in it. Then, we depict the text understanding algorithm using the SB. The process starts with morphological and dependency analyses by the non-SFL-based existing parser, followed by looking up the dictionary to enrich the input for SFL-based analysis. After mapping the pre-processing results onto systemic features, the path identification of selected features and unification based on O'Donnell are conducted with reference to the linguistic resource represented in the system networks. Consequently, we obtain graphological, lexicogrammatical, semantic and conceptual annotations of a given text.

1 Introduction

The purpose of this research is to implement a natural language processing system that follows the theoretical model of *systemic functional linguistics* (SFL). SFL aims at describing a language comprehensively and provides a unified way of modeling language use in context [1]. While SFL has been used as the basis for many natural language generation systems (e.g., [2]), less work has been done for natural language understanding systems (e.g., [3]).

Sugimoto [4] proposed the data structure of the *Semiotic Base* (SB), which stores SFL-based linguistic knowledge in computational form, and investigated how to incorporate the SB into a dialogue management model in order to enable an intelligent agent system to identify the current dialogue context and behave appropriately according to it. By elaborating their idea and combining the existing parser and dictionary with systemic resources, we implemented a Japanese text processing system that can conduct both understanding and generation of Japanese text.

In this paper, we explain the text understanding algorithm of our text processing system that utilizes the various linguistic resources in the SB. First, we describe the structure of the SB and the linguistic resources stored in it. Then, we depict the text understanding algorithm using the SB and the outputs of the process.

A. Gelbukh (Ed.): CICLing 2004, LNCS 2945, pp. 26–37, 2004.
© Springer-Verlag Berlin Heidelberg 2004

2 The Semiotic Base

According to [4], the SB consists of four main and two subsidiary components as shown in Table 1.[1]

Table 1. Structure of the Semiotic Base

Main components	Context Base (CB)	Situation Base
		Stage Base
		Concept Repository (CR)
	Meaning Base (MB)	
	Wording Base (WB)	
	Expression Base (EB)	
Subsidiary components	Machine readable dictionary	General Dictionary (GD)
		Situation-Specific Dictionary
	Corpus Base (texts with annotations)	

Following SFL, they in [4] employed distinctive perspectives in their design of the SB. One of them is the stratificational organization of a language in context. Corresponding to this, the main components are: *Context Base* (CB), which stores the features characterizing a given situation of dialogue and selection constraints on semantics specifying which semantic features are relevant to a given situation type; *Meaning Base* (MB), which stores features depicting the meanings associated with a situation type and constraints on lexicogrammar specifying which lexicogrammatical features are available in realizing a particular meaning in a situation type; *Wording Base* (WB), which stores the features to describe dialogue in terms of Japanese lexicogrammar and constraints specifying which graphological features are available for realizing a particular lexicogrammatical features in a situation type; and *Expression Base* (EB), which is currently designed to deal with written texts and stores graphological features associated with rules to lay out the word list using a conventional publication language, e.g., HTML.

Another characteristic is that the linguistic features in these bases and the influences of feature selection on the structure, on the feature of other units in the structure and on the relation between the units generated within and across the strata and the ranks are represented in the same manner, i.e., as *system networks* and *realization statements*. Fig. 1 shows an example of a system network and the associated realization statements extracted from WB.

A system network is a directed graph that consists of systems whose terms are represented by linguistic features. In each system, only one feature can be selected. The selected feature may be an entry condition for other systems. In Fig. 1, 'major-clause' is the entry condition for two systems. If this feature is selected, of the first system, either 'effective' or 'middle' must be chosen, and of the second system, either'material', 'mental', 'verbal-process' or 'relational' must be selected. If 'effective' and 'material' are selected, 'mat-doing' is selected.

---

[1] In the table, the dotted cell indicates the contents that are not relevant to the process explained in this paper.

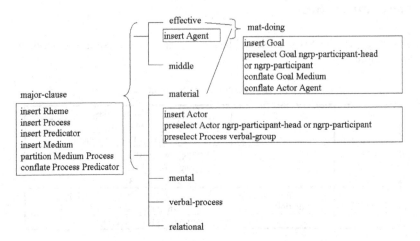

Fig. 1. Fragment of a system network and associated realization statements

Some features are associated with realization statements, which are used to specify instance structures containing these features. We assume that an instance structure is a tree whose nodes are called units. A unit consists of a feature selection path of SFL features from the root feature of the system network and a set of roles that this unit is considered to play for the parent unit. In Fig. 1, 'insert Agent', which is associated with 'effective', is a realization statement that means a unit containing 'effective' should have a child unit whose role is 'Agent'. 'Preselect Process verbal-group', which is associated with 'material', requires that if a unit containing 'material' has a child unit whose role is 'Process', this child unit should contain a feature 'verbal-group'. 'Conflate Goal Medium' associated with 'mat-doing' indicates the child units whose role is 'Goal' and 'Medium' must be unified.

The realization statements are precompiled in what O'Donnell [3] calls *partial-structure* and used in lexicogrammatical and semantic analyses explained below. A *linking partial-structure* represents a possible pattern of parent/child unit pairs, and is compiled from a combination of insert, conflate and preselect realization statements in the WB and MB networks. An *ordering partial-structure* specifies a constraint on the ordering of child units of a parent/child unit pair, and is compiled from insert, conflate and order statements. Fig. 2 represents the partial structures converted from the realization statements shown in Fig. 1.

We divide CB into three sub-components: *Situation Base*, *Stage Base*, and *Concept Repository* (CR).[2] In CR we provide the concepts in the form of frame representation, associated systemic features and roles, and EDR concept identifier [5]. Table 2 shows an example of a CR record.

---

[2] The contents of CB mentioned in [4] are stored in what we call Situation Base. The contents of Stage Base and CR here roughly correspond to interaction plans in Plan Library and concept frames in Knowledge Base proposed in [4]. We assume that these are part of linguistic knowledge, hence we include them in the SB.

link_Actor_1

```
(:and wb clause clause-simplex major-clause
effective material mat-doing)
                                    | Actor/Agent
(:and wb group-phrase groups nominal-group
   (:or (:and ngrp-simplex nominal-head
         ngrp-participant-head)
        (:and ngrp-complex ngrp-hypotactic
         ngrp-participant)))
```

link_Actor_2

```
(:and wb clause clause-simplex major-clause material)
                                    | Actor
(:and wb group-phrase groups nominal-group
   (:or (:and ngrp-simplex nominal-head
         ngrp-participant-head)
        (:and ngrp-complex ngrp-hypotactic
         ngrp-participant)))
```

link_Goal_3

```
(:and wb clause clause-simplex major-clause
   effective material mat-doing)
                                    | Goal/Medium
(:and wb group-phrase groups nominal-group
   (:or (:and ngrp-simplex nominal-head
         ngrp-participant-head)
        (:and ngrp-complex ngrp-hypotactic
         ngrp-participant)))
```

link_Process_4

```
(:and wb clause clause-simplex major-clause)
                                    | Process/Predicator
(:and wb group-phrase groups verbal-group)
```

order_Medium#Process_5

```
(:and wb clause clause-simplex major-clause)
                     |
              Medium#Process/Predicator
```

Fig. 2. Examples of partial-structures

The records in CR are sorted according to a situation type to which a given concept is relevant. In this sense, CR is different from EDR concept dictionary, which is designed to serve as a general taxonomy.

In addition to the main bases, the SB accommodates *Corpus Base* and a machine-readable dictionary. We provide two types of machine-readable dictionary: *General Dictionary* (GD) and *Situation-Specific Dictionary*. Both store ordinary dictionary information on lexical items, associated systemic features and roles, and EDR concept identifier and concept relation label. Table 3 shows an example of GD record.

Table 2. Example of Concept Repository record

Head Concept Name		writing	
Concept Type		class	
EDR Concept Identifier		0fe07c	
MB Features		fg-creative	
WB Features		creative	
Upper Concept Name		domain-action	
	Slot Name	Slot Value Type	SFL Role
1	agent	agent	Actor
2	object	document	Goal
3	instrument	word-processor	Means

Table 3. Example of General Dictionary record

Headword		書く "writing"
Kana		カク "kaku"
EDR Part of Speech		JVE (i.e., verb)
EDR Concept Identifier		0fe07c
MB Features		fg-creative
WB Features		creative&lg-concrete or creative&lg-abstract
SFL Roles for Headword		Event
	EDR Concept Relation Label	SFL Roles
1	agent	Actor&Agent
2	object	Goal&Medium
3	instrument	Means

3   Text Understanding Algorithms

Fig. 3 shows the flow of the text understanding process with the SB. In this section, we briefly explain each phase in this diagram using an example output of our system shown partly in Table 4.

3.1 Graphological Analysis

In this phase, the graphological instance structure of the text is constructed referring to EB. All that the current system does is to recognize sentence boundary based on punctuation. This process is independent of the other processes.

3.2 Preprocessing

After the morphological analysis and the dependency structure analyses [6] and the GD lookup are done, EDR concept identifiers are assigned to each word segment and EDR concept relation labels to each dependency pair of bunsetsu (i.e., phrase) segments by looking up the EDR dictionary of selectional restrictions for Japanese

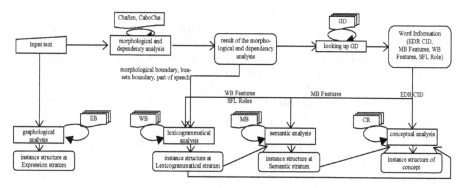

Fig. 3. Overview of text understanding process

Table 4. Example of the output of text understanding process (in part)

		translation	I want to write a business trip report with a word processor.										
		gloss	I	THEME	business trip	GENITIVE	report	document	ACCUSATIVE	wordprocessor	INSTRUMENTAL	writing	OPTATIVE
Preprocessing		morphological and dependency analyses	watasi	wa	syuttyoo	no	hookoku	syo	o	waapuro	de	kaki	tai	.
			0 4D		1 2D		2 4D			3 4D		4~10		
		GD search	0e7e95, 2dc301	-	0f5926	-	444e21		-	3cdcc5	-	0fe07c	2621c8	-
		CID CRL	agent		scene		object			implement			-	
Graphological analysis		sentence	eb-graphology-base sentence										
		comma unit	Head										Tail full-stop
			eb-graphology-base comma-unit										
		letter	Head	2	3-4	5	6-7	8	9	10-13	14	15-16	17-Tail
			j-characters...	j-characters...	j-characters...	j-characters...	j-characters...	j-characters...	j-characters...	j-characters...	j-characters...	j-characters...	j-characters...
Lexicogrammatical analysis		clause simplex rank	clause clause-simplex major-clause independent-clause non-conjunct cls-neutral cir-specified cir-expansion cir-enhancement cir-manner cir-means material mat-doing creative lg-concrete effective thematic-agent-subject operative-voice thematic relative-theme unmarked-theme explicit-topical-theme free cls-positive cls-non-default cls-informal obj-explicit md-interactant md-non-addressee md-speaker non-addressee-ophon non-indicative cls-optative unkeyed ... md-speaker non-addressee-ophon non-indicative cls-optative unkeyed ...										-
		group complex rank	-		Goal/ Medium/ Complement/ Rheme1								-
					ngrp-complex ngrp-projection ngrp-hypotactic ngrp-matter...								
		group simplex rank	Actor/ Agent/ Subject/ Topical Theme		Qualifier/ Modifier1		Thing/ Head1			Means/ Adjunct/ Rheme2		Process/ Predicator/ Rheme3	-
			ngrp-simplex specific determinative nominal-head thematic-ngrp personal pronominal ngrp-participant-head general-theme-marker speaker ngrp-part-ga non-qualified ...		ngrp-simplex non-specific nominal ngrp-abstract non-thematic-ngrp ngrp-qualifier noun-qualifier non-qualified ...		ngrp-simplex non-thematic-ngrp nominal-head non-specific ngrp-participant-head nominal ngrp-part-o ngrp-concrete qualified ...			ngrp-simplex non-specific nominal ngrp-concrete non-thematic-ngrp nominal-head ngrp-circumstance-head ngrp-cir-de ...		vgrp-simplex ngrp-positive temporal non-past modal modulation redness-inclination optative ophon-tai non-causative active-voice ...	-
		word simplex rank	Thing/ Head1	Thematic-marker/ Nominal-marker/ Modifier1	Thing/ Head1	Binder/ Modifier1	Thing/ Head1		Nominal-marker/ Modifier1	Thing/ Head1	Nominal-marker/ Modifier1	Event/ Head1	Tense/ Modality/ Modifier1
			pronoun-ippan	j-kakari-zyoshi kakari-wa ...	common-sahen-setuzoku-noun ...	j-zyoshi-rentai-ka ...	common-noun-ippan hasei-go suffixation ...		j-case-marker case-o ...	common-noun-ippan ...	j-case-marker case-de ...	lexical-verb ...	auxiliary-verb aux-tai ...
		morpheme rank	1	1	1	1	Head1	Modifier1	1	1	1	1	1
			base ...	base ...	base ...	base ...	base ...	suffix ...	base ...	base ...	base ...	base ...	base ...
Semantic analysis		figure/move	ph-figure fig-non-projected fig-doing-to-with fig-creative agentive move-simplex role-assigning mb-goods-and-services command mb-demanding initiating ...										-
		sequence	-		Goal/ Medium								-
					sq-element sq-unequal sq-projection sq-locution ...								
		element	Actor/ Agent		Qualifier/ Modifier1		Thing/ Head1			Means		Process	-
			ph-participant simple-thing mb-conscious ...		ph-participant macro-thing ...		ph-participant simple-thing mb-non-conscious mb-material-object...			ph-circumstance...		ph-process...	-
Concept analysis			want-action(speaker = user, hearer = system, content = writing(agent = user, object = report(concern = business-trip()), instrument = word-processer())))										

verbs, the Japanese co-occurrence dictionary and the concept dictionary. Some word sense ambiguities may also be resolved in this phase. For instance, there are four records whose headword is "kaku" in GD. Each record has different concept identifier. After looking up EDR dictionary of selectional restrictions for Japanese verbs with reference to the concept identifier given to the verb record, we obtain specification of selectional restriction. By checking the consistency of the selectional restriction with the concept identifiers assigned to each word in the input sentence, we can reduce the four to one. Then, candidates of the SFL roles of each segment are obtained from the concept relation labels by referring to the mapping table in the GD record. For example, the 'implement' concept relation label is assigned to the fourth segment "waapuro-de" by looking up the concept dictionary, and this segment is identified to play 'Means' role for the fifth segment "kaki-tai" on which it depends.

3.3 Lexicogrammatical Analysis

The goal of this phase is the construction of the lexicogrammatical instance structure of the text. A lexicogrammatical instance structure is constructed by referring to the WB resource, i.e., the system networks and the realization statements. Our method is based on O'Donnell's idea realized in his WAG systemic parser [3], which uses data structures called partial-structures and a bottom-up chart parsing strategy. The phase can be divided into five steps as indicated in Fig. 4. We will explain each step in the following subsections.

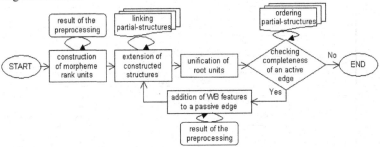

Fig. 4. Flow of lexicogrammatical analysis

3.3.1 Construction of Morpheme Rank Units
The first step is to construct morpheme rank units based on the result of the preprocessing. Of the lexicogrammatical features drawn from the preprocessing, the features that are located at the morpheme rank system network are assigned to each morpheme unit. For example, the fifth morpheme unit "hookoku" and the sixth "syo" are given WB feature "base" and "suffix" respectively.

3.3.2 Extension of the Constructed Instance Structure
The second step involves looking up the precompiled linking partial-structures explained in Section 2 and collecting the partial-structures that have compatible selection paths with the root unit of the constructed structures. We can find the partial-structures whose child unit contains "base" or "suffix" as shown below.

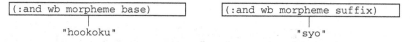

Fig. 5. Morpheme rank instance structures

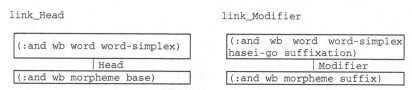

Fig. 6. Linking partial-structures for "base" and "suffix"

Fig. 7 shows the result of unification of the morpheme units into each of these linking partial-structures.

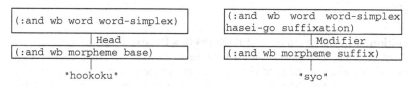

Fig. 7. Two morpheme and word rank instance structures

3.3.3 Unification of the Root Units of the Constructed Instance Structures

The third step is to attempt to unify the root units of the constructed instance structures. As indicated in Fig. 7, the parent units of "hookoku" and "syo" have compatible selection paths. Thus, we can unify these units, and this new unit corresponds to a word "hookokusyo". The units that have succeeded in unification are incorporated into the parse-chart as an active edge.

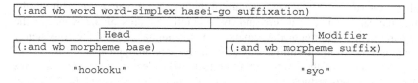

Fig. 8. One unified morpheme and word rank instance structure

3.3.4 Checking Completeness of an Active Edge

The fourth step involves looking up the precompiled ordering partial-structures explained in Section 2 and collecting the partial structures that contain the same features with the root unit of the active edge. Suppose the instance structure shown in Fig. 8 is currently in the chart as an active edge. In order to see whether this is completed or not, the following ordering partial-structure, which has the same selection path with "hookokusyo" unit, is relevant.

```
order_Head#Modifier
```

```
(:and wb word word-simplex hasei-go suffixation)
```
                              Head # Modifier

Fig. 9. Ordering partial-structure

This tells us that a given unit can have two child units, the one has Head role and the other has Modifier role, and the Head unit precedes the Modifier. As shown in Fig. 8, "hookokusyo" unit has two child units that meet such role restrictions. Therefore, the active edge in question can be regarded as completed. Then, this is incorporated into the chart as a passive edge and the fifth step is conducted.

If a given active edge is not completed, it needs to wait for other units to unify. The process starts reading the next morpheme boundary and constructing a new morpheme unit. As each morpheme unit is incorporated into the parse-chart, the parser then moves on to incorporate the next morpheme unit, until all morpheme units are incorporated.

3.3.5   Addition of Lexicogrammatical Features to a Passive Edge

The fifth step is to add lexicogrammatical features to the root unit of a passive edge by referring to the result of the preprocessing. Suppose the instance structure shown in Fig. 8 is currently in the chart as a passive edge. By referring to the result of GD lookup, we can add word rank features such as "common-noun" to the root unit "hookokusyo." Then, we go back to the second step, searching linking partial-structures whose child unit has compatible selection paths with the root of the passive edge to unify the edge with appropriate linking partial-structures.

Using these data structures and a unification algorithm for units, an instance structure is constructed from morpheme rank units in a bottom-up manner.

3.4   Semantic Analysis

In this phase, the semantic instance structure of the text is constructed referring to the lexicogrammatical instance structure and the semantic features of the words in the text. The parent/child relation of the semantic units is augmented and the consistency among them is verified in the similar way as in the lexicogrammatical analysis.

The current version of the implementation deals with *ideational* semantic features that characterize a proposition of a text [7], *interpersonal* semantic features that characterize a speech act [8], and *textual* features that characterize a rhetorical structure [9].

3.5   Conceptual Analysis

Finally, the conceptual analysis is conducted to create an instance concept frame representing the conceptual content of the input text. Slots of the instance concept are filled recursively by other instance concepts, which correspond to child segments of the text. Type constraints on slot fillers are checked according to both the class hierarchy of the concept repository and the EDR concept classification hierarchy that has richer contents for general concepts.

4 Discussion

SFL has been used successfully in text generation systems, e.g., [2, 10]. On the other hand, only several SFL-based text understanding systems have been developed. Most of them deal with small fragments of the whole theory due to implementation constraints [11, 12]. Others are approaches where systemic description of language is converted into the representation proposed by other grammatical theory such as HPSG [13, 14]. It does not seem that these systems fully utilize the theoretical features of SFL. One exception is WAG system [3], where a text is analyzed directly using SFL resources carefully compiled to cope with efficiency problems.

We extend the parsing method described in [3] in several significant ways. In particular, we incorporate the results of the preprocessing phase to add information to instance structures and filter out implausible interpretations. When a new inactive edge is added to the chart, an import of word information into the root unit of the edge is attempted. When an attempt to create a larger active edge by unifying the root unit of an inactive edge with a unit contained in a partial-structure or an active edge, unifications of feature/role information and a verification of consistency between the current instance structure and the dependency structure identified in the preprocessing phase, as well as the standard unification of feature selection paths [15] are performed. For example, as for nominal groups with a case particle "de", four linking partial-structures with role 'Means', 'Quality', 'TemporalLocation' and 'SpatialLocation' are compiled from the current WB network. However, only the first one is consistent with the preprocessing result and is used to construct the instance structure for this sentence.

We introduce *inter-stratal linking partial-structures* that declaratively represent the relationship between lexicogrammatical units and semantic ones. They are used to map instance structures from the lexicogrammatical stratum to the semantic stratum. Fig. 9 represents an example of inter-stratal linking partial-structures.

```
wblink_1
```

```
(:and mb grammatical-semantics non-rhetorical-unit
exchange move-simplex role-assigning initiating
mb-demanding mb-goods-and-services command)
```
```
(:and wb clause clause-simplex major-clause free
non-indicative cls-optative md-interactant
md-non-addressee non-addressee-option)
```

Fig. 10. Example of inter-stratal linking partial-structures

Moreover, we incorporate a forward chaining style of inferences to deal with *co-selection constraints* [2], a *gate* having only one feature and default feature selections.

5 Conclusion

The SB and the text understanding algorithm illustrated in this paper have been implemented in Java, and the results of the analyses are output as XML annotations on the input texts. The current version of the SB has approximately 700 systems, 1600 features, 1100 realization statements, 130 records in CR, and 70 records in GD. The system can analyze a nominal group complex that consists of more than one nominal group combined by particle "no," like "syuttyoo-no hookokusyo-o", a clause where obligatory unit, i.e., "watasi wa" in "watasi-wa syuttyoo-no hookokusyo-o waapuro-de kaki-tai," is elliptical, and a clause that contains optional unit "waapuro-de" in "watasi-wa syuttyoo-no hookokusyo-o waapuro-de kaki-tai." We have also implemented text generation system that utilizes the resources in the SB, and this assures us that the resources are reusable [16].

We extend O'Donnell's idea by adding a method for unifying the results of non-SFL-based NLP tools, and this enables us to deal with Japanese text. Our system can be regarded as a hybrid parser. Adopting SFL as the basis for the system enables us to deal with a wider range of language for linguistic analysis. By combining the existing parser and dictionary with the systemic resource, we aim at reducing the cost for system development and keeping the standard accuracy of the analysis.

We remark on limitations of the current work and future works. Regarding lexicogrammatical analysis, the resource for rankshift and grammatical metaphor is under construction, so the system may not construct appropriate instance structures of an input text with adnominal clause, embedded clause or nominalization. As for contextual analysis, the system can deal with concepts manifested in a text referring to CR. Algorithm for inferring contextual configuration from linguistic behavior with reference to the entire SB has been under design. These points will be resolved in future works.

References

1. Halliday, M. A. K.: An Introduction to Functional Grammar. 2nd edn. Edward Arnold, London (1994)
2. Matthiessen, C. M. I. M., Bateman, J. A.: Text Generation and Systemic-Functional Linguistics: Experiences from English and Japanese. Pinter, London (1991)
3. O'Donnell, M.: Sentence Analysis and Generation: A Systemic Perspective. PhD dissertation, Department of Linguistics, University of Sydney, Sydney (1994)
4. Sugimoto, T., Ito, N., Fujishiro, H., Sugeno, M.: Dialogue Management with the Semiotic Base: A Systemic Functional Linguistic Approach. Proc. of 1st International Conference on Soft Computing and Intelligent Systems (SCIS 2002), Tsukuba (2002)
5. Japan Electronic Dictionary Research Institute Ltd.: EDR Dictionary. Japan Electronic Dictionary Research Institute, Ltd., Tokyo, Japan (2001)
6. Kudo, T., Matsumoto, Y.: Japanese Dependency Analysis Using Cascaded Chunking. Proc. of 6th Conference on Natural Language Learning, Taipei, Taiwan (2002)
7. Halliday, M. A. K., Matthiessen, C. M. I. M.: Construing Experience through Meaning: A Language-Based Approach to Cognition. Cassell, London (1999)
8. Matthiessen, C. M. I. M.: Lexicogrammatical Cartography: English Systems. International Language Science Publishers, Tokyo (1995)

9. Mann, W. C., Matthiessen, C. M. I. M., Thompson, S. A.: Rhetorical Structure Theory and Text Analysis. In: Mann, W., Thomson, S. A. (eds.): Discourse Description: Diverse Linguistic Analyses of a Fund-Raising Text. Amsterdam, John Benjamins (1992) 39-78

10. Fawcett, R. P., Gordon, T. H., Lin, Y. Q.: How Systemic Functional Grammar Works: The Role of Realization in Realization. In: Horacek, H., Zock, M. (eds.): New Concepts in Natural Language Generation: Planning, Realization and Systems. London, Pinter (1993) 114-186

11. Winograd, T.: Understanding Natural Language. Academic Press (1972)

12. O'Donoghue, T. F.: Semantic Interpretation in a Systemic Functional Grammar. In: Strzalkowski, T. (ed.): Reversible Grammar in Natural Language Processing. Boston, Kluwer Academic Publishers (1994) 415-447

13. Kasper, R. T.: An Experimental Parser for Systemic Grammars. Proc. of COLING-88 (1988)

14. Bateman, J. A., Emele, M., Momma, S.: The Nondirectional Representation of Systemic Functional Grammars and Semantics as Typed Feature Structures. Proc. of COLING-92 (1992)

15. Kasper, R. T.: A Unification Method for Disjunctive Feature Descriptions. Proc. of 26th annual meeting of ACL (1987)

16. Ito, N., Sugimoto, T., Takahashi, Y., Kobayashi, I.: Algorithms for Text Processing with the Semiotic Base. Proc. of 17th annual conference of the Japanese Society for Artificial Intelligence, Niigata (2003)

Building and Using
a Russian Resource Grammar in GF

Janna Khegai and Aarne Ranta

Department of Computing Science
Chalmers University of Technology and Gothenburg University
SE-41296, Gothenburg, Sweden
{janna, aarne}@cs.chalmers.se

Abstract. Grammatical Framework (GF) [5] is a grammar formalism
for describing formal and natural languages. An application grammar
in GF is usually written for a restricted language domain, e.g. to map
a formal language to a natural language. A resource grammar, on the
other hand, aims at a complete description of a natural languages. The
language-independent grammar API (Application Programmer's Interface) allows the user of a resource grammar to build application grammars in the same way as a programmer writes programs using a standard library. In an ongoing project, we have developed an API suitable
for technical language, and implemented it for English, Finnish, French,
German, Italian, Russian, and Swedish. This paper gives an outline of
the project using Russian as an example.

1 The GF Resource Grammar Library

The Grammatical Framework (GF) is a grammar formalism based on type theory
[5]. GF grammars can be considered as programs written in the GF grammar
language, which can be compiled by the GF program. Just as with ordinary
programming languages, the efficiency of programming labor can be increased by
reusing previously written code. For that purpose standard libraries are usually
used. To use the library a programmer only needs to know the type signatures
of the library functions. Implementation details are hidden from the user.

The GF resource grammar library [4] is aimed to serve as a standard library
for the GF grammar language. It aims at fairly complete descriptions of different
natural languages, starting from the perspective of linguistics structure rather
the logical structure of applications. The current coverage is comparable with,
but still smaller than, the Core Language Engine (CLE) project [2].

Since GF is a multilingual system the library structure has an additional
dimension for different languages. Each language has its own layer, produced by
visible to the linguist grammarian. What is visible to the application grammarian
is a an API (Application Programmer's Interface), which abstracts away from
linguistic details and is therefore, to a large extent, language-independent. The
module structure of a resource grammar layer corresponding to one language is
shown in Fig. 1. Arrows indicate the dependencies among the modules.

A. Gelbukh (Ed.): CICLing 2004, LNCS 2945, pp. 38–41, 2004.
© Springer-Verlag Berlin Heidelberg 2004

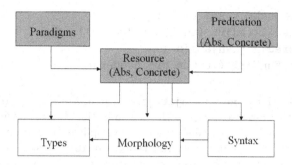

Fig. 1. The resource grammar structure (main modules). One language layer. Shadowed boxes represent high-level of interface modules. White boxes represent low-level or implementation modules. Arrows show the dependencies.

The Russian grammar was written after grammars for English, Swedish, French and German. The language-independent modules, defining the coverage of the resource library, were therefore ready. The task was to instantiate these modules for Russian. As a reference for Russian language, [3,6,7] were used.

2   An Example: Arithmetic Grammar

Here we consider some fragments from a simple arithmetic grammar written using the Russian resource grammar library, which allows us to construct statements like *one is even* or *the product of zero and one equals zero*.

The abstract part describes the meaning captured in this arithmetic grammar. This is done by defining some categories and functions:

```
cat
  Prop ;                        -- proposition
  Dom ;                         -- domain of quantification
  Elem Dom ;                    -- individual element of a domain
fun
  zero : Elem Nat ;                  -- zero constructor
  Even : Elem Nat -> Prop ;          -- evenness predicate
  EqNat : (m,n : Elem Nat) -> Prop ; -- equality predicate
  prod : (m,n : Elem Nat) -> Elem Nat ; -- product function
```

To linearize the semantic categories and functions of the application grammar, we use grammatical categories and functions from the resource grammar:

```
lincat
  Dom = N ; -- Common Noun category
  Prop = S ; -- Sentence category
  Elem = NP ; -- Noun Phrase category
lin
```

```
zero = DefOneNP (UseN nol) ;
Even = predA1 (AdjP1 (adj1Star "четн"));
EqNat = predV2 ravnjatsja ;
prod = appFunColl (funGen proizvedenie) ;
```

Some of the functions—nol, ravnjatsja, and proizvedenie—are lexical entities defined in the resource, ready with their inflectional forms ((which can mean
dozens of forms in Russian), gender, etc. The application grammarian just has
to pick the right ones. Some other functions—adj1Star—are lexical inflection
patterns. To use them, one has to provide the word stem and choose the correct
pattern.

The rest of the functions are from the language-independent API. Here are
their type signatures:

```
AdjP1 : Adj1 -> AP ;                      -- adjective from lexicon
predA1 : AP -> VP ;                       -- adjectival predication
DefOneNP : CN -> NP ;                     -- singular definite phrase
UseN : N -> CN ;                          -- noun from lexicon
appFamColl : Fun -> NP -> NP -> NP ; -- collective function appl
predV2 : V2 -> NP -> NP -> NP -> S ; -- two-place verb predic
```

The user of the library has to be familiar with notions of constituency, but not
with linguistic details such as inflection, agreement, and word order.

Writing even a small grammar in inflectionally rich language like Russian
requires a lot of work on morphology. This is the part where using the resource
grammar library really helps to speed up, since the resource functions for adding
new lexical entries are relatively easy to use.

Syntactic rules are more tricky and require fair knowledge of the type system
used. However, they heighten the level of the code written by using only function
application. The resource style is also less error prone, since the correctness of
the library functions is presupposed.

Using the resource grammar API, an application grammar can be implemented for different languages in a similar manner, since there is a shared
language-independent API part and also because the libraries for different languages have similar structures. Often the same API functions can be used in
different languages; but it may also happen that e.g. adjectival predication in
one language is replaced by verbal predication in another.

Fig. 2 shows a simple theorem proof constructed by using the arithmetic
grammars for Russian and English. The example was built with help of GF
Syntax Editor [1].

3   Conclusion

A library of resource grammars is essential for a wider use of GF. In a grammar formalism, libraries are even more important than in a general-purpose
programming language, since writing grammars for natural languages is such a

/* Теорема . Для любого числа x , x - четный или x - нечетный . Доказательство .
Доказательство по индукции. Базис, Согласно первой аксиоме четности , ноль - четное число .
Тем более , ноль - четный или ноль - нечетный . Шаг индукции, рассмотрим число x и
предположим x - четный или x - нечетный (h) . h . Возможно два случая . Первый случай,
допустим x - четный (a) . a . Согласно второй аксиоме четности, число, следующее за x -
нечетное . Тем более , число , следующее за x - четное или число , следующее за x - нечетное .
Второй случай, допустим x - нечетный (b) . b . Согласно третьей аксиоме четности, число,
следующее за x - четное . Тем более , число , следующее за x - четное или число , следующее
за x - нечетное . Т.о. число , следующее за x - четное или число , следующее за x - нечетное В
обоих случаях. Следовательно, для всех чисел x , x - четный или x - нечетный . */

****

Theorem. For all numbers x, x is even or x is odd.

Proof. We proceed by induction. For the basis, by the first axiom of evenness, zero is even. A
fortiori, zero is even or zero is odd. For the induction step, consider a number x and assume x is even
or x is odd (h). By the hypothesis h, x is even or x is odd. There are two possibilities. First, assume x
is even (a). By the hypothesis a, x is even. By the second axiom of evenness, the successor of x is
odd. A fortiori, the successor of x is even or the successor of x is odd. Second, assume x is odd (b).
By the hypothesis b, x is odd. By the third axiom of evenness, the successor of x is even. A fortiori, the
successor of x is even or the successor of x is odd. Thus the successor of x is even or the successor
of x is odd in both cases Hence, for all numbers x, x is even or x is odd.

Text

Fig. 2. Example of a theorem proof constructed using arithmetic grammars in Russian and English.

special kind of programming: it is easier to find a programmer who knows how to write a sorting algorithm than one who knows how to write a grammar for Russian relative clauses. To make GF widely used outside the latter group of programmers, resource grammars have to be created. Experience has shown that resource grammars for seemingly very different languages can share an API by which different grammars can be accessed in the same way. As a part of future work on the resource libraries, it remains to see how much divergent extensions of the common API are needed for different languages.

References

1. J. Khegai, B. Nordström, and A. Ranta. Multilingual syntax editing in GF. In A. Gelbukh, editor, *CICLing-2003, Mexico City, Mexico*, LNCS, pages 453–464. Springer, 2003.
2. M. Rayner, D. Carter, P. Bouillon, V. Digalakis, and M. Wirén. *The spoken language translator.* Cambridge University Press, 2000.
3. I.M. Pulkina. *A Short Russian Reference Grammar.* Russky Yazyk, Moscow, 1984.
4. A. Ranta. The GF Resource grammar library, 2002. http://tournesol.cs.chalmers.se/aarne/GF/resource/.
5. A. Ranta. Grammatical Framework: A Type-theoretical Grammar Formalism. *The Journal of Functional Programming*, to appear.
6. M.A. Shelyakin. *Spravochnik po russkoj grammatike* (in Russian). Russky Yazyk, Moscow, 2000.
7. T. Wade. *A Comprehensive Russian Grammar.* Blackwell Publishing, 2000.

An Application of a Semantic Framework for the Analysis of Chinese Sentences

Li Tang, Donghong Ji, Yu Nie, and Lingpeng Yang

Institute for Infocomm Research
21 Heng Mui Keng Terrace, Singapore 119613
{tangli, dhji, niey, lpying}@ i2r.a-star.edu.sg

Abstract. Analyzing the semantic representations of 10000 Chinese sentences and describing a new sentence analysis method that evaluates semantic preference knowledge, we create a model of semantic representation analysis based on the correspondence between lexical meanings and conceptual structures, and relations that underlie those lexical meanings. We also propose a semantical argument-head relation that combines 'basic conceptual structure' and 'Head-Driven Principle'. With this framework which is different from Fillmore's case theory (1968) and HPSG among other, we can successfully disambiguate some troublesome sentences, and minimize the redundancy in language knowledge description for natural language processing.

1   Introduction

To enable computer-based analysis of Chinese sentences in natural language texts we have developed a semantic framework, using the English language framework created by C. Fillmore et al. at UC Berkeley as a starting point. The theoretical framework developed in this paper is different from other syntactic and semantic frameworks (e.g. Case Grammer and HPSG). First, those syntactic and semantic frameworks in the literature are either purely syntactic or purely semantic. Our framework is largely a semantic one, but it has adopted some crucial principles of syntactic analysis in the semantic structure analysis. Secondly, some crucial semantic relationships as exemplified in (1) below are reasonably represented which are often neglected in Case Grammar and HPSP. Third, our proposal is based mainly on our own practical large scale analysis of Chinese data. We are planning to apply the same framework to analyze other languages. The overall goal is to offer for each natural sentence a representation of semantic relation labeling.

2   Semantic Relation Labeling

This workflow includes linking and manual labeling of each relation between direct semantic units in single sentences, which reflects different semantic representation of the potential realization patterns identified in the formula, and descriptions of the relations of each frame's basic conceptual structure in terms of semantic actions. For

A. Gelbukh (Ed.): CICLing 2004, LNCS 2945, pp. 42–45, 2004.
© Springer-Verlag Berlin Heidelberg 2004

example, the direct relationships of different semantic units in sentence (1) below can be labeled as follows:

(1) Ta   xiao   tong-le   duzi
     He   laugh   painful -ASP belly
     'He laughed so much that his belly was painful.'

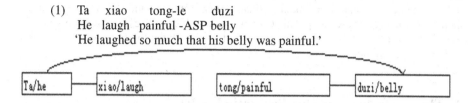

Within the Case Grammar model, the main verb 'laugh' will be taken as the core semantic unit and all other noun units are directly associated with this verb. Note an analysis in that framework mistakenly neglects the immediate relationship between 'he' as a possessor and 'belly' as a possession and that between 'belly' as entity and 'painful' as description. Our approach clearly recognizes those relationships while the central nature of the verb is also specified.

Link rule 1: Direct Relations Determination. The basic link is the direct link between two semantic units. In addition, a set of general rules for determining the direct relations has been identified. There are summarized into three major conditions. 1. A case of direct relationship between head and its modifier; 2. A case of direct relationship between an action verb and its patient; 3. Other cases of direct relationships.

Link rule 2: 'Head' Determination. We have proposed an approach that combines 'basic conceptual structure' and 'Head-Driven Principle'. By 'Head-Driven Principle', most structures are analyzed as having a 'Head' modified. The exceptions are 'Subject-Predicate Structure' and 'Verb-Object Structure'. Employing the 'Head-Driven Principle' for the construction of semantic model, some ambiguous sentences can be clearly represented.

3 Feature Labeling

Based on the analysis of semantic relationships, we have been parsing feature structures to express dependencies between semantic features. To avoid the confusion of feature classification, we use the features directly included in the sentences. By abstracting, we take the features exemplified in sentences directly as semantic features that link different semantic units in those sentences. For example:

(3) Ta gezi bu gao.
    His stature isn't tall.
    He isn't tall.

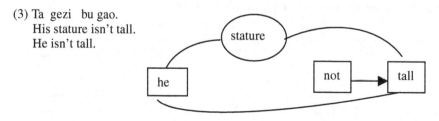

In traditional analysis, 'stature' is just a syntactic constituent in a sentence. However, the essential meaning of the sentence is 'he is not tall', 'stature' is semantic feature linking 'he' and 'tall' together, thus in our semantic analysis we link only 'he' and 'tall' semantically, 'stature' is taken as feature marking a semantic relationship, rather than an immediate constituent. This Chinese semantic structure, after feature abstraction, is very similar to its English counterpart. It facilitates the translation from one language into another.

4   The Advantages of Our Semantic Model

In developing our semantic tree bank, we also have articulated a framework of 'Noun-Centrality' as a supplement to the widely assumed 'Verb-Centrality' practice. We can successfully disambiguate some troublesome sentences, and minimize the redundancy in language knowledge description for natural language processing. We automatically learn a simpler, less redundant representation of the same information. First, one semantic structure may correspond to more syntactic structures in Chinese, and this correspondence can be made specifically clear using our approach.

(4) Ta da po-le beizi   (5) Ta ba beizi da po-le   (6) Beizi BEI Ta da po-le
    She broke up the cup   She BA cup broke up   cup BEI she broke up
    'She broke up the cup.'   'She broke up the cup.'   'The cup has been broken
                                                                     up by her.'

The syntactic structures of the above three sentences are clearly different from each other. But they nevertheless share the same basic semantic structure: 'he' is the AGENT, 'cup' is the PATIENT, and 'break up' is the ACTION verb.

On the other hand, one syntactic structure may correspond to two or more semantic structures, that is, various forms of structural ambiguity are widely observed in Chinese. Disregarding the semantic types will cause syntactic ambiguity. If this type of information is not available during parsing, important clues will be missing, and loss of accuracy will result. Consider (5) below.

(5) Ta de yifu zuo de piaoliang.
    Her cloth do DE beautiful
    Reading 1: 'She has made the cloth beautifully
    Reading 2: (Somebody) has made her cloth beautifully.'

Syntactically, the sentence, with either one of the above two semantic interpretations, should be analyzed having 'her cloth' as a subject, 'do' as a verb, and 'beautiful' as a complement. But the two semantic structures have to be properly represented in a semantics-oriented Treebank. Under our proposal, the above two different types of semantic relations can be clearly represented as follows.

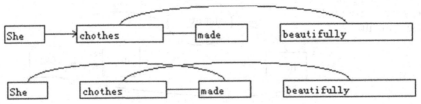

5 Conclusion

We have demonstrated several key advantages of our semantic model, which are: a) many ambiguous sentences can be clearly represented, b) minimal redundancy in language knowledge description for natural language processing.

References

1. Baker C, Fillmore C, Lower J 1998 The Berkeley FrameNet Project, In *Proc. of ACL/COLING 1998.*
2. Brew C 1995 Stochastic HPSG. In *Proc. of 7th Conf. of the Europ. Chapter of the Assoc. for Comput. Linguistics (EACL 95)*, pp. 83–89.

A Modal Logic Framework for Human-Computer Spoken Interaction

Luis Villaseñor-Pineda[1], Manuel Montes-y-Gómez[1], and Jean Caelen[2]

[1] Instituto Nacional de Astrofísica, Óptica y Electrónica (INAOE), Mexico.
{villasen,mmontesg}@inaoep.mx
[2] Laboratoire CLIPS-IMAG, Université Joseph Fourier, France.
jean.caelen@imag.fr

Abstract. One major goal of human computer interfaces is to simplify the communication task. Traditionally, users have been restricted to the language of computers for this task. With the emerging of the graphical and multimodal interfaces the effort required for working with a computer is decreasing. However, the problem of communication is still present, and users continue caring about the communication task when they deal with a computer. Our work focuses on improving the communication between the human and the computer. This paper presents the foundations of a multimodal dialog model based on a modal logic, which integrates the speech and the action under the same framework.

Keywords: Human computer spoken interaction, speech acts, multimodal interaction, and modal logic.

1 Introduction

The first dialog systems used the speech as the unique communication channel. However, the human communication is strongly *multimodal*. The lips movement, the facial expressions, and the gestures are all of them key elements in the human interchange of information.

Current multimodal dialog systems attempt to integrate several communication modalities along with the speech. The construction of this kind of systems is a complex task [8, 10, 13]. It considers several problems such as: speech recognition, natural language understanding, knowledge representation, fusion of the different input modalities in a coherent message, the definition of a dialog model and others.

This paper focuses on the definition of a dialog model. It presents the foundations of a *multimodal dialog model* based on a modal logic, which represent the rules of the conversation and integrates in the same framework the direct actions (those accomplished with a device of direct designation such as the mouse) and the spoken ones (those orally requested by the user to the machine). This consideration is of great relevance because the spoken actions are not performed immediately such as the direct ones. Thus, the evolution of a spoken action must be controlled during the dialog: from the moment it is proposed until the time it is satisfied.

The proposed model is supported by the theory of speech acts [1, 12]. It is based on the hypothesis that the dialog is conduced by the mental states that maintain the beliefs, desires and intentions of the user. Nevertheless, this model does not attempt to

A. Gelbukh (Ed.): CICLing 2004, LNCS 2945, pp. 46–55, 2004.
© Springer-Verlag Berlin Heidelberg 2004

set a human behavior to the machine, but only to give it the logical elements to hold its actions [2]. The idea of treating the speech as an action is not original (see for instance [3–6, 9]), however our logic implements a general mechanism in which the spoken action is controlled over all the dialogic interchange. This way, it models the *convergence* of a cooperative dialog [18].

The paper is organized as follows. Section 2 presents the complete logic framework. Section 3 shows a short but illustrative example of a dialog conduced by the proposed logic. Finally, Section 4 discusses our conclusions and future work.

2 A Logic for the Dialog

This section presents the basis of a logic that models the information interchange between a user and a machine. This logic, inspired by previous works [2, 4, 7, 11, 14–17], proposes the integration of the *dialog acts* in a framework based on the action. It contains elements of an epistemological logic – to represent the knowledge, a dynamic logic – to describe the action and its effects, and a dialogical logic – to represent the obligations and intentions expressed during the dialog.

2.1 Basic Concepts

This subsection defines the three basic concepts of our logic: knowledge, action and intention.

The *knowledge* is represented by the operator s (to know). For instance, the formula $Us\ \varphi$ expresses that the user knows the proposition φ (to make the distinction between the user and the machine, the two possible agents of our logic, we used the letter U for the user and M for the machine).

In order to represent the *action*, we introduce the notion of an event. An event $Uf\ \alpha$ is the achievement of the action α by the user (or $Mf\ \alpha$ in the case of the machine), which has the proposition φ as result. Using the notation of a dynamic logic we have the following formula $[Uf\ \alpha\ ]\ \varphi$. This formula indicates that after the execution of α by the user, φ is true. An action can be a base action, i.e., an elemental instruction, or even a task, i.e., a sequence of actions organized by a plan.

The *intention* is represented by the operator i. Only the user is capable of having intentions, thus the formula $Ui\ \varphi$ expresses the intention of the user to make φ true.

2.2 Dialog Acts

A *dialog act* is an action causing a change in, on one hand, the task or the machine knowledge about the task, and on the other hand, the dialog itself. Hence, a dialog act is defined as an event $[Uf\ \alpha](\ \varphi_a \wedge \varphi_d\ )$, where the result is the set of changes related with the task φ_a and with the dialog φ_d.

The changes related with the task are the own effects of the action (φ_a), while the changes related with the dialog φ_d shows the progress in the dialog state after each interchange of information. In our case, the goal of any dialog is to complete the task intended by the user. This way, each dialog act produces an effect over the goal (φ_d).

Further, the effects of a spoken action depend on the comprehension of the action by the receptor (who may not understand or even perform an erroneous operation), and consequently, they are not always predictable. In other words, the effects of a spoken action only make sense when they are related with the intentions of the speaker. Thus, the evolution of a spoken action must be controlled during the dialog: from the moment it is *proposed* until the time it is *satisfied*. For this reason we define the following states for an action:

?   Proposed goal; an action to be perform it.
+   Reached goal; an accomplished action with no confirmation.
++   Satisfied goal; a completed (and correct) action.
@   Aborted goal.

The dialog acts are expressed, by means of direct and spoken actions, as follows:

Uf α, *Mf* α	the user or the machine performs α.
Uff α, *Mff* α	the user asks the machine to perform the action α (or vice versa)
Ufs ϕ, *Mfs* ϕ	the user informs ϕ to the machine (or vice versa)
Uffs ϕ, *Mffs* ϕ	the user asks the machine to inform ϕ (or vice versa)

where the action *fs* is an abbreviation of the base action *to share*: *Ufs* $\phi \equiv$ *Uf share* ϕ.

2.3 Definition of the Language L_d

Definition 1. If T is the set of propositional symbols, *Ab* a finite set of base actions, U the symbol to named the user and M the machine, then the language L_d is defined as follows:

L_d is the smallest subset of T such that:
- if φ, $\psi \in L_d$ then $\neg\varphi$, $\varphi \vee \psi \in L_d$
- if $\alpha \in Ac$, y $\varphi \in L_d$ then
-     $Us\ \varphi$, $Ms\ \varphi$, $[Uf\ \alpha]\varphi$, $[Mf\ \alpha]\varphi$, $Ui\ \varphi \in L_d$

where *Ac* is the smallest subset of *Ab*, such that:
- if $\alpha \in Ab$ then $\alpha \in Ac$
- if $\varphi \in L_d$ then *verify*$(\varphi) \in Ac$
- if $\alpha \in Ac$ and $\beta \in Ac$ then α ;$\beta \in Ac$

We use the abbreviated notations $\varphi \wedge \psi$ for $\neg(\neg\varphi \vee \neg\psi)$ and $\varphi \supset \psi$ for $\neg(\varphi \wedge \neg\psi)$. The *true* abbreviation is considered as a valid formula, e.g. $\varphi \vee \neg\varphi$, and *false* as an abbreviation of $\neg true$.

Definition 2. The semantic of the language L_d. The class **M** of the models of Kripke contains all the tuples $M = <S, \pi, R_U, R_M, I_U, r_U, r_M>$ such that:

i) S is the set of possible worlds, or states.

ii) π is a function that assigns truth values to the propositional symbols of T in a possible state s ($\pi(s) : T \rightarrow \{1,0\}$ for all $s \in S$).

iii) R_U is a binary relation among the possible states of S. It is the relation of accessibility to the user knowledge ($R_U \subseteq S \times S$)

iv) R_M is a binary relation among the possible states of S. It is the relation of accessibility to the machine knowledge ($R_M \subseteq S \times S$)

v) I_U is a binary relation among the possible states of S. It is the relation of accessibility to the user intentions ($I_U \subseteq S \times S$)

vi) r_U is a relation among the set of possible states caused by the accomplishment of the action α by the user in a possible state s, ($r_U : Ac \times S \rightarrow \wp(S)$)

vii) r_M is a relation among the set of possible states caused by the accomplishment of the action α by the machine in a possible state s, ($r_M : Ac \times S \rightarrow \wp(S)$)

Definition 3. Let $M = <S, \pi, R_U, R_M, I_U, r_U, r_M>$ be a Kripke model of class **M**. The truth value of a proposition ($\models$) in a possible state s, based on the model M, is inductively defined as follows:

$$
\begin{aligned}
&M, s \models \varphi &&\text{iff } \pi(s)(\varphi) = 1 \text{ for } \varphi \in T \\
&M, s \models \neg\varphi &&\text{iff } M, s \not\models \varphi \\
&M, s \models \varphi \vee \phi &&\text{iff } M, s \models \varphi \text{ or } M, s \models \phi \\
&M, s \models [Uf\,\alpha]\,\varphi &&\text{iff } \forall s' \, [s' \in r_U(\alpha, s) \Rightarrow M, s' \models \varphi\,] \\
&M, s \models [Mf\,\alpha]\,\varphi &&\text{iff } \forall s' \, [s' \in r_M(\alpha, s) \Rightarrow M, s' \models \varphi\,] \\
&M, s \models Us\,\varphi &&\text{iff } \forall s' \, [(s, s') \in R_U \Rightarrow M, s' \models \varphi\,] \\
&M, s \models Ms\,\varphi &&\text{iff } \forall s' \, [(s, s') \in R_M \Rightarrow M, s' \models \varphi\,] \\
&M, s \models Ui\,\varphi &&\text{iff } \forall s' \, [(s, s') \in I_U \Rightarrow M, s' \models \varphi\,]
\end{aligned}
$$

where r_U and r_M, denoted as r_A for their equivalence and shake of simplicity, are defined by:

$$
\begin{aligned}
r_A(\,\text{verify}(\varphi), s) \quad &= \{s\} \text{ if } M, s \models \varphi \\
&= \varnothing \text{ in other case} \\
r_A(\,(\alpha; \beta), s) \quad &= r_A(\beta, r_A(\alpha, s))
\end{aligned}
$$

2.4   Definition of the Axioms

This subsection presents the main axioms of our logic. The first part describes the axioms about the knowledge, the second part introduces some concepts related with the goal evolution, and the third part explains the axioms about the cooperative dialog.

2.4.1   Knowledge Characterization

The following axioms describe the machine and the user knowledge, and for the case of the machine, they characterize it knowledge about the user intentions.

Let $A = \{U, M\}$:

(A1) $As\,\varphi \wedge As(\varphi \supset \phi) \supset As\,\phi$ axiom K

(A2) $As \; \varphi \supset \varphi$
The user and the machine just know true facts

(A3) $As \; \varphi \supset As \; As \; \varphi$ *positive introspection*
The user and the machine know the facts that they know

(A4) $\neg As \; \varphi \supset As \; \neg As \; \varphi$ *negative introspection*
The user and the machine know the facts they do not know

2.4.2   Goal Evolution

In our model, the structure of the dialog is based on the user intention. This intention is expresses as an action (or plan), which its effect is the desired final state. Thus, the realization of a dialog act generally produces a movement to the goal. This movement depends on the current situation and in the dialog act. It is represented by three states: (i) *a proposed goal*, when the user orders the machine the execution of an action (*Uff*), or asks it for an information (*Uffs*); (ii) a *reached goal*, when the machine responds (*Mfs*), or execute the requested action (*Mf*); (iii) finally, a *satisfied goal*, when the user is pleased with the machine response. Of course, the user can abort a goal at any moment. The following paragraphs describe this evolution at detail.

The User Asks the Machine to Perform an Action

i)   A *proposed goal* is the effect of a user request. It is expressed as a user intention (that the machine performs some action) integrated with the machine knowledge.

$$[Uff \; \alpha] \; (\; Ms \; Ui \; [Mf \; \alpha] \varphi) \; \equiv \; [Uff \; \alpha] \; (\; ? \; [Mf \; \alpha] \varphi)$$

Here the abbreviation *?Mf α* designates the action *Mf α* as a proposed goal.

ii)   A *reached goal* emerges when the action requested by the user becomes true.

$$Ms \; Ui \; [Mf \; \alpha] \varphi \wedge [Mf \; \alpha] \varphi$$
$$\equiv \; ? \; [Mf \; \alpha] \varphi \wedge [Mf \; \alpha] \varphi$$
$$\equiv \; + [Mf \; \alpha] \varphi$$

where the abbreviation *+Mf α* designates the action *Mf α* as a reached goal.

iii) A *satisfied goal* materializes when the user admits the action of the machine as acceptable. This acceptation can be explicit (when the user informs that his intention is no more related with the proposed action), or even implicit (when the user asks the machine to perform a different action – not related with the previous one).

$$Ms \; Ui \; [Mf \; \alpha] \varphi \wedge ([Ufs \; U\neg i \; [Mf \; \alpha] \varphi] \phi \vee ([Uff \; \beta] \gamma \wedge \neg rel(\varphi,\beta)))$$
$$\equiv \; ? \; [Mf \; \alpha] \varphi \; \wedge ([Ufs \; U\neg i \; [Mf \; \alpha] \varphi] \phi \vee ([Uff \; \beta] \gamma \wedge \neg \; rel(\varphi,\beta)))$$
$$\equiv \; ++ [Mf \; \alpha] \varphi$$

Here, the abbreviation *++Mf α* designates the action *Mf α* as a satisfied goal.

iv) An *aborted goal* occurs when the user informs the machine that his desire is no more the achievement of the action in progress.

$$Ms \; Ui \; [Mf \; \alpha] \varphi \wedge (Ufs \; Ui \; [M \neg f \; \alpha] \varphi)$$

$$\equiv \ ? \ [Mf \ \alpha] \varphi \wedge (Ufs \ Ui \ [M\neg f \ \alpha] \varphi)$$
$$\equiv \ @ \ [Mf \ \alpha] \varphi$$

Here, the abbreviation @$Mf \ \alpha$ designates the action $Mf \ \alpha$ as an aborted goal.

The User Asks the Machine to Inform Something

In this case (a question $Uffs$), the goal has the same evolution that in the previous one, but the machine response is of the type Mfs. It is necessary to remember that ffs is a short form for ff *share*, where to share is a base action.

$$[Uffs \ \phi] \ (Ms \ Ui \ [Mfs \ \phi])$$
$$\equiv \ [Uffs \ \phi] \ (? \ [Mfs \ \phi] \varphi)$$

Here the abbreviation ?$Mfs \ \phi$ designates the sharing of information $Mfs \ \phi$ as a proposed goal.

The Machine Asks the User to Inform Something

In this framework for human computer interaction, the machine has no intentions. However, it can take some initiative when the information required to complete a task is incomplete. Basically, the machine can generate a subdialog in order to request some complementary information to the user. Different to a user request, the evolution of a subgoal proposed by the machine has just the following two stages.

i) A *proposed subgoal* is the effect of a machine request for complementary information to the user.

$$[Mffs \ \phi] \ (Ms \ Ui \ [Ufs \ \phi] \varphi) \ \equiv \ [Mffs \ \phi] \ (\ ? \ [Ufs \ \phi] \varphi)$$

Here the abbreviation ?$Ufs \ \phi$ designates the action $Ufs \ \phi$ as a proposed subgoal.

ii) A *reached*, and consequently, *satisfied subgoal* materializes when the answer waited for the machine is true.

$$Ms \ Ui \ [Ufs \ \phi] \varphi \wedge [Ufs \ \phi] \varphi$$
$$\equiv \ ? \ [Ufs \ \phi] \varphi \wedge [Ufs \ \phi] \varphi$$
$$\equiv \ ++ \ [Ufs \ \phi] \varphi$$

Here the abbreviation ++$Ufs \ \phi$ designates the action $Ufs \ \phi$ as a satisfied subgoal.

iii) An aborted subgoal occurs when the user informs the machine that he will not answer the given request.

$$Ms \ Ui \ [Ufs \ \phi] \varphi \wedge [Ufs \ [U\neg fs \ \phi] \ \varphi] \ ?$$
$$\equiv \ ? \ [Ufs \ \phi] \varphi \ \wedge [Ufs \ [U\neg fs \ \phi] \varphi] ?$$
$$\equiv \ @ \ [Ufs \ \phi] \varphi$$

Here, the abbreviation @ $Ufs \ \phi$ designates the action $Ufs \ \phi$ as an aborted goal.

2.4.3 Cooperative Dialog

As explained in the above sections, the cooperative dialog is produced around a task, where the machine is just a collaborator in it achievement. In our case, the machine has the obligation to resolve the proposed goal, for that it will be necessary its spoken intervention when lack the information to complete the task. The following axioms describe the cooperative dialog under these considerations.

The Machine Is Obligated to Reach the Proposed Goal

If the user orders the realization of a task, and the machine knows the plan (*Msf*, knows how to do it), then the machine executes this plan

(A5.i) $? [Mf\,\alpha]\varphi \,\wedge\, Msf\,\alpha \wedge \alpha \in Ab \supset [Mf\,\alpha]\,\varphi$
   for a base action (i.e. elementary instruction)

(A5.ii) $? [Mf(\beta_1; \beta_2)](\,\varphi_1 \wedge \varphi_2\,) \wedge Msf\,\beta_1 \supset [Mf\,\beta_1]\,(\varphi_1 \wedge [Uff\,\beta_2]\,(\,? [Mf\,\beta_2]\varphi_2))$
   for a complex task (i.e. a sequence of basic actions)

The Ignorance of the Machine Generates a Question

In this case, the machine knows the proposed task, but requires more information to accomplish it. Consequently, the task must be stopped until the information is completed. The machine executes two complementary actions before the tasks: (1) it asks the user about the required information, and (2) it verifies the user answer.

(A6) $? [Mf\,\alpha]\varphi \,\wedge\, Msf\,\alpha \wedge M\neg s\; parameter(\alpha,\, \phi) \supset$
       $? [Mffs\; parameter(\alpha,\, \phi)]$
             $(? [Ufs\; parameter(\alpha,\, \phi)]\; ;$
               $verify(++Ufs\; parameter(\alpha,\, \phi); [Mf\,\alpha]\,\varphi)$

3   A Brief Example

The following example shows the structure of a short dialog where the interchanges of information converge to a goal in a world of design. For this example, we take a small fragment of a dialog from the DIME corpus [19]. This corpus was constructed for studying the multimodal interaction in the domain of kitchen design. In the selected fragment the user asks the system to reallocate the kitchen sink. However, he does not specify the new position, causing a subdialog (see step 4) by the system in order to obtain such information.

The knowledge of the system at this moment:
(C1)   *Msf move*(**Obj**, **NewLocation**)   The machine knows the base action *to move*

utt259: u: now move the kitchen sink   (ahora a recorrer el fregadero)
[*Uff move*(obj53, χ)]

1. $[Uff\,move(obj53, \chi)](\,? Mf\,move(obj53, \chi))$
         Definition of *Uff*   *the proposed goal*

2. $? [Mffs\; parameter(move(obj53, \chi), \chi)]$
         $(? [Ufs\; parameter(move(obj53, \chi), \chi)];$

> $verify(++Ufs\ parameter(move(obj53, \chi), \chi);$
> $Mf\ move(obj53, \chi))$
> 1, C1, A6   *a generated subgoal*

3. $[Mffs\ parameter(move(obj53, \chi), \chi)]$
      $(?\ [Ufs\ parameter(move(obj53, \chi), \chi)];$
        $verify(++Ufs\ parameter(move(obj53, \chi), \chi);$
        $Mf\ move(obj53, \chi)\ )$
      2, A5.i

$[Mffs\ parameter(move(obj53, \chi), \chi)]$
utt260: s: where do you want it?   (¿a dónde quieres que lo ponga?)

4. $(?\ [Ufs\ parameter(move(obj53, \chi), \chi)];$
        $verify(++Ufs\ parameter(move(obj53, \chi), \chi);$
        $Mf\ move(obj53, \chi)\ )$
      Definition of *Mffs*   *proposed subgoal*

utt261: u: move it to the dishwasher   (recorrerlo hacia la máquina lava trastes)
$[Ufs\ parameter(move(obj53, loc45), loc45)]$

5. $[Ufs\ parameter(move(obj53, loc45), loc45)]$
      $(\ Ms\ parameter(move(obj53, loc45), loc45)$
      Definition of *Ufs*

6. $++\ Ufs\ parameter(move(obj53, loc45), loc45)$
      4, 5   *satisfied subgoal*

7. $[Mf\ move(obj53, loc45)](hold(location(obj53, loc45)))$
      3, 6, and the definition of *move*

$[Mf\ move(obj53, loc45)]$
M: <*reallocation of the kitchen sink to the new position in the graphical context*>

8. $+[Mf\ move(obj53, loc45)]$
      1, 7   *reached goal*

4   Conclusions

This paper establishes the basis of a *multimodal dialog model*. In this model, the user activities are characterized by his goals, which at the same time give a structure to the dialog.

The proposed dialog model is based on *a modal logic framework*. This logic framework considers the *action* its central element. Thus, a spoken intervention is contemplated just as another form of action. This way, the dialog conduces the execution of an action, and the action causes the dialog.

In addition, our logic framework describes the dialog (i.e., the interchange of information) as the *evolution of the goal* proposed by the user. This evolution is a sequence of *spoken and direct actions* defined by the user intentions and the machine knowledge.

As future work, we plan to define new axioms that allow describing other phenomenon of the multimodal conversations, such as the resolution of the incomprehension related with the problems of communication.

Acknowledgements. This work has been partly supported by the CONACYT (project 31128-A), the *Laboratorio Franco-Mexicano de Informática* /LAFMI (project "Interaction Parlée Homme-Machine") and the Human Language Technologies Laboratory of INAOE.

References

1. Austin, J., *How to Do Things with Words*. Harvard University Press, 1962.
2. Caelen, J. Vers une logique dialogique. *Séminaire International de Pragmatique*, Jerusalem, 1995.
3. Calvo, H., A. Gelbukh . *Action-request dialogue understanding system*. J. U. Sossa Azuela *et al.* (Eds.) Avances en Ciencias de la Computación e Ingeniería de Cómputo. (CIC'2002, XI Congreso Internacional de Computación, 2002, CIC-IPN, Mexico, v. II, p. 231–242.
4. Cohen, P. R. & Levesque, H.J. Persistence, Intention and Commitment. *Intentions in Communication*. (eds.) P. R. Cohen, J. Morgan & M. E. Pollack. The MIT Press. 1990.
5. Cohen, P. R., Levesque, H. J. Rational interaction as the basis for communication. In *Intentions in Communication*. P.R. Cohen, J. Morgan et M. Pollack. (eds.) MIT Press. 1990.
6. Cohen, P. R., Perrault, C. R. Elements of a Plan-Based Theory of Speech Acts. *Cognitive Science*, 3(3) : 177-212, 1979.
7. Halpern, J.Y. & Moses, Y. A guide to completeness and complexity for modal logics of knowledge and belief. *Artificial Intelligence* 54, 319-379. Elsevier Science Publ. 1992.
8. McTear, M. Spoken Dialogue Technology: Enabling the Conversational User Interface. *ACM Computing Surveys*, Vol. 34, No. 1, March 2002, pp 90-169.
9. Sadek, D. Logical task modelling for man-machine dialogue. AAAI-90 Proceedings. Eighth National Conference on Artificial Intelligence. pp 970-5 vol.2
10. Oviatt, S.L. "Breaking the Robustness Barrier: Recent Progress on the Design of Robust Multimodal Systems," *Advances in Computers* (ed. by M. Zelkowitz), Academic Press, 2002, vol. 56, 305-341.
11. Prendinger, H. & Schurz, G. Reasoning about Action and Change. A Dynamic Logic Approach. *Journal of Logic, Language, and Information*, 5:209-245, 1996.
12. Searle, J.R. *Actes de Langage*, Hermann ed., Paris, 1972.
13. Taylor, M., Néel, F. & Bouwhuis, D. (eds.) The Structure Of Multimodal Dialogue II. John Benjamins Publishing Company. 2000.
14. van der Hoek, W., van Linder, B. & Meyer, Ch. J.-J. A Logic of Capabilities (extended abstract). *Proceedings of the Third International Symposium of Logic Foundations of Computer Science*. LFCS, 94. (eds.) A. Nerode & Yu. V. Matiyasevich. San. Petersburg, Russia, July 11-14, Springer-Verlag, 1994.
15. van der Hoek, W., van Linder, B. & Meyer, Ch. J.-J. 1994. Unraveling Nondeterminism: On having the Ability to Choose (extended abstract). *Proceedings of the sixth International Conference on Artificial Intelligence: Methodology, Systems, Applications* AIMSA'94. (eds.) P. Jorrand & V. Sgurev. Sofia, Bulgaria, September 21-24, 1994. World Scientific. 1994.

16. van Linder, B., van der Hoek, W. & Meyer, Ch. J.-J. Communicating Rational Agents. *Proceedings of the 18th German Annual Conference on Artificial Intelligence* KI-94 : Advances in Artificial Intelligence. (eds.) B. Nebel & L. Dreschler-Fischer. Saarbrücken, Alemania, Septiembre 18-23, 1994. Springer-Verlag 1994.

17. Vanderveken, D. *La logique illocutoire.* Mandarga éd. Bruselas, 1990.

18. Vernant, D. Modèle projectif et structure actionnelle du dialogue informatif. *Du dialogue, Recherches sur la philosophie du langage,* Vrin éd., París, n°14, p. 295-314, 1992.

19. Villaseñor, L., Massé, A. & Pineda, L.A. *The DIME corpus.* ENC01, 3er Encuentro Internacional de Ciencias de la Computación, Aguascalientes, México, SMCC-INEGI 2001.

Agents Interpreting Imperative Sentences

Miguel Pérez-Ramírez[1] and Chris Fox[2]

[1]Instituto de Investigaciones Eléctricas.
Reforma 113. Cuernavaca Mor., México. CP 62490.
mperez@iie.org.mx
[2]University of Essex. Computer Science Department
Wivenhoe Park, Colchester CO4 3SQ, Essex, UK.
foxcj@essex.ac.uk

Abstract. The aim of this paper is to present a model for the interpretation of imperative sentences in which reasoning agents play the role of speakers and hearers. A requirement is associated with both the person who makes and the person who receives the order, which prevents the hearer coming to inappropriate conclusions about the actions s/he has been commanded to do. By relating imperatives with the actions they prescribe, the dynamic aspect of imperatives is captured. Further, by using the idea of *encapsulation*, it is possible to distinguish what is demanded by an imperative from the inferential consequences of the imperative. These two ingredients provide agents with the tools to avoid inferential problems in interpretation.

1 Introduction

There is a move to produce formal theories which attempt to capture different aspects of agents, such as the ability to reason, plan, and interpret language. Some such theories seek to formalize power relations between agents, where an agent can make other agents satisfy his/her goals (e.g. [10;11]). Here we present a model in which agents represent speakers and hearers. Once an agent has uttered an order, the main role of the agent addressed is to interpret it and decide what course of actions s/he needs to follow, so that the order given can be satisfied. Nevertheless, without care, such autonomous reasoning behavior might lead to inappropriate inferences, as we shall see. In the specific case of the interpretation of imperatives, there is an additional problem: imperatives do not denote truth values. The term *practical inference* has been used to refer inferential patterns involving imperatives. For instance, if an agent A is addressed with the order *Love your neighbours as yourself!* and A realizes that Alison, is one of those object referred as his/her neighbours, then A could infer *Love Alison as yourself.* Even though the order given cannot be *true* or *false* [9; 13; 18].

Formalizations in which imperatives are translated into statements of classical logic are problematic as they can lead an agent to draw inappropriate conclusions. In those approaches, if an agent A is given the order *Post the letter!*, s/he can erroneously infer that s/he has been ordered to *Post the letter or burn the letter!* by using the rule of introduction for disjunction. Thus, having a choice, agent A might decide to burn the letter. In deontic approaches this is known as the Paradox of Free

A. Gelbukh (Ed.): CICLing 2004, LNCS 2945, pp. 56–67, 2004.
© Springer-Verlag Berlin Heidelberg 2004

Choice Permission, which was thought to be an unsolved problem as recently as 1999 [17].

Here we present a model which does not suffer from this kind of paradoxical behaviour. It involves the following ingredients a) *agents* with the ability to interpret imperative sentences within b) a *context*. It also captures c) *the dynamic aspect of imperatives*, so that imperatives are not translated into truth-denoting statements. Finally, d) *encapsulation* makes agents capable of distinguishing what is uttered from what is not, so avoiding 'putting words in the mouth of the speaker'.

The rest of the paper is organized as follows. First as a preamble to the model, the concepts of imperative, context and requirement are defined. Then a formalization is presented followed by examples illustrating that the model overcomes inferential problems in the interpretation of imperatives. The paper ends with some conclusions.

2 Analysis

In this section, we describe some of the main concepts which need to be addressed by the model in which agents interpret imperatives. As a first step we define imperative sentences as they are considered in this paper.

Definition: Imperative
> Imperatives are sentences used to ask someone to do or not to do something and that do not denote truth-values.

This definition introduces a distinction between different sentences used to ask someone to do something. Following the definition, *Come here!* might convey the same request than *I would like you to come here*. However the former does not denote a truth value, whereas the latter does it. The former provides an example of the kind of sentences that we shall address here. It is worth to mention that the 'something' which is requested in an imperative shall be called a *requirement*. Other examples of imperatives are: a) direct: *Come here!* ; b) negative: *Don't do that!*; c) conjunctive: *Sit down and listen carefully!*; d) disjunctive: *Shut up or get out of here!*; e) conditional: *If it is raining, close the window!*

2.1 Context

It is widely accepted that the interpretation of utterances is context dependent. For instance the imperative *Eat!*, said by a mother to her son, might be an order. However said to a guest it might be only an invitation to start eating. The real meaning depend on context.

Many authors, agree that context is related to people's view or perception of the world or a particular situation rather than the world or the situation themselves [2; 15]. That is, context is conceived in terms of what agents have in their minds. After all this is what an agent uses to interpret a sentence. This might include intentions, beliefs, knowledge etc. However we will subscribe to the following definition.

Definition: Context

> A context is a consistent collection of propositions that reflects a relevant subset of agents' beliefs.

This view will not commit us here to an ontology or classification of components or to the use of operators such as **B** for beliefs and **K** for knowledge (Turner [16]). We simply assume that all that which constitutes a context can be represented in terms of propositions so the context is viewed as a consistent set of propositions [3].

2.2 Dynamic Aspect of Imperatives

Different authors have related imperatives and actions (Ross [13], von Wright [17], Hamblin [6] p. 45 and Segerberg [14] among others). Sometimes it is said that imperatives prescribe actions. Nevertheless, it would be more precise to say that imperatives posses a dynamic aspect. For instance, *I would like you to open the door*, and *Open the door!* might convey the same request. However the former is a statement which defines a truth value. It can be true or false within a state of affairs, but there is not a dynamic aspect in it. However the latter, does not denote a truth value, but if we assume that is uttered in a state of affairs in which the door is closed, it demands another future and wished state of affairs in which the door is open. That is, it demands a change of states, it involves a dynamic aspect (Fig. 1). This suggests that translating imperatives into statements is the wrong approach; it does not model a basic aspect of imperatives.

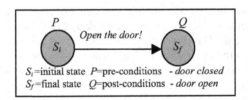

S_i=initial state P=pre-conditions - *door closed*
S_f=final state Q=post-conditions - *door open*

Fig. 1. Dynamic aspect of imperatives

2.3 Evaluation of Imperatives and Correctness

When an agent interprets an imperative, s/he also evaluates it. For instance in the example above, *Open the door!* would not make sense in a state of affairs where the door is already open. It seems that imperatives impose some pre-conditions that the agent verifies during the process of interpretation; the door must be closed. Complying with an imperative will produce a result, a post-condition which shall indicate that the order has been satisfied; the door will be open. Thus, the dynamic aspect of imperatives provides us with at least three components, namely pre-conditions, imperative, and post-conditions. This resembles what is known as Hoare's triple [8]. In 1969 Hoare proposed a logic to verify correctness of programs. He proposed to evaluate triples $P\{S\}Q$, where S is a program, P are its pre-conditions, and Q are its post-conditions. According to Hoare, the program S is correct iff the assertion P is *true* before initiation of S, and then the assertion Q is *true* on its completion. Since the interpretation of imperatives can be construed as involving a verification process, here we adopt the concept of *correctness of an imperative* which is defined analogously by using Hoare's triple $P\{Imp\}Q$.

Definition: Correctness of an Imperative
> The imperative *Imp* is correct with respect to a state of affairs *Si* iff *P* is the case in S_i and *Q* is the case in the state S_j reached after the imperative is satisfied.

An imperative is satisfied when the agent addressed, complies with the imperative, reaching the state wished by the speaker.

2.4 Encapsulation

A program is a sequence of instructions encapsulated in a file. The file contains the instructions that a programmer wants a computer to perform. Hoare logic would allow us to verify the correctness of such program, and make derivations but it will not derive a new program. That is, it is not assumed that the programmer wants the computer to perform any derivation during the verification of the correctness of a program. We shall use this idea to distinguish what an agent is commanded to do, so that, logical derivations will not be considered new imperatives. In fact this also corresponds to the use of imperatives. If an agent is given the order *Close all the windows!* while being in a house, and s/he realizes that the kitchen's window is open, then the agent might conclude that s/he should close that windows, as a derivation of the order given. However the agent will not assume that his/her inferential derivation *Close the kitchen's window*, means that is an imperative uttered by the speaker.

Now we present the model, illustrating how it is able to describe the main features of imperatives and how it overcomes the paradoxical behavior faced by other approaches.

3 Model

L_{ImpA} is a dynamic language, defined along the lines of first-order dynamic logic as in Harel [7]. In this language Hoare's triples can be represented and, therefore, so can the concept of requirement. The ability of an agent (the actions that an agent is able to perform) can also be represented. Its interpretation will allow us to verify validity with respect to a context.

3.1 Definition of Sets

We define the following sets. $C=\{c, c_1, c_2,...\}$ is a set of constant symbols. Analogously we define set for variable symbols (V); function symbols (F); regular constant symbols (C); speaker constant symbols (CS); speaker variable symbols (S); hearer constant symbols (CH); hearer variable symbols (H); atomic actions ($AtAct$);

atomic predicate symbols (*AtPred*); and we assume that $AC = C \cup CS \cup CH$ and $AV = V \cup S \cup H$.

3.2 Definition of Terms

Terms are defined recursively by: $t ::= c|cs|ch|v|s|h|f(t_1, t_2, ..., t_n)$. Thus, a term is a regular constant (c), a speaker constant (cs), a hearer constant (ch), a regular variable (v), a speaker variable (s), a hearer variable (h) or a function ($f(t_1, t_2, ..., t_n)$) of arity n (n arguments), where $t_1, t_2, ..., t_n$ are terms. The expressions $ts ::= cs|s$ and $th ::= ch|h$ define the terms for speaker and hearers respectively as constants or variables.

3.3 Definition of wff of the Language L_{ImpA}

The set *FOR* contains all possible wffs in L_{ImpA} and the set *Act* contains all possible actions defined in the category of actions. The definition of the language L_{ImpA} is given by $\phi ::= p(t_1, t_2, ..., t_n)|t_1=t_2|\neg\phi\ |\phi_1 \wedge \phi_2 |\exists x\phi\ |[\alpha]\phi$. In other words, if $p \in AtPred$, $t_1, t_2, ..., t_n$ are terms, $x \in V$, and $\alpha \in Act$, then $p(t_1, t_2, ..., t_n)$ is an atomic predicate, with arity n. $t_1=t_2$ is the equality test (=). $\neg\phi$ is the negation of ϕ. $\phi_1 \wedge \phi_2$ is the conjunction of ϕ and ψ. $\exists x\phi$ is the existential quantifier. $[\alpha]\phi$ is a modal expression indicating that ϕ holds after the action α is performed. The usual abbreviations are assumed: $\phi_1 \vee \phi_2 = \neg(\neg\phi_1 \wedge \neg\phi_2)$, $\phi_1 \rightarrow \phi_2 = \neg\phi_1 \vee \phi_2$, $\phi_1 \leftrightarrow \phi_2 = \phi_1 \rightarrow \phi_2 \wedge \phi_2 \rightarrow \phi_1$, $\forall x\phi = \neg\exists x\neg\phi$ and $<\alpha>\phi = \neg[\alpha]\neg\phi$.

3.4 Category of Actions

The set *Act* of actions is defined as follows: $\alpha ::= a(t_1, t_2, ..., t_n)|\phi?|\alpha_1;\alpha_2|\alpha_1+\alpha_2|(\alpha)_{ts,th}|(\alpha)_{th}$. In other words, if $\alpha, \alpha_1, \alpha_2 \in Act$, $t_1, t_2, ..., t_n$ are terms and ts, th are terms for speaker and hearer respectively then $a(t_1, t_2, ..., t_n)$ is the atomic action. $\alpha_1;\alpha_2$ is the sequential composition of actions. $\alpha_1+\alpha_2$ is the disjunction of actions. $\phi?$ is a test and it just verifies whether ϕ holds or not. $(\alpha)_{ts,th}$ is a *requirement*, an action requested directly or derived from a requested one by a speaker ts to a hearer th. $(\alpha)_{th}$ is an action that a hearer th is able to do. In this way, we keep track of the agents involved in a requirement, both uttered or derived.

3.5 Representation of Requirements

Requirements are represented in terms of the actions prescribed, with explicit reference to the speaker who demands, and the hearer who is being addressed.

Because of the dynamic aspect of imperatives, they are associated with the actions they prescribe, therefore the dynamic operators must be used between them. Thus, the sequencing operator (;) models a conjunction of requirements the choice operator (+) models a disjunction of requirements, and a conditional requirement is represented by using the symbol '$\Rightarrow$', where $(\phi \Rightarrow \alpha) = (\phi?;\alpha)$. Following Harel [7] and Gries [5] a

Hoare´s triple P{α}Q can be represented in L_{ImpA} as P→[α]Q. Thus, $P→[(a)_{ts,th}]Q$ is an atomic requirement, $P→[(α_1;α_2)_{ts,th}]Q$ is a conjunction of requirements, $P→[(α_1+α_2)_{ts,th}]Q$ is a disjunction of requirements, and $P→[(φ?;α)_{ts,th}]Q$ is a conditional requirement.

3.6 Axioms

A0) T (any tautology); **A1)** $[φ?;α]ψ ↔ φ→[α]ψ$; **A2)** $[(φ?;α)_{ts,th}]ψ ↔ φ→[(α)_{ts,th}]ψ$; **A3)** $[(φ?;α)_{th}]ψ ↔ φ→[(α)_{th}]ψ$;   **A4)** $[α_1;α_2]φ ↔ [α_1]([α_2])φ$; **A5)** $[α_1+α_2]φ ↔ [α_1]φ∧[α_2]φ$; **A6)** $[φ?]ψ ↔ φ→ψ$; **A7)** $[α](φ→ψ) → [α]φ→[α]ψ$; **A8)** $∀xφ(x) → φ(t)$ provided that t is free in $φ(x)$; **A9)** $∀x(φ→ψ) → φ→∀xψ$ provided that x is not free in $φ$. Furthermore we can relate requirements and ability of hearers: **shA1)** $[(α)_{ts,th}]ψ → [(α)_{th}]ψ$; **hA2)** $[(α)_{th}]ψ → [α]ψ$.

Axioms, from A0)-A7) are standard in Dynamic Logic, A2) and A3) explicitly include speakers and hearers and A8)-A9) are standard in predicate logic respectively. shA1) is analogous to Chellas (1971: p. 125) axiom where 'ought' implies 'can' in his model of imperatives through Obligation and Permission. Here shA1) expresses that if α is demanded for *ts* to *th*, is correct, that implies that there is some action, usually a sequence $α=a_1;a_2; ... ;a_n$ of actions, such that hearer is able to perform it, so that α can be satisfied. hA2) emphasise that any action a hearer is able to do is simply an action in the nature.

3.7 Inference Rules

a) Modus Ponens (**MP**): If $φ$ and $φ→φ$ then $φ$; b) Necessitation rule (**Nec**): If $φ$ then $[α]φ$ y c) Universal generalization (**UG**): If $φ$ then $∀x φ$ provided x is not free in $φ$.

3.8 Semantics

The semantics for L_{ImpA} is given as a possible worlds semantics. Formally, a model M is defined to be the structure $<W, D, Val, Λ, δ, η, ν, τ, κ>$, where $W = \{w_0, w_1, ... w_n, ...\}$ is a set of worlds or states. D is a non empty set called domain composed by a) *Sp* a set of agents playing the role of speakers, b) *Hr* a set of agents playing the role of hearers and c) a set D' of objects such that $D = D'∪Sp∪Hr$. *Val* is a function assigning a semantic value to each non-logical constant of L_{ImpA}, where such constants correspond to standard constants, functions, predicates and actions. $Λ: AtAct×D^n ⇒ 2^{W×W}$, defines a set of pairs (w, w') describing actions $α(d^n)$ such that starting in w the occurrence of the action would lead to the state w', where $d^n = (d_1, d_2, ... d_n)$ and $d_i∈D$. ($i=1, n$). $δ: AtAct×D^n×Sp×Hr⇒2^{W×W}$, defines a set of pairs of states (w, w') describing requirements such that in the state w a speaker is demanding some request to some hearer who is able to get the state w' where the request is considered satisfied. $η: AtAct×D^n×Hr ⇒ 2^{W×W}$, defines a set of pairs of states (w, w') describing actions such that starting in w an agent (hearer) would be able to perform the action and so reach the state w'. ν is a valuation that assigns a semantic value (*true* or *false*) to predicates and formulae. τ is the environment function that assigns to each variable x and world w an element d from D. τ is defined in the next Section below. κ provides the valuation for terms by using the environment function τ and *Val*.

3.9 Semantics for Non-logical Constants

Val assigns values to the different kind of constants as follows. If c is a standard constant then $Val(c) = c_{Val} = d$ where $d \in D$. If cs is a standard speaker constant then $Val(cs) = cs_{Val} = os$ where $os \in Sp$. If ch is a standard hearer constant then $Val(ch) = ch_{Val} = oh$ where $oh \in Hr$. If p is a predicate constant then $Val(p) = p_{Val}$ where $p_{Val} \subseteq D^n$. If a^n is a n-ary action constant then $Val(a^n) = a^n_{Val}$ where $a^n_{Val} \subseteq W \times W \times D^n$. If f^n is a function from D^n to D, $Val(f^n) = f^n_{Val}$ where $f^n_{Val} \subseteq D^{n+1}$.

3.10 Semantics for Terms

a) Environment Function
   Let τ be the semantic function for variables defined as follows. $\tau: V \times W \Rightarrow D$, such that $\tau(x/d, w)$ is exactly like τ, except that $\tau(x/d, w)$ assign d to x in w.

b) Semantic for Terms
   - If x is a variable symbol then $\qquad \kappa(x)_{\tau,w} = \tau(x, w) = d$ such that $d \in D$
   - If c is a constant symbol then $\qquad \kappa(c)_{\tau,w} = Val(c) = d$ such that $d \in D$
   - If s is a speaker variable symbol then $\kappa(s)_{\tau,w} = \tau(s, w) = os$ such that $os \in Sp$
   - If h is a hearer variable symbol then $\kappa(h)_{\tau,w} = \tau(h, w) = oh$ such that $oh \in Hr$
   - If cs is a speaker constant symbol then $\kappa(cs)_{\tau,w} = Val(cs) = os$ such that $os \in Sp$
   - If ch is a hearer constant symbol then $\kappa(ch)_{\tau,w} = Val(ch) = oh$ such that $oh \in Hr$
   - If $f(t_1, t_2, ..., t_n)$ is a function symbol from D^n to D, then $\kappa(f(t_1, t_2, ..., t_n))_{\tau,w} =$
     $$Val(f)(\kappa(t_1)_{\tau,w}, \kappa(t_2)_{\tau,w}, ..., \kappa(t_n)_{\tau,w})$$

3.11 Semantics for Actions

If ts is a speaker term, th is a hearer term and α, α_1, and α_2 are actions with no references to speakers and hearers, we define the following semantic functions δ, η. In order to avoid subscripts of subscripts we use the following notation.
$$\delta((\alpha)_{ts,th})_{\tau,w} = \delta(\alpha, ts, th)_{\tau,w} \quad \text{and} \quad \eta((\alpha)_{th})_{\tau,w} = \eta(\alpha, th)_{\tau,w}.$$

a) Semantics for Requirements (Triples Involving Speaker-Action-Hearer)
- Atomic requirements:
   If $a(t_1, t_2, ..., t_n) \in AtAct$ then $\delta((a(t_1, t_2, ..., t_n))_{ts,th})_{\tau,w} = \delta(a(t_1, t_2, ..., t_n), ts, th)_{\tau,w} =$
   $\{(w_h, w_i) \mid (w_h, w_i) \in Val(a) \, (\kappa(t_1)_{\tau,w}, \kappa(t_2)_{\tau,w}, ..., \kappa(t_n)_{\tau,w}), \kappa(ts)_{\tau,w}, \kappa(th)_{\tau,w})\}$
- Composition of requirements:
   $\delta((\alpha_1;\alpha_2)_{ts,th})_{\tau,w} = \delta((\alpha_1;\alpha_2), ts, th)_{\tau,w} = \delta((\alpha_1), ts, th)_{\tau,w} \circ \delta((\alpha_2), ts, th)_{\tau,w} =$

$\{(w_h, w_j)|\text{There exists } w/(w_h, w_i)\in\delta(\alpha_1, \kappa(ts)_{\tau,w}, \kappa(th)_{\tau,w})_{\tau,w}$ and

$(w_i, w_j)\in\delta(\alpha_2, \kappa(ts)_{\tau,w}, \kappa(th)_{\tau,w})_{\tau,w}\}$

- Disjunction of requirements:

$\delta((\alpha_1+\alpha_2)_{ts,th})_{\tau,w} = \delta(\alpha_1+\alpha_2, ts, th)_{\tau,w} = \delta(\alpha_1, ts, th)_{\tau,w} \cup \delta(\alpha_2, ts, th)_{\tau,w} =$
$\{(w_i, w_j)| (w_i, w_j)\in\delta(\alpha_1, \kappa(ts)_{\tau,w}, \kappa(th)_{\tau,w})_{\tau,w}$ or $(w_i, w_j)\in\delta(\alpha_2, \kappa(ts)_{\tau,w}, \kappa(th)_{\tau,w})_{\tau,w}\}$

The semantic functions, (η) for ability of agents and (Λ) for actions, are defined analogously, with the corresponding number of arguments.

b) Mixing Requirements ($(\alpha)_{ts,th}$), Ability ($(\alpha)_{th}$) and Actions (α)

If α, α_1 and α_2 are actions with no references to speakers and hearers then we define the semantic function Γ as follows: a) $\Gamma(\alpha)_{\tau,w} = \Lambda(\alpha)_{\tau,w}$, b) $\Gamma((\alpha)_{th})_{\tau,w} = \eta((\alpha)_{th})_{\tau,w}$ and c) $\Gamma((\alpha)_{ts,th})_{\tau,w} = \delta((\alpha)_{ts,th})_{\tau,w}$. Now for any actions α, α_1 and α_2 in *Act*, even involving reference to speakers and hearers, Γ is defined as follows. *i)* $\Gamma(\alpha_1;\alpha_2)_{\tau,w} = \Gamma(\alpha_1)_{\tau,w}{}^{\circ}\Gamma(\alpha_2)_{\tau,w} = \{(w,w')|\exists w''$ such that $(w,w'')\in\Gamma(\alpha_1)_{\tau,w}$ and $(w'',w')\in\Gamma(\alpha_2)_{\tau,w''}\}$. *ii)* $\Gamma(\alpha_1+\alpha_2)_{\tau,w} = \Gamma(\alpha_1)_{\tau,w} \cup \Gamma(\alpha_2)_{\tau,w} = \{(w, w')| (w, w')\in\Gamma(\alpha_1)_{\tau,w}$ or $(w, w')\in\Gamma(\alpha_2)_{\tau,w}\}$

3.12 Semantics Expressions in the Language L_{ImpA}

- $\mathcal{V}(p(t_1, t_2, ..., t_n))_{\tau,w} = true$ iff $<\kappa(t_1)_{\tau,w}, \kappa(t_2)_{\tau,w}, ..., \kappa(t_n)_{\tau,w}>\in Val(p)$.

  $\mathcal{V}$ defines the set of states where the predicate $p(t_1, t_2, ..., t_n)$ is *true* and $Val(p)\subseteq D^n$.

- $\mathcal{V}(t_1 = t_2)_{\tau,w}$ = *true*   iff $\kappa(t_1)_{\tau,w} = \kappa(t_2)_{\tau,w}$

- $\mathcal{V}(\neg\phi)_{\tau,w}$ = *true*   iff $\mathcal{V}(\phi)_{\tau,w} = false$

- $\mathcal{V}(\phi_1 \wedge \phi_2)_{\tau,w}$ = *true*   iff $\mathcal{V}(\phi_1)_{\tau,w} = true$ and $\mathcal{V}(\phi_2)_{\tau,w} = true$

- $\mathcal{V}(\exists x\phi)_{\tau,w}$ = *true* iff there exists an element d in D such that $\mathcal{V}(\phi)_{\tau(x/d,w),w} = true$

  $\tau(x/d,w)$ is exactly like τ except that $\tau(x/d,w)$ assigns d to x.

- $\mathcal{V}[\alpha]\phi)_{\tau,w}$ = *true*   iff For every w' (if $(w, w')\in\Gamma(\alpha)_{\tau,w}$ then $\mathcal{V}(\phi)_{\tau,w} = true$)

- $\mathcal{V}(<\alpha>\phi)_{\tau,w}$ = *true*   iff There exists $w'| ((w, w')\in\Gamma(\alpha)_{\tau,w}$ and $\mathcal{V}(\phi)_{\tau,w'} = true)$

3.13 Soundness

Soundness of L_{ImpA} follows from the soundness of first order dynamic logic as defined by Harel [7].

Notation: Truth at state w of an arbitrary formula ϕ under L_{ImpA} for any valuation τ and the model $\mathcal{M}$ is inductively defined using the notation $w\in\mathcal{V}(\phi)_{\tau,w}$ and simply abbreviated as $w\vDash\phi$. When ϕ is not true at w under L_{ImpA} we can write $w\nvDash\phi$. If ϕ is valid in $\mathcal{M}$ we write simply $\vDash\phi$.

3.14   Truth with Respect to a Context

If we have a description of a context, that is, a collection of consistent propositions, we can define the truth of a proposition (ϕ) with respect to context as follows. Let $k=\{\phi_0, \phi_1, ..., \phi_n\}$ represent our context, where for $i=1,n$, $\phi_i \in FOR$. We may also identify the set of states defined by our context as follows. $\nu'(k) = \{w|$ For every $\phi \in k$, $w \vDash \phi\}$. Now we can define truth with respect to a context. If k represents a context and $\phi \in FOR$, we use the symbol '$\vDash$' and the notation $k \vDash_M \phi$ to indicate that ϕ is *true* in the model M with respect to context k, for any assignment τ. We abbreviate $k \vDash_M \phi$ simply as $k \vDash \phi$. When ϕ is *not true* at k under L_{ImpA} we can write $k \nvDash \phi$. Thus, if $\phi \in FOR$, $k \vDash \phi$ iff for every w if $w \in \nu'(k)$ then $w \vDash \phi$. In this model we assume that in expressions involving more than one agent, context represents a common set of beliefs shared by the agents involved.

3.15   Hoare Style Rules

The following are derived rules, which operate between actions, which might or might not make reference to speakers and hearers. *Pre* usually indicates pre-conditions and *Pos* post-conditions. We assume the equality $Pre\{\alpha\}Pos = Pre \rightarrow [\alpha]$. The derived rules, (I;) Introduction for composition, (I+) Introduction for disjunction and (I⇒) Introduction for conditional are given below.

(I;)   If $\vdash Pre \rightarrow [\alpha_1]Pos'$ and $\vdash Pos' \rightarrow [\alpha_2]Pos$ then $\vdash Pre \rightarrow [\alpha_1;\alpha_2]Pos$.

(I+)   If $\vdash Pre \rightarrow [\alpha_1]Pos$ and $\vdash Pre \rightarrow [\alpha_2]Pos$ then $\vdash Pre \rightarrow [\alpha_1 + \alpha_2]Pos$.

(I⇒)   If $\vdash (Pre \wedge \phi) \rightarrow [\alpha]Pos$ and $\vdash (Pre \wedge \neg\phi) \rightarrow Pos$ then $\vdash Pre \rightarrow [\phi?;\alpha]Pos$.

3.16   Correctness for Imperatives

Having all this infrastructure to represent and verify requirement, we can formalize the definition of correctness for imperatives.

Definition: Correctness of an Imperative

Given a requirement $(\alpha)_{s,h}$, prescribed by an imperative utterance Imp(k, P, $(\alpha)_{s,h}$, Q) we say that Imp is correct w.r.t context k iff $k \vDash P \rightarrow [(\alpha)_{s,h}]Q$ for appropriate pre and post-conditions P and Q.

Note that this definition of correctness is only a case of the more general definition $k \vDash P \rightarrow [\alpha]Q$, which defines the correctness of any action in L_{ImpA}. This includes requirements, ability of agents and actions in general.

3.17 Encapsulating Uttered Requirements

In order for an agent to distinguish what is uttered from what is not, we encapsulate as follows.

Definition: Set of Requirements

Let be $\sigma_k = <(\alpha_1)_{s,h}, (\alpha_2)_{s,h}, ..., (\alpha_n)_{s,h}>$ a set of requirements demanded in context k, such that α_1, α_2, ..., α_n represent actions prescribed by imperatives sentences. s and h represents the agents playing the role of speakers and hearer respectively.

Note that σ_k allows the distinction between demanded and derived actions. On the other hand, there is the implicit assumption that all requirements in σ_k are supposed to be satisfied as long as σ_k is correct.

Definition: Correctness of a Set of Requirements

A set σ_k is correct with respect to context k iff $k \vDash P\{(\alpha_1)_{s,h};(\alpha_2)_{s,h}; ...;(\alpha_n)_{s,h}\}Q$ for appropriate pre and post-conditions P and Q.

4 Model at Work

In the example below we assume that k the context, represent not the set of beliefs of a particular agent, but rather a subset, such that it represents a set of common beliefs of the hearer and speaker involved.

a) Uttered and Derived Requirements

Let us assume that Helen says to Betty, *Love your neighbour as yourself!* Betty should be able to encapsulate the requirement such that $\sigma_k =<$*Love your neighbour as yourself!*$)_{\text{Helen, Betty}}>$. We can paraphrase the order as a conditional requirement, where $\alpha(x) = $ *Love x as yourself*, $\phi(x) = x$ *is your neighbour*, $Q(x) = $ *You love x as yourself* and $P(x)=\neg Q(x)$. Thus, the Hoare's triple of the imperative is $\forall x P(x) \rightarrow [(\phi(x) \Rightarrow \alpha(x))_{\text{Helen, Betty}}]Q(x)$. If we assume that the requirement is correct w.r.t. k, then $k \vDash \forall x P(x) \rightarrow [(\phi(x) \Rightarrow \alpha(x))_{\text{Helen, Betty}}]Q(x)$. This means that for both Helen and Betty, the requirement according to their beliefs is acceptable. If furthermore it is the case that $\phi(Alison) = $ *Alison is your neighbour*, then we can derive as follows.

1) $k \vDash \forall x P(x) \rightarrow [(\phi(x) \Rightarrow \alpha(x))_{\text{Helen, Betty}}]Q(x)$ assumption

2) $k \vDash \forall x (P(x) \wedge \phi(x)) \rightarrow [(\alpha(x))_{\text{Helen, Betty}}]Q(x)$ 1), axiom A1)

3) $k \vDash \phi(Alison)$ assumption

4) $k \vDash (P(Alison) \wedge \phi(Alison)) \rightarrow [(\alpha(Alison))_{\text{Helen, Betty}}]Q(Alison)$ 2), Univ. Inst.

5) $k \vDash P(Alison) \wedge \phi(Alison)$ 3), 4), Int Conj.

6) $k \vDash [(\alpha(Alison))_{\text{Helen, Betty}}]Q(Alison)$ 4), 5), MP

In 6) Betty would derive the requirement of loving Alison, from the original request by Helen, given that she is one of her neighbors. However that is not an uttered requirement, $(\alpha(Alison))_{\text{Helen, Betty}} \notin \sigma_k$.

b) No Choice
Let us assume that now Helen says to Betty, *Talk to the president!* Betty would distinguish this uttered requirement as follows $\sigma_k = <(\textit{Talk to the president})_{\text{Helen, Betty}}>$. We can paraphrase the order, such that $\alpha = \textit{Talk to the president}$, $Q = \textit{You have talked to the president}$ and $P = \neg Q$. Thus, the Hoare's triple of the imperative is $P \to [(\alpha)_{\text{Helen, Betty}}]Q$. If we assume that the requirement is correct w.r.t. k, then $k \vDash P \to [(\alpha)_{\text{Helen, Betty}}]Q$. This means that for both Helen and Betty, it is acceptable the requirement of talking to the president, according to their beliefs.

If we assume that $\beta = \textit{Kill the president}$, Betty and Helen cannot introduce a disjunction such that Betty believes that a choice has been uttered and given to her, That is $\sigma_k = <(\alpha)_{\text{Helen, Betty}} + (\beta)_{\text{Helen, Betty}}>$. On the other hand, even a verification of a choice might be incorrect, that is $k \nvDash P \to [(\alpha)_{\text{Helen, Betty}} + (\beta)_{\text{Helen, Betty}}]Q$. There might be a clash between this verification and Betty's beliefs.

c) Impossible Requirements
Let us assume that now Helen says to Betty, *Have three arms!* Betty would distinguish this uttered requirement as follows $\sigma_k = <(\textit{Have three arms})_{\text{Helen, Betty}}>$. We can paraphrase the order, such that $\alpha = \textit{Have three arms}$, $Q = \textit{You have three}$ and $P = \neg Q$. Thus, the Hoare's triple of the imperative is $P \to [(\alpha)_{\text{Helen, Betty}}]Q$. In this case, and under normal circumstances, there would be a clash between this verification and Betty's beliefs. In this case Betty's clash can be represented by the following expression, $k \nvDash P \to <(\alpha)_{\text{Helen, Betty}}>Q$, which means that there is not a state she can reach by doing something so that she can have three arms. In terms of ability we can express this as $k \nvDash P \to <(\alpha)_{\text{Betty}}>Q$, which means that Betty does not believe that she is able to perform the action of having three arms.

5 Conclusions and Future Work

We have presented a model in which agents that possess a reasoning ability are able to interpret imperative sentences. This does not suffer from the inferential problems faced by other approaches to the interpretation of imperatives.

It is assumed that by various means (order, advice, request, etc.) imperatives convey *requirements*. The dynamic aspect of imperatives allows us to envisage that the connectives between imperatives behave similarly but not identically to classical logic connectives. A set of dynamic operators is used instead (disjunction (+), composition (;), conditional imperative ($\Rightarrow$)). Following Hoare, an introduction rule is provided for each of these operators.

The features of the model presented here, are that it captures the main aspects of imperatives (including the lack of truth-values), and that it corresponds to our intuitions about behavior of imperative sentences.

The model presented here is useful for verifying imperatives or sequences of imperatives, but it is not able to infer new utterances. This distinction between derived and uttered requirements allows us to avoid certain paradoxes.

Propositions and imperatives interact within the model. It allows us to verify the appropriate use of imperatives (correctness). Verification of correctness provides a *legitimation procedure*, and it is able to detect impossible requirements.

There are many possible extension for this model, for instance the explicit inclusion of time. The introduction of "contrary to duty" imperatives (Prakken and Sergot [12]; Alarcón-Cabrera [1]), would be another example.

In a near future we want to implement this model in a computer system so that it can be used in natural language interfaces. At the moment we are working on the syntactic analysis of imperatives.

References

1. Alarcón Cabrera Carlos, 1998. *"Von Wright's Deontic Logics and 'Contrary-to-Duty Imperatives.'"* Ratio Juris. Vol 11. No. 1 March 1998. 67-79.
2. Bunt. Harry *"Dialogue pragmatics and context specification"* in *"Abduction, Belief and Context in Dialogue;"* Studies in Computational Pragmatics, Amsterdam: Benjamins, Natural Language. Processing Series No. 1, 2000. P. 81-150.
3. Buvac, Sasa. 1995. *"Resolving Lexical Ambiguity Using a Formal Theory of Context."* Visited in October 1998 in http://www-formal.Stanford.EDU/buvac/
4. Chellas, B., 1971. *"Imperatives."* Theoria. Vol 37, 114-129. 1971
5. Gries, David, 1983. *"The Science of programming."* Department of Computer Science. Cornell University. Upson Hall Ithaca, NY. 1983.
6. Hamblin, C. L, 1987. *"Imperatives."* Basil Blackwell. USA. 1987
7. Harel David, 1979. *"First-Order Dynamic Logic."* Lecture Notes in Computer Science. Edited by Goos and Hartmanis. 68. Springer-Verlag. Yorktown Heights, NY. 1979.
8. Hoare. C. A. R., 1969. *"An Axiomatic Basis for Computer Programming."* Communications of the ACM, Vol. 12, No 10. October 1969. pp. 576 -580, 583.
9. Jorgensen J, 1937. *"Imperatives and logic."* Erkenntnis. Vol. 7, (1937-1938), pp. 288-296.
10. Lopez F. and Luck M., 2002. *"Empowered situations of autonomous agents"* Iberamia 2002, pp585-595. Springer Verlag.
11. Piwek, P., 2000. *"Imperatives, Commitment and Action: Towards a Constraint-based Model."* In: LDV Forum: Journal for Computational Linguistics and Language Technology, Special Issue on Communicating Agents, 2000.
12. Prakken, Henry and Sergot, Marek, 1996. *"Contrary-to-duty Obligations."* Studia Logica 57(1/2):91-115 (1996)
13. Ross A., 1941. *"Imperatives and Logic."* Theoria (journal). Vol. 7. 53-71. 1941.
14. Segerberg Krister, 1990. *"Validity and Satisfaction in Imperative Logic."* Notre Dame Journal of Formal Logic. Volume 31, Number 2, Spring 1990. 203-221.
15. Sperber Dan and Wilson Deirdre, 1986. *"Relevance."* Communication and Cognition. Great Britain London. 1986.
16. Turner Raymond. *"Properties, Propositions and Semantic Theory. In Computational Linguistics and Formal Semantics."* Edited by Michael Rosner and Roderick Johnson. Cambridge University Press. Cambridge. 159-180. 1992
17. von Wright, Henrik G. *"Deontic Logic: A personal View"* Ratio Juris. 1999. 26-38. 1999
18. Walter Robert, 1996. *"Jorgensen's Dilemma and How to Face It."* Ratio Juris. Vol 9. No. 2 June 1996. 168-71.

Intention Retrieval
with a Socially-Supported Belief System

Naoko Matsumoto and Akifumi Tokosum

Department of Value and Decision Science, Tokyo Institute of Technology,
2-12-1 Oookayama, Meguro-ku, Tokyo, 152-8552, Japan
{matsun, akt}@valdes.titech.ac.jp
http://www.valdes.titech.ac.jp/~matsun/

Abstract. This paper proposes a dynamically-changed knowledge system. Each belief in the system has a component reflecting the strength of support from other people. The system is capable of adapting to a contextual situation by means of the continuous revision of belief strengths through interaction with others. As a paradigmatic application of the proposed socially-supported belief system, a parser was designed and implemented in CLOS. The parser outputs (a) speaker intention, (b) conveyed meaning, and (c) hearer's emotion.

1 Introduction

A language user's belief structure is one of the important cues for 'proper' utterance interpretation. In this paper, we defined the belief structure as a knowledge structure with a degree of subjective confidence. To understand an utterance 'properly' means to infer 'as exactly as possible' what the speaker intends to. Of course, contextual information is also important to proper utterance interpretation. However, we often cannot properly interpret utterances even when provided with considerable contextual information. Reference to the belief structure enables an utterance's meaning to be properly interpreted with little or no reference to the situation. For example, when the speaker utters *"This dish tastes good,"* there are possible interpretations for the hearer, such as *"Father thinks mother has cooked a good meal and praises her,"* or *"A man thinks the restaurant has served a good meal and requests one more."* To retrieve the speaker's intention, the first interpretation is automatically decided in the speaker's mind by referring to his/her belief. In analyzing such phenomena we focus on the role of each language user's belief structure and propose that the belief structure is built up by reflecting the other people's beliefs through social interactions.

2 How to Treat the Proper Context

Although contextual information is considered as essential for utterance interpretation in traditional pragmatics, the problem how the hearer infers the appropriate context of

A. Gelbukh (Ed.): CICLing 2004, LNCS 2945, pp. 68–71, 2004.
© Springer-Verlag Berlin Heidelberg 2004

the utterance is not addressed. In Gricean theory (e.g. [2]), context is dealt with only as the obvious and given information. Computational pragmatics decomposes the problem into the steps involved in plan-recognition (e.g. [1]), therefore context is defined in terms of data structures. Relevance Theory ([5]) takes a more satisfying approach; asserting that assumption is the major cue for utterance interpretation. They state that assumptions are built on the basis of cognition for optimal relevance. This approach is similar to ours, but it downplays the fact that the cognitive computation for building the assumption has not been described yet in detail. This is a point we address.

We also introduce the new idea of meaning being supported collectively with the help of other language users in the community ([3]). In our approach, context is not merely a data structure or given information, but rather a support mechanism existing between the cognitive systems of the members of a particular linguistic community.

3 The Socially-Supported Belief System

The Socially-supported Belief System (SBS) is a computational model of utterance interpretation which incorporates the dynamical revision of the belief system of a given language user ([4]). The belief revising system models the user's linguistic and world knowledge with a component representing the degree of support from others in the community. A key concept in this system is the socially-supported belief (sb).

As a hearer model, the task for SBS is to disambiguate the intention of the speaker by using its sb database. The hearer builds his/her own belief structure in the form of sbs. Each sb has a value, representing the strength of support from others. The belief which has the highest level of support is considered as the most likely interpretation of a message, with the ranking order of a knowledge-belief, revised dynamically through interaction. Figure 1 depicts the general architecture of the SBS model (Figure 1). Ordinary models of utterance interpretation do not include the emotional responses of the hearer, although many utterances elicit emotional reactions. We believe that emotional reactions are an inherent function of utterance exchange and the process is best captured as a socially-supported belief processing. In our system, emotions are evoked by sbs activated by input words. When the SSB determines the final utterance function as a speaker's intention, it extracts the associated emotions from the utterance function. From the utterance function "praise", the SBP (Socially-supported Belief Parser) searches the emotion knowledge for the word "praise," it extracts the emotion "happy."

The SBS has its roots in Web searching research. In Web searching situation, little or no information concerning the context of the search or concerning the searcher is available, yet a searching engine is expected to function as if it knew all the contextual information surrounding the target words. The main similarity between the SBS and search engines is in the weighed ordering of the utterance's meaning built by the system and the presumed ordering of found URLs by the search engines. Support from others (other sites, in the case of Web searching) is the key idea in both cases ([4]).

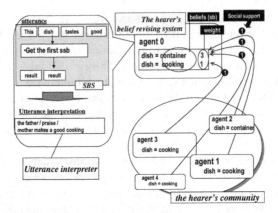

Fig. 1. The general architecture of Socially-supported Belief System: the bottom of the right part of the figure represents "the hearer's community (for instance, community of language, gender, or generation, etc.). The right upper part shows the belief structure of the hearer. The hearer communicates with the member of the community, and he/she takes its belief into his/her belief structure. Each belief has weight and the hearer's belief structure is revised at each communication. The left part of the figure represents the utterance interpreter (whose work is explained in detail in 6.)

4 Metaphor Comprehension

We will discuss the analysis about the description concerning the comprehension for the metaphor "Life is a journey (in Japanese)." We deal with 302 propositions for 15 descriptions. The participants, who are college students, ware instructed to describe interpretations, thought, emotions, and associations in reading the metaphor "Life is a journey." After extracting propositions from the descriptions, we categorized them depending on their content. According to the analysis ([3]), there are some agreements in participants' cognitive processes. In the data, we can find some utterances which show that the reader refers to his/her belief structure. Some readers describe having seen the metaphor in Japanese textbook, and they tend to consider the metaphor as a 'lesson' or a 'moral' ([3]). Considering that there is no contextual information about the metaphor in this experiment, this description suggests that the reader interprets the metaphor according to his/her own belief structure.

5 Implementation

Our intention inference parser has been implemented in Common Lisp Object System (CLOS). We designed the SBS as a word-based parser, which can deal with various types of data structures. This system has its own belief database, and revises the belief database dynamically based on the input beliefs. The SBS processes a sequence of input words by using its word knowledge which consists of three types of knowledge: (a) grammatical knowledge (controls the current word's syntactic behavior), (b) semantic knowledge (deals with the maintenance of the sb database derived from the current word), (c) discourse knowledge (accommodates information about speakers and utterance functions). Each knowledge type is represented as a daemon, a unit of program code executable in a constraint-satisfaction mechanism. The SBS parses each input word using the sb, which connects to the word. It can retrieve the intention from even the incomplete utterances, because the proposed parser is strictly a word-based parser. If any interaction occurs with other language users, the weight of each sb would be revised constantly, and the hearer can revise his/her own belief system, and check it for utterance interpretation.

In result, the SBS determines (i) word meaning, (ii) utterance meaning, (iii) utterance function, (iv) utterance function, (v) the speaker, and (vi) the hearer's emotion. Without any contextual information, it can do them all because it construct context by socially-supported beliefs in its system. Because of the reference to other's beliefs, in addition, it can always gain a stable state of meaning within the particular community which the hearer belongs to.

Acknowledgement. The work presented here is part of a larger project ("Framework for Systematization and Application of Large-scale Knowledge Resources"), defined by Sadaoki Furui and financially supported by the "Japanese Ministry of Education, Culture, Sports, Science and Technology" within the "21st Century COE (Center of Excellence) Program" framework. The authors are greatly indebted to Professor Furui for his continuous support. We would also like to thank Dr. Tony Mullen and two anonymous referees for their helpful comments.

References

1. Cohen, P. R. Levesque, H. J. :Persistence, Intention and Commitment. In: Cohen, P. R., Morgan, J., Pollack, M. (eds.): Intentions in Communication. MIT Press, Cambridge, Mass. (1990) 33-70
2. Grice, H. P.: Logic and Conversation. In: Cole, P., Morgan, J. L. (eds.): Syntax and Semantics; vol. 3. Speech Acts. Academic Press, New York (1975) 45-58
3. Matsumoto, Naoko, and Tokosumi, Akifumi. (2003). "Belief supporting in metaphor comprehension: A case study in 'Life is a journey'" iwLCC (Literature Symposium) in The 4th International Conference on Cognitive Science ICCS/ASCS 2003.
4. Matsumoto, N., and Tokosumi, A., "A Socially Supported Knowledge-belief System and Its Application to a Dialogue Parser." Proceedings of the Seventh International Conference on Knowledge-Based Intelligent Information & Engineering. KES2003, Springer Press, (2003). 778-784.
5. Sperber, D., Wilson, D.: Relevance; Communication and Cognition. Harvard Univ. Press, Cambridge, Mass. (1986)

Extracting Domain Knowledge for
Dialogue Model Adaptation

Kuei-Kuang Lin and Hsin-Hsi Chen

Department of Computer Science and Information Engineering
National Taiwan University
Taipei, Taiwan
hh_chen@csie.ntu.edu.tw

Abstract. Domain shift is a challenging issue in dialogue management. This paper shows how to extract domain knowledge for dialogue model adaptation. The basic semantic concepts are derived from domain corpus by iterative token combination and contextual clustering. Speech act is identified by using semantic clues within an utterance. Frame states summarize current dialogue condition and state transition captures the mental agreement between users and system. Both Bayesian and machine learning approaches are experimented in identification of speech act and prediction of next state. To test the feasibility of this model adaptation approach, four corpora from domains of hospital registration service, telephone inquiring service, railway information service and air traveling information service are adopted. The experimental results demonstrate good portability in different domains.

1 Introduction

Dialogue management provides a rich human-computer interaction which allows users to convey more complex information than a single utterance. Despite of the recent significant progress in the areas of human language processing, building successful dialogue systems still requires large amounts of development time and human expertise [1]. The major challenging issue is the introduction of the new domain knowledge to the dialogue model when domain is shifted. That usually takes time to handcraft the domain knowledge that a dialogue manager needs. In the past, some papers [2,6] dealt with acquisition and clustering of grammatical fragments for natural language understanding; and some papers [4,9] employed statistical techniques for recognizing speech intentions. This paper emphasizes on how to extract crucial domain knowledge, including semantic concept extraction, speech act identification and formulation of dialogue state transition. Four corpora from different domains are employed to test the feasibility.

A. Gelbukh (Ed.): CICLing 2004, LNCS 2945, pp. 72–80, 2004.
© Springer-Verlag Berlin Heidelberg 2004

2 Corpora of Different Domains

Two dialogue corpora and two single query corpora were studied. They belong to domains of hospital registration service, telephone inquiring service, railway information service and air traveling information service. Tables 1 and 2 summarize the statistics of the materials. The dialogues in NTUH corpus, which were transcribed from face to face conversation in Chinese, deal with tasks in a registration counter of NTU hospital, including registration, cancellation, information seeking, *etc.* The Chinese CHT corpus was transcribed from Chun-Hwa Telecom phone number inquiring system through telephone. Compared with NTUH corpus, most of the utterances in CHT corpus are very short and incomplete due to the fact that people often address the targets directly when using phone number inquiring service.

Table 1. Dialogue Corpora

Corpus name	NTU Hospital (NTUH)	Chun-Hwa Telecom (CHT)
Content	Register (make appointment), cancel, inquire info	Inquire phone number or other info
Number of dialogues	13	98
Number of utterances	440	1923
Average length	33.5	16.4

Besides the dialogue corpora, two Chinese query corpora, Taiwan Railway Corpus (TWR) and Air Traveling Information Service corpus (CATIS), which include queries about train timetable and air traveling information, respectively, were employed. CATIS is a Chinese version of ATIS [7]. All the airline booking information, e.g., location names, airline names, *etc.*, are translated into Chinese. CATIS is much larger, and it contains more unknown words than TWR corpus.

Table 2. Corpora of Single Utterances

Corpus name	Taiwan Railway (TWR)	Air Traveling (CATIS)
Content	Train timetable queries	Airline booking queries
Number of utterances	200	5517
Average length	29	32

3 Acquisition of Semantic Concepts

Semantic concept refers to key entities in a domain that users have to fill, answer or mention to accomplish the desired tasks. Concepts come with different forms, e.g., they could be database attributes, certain key verbs, or some types of named entities. A concept may have several values, e.g., a destination station in railway corpus may be any location names. In the proposed data-driven methodology, token combination is performed first to combine tokens, and then contextual cluster is employed to gather terms with similar context. The combined tokens are labeled to create a modified corpus for another iteration of token combination and contextual clustering.

NTUH dialogue corpus is adopted for experiment. The Chinese corpus is segmented and tagged with parts of speech. Unseen words like person names are often the major source of segmentation errors. For example, a doctor's name "楊士毅" (Yang Shi Yi) was segmented to three individual characters. Named entity recognition [3] attempts to merge such individual characters. Besides named entities, certain word strings denote potential semantic concepts. We group terms that tend to co-occur in NTUH corpus by mutual information shown as follows. They form phrases or multi-word entities.

$$MI\ (e_1, e_2) = P\left(e_1 | e_2\right)\log\ \frac{P\left(e_1, e_2\right)}{P\left(e_1\right)P\left(e_2\right)} \tag{1}$$

Terms of the same semantic concepts are often represented with similar utterance structure and neighbor context. For example, "我要查第一銀行的電話" (I want the phone number of First Bank) and "我要查台灣大學的電話" (I want the telephone number of National Taiwan University) are used in CHT corpus. The two target elements "第一銀行" (First Bank) and "台灣大學" (National Taiwan University) have similar left and right contexts, which show that two different names denote the similar concepts. Kullback-Leibler distance [5] is used to measure the similarity between two contexts, where V denotes the vocabulary used in contexts.

$$D\ (p_1 \| p_2) = \sum_{i=1}^{V}\ p_1(i)\log\ \frac{p_1(i)}{p_2(i)} \tag{2}$$

$D(p_1 \| p_2) = 0$ if p_1 and p_2 are equivalent, i.e., they have exactly the same neighboring context. Terms with large MI are merged into a larger term and terms with small KL distance are grouped into the same cluster.

Experimental results are judged by human assessors. The results of token combination are rated as four levels – say, *correct word*, *correct phrase*, *nonsense* (i.e., wrong combination) and *longer* (i.e., terms contains both correct and incorrect combinations of previous iterations). Figure 1 shows that formulation of *words* starts from the beginning of token combination, and grows steadily until middle of process (around iteration 30). Phrase combinations occur later at the 15th iteration and the number does not increase as fast as word combinations do. Because the number of phrases is smaller and the meaningful combinations are formulated from word level to phrase level, the number of nonsense and longer combinations increases rapidly in the later iterations. Error propagations exist after 10-15 iterations and result in most nonsense combinations as the curve goes approximately along with nonsense curve.

Contextual clusters are rated as three levels – say, *correct* (i.e., all the clustered terms belong to the same semantic concept), *wrong* (i.e., all the terms are unrelated to one another), and *part* (i.e., some of the clustered items belong to same concept, and some are not.) Figure 2 shows that the curves of correct (meaningful) and wrong (meaningless) clusters have same tendency. They all increase rapidly in the first 5 iterations, and then the increase speed slows down. As the iteration proceeds, a cluster containing totally unrelated terms would seldom occur because terms with clear evidence have been correctly or partly clustered in the previous iterations. Error

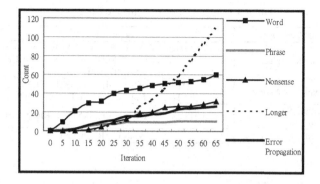

Fig. 1. Quantitative Result of Token Combination

propagation begins at the 10th iteration and grows with the number of "part" clusters. The number of "part" clusters stops growing after 30 iterations. These clusters are in fact unrecognizable for human to make judgment. We can see that the meaningful clusters are proposed in the first half of iterations, and most of the later iterations provide useless clusters. Therefore a reasonable number of iterations should be inspected to stop the clustering algorithm.

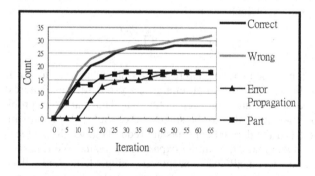

Fig. 2. Quantitative Result of Contextual Clustering

A concept category groups semantic concepts that serve similar roles or present similar intentions in an utterance. At this time, the meanings of the clusters generated from previous experiments are undefined. After the clustering results are examined, total 44 concepts are identified. We re-label the original corpus with these concepts and cluster the corpus again. Table 3 shows some examples of the result.

Although the number of meaningful categories is only few, the result indeed indicates that some concepts can be grouped to proper categories. A complete concept set is formulated by using the proposed semi-automatic algorithm. The experiments show the algorithm is helpful for human to craft domain knowledge. The extracted semantic concepts will be used in the following sections.

Table 3. Categorization of Semantic Concepts

Concept Category	Semantic Concept
Domain Slot Values	(BIRTHDATE_VALUE), (IDNUMBER_VALUE), (RECORDNUM_VALUE), (DATE_VALUE), (TIME_VALUE)
Domain Slot Names	(DATA), (ID_NUM), (RECORD_NUM), (PATIENT_TYPE), (DEPARTMENT_TYPE)
Domain Specific Actions	(CHECK), (CANCEL), (CHANGE), (REGISTER)
Frequently Used Verbs	(WANT), (REQUEST)

4 Identification of Speech Act

Speech acts represent the mental state of the participants in a dialogue. Some words in each utterance are replaced with the semantic concepts derived in last section. A set of speech acts are defined, including *Request-ref, Answer-ref, Request-if, Answer-if, Request-fact, Answer-fact, Greeting, Prompt, Clarify, Accept,* and *Reject* [4]. Four trained annotators were asked to tag corpora with these speech acts. That will serve as an answer set for evaluation. Formula 3 defines the Bayesian identification. Given a set of conceptual features in an utterance, which are denoted by semantic tags C_k, we try to find the speech act with the largest probability. Here we assume that each concept is independent of each other.

$$P\left(\hat{A} \middle| \vec{C} \right) = \arg \max_{A_i} \; P\left(A_i\right) \prod_{k=1}^{M} \frac{P\left(C_k = c_k \middle| A_i\right)}{P\left(C_k = c_k\right)} \tag{3}$$

The precision of the experimental result is 57%. Compared to raw material (i.e., words with the N highest *tf*idf* in an utterance are regarded as features), which has only 18% of precision, semantic concepts eliminate data sparseness problem. The bad performance of raw data is due to the small size of the corpus from which *tf* and *idf* are trained. To tell if the derived concepts are redundant, we divide the concepts into several subgroups and make the similar experiments again. We find out that the best performance occurs when all the concepts are adopted. It shows that the derived semantic concepts do capture specific features of domain utterances and are not redundant.

See5 [8], a machine learning tool, is also adopted to identify speech act. Semantic tags extracted from each utterance are used as attributes to identify speech act. The precision is 65% when all the concepts are considered as clues. Compared to the performance of using the raw material, i.e., 53%, semantic concepts got less gain than Bayesian method.

5 Dialogue Modeling

We adopted frame-based model to formulate the dialogue behavior in this paper. The agreements of contexts between participants in a dialogue are based on the content of frame slots. Predicting the condition of each frame slot could capture the transition process of dialogues. An information state consists of several semantic slots selected from the semantic concepts computed in Section 3. Besides, several conditions are defined to represent each slot state, including *in question*, *mentioned*, *with value*, and *empty*, which are denoted by symbols *, +, 1, and 0, respectively, in Table 4. Originally, all the frame slots are set to 0. An algorithm shown as follows determines the state of each frame slot.

1. Check if any slot value is confirmed. If so, fill the slot with value and set the state to 1.
2. Determine if any questioning clues exist. If yes, tag each slot name mentioned along with questioning clues, and set the state to *.
3. Tag all mentioned slot names as mentioned, and set the state to +.

Using this algorithm, an input utterance will be transformed into information state representation. Total 13 slots, including *branch name, service type, department type, doctor name, week date, time, birth date, ID number, medical record number, patient name, number of times coming*, and *general number*, are selected from the derived semantic concepts, and form the set of frame states. Not all slots are presented in the Table 4. Numbers 1-5 show the first five slots illustrated above.

Table 4. Examples of Transformation of Information State

Original Utterance	U: 我要掛眼科門診。(I want to register outpatient service of ophthalmology department.)	U: 不知道星期幾有呢？(I wonder on what day there is such a service?)	S: 請問要在總院看還是公館分院看？(Would you like to go to main hospital or Gong-gwan branch?
Concepts chunked	(department_type) (service_type) (person) (want) (register)	(week) (question_word)	(branch_name1) (branch_name2) (request) (at) (see_doctor) (question_word)
Slot	User	User	System
1	0	0	+
2	1	1	1
3	1	1	1
4	0	0	0
5	0	*	*

Following the above procedure, a dialogue corpus could be transformed into transitions of a sequence of information states. By using an information state as a clue, we have transformed the problem from modeling a complete dialogue into predicting next information state. Because the history of dialogue is accumulated in terms of state transition, every prediction to the next state actually concerns about all the previous dialogue history.

Due to the sparseness and small amount of corpus, Bayesian prediction is divided into two phases: 1) Predict the entire set of states when the previous state actually occurred in the training corpus; and 2) If not, assume that each slot is independent, and predict each individually. In Formulas 4, 5, 6 and 7, S_{i+1} is the whole frame state in time i+1; s_{i+1} is a candidate of the next slot state; s_i is the current slot state; f_j is a feature presented in the current utterance; and K is the number of features.

$$P\left(S_{i+1}|S_i\right) = P\left(S_{i+1}\right)\frac{P\left(S_i|S_{i+1}\right)}{P\left(S_i\right)} \tag{4}$$

$$P\left(s_{i+1}|s_i\right) = P\left(s_{i+1}\right)\frac{P\left(s_i|s_{i+1}\right)}{P\left(s_i\right)} \tag{5}$$

$$P\left(s_{i+1}|\vec{F}\right) = P\left(s_i\right)\prod_{j=1}^{K}\frac{P\left(F_j = f_j|s_{i+1}\right)}{P\left(F_j = f_j\right)} \tag{6}$$

$$score\left(s_{i+1}\right) = P\left(s_{i+1}|s_i\right)* P\left(s_{i+1}|\vec{F}\right) \tag{7}$$

In the experiment, there are 440 transitions. In 209 of these transitions, the previous frame state occurred in the training corpus. The predictions are done trivially in phase 1. In the other 231 transitions, each slot state is predicted in phase 2. The next frame slots can be predicted from the training experience in about 60% (i.e., 127 correct among 209 example frames) of the transitions. If the determination is relaxed to determining if a slot state should appear, the precision is up to 82%. Table 5 summarizes the experimental results of phase 1. It shows that if there is a large enough training corpus to obtain more reliable dialogue states, the prediction of next frame state is feasible. For those not seen in the training set, phase 2 predicts each slot state respectively. Table 6 shows the result. Each frame contains 13 slots to be predicted. The overall precision is 91.2%. After further analyzing the distribution of slot state, we found that most of the slot states (i.e., 97.4%) are not change through transitions. In other words, it is much easier to predict an unchanged slot state than a changed one. In our experiment, 50.6% of slot states which are changed can be correctly predicted, on the other hand, 92.34% of slot states which are not changed can be predicted correctly.

Table 5. Phase 1 Result

Number of frame	209
Correct	127
Plain Correct	45
Incorrect	37
Precision	82.3%

Machine learning method is also applied to predict each slot state. Semantic features, the previous slot state, the role and the speech act of current utterance are considered as the attributes for each slot state. The result shows that the most important attributes are the previous slot states. The precision drops from 98% to 7% without consideration of the previous slots.

Table 6. Phase 2 Result

Number of frame	231
Number of slots	3003
Correct	2740
Incorrect	263
Precision	91.2%

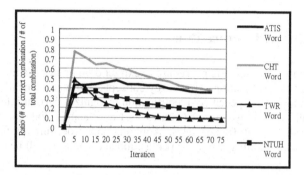

Fig. 3. Results of Word Combination in Different Corpora

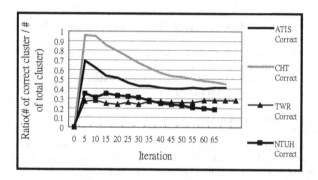

Fig. 4. Results of Clustering in Different Corpora

6 Shifting Domain

The proposed method is experimented on the NTUH service domain in the previous sections. To test its portability, the method is also applied to the other three different domains.

In semantic concept acquisition, we can see that each domain presents similar tendency, as shown in Figures 3 and 4. The difference lies mainly in different sizes and characteristics of corpora. For example, CHT corpus contains many named entities and special representations, so that the proportion of correct combinations is higher.

In speech act identification, the precision rates in CHT corpus are 77% with machine learning method and 57% with Bayesian method. CHT is comparatively a simpler domain than NTUH. The most frequent speech acts in CHT corpus are *Request-ref* and *Answer-ref*. In dialogue modeling, average frame state prediction (phase 1) is 85%, and slot state prediction (phase 2) is 87%.

7 Conclusions and Future Work

This paper proposes a systematic procedure to extract domain knowledge for dialogue adaptation. Semantic acquisition extracts key concepts semi-automatically to decrease human intervening cost. Speech act identification recognizes current intent and focus of an utterance. Regarding derived features as frame states, dialogue transition is modeled as prediction of frame states. Applying the procedure to four different domains shows its portability. More data collection and domains will be experimented in future work.

References

1. Allen, J.F *et al.*: Towards Conversational Human-Computer Interaction. In AI Magazine, (2001)
2. Arai, K. *et al.*: Grammar Fragment Acquisition using Syntactic and Semantic Clustering. In Speech Communication, Vol. 27, No. 1, (1999)
3. Chen, H.H., Ding, Y.W. and Tsai, S.C.: Named Entity Extraction for Information Retrieval. In Computer Processing of Oriental Languages, Vol. 12, No. 1, (1998) 75-85.
4. Chu-Carrol, J.: A Statistical Model for Discourse Act Recognition in Dialogue Interactions. In Proceedings of AAAI Spring Symposium on Applying Machine Learning to Discourse Processing (1998)
5. Kullback, S.: Information Theory and Statistics. John Wiley and Sons, New York (1959)
6. Meng, Helen and Siu, K.C.: Semiautomatic Acquisition of Semantic Structures. In IEEE Transaction Knowledge and Data Engineering, Vol. 14, (2001)
7. Price, P.: Evaluation of Spoken Language Systems: The ATIS Domain. In Proceedings of ARPA Human Language Technology Workshop (1990)
8. Quinlan, R.: See5. URL: www.rulequest.com (2002)
9. Stolcke, A. and Shriberg, E.: Dialog Act Modeling for Conversational Speech. In Proceedings of AAAI Spring Symposium on Applying Machine Learning to Discourse Processing (1998)

A Probabilistic Chart Parser Implemented with an Evolutionary Algorithm*

Lourdes Araujo

Dpto. Sistemas Informáticos y Programación. Universidad Complutense de Madrid.
Spain. `lurdes@sip.ucm.es`

Abstract. Classic parsing methods use complete search techniques to find the different interpretations of a sentence. However, the size of the search space increases exponentially with the length of the sentence or text to be parsed and the size of the grammar, so that exhaustive search methods can fail to reach a solution in a reasonable time. Nevertheless, large problems can be solved approximately by some kind of stochastic techniques, which do not guarantee the optimum value, but allow adjusting the probability of error by increasing the number of points explored. Evolutionary Algorithms are among such techniques. This paper presents a stochastic chart parser based on an evolutionary algorithm which works with a population of partial parsings. The paper describes the relationships between the elements of a classic chart parser and those of the evolutionary algorithm. The model has been implemented, and the results obtained for texts extracted from the Susanne corpus are presented.

Keywords: Evolutionary programming, Partial Parsing, Probabilistic Grammars

1 Introduction

Parsing a sentence can be sought as a procedure that searches for different ways of combining grammatical rules to find a combination which could be the structure of the sentence. A bottom-up parser starts with the sequence of lexical classes of the words and its basic operation is to take a sequence of symbols to match it to the right-hand side of the rules. Thus, this parser can be implemented simply as a search procedure for this matching process. However, such implementation would be extremely expensive because the parser would try the same matches again and again. This problem is avoided in the chart parsing algorithms by introducing a data structure called *chart* [1]. This structure stores the partial results of the matchings already done.

Classical parsing methods are based on complete search techniques to find the different interpretations of a sentence. However, experiments on human parsing suggest that people do not perform a complete search of the grammar while

---

* Supported by projects TIC2003-09481-C04 and 07T/0030/2003.

A. Gelbukh (Ed.): CICLing 2004, LNCS 2945, pp. 81–92, 2004.
© Springer-Verlag Berlin Heidelberg 2004

parsing. On the contrary, human parsing seems to be closer to a heuristic process with some random component. This suggests exploring alternative search methods. Another central point when parsing is the need of selecting the "most" correct parsing from the multitude of possible parsings consistent with the grammar. In such a situation, some kind of disambiguation is required. Statistical parsing provides a way of dealing with disambiguation. Stochastic grammars [4], obtained by supplementing the elements of algebraic grammars with probabilities, represent an important part of the statistical methods in computational linguistics and have allowed important advances in areas such as disambiguation and error correction. A probabilistic context free grammar, PCFG, is defined as a CFG along with a set of probabilities on the rules such that

$$\sum_j P(N^i \rightarrow \eta^j) = 1$$

for all i, where N^i is a nonterminal and η^j is a sequence of terminals and nonterminals.

In order to improve the efficiency of a parser based on a PCFG, we can develop algorithms that attempt to explore the high-probability components first. These are called *best-first parsing* algorithms. The goal is to find the best parse quickly and thus to avoid exploring much of the search space. Chart parsing algorithms can be easily modified to consider the most likely components first.

Another alternative to search the parses are evolutionary algorithms (EAs). EAs have already been applied to some issues of natural language processing [8], such as query translation [10], inference of context-free grammars [13,12,9, 7], tagging [3], parsing [2], word sense disambiguation [5], and information retrieval [6]. In the system described in [2] parse trees are randomly generated and combined. The evolutionary process is in charge of giving low rates of probability of surviving to those trees which do not match the grammar rules properly. This system has been tested on a set of simple sentences, but the size of the population required to parse real sentences with real grammars, as those extracted from a linguistic corpus, is too large for the system to work properly.

This paper presents the implementation of a stochastic bottom-up chart parser based on an evolutionary algorithm which works with a population of partial parsings. The algorithm produces successive generations of individuals, computing their quality or "fitness" at each step and selecting the best of them for the next generation. The purpose of most EAs is to find a good solution and not necessarily the best solution, and this is enough for most natural language statistical processes. EAs provide at the same time a reasonable accuracy as well as a unified scheme of algorithm applicable to different problems.

The rest of the paper proceeds as follows: Section 2 describes the evolutionary parser, presenting the main elements of the evolutionary algorithm; section 3 presents and discusses the experimental results, and section 4 draws the main conclusions of this work.

```
function Arc-Extension(chart, agenda, grammar, C, p₁, p₂)
    Insert(chart, C, p1, p2);
    for each active arc X → X₁, ···, ∘C, Xₙ from p₀ to p₁do{
        AddNewActiveArc(chart, X → X₁, ···, C ∘ Xₙ, p₀, p₂);
    }
    for each active arc X → X₁, ···, Xₙ ∘ C from p₀ to p₁do{
        AddNewComponent(agenda, X, p₀, p₂);
    }
end
```

Fig. 1. Arc extension algorithm to add a component from position p1 to position p2

2 Evolutionary Algorithm for Chart Parsing

The algorithm can be view as a probabilistic implementation of a bottom-up chart parser. In a chart parser, the *chart* structure stores the partial results of the matchings already done. Matches are always attempted from one component, called *key*. To find rules that match a string involving the key, the algorithm looks for rules which start with the key, or for rules which have already been started by early keys and require the present key either to extend or to complete the rule. The chart records all components derived from the sentence so far in the parse. It also maintains the record of rules that have partially matched but are incomplete. These are called *active arcs*. The basic operation of a chart parser consists in combining an active arc with a completed component. The result is either a new completed component or a new active arc that is an extension of the original active arc. Completed components are stored in a list called *agenda* until being added to the chart. This process is called *arc extension algorithm*, of which Figure 1 shows an scheme. To add a component C into the chart from position p_1 to position p_2, C is inserted into the chart between those positions. Then, for any active arc of the form $X \rightarrow X_1, \cdots, \circ C, X_n$ (where $\circ$ denotes the key position) from p_0 to p_1, a new active arc $X \rightarrow X_1, \cdots, C \circ X_n$ is added from position p_0 to p_2. Finally, for each active arc $X \rightarrow X_1, \cdots, X_n \circ C$ from position p_0 to p_1, which only requires C to be completed, a new component of type X is added to the agenda from position p_0 to p_1. Figure 2 shows a scheme of the chart parsing algorithm. It consists in a loop repeated until there is no input left. At each iteration, if the agenda is empty, the lexical categories for the next word of the sentence are added to the agenda. Then a component C is selected from the agenda. Let us assume it goes from position p_1 to p_2. For each grammar rule of the form $X \rightarrow C X_1, \cdots, X_n$, a new active arc $X \rightarrow \circ C X_1, \cdots, X_n$ from p_1 to p_2 is added from position p_1 to p_2. Finally, C is added to the chart by means of the arc extension algorithm.

Probabilistic Chart parsing algorithms consider the most likely components first. The main idea is to implement the agenda as a *priority queue* — where the highest-rate elements are always first in the queue. Accordingly, the parser always removes the highest-ranked component from the agenda and adds it to the chart.

```
function ChartParser(sentence, chart)
    while cont < Length(sentence) do{
    if Empty(agenda) {
        AddInterpretation(sentence[cont]);
        cont++;
    }
    SelectComponent(agenda, C, p₁, p₂);
    for each grammar rule X → CX₁ ··· Xₙ from p₁ to p₂do{
        AddNewActiveArc(chart, X → ∘CX₁ ··· Xₙ, p₁, p₂);
    }
    ArcExtension(chart, agenda, grammar, C, p₁, p₂);
end
```

Fig. 2. Bottom-up chart parsing algorithm

In the evolutionary parser (EP), the population is composed of partial parses of different sequences of words of the sentence, that are randomly combined to produce new parses for longer sequences of words. Thus, the *agenda* of a chart parser, which stores completed components, is represented by the population of the EA. The algorithm of arc extension is represented by the crossover operator, which combines partial parses until completing the categories requires by the right-hand side of a rule, so as to produce a new completed component of the classes given by the left-hand side of the rule. At this point, the EP differs of the chart parsing because the arc extension algorithm is continuously applied until completing a component. Thus, in the EA active arcs only exist during the crossover operation, because when this finishes every arc explored has been completed. Another difference comes from the way of selecting the rules to be applied. A *best-first parsing* algorithm always selects the most likely rule, while the EA, can select any rule, though those of higher probability have more chances to be selected.

Finally, the input data for the EA are those of the classic chart parser: the sentence to be parsed, the dictionary from which the lexical tags of the words can be obtained along with their frequencies, and the PCFG, together with the genetic parameters (population size, crossover and mutation rates, etc.).

Let us now consider each element of the algorithm separately.

2.1   Chart Representation: The EA Population

The chart data structure stores all intermediate results of the parsing, that is, any valid parse of the substrings of the input. This intermediate results are the *edges* of the chart. Thus, each edge stores three things: the grammar rule, the parse subtree and the corresponding locations in the sentence.

Individuals in our system can be view as edges, directly represented by subtrees. They are parses of segments of the sentence, that is, they are trees obtained by applying the probabilistic CFG to a sequence of words of the sentence. Each

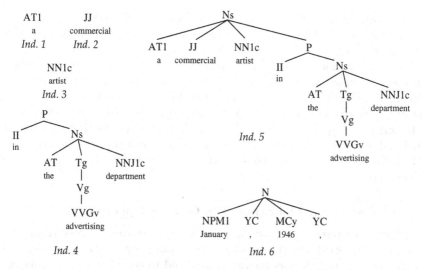

Fig. 3. Examples of individuals for the sentence *The new promotion manager has been employed by the company since January +, 1946 +, as a commercial artist in the advertising department +.*

individual is assigned a syntactic category: the left-hand side of the top-level rule in the parse. The probability of this rule is also registered. The first word of the sequence parsed by the tree, the number of words of that sequence and the number of nodes of the tree are also registered. Each tree is composed of a number of subtrees, each of them corresponding to the required syntactic category of the right-hand side of the rule. Figure 3 shows some individuals for the sentence *The new promotion manager has been employed by the company since January +, 1946 +, as a commercial artist in the advertising department +.*, used as a running example, which has been extracted from the Susanne corpus. We can see that there are individuals composed of a single word, such as *1*, while others, such as *5*, are a parse tree obtained by applying different grammar rules. For the former, the category is the chosen lexical category of the word (a word can belong to more than one lexical class); e.g., the category of *1* is *AT1*. For the latter, the category is the left hand-side of the top level rule; e.g., the category of *5* is *Ns*.

Chart Initialization: The Initial Population. The first step in parsing a sentence with a bottom-up chart parser is to initialize the chart with word edges. For each lexical rule which expands to a given word, a corresponding edge is created. This edge stores a leaf tree and a location equal to the location of the word in the sentence.

Lexical rules can be obtained by finding the possible lexical tags of each word. For example, for the word *as*, which has the tags *CSA*, *IIa* and *RGa* in the

Susanne corpus, we will include in the grammar the rules $CSA \longrightarrow as$, $IIa \longrightarrow as$ and $RGa \longrightarrow as$. The lexical tags are obtained, along with their frequencies, from a dictionary.

The initialization of our system amounts to creating the initial population of the evolutionary algorithm which, like for the chart parser, is composed of individuals that are leave trees formed only by a lexical category of the word. The system generates a different individual for each lexical category of the word.

In order to improve the performance, the initial population also includes individuals obtained by applying a grammar rule provided that all the categories of the right-hand side of the rule are lexical. The individual 6 of Figure 3 is one such example.

2.2   Arc-Extension Algorithm: The Genetic Operators

The edge set represents the state of a chart parser during processing, and new edges can be inserted into the set at any time. Once entered, an edge cannot be modified or removed. New edges can correspond to complete components or to active arcs, pending of further extension to be completed.

In our system, active arcs only have a temporary existence and they do not appear in the population, which is only composed of complete components. The process of extending an arc is not partitioned in a number of steps, but is done as a whole in the crossover operation. New individuals are created by means of two genetic operators: *crossover* and *cut*. The crossover operator combines a parse with other parses present in the population to satisfy a grammar rule; cut creates a new parse by randomly selecting a subtree from an individual of the population. The rates of crossover and cut operations performed at each step are input parameters, to which the algorithm is very sensitive.

At each generation genetic operators produce new individuals which are added to the previous population that in this way is enlarged. The selection process is in charge of reducing the population size down to the size specified as an input parameter. Selection is performed with respect to the relative fitness of the individuals, but it also takes into account other factors to ensure the presence in the population of parses containing words that can be needed in later generations.

Reproduction. The crossover operator produces a new individual by combining an individual selected from the population with an arbitrary number of other ones. Notice that the crossover in this case does not necessarily occurs in pairs. The operator repeatedly applies the arc-extension algorithm until completed components are obtained. The individuals to be crossed are randomly selected. This selection does not consider the fitness of the individuals because some grammar rules may require, to be completed, individuals of some particular syntactic category for which there are not higher fitness representatives.

Crossover begins by selecting an individual from the population. For example, let us assume that the individual 1 of Figure 3 is selected. Then the process continues as follows:

- Identify the syntactic category of the root of the tree to be combined. For *Ind1* it is *AT1*.
- Select among the grammar rules those whose right-hand side begins with this syntactic category. For the grammar used in this work, some examples of these rules for the *AT1* category are:

$$Ns \rightarrow AT1\ JJ\ NN1c\ P$$
$$Ns \rightarrow AT1\ JJ\ NN1n\ P$$
$$Ns \rightarrow AT1\ JJ\ Tg\ NN1c\ P$$
$$Ns \rightarrow AT1\ NN1c\ Po$$
$$Ns \rightarrow AT1\ NN1c\ YC\ Nns\ YC\ MCn$$
$$Ns \rightarrow AT1\ NN1n\ Po$$

Let us assume that the first rule is the selected one.

- For each category of the right hand side of the rule after the first one, search in the population for an individual whose syntactic category matches the considered category, and whose sequence of words is the continuation of the words of the previous individual. In the example, we look for an individual of category *JJ*, other of category *NN1c* and other of category *P*. The sequence of words of the individual of category *JJ* must begin with the word *commercial*, the word which follows those of the individual *1*. Accordingly, the individual *2* of Figure 3 is a valid one (likewise, individuals *3* and *4* are also chosen for the crossover).
- Construct a new individual which has in its root the syntactic category of the rule (Ns) and is composed of the subtrees selected in the previous step, what produces the individual *5* of Figure 3.
- Add the new individual to the population.

With this scheme, the crossover of one individual may produce no descendant at all, or may produce more than one descendant. In this latter case all descendants are added to the population. The process of selection is in charge of reducing the population down to the specified size. Figure 4 shows a scheme of the operator. For each individual in the population the operator is applied according to the crossover rate. If a individual is selected to be crossed, the function *Search-GrammarRules* returns the set of grammar rules whose right-hand side begins with the category of the individual. Then, for each of these rules, the function *SearchIndividuals* searches the population for individuals to complete the right-side of the rule. If they are found, new individuals are created for each possible combination (*CreateTree*) and added to the population. If crossover is applied alone, the mean size of the individuals increases at each generation. Though this is advantageous because at the end we are interested in providing as solutions individuals which cover the whole sentence, it may also induce some problems. If the selection process removes small individuals which can only can be combined in later generations, the parses of these combinations will be never produced. This situation is prevented by applying some constraints in the selection process, as well as by means of the *cut* operator.

```
function Crossover(Population, per_crossover)
    for each individual in Population do{
        prob = random(100);
        if (prob < per_crossover) {
            Rules = SearchGrammarRules(individual);
            for each rule in Rules do{
                Trees = SearchIndividuals(Population, rule, individual);
                for each selection in Trees do{
                    new_individual = CreateTree(rule, individual, selection);
                    population.add(new_individual);
                }
            }
        }
    }
end
```

Fig. 4. Scheme of the crossover operator

The Cut operator. Because our chart representation does not ensures the presence of any edge previously produced, we include the *cut* operator, which allows extracting a part of a parse from an individual. The rate of application of the cut operator increases with the length of the individuals, while crossover is applied at a fixed rate. Thus, in the beginning of the evolution process, crossover is applied almost alone, and so the length of the individuals increases. Later on, when the length of the individuals is long enough, cut and crossover are applied together. Accordingly, the application of the cut operator depends on two parameters, *per_cut* and *threshold_cut*. *Per_cut* is the percentage of application of cut, while *threshold_cut* is the minimum number of words of the individual required to allow the application of *cut*. It is given as a percentage of the length of the sentence being parsed. Figure 5 shows a scheme of this operator. For each individual in the population, the conditions to apply cut are checked. If they are fulfilled, a subtree of the parse tree of the individual is randomly selected and added to the population.

```
function Cut(Population, per_cut, threshold_cut)
    for each individual in Population do{
        if number_words(individual > threshold_cut){
            prob = random(100);
            if (prob < per_cut) {
                new_individual = choose_random_subtree(individual);
                population.add(new_individual);
            }
        }
    }
end
```

Fig. 5. Scheme of the cut operator

2.3   Selection of Components: Fitness Evaluation

A classic parser produces any valid parse of the substrings of the input. This is not guaranteed in an evolutionary algorithm, which tends to generate highly probable individuals, though individuals with low probability also have some opportunities to be produced and survive. Thus, we need a measure of the individual quality or fitness.

The fitness function is basically a measure of the probability of the parse. It is computed as the average probability of the grammar rules used to construct the parse:

$$fitness = \frac{\sum\limits_{\forall s_i \in T} prob(s_i)}{nn(T)}$$

where T is the tree to evaluate, s_i each of its nodes and $nn(T)$ is the number of nodes. For the lexical category, the probability is the relative frequency of the chosen tag.

2.4   The Selection Process

Selection usually replaces some individuals of the population (preferably those with lower fitness) by others generated by the genetic operators. However, there are two issues that make selection a bit different in our case. First at all, our genetic operators include every new individual in the population, that in this way grows arbitrarily and therefore needs to be reduced to a suitable size. And secondly, if fitness were the only criterion to select the individuals to be eliminated, individuals that are the only ones parsing a particular word of the sentence could disappear, thus making impossible to generate a complete parse of the sentence in later generations. Accordingly, our selection process reduces the size of the population by erasing individuals according to their fitness but always ensuring that each of their words are present in at least other individual. If the population size *popu_size* is not enough to allow this, the parsing process is halted. However, this situation is not to be expected because any population size larger than the length of the sentence is enough to guarantee this condition. Figure 6 presents an scheme of the selection process. First at all, in order to improve diversity, duplicated individuals are erased from the population (*Eliminate_duplicate*). The function *ChooseToErase* returns the sequence with the tentative order in which the individuals must be erased. This order is randomly determined with probability inversely proportional to the fitness. Then a loop which erases individuals is repeated until the population is sufficiently reduced. The function *SequencePresent* checks that every of word in the sequence parsed by the individual *ToErase[i]* is present in at least another individual.

3   Experimental Results

The algorithm has been implemented using C++ language and run on a Pentium III processor. In order to evaluate its performance we have considered the

```
function Selection(Population, popu_size)
    Eliminate_duplicate(Population);
    ChooseToErase(Population, ToErase);
    i = 0;
    while Size(Population) > popu_size do{
        if SequencePresent(Population, ToErase[i]){
            Erase(Population, ToErase[i]);
            i++;
        }
    }
end
```

Fig. 6. Scheme of the selection process

parsing of the sentences extracted from the Susanne corpus [11], a database of annotated sentences from the Brown Corpus of written American English manually annotated with syntactic information. The Susanne analytic scheme has been developed on the basis of samples of both British and American English. The corpus comprises 64 files of annotated text and a lexicon. Each file has a line for each word of the original text. In this corpus, punctuation marks and the apostrophe-s suffix are treated as separate words and assigned separate lines. Each line has six fields, which contain at least one character. Figure 7 shows some lines of one Susanne file.

```
A01:0120.21    -    AT      the      the      [Ns-.
A01:0120.24    -    NN1c    number   number   .
A01:0120.27    -    IO      of       of       [Po.
A01:0120.30    -    NN2     voters   voter    .Po]Ns-]
```

Fig. 7. Sequence of lines extracted from the file A01 of the Susanne corpus. The fields of each line are *reference*, *status*, *wordtag*, *word*, *lemma* and *parse*.

The grammar used herein has been read off the parsed sentences of the Susanne corpus. In order to simplify the process, those sentences which make reference to elements outside them (*trace* sentences) have not been used to extract the grammar. Each grammar rule is assigned a probability computed as its relative frequency with respect other rules with the same left-hand side[1].

---

[1] That is, if we are considering the rule r of the form $A \rightarrow \cdots$, the probability of r is computed as:

$$P(r) = \frac{\#r}{\sum_{r' = A \rightarrow \cdots} \#r'}$$

where $\#r$ is the number of occurrences of r

3.1   Recall, Precision, and Accuracy

Recall, precision and accuracy are the most commonly measures used for parsing evaluation. *Precision* is given by the number of brackets in the parse to evaluate which match those in the correct tree; *recall* measures how many of the brackets in the correct tree are in the parse, and *accuracy* is the percentage of brackets from the parse which do not cross over the brackets in the correct parse.

One of the several reasons why a parser can produce a wrong parse for a sentence is that the necessary rules are not present in the grammar due to lack of statistics in the corpus. It is a serious problem when using the Susanne corpus because of its large tag sets. However, if we are mainly interested in evaluating a parser, this problem can be circumvented by applying the parser to sentences from the training corpus. Thus we have tested the parser on a set of 17 sentences from the training corpus (the average length of the sentences is 30 words). In order to compare the EA with a classic parser, we have implemented a classic *best-first chart parsing* (BFCP) algorithm. Table 1 shows the precision, recall, accuracy and tagging results obtained for grammars of different size (best results achieved in ten runs). We can observe that the results of the EP improve those of a classic chart parser for the first grammar. Though these results get a bit worse when the size of the grammar is enlarged, they can be improved again by modifying the parameters of the evolutionary algorithm (those employed are suitable for the grammar of 225 rules). Anyway, the Susanne corpus produces too large grammars, inappropriate for the EP, so we expect to improve the results by using more appropriate corpus.

What is most relevant in the obtained results is that the EP is able to reach a 100% in any of the three measures, while the probabilistic chart parsing does not reach this value simply because the correct parse of some sentences is not the most probable one. In this way the heuristic component of the evolutionary algorithm shows its usefulness for parsing.

Table 1. Results obtained for different sizes of the grammar with a best-first chart parser (BFCP) and with the evolutionary parser (EP).

	225 r.		446 r.		795 r.	
	BFCP	EP	BFCP	EP	BFCP	EP
Precision	99.23	100	99.23	99.01	99.23	97.48
Recall	99.23	100	99.23	99.01	99.23	94.86
Accuracy	98.20	100	98.20	99.01	98.20	97.42
Tag. accuracy	100	100	100	100	100	99.61

4   Conclusions

This paper presents an implementation of a probabilistic chart parser by means of an evolutionary algorithm. It works with a population of partial parses for a given input sentence and a given grammar. Evolutionary algorithms allow a statistical treatment of the parsing process, providing at the same time the typical generality of the evolutionary methods, which allows to use the same algorithm scheme to tackle different problems.

The grammar and sentences used to evaluate the system have been extracted from the Susanne corpus. Measures of precision, recall and accuracy have been provided, obtaining results which improve those of a classic chart parser, thus indicating that the evolutionary algorithms are a robust approach for natural language parsing. Moreover, the heuristic component of these algorithms seems to harmonize with the non deterministic nature of the natural language tasks.

Another conclusion of this work is the inappropriateness of the Susanne corpus for statistical processing. The sets of lexical and syntactic tags used in this corpus are too large to get significant statistics. We thus plan to test the system on other corpora.

References

1. J. Allen. *Natural Language Understanding*. Benjamin/Cumming Publ., 1994.
2. L. Araujo. A parallel evolutionary algorithm for stochastic natural language parsing. In *Proc. of Int. Conf. Parallel Problem Solving from Nature (PPSNVII)*, 2002.
3. L. Araujo. Part-of-speech tagging with evolutionary algorithms. In *Proc. of the Int. Conf. on Intelligent Text Processing and Computational Linguistics (CICLing-2002), Lecture Notes in Computer Science 2276*, p. 230–239. Springer-Verlag, 2002.
4. E. Charniak. *Statistical Language Learning*. MIT press, 1993.
5. A. Gelbukh, G. Sidorov, and S.-Y. Han. Evolutionary Approach to Natural Language Word Sense Disambiguation Through Global Coherence Optimization. In *WSEAS Transaction on Communications*, 1(2), 2003, pp 11-19.
6. A. Gelbukh, S. Han, G. Sidorov. Compression of Boolean inverted files by document ordering. In *NLPKE-2003, Nat. Lang. Proc. & Knowl. Eng.*, IEEE Comp., 2003.
7. B. Keller and R. Lutz. Evolving stochastic context-free grammars from examples using a minimum description length principle. In *In Worksop on Automata Induction, Grammatical Inference and Language Acquisition. ICML097*. ICML, 1997.
8. Anne Kool. Literature survey, 2000.
9. Robert M. Losee. Learning syntactic rules and tags with genetic algorithms for information retrieval and filtering: an empirical basis for grammatical rules. *Information Processing & Management*, 32(2):185–197, 1996.
10. T. Dunning M. Davis. Query translation using evolutionary programming for multilingual information retrieval II. In *Proc. of the Fifth Annual Conf. on Evolutionary Programming*. Evolutionary Programming Society, 1996.
11. G. Sampson. *English for the Computer*. Clarendon Press, Oxford, 1995.
12. T.C. Smith and I.H. Witten. A genetic algorithm for the induction of natural language grammars. In *Proc. IJCAI-95 Workshop on New Approaches to Learning Natural Language*, pages 17–24, Montreal, Canada, 1995.
13. P. Wyard. Context free grammar induction using genetic algorithms. In *Proc. of the 4th Int. Conf. on Genetic Algorithms*, pages 514–518, 1991.

Probabilistic Shift-Reduce Parsing Model Using Rich Contextual Information

Yong-Jae Kwak, So-Young Park, Joon-Ho Lim, and Hae-Chang Rim

Natural Language Processing Lab., Dept. of CSE,
Korea University, Anam-dong 5-ga, Seongbuk-gu, 136-701, Seoul, Korea
{yjkwak,ssoya,jhlim,rim}@nlp.korea.ac.kr

Abstract. In this paper, we present a probabilistic shift-reduce parsing model which can overcome low context-sensitivity of previous LR parsing models. Since previous models are restricted by LR parsing framework, they can utilize only a lookahead and a LR state (stack). The proposed model is not restricted by LR parsing framework, and is able to add rich contextual information as needed. To show an example of contextual information designed for applying the proposed model to Korean, we devise a new context scheme named "*surface-context-types*" which uses syntactic structures, sentential forms, and selective lexicals. Experimental results show that rich contextual information used by our model can improve the parsing accuracy, and our model outperforms the previous models even when using a lookahead alone.

1 Probabilistic Shift-Reduce Parsing Model

Since the first approach [1] and [2] of integrating a probabilistic method with the LR parsing technique, some standard probabilistic LR parsing models have been implemented. [3] and [4] (or [5]) defined a parse tree candidate T as a transition sequence of LR state [3] or LR stack [4] that is driven by an action and a lookahead, as follows:

$$s_0 \overset{l_1,a_1}{\Rightarrow} s_1 \overset{l_1,a_1}{\Rightarrow} \ldots \overset{l_{m-1},a_{m-1}}{\Rightarrow} \overset{l_m,a_m}{\Rightarrow} s_{n-1} \Rightarrow s_m \text{ [3]} \quad \sigma_0 \overset{l_1,a_1}{\Rightarrow} \sigma_1 \overset{l_1,a_1}{\Rightarrow} \ldots \overset{l_{m-1},a_{m-1}}{\Rightarrow} \overset{l_m,a_m}{\Rightarrow} \sigma_{n-1} \Rightarrow \sigma_m \text{ [4]} \tag{1}$$

where s_i and σ_i are the i-th state [3] and stack [4], l_i is the i-th lookahead, a_i is the action that can be performed for the lookahead and the state (or the stack), and m is the number of actions to complete parsing procedure. A state/stack transition sequence gives the following probabilistic model:

$$P(T) = \prod_{i=1\ldots n} P(l_i, a_i, s_i \mid s_{i-i}) \text{ [3]} \quad P(T) = \prod_{i=1\ldots n} P(l_i, a_i, \sigma_i \mid \sigma_{i-i}) \text{ [4]} \tag{2}$$

These models are less context-sensitive, because the selection of action can be affected by information beyond the LR parsing framework, such as LR parsing table, LR stack, lookahead.

As actions are performed, not only the stack but also the input are changed. We propose a probabilistic shift-reduce parsing model considering both of the stack and the input word sequence $W = w_1 \ldots w_n$, as follows:

A. Gelbukh (Ed.): CICLing 2004, LNCS 2945, pp. 93–96, 2004.
© Springer-Verlag Berlin Heidelberg 2004

$$P(T \mid W) = P(T \mid w_{1...n}, a_0, \sigma_0, l_0) = P(a_{1...m}, \sigma_{1...m}, l_{1...m} \mid w_{1...m}, a_0, \sigma_0, l_0) \tag{3}$$

where a_0, σ_0, and l_0 are the initial action, stack[1], and lookahead introduced for satisfying the formula. This equation is decomposed as follows:

$$
\begin{aligned}
& P(a_{1...m}, \sigma_{1...m}, l_{1...m} \mid w_{1...n}, a_0, \sigma_0, l_0) \\
& = \prod_{i=1...m} P(a_i, \sigma_i, l_i \mid w_{1...n}, a_{0...i-1}, \sigma_{0...i-1}, l_{0...i-1}) \\
& = \prod_{i=1...m} \begin{aligned}[t] & P(l_i \mid w_{1...n}, a_{0...i-1}, \sigma_{0...i-1}, l_{0...i-1}) \\ & \times P(a_i \mid w_{1...n}, a_{0...i-1}, \sigma_{0...i-1}, l_{0...i-1}, l_i) \times P(\sigma_i \mid w_{1...n}, a_{0...i-1}, \sigma_{0...i-1}, l_{0...i-1}, a_i, l_i) \end{aligned}
\end{aligned}
\tag{4}
$$

We assume that the history of action $a_{0...i-1}$ (until a_{i-1}) is not influential, and the latest action, stack and lookahead have any effect on the next action, stack, and lookahead, namely:

$$
\begin{aligned}
& P(P \mid W) \\
& = \prod_{i=1...m} \begin{aligned}[t] & P(l_i \mid w_{1...n}, a_{0...i-1}, \sigma_{0...i-1}, l_{0...i-1}) \\ & \times P(a_i \mid w_{1...n}, a_{0...i-1}, \sigma_{0...i-1}, l_{0...i-1}, l_i) \times P(\sigma_i \mid w_{1...n}, a_{0...i-1}, \sigma_{0...i-1}, l_{0...i-1}, a_i, l_i) \end{aligned} \\
& = \prod_{i=1...m} P(l_i \mid w_{1...n}, \sigma_{i-1}, l_{i-1}) \times P(a_i \mid w_{1...n}, \sigma_{i-1}, l_i) \times P(\sigma_i \mid w_{1...n}, a_i, \sigma_{i-1}, l_i)
\end{aligned}
\tag{5}
$$

In the above equation, the second factor can be estimated such that $\sum_{a \in \{shift, reduce\}} P(a_i \mid w_{1...n}, \sigma_{i-1}, l_i) = 1$. The first and the third factor are deterministically 1, because l_i is naturally determined by $w_{1...n}$, σ_{i-1}, and l_{i-1}, and σ_i can be uniquely determined by a_i, σ_{i-1}, and l_i. As a result, the parse probability can be summarized as follows:

$$P(T \mid W) = \prod_{i=1...m} P(a_i \mid w_{1...n}, \sigma_{i-1}, l_i) \tag{6}$$

Here, a lookahead l_i, an element of W, also indicates a stack-input boundary which is an imaginary border line between the stack and the input. Our model is not necessarily restricted by LR parsing framework and can use rich contextual information by proper assumption. Moreover, it is more intuitive than the previous models in that it evaluates the probability of action for the given conditional (contextual) information.

2 Contextual Information for Shift-Reduce Parsing of Korean

We show an example of contextual information designed for applying the proposed shift-reduce parsing model to Korean. Using a shift-reduce parser, we generate binary-branching phrase structure. Based on the observation of characteristics of Korean that the functional words are so developed that they can represent the structure of a phrase or a sentential form by themselves, we have devised the context schemes using mainly functional words named *surface-context-types* that is composed of following three components:

• **Surface-Phrasal-Type (SPT)** represents the abbreviated syntactic structures of the two sub-trees to be reduced or not on the top of the stack σ_i (we call them *stack-*

---

[1] Unlike [3] and [4], we assume that stack transition starts from σ_1, not σ_0.

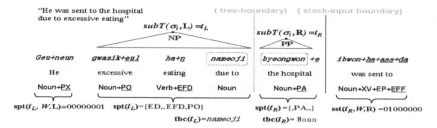

Fig. 1. Contextual information used in the proposed model

top sub-trees from now on).. We represent SPT as a generalized sequence of the terminal functional words consisting of a quadruple {nvfm_c, head_f, midp_f, rest_f}. nvfm_c is the mnemonic selected among the mnemonic sequence for noun/verb phrase [6]. The next three members correspond the right-most three functional word. In Fig.1, SPT representations of the left sub-tree NP ($subT(\sigma_i,L)$) and the right sub-tree PP ($subT(\sigma_i,R)$) are provided, where $subT(\sigma_i,L/R)$ is the left/right stack-top sub-tree for the stack σ_i and $spt(t)$ is the SPT representation of tree t.

• **Surface-Sentential-Type (SST)** represents the sub-sentential forms outside the stack-top sub-trees. We represent SST as a bit-string which is constructed by turning on/off the bit-field according to whether specific functional words exist. In Fig.1, SST representations of the left area and the right area outside NP and PP are provided, where $sst(t,W,L/R)$ is the SST representation of the area left/right to t for the given input word sequence W.

Table 1. Parsing accuracies as the contextual information is accumulated, compared with previous models. <1>~<4> denote contextual information used in our model.

	State transition [3]	Stack transition [4]	<1> lh	<2> <1>+spt	<3> <2>+sst	<4> <3>+tbc
Labeled Recall	71.22	74.27%	75.57%	83.78%	83.98%	85.77%
Labeled Precision	71.30	74.39%	75.59%	83.86%	84.06%	85.80%
Exact Matching	1.70%	3.77%	5.18%	14.81%	15.13%	16.65%

• **Tree-Boundary-Contentword (TBC)** is the right-most terminal content word of each stack-top sub-tree. They are adjacent to the boundary between the stack-top sub-trees (called 'tree-boundary') and are similar to content phrasal heads. Among all the content words, we selectively lexicalise some content words especially contributing to sentence segmentation. Other words are replaced by part-of-speeches. Such words are effective in promoting shift probability for the sub-trees that are likely to be reduced. In Fig.1, the left/right content word for the tree-boundary between NP and PP are provided, where $tbc(t)$ is the TBC for the tree t.

For our probabilistic shift-reduce parsing model, we assume that the contextual information is represented by using the surface-context-types and a lookahead, namely:

$$P(T) = \prod_{i=1..m} P(a_i \mid W, \sigma_{i-1}, l_i) \cong \prod_{i=1..m} P(a_i \mid spt(t_L), spt(t_R), sst(t_L, W, L), sst(t_R, W, R), tbc(t_L), tbc(t_R), l_i) \qquad (7)$$

, where $t_L = subT(\sigma_i, L)$ and $t_L = subT(\sigma_i, R)$

For calculating the action probabilities we use the maximum-likelihood estimation, and for handling the sparse-data problem we use a deleted interpolation method with a backing-off strategy similar to [6].

3 Experimental Results

We used the treebank with 12,084 sentences annotated using the binary-branching CFG [7]. We have used 10,906 sentences for the training data and 1,178 sentences for the test data. Average morpheme length per sentence is 22.5. Table 1 shows parsing accuracies as contextual information is accumulated. The rich contextual information used by our model improves the parsing accuracy by about 11–14 % over the previous models. Besides, we observe that the proposed shift-reduce parsing model outper forms the previous LR parsing models even when using a lookahead alone (<1>). The reason is that our model needs not have a lookahead as requisite information, thus it can be more flexible and robust against the data sparseness problem than the previous models.

Acknowledgement. This work was supported by Korea Research Foundation Grant (KRF-2002-042-D00485).

References

1. Wright, J. H. and Wrigley, E. N.: GLR Parsing with Probability. In Generalized LR Parsing. Kluwer Academic Publishers (1991)
2. Su, Keh-Yi, Wang, Jong-Nae, Su, Mei-Hui, and Chang, Jing-Shin: GLR Parsing with Scoring. In Generalized LR Parsing, Kluwer Academic Publishers (1991) 93-112
3. Briscoe, Ted and Carroll, John: Generalized Probabilistic LR Parsing of Natural Language with Unification-Based Grammars. In Computational Linguistics,19(1) (1993) 25-59
4. Kentaro, Inui, Sornlertlamvanich,Virach, Hozumi, Tanaka and Takenobu, Tokunaga: Probabilistic GLR parsing: a new formalization and its impact on parsing performance. In Journal of Natural Language Processing, Vol. 5, No. 3 (1998) 33-52
5. Prolo, Carlos A.: "Fast LR Parsing Using Rich (Tree Adjoining) Grammars", In Proceedings of the Conference on EMNLP 2002 (2002)
6. Kwak, Yong-Jae, Park, So-Young, Chung, Hoojung, Hwang, Young-Sook, and Rim, Hae-Chang: GLR Parser with Conditional Action Model using Surface Phrasal Types For Korean. In Proceedings of the 8th IWPT (2003) 213-214
7. Park, So-Young, Hwang, Young-Sook, Chung, Hoojung, Kwak, Yong-Jae, and Rim, Hae-Chang: A Feature-based Grammar for Korean Parsing. In proceedings of 5th Natural Language Processing Pacific Rim Symposium (1999) 167-171

Evaluation of Feature Combination
for Effective Structural Disambiguation

So-Young Park, Yong-Jae Kwak, Joon-Ho Lim, and Hae-Chang Rim

NLP Lab., Dept. of CSE, Korea University,
5-ka 1, Anam-dong, Seongbuk-ku, SEOUL, 136-701, KOREA
{ssoya,yjkwak,jhlim,rim}@nlp.korea.ac.kr

Abstract. In this paper, we present the useful features of a syntactic constituent for a probabilistic parsing model and analyze the combination of the features in order to disambiguate parse trees effectively. Unlike most of previous works focusing on the features of a single head, the features of a functional head, the features of a content head, and the features of size are utilized in this study. Experimental results show that the combination of different features such as the functional head feature and the size feature is prefered to the combination of similar features such as the functional head feature and the content head feature. Besides, it is remarkable that the function feature is more useful than the combination of the content feature and the size feature.

1   Introduction

Natural language parsing is regarded as a task of finding the parse tree for a given sentence. A probabilistic approach such as PCFG selects the best parse tree with the highest probability, which is generated by the production rules. However, it cannot select the best parse tree between the parse trees in Figure 1 because of the same CFG rules.

In order to improve the syntactic disambiguation, most of recent parsing models have been lexicalized[1,2,3,4] so that they can discriminate between $P(NP/mother$
$\rightarrow NP/mother\ PP/in)$ and $P(NP/portrait \rightarrow NP/portrait\ PP/in)$. Besides, some of them also utilize the inner contexts[2,5], the outer contexts[3] or the derivational history[4,6]. Still, the parse tree type selected in Figure 1 is the same as

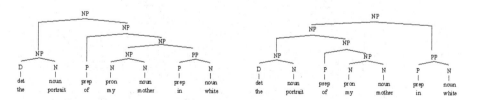

Fig. 1. Syntactic Ambiguities of a Noun Phrase by the Syntactic Tag

A. Gelbukh (Ed.): CICLing 2004, LNCS 2945, pp. 97–101, 2004.
© Springer-Verlag Berlin Heidelberg 2004

the parse tree type selected for a noun phrase "the portrait of my mother in oil" since the previous models don't consider the relationship between "portrait" and "oil". Besides, the lexicalized model using the derivational history cannot calculate the probability without a completed parse because it cannot know what word is the head word of a parent or a grandparent in a partial parse tree[4].

In this paper, we provide the useful features of a syntactic constituent for a parsing model and analyze the combination of the features in order to disambiguate parse trees effectively. The rest of this paper is organized as follows. Section 2 explains a parsing model using the feature structure, and Section 3 shows the experimental results of the feature combination. Finally, we conclude this paper in Section 4.

2   A Parsing Model Using the Feature Structure

Given a part-of-speech tagged sentence $w_1 w_2 ... w_k$, the best parse tree is selected based on the probability of generating a parse tree, which is calculated by multiplying the probabilities of all rules in the parse tree as follows.

$$T_{best}(w_{1k}) = \underset{T}{argmax}\, P(T) = \underset{T}{argmax}\, \prod_{i=1}^{k} P(n^{P_i} \to w_i) \prod_{i=k+1}^{j} P(n^{P_i} \to n^{L_i} n^{R_i})$$

where k is the number of unary rules, j is the number of all rules in the parse tree, n^{P_i} is the parent feature structure of the i-th rule, n^{L_i} is its left child, n^{R_i} is its right child, and w_i is the i-th part-of-speech tagged word.

A feature structure n includes the following seven features as shown in Figure 2. $_{syn}n$ describes the syntactic tag. $^{func}_{pos}n / ^{func}_{word}n$ represent the part-of-speech tag and the word of its functional head. $^{cont}_{pos}n / ^{cont}_{word}n$ express the part-of-speech tag and the word of its content head. $^{size}_{sect}n / ^{size}_{int}n$ mean the number of terminal words and the section tag such as S(small), M(medium) or L(large). For example, a feature structure for a prepositional phrase "in white" contains "P"

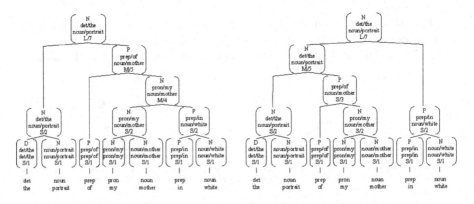

Fig. 2. Syntactic Ambiguities of a Noun Phrase by the Feature Structure

as $_{syn}n$, "prep/in" as $^{func}_{pos}n/^{func}_{word}n$, "noun/white" as $^{cont}_{pos}n/^{cont}_{word}n$, and "S/2" as $^{size}_{sect}n/^{size}_{int}n$.

In Figure 2 that shows the parse trees generated for a noun phrase "the portrait of my mother in white", a probabilistic parsing model can discriminate between $P(N/my/mother \rightarrow N/my/mother\ P/in/white)$ and $P(N/the/portrait \rightarrow N/the/portrait\ P/in/white)$. While the syntactic tag NP of "my mother" is identical with the syntactic tag NP of "my mother in white" in Figure 1, the feature structure of "my mother" represented by N/2 is not equal to the feature structure of "my mother in white" represented by N/4 in Figure 2 according to $_{syn}n/^{size}_{int}n$. In addition, the parse trees selected in Figure 2 is not the same as the parse tree for "the portrait of my mother in oil" because $P(\ N/my/mother \rightarrow N/my/mother\ P/in/white\ )$ is different from $P(\ N/my/mother \rightarrow N/my/mother\ P/in/oil\ )$.

3   Evaluation of Feature Combination

In order to evaluate the disambiguating power of each feature combination, we select some features as elements of a nonterminal as shown in Figure 3 where func describes the functional head feature, cont expresses the content head feature, and size means the size feature. And then, we measure the labeled precision, the labeled recall, the cross brackets, and the exact matching of the model using the feature combination[7]. The treebank of 31,080 Korean sentences that includes

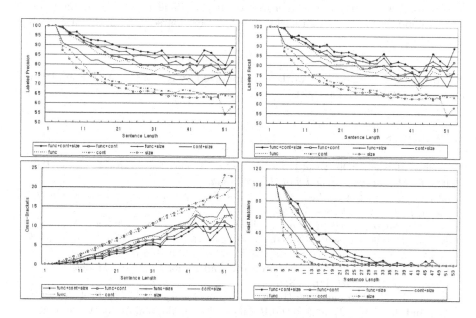

Fig. 3. The Experimental Results of the Feature Combination

the wide variety of Korean sentences are divided into 90% for the training set and 10% for the test set for experimentation. Also, the test set is sorted according to the number of morphemes per sentence.

Figure 3 shows that the combination of the content feature, the function feature, and the size feature performs best. Although the function feature is best and the size feature is worst on the performance of a single feature, the combination of them is better than the combination of the function feature and the content feature. The reason is that the effect of the function feature may overlap the effect of the content feature because the former represented by a word and its part-of-speech is similar to the latter. Therefore, we can say that the combination of different features is prefered to the combination of similar features. Besides, it is remarkable that the function feature is more useful than the combination of the content feature and the size feature.

4   Conclusion

In this paper, we represent a syntactic constituent as the combination of a syntactic feature, content features, functional features, and size features. And then, we analyze the disambiguating power of each feature combination for a probabilistic parsing model. Experimental results show that the combination of different features such as the functional head feature and the size feature is prefered to the combination of similar features such as the functional head feature and the content head feature. Besides, it is remarkable that the function feature is more useful than the combination of the content feature and the size feature. For the future work, we will try to consider improving the efficiency of the parsing model and profoundly analyze the relationship between sparse data problem and the word frequency.

Acknowledgements. This work was supported by Korea Research Foundation Grant(KRF-2002-042-D00485).

References

1. Collins, Michael. 1999. Head-Driven Statistical Models for Natural Language Parsing. *Ph.D. Thesis, University of Pennsylvania.*
2. Magerman, David M. 1995. Statistical Decision-Tree Models for Parsing. *In Proceedings of ACL 1995*, pp.276–283.
3. Lee, Kong-Joo, Jae-Hoon Kim, and Kil-Chang Kim. 1998. Syntactic Analysis of Korean Sentences based on Restricted Phrase Structure Grammar. *Journal of the Korea Information Science Society*, 25(4):722–732. (written in Korean)
4. Charniak, Eugene. 2001. Immediate-Head Parsing for Language Models. *In Proceedings of ACL 2001*, 116–123.
5. Kwak, Yong-Jae, Young-Sook Hwang, Hoo-Jung Chung, So-Young Park, Sang-Zoo Lee, and Hae-Chang Rim. 2001. GLR Parser with Conditional Action Model(CAM). *In Proceedings of NLPRS 2001*, pp.359–366.

6. Black, Ezra, Fred Jelinek, John Lafferty, David M. Magerman, Robert Mercer, and Salim Roukos. 1993. Towards History-based Grammars: Using Richer Models for Probabilistic Parsing *In Proceedings of In Proceedings of ACL 1993*, pp.31–37.
7. Goodman, Joshua. 1996. Parsing Algorithms and Metrics. *In Proceedings of In Proceedings of ACL 1996*, pp.177–183.

Parsing Incomplete Sentences Revisited*

Manuel Vilares[1], Victor M. Darriba[1], and Jesús Vilares[2]

[1] Department of Computer Science, University of Vigo
Campus As Lagoas s/n, 32004 Ourense, Spain
{vilares,darriba}@uvigo.es
[2] Department of Computer Science, University of A Coruña
Campus de Elviña s/n, 15071 A Coruña, Spain
jvilares@mail2.udc.es

Abstract. We describe a context-free parsing algorithm to deal with incomplete sentences, including unknown parts of unknown length. It produces a finite shared-forest compiling all parses, often infinite in number, that could account for both the error and the missing parts.
In contrast to previous works, we derive profit from a finer dynamic programming construction, leading to an improved computational behavior. We also introduce a deductive construction, which has the advantage of simplifying the task of description.

1 Introduction

An ongoing question in the design of dialogue systems is how to provide the maximal coverage and understanding of the language, finding the interpretations that have maximal thresholds, when the computational process must be prompted immediately at the onset of new input. This is largely due to the fact that the user often does not know the type of questions that the system answers. In this sense, it is often better to have a system that tries to guess a specific interpretation in case of ambiguity rather than ask the user for a clarification. As a consequence, analysis of the utterance should continuously anticipate the interaction with the user, based on the expectations of the system.

To comply with these requests, we need a parser which analyses the input simultaneously as it is entered, even when current data are only partially known. Two factors are at the origin of this behavior in natural language man-machine interfaces, whether text or speech-based. In the case of the former, the input language can only be approximately defined and individual inputs can vary widely from the norm [6] due to ungrammatical spontaneous phenomena. In the case of the latter [7], inputs can only often be considered as a distorted version of any of several possible patterns resulting from an erroneous recognition process.

In this context, our aim is computational. We restrict interaction types to only those necessary for immediate understanding using a predictive model

---

* Research partially supported by the Spanish Government under projects TIC2000-0370-C02-01 and HP2002-0081, and the Autonomous Government of Galicia under projects PGIDT01PXI10506PN, PGIDIT02PXIB30501PR and PGIDIT02SIN01E.

A. Gelbukh (Ed.): CICLing 2004, LNCS 2945, pp. 102–111, 2004.
© Springer-Verlag Berlin Heidelberg 2004

based on the parsing algorithm for unrestricted context-free grammars (CFG's) proposed by Vilares in [9]. In relation to previous works [8,3], our proposal provides a formal definition framework and an improved computational behavior.

2 The Standard Parser

Our aim is to parse a sentence $w_{1...n} = w_1 \ldots w_n$ according to an unrestricted CFG $\mathcal{G} = (N, \Sigma, P, S)$, where the empty string is represented by ε. We generate from $\mathcal{G}$ a *push-down transducer* (PDA) for the language $\mathcal{L}(\mathcal{G})$. In practice, we choose an LALR(1) device generated by ICE [9], although any shift-reduce strategy is adequate. A PDA is a 7-tuple $\mathcal{A} = (\mathcal{Q}, \Sigma, \Delta, \delta, q_0, Z_0, \mathcal{Q}_f)$ where: $\mathcal{Q}$ is the set of states, Σ the set of input symbols, Δ the set of stack symbols, q_0 the initial state, Z_0 the initial stack symbol, $\mathcal{Q}_f$ the set of final states, and δ a finite set of transitions of the form $\delta(p, X, a) \ni (q, Y)$ with $p, q \in \mathcal{Q}$, $a \in \Sigma \cup \{\varepsilon\}$ and $X, Y \in \Delta \cup \{\varepsilon\}$. Let the PDA be in a configuration $(p, X\alpha, ax)$, where p is the current state, $X\alpha$ is the stack contents with X on the top, and ax is the remaining input where the symbol a is the next to be shifted, $x \in \Sigma^*$. The application of $\delta(p, X, a) \ni (q, Y)$ results in a new configuration $(q, Y\alpha, x)$ where a has been scanned, X has been popped, and Y has been pushed.

To get polynomial complexity, we avoid duplicating stack contents when ambiguity arises. We determine the information we need to trace in order to retrieve it [4]. This information is stored in a table $\mathcal{I}$ of *items*, $\mathcal{I} = \{[q, X, i, j], q \in \mathcal{Q}, X \in \{\varepsilon\} \cup \{\nabla_{r,s}\}, 0 \le i \le j\}$; where q is the current state, X is the top of the stack, and the positions i and j indicate the substring $w_{i+1} \ldots w_j$ spanned by the last terminal shifted to the stack or by the last production reduced. The symbol $\nabla_{r,s}$ indicates that the part $A_{r,s+1} \ldots A_{r,n_r}$ of a rule $A_{r,0} \to A_{r,1} \ldots A_{r,n_r}$ has been recognized.

We describe the parser using *parsing schemata* [5]; a triple $\langle \mathcal{I}, \mathcal{H}, \mathcal{D} \rangle$, with $\mathcal{I}$ the table of items previously defined, $\mathcal{H} = \{[a, i, i+1], a = w_i\}$ an initial set of triples called *hypotheses* that encodes the sentence to be parsed[1], and $\mathcal{D}$ a set of *deduction steps* that allow new items to be derived from already known items. Deduction steps are of the form $\{\eta_1, \ldots, \eta_k \vdash \xi / conds\}$, meaning that if all antecedents $\eta_i \in \mathcal{I}$ are present and the conditions *conds* are satisfied, then the consequent $\xi \in \mathcal{I}$ should be generated. In the case of ICE, $\mathcal{D} = \mathcal{D}^{Init} \cup \mathcal{D}^{Shift} \cup \mathcal{D}^{Sel} \cup \mathcal{D}^{Red} \cup \mathcal{D}^{Head}$, where:

$$\mathcal{D}^{Shift} = \{[q, X, i, j] \vdash [q', \varepsilon, j, j+1] \left/ \begin{array}{l} \exists\, [a, j, j+1] \in \mathcal{H} \\ shift_{q'} \in action(q, a) \end{array} \right. \}$$

$$\mathcal{D}^{Sel} = \{[q, \varepsilon, i, j] \vdash [q, \nabla_{r,n_r}, j, j] \left/ \begin{array}{l} \exists\, [a, j, j+1] \in \mathcal{H} \\ reduce_r \in action(q, a) \end{array} \right. \}$$

$$\mathcal{D}^{Red} = \{[q, \nabla_{r,s}, k, j][q, \varepsilon, i, k] \vdash [q', \nabla_{r,s-1}, i, j] / q' \in reveal(q)\}$$

$$\mathcal{D}^{Init} = \{\vdash [q_0, \varepsilon, 0, 0]\} \qquad \mathcal{D}^{Head} = \{[q, \nabla_{r,0}, i, j] \vdash [q', \varepsilon, i, j] / q' \in goto(q, A_{r,0})\}$$

---

[1] The empty string, ε, is represented by the empty set of hypothesis, $\emptyset$. An input string $w_{1...n}$, $n \ge 1$ is represented by $\{[w_1, 0, 1], [w_2, 1, 2], \ldots, [w_n, n-1, n]\}$.

with $q_0 \in \mathcal{Q}$ the initial state, and *action* and *goto* entries in the PDA tables [1]. We say that $q' \in reveal(q)$ iff $\exists \, Y \in N \cup \Sigma$ such that $shift_q \in action(q', Y)$ or $q \in goto(q', Y)$, that is, when there exists a transition from q' to q in $\mathcal{A}$. This set is equivalent to the dynamic interpretation of non-deterministic PDA's:

- A deduction step *Init* is in charge of starting the parsing process.
- A deduction step *Shift* corresponds to pushing a terminal a onto the top of the stack when the action to be performed is a shift to state st'.
- A step *Sel* corresponds to pushing the ∇_{r,n_r} symbol onto the top of the stack in order to start the reduction of a rule r.
- The reduction of a rule of length $n_r > 0$ is performed by a set of n_r steps *Red*, each of them corresponding to a pop transition replacing the two elements $\nabla_{r,s} \, X_{r,s}$ placed on the top of the stack by the element $\nabla_{r,s-1}$.
- The reduction of a rule r is finished by a step *Head* corresponding to a swap transition that recognizes the top element $\nabla_{r,0}$ as equivalent to the left-hand side $A_{r,0}$ of that rule, and performs the corresponding change of state.

These steps are applied until new items cannot be generated. The splitting of reductions into a set of *Red* steps allows us to share computations corresponding to partial reductions, attaining a worst case time (resp. space) complexity $\mathcal{O}(n^3)$ (resp. $\mathcal{O}(n^2)$) with respect to the length n of the input string [9]. The input string is recognized iff the final item $[q_f, \nabla_{0,0}, 0, n+1]$, $q_f \in \mathcal{Q}_f$, is generated.

When the sentence has several distinct parses, the set of all possible parse chains is represented in finite shared form by a CFG that generates that possibly infinite set, which is equivalent to using an AND-OR graph. In this graph, AND-nodes correspond to the usual parse-tree nodes, while OR-nodes correspond to ambiguities. Sharing of structures is represented by nodes accessed by more than one other node, and may correspond to sharing of a complete subtree, but also to sharing of a part of the descendants of a given node.

3 Parsing Incomplete Sentences

In order to handle incomplete sentences, we extend the input alphabet. Following Lang in [3], we introduce two new symbols. So, "?" stands for one unknown word symbol, and "∗" stands for an unknown sequence of input word symbols.

3.1 The Parsing Algorithm

Once the parser detects that the next input symbol to be shifted is one of these two extra symbols, we apply the set of deduction steps $\mathcal{D}_{\text{incomplete}}$, which includes the following two sets of deduction steps:

$$\mathcal{D}^{\text{Shift}}_{\text{incomplete}} = \{[q, \varepsilon, i, j] \vdash [q', \varepsilon, j, j+1] \; \Big/ \; \begin{array}{l} \exists \, [?, j, j+1] \in \mathcal{H} \\ shift_{q'} \in action(q, a) \\ a \in \Sigma \end{array} \}$$

$$\mathcal{D}^{\text{Loop\_shift}}_{\text{incomplete}} = \{[q, \varepsilon, i, j] \vdash [q', \varepsilon, j, j] \; \Big/ \; \begin{array}{l} \exists \, [*, j, j+1] \in \mathcal{H} \\ shift_{q'} \in action(q, X) \\ X \in N \cup \Sigma \end{array} \}$$

while we maintain the rest of the deduction steps in $\mathcal{D}^{\text{Init}}$, $\mathcal{D}^{\text{Shift}}$, $\mathcal{D}^{\text{Sel}}$, $\mathcal{D}^{\text{Red}}$, and $\mathcal{D}^{\text{Head}}$. From an intuitive point of view, $\mathcal{D}^{\text{Shift}}_{\text{incomplete}}$ applies any shift transition independently of the current lookahead available, provided that this transition is applicable with respect to the PDA configuration and that the next input symbol is an unknown token. In relation to $\mathcal{D}^{\text{Loop\_shift}}_{\text{incomplete}}$, it applies any valid shift action on terminals or variables to items corresponding to PDA configurations for which the next input symbol denotes an unknown sequence of tokens. Given that in this latter case new items are created in the same starting itemset, shift transitions may be applied any number of times to the same computation thread, without scanning the input string.

All deduction steps in dealing with incomplete sentences are applied until a parse branch links up to the right-context by using a standard shift action, resuming the standard parse mode. In this process, when we deal with sequences of unknown tokens, we can generate nodes deriving only "$*$" symbols. This over-generation is of no interest in most practical applications and introduces additional computational work, which supposes an extra loss of parse efficiency. So, our goal is to replace these variables with the unknown subsequence terminal, "$*$". We solve this problem by extending the item structure in order to consider an insertion counter to tabulate the number of syntactic and lexical categories used to rebuild the incomplete sentence. When several items representing the same node are generated, only those with minimal number of insertions are saved, eliminating the rest, which are pruned from the output parse shared-forest.

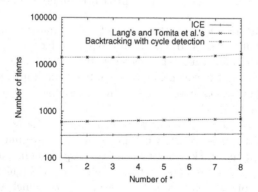

Fig. 1. Number of items for the *noun*'s example

Formally, items extended with counters, e, are of the form $[p, X, i, j, e]$ and, to deal with them, we should redefine the set of deduction steps $\mathcal{D}_{\text{incomplete}}$ as follows:

$$\mathcal{D}_{\text{incomplete}}^{\text{Shift}} = \{[q,\varepsilon,i,j,e] \vdash [q',\varepsilon,j,j+1,e+I(a)] \left/ \begin{array}{l} \exists\,[?,j,j+1] \in \mathcal{H} \\ shift_{q'} \in action(q,a) \\ a \in \Sigma \end{array} \right. \}$$

$$\mathcal{D}_{\text{incomplete}}^{\text{Loop\_shift}} = \{[q,\varepsilon,i,j,e] \vdash [q',\varepsilon,j,j,e+I(X)] \left/ \begin{array}{l} \exists\,[*,j,j+1] \in \mathcal{H} \\ shift_{q'} \in action(q,X) \\ X \in N \cup \Sigma \end{array} \right. \}$$

where $I(X)$ is the insertion cost for $X \in N \cup \Sigma$, and we have to adapt the previous deduction steps to deal with counters:

$$\mathcal{D}_{\text{count}}^{\text{Init}} = \{\vdash [q_0,\varepsilon,0,0,0]\}$$

$$\mathcal{D}_{\text{count}}^{\text{Shift}} = \{[q,X,i,j] \vdash [q',\varepsilon,j,j+1] \left/ \begin{array}{l} \exists\,[a,j,j+1] \in \mathcal{H} \\ shift_{q'} \in action(q,a) \end{array} \right. \}$$

$$\mathcal{D}_{\text{count}}^{\text{Sel}} = \{[q,\varepsilon,i,j,e] \vdash [q,\nabla_{r,n_r},j,j,e] \left/ \begin{array}{l} \exists\,[a,j,j+1] \in \mathcal{H} \\ reduce_r \in action(q,a) \end{array} \right. \}$$

$$\mathcal{D}_{\text{count}}^{\text{Red}} = \{[q,\nabla_{r,s},k,j,e][q',\varepsilon,i,k,e'] \vdash [q',\nabla_{r,s-1},i,j,e+e'] / q' \in reveal(q)\}$$

$$\mathcal{D}_{\text{count}}^{\text{Head}} = \{[q,\nabla_{r,0},i,j,e] \vdash [q',\varepsilon,i,j,e] / q' \in goto(q,A_{r,0})\}$$

As for the standard mode, these steps are applied until new items cannot be generated. The resulting complexity bounds are also, in the worst case, $\mathcal{O}(n^3)$ and $\mathcal{O}(n^2)$ for time and space, respectively, with respect to the length n of the input string. The parse is defined by the final item $[q_f, \nabla_{0,0}, 0, n+1, e]$, $q_f \in \mathcal{Q}_f$.

3.2   Previous Works

Both, Tomita et al. [8] and Lang [3], apply dynamic programming techniques to deal with no determinism in order to reduce space complexity and improve computational efficiency. However, the approach is different in each case:

- From the point of view of the descriptive formalism, Lang's proposal generalizes Tomita et al.'s. In effect, in order to solve the problems derived from grammatical constraints, Earley's construction [2] is extended by Lang to PDA's, separating the execution strategy from the implementation of the interpreter. Tomita et al.'s work can be interpreted as simply a specification of Lang's for LR(0) PDA's.
- From the point of view of the operational formalism, Lang introduces items as fragments of the possible PDA computations that are independent of the initial content of the stack, except for its two top elements, allowing partial sharing of common fragments in the presence of ambiguities. This relies on the concept of *dynamic frame* for CFG's [9], for which the transitional mechanism is adapted to be applied over these items. Tomita et al. use a shared-graph based structure to represent the stack forest, which improves the computational efficiency at the expense of practical space cost.
- Neither Lang nor Tomita et al., avoid over-generation in nodes deriving only "*" symbols. In relation with this, only Lang includes a complementary simplification phase to eliminate these nodes from the output parse shared forest. In addition, these authors do not provide details about how to deal

with these nodes when they are generated from more than one parse branch, which is usual in a non-deterministic frame.

Our proposal applies Lang's descriptive formalism to the particular case of an LALR(1) parsing scheme, which makes lookahead computation easier, whilst maintaining the state splitting phenomenon at reasonable levels. This ensures a good sharing of computation and parsing structures, leading to an increase in efficiency. In relation to Tomita *et al.*'s strategy, our deterministic domain is larger and, in consequence, the time complexity for the parser is linear on a larger number of grammars.

With regard to the operational formalism, we work in a dynamic frame S^1, which means that our items only represent the top of the stack. This implies a difference with Lang's proposal, or implicitly Tomita *et al.*'s, which used S^2. From a practical point of view, S^1 translates in a better sharing for both syntactic structures and computations, and improved performance.

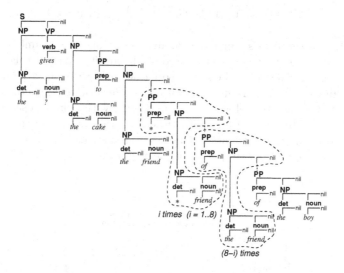

Fig. 2. Shared-forest for the *noun*'s example

Finally, we solve both the consideration of an extra simplification phase and the over-generation on unknown sequences by considering a simple subsumption criteria over items including error counters.

4   Experimental Results

We consider the language of pico-English to illustrate our discussion, comparing our proposal on ICE [9], with Lang [3] and Tomita *et al.*'s algorithm [8]. As grammatical formalism, we take the following set of rules:

$$S \to NP\ VP \qquad NP \to det\ noun \qquad VP \to verb\ NP$$
$$S \to S\ PP \qquad NP \to NP\ PP \qquad PP \to prep\ NP$$

generating the language. Tests have been applied on input strings of two types:

$$det\ ?\ verb\ det\ noun\ prep\ det\ noun\ \{*\ noun\}^i\ \{prep\ det\ noun\}^{8-i}\ prep\ det\ noun \qquad (1)$$
$$det\ ?\ verb\ det\ noun\ prep\ \{*\ prep\}^i\ \{det\ noun\ prep\}^{8-i}\ det\ noun \qquad (2)$$

where i represents the number of tokens "*", that is, the number of unknown sentences in the corresponding input string. This could correspond, for example, to concrete input strings of the form:

$$\text{The ? gives the cake to the friend } \{*\ friend\}^i\ \{of\ the\ friend\}^{8-i}\ of\ the\ boy \qquad (3)$$
$$\text{The ? gives the cake to } \{*\ of\}^i\ \{the\ friend\ of\}^{8-i}\ the\ boy \qquad (4)$$

respectively. As our running grammar contains rules "NP $\to$ NP PP" and "PP $\to$ prep NP", these incomplete sentences have a number of cyclic parses which grows exponentially with i. This number is:

$$C_0 = C_1 = 1 \quad \text{and} \quad C_i = \binom{2i}{i} \frac{1}{i+1}, \text{ if } i > 1$$

In effect, the parser must simulate the analysis of an arbitrary number of tokens and, in consequence, it is no longer limited by the input string. At this point, the parser may apply repeatedly the same reductions over the same grammar rules. So, although the running grammar is not cyclic, the situation generated is close to this kind of framework. More exactly, in dealing with unknown sentences, we can derive a non-terminal from itself without extra scan actions on the input string. This allows us to evaluate our proposal in a strongly ambiguous context with cycles, in spite of the simplicity of the grammar.

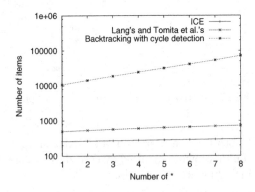

Fig. 3. Number of items for the *prep*'s example

The essential experimental results are shown in Fig. 1 (resp. Fig. 3) in relation to running example 1 (resp. example 2), for which the output shared-forests are shown in Fig. 2 (resp. Fig. 4). Since the number of possible tree combinations in these forests is exponential, these figures focus only on particular examples. In all cases our reference for measuring efficiency is the number of items generated by the system during the parsing process, rather than of pure temporal criteria, which are more dependent on the implementation. The shared-forests represented clearly show the existence of a cyclic behavior and ambiguous analyses.

At this point, we are comparing three dynamic frames. The classic one, S^T, is comparable to parse methods based on backtracking and including some kind of mechanism to detect cycles. In this case, no sharing of computations and structures is possible, and it is of only theoretical interest. The other two dynamic frames, S^1 and S^2, are of real practical interest. The first one is considered by ICE, while S^2 can be identified in these tests with Lang's and Tomita et al.'s results.

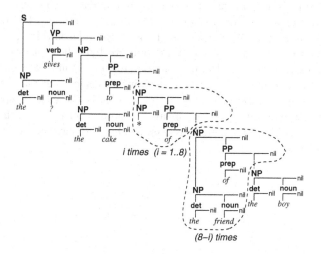

Fig. 4. Shared-forest for the *prep*'s example

In order to allow an objective comparison to be made between all proposals considered, we have made the parsing schema used uniform. So, although Lang's algorithm can be applied to any parse strategy, and Tomita et al.'s was originally intended for LR(0) PDA'S, we have adapted both of them to deal with an LALR(1) scheme, as used by ICE. In all cases, these experimental results illustrate the superior performance of our proposal, ICE, in relation to previous strategies. This is due to the following causes:

— We do not need a supplementary simplification phase in order to eliminate nodes deriving only sequences of unknown sequences, "*", from the output structure.

 – The choice of S^1 instead of S^2 as dynamic frame provides a better sharing
   efficiency for both structures and computations. As a consequence, the
   number of items generated is smaller.

In order to illustrate the cost of the previously mentioned simplification phase
used by Lang and Tomita *et al.*, Fig. 5 shows the number of items to be
eliminated in this process for both examples, noun's and prep's. We include
this estimation for S^2, the original dynamic frame for these proposals, and S^1.
In this last case, we have previously adapted the original methods of Lang's and
Tomita *et al.*.

5   Conclusions

Dialogue systems should provide total understanding of the input. However,
in practice, this is not always possible with current technology, even when
we restrict ourselves to the treatment of a limited domain of knowledge. In
consequence, robustness becomes crucial in order to find a suitable interpretation
for the utterance, and we are forced to compute hypotheses to guarantee the
interactivity in this kind of frames. So, parsing of incomplete sentences is a
fundamental task in a variety of man-machine interfaces, as part of the more
general and complex robust parsing activity. This is the case of speech-based
systems, where the language often appears to contain noise derived from human
causes such as a stutter or a cough; or even mechanical ones due to an imperfect
signal recognition.

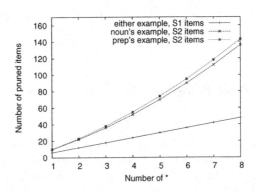

Fig. 5. Items to be pruned in the simplification phase

In this context, our proposal provides an improved treatment of the
computation, avoiding extra simplification phases used in previous proposals
and profiting from the concept of dynamic frame. In particular, this allows the
sharing of computations and structures, reducing the amount of data to be taken
into account as well as the work necessary to manipulate them.

References

1. A.V. Aho, R. Sethi, and J.D. Ullman. *Compilers: Principles, Techniques and Tools*. Addison-Wesley Publishing Company, Inc., Reading, Massachusetts, U.S.A., 1986.
2. J. Earley. An efficient context-free parsing algorithm. *Communications of the ACM*, 13(2):94–102, 1970.
3. B. Lang. Parsing incomplete sentences. In D. Vargha (ed.), editor, *COLING'88*, pages 365–371, Budapest, Hungary, 1988. vol. 1.
4. Bernard Lang. Deterministic techniques for efficient non-deterministic parsers. In J. Loeckx, editor, *Automata, Languages and Programming*, number 14 in Lecture Notes in Computer Science, pages 255–269. Springer, Berlin, DE, 1974.
5. K. Sikkel. *Parsing Schemata*. PhD thesis, Univ. of Twente, The Netherlands, 1993.
6. Robert S. Stainton. The meaning of 'sentences'. *Noûs*, 34(3):441–454, 2000.
7. Andreas Stolcke. Linguistic knowledge and empirical methods in speech recognition. *The AI Magazine*, 18(4):25–31, 1998.
8. M. Tomita and H. Saito. Parsing noisy sentences. In *COLING'88*, pages 561–566, Budapest, Hungary, 1988.
9. M. Vilares. *Efficient Incremental Parsing for Context-Free Languages*. PhD thesis, University of Nice. ISBN 2-7261-0768-0, France, 1992.

Unlexicalized Dependency Parser
for Variable Word Order Languages
Based on Local Contextual Pattern

Hoojung Chung and Hae-Chang Rim

Department of Computer Science
Korea University, Seoul 136-701 Korea
{hjchung, rim}@nlp.korea.ac.kr

Abstract. We investigate the effect of unlexicalization in a dependency parser for variable word order languages and propose an unlexicalized parser which can utilize some contextual information in order to achieve performance comparable to that of lexicalized parsers. Unlexicalization of an early dependency parser makes performance decrease by 3.6%. However, when we modify the unlexicalized parser into the one which can consider additional contextual information, the parser performs better than some lexicalized dependency parsers, while it requires simpler smoothing processes, less time and space for parsing.

1 Introduction

Lexical information has been widely used to achieve a high degree of parsing accuracy, and parsers with lexicalized language models [1,2,3] have shown the state-of-the-art performances in analyzing English. Most of parsers developed recently use lexical features for syntactic disambiguation, whether they use a phrase structure grammar or a dependency grammar, regardless of languages they deal with.

However, some researchers recently insisted that the lexicalization did not play a big role in parsing with probabilistic context-free grammars (PCFG). [4] showed that the lexical bigram information does not contribute to the performance improvement of a parser. [5] concluded that the fundamental sparseness of the lexical dependency information from parsed training corpora is not helpful to the lexicalized parser, and proposed an accurate unlexicalized parsing model.

This is the story of analyzing fixed word order languages, e.g. English, with a phrase structure grammar. What about parsing other type of languages with other type of grammars, without lexical dependency information? For instance, can an unlexicalized dependency parser for languages with variable word order achieve high accuracy as the unlexicalized PCFG parser for English does?

This paper investigates the effect of the unlexicalization in a dependency parser for variable word order languages and suggests a new unlexicalized parser which can solve the problems of the unlexicalized dependency parser.

A. Gelbukh (Ed.): CICLing 2004, LNCS 2945, pp. 112–123, 2004.
© Springer-Verlag Berlin Heidelberg 2004

Table 1. Effect of unlexicalization. The lexicalized parser uses Equation (2), while the unlexicalized parser uses Equation (3)

	Lexicalized (F_1-score)	Unlexicalized (F_1-score)
Training Set	0.996	0.801
Testing Set	0.837	0.801

2   The Effect of Unlexicalizing Dependency Parser

It seems that lexicalization may play more role in dependency parsing for variable word order languages than in parsing fixed word order languages with a phrase structure grammar. There are some reasons: dependency parsers cannot use information on constituents because the grammar is based on the word unit, not on the constituent. Therefore, the disambiguation depends more on the lexical dependency between words. Secondly, since the word order is variable, which means there is less restriction, it requires higher level information such as semantic constraint or lexical preference to offset inexistency of word order information.

To investigate the effect of unlexicalization, we implemented [6]-style parser, which uses bigram lexical dependencies and distance measure for syntactic disambiguation. The parsing model for a sentence S is :

$$P(t|S) \approx \prod_{i=1}^{|S|-1} P(dep_i = h(i)|S) \tag{1}$$

where $|S|$ is a number of words in S, $h(i)$ is the modifyee of w_i, the ith word of S, and dep_i is a dependency relation from w_i to $w_{h(i)}$. The modifyees for each word are stated in the tree t, which is a set of modifyees. The probability of each dependency relation is :

$$P(dep_i = h(i)|S) \approx P(link(i, h(i)) = Yes|w_i \ w_{h(i)} \ \Delta_{i,j}) \tag{2}$$

$$link(x, y) = \begin{cases} Yes & \text{if } w_x \text{ modifies } w_y \\ No & else. \end{cases}$$

where Δ is a number of features to consider the distance between the two depending words. The unlexicalized model is induced by substituting part-of-speech (POS) tags t for all lexical words w in (2) :

$$P(dep_i = h(i)|S) \approx P(link(i, h(i)) = Yes|t_i \ t_{h(i)} \ \Delta_{i,j}) \tag{3}$$

We trained both model (2) and (3) on about 27,000 sentences and tested their performance on held-out testing data. The result is on Table 1.

Overfitting causes the lexicalized parser performs extremely well in the training data. On the testing set, unlexicalization hurts the parsing performance by

3.6% absolute, which is a sharper drop than the decrease by the unlexicalization of PCFG parser for English, which was reported in [4].

Despite the poor performance of the unlexicalized dependency parser for variable word order language, using unlexicalized parser have considerable advantages. First, we can simplify smoothing processes for estimating probabilities that are designed to alleviate lexical data sparseness problems. Consequently, it increases parsing speed. And eliminating lexical data reduces the space complexity.

So we designed a new unlexicalized parser that considers more contexts for syntactic disambiguation, yet can parse more accurately.

3   Revising the Unlexicalized Parser

We observed that even a variable word order language generates some fixed POS tag sequence pattern in a local context. Based on this observation, we use local contexts of modifier and modifyee in estimating the likelihood of dependency between the two POS tags, and the likelihood of a length of modification relation from the modifier. We use the Korean language[1], which allows variable word order, for explaining our ideas.

3.1   Word Dependency Probability with Local Context

In the research on a phrase structural parsing model for Korean [7], the outer contexts of constituents were found to be useful for syntactic disambiguation. We use similar method for our dependency parser. In other words, we consider outer contexts of a dependency relation, instead of the constituent, when we estimate the *word dependency probability*:

$$P(link(i,j) = Yes|w_i \ w_j \ \Phi_i\Phi_j) \approx P(link(i,j) = Yes|t_i \ t_j \ \Phi_i \ \Phi_j) \quad (4)$$
$$\approx P(link(i,j) = Yes|t_i \ t_j \ t_{i-1} \ t_{j+1}) \quad (5)$$

where Φ_i is contextual information of w_i. According to [7], considering two POS tags, one at the left and one at the right of a constituent, was sufficient for improving parsing performance. So we substitute a single POS tag for each context Φ. i.e. (5).

3.2   Modification Distance Probability Based on Local Contextual Pattern

We observed that a word has the tendency to have a fixed modification distance in a certain context. Let's see an example with Figure 1. The word *na-ui*

---

[1] Readers who are unfamiliar with the Korean syntax may refer Appendix at the end of this paper for a brief introduction to the Korean syntax.

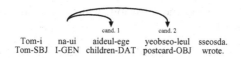

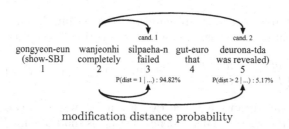

	cand. 1		cand. 2	
Tom-i	na-ui	aideul-ege	yeobseo-leul	sseosda.
Tom-SBJ	I-GEN	children-DAT	postcard-OBJ	wrote.

Fig. 1. The sentence means *Tom wrote a postcard to my children*. The word *na-ui* has two alternative modifyee candidates

	cand. 1			cand. 2
gongyeon-eun	wanjeonhi	silpaeha-n	gut-euro	deurona-tda
(show-SBJ	completely	failed	that	was revealed)
1	2	3	4	5

P(dist = 1 | ...) : 94.82%   P(dist > 2 | ...) : 5.17%

modification distance probability

Fig. 2. The sentence interpreted as *It was revealed that the show was completely failed.* in English. The arcs at the bottom of the sentence show modification distance probability, which is proposed in this paper

(I-GEN[2]), which is a noun modifier, has two alternative noun modifyee candidates: *aideul-ege* (children-DAT) and *yeobseo-leul* (postcard-OBJ). Here, the first candidate is the correct modifyee for the modifier. It is well known to Korean users that the word ends with the morpheme *-ui* (genitive postposition) usually modifies the right next word. In other words, the word ends with the genitive marker *-ui* prefers modification distance of 1 in general context. Some rule-based or heuristic-based parsers encoded this preference into a rule for syntactic disambiguation.

Let's see another similar, but more complex example in Figure 2. The adverb *wanjeonhi* (completely) has two alternative modifyee candidates in this sentence. They are *silpaeha-n* (failed) and *derona-tda* (was revealed), and the former is the correct modifyee of the adverb. Finding the correct modifyee is tough in this case, even though we consider lexical or semantic information, because the lexical or semantic preference of the adverb *wanjeonhi* to both modifyee candidates are similar.

We define a *modification distance probability* to solve the problem. It is the likelihood of the preferred length of a modification relation for a certain modifier in a certain context, which reflects the following two preferences:

1. Whether a modifier prefers long distance modification or local (short distance) modification.

---

[2] SBJ, GEN, DAT, and OBJ stand for a subjective, genitive, dative and objective case marker, respectively.

2. If a modifier prefers local modification, which word in the local context is preferred as its modifyee.

The probability of a certain modification distance x for the given modifier word w_i and its surrounding context Φ_i is :

$$P(len = x \mid w_i \ \Phi_i) \approx P(len = x \mid w_{i-m} \ \cdots \ w_{i+n})$$
$$\approx P(len = x \mid t_{i+m} \ \cdots \ t_{i+n}) \tag{6}$$

where the constants m and n are empirically determined. The length of the modification relation x is calculated with the function $\Psi(ld)$, that is

$$\Psi(ld) = \begin{cases} ld & \text{if} \quad ld < k \\ long & \text{if} \quad ld \geq k \end{cases}, \qquad \Psi(ld) \in Dist = \{1, \cdots, k-1, long\}.$$

when ld is a linear distance between two depending words. A constant k is the yardstick to decide whether a dependency relation is short or long. We named (6) the modification distant probability and used this probability instead of using the distance measure as in (3).

To see an example that uses this probability, revisit Figure 2 which is showing the probabilities for each modification distance[3]. The probabilities are calculated with the modification distance probability.[4].

$$P(len = 1 | mag \ pvg\text{-}etm \ nbn\text{-}jca) = 94.82$$
$$P(len = 2 | mag \ pvg\text{-}etm \ nbn\text{-}jca) = 0$$
$$P(len = long | mag \ pvg\text{-}etm \ nbn\text{-}jca) = 5.17$$

3.3   The Probabilistic Dependency Parsing Model

A dependency parsing model estimates the probability of a parsing tree t for a given sentence S.

$$P(t|S) \approx \prod_{i < |S|} P(dep_i = h(i)|S) \tag{7}$$

We assume a dependency relation depends only on the two words that is linked by the relation and their local context. This makes (7) become (8).

$$P(dep_i = h(i)|S) \approx \frac{P(link(i, h(i)) = Yes \ len = \Psi(h(i) - i) | w_i \Phi_i w_{h(i)} \Phi_{h(i)})}{\sum_{k > i, x \in \{Yes, No\}, y \in Dist} P(link(i, k) = x \ len = y | w_i \Phi_i w_{h(i)} \Phi_{h(i)})} \tag{8}$$

$$= P(link(i, h(i)) = Yes | w_i \ \Phi_i \ w_{h(i)} \ \Phi_{h(i)})$$
$$\cdot P(len = \Psi(h(i) - i) | link(i, h(i)) = Yes \ w_i \ \Phi_i \ w_{h(i)} \ \Phi_{h(i)}) \tag{9}$$

---

[3] The probabilities for distance 2 is not shown in the figure, and the probabilities for *long* distance modification is marked as *dist* > 2.

[4] m, n, and k are 0, 2, and 3 here. *mag*, *pvg-etm* and *nbn-jca* are POS tags for w_1, w_2, and w_3 in Figure 2.

Since the denominator of (8) is constant, and by a using chain rule, we can get (9). The latter term of (9) is a probability of a certain modification length. Since we assume that the modification length only depends on a modifier and its context, and since we exclude all lexical information from the model, the whole parsing model becomes as :

$$P(dep_i = h(i)|S) \approx P(link(i, h(i)) = Yes|w_i \; \Phi_i \; w_{h(i)} \; \Phi_{h(i)})$$
$$\cdot \; P(len = \Psi(h(i) - i)|w_i \; \Phi_i)$$
$$\approx P(link(i, h(i)) = Yes|t_i \; \Phi_i \; t_{h(i)} \; \Phi_{h(i)}) \cdot P(len = \Psi(h(i) - i)|t_i \; \Phi_i)$$

As you see, it becomes a product of the probability of word dependency between modifier and modifyee, and the probability of length of modification relation for the modifier based on the local contextual pattern of it.

4   Related Works

There has been little work done on unlexicalizing the parsing model. Instead, many studies tried to combine various features including lexicalized information. The distance measure is one of widely used feature in dependency parsing. As shown earlier, [6] proposed a statistical parsing model for English, based on bigram lexical dependencies and distance between the two depending words. [8, 9,10] proposed similar models for parsing Korean and Japanese.

However, using the distance features in the conditional part of the probability equation[5] as [6] assumes that the dependency relation of a certain length is different from dependency relations with different lengths. This assumption may cause sparse data problem in estimating word dependencies for the languages allowing variable word order. The sparseness would be more serious for the model that uses lexical dependencies, such as [9,10].

There were another approaches that used modification distance as we do, but in a different way. [11,12] utilized handcrafted HPSG for dependency analysis of Japanese. HPSG is used to find three alternative modifyee candidates: the nearest, the second nearest, and the farthest candidates from a certain modifier. Then, the probabilistic models choose an appropriate modifyee among three candidates. These models seem to work well for Japanese, however, it is doubtful that the parsing models can be applied to other languages well. The parsing models are restricted to consider only three head candidates at most, based on the statistics from Japanese corpora. So they may fit for Japanese parsing but would cause problems for parsing other languages. And these approaches require handcrafted grammars which usually demands excessive manual labors. These features can be obstacles when someone uses these models to develop a new parser for other languages.

In contrast, our model splits probability of a dependency relation into the word dependency probability and the modifying distance probability to alleviate sparse data problem. And proposed model does not depend on language

---

[5] See Equation (2)

specific features, and does not require any language-specific manual rules – such as heuristic constraints or HPSG – either. So it can be adapted to other languages easily. Of course, our model does not ignore any grammatically correct modifyee candidates at all, while [11] and [12] ignore less likely grammatical modifyee candidates.

5   Experimental Results

We implemented a probabilistic parser that uses the proposed parsing model and performed some experiments to evaluate our method empirically. We used a backward beam search algorithm, which was originally designed to analyze Japanese with dependency probabilities[15].

The parser was trained on 27,694 sentences and tested on heldout 3,386 sentences of dependency tagged sections of KAIST LANGUAGE RESOURCES[14]. All sentences are POS tagged, and this information was used as an input for the parser.

5.1   Deciding Length of Modification Relation with the Modification Distance Probability

First of all, we evaluate our assumption, that is *length of a modification relation can be determined by a modifier and its local contextual pattern*. To do this, we made a classifier using the modification distance probability that models our assumption statistically. The classifier decide the length of a modification relation for the given modifier t_i and its context Φ_i.

$$\text{modification distance} = argmax_{d \in Dist}P(len = d \,|t_i \; \Phi_i) \qquad (10)$$
$$= argmax_{d \in Dist}P(len = d \,|t_{i-n} \cdots t_i \cdots t_{i+m})$$

We experiment with changing n and m from 0 to 2, while k changes from 1 to 3. We used F_1 measure for evaluating the classifier. The experimental result is on Table 2. It tells that considering wider context does not always induce more accurate classification. The best result is acquired when m and n are 0 and 2. This means the left context hardly affect the performance of deciding modification distances[6]. Right context size bigger than 3 does not help the classification too.

Meanwhile, the performance of the classifier increases as the value of k decreases. It is because a smaller k decreases the number of distance class, which is k, and classification becomes easier for smaller and more generic class. We selected the values for m, and n as 0 and 2 through this experiment, but could not decide the value for k. Although the performance of classifier with bigger k is worse, it might be more helpful for the parser to have probabilities for more subdivided distances.

---

[6] [13] reported that similar characteristic is observed for Japanese too. Based on his experiment with humans, it is true more than 90% of the time for Japanese.

Table 2. Experimental result (in F_1-score) for the modification distance classifier, with various m (left context size) , n (right context size) , and k (class size) values

context size		Dist		
m	n	{1, long} $(k{=}2)$	{1,2, long} $(k{=}3)$	{1,2,3, long} $(k{=}4)$
1	0	0.916	0.750	0.722
2	0	0.787	0.747	0.721
0	1	0.916	0.855	0.817
1	1	0.898	0.835	0.799
2	1	0.847	0.793	0.761
0	2	0.926	0.879	0.838
1	2	0.894	0.851	0.814
2	2	0.816	0.775	0.748
0	3	0.872	0.831	0.800
1	3	0.831	0.793	0.770
2	3	0.794	0.755	0.731

Figure 3 is an example that shows the effect of different k makes. The upper arcs show modification distance probability when k is 2. The lower arcs show the probability when k is 3. When k is 2, the only information we can get from the modification distance probability is that the modifier *norae-reul* (song-OBJ) does not modify the next word *jal* (well) . However, this independency can be known by simple dependency rule probability because an object noun never modifies an adverb. So the modification distance probability is not helpful when k is 2. However, when the value of k is 3, the modification distance probability assigns higher probability for length 2 modification relation, which cannot be considered with the simple dependency probability. So we will not determine the value k here, but use all k for the following experiments.

5.2 Experiment with Richer Context

We used modification distance probability and added a little more context information to the bare word dependency probability to achieve higher parser performance. Here, we are going to evaluate the effect of information we have added to the vanilla dependency probability.

To evaluate the performance of the parser, we used arc-based F_1 measure and sentence-based exact matching rate. The results are shown in Table 3. It shows both additional contextual information (OC & MDP) contribute to the parser performance. Interesting point here is the increase of parser performance as k gets bigger. In the previous experiments, classifier performs worse for bigger k values. This change is due to the effect of larger k, which is more helpful for a parser to decide appropriate modifyee as we discussed in the previous experiment with Figure 3. The table also shows that using the modification distance probability (BM-Δ+MDP) is better than using the distance measure as in [6] (BM). This

when $k = 2 : Dist = \{1, long\}$

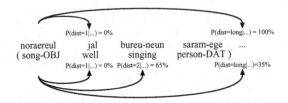

when $k = 3 : Dist = \{1, 2, long\}$

Fig. 3. Comparison of the modification distance probability from the word *norae-reul*, when $k = 2$ and $k = 3$. As k gets bigger, the modification distance probability may be more helpful.

Table 3. Effect of considering outer context and modification distance. BM stands for the unlexicalized parser with the model (3). Δ, OC, and MDP stands for distance measure used in [6], outer context, and modification distance probability

	Measures	BM	BM -Δ	BM-Δ +OC	BM-Δ+MDP			BM-Δ+OC+MDP		
					$k=2$	$k=3$	$k=4$	$k=2$	$k=3$	$k=4$
Training	Arc Prec.	0.801	0.748	0.783	0.812	0.824	0.831	0.854	0.862	0.865
Set	Exact Match	0.212	0.181	0.242	0.246	0.273	0.291	0.336	0.350	0.354
Testing	Arc Prec.	0.801	0.747	0.762	0.807	0.819	0.826	0.842	0.853	0.856
Set	Exact Match	0.200	0.178	0.223	0.225	0.246	0.266	0.310	0.321	0.322

means using the distance measure as in our paper is better than method in others.

5.3   Comparison with Other Parsers

We compared our parser with some lexicalized parsers. They are parsers from [6] and [11][7]. The results are shown in Table 4.

In the training set, the parser from [6] shows almost 100% F_1 score It is because the parser is highly lexicalized. The parser from [11] using triplet/quadruplet model assumes that a modifyee of a word is one among the nearest, second nearest, or the last modifyee candidate. Unfortunately, according to our investigation, only 91.48% of modifyees are among the three candidates in the training data. This restriction causes the poor performance in the training data even the model is lexicalized.

---

[7] [11] parser requires handcrafted grammar(HPSG). Instead of HPSG, we used a set of dependency rules whose frequency is more than one in the training corpus as the grammar. (e.g. *Treebank grammar* [16])

Table 4. Result of the comparison with other lexicalized models. Many statistical parsing models dealing with distance measure, such as [9,10], resemble the model of [6]

	Measures	Parser from [6]	Parser from [11]	This Paper ($k{=}4$)
Training Set	Arc F_1 score	0.996	0.908	0.865
	Exact Matching	0.966	0.555	0.354
Testing Set	Arc F_1 score	0.837	0.843	0.856
	Exact Matching	0.256	0.303	0.322

In contrast, our model performs better than other lexicalized models in the experiment for the testing data. The improvements (+1.9% from [6]'s and +1.3% from [11]'s, absolute) in the arc-level performance are statistically meaningful.

This result is showing that the lexical dependency information may be useful for accurate parsing, but the proper use of other contextual information may be more helpful[8]. And it means the method we used to deal with the length of modification relation is effective for syntactic disambiguation.

6 Conclusion

We investigate the effect of unlexicalization of dependency parser for variable word order languages and propose a new parser, which is unlexicalized to keep the parser light, simple, and robust from the data sparseness problem. It utilizes some POS-level information to keep accuracy high as lexicalized parsers. In particular, we suggest using the modification distance probability to reflect the preference on a length of a modification relation for a given modifier and its contextual pattern. The experimental results show our model outperformed other lexicalized models for parsing Korean, which is a free word order language. Since it does not use any language specific predefined rules, the proposed parser can be easily adapted to other variable word order languages.

We don't say lexical information is unworthy. However, ignoring lexical information in a parser can give some advatages – simpler parser implementation, smaller disk space and shorter processing time – without sacrificing much accuracy, and this advatages may be useful for some cases, i.e. developing a parser for the system with limited memory size or processing speed.

We found out that the lexicalization plays a bigger role in parsing with probabilistic dependency grammar, but we haven't deeply investigated the cause of it yet. We will continue to investigate it. And there are some works that does not assume independency between dependency relations, such as [17]. We are

---

[8] In addition, our unlexicalized parser requires much smaller size of frequency data for estimating the probabilities. While the lexicalized parsers require 643M ([6]'s) and 540M, ([11]'s) bytes for storing the data, our parser uses only 18M bytes of data. We haven't trie to optimize the data structure. But taking that into account, the huge difference of the required resource size gives some ideas why unlexicalized parser is preferable.

going to reconstruct our parsing model without the independency assumption in the future.

References

1. Collins, M.: Head-Driven Statistical Models for Natural Language Parsing. PhD thesis, University of Pennsylvania (1999)
2. Charniak, E.: A maximum-entropy-inspired parser. Technical Report CS-99-12, Department of Computer Science, Brown University (1999)
3. Charniak, E.: Immediate-head parsing for language models. In: Meeting of the Association for Computational Linguistics. (2001) 116–123
4. Gildea, D.: Corpus variation and parser performance. In: Proceedings of Conference on Empirical Methods in Natural Language Processing. (2001)
5. Klein, D., Manning, C.D.: Accurate unlexicalized parsing. In: Proceedings of the 41st Meeting of the Association for Computational Linguistics. (2003) 310–315
6. Collins, M.J.: A new statistical parser based on bigram lexical dependencies. In: Proceedings of the 34th Annual Meeting of the ACL. (1996)
7. Lee, K.J.: Probabilistic Parsing of Korean based on Language-Specific Properties. PhD thesis, Dept. of Computer Science. KAIST (1997)
8. Haruno, M., Shirai, S., Ooyama, Y.: Using decision trees to construct a practical parser. In: Proceedings of COLING-ACL 98. (1998) 505–512
9. Kim, H., Seo, J.: A statistical Korean parser based on lexical dependencies. In: Spring Proceedings of Conference on Korea AI Society. (1997)
10. Uchimoto, K., Sekine, S., Isahara, H.: Japanese dependency structure analysis based on maximum entropy models. In: Proceedings of 13th EACL. (1999) 196–203
11. Kanayama, H., Torisawa, K., Mitsuichi, Y., Tsujii, J.: Statistical dependency analysis with an HPSG-based Japanese grammar. In: Proceedings of 5th Natural Language Processing Pacific Rim Symposium. (1999) 138–143
12. Kanayama, H., Torisawa, K., Mitsuichi, Y., Tsujii, J.: A hybrid Japanese parser with an hand-crafted grammar and statistics. In: Proceedings of the COLING 2000. (2000) 411–417
13. Sekine, S., Uchimoto, K., Isahara, H.: Backward beam search algorithm for dependency analysis of japanese. In: Proceedings of the COLING 2000. (2000) 745–760
14. Choi, K.S.: KAIST Language Resources v.2001. Result of Core Software Project from Ministry of Science and Technology, Korea (http://kibs.kaist.ac.kr) (2001)
15. Sekine, S.: Japanese dependency analysis using a deterministic definite state transducer. In: Proceedings of the COLING 2000. (2000) 761–767
16. Charniak, E.: Tree-bank grammars. Technical Report CS-96-02, Department of Computer Science, Brown University (1996)
17. Seo, K.J., Nam, K.C., Choi, K.S.: A probabilistic model of the dependency parse for the variable-word-order languages by using ascending dependency. Computer Processing of Oriental Languages 12 (1999) 309–322

Appendix

Brief Introduction to Korean Syntax

Two prominent characteristics of Korean are agglutinative morphology, and rather free word order with explicit case marking [7].

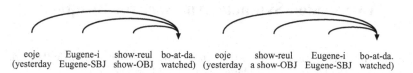

eoje   Eugene-i   show-reul bo-at-da.   eoje   show-reul   Eugene-i   bo-at-da.
(yesterday Eugene-SBJ show-OBJ watched)   (yesterday a show-OBJ Eugene-SBJ watched)

Fig. 4. Dependency trees for Korean sentences which have identical meaning, *Eugene watched a show yesterday.*

Korean is an agglutinative language, in which a word[9] is in a composition of more than one morpheme, in general. There are two types of morpheme: a content morpheme and a functional morpheme. A content morpheme contains the meaning of the word, while a functional morpheme plays a role as a grammatical information marker, which indicates a grammatical role, tense, modality, voice, etc. of the word.

The order of words is relatively weak in Korean compared to the fixed-order languages such as English. The grammatical information conveyed from a functional morpheme makes a word order be free. The following example is a Korean sentence consists of 4 words. Let's see a simple example[10].

eoje	*Eugene-i*	*show-reul*	*bo-at-da.*
yesterday	Eugene-SBJ	a show-OBJ	watched
Eugene watched a show yesterday.			

The second word in the sentence is *Eugene-i*. It consists of a content morpheme *Eugene* and a functional morpheme *i* which is a subject case marking postposition. The sentence can be rewritten as :

eoje	*show-reul*	*Eugene-i*	*bo-at-da.*
yesterday	a show-ACC	Eugene-NUM	watch-PAST-END
Eugene watched a show yesterday.			

Though the subject and the object exchange their position, the two sentences have identical meaning. Because of this property of Korean, dependency grammar is widely used for analyzing syntactic structure of the Korean language.

The grammatical relation of a dependency relation can be specified by the functional morpheme of the modifier for the most case, selecting modifyee word for the modifier is the main concern for dependency parsing with Korean. Figure 4 shows dependency structure trees for the Korean sentences shown above.

---

[9] The exact term for the word is *eojeol*. However we use the term *word* for easier understanding.

[10] SBJ and OBJ stand for subjective and objective case.

A Cascaded Syntactic Analyser for Basque

Itziar Aduriz*, Maxux J. Aranzabe, Jose Maria Arriola, Arantza Díaz de Ilarraza,
Koldo Gojenola, Maite Oronoz, and Larraitz Uria

IXA Group (http://ixa.si.ehu.es)
Department of Computer Languages and Systems
University of the Basque Country
P.O. box 649, E-20080 Donostia
jiporanm@si.ehu.es
* Department of General Linguistics
University of Barcelona
Gran Via de las Corts Catalans, 585, 08007 Barcelona
itziar@fil.ub.es

Abstract. This article presents a robust syntactic analyser for Basque and the different modules it contains. Each module is structured in different analysis layers for which each layer takes the information provided by the previous layer as its input; thus creating a gradually deeper syntactic analysis in cascade. This analysis is carried out using the Constraint Grammar (CG) formalism. Moreover, the article describes the standardisation process of the parsing formats using XML.

1 Introduction

This article describes the steps we have followed for the construction of a robust cascaded syntactic analyser for Basque. Robust parsing is understood as *"the ability of a language analyser to provide useful analyses for real-world input texts. By useful analyses, we mean analyses that are (at least partially) correct and usable in some automatic task or application"* (Ait-Mokhtar et al., 2002). The creation of the robust analyser is performed based on a shallow parser. In this approach, incomplete syntactic structures are produced and thus the process goes beyond shallow parsing to a deeper language analysis in an incremental fashion. This allows us to tackle unrestricted text parsing through descriptions that are organized in ordered modules, depending on the depth level of the analysis (see Fig. 1).

In agglutinative languages like Basque, it is difficult to separate morphology from syntax. That is why we consider morphosyntactic parsing for the first phase of the shallow syntactic analyser, which, in turn, will provide the basis for a deeper syntactic analysis.

In section 2 we briefly describe the main features of Basque. The steps followed in the process of creation of the cascaded parser are presented in section 3. Section 4 explains how the information is encoded in XML following the Text Encoding Initiative (TEI) guidelines. Finally, some conclusions and objectives for future work are presented.

A. Gelbukh (Ed.): CICLing 2004, LNCS 2945, pp. 124–134, 2004.
© Springer-Verlag Berlin Heidelberg 2004

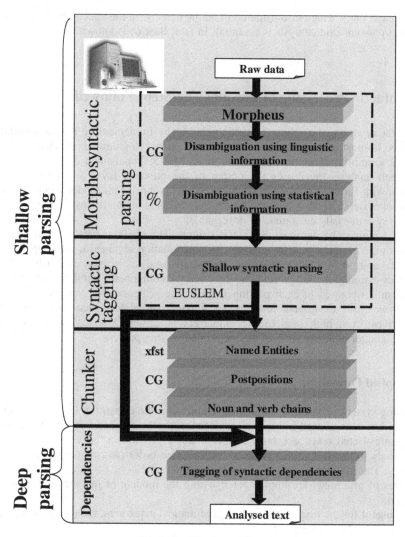

Fig. 1. Architecture of the system

2   Main Features of Basque

Basque is not an Indo-European language and differs considerably in grammar from the languages spoken in surrounding regions. It is an inflectional language in which grammatical relations between components within a clause are represented by suffixes. This is a distinguishing feature since the morphological information that words contain is richer than in surrounding languages. Given that Basque is a head final language at the syntactic level, the morphological information of the phrase (number, case, etc.), which is considered to be the head, is in the attached suffix. That is why morphosyntactic analysis is essential. In fact, Basque is known as a free-order language.

3   Syntactic Processing of Basque: The Steps Followed

We face the creation of a robust syntactic analyser by implementing it in sequential rule layers. In most of the cases, these layers are realized in grammars defined by the Constraint Grammar formalism (Karlsson *et al.*, 1995; Tapanainen & Voutilainen, 1994). Each analysis layer uses the output of the previous layer as its input and enriches it with further information. Rule layers are grouped into modules depending on the level of depth of their analysis. Modularity helps to maintain linguistic data and makes the system easily customisable or reusable.

Figure 1 shows the architecture of the system. The shallow parsing of the text begins with the morphosyntactic analysis. The information obtained is then separated into noun and verb chains. Finally, the deep analysis phase establishes the dependency-based grammatical relations between the components within the clause.

The results obtained in each parsing level of the sentence *Noizean behin itsaso aldetik Donostiako Ondarreta hondartzara enbata iristen da* 'Once in a while, a storm arrives from high seas to the Ondarreta beach in Donostia' will help in providing a better understanding of the mentioned parsing process.

3.1   Applied Formalism

The parsing system is based on finite state grammars. The Constraint Grammar (CG) formalism has been chosen in most cases because, on the one hand, it is suitable for treating unrestricted texts and, on the other hand, it provides a useful methodology and the tools to tackle morphosyntax as well as free order phrase components in a direct way. The analyser used is CG-2 (www.conexor.com).

A series of grammars are implemented within the module of the shallow parsing which aim:

1. To be useful for the disambiguation of grammatical categories, removing incorrect tags based on the context;
2. To assign and disambiguate partial syntactic functions;
3. To assign the corresponding tags to delimit verb and noun chains.

Besides, dependency-based parsing is made explicit in the deep parsing module by means of grammars similar to those used in the shallow parsing module.

Even though CG originally uses mapping rules to assign the syntactic functions of grammatical categories defined by the context, in the above-mentioned modules these rules assign the corresponding syntactic tags to each analysis level. An example of a rule defined to detect the beginning of noun chains is shown below:

```
MAP (%INIT_NCH) TARGET (NOUN) IF (0 (GEN-GEL) + (@NC))
                               (-1 PUNCT)
                               (1 NOUN OR ADJ OR DET);
```

This rule assigns the noun-chain-initial tag (%INIT_NCH) to the noun if the following conditions are satisfied: a) the word is in any of both genitives (0 (GEN-GEL) + (@NC[1])); b) it has a punctuation mark on its left side (-1 PUNCT); c) there is a noun, an adjective or a determiner (1 N OR ADJ OR DET) on its right side.

3.2 Shallow Syntactic Analyser

The parsing process starts with the outcome of the morphosyntactic analyser MORFEUS (Aduriz *et al.*, 1998), which was created following a two-level morphology (Koskenniemi, 1983) and it deals with the parsing of all the lexical units of a text, both simple words and multiword units as a Complex Lexical Unit (CLU).

>From the obtained results, grammatical categories and lemmas are disambiguated. The disambiguation process is carried out by means of linguistic rules (CG grammar) and stochastic rules based on markovian models (Ezeiza, 2003) with the aim of improving the parsing tags in which the linguistic information obtained is not accurate enough. Once morphosyntactic disambiguation has been performed, we should, ideally, be working on a morphosyntactically fully disambiguated text when assigning syntactic functions.

3.2.1 Disambiguation of Shallow Syntactic Functions

The aim of the syntactic disambiguation rules is to assign a single syntactic function to each word. This process is performed in two steps:

1. Assignment of syntactic functions. Words inherit their syntactic function from the EDBL database for Basque (Aldezabal *et al.*, 2001). Nevertheless, not all the syntactic functions derive from EDBL but some are inherited from CG syntactic and *mapping* rules due to the fact that they depend on the context.
2. Reduction of syntactic ambiguity by means of constrains.

The syntactic functions that are determined in the partial analysis are based on those given in Aduriz *et al.* (2000). The syntactic functions employed basically follow the same approach to syntactic tags found in ENGCG, although some decisions and a few changes were necessary. Basically, there are three types of syntactic functions:

1. Those that represent the dependencies within noun chains (@CM>[2], @NC> etc.).
2. Non-dependent or main syntactic functions (@SUBJ, @OBJ, etc.).
3. Syntactic functions of the components of verb chains (@-FMAINVERB[3], @+FMAINVERB, etc.).

The distinction of these three groups is essential when designing the rules, which assign the function tags for verb and noun chains detection.

Figure 2 shows the parsing of the sample sentence at this level.

For instance, the syntactic function of the noun phrase *enbata* 'storm' (absolutive) is ambiguous because three syntactic analyses are possible (@SUBJ, @OBJ @PRED). Given that CG aims to assign a single function to each word, we need to choose whether to assign @SUBJ, @OBJ or @PRED to *enbata*. In this case, we

---

[1] @NC> noun complement

[2] @CM> modifier of the word carrying case in the noun chain

[3] @-FMAINVERB non finite main verb

choose the @SUBJ syntactic function by means of a CG rule that select it provided that there is agreement between *enbata* and the finite auxiliary verb *da*.

```
/<Noizean_behin>/<CLU_EDBL>/
    ("noizean_behin" ADV ADVCOM @VC)
/<itsaso>/
    ("itsaso" NOUN COM @CM>)
/<aldetik>/
    ("alde" NOUN COM DEC NUMS DET DEC ABL @VC)
/<Donostiako>/<BEG_WC>/
  ("Donostia" NOUN LPN PLU- DEC NUMS DET DEC GEL @NC> @<NC)
/<Ondarreta>/<BEG_WC>/
    ("Ondarreta" NOUN LPN PLU- @CM>)
/<hondartzara>/
    ("hondartza" NOUN COM DEC NUMS DET DEC ALA @VC)
/<enbata>/
    ("enbat" NOUN COM DEC ABS NUMS DET  @OBJ @SUBJ @PRED)
    ("enbata" NOUN COM DEC ABS NDET  @OBJ @SUBJ @PRED)
    ("enbata" NOUN COM DEC ABS NUMS DET  @OBJ @SUBJ @PRED)
/<iristen>/
    ("iritsi" VERB SIM MVC INF ASP NF @-FMAINVERB)
/<da>/
    ("izan" AUXV A1 NR_HU  @+FAUXVERB)
/<.>/<PUNC_FS>/
```

Fig. 2. Morphosyntactic analysis

3.2.2   Delimiting Chains (*chunker*)

In the recognition process of entity names and postpositional phrases morphosyntactic information must be provided. Verb and noun chains make use of the syntactic functions provided by each word-form.

Entity Names

For the recognition and categorization of entity names (person, organization and location) a combined system has been created. Firstly, the system applies a grammar that has been developed using an XFST tool (Xerox Finite State Transducer) (Karttunen *et al.* 1997) which detects the entity names using the morphological information. Then, entity names are classified through the application of a heuristic, which combines textual information and *gazetteers* (Alegria *et al.*, 2003).

The function tags defining the initial and final elements of entity names are: %INIT_ENTI_*, %FIN_ENTI_*, where "*" may be either LOC (location), PER (person) or ORG (organization).

Complex Postpositions

Another characteristic feature of Basque is its postpositional system. The complex postpositions the system recognizes in this phase consist of both a case suffix followed by an independent word. For example: *gizonaren aurrean* 'in front of the man'. This type of complex postposition is taken into account in the recognition of noun chains (these noun chains also represent a postpositional system even though the postposition, in this case, consists of a single suffix). The function tags %INIT_POS and %FIN_POS define the beginning and the end of postpositional phrases.

Verb Chains
The identification of verb chains is based on both the verb function tags (@+FAUXVERB, @-FAUXVERB, @-FMAINVERB, @+FMAINVERB, etc.) and some particles (the negative particle, modal particles, etc.).

There are two types of verb chains: continuous and dispersed verb chains (the latter consisting of three components at most). The following function tags have been defined:

- %VCH: this tag is attached to a verb chain consisting of a single element.
- %INIT_VCH: this tag is attached to the initial element of a complex verb chain.
- %FIN_VCH: this tag is attached to the final element of a complex verb chain.
  The tags used to mark-up dispersed verb chains are:
- %INIT_NCVCH: this tag is attached to the initial element of a non-continuous verb chain.
- %SEC_NCVCH: this tag is attached to the second element of a non-continuous verb chain.
- %FIN_NCVCH: this tag is attached to the final element of a non-continuous verb chain.

Noun Chains
This module is based on the following assumption: any word having a modifier function tag has to be linked to some word or words with a main syntactic function tag. Moreover, a word with a main syntactic function tag can, by itself, constitute a phrase unit. Taking into account this assumption, we recognise simple and coordinated noun chains, for which these three function tags have been established:

- %NCH: this tag is attached to words with main syntactic function tags that constitute a noun phrase unit by themselves.
- %INIT_NCH: this tag is attached to the initial element of a noun phrase unit.
- %FIN_NCH: this tag is attached to the final element of a noun phrase unit.

Figure 3 shows the parsing of the sample sentence with its corresponding chains. In it we can distinguish:

1. A complex lexical unit: *Noizean_behin* 'once in a while'
2. A complex postposition: *itsaso aldetik* 'from high seas'
3. An entity name: *Donostiako Ondarreta* 'Ondarreta in Donostia'
4. Noun chains: *Donostiako Ondarreta hondartzara* 'to the Ondarreta beach in Donostia', and *enbata* 'storm'

It is important to highlight that this process is parametrizable, allowing the user to choose to mark entity names but not postpositional phrases, etc.

3.3   Deep Syntactic Analysis

The aim of the deep syntactic analysis is to establish the dependency relations among the components of the sentence. This process is performed by means of CG rules.

```
/<Noizean_behin>/<CLU_EDBL>/
   ("noizean_behin"  ADV ADVCOM @VC %NCH)
/<itsaso>/
   ("itsaso"  NOUN COM @CM> %INIT POS %INIT_NCH)
/<aldetik>/
   ("alde" NOUN COM DEC NUMS DET DEC ABL @VC
            %FIN POS %FIN_NCH)
/<Donostiako>/<BEG_WC>/
   ("Donostia" NOUN LPN PLU- DEC NUMS DET DEC GEL
            %INIT ENTI LOC @NC> @<NC %INIT_NCH)
/<Ondarreta>/<BEG_WC>/
   ("Ondarreta"  NOUN LPN PLU- %FIN ENTI LOC @CM>)
/<hondartzara>/
   ("hondartza" NOUN COM DEC NUMS DET DEC ALA @VC
            %FIN_NCH)
/<enbata>/
   ("enbat" NOUN COM DEC ABS NUMS DET @OBJ @SUBJ @PRED %NCH)
   ("enbata" NOUN COM DEC ABS NDET @OBJ @SUBJ @PRED %NCH)
   ("enbata" NOUN COM DEC ABS NUMS DET @OBJ @SUBJ @PRED %NCH)
/<iristen>/
   ("iritsi"  VERB SIM MVC INF ASP NF @-NFMV %INIT_VCH)
/<da>/
   ("izan"  AUXV A1 NR_HU  @+NFAV %FIN_VCH)
/<.>/<PUNC_FS>/
```

Fig. 3. Analysis of chains

After considering several choices in the field of syntactic tagging, and taking into account the mentioned morphological and syntactic peculiarities of Basque, we decided to adopt the framework presented in Carroll *et al.* (1998, 1999). The dependencies we have defined, constitute a hierarchy that describes the most important grammatical structures such as relative clauses, causative sentences, coordination, discontinuous elements, elliptic elements and so on (Aduriz et al. 2002).

Figures 4 and 5 show an example of the adopted schema for the syntactic analysis as well as its corresponding syntactic tree. Notice that the nodes of the trees can be either single words or word-chains.

The syntactic dependencies between the components within the sentence are represented by tags starting with "&". The symbols ">" and "<" attached to each dependency-tag represent the direction in which we find the sentence component whose dependant is the target word.

In the example we can see that the postpositional phrase *itsaso aldetik* 'from high seas' depends on the verb *iristen* 'arrives', which is on its right side. A post-process will make this link explicit.

4   Representation of All the Phases of the Analysis Using XML

Figure 1 shows the global architecture of the robust syntactic analyser. The information to be exchanged among the different tools which constitute the parsing

```
/<Noizean_behin>/<CLU_EDBL>/
    ("noizean_behin"  ADV ADVCOM @VC %NCH &NCMOD-CLU>)
/<itsaso>/
    ("itsaso"  NOUN COM @CM> %INIT_POS %INIT_NCH
              &NCMOD-POS12>)
/<aldetik>/
    ("alde"  NOUN COM DEC NUMS DET DEC ABL @VC
            %FIN_POS %FIN_NCH &NCMOD-POS22>)
/<Donostiako>/<BEG_WC>/
    ("Donostia"  NOUN LPN PLU- DEC NUMS DET DEC GEL
            %INIT ENTI LOC @NC> @<NC %INIT_NCH
            &NCMOD-GEL>)
/<Ondarreta>/<BEG_WC>/
    ("Ondarreta"  NOUN LPN PLU- %FIN ENTI LOC @CM> &NCMOD>)
/<hondartzara>/
    ("hondartza"  NOUN COM DEC NUMS DET DEC ALA @VC %FIN_NCH
            &NCMOD-ALA>)
/<enbata>/
    ("enbat"  NOUN COM DEC ABS NUMS DET @OBJ @SUBJ @PRED
            %NCH &NCSUBJ>)
    ("enbata"  NOUN COM DEC ABS NDET @OBJ @SUBJ @PRED
            %NCH &NCSUBJ>)
    ("enbata"  NOUN COM DEC ABS NUMS DET @OBJ @SUBJ @PRED
            %NCH &NCSUBJ>)
/<iristen>/
    ("iritsi"  VERB SIM MVC INF ASP NF @-NFMV %INIT_VCH)
/<da>/
    ("izan"  AUXV A1 NR_HU  @+NFAV %FIN_VCH &<AUXMOD)
/<.>/<PUNC_FS>/
```

Fig. 4. Dependency-based analysis

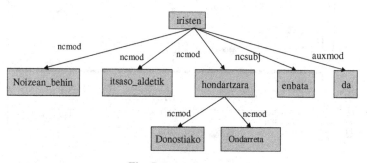

Fig. 5. Dependency tree

system is complex and diverse. Because of this complexity, we decided to use Feature Structures (FSs) to represent this information (Artola *et al.*, 2002). Feature structures are coded following the TEI's DTD for FSs (Sperberg-McQueen *et al.*, 1994), and Feature Structure Definition descriptions (FSD) have been thoroughly defined for each document created. The documents created as input and output of the different tools are coded in XML. The use of XML for encoding the information flowing between programs forces us to describe each document in a formal way, with the advantages it offers to keep coherence, reliability and maintenance.

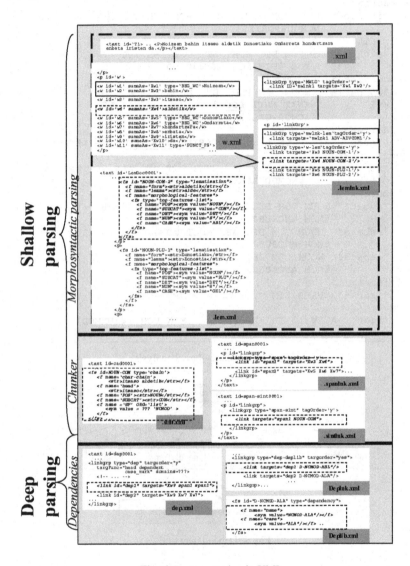

Fig. 6. Representation in XML

Figure 6 shows the representation of the sample sentence in XML format. The files described at the bottom constitute the tree of the above described analysis: *.dep.xml* (structure that establishes the syntactic relation between the head and its dependants), *.deplib.xml* (description of syntactic dependencies), *.deplnk.xml* (link between the two previous components).

5   Conclusions and Future Work

The present article outlines the process of the creation of a robust syntactic analyser for Basque. We want to remark that the morphosyntactic analyser has been widely used and tested in different projects (Verdejo *et al.*, 2002). Regarding evaluation, we assessed the chain delimiter grammars according to Carroll (2003). We measured the correctness of the identified chunk boundaries, including ambiguous and unambiguous analyses. To achieve this, we based our analysis on a sample consisting of 260 sentences (totalling 4,873 words), where phrase boundaries have been marked. As a result we achieved an 83% precision rate (correctly selected chunks / number of chunks returned) and 81.4% recall rate (correctly selected chunks / actual chunks in the sentence).

As far as the deep syntactic analyser is concerned, we have defined a hierarchy of dependencies that describes the most important grammatical structures, such as relative clauses, causative sentences, coordination, discontinuous elements, elliptic elements and so on. To the present time, 150 CG rules have been defined and are currently being evaluated.

Moreover, we have already defined the structure of all the documents to be used in the syntactic analysis process in XML, but we are still working on the process for the automatic extraction of these documents. A library in C++ has been created in order to implement the whole internal structure of XML documents. No specific knowledge about XML is required in order to define this kind of document.

Acknowledgements. This research is being supported by the University of the Basque Country (9/UPV00141.226-14601/2002), the Ministry of Industry of the Basque Government (XUXENG project, OD02UN52), the Interministerial Commission for Science and Technology of the Spanish Government (FIT-150500-2002-244), and the European Community (MEANING project, IST-2001-34460).

We would especially like to thank Itsaso Esparza for helping us write the final version of the paper.

References

Aduriz I, Agirre E, Aldezabal I, Alegria I, Ansa O, Arregi X, Arriola J.M, Artola X, Díaz de Ilarraza A, Ezeiza N, Gojenola K, Maritxalar A, Maritxalar M, Oronoz M, Sarasola K, Soroa A, Urizar R, Urkia M 1998. A Framework for the Automatic Processing of Basque. In *Proceedings of the First International Conference on Language Resources and Evaluation*, Granada.

Aduriz I, Aldezabal I, Aranzabe M, Arrieta B, Arriola J, Atutxa A, Díaz de Ilarraza A, Gojenola K, Oronoz M, Sarasola K 2002. Construcción de un corpus etiquetado sintácticamente para el euskera. *Actas del XVIII Congreso de la SEPLN*, Valladolid, Spain.

Aduriz I, Díaz de Ilarraza A 2003. Morphosyntactic Disambiguation and Shallow Parsing in Computational Processing of Basque. Oyharçabal, B (Ed.) In *Inquiries into the lexicon-syntax relations in Basque (forthcoming)*.

Ait-Mokhtar S,.Chanod J.-P, Roux C. 2002. Robustness beyond shallowness: incremental deep parsing. *Natural Language Engineering, 8: 121-144*. Cambridge University Press.

Aldezabal I, Ansa O, Arrieta B, Artola X, Ezeiza A, Hernández G, Lersundi M 2001. EDBL: a General Lexical Basis for the Automatic Processing of Basque. *IRCS Workshop onLinguistic Databases*, Philadelphia (USA).

Alegria I.,Balza I.,Ezeiza N.,Fernandez I.,Urizar R. 2003. Named Entity Recognition and Classification for texts in Basque. *II Jornadas de Tratamiento y Recuperación de Información, JOTRI, Madrid. Spain.*

Artola X, Díaz de Ilarraza A, Ezeiza N, Gojenola K, Hernández G, Soroa A 2002. A Class Library for the Integration of NLP Tools: Definition and implementation of an Abstract Data Type Collection for the manipulation of SGML documents in a context of stand-off linguistic annotation. In *Proceedings of the Third International Conference on Language Resources and Evaluation*, Las Palmas de Gran Canaria, Spain.

Carroll, J. 2003. `Parsing'. In R. Mitkov (ed.), *The Oxford Handbook of Computational Linguistics*, Oxford, UK: OUP. 233-248.

Ezeiza, N 2003. Corpusak ustiatzeko tresna linguistikoak. Euskararen etiketatzaile sintaktiko sendo eta malgua. PhD thesis, University of the Basque Country.

Karlsson F, Voutilainen A, Heikkila J, Anttila A. 1995. Constraint Grammar: Language-independent System for Parsing Unrestricted Text. *Mouton de Gruyter*, Berlin.

Karttunen L., Chanod J-P., Grefenstette G., Schiller A. 1997. *Regular Expressions For Language Engineering*. Journal of Natural Language Engineering.

Koskenniemi K 1983. *Two-level Morphology: A general Computational Model for Word-Form Recognition and Production.* University of Helsinki, Department of General Linguistics. Publications 11.

Sperberg-McQueen C.M., Burnard L., 1994. *Guidelines for Electronic Text Encoding and Interchange.* TEI P3 Text Encoding Initiative.

Tapanainen P, Voutilainen A 1994. Tagging Accurately-Don´t guess if you know. In Proceedings of the 4th Conference on Applied Natural Language Processing, Washington.

Verdejo M.F., Gonzalo J., Màrquez LL., Padró LL., Rodríguez H., Agirre E. 2002. *HERMES, Hemerotecas electrónicas: Recuperación multilingüe y extracción semántica*, TIC2000-0335-C03. Jornada de Seguimiento de Proyectos en Tecnologías del Software. Programa Nacional de Tecnologías de la Información y las Comunicaciones.

An Analysis of Sentence Boundary Detection Systems for English and Portuguese Documents*

Carlos N. Silla Jr. and Celso A.A. Kaestner

Pontifical Catholic University of Parana
Rua Imaculada Conceicao, 1155 - 80.215-901
Curitiba – Parana – BRAZIL
{silla, kaestner}@ppgia.pucpr.br

Abstract. In this paper we present a study comparing the performance of different systems found in the literature that perform the task of automatic text segmentation in sentences for English documents. We also show the difficulties found to adapt these systems to make them work with Portuguese documents and the results obtained after the adaptation. We analyzed two systems that use a machine learning approach: MxTerminator and Satz, and a customized system based on fixed rules expressed by Regular Expressions. The results achieved by the Satz system were surprisingly positive for Portuguese documents.

1 Introduction

When dealing with tasks related to the automatic processing of documents like summarization, translation, etc. one of the procedures that frequently occur is the segmentation of the text in sentences. This task is usually included in the pre-processing stage, and uses a simple criterion, tagged documents, or one of the approaches found in the literature.

The systems found in the literature can be grouped in two classes: the ones that use fixed rules to identify what is and what is not a sentence, and the ones that use a machine learning approach. In this work we evaluate the performance of one customized system that uses fixed rules, and two systems that use a machine learning approach: MxTerminator [1] and Satz [2]. The first system uses templates based on Regular Expressions, considering the context where a punctuation mark appears, and will be refered to as RE (Regular Expressions) [3]. The MxTerminator uses a Maximum Entropy Model to detect the sentence boundaries, while Satz considers the context where a possible punctuation mark appears and can be used with any machine learning algorithm; in this work, it was used with the C4.5 classifier [4].

The remaining part of the article is divided as follows: section 2 presents a general view of the systems used for comparison and how they were adapted to Brazilian Portuguese; section 3 describes the methodology used in the experiments and presents the corresponding results for two sets of documents, in

---

* This research was supported by the Brazilian PIBIC-CNPq Agency.

A. Gelbukh (Ed.): CICLing 2004, LNCS 2945, pp. 135–141, 2004.
© Springer-Verlag Berlin Heidelberg 2004

English and Portuguese; and finally, in section 4 we draw the conclusions and perspectives of this work.

2   The Different Approaches to Detect Sentence Boundaries

In this section we present an overview of the three different systems used in this work.

2.1   RE SYSTEM

As a representative of the fixed rules approach, we used a system that encode the rules as regular expressions, and considers the context where each possible end of sentence occurs within the document. This system was chosen because it has achieved results close to the MxTerminator system in a dataset of the TIPSTER collection in recent experiments [3].

The system uses a database of regular expressions which denote chains that contain punctuation marks but don't indicate the end of a sentence, like abbreviations and other sequences like e-mails, www addresses, etc. The database of regular expressions is kept on a text file, which allows easy manipulation of the existing rules.

To identify the sentences, the system scans the text until it finds the first period (.); after that, it analyzes the preceding string; if this string matches some regular expression, then the system concludes that this is not an end of sentence and advances to the next period. If the preceding string doesn't match any regular expression, the system verifies the string after the period, which might be one of the special cases and need a different treatment. If the system doesn't find any matching regular expression for the current string, it concludes that the period indicates an end of sentence, and tags the text with the appropriate marks, in this case: <S> and </S>. The procedure is repeated until the entire document has been analyzed.

The following special cases are treated by the system:

- Decimal Numbers: the system verifies if what comes before the period is a number, and if it is, it also verifies if the word after the dot is a number. That way it can distinguish between: "...2003." and "...US$ 50.25".
- Parenthesis at the end of a sentence: one characteristic of the English language is that sentences like "(...that night.)" are correct, unlike the Portuguese language, in which the correct form is "(...that night).".
- Ellipsis: The last special case treated by the system is related to the occurrence of ellipsis ("..."). In this case, the system verifies the occurrences of successive dots until it finds the last one of them, which indicates the end of the sentence.

To adapt the system to the Brazilian Portuguese it was necessary to add 240 new regular expressions that basically denote abbreviations of the language.

Since a text file describes the regular expressions, it was easy, although time consuming, to adapt the system.

2.2 MxTerminator

The system MxTerminator was developed by Reynar and Ratnaparkhi[1] in the Pennsylvania University and uses an approach which is independent of language or text genre. MxTerminator uses a machine learning algorithm named Maximum Entropy Model to identify the sentences of a document.

From a Corpus with the sentences already identified (training set) the model learns to classify each instance of period (.), exclamation mark (!) and question mark (?) as elements that identify what is a sentence end and what is not.

The training process is robust and doesn't need any type of fixed rules or some other linguistic information, like part-of-speech frequencies, or even specific information about the genre or domain of the texts, because during the training the system creates a list of induced abbreviations. This list is obtained considering an abbreviation as every word in the training set that has a white space before and after its occurrence and contains a possible end of sentence symbol (.,!,?), but doesn't indicate an end of sentence.

The possible sentences of the document are identified by scanning the text for sequences of characters separated by a blank space (token) containing one of the symbols that indicate a possible end of sentence (.,?,!).

The token that contains the symbol which denotes a possible end of sentence is called Candidate. The system then uses the contextual information where each Candidate occurs. The contextual information is represented by a set of features like the prefix, the suffix, etc.

The main idea of the Maximum Entropy Model is that the probability of a certain class in this case - the sentence boundaries - in a given context, can be estimated by the joint probability distribution using a maximum entropy model.

To adapt the MxTerminator to the Brazilian Portuguese language the procedure was very simple, because the system uses, for training a text file of any size that must contain one sentence per line. Another interesting factor is that, besides the training files, no other type of information was needed. For this reason, the MxTerminator was considered the simplest of the analyzed methods to use and adapt and use in new language.

2.3 Satz

The Satz system was developed by Palmer and Hearst[2] and uses an approach that considers the context where each punctuation mark occurs; it can be used with any machine learning algorithm, and the original results were tested using Neural Networks [5] and the C4.5 Decision Tree Classifier [2].

The Satz system represents the context around a possible end of sentence symbol constructing a series of descriptor arrays, that represent an estimative of the part-of-speech distribution for each word.

Table 1. Mapped Classes

Grammatical Class	Mapped Tags
Miscellaneous	CUR; IN; OTHER; PDEN;
Noun	N; N/N; N/N/N; N/V
Verb	V; VAUX; V|PASS; V/V
Article	ART
Modifier	PCP; PCP/PCP; ADV; ADV/ADJ; ADV/ADV; ADV/KC; ADV/KS; ADV-KS-REL; ADV-KS-REL/ADV-KS-REL; ADV/PREP; ADV/PROADJ; ADV/PROSUB; ADJ; ADJ/ADJ; ADJ/V
Conjunction	KS; KS/ADJ; KC; CC
Pronoun	PROADJ; PROADJ/ADJ; PRO-KS; PRO-KS/PRO-KS; PROPESS; PROPESS/PROPESS; PROSUB
Preposition	PREP; PREP/ADJ; PREP/V
Proper Noun	PROP; NPROP; NPROP/NPROP
Number	NUM
Comma or Semicolon	, ;
Left Parentheses	QUOTEL; (
Right Parentheses	QUOTER;)
Non Punctuation Character	=; *; #;
Possessive	$
Colon or Dash	-; :; –;
Abbreviation	AB
Sentence Ending Punctuation	.; ..; !; ?;

The use of a part-of-speech estimative considers the context in which the word occurred rather than just the word itself. This is a unique aspect of the Satz system, and according to its authors is the main factor for the high efficiency of the system. The part-of-speech frequencies are stored in a lexicon. If a word is not present in the lexicon, a series of heuristics are used in order to define the corresponding frequency.

The context vector contains the descriptor arrays for each word surrounding the possible end of sentence, and is the input for the machine-learning algorithm. The output is used to indicate if a possible end of sentence mark corresponds to an end of sentence or not.

To adapt the Satz system to Portuguese it was necessary to re-implement the system, because the version available at the UCI Repository presents problems when dealing with accented characters, which are very common in Brazilian Portuguese. For example, a word like "agrícola" (agricultural) would be identified as two tokens: "agr" and "cola".

In order to re-implement the Satz system, we developed a Java-based version of the system that produces the descriptor arrays and integrated it with the Weka Data Mining Tool [6]. We used the J4.8 (which is a Java implementation of the C4.5 algorithm) in the tests. However, this procedure alone was not enough to adapt the system. We had to create a new lexicon using the part-of-speech information which is present in the Corpus. We also needed to map the Brazilian Portuguese Corpus tags to the 18 general categories of the system. Table 1 shows the tags mapped to each category.

3   Experiments and Obtained Results

In order to perform a comparison between the different systems using documents in English, we used one of the databases that contains news from the Wall Street Journal, which belongs to the TIPSTER document collection, from the Text Retrieval Conference (TREC - Reference number of the database: WSJ-910130).

The database contains 156 documents at different sizes, totalizing 3.554 sentences. To perform the experiments, each of the documents had their sentences detected and tagged manually. To evaluate the performance of the systems described in section 2, we also compared their results with the baseline proposed by Palmer[5]: where each sentence is obtained using the simple criterion period (.).

The results achieved by each system are presented in Table 2, where:

Table 2. Results achieved by the different systems in the TIPSTER (English) document collection

System	Precision	Recall	F-Measure
Baseline	30,29%	50,61%	37,89%
RE	92,39%	91,18%	91,78%
MxTerminator	91,19%	91,25%	91,22%
Satz	98,67%	85,98%	91,88%

- "Precision" indicates the percentage of correctly classified sentences of the documents (Number of sentence endings correctly identified / Number of sentences identified);
- "Recall" indicates the percentage of correctly classified sentences of the documents regarding the number of sentences present in the original document (Number of sentence endings correctly identified / Number of sentences present in the original database);
- "F-measure" is a unique evaluation measurement, which combines precision and recall in a single metric: the harmonic mean.

The results achieved by the different systems show that although the RE system uses a fixed rule approach, its results are close to the other systems. This indicates that when the domain of the documents is well known, and no training Corpus is available, the use of a fixed rule system might be a good option.

In order to evaluate the performance of the systems with Portuguese Documents, we used a version of the Lacio-Web Corpus [7], that contains 21.822 sentences.

To evaluate the robustness of each one of the systems, i.e. their performance using their original configuration, without any modification in the regular expressions nor any re-training, we used the Lacio-Web Corpus with unidentified sentences. The results achieved by each system are presented in Table 3. For the Satz system which is dependent on part-of-speech frequencies, the test was performed using only the original heuristics of the system.

Table 3. Robustness of the different systems using the Lacio-Web (Portuguese) document collection (uncustomized versions)

System	Precision	Recall	F-Measure
Baseline	85,40%	92,25%	88,69%
RE	91,80%	88,02%	89,87%
MxTerminator	94,29%	95,84%	95,05%
Satz	99,48%	98,81%	99,14%

Finally, in order to evaluate the performance of each of the systems when customized, they were adapted to Brazilian Portuguese by providing the needed information about the language. The MxTerminator was trained using the Lacio-Web Corpus using 10-fold cross-validation [8]. To the RE system we added 240 new regular expressions mostly containing abbreviations of Brazilian Portuguese words. The Satz system was also trained using 10-fold cross-validation, but a complete lexicon was created using the part-of-speech frequencies available within the Corpus. The results achieved by each system can be seen in Table 4.

Table 4. Results achieved by the different systems in the Lacio-Web (Portuguese) document collection (customized versions)

System	Precision	Recall	F-Measure
Baseline	85,40%	92,25%	88,69%
RE	91,80%	88,02%	89,87%
MxTerminator	96,31%	96,63%	96,46%
Satz	99,59%	98,74%	99,16%

Table 3 shows that the results achieved by the MxTerminator are surprisingly good, but not as impressive as the ones achieved by Satz. The results indicate that the MxTerminator and Satz are robust methods, although the results achieved by Satz are surprisingly positive. The results also indicate that the fixed rule approach, even in the form of regular expressions, is not well suited if the domain and genre of the texts are unknown.

Table 4 shows that after being adapted to Brazilian Portuguese, both machine learning methods improved their performance, except for the fixed rule approach. However, the results achieved by Satz even without the lexicon with part-of-speech information for all the words in the documents are outstanding.

4   Conclusions

In this work, we analyzed three different systems for the task of automatic text segmentation, in order to identify the sentence boundaries in a document. We performed experiments for both English and Portuguese documents, using a fixed regular expression rules system, the Satz decision tree approach and the MxTerminator maximum entropy approach. The best results were achieved by the Satz system: 91,88% of F-measure in the English document database; 99,14% in the Portuguese document database without retraining, using only heuristics and 99,16% in the same collection with retraining.

These results indicate that the part-of-speech frequencies, in the case of Brazilian Portuguese, are not as important as it is when working with English. This is explained by the fact that English sentence construction follows more restrictive construction patterns than the sentences in Portuguese, which is a Latin language. The adaptability and robustness of each system were also evaluated.

Although the RE system achieved results similar to the ones achieved by the other two systems, this was one specific case where the domain and genre of the text was well known. The MxTerminator achieved good results and was also the easiest system to adapt to the Brazilian Portuguese language. The Satz system had an outstanding performance showing that the part-of-speech information does not matter to identify the sentences in Brazilian Portuguese Documents.

Acknowledgments. We would like to thank Dr. Adwait Ratnaparkhi from the Pennsylvania University for sending us the MxTerminator system, and to Dr. Marti A. Hearst from the Berkeley University for kindly sending us the original files used by Satz.

References

1. Reynar, J., Ratnaparkhi, A.: A maximum entropy approach to identifying sentence boundaries. In: Proceedings of the Fifth Conference on Applied Natural Language Processing. (1997) 16–19
2. Palmer, D.D., Hearst, M.A.: Adaptive multilingual sentence boundary disambiguation. Computational Linguistics **23** (1997) 241–267
3. Silla Jr., C.N., Valle Jr., J.D., Kaestner, C.A.A.: Automatic sentence detection using regulares expressions (in portuguese). In: Proceedings of the 3rd Brazilian Computer Science Congress, Itajaí, SC, Brazil (2003) 548–560
4. Quinlan, J.R.: C4.5: Programs for Machine Learning. Morgan Kaufmann (1993)
5. Palmer, D.D.: SATZ - an adaptive sentence segmentation system. Master's thesis (1994)
6. Witten, I.H., Frank, B.: Data Mining: Practical Machine Learning Tools and Techniques with Java Implementations. Wiley-Interscience, San Francisco (1999)
7. Aluisio, S.M., Pinheiro, G.M., Finger, Nunes, M.G.V., Tagnin, S.E.: The lacio-web project: overview and issues in brazilian portuguese corpora creation. In: Proceedings of the Corpus Linguistics 2003. Volume 16. (2003) 14–21
8. Mitchell, T.M.: Machine Learning. McGraw-Hill (1997)

Towards Language-Independent Sentence Boundary Detection

Do-Gil Lee and Hae-Chang Rim

Dept. of Computer Science & Engineering, Korea University
1, 5-ka, Anam-dong, Seongbuk-ku, SEOUL 136-701, Korea
{dglee, rim}@nlp.korea.ac.kr

Abstract. We propose a machine learning approach for language-independent sentence boundary detection. The proposed method requires no heuristic rules and language-specific features, such as Part-of-Speech (POS) information, a list of abbreviations or proper names. With only the language-independent features, we perform experiments on not only an inflectional language but also an agglutinative language, having fairly different characteristics (in this paper, English and Korean, respectively). In addition, we obtain good performances in both languages.

1 Introduction

Sentence boundary detection (SBD) is the first step of natural language processing applications. Most of them, including POS taggers and parsers regard sentence as input. Many researchers have considered the SBD task as an easy one so that they have not stated the accurate algorithms for the job.

A sentence usually ends with a punctuation mark such as '.', '?', or '!'. So, identifying sentence boundaries can be done by comparatively simple heuristic rules. The punctuation marks, however, are not always used as a sentence final. Moreover, some sentences may not have any punctuation mark. For example, output texts from automatic speech recognition (ASR) systems are unpunctuated. Even a phrase or a single word would be a sentence by itself. Therefore, in order to acquire accurate results, it is required more and more complicated rules. Writing such rules are both labour-intensive and time-consuming. For these reasons, recently, various machine learning techniques, such as decision tree, neural network, and maximum entropy, have been successfully applied to the SBD task[1][2].

The previous works have been made mainly on English and European languages such as German and French[1]. Few researches have been done for languages other than Roman-alphabet languages. To our knowledge, a recent SBD work about Korean language is only [3]'s. They take a hybrid method (regular expressions, heuristic rules, and decision tree learning), but cannot be applied to languages other than Korean because language-specific features are used (such as a functional syllable list, a sentence-end syllable list, and POS information).

There are at least three main differences between English and Korean when considering SBD: firstly, Korean has no capitalization information, which is very

A. Gelbukh (Ed.): CICLing 2004, LNCS 2945, pp. 142–145, 2004.
© Springer-Verlag Berlin Heidelberg 2004

important for English SBD. Secondly, Korean has no sentence boundary ambiguity in abbreviation because no punctuation mark is attached at the end of abbreviations. Finally, Korean is a verb-final language: although Korean is relatively a free word-order language, preferred word order is "subject-object-verb". So, a verb would be the last constituent of the sentence, and is always followed by verbal suffixes. The first difference makes the Korean SBD task difficult but the last two differences easy against the English SBD task.

Despite these and more linguistic differences, we argue that the surrounding context of the sentence boundary can be an important feature. In this paper, we deal with a language-independent SBD method using machine learning approach. Without language-specific information, we investigate whether using only language-independent features can be successfully applied to the SBD task.

2   Language-Independent Sentence Boundary Detection

We use two publicly available machine learning systems in the experiments: TiMBL[4], a memory-based learner, and SVM light[5], an implementation of support vector machine.[1] They have been successfully applied to a number of NLP problems.

As mentioned earlier, because there may be sentences that include no punctuation mark, we regard all words delimited by a whitespace as potential sentence boundaries, and classifies the words. Each instance consists of a feature vector representing the context of the candidate word. We use three types of features as follows:

1. **Character features**, which denote the character itself.
2. **Character type features**, which denote the type of a character. We distinguish seven kinds of character types as follows[2]: uppercase letters (U), lowercase letters (L), digits (D), ASCII symbols, which are one-byte symbols (S), Korean characters (K), Chinese characters (C), and non-ASCII symbols, which are two-byte symbols (F).
3. **Word features**, which denote the word itself.
4. **Word type features**, which denote the type of word. The type of a word is determined by the types of characters in the word. However, the type of successive characters that have the same character type is represented by the type of one of the characters. For example, the type of a word "We're" is "ULSL".

We apply the character type and word type features to reduce the data sparseness problem. All features used in TiMBL and SVM light are listed in Table 1.

---

[1] All experiments using TiMBL and SVM light have been performed with the default settings of the systems.

[2] Only the first four character types will usually appear in English texts.

Table 1. Features used in TiMBL and SVM light

Feature	No.	Description
Character Feature (CF)	1	last character of the current word
	2	second last character of the current word
	3	last two characters of the current word
	4	first character of the following word
	5	last character of the following word
Character Type Feature (CTF)	6	type of the last character of the current word
	7	type of the second last character of the current word
	8	type of the first character of the following word
	9	type of the last character of the following word
Word Feature (WF)	10	current word
	11	previous word
	12	following word
Word Type Feature (WTF)	13	type of the current word
	14	type of the previous word
	15	type of the following word

3   Experiments

3.1   Experimental Environments

For the English experiments, randomly selected 50,000 sentences from WSJ articles of year 1988 are used as training data. For testing, two data sets are used: one is the Penn WSJ Treebank and the other is a collection of 50,000 sentences from WSJ articles of year 1987. The Korean Experiments are carried out by the 10-fold cross validation on ETRI POS tagged corpus of 27,855 sentences.

Previous works regard a punctuation mark as a potential sentence boundary and classify whether the punctuation mark is the sentence final or not, and then evaluate the accuracy of the classifier. However, this is not appropriate for evaluating the SBD task. This is "punctuation disambiguation" rather than "sentence boundary detection". What we are interested in is how "well" does the system identify the sentences in a document. Such requirement can be fulfilled by precision and recall.

3.2   Experimental Results

The results of English and Korean experiments are listed in Table 2 and Table 3, respectively. In the tables, the baseline method is just to classify every word including the punctuation marks (., !, and ?) at the end as a sentence boundary. ME refers to [2]'s system, "MXTERMINATOR"[3], and MBL refers to TiMBL.

According to the results, the machine learning methods significantly outperform the baseline. In addition, our approaches (MLB and SVM) outperform MXTERMINATER in both languages and achieve considerable improvements

---

[3] It is trained and tested under the same conditions.

Table 2. Results of English SBD experiments: tested with Penn Treebank WSJ corpus (left) and WSJ 1987 corpus (right)

	Baseline	ME	MBL	SVM
Precision	70.99 / 74.49	91.09 / 98.91	91.35 / 99.04	**91.69 / 99.47**
Recall	93.15 / 91.95	96.49 / 98.31	96.79 / 98.66	**97.24 / 98.93**
F-measure	80.58 / 82.30	93.71 / 98.61	93.99 / 98.85	**94.38 / 99.20**

Table 3. Results of Korean SBD experiments (ten-fold cross validation)

	Baseline	ME	MBL	SVM
Precision	78.73	88.57	93.89	**95.42**
Recall	72.97	93.79	**94.48**	93.68
F-measure	75.74	91.10	94.18	**94.54**

in the Korean experiment. Among the learning approaches, SVM shows the best performance.

4 Conclusion

We have presented a machine learning approach for language-independent SBD. The proposed method does not require heuristic rules and language-specific features, such as POS tag information, a list of abbreviations or proper names.

With only the local context and language-independent features, we achieve good performances in both English and Korean. The approach is easily applicable to other languages.

References

1. David D. Palmer and Marti A. Hearst: Adaptive Multilingual Sentence Boundary Disambiguation. Computational Linguistics, Vol. 23. No. 2. (1997) 241–267
2. J. Reynar and A. Ratnaparkhi: A Maximum Entropy Approach to Identifying Sentence Boundaries. In Proceedings of the Fifth Conference on Applied Natural Language Processing, (1997) 16–19
3. Junhyeok Shim, Dongseok Kim, Jeongwon Cha, Geunbae Lee, and Jungyun Seo: Multi-strategic integrated web document pre-processing for sentence and word boundary detection. Information Processing and Management, Vol. 38. No. 4. (2002) 509–527
4. Walter Daelemans, Jakub Zavrel, Ko van der Sloot, and Antal van den Bosch: TiMBL: Tilburg Memory Based Learner, version 4.3, Reference Guide. ILK Technical Report 02-10 (2002)
5. T. Joachims: Making large-Scale SVM Learning Practical. Advances in Kernel Methods - Support Vector Learning. In: B. Scholkopf and C. Burges and A. Smola (eds.): MIT-Press (1999)

Korean Compound Noun Decomposition Using Syllabic Information Only

Seong-Bae Park, Jeong-Ho Chang, and Byoung-Tak Zhang

School of Computer Science and Engineering
Seoul National University
151-744 Seoul, Korea
{sbpark,jhchang,btzhang}@bi.snu.ac.kr

Abstract. The compound nouns are freely composed in Korean, since it is possible to concatenate independent nouns without a postposition. Therefore, the systems that handle compound nouns such as machine translation and information retrieval have to decompose them into single nouns for the further correct analysis of texts. This paper proposes the GECORAM (GEneralized COmbination of Rule-based learning And Memory-based learning) algorithm for Korean compound noun decomposition using only syllabic information. The merit of rule-based learning algorithms is high comprehensibility, but they shows low performance in many application tasks. To tackle this problem, GECORAM combines the rule-based learning and memory-based learning. According to the experimental results, GECORAM shows higher accuracy than rule-based learning or memory-based learning alone.

1 Introduction

The nouns that appear successively without a postposition can be concatenated to compose a compound noun in Korean. Such compound nouns have more contextual information compared to single nouns [15], and play important role in natural language processing. The critical issue in handling compound nouns is that the number of possible compound nouns is infinite. Because all compound nouns can not be listed in the dictionary, it is required to decompose given a compound noun into single nouns.

When a compound noun is composed of n syllables, there are theoretically 2^{n-1} kinds of decompositions. Thus, the easiest way to decompose a compound noun is to take the most plausible one among 2^{n-1} decompositions. Many previous studies have been proposed based on this idea. Shim used composite mutual information trained from about a corpus of 1.1 million word size [15]. Lee et al. considered this task as part-of-speech tagging, and applied a Markov model [11].

The main drawback of such statistics-based methods is that it is difficult for human to understand the trained results. On the other hand, the rules, whether they are made manually or automatically, have high comprehensibility. Thus, there have been a number of studies that apply rules to compound noun decomposition. For instance, Kang designed four decomposition rules and two

A. Gelbukh (Ed.): CICLing 2004, LNCS 2945, pp. 146–157, 2004.
© Springer-Verlag Berlin Heidelberg 2004

exception rules [10]. Yoon used both statistics and heuristic rules [16], where the heuristic rules take charge of the nouns with unknown single nouns.

The rule-based methods need a human expert who writes the accurate rules. Since the performance of the rule-based methods depends on the quality of the rules, the rule writer must have profound knowledge about a target task. However, it is very expensive to work with such an expert. Thus, in machine learning community, a number of methods have been proposed that learn the rules from data represented as vectors of feature-value pairs. Clark and Niblett proposed the CN2 program that uses the general-to-specific beam search [3], and Fürnkranz and Widmar proposed the IREP algorithm [9]. Cohen improved the IREP to produce the RIPPER algorithm [4], while Cohen and Singer presented the SILPPER algorithm [5] which adopted a boosting into rule leanring.

The problem of automatically learned rules is low performance compared with other supervised learning algorithms. In our previous work, it is shown that a combination of rules and memory-based learning achieves high accuracy [12]. To apply this idea to the tasks without the previously designed rules, we propose in this paper the *GECORAM* (GEneralized COmbination of Rule-based learning And Memory-based learning) *algorithm* that effectively combines rule-based learning and memory-based learning. Because the rules are basic approach to ILP (Inductive Logic Programming), the improvement of the rules is important not only in natural language processing but also in machine learning.

The rest of this paper is organized as follows. Section 2 surveys the previous rule-based learning algorithms. Section 3 describes the GECORAM algorithm, and Section 4 presents the experimental results. Finally, section 5 draws conclusions.

2   Previous Work on Rule-Based Learning Algorithms

2.1   The IREP Algorithm

Since the GECORAM algorithm is primarily based on the IREP (Incremental Reduced Error Pruning) algorithm, the IREP should be first explained for understanding of the GECORAM algorithm. The algorithm of the IREP is summarized in Figure 1 and consists of two greedy algorithms. The first greedy algorithm constructs a rule at a time, and then removes from the training set all examples covered by a new rule. The principle used in constructing a rule is that more positive examples and less negative examples should be covered by the rule. For this purpose, it partitions given a training set **data** into two subsets: **grow** and **prune**. In general, **grow** is two-thirds of **data**, and **prune** is one-third. **grow** is used to first construct a rule, and **prune** is used to simplify it. The step to grow a rule (function **GrowRule** in Figure 1) repeatedly adds conditions to rule r_0 with an empty antecedent. In each i-th stage, a more specialized rule r_{i+1} is made by adding single condition to r_i. The added condition in constructing r_{i+1} is the one with the largest *information gain* [13] relative to r_i, where the

```
function IREP(data)
begin
   RuleSet := φ
   while ∃ positive examples ∈ data do
      Split data into grow and prune.
      rule := GrowRule(grow)
      rule := PruneRule(prune)
      Add rule to RuleSet.
      Remove examples covered by rule from data.
      if Accuracy(rule) ≤ P/(P+N) then
         return RuleSet
      endif
   endwhile
   return RuleSet
end
```

Fig. 1. The IREP algorithm. P is the number of positive examples in data and N is that of negative examples

information gain is defined as

$$
Gain\left(r_{i+1}, r_i\right) = T_{i+1}^{+} \cdot \left(-\log \frac{T_i^{+}}{T_i^{+} + T_i^{-}} + \log \frac{T_{i+1}^{+}}{T_{i+1}^{+} + T_{i+1}^{-}} \right).
$$

Here, T_i^{+} and T_i^{-} are the number of positive and negative examples covered by r_i accordingly. The conditions are added until the information gain becomes 0.

In the second step, the rule constructed in the function GrowRule is simplified by removing the conditions one by one. In the function PruneRule, the condition that maximizes the function $f(r_{i+1}) = \frac{T_{i+1}^{+} - T_{i+1}^{-}}{T_{i+1}^{+} + T_{i+1}^{-}}$ is removed. After simplifying the rule, the pruned rule is added to RuleSet, and all examples covered by it are removed from data.

The information gain used in constructing a rule is larger than or equal to 0. Thus, all the generated rules always cover some positive examples in data and it guarantees that the algorithm will eventually terminate. However, it is possible that there could be a number of rules that cover only a few positive examples, which causes too much computation for noisy data. To keep these rules from being added to RuleSet, the learning process stops if the accuracy of the generated rule is less than $P/(P+N)$, where P is the number of positive examples in data, and N is that of negative examples.

2.2   The RIPPER Algorithm

The RIPPER(Repeated Incremental Pruning to Produce Error Reduction) algorithm is an improved model of the IREP algorithm, and Figure 2 gives its pseudo-code. After adding rules by running IREP, the RIPPER optimizes the rule set RuleSet to reduce the number of the rules within RuleSet and improve

```
function Optimize(RuleSet, data)
begin
    for each rule c ∈ RuleSet do
        Split data into grow and prune.
        c' := GrowRule(grow)
        c' := PruneRule(c', data) with RuleSet−c + c'
        c'' := GrowRule(c, grow)
        c'' := PruneRule(c'', prune) with RuleSet−c + c''
        Replace c in RuleSet with best of c, c', and c''.
    endfor
    return RuleSet
end

function RIPPER(data)
begin
    RuleSet := IREP(data)
    repeat twice:
        RuleSet := Optimize(RuleSet, data)
        UncovData := examples ∈ data not covered by the rules in RuleSet
        RuleSet := RuleSet + IREP(UncovData)
    endrepeat
end
```

Fig. 2. The RIPPER algorithm.

performance. In the function Optimize, each rule is tested one by one in the order in which they were added. For each rule $c \in$ RuleSet, two alternative rules are constructed: c' and c''. c' is made by growing and pruning, where pruning is guided so as to minimize error not of prune but of the entire rule set with c' replacing c. c'' is constructed in a similar way except that it is grown from c not empty antecedent. Finally, the best of c, c' and c'' is added to RuleSet. Then, which of them is best? To determine this, RIPPER uses the MDL (Minimum Description Length) principle. According to MDL, the best rule is the one with the shortest DL (description length). To measure the DL of a rule, the RIPPER adopts the method proposed by Quinlan [14]. After optimization, because it is highly possible for RuleSet to cover less number of positive examples than the original RuleSet, new rules are added to RuleSet by running the IREP over UncovData that contains the examples uncovered by RuleSet. This process is performed twice, because the empirical performance is increased when it is repeated twice.

3   GECORAM Algorithm

3.1   Basic Idea

Korean compound noun decomposition can be regarded as a classification task in the viewpoint of machine learning. That is, it is a binary classification task

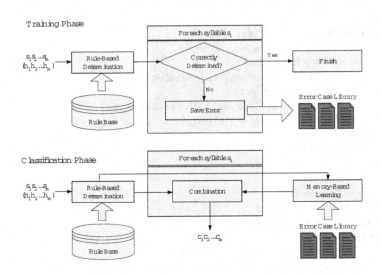

Fig. 3. The basic idea of the GECORAM algorithm.

to determine whether a space is put after a syllable s_i of a compound noun $w = s_1, \ldots, s_m$. The context information h_i of s_i is usually used to determine it. In this paper, n ($n \leq m/2$) syllables in left and right positions are used as context information.

The GECORAM algorithm combines rule-based learning and memory-based learning efficiently to solve classification tasks. The basic idea of this algorithm is expressed in Figure 3. In the training phase, each compound noun is analyzed by the rules trained by a rule-learning algorithm and the classification results are compared with the true labels[1]. In case of misclassification, the errors are stored in the *error case library* with their true labels. Since the error case library accumulates only the exceptions of the rules, the number of examples in it is small if the rules are general and accurate enough to represent the instance space well.

The classification phase determines the decomposition of s_i given with the context h_i. First, the rules are applied to decide whether a space is put after s_i. Then, it is checked if the current context h_i of s_i is an exception of the rules. If it is, the decomposition determined by the rules is discarded and then is determined again by the memory-based classifier trained with the error case library. This is because the rules tend to make errors if h_i is an exception of the

---

[1] When a space should be put after s_i, the label is 'True'. Otherwise, it is 'False'.

```
function Support(RuleSet, data)
begin
  Err := φ
  for each (⟨s_i, h_i⟩, c_i) ∈ data do
    if RuleSet(⟨s_i, h_i⟩) ≠ c_i then
      Add (⟨s_i, h_i⟩, c_i) into Err.
    endif
  endfor
  MBL := Memory-Based-Learning(Err)
  return MBL
end

function Training-GECORAM(data)
begin
  RuleSet := MODIFIED-IREP(data)
  MBL := Support(RuleSet, data)
  θ := Get-Threshold-MBL(RuleSet, MBL, HeldOutData)
  return RuleSet + MBL + θ
end
```

Fig. 4. The training algorithm of the GECORAM. c_i is the true label for $\langle s_i, h_i \rangle$.

rules. Thus, memory-based learning is a component that handles the errors of the rules.

3.2 GECORAM Algorithm

Figure 4 shows the training phrase of the GECORAM. The first step of GECORAM is to train the rules from a training set data. For this purpose, GECORAM uses MODIFIED-IREP, a modified version of the IREP. The only difference between MODIFIED-IREP and the IREP is that MODIFIED-IREP does not have a PruneRule function. That is, in MODIFIED-IREP, the rules only grow and are never simplified. The role of the function PruneRule is played by the memory-based learning explained later. In the next step, the examples that are uncovered by MODIFIED-IREP are gathered, and the memory-based learner is trained with them.

Memory-based learning is a direct descent of the k-Nearest Neighbor (k-NN) algorithm [6]. Since many natural language processing tasks have constraints of a large number of examples and many attributes with different relevance, memory-based learning uses more complex data structure and different speedup optimization from k-NN.

The learning process in memory-based learning is simply to store the examples into memory, where all examples are assumed to be fixed-length vectors of n attributes. The similarity between an instance $\mathbf{x}$ and all examples $\mathbf{y}$ in memory is computed using a *distance metric*, $D(\mathbf{x}, \mathbf{y})$. The class of $\mathbf{x}$ is then determined by assigning the most frequent category within the k most similar examples of $\mathbf{x}$.

```
function Classify-GECORAM(x, θ, RuleSet, MBL)
begin
    c := RuleSet(x)
    y := the nearest instance of x in Err.
    if D(x, y) ≥ θ then
        c := MBL(x)
    endif
    return c
end
```

Fig. 5. The classification algorithm of the GECORAM.

The distance from $\mathbf{x}$ and $\mathbf{y}$, $D(\mathbf{x}, \mathbf{y})$ is defined to be

$$D(\mathbf{x}, \mathbf{y}) \equiv \sum_{i=1}^{n} \alpha_i \delta(x_i, y_i),$$

where α_i is the weight of i-th attribute and

$$\delta(x_i, y_i) = \begin{cases} 0 \text{ if } x_i \neq y_i, \\ 1 \text{ if } x_i = y_i. \end{cases}$$

When α_i is determined by *information gain* [13], the k-NN algorithm with this metric is called *IB1-IG* [7]. All the experiments performed by memory-based learning in this paper are done with IB1-IG.

Since both rules and memory-based learning are used in the GECORAM, it is important to determine when to use rules and when to use memory-based classifier. To determine this, GECORAM has a threshold θ. The optimal value for θ is found by the following procedure. Assume that we have an independent held-out data set HeldOutData. Various value for θ is applied to the classification algorithm of the GECORAM described in Figure 5. The optimal value for θ is the one that outputs the best performance over HeldOutData.

In Classify-GECORAM, if $\mathbf{x}$ and $\mathbf{y}$ are simlar, $\mathbf{x}$ is considered to be an exception of the rules. Since the instances in memory are the ones with which the rules make an error, large $D(\mathbf{x}, \mathbf{y})$ implies that $\mathbf{x}$ is highly possible to be an exception of the rules. Thus, if $D(\mathbf{x}, \mathbf{y})$ is larger than the predefined threshold θ, the rules should not be applied.

Since θ is a threshold value for $D(\mathbf{x}, \mathbf{y})$, $0 \leq \theta \leq \beta$ is always satisfied when $\beta \equiv \sum_{j=1}^{m} \alpha_j$. When $\theta = 0$, the rules are always ignored. In this case, the generalization is done by only memory-based classifier trained with the errors of the rules. Thus, it will show low performance due to data sparseness. In contrast, only the rules are applied when $\theta = \beta$. In this case, the performance of GECORAM is equivalent to that of the rules.

3.3 Comparison to Other Algorithms

The GECORAM algorithm is similar to the RIPPER in that both algorithms are based on the IREP. While the RIPPER is a pure memory-based learning algorithm for ILP, the GECORAM is a kind of mixture model that combines rule-based learning and memory-based learning. Thus, RIPPER prepares an Optimize function to keep too specific rules from being added into a rule set, but the optimizing process is substituted by memory-based learning in the GEC-ORAM. Since memory-based learning is a lazy learning, the GECORAM does not use even a PruneRule function in the IREP.

In addition, the GECORAM shares similarities with transformation-based learning (TBL) [2] and AdaBoost [8]. Both methods build classifiers by combining simple rules. However, AdaBoost rests on the firm theoretical foundations while TBL does not. In addition, AdaBoost outperforms TBL in many applications of NLP [1].

The drawbacks of TBL can be summarized by three problems. The first problem is that it is easy to overfit to the training data. In addition, it is sensitive to noise, since it always tries to minimize the number of errors made by the current transformation list by adding an additional transformation. Finally, there is no theoretical foundation which supports that the added transformation improves the performance in the applications.

AdaBoost is similar to TBL in that the learning process is derived by the errors of current classifier. But, it is based on more theoretical background. Assume each $\epsilon_t \leq 1/2$, and let $\gamma_t = 1/2 - \epsilon_t$. Then, it is proven that the error of the final hypothesis h_{fin} has the following upper bound:

$$\frac{1}{N}|\{i : h_{fin}(\mathbf{x}_i) \neq y_i\}| \leq \exp\left(-2\sum_{t=1}^{T}\gamma_t^2\right),$$

where N is the number of training examples and T is the number of weak learners within AdaBoost. It is different from the proposed method in that each weak learner behaves in the same way and more than one learner is used.

The convergence speed of AdaBoost rests on the performance of weak learner. Though the only convergence condition of AdaBoost is that the accuracy of the weak learner is larger than $1/2$, the convergence speed depends on the performance of weak learners. The early convergence can be obtained if the weak learners in early stage are strong with the help of prior knowledge. Thus, the proposed method can be considered to be a variation of AdaBoost, where first $(T-1)$ weak learners is substituted by the rules and the last one is substituted by memory-based learning. And, the threshold θ corresponds to weights of the weak learners. Therefore, it is important to design the rules to be strong enough to explain the problem space well. In addition, since the proposed method consists of only two steps rather than T steps, the computational cost is much decreased compared to TBL and AdaBoost.

4   Dataset

4.1   Data Set

In this paper, two kinds of standard data sets are used. The first data set (shim) is designed by Shim and used in [15], and the other (yoon) is the one used in [16].

Table 1. Statistics on data sets for Korean compound noun decomposition.

Data Set	shim	yoon
Number of examples	9,863	15,096
Number of syllables used	562	557
Average length of compound noun	7.26	4.92

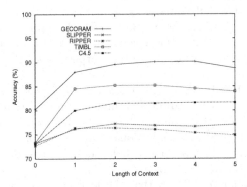

Fig. 6. The accuracy according to the context length on shim data set.

Table 1 summarizes the simple statistics on these two data sets. Each data set is divided into three parts: *training* (80%), *held-out* (10%), and *test* (10%). Since there are not enough examples in both data sets, the 10-fold cross validation is performed.

4.2   Experimental Results

In order to evaluate the performance of the GECORAM, we compare it with RIPPER [4], SLIPPER [5], C4.5 [13], and TiMBL [7]. RIPPER, SLIPPER, and C4.5 are rule-based learning algorithms, and TiMBL is a memory-based learning algorithm.

Figure 6 and Figure 7 shows the accuracy change according to the context length. The GECORAM shows the best performance for both data sets. TiMBL shows higher performance than rule-based learning algorithms such as RIPPER and SLIPPER. In general, the rule-based learning algorithms focus on the comprehensibility, and they have tendency to give lower performance than other supervised learning algorithms.

When the length of context is zero, the context information h_i is not used but only a syllable s_i is used to decompose a compound noun. Even in this case, all algorithms shows over 70% of accuracy. It implies that syllable is very important information for compound noun decomposition. The average syllable length in shim data set is 7.26. When three syllables in left and right context are considered, we will see seven syllables altogether. Thus, when the context length is three, the best performance is obtained. More context information plays role of noise in this data set. Since the average syllable length in yoon data set is 4.92, it

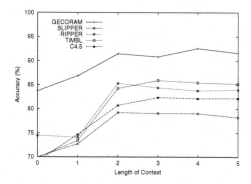

Fig. 7. The accuracy according to the context length on yoon data set.

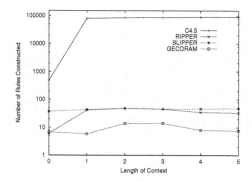

Fig. 8. The number of rules constructed according to the context length on shim data set.

is expected that the best performance is obtained when the context length is two. However, the best performance is actually obtained when it is four. Nevertheless, the difference between them is slight and statistically indistinguishable.

Figure 8 and Figure 9 illustrate the number of rules generated according to the context length. C4.5 constructs the most number of rules, while GECORAM generates the least number of rules. RIPPER and SLIPPER produce less than 100 rules. In the other hand, GECORAM makes only about 20 rules. This is because the errors of the rules are handled by memory-based learning in GECORAM and GECORAM does not have the optimizing process of RIPPER. In the result, GECORAM shows high performance with low computational cost.

Finally, Table 2 gives the accuracy when each algorithm shows the best performance. The GECORAM algorithm shows 90.13% of accuracy for shim data set and 92.57% for yoon data set. This is, on the average, higher than C4.5 by 9.3%, RIPPER by 10.5%, SLIPPER by 13.1%, and TiMBL by 5.8%. Therefore, GECORAM shows higher performance than rule-based learning or memory-based learning alone.

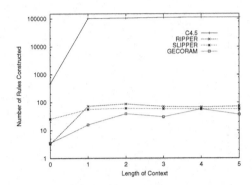

Fig. 9. The number of rules constructed according to the context length on yoon data set.

Table 2. The best accuracy of each algorithm.

Data Set	shim	yoon
C4.5	81.67%	82.37%
TiMBL	85.24%	85.89%
RIPPER	76.36%	85.27%
SLIPPER	77.22%	79.23%
GECORAM	**90.13%**	**92.57%**

5   Conclusions

In this paper we have proposed a new learning algorithm, GECORAM, that combines rule-based learning and memory-based learning. It first learns the rules, and then memory-based learning is performed with the errors of the trained rules. In classification, it is basically based on the rules, and its estimates are verified by a memory-based classifier. Since the memory-based learning is an efficient method to handle exceptional cases of the rules, it supports the rules by making decisions only for the exceptions of the rules. That is, the memory-based learning enhances the trained rules by efficiently handling their exceptions.

We have applied the GECORAM algorithm to Korean compound noun decomposition. The experimental results on two standard data sets showed that it improves the accuracy of RIPPER by 10.5%, SLIPPER by 13.1%, and TiMBL by 5.8%, where RIPPER and SLIPPER are rule-based learning algorithms and TiMBL is a memory-based learning algorithm. Therefore, the proposed algorithm, GECORAM is more efficient than rule-based learning or memory-based learning alone.

In this paper, only syllabic information is used for decomposing compound nouns. Thus, the overall accuracy is lower than that of the previous studies [10, 11,15,16] that use external information such as dictionary and thesaurus. As a future work, we will study how to use such information with the GECORAM algorithm.

Acknowledgements. This research was supported by the Korean Ministry of Education under the BK21-IT Program, by BrainTech and NRL programs sponsored by the Korean Ministry of Science and Technology.

References

1. S. Abney, R. Schapire, and Y. Singer, "Boosting Applied to Tagging and PP Attachment," In *Proceedings of the Conference on Empirical Methods in Natural Language Processing and Very Large Corpora*, pp. 38–45, 1999.
2. E. Brill, "Transformation-Based Error-Driven Learning and Natural Language Processing: A Case Study in Part of Speech Tagging," *Computational Linguistics*, Vol. 21, No. 4, pp. 543–566, 1995.
3. P. Clark and T. Niblett, "The CN2 Induction Algorithm," *Machine Learning*, Vol. 3, No. 1, pp. 261–284, 1989.
4. W. Cohen, "Fast Effective Rule Induction," In *Proceedings of the 12th International Conference on Mahcine Learning*, pp. 115–123, 1995.
5. W. Cohen and Y. Singer, "A Simple, Fast, and Effective Rule Learner," In *Proceedings of the 16th National Conference on Artificial Intelligence*, pp. 335–342, 1999.
6. T. Cover and P. Hart, "Nearest Neighbor Pattern Classification," *IEEE Transactions on Information Theory*, Vol. 13, pp. 21–27, 1967.
7. W. Daelemans, J. Zavrel, K. Sloot, and A. Bosch, *TiMBL: Tilburg Memory Based Learner, version 4.1, Reference Guide*, ILK 01-04, Tilburg University, 2001.
8. Y. Freund and R. Schapire, "Experiments with a New Boosting Algorithm," In *Proceedings of the 13th International Conference on Machine Learning*, pp. 148–156, 1996.
9. J. Fürnkranz and G. Widmar, "Incremental Reduced Error Pruning," In *Proceedings of the 11th International Conference on Machine Learning*, pp. 70–77, 1994.
10. S.-S. Kang, "Korean Compound Noun Decomposition Algorithm," *Journal of KISS (B)*, Vol. 25, No. 1, pp. 172–182, 1998.
11. J.-W. Lee, B.-T. Zhang, and Y.-T. Kim, "Compound Noun Decomposition Using a Markov Model," In *Proceedings of MT Summit VII*, pp. 427–431, 1999.
12. S.-B. Park and B.-T. Zhang, "Text Chunking by Combining Hand-Crafted Rules and Memory-Based Learning," In *Proceedings of the 41st Annual Meeting of the Association for Computational Linguistics*, pp. 497–504, 2003.
13. R. Quinlan, *C4.5: Programs for Machine Learning*, Morgan Kaufmann Publisher, 1993.
14. R. Quinlan, "MDL and Categorical Theories (continued)," In *Proceedings of the 12th International Conference on Machine Learning*, pp. 464–470, 1995.
15. K.-S. Shim, "Segmentation of Compound Nouns using Composite Mutual Information," In *Proceedings of the 3rd Chinese-Korea Joint Symposium on Oriental Language Processing and Character Recognition*, pp. 106–113, 1999.
16. B.-H. Yoon, M.-J. Cho, and H.-C. Rim, "Segmenting Korean Compound Nouns Using Statistical Information and a Preference Rule," *KISS Journal (B)*, Vol. 24, No. 8, pp. 900–909, 1997.

Learning Named Entity Classifiers
Using Support Vector Machines

Thamar Solorio and Aurelio López López

Computer Science Department
Instituto Nacional de Astrofísica, Óptica y Electrónica
Luis Enrique Erro #1, 72840 Puebla, México

Abstract. Traditional methods for named entity classification are based on hand-coded grammars, lists of trigger words and gazetteers. While these methods have acceptable accuracies they present a serious drawback: if we need a wider coverage of named entities, or a more domain specific coverage we will probably need a lot of human effort to redesign our grammars and revise the lists of trigger words or gazetteers. We present here a method for improving the accuracy of a traditionally-built named entity extractor. Support vector machines are used to train a classifier based on the output of an existing extractor system. Experimental results show that this approach can be a very practical solution, increasing precision by up to 11.94% and recall by up to 27.83% without considerable human effort.

1 Introduction

While hand-coded grammars, gazetteers, chunkers, contextual rules and lists of trigger words provide a valuable source of information useful for building NE extractors, [1,2,3,4,5], they can become obsolete if no updating is performed. Another disadvantage of relying on this information is that the coverage of these tools might be too general or overly specific, thus achieving poor precision and recall when applied to more specific or different domains. However, they can present a useful starting point in building accurate Named Entity (NE) classifiers. We believe that machine learning techniques can be used to build automated classifiers trained on traditional hand-built NE extractors. Then, instead of manually redesigning the NE extractors we can allow the classifiers to learn from tags assigned by the NE extractor. Hopefully the NEs not covered by the extractor will be successfully classified by the learner.

We present here a new methodology for NE classification that uses Support Vector Machines (SVM) in order to enhance the accuracy of a NE Extractor System (NEES). The NEES is considered as a black box, we are only interested in its output, which is used as one of the attributes in our learning scenario. Our proposed solution can be considered as a stack of classifiers where in the first stage a traditional hand-built NEES is used to assign possible tags to the corpus, then these tags are used by a SVM classifier to obtain the final NE tags. In addition, other attribute information used are the class values assigned to

A. Gelbukh (Ed.): CICLing 2004, LNCS 2945, pp. 158–167, 2004.
© Springer-Verlag Berlin Heidelberg 2004

the 2 words to the left and right of the instance. Experimental results show that Support Vector Machines are successfully applied to this learning task increasing F-measure and accuracy.

The organization of this paper is as follows: the next section describes some of the most recent work in NE classification. Section 3 describes our learning scenario and provides a brief introduction to Support Vector Machines. In Section 4 we present some experimental results and Section 5 summarizes our conclusions and discusses possible future work.

2   Related Work

In [6] a new method for automating the task of extending a proper noun dictionary is presented. The method combines two learning approaches: an inductive decision-tree classifier and unsupervised probabilistic learning of syntactic and semantic context. The decision tree learns to assign semantic categories to named entities using a dictionary and a training corpus. In this stage only high confidence classifications are accepted. On a second stage, unsupervised learning is used to improve recall. The attribute information selected for the experiments uses POS tags as well as morphological information whenever available. Also, in this work the original named entity words are not used, at least not completely. This method uses the first two and last two words of the NE, along with contextual information (two words to the left of the NE and two words to the right).

A very interesting system for NE recognition based on Hidden Markov Models was proposed by Zhou and Su [2]. The novelty in this system being the combination of information used to build the HMM-based tagger: they use a combination of internal and external sub-features. The system considers three internal sub-features: in the first one they consider information relevant to discriminate between dates, percentages, times, monetary amounts and capitalization information; the second sub-feature consists of triggers that the authors consider useful for NE recognition; the last internal sub-feature contains gazetteer information, gathered from look-up gazetteers that contain lists of names of people, organizations, locations and other kinds of named entities. The external evidence considered is about context of other NEs already recognized. A list is updated with every named entity that has been recognized so far; when a new candidate is found an alias algorithm is invoked to determine its relation with the NE on the list.

Sekine et al. presented a named entity hierarchy containing 150 NE types [7]. They build the hierarchy in three steps: initially they build three different hierarchies, corpus-based, based on previous systems and tasks and based on thesauri; then they merge the three hierarchies (in this stage three experts are involved in the procedure); in the final step the final hierarchy is refined by tagging additional corpora and developing automatic taggers.

One work focused in NE recognition for Spanish is based on discriminating among different kinds of named entities: core NEs, which contain a trigger word as nucleus, syntactically simple weak NEs, formed by single noun phrases, and syntactically complex named entities, formed by complex noun phases. Arévalo et al. focused on the first two kinds of NEs [1]. The method is a sequence of processes that uses simple attributes combined with external information provided by gazetteers and lists of trigger words. A context free grammar, manually coded, is used for recognizing syntactic patterns.

In [8] the authors experimented with a risk minimization approach. They performed several experiments, combining different features. Their best performance for NE recognition in English is achieved by a system that combines dictionaries and trigger word lists with linguistic features extracted directly from the text, such as case information, token prefix and suffix. However, in the German data set the improvement from using additional information was not that great, the authors believe that this difference between the English and German data sets may be due to the fact that for English there is a higher availability of good quality dictionaries.

3   Learning NE Classifiers

In this section we describe the setting of our learning scenario and present a brief introduction to Support Vector Machines.

As mentioned previously, we build our NE classifiers using the output of a NEES. Our assumption is that by using machine learning algorithms we can improve performance of NE extractors without a considerable effort, as opposed to that involved in extending or redesigning grammars and lists of trigger words and gazetteers. Another assumption underlying this approach is that of believing that the misclassifications of the NEES will not affect the learner. Intuitively, one may consider the incorrectly classified instances as noisy. However we believe that by having available the correct NE classes in the training corpus, the learner will be capable of generalizing error patterns that will be used to assign the correct NE. If this assumption holds, learning from other's mistakes, the learner will end up outperforming the NEES.

In this work we are considering that all the possible named entities are already identified, that is, we are not dealing with the problem of recognizing which parts of the text are NEs. Named Entities are recognized and segmented by the NEES, our only concern being the NE classification in the same four types defined in the CoNLL 2002 competition: Person (Per), Location (Loc), Organization (Org) and Miscellaneous ($Misc$).

In order to build a training set for the learner, each instance n is described by a vector of six attributes, $\langle a_1, a_2, ..., a_6 \rangle$, where a_1 and a_2 are the classes assigned by the NEES to the first two words to the left of n, a_3 and a_4 are the classes for the first two words to the right of n, a_5 is the class value of n predicted by the NEES and a_6 is the true class value of n. Note that a_5 and a_6 will differ only when the base NEES misclassifies a named entity. There are two types of possible errors from the NEES that the learner will try to overcome. The first type occurs when the NEES assigns the wrong NE class to the NE; the other type occurs when the NEES fails to recognize the NE. When this is the case the NEES assigns a Part Of Speech (POS) tag to the NE, although the same thing happens when the NEES needs to classify a non-NE word. It follows that the possible values for attributes a_1 to a_5 can take any value from the set of possible NEs, this is $NE = \{Per, Loc, Org, Misc\}$, plus the set of possible POS tags, which has over one hundred different tags; so the size of the feature space of our NE classification task is 5×10^{10}.

A graphical representation of our proposed NE classifier is given in Figure 1. We can see that a NEES is used as a black box, the output of which is fed to the SVM classifier. The SVM classifier uses this information (in some cases also additional information such as POS tags, capitalization information and lemmas) and assigns the final NE classification.

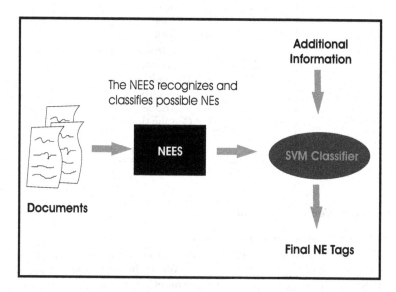

Fig. 1. A graphical representation of our NE classifier. The possible NEs together with the tags given by the NEES are used as input to the SVM classifier.

3.1   Low-Dimensionality Features

Having the high-dimensionality feature space described above has some serious drawbacks: the number of training examples needed in order to achieve good accuracy is proportional to the size of the feature space; but increasing the amount of training examples to meet this requirement might be unfeasible. Another disadvantage is the high computational resources needed to use SVM with a feature space such as this.

In order to overcome these difficulties we decided to reduce the size of the feature space. We achieve this by generalizing the POS tags, i.e. instead of having tags for all the possible kinds of pronouns, we kept one tag P that encapsulates the set of pronouns. We did the same for each POS. Table 1 shows the resulting reduced set of feature values. By doing this our reduced feature space has a size of $16^5 * 4 = 4,194,304$.

Table 1. Reduced Feature Values Set

Feature Value	Description
Per	Person
Org	Organization
Loc	Location
Misc	Miscelaneous
N	Noun
A	Adjective
P	Pronoun
F	Punctuation mark
D	Determiner
V	Verb
S	Preposition
R	Adverb
T	Article
C	Conjunction
M	Numeral
I	Interjection

3.2 Support Vector Machines

SVM have been successfully used in classification and regression tasks. This technique uses geometrical properties in order to compute the hyperplane that best separates a set of training examples [9]. When the input space is not linearly separable SVM can map, by using a kernel function, the original input space to a high-dimensional feature space where the optimal separable hyperplane can be easily calculated. This is a very powerful feature, because it allows SVM to overcome the limitations of linear boundaries. They also can avoid the over-fitting problems of neural networks as they are based on the structural risk minimization principle. The foundations of these machines were developed by Vapnik, for more information about this algorithm we refer the reader to [10].

4   Experimental Results

Having introduced our proposed solution we continue describing in this section the experimental setting used to evaluate it. We begin by describing the data sets used, and continue presenting the results achieved. In our experiments we used the WEKA implementation of SVM [11]. In this setting multi-class problems are solved using pairwise classification. The optimization algorithm used for training the support vector classifier is an implementation of Platt's sequential minimal optimization algorithm [12]. The kernel function used for mapping the input space was a polynomial of exponent one.

Two data sets were used in the experiments, one was gathered by people in the NLP lab at our Institution. It consists of news in Spanish acquired from different newspapers from Mexico that cover disaster-related events. This collection contains a total of 285 NEs. Although it is a small corpus (which is not so bad as it gives us the opportunity of manual revision) it is large enough for our experimental evaluation. The other corpus is that used in the CoNLL 2002 competitions for the Spanish NE extraction task. This corpus is divided in three sets: a training set consisting of 20,308 NEs and two different sets for testing, *testa* which has 4,634 NEs and *testb* with 3,948 NEs, the former was designated to tune the parameters of the classifiers (development set), while *testb* was designated as the one used to compare the results of the competitors. As in our setting there is no parameter tuning we performed experiments with the two sets.

In order to evaluate our solution we used the Named Entity extractor developed by Carreras and Padró [13]. They have developed a set of NLP analyzers for Spanish, English and Catalan that include practical tools such as POS taggers, semantic analyzers and NE extractors. This NEES is based on hand-coded grammars and lists of trigger words and gazetteer information.

Table 2. Results of NE categorization with our data set. The last row shows the percentage of highest improvement comparing the best result with SVM, marked with "*", against the baseline.

Data Sets	Precision	Recall	F_1	Accuracy
Baseline	**90.80%**	66.2%	76.62%	62.10%
SVM Features	78.60%	89.95%	83.91%	73.38%
SVM Features+NEE	87.02%	90.83%	88.88%	80.00%
SVM NEE (*)	88.30%	**91.73%**	**89.96%**	**81.75%**
% of improvement (best vs baseline)	-2.83%	27.83%	14.83%	24.04%

We begin describing the results using our disaster corpus. We perform four different experiments and report the results in Table 2. We experimented here using 10-fold cross-validation. The first experiment, labeled Baseline is the result of the NEES. As can be seen, it has very high precision, while recall and thus F-measure, are not so good. The Baseline system achieved an accuracy of 62.10%. A different experiment was performed using SVM trained on features like POS tags, lemma and capitalization information. These features are acquired automatically from the text using the Spanish analyzers mentioned above. We used a five word window, where we consider 2 words to the left and 2 words to the right of the target word, each of these words is described by its POS tag, its lemma and the capitalization of the word (all letters capitalized, first letter capitalized, digits or other when non of these is true). Each target word is then described by a vector of 16 attributes: 5 times 3 features plus the real class value. Results from this experiment are also in Table 2 under label SVM Features. We can see that even though we are not using the NEES tags we achieve higher recall, F-measure and accuracy than the NEES.

The results named SVM Features+NEE were obtained using the same features described in the previous experiment plus the NE tags assigned by the extractor system. This combination of features outperformed the previous results in all but one figure, achieving an accuracy of 80%. The last experiment performed with this corpus uses as features the output of the NEES, it does not use POS tags or additional information. Results are labeled SVM NEE, also shown in Table 2. As we can see, the methods using SVM outperformed the NEES in recall, F-measure and accuracy, the best results being those from training SVM on the extractor system tags. Precision of the NEES was the only figure that remained higher. However the improvements achieved by using SVM are as high as 27% in recall, 14.83% in F-measure and 24.04% in accuracy.

In Tables 3 and 4 we present results using the corpora from the CoNLL 2002 competition. In both tables we used the designated training set to build the classifiers. The first table shows the results of using the development set for testing. It can be seen that we achieve higher precision, F-measure and accuracy by using the NEES tags and additional features (POS tags, capitalization and lemmas), while the NEES by itself has the highest recall for this set. Table 4 shows the results of testing with the test set of CoNLL 2002, the SVM Feature+NEES classifier outperformed the Baseline method in three figures: precision, F-measure and accuracy.

Table 3. Results of NE categorization for CoNLL 2002 *development* set. The last row shows the percentage of highest improvement comparing the best result with SVM, marked with "*", against the baseline.

Data Sets	Precision	Recall	F_1	Accuracy
Baseline	77.4%	**95.49%**	85.48%	74.64%
SVM Features+NEE (*)	**86.00%**	92.27%	**88.97%**	**80.14%**
SVM Features	67.00%	83.02%	74.12%	58.89%
SVM NEE	85.60%	91.31%	88.36%	79.15%
% of improvement (best vs baseline)	10%	-3.49%	3.92%	6.86%

By comparing the results from the three tables it is interesting to note that for the CoNLL 2002 test sets the best results are achieved by combining features such as POS tags, capitalization and lemma information with the output of the NEES. While in our disaster data set the best results are achieved by using only the output of the extractor system. This is not surprising if we consider an important difference between our corpus and those from the CoNLL 2002: as our disaster-related corpus was carefully checked the NE tags are nearly error-free, while the other corpora are very large, which makes it unfeasible to manually

Table 4. Results of NE categorization for CoNLL 2002 *test* set. The last row shows the percentage of highest improvement comparing the best result with SVM, marked with "*", against the baseline.

Data Sets	Precision	Recall	F_1	Accuracy
Baseline	70.50%	**88.08%**	78.33%	64.38%
SVM Features+NEE (*)	80.06%	87.40%	**83.86%**	**72.21%**
SVM Features	71.60%	81.55%	76.23%	61.60%
SVM NEE	**80.20%**	86.57%	83.28%	71.35%
% of improvement (best vs baseline)	11.94%	-0.78%	6.59%	10.84%

correct any misclassification. There are some inconsistencies in these corpora that we were unable to correct. We believe that, by using additional information, SVM can achieve better results when there may be noise in the examples, as we suspect is the case. However, the three learning tasks share a common characteristic, the average best results were achieved by a method using SVM. The NE extractor system was always outperformed by some method based on machine learning in at least three out of the four measures.

5 Discussion

Most approaches to NE classification involve the use of hand-coded grammars, lists of trigger words and gazetteers, as observed by [8] in their introduction to the CoNLL-2003 Shared Task. While the accuracies of such systems may be acceptable in some domains, i.e. the domains covered by those lists and grammars, it is very likely that their accuracy will suffer when used to classify NEs in documents from a more specific subject. Consider then the effort of extending the coverage of these approaches: we need to revise the grammar, or regular expressions, to adapt them in order to cover new NE instances. In addition, it is very likely that the lists of trigger words will need some changes, together with gazetteers. We have presented here an alternate solution where instead of redesigning internally the NEES for new instances we need only to use a machine learning classifier, a SVM in this case, using the outputs of the current NEES correcting them if pertinent and retrain. In this way, we can take advantage of previous efforts to build the extractor. Our experimental results show that we can increase the overall performance of the NEES with this approach as assessed by F-measure and accuracy. We observed from the experiments that there is a minor penalty either in precision or recall although it is easily override by the improvement in the other measures.

We have presented here an alternative, based on machine learning techniques, for NE classification. This alternative can be applied when we need to have a wider coverage of named entities, i.e. if the NEES was built from a very specific domain and we want to extend its usability, or if the NEES is very general and we need a more specified coverage of NEs, such as the case of our disaster related corpus. We believe that NE recognition can also be improved by using a similar approach. Some interesting possibilities of future work include:

- *Evaluating this approach with a NEES for English* We believe that this solution can be applied with similar success to the problem of NE classification for English. We are working now in finding a NEES that we can use in order to experiment.
- *Automatic Correction of Errors in Corpus* A major difficulty of doing research related with natural language processing is the lack of error-free annotated corpora. It can be a very extenuating task to verify the correctness of the tagging. We believe that machine learning can be used for building error detectors in corpora, and we are planning to explore this topic.
- *Using Unlabeled Data* Given that unlabeled data are more easily gathered, as opposed to labeled, there have been some interesting methods proposed in problems such as text categorization that exploit information contained in unlabeled data. We believe that using unlabeled data can benefit NE categorization and that machine learning algorithms such as SVM can be an interesting alternative in this direction.

Acknowledgements. We would like to thank CONACYT for partially supporting this work under grants 166934 and U39957-Y.

References

1. M. Arévalo, L. Márquez, M.A. Martí, L. Padró, and M. J. Simón. A proposal for wide-coverage spanish named entity recognition. *Sociedad Española para el Procesamiento del Lenguaje Natural*, 28, May 2002.
2. G. Zhou and J. Su. Named entity recognition using an HMM-based chunk tagger. In *Proceedings of ACL'02*, pages 473–480, 2002.
3. R. Florian. Named entity recognition as a house of cards: Classifier stacking. In *Proceedings of CoNLL-2002*, pages 175–178, 2002.
4. T. Zhang and D. Johnson. A robust risk minimization based named entity recognition system. In *Proceedings of CoNLL-2003*, 2003.
5. S. N. Galicia-Haro, A. Gelbukh, and I. A. Bolshakov. Recognition of Named Entities in Spanish Texts. In *Mexican Internactional Conference on Artificial Intelligence (MICAI-2004)*. Lecture Notes in Artificial Intelligence, N 2972, Springer-Verlag, 2004.
6. G. Petasis, A. Cucchiarelli, P. Velardi, G. Paliouras, V. Karkaletsis, and C. D. Spyropoulos. Automatic adaptation of proper noun dictionaries through cooperation of machine learning and probabilistic methods. In *Proceedings of the 23rd Annual International ACM SIGIR conference on Research and development in information retrieval*, pages 128–135. ACM Press, 2000.
7. C. Nobata S. Sekine, K. Sudo. Extended named entity hierarchy. In *Proceedings of the Third International Conference on Language Resources and Evaluation (LREC 2002)*, 2002.
8. E. F. Tjong Kim Zhang and F. De Meulder. Introduction to the CoNLL-2003 shared task: Language-independent named entity recognition. In *Proceedings of the CoNLL-2003*, 2003.

9. M. O. Stitson, J. A. E. Wetson, A. Gammerman, V. Vovk, and V. Vapnik. Theory of support vector machines. Technical Report CSD-TR-96-17, Royal Holloway University of London, England, December 1996.

10. V. Vapnik. *The Nature of Statistical Learning Theory.* ISBN 0-387-94559-8. Springer, N.Y., 1995.

11. I. H. Witten and E. Frank. *Data Mining, Practical Machine Learning Tools and Techniques with Java Implementations.* The Morgan Kaufmann Series in Data Management Systems. Morgan Kaufmann, 1999.

12. J. Platt. Fast training of support vector machines using sequential minimal optimization. In *Advances in Kernel Methods-Support Vector Learning, (B. Scholkopf, C. J. C. Burges, A. J. Smola, eds.)*, pages 185–208, Cambridge, Massachusetts, 1999. MIT Press.

13. X. Carreras and L. Padró. A exible distributed architecture for natural language analyzers. In *Proceedings of LREC'02*, Las Palmas de Gran Canaria, Spain, 2002.

An Internet-Based Method for Verification of Extracted Proper Names

Angelo Dalli

NLP Research Group
Department of Computer Science
University of Sheffield
angelo@dcs.shef.ac.uk

Abstract. Identification and extraction of proper names from Internet-based sources currently suffers from a lack of verification methods that check the validity of these extracted names. A language-independent method for assigning probabilities to extracted proper names using frequency data harvested from the Internet is presented. Verification mechanisms are built on top of this technique to exclude misidentified proper names automatically.

1 Introduction

The task of automatically identifying proper names in text is often aided through gazetteer lists obtained from telephone directories, government records, and additional sources together with additional heuristics. Although traditional publication sources provide acceptably large gazetteer lists for a single language, it may prove difficult to integrate different data sources to produce a comprehensive multi-lingual gazetteer list.

An innovative approach to gathering a large set of proper names was adopted by having a small custom-built information extraction system analyse a large corpus of multi-lingual text crawled over the Internet. Simple capitalisation rules together with the presence of various personal titles such as Mr., Ms., and so on were used to identify likely proper names in the texts. Additional hints were provided by the presence of anaphora in the same sentence or the following sentence as the suspected proper name. A manually compiled list of anaphora was used to detect their presence. The gender of every title and anaphora was manually noted and this information was used to keep a count of the number of male or female titles and anaphors associated with a particular name. This enabled the list of names to be organised by gender. Although this is not the most sophisticated form of multi-lingual anaphora detection and resolution, acceptable results were obtained since the task was only to assign a rough probability to suspect words [1–7].

One of the main problems encountered in this approach were the numerous nicknames used in online chat rooms, forums and other communications that were often incorrectly identified as proper names. This problem was solved partially by removing names that had unusual punctuation marks or numeric digits.

A. Gelbukh (Ed.): CICLing 2004, LNCS 2945, pp. 168–171, 2004.
© Springer-Verlag Berlin Heidelberg 2004

A list of over 592,000 proper names was thus obtained by this method with around 284,000 names being identified as male and 308,000 names identified as female. The large size of this list compares favourably with previously compiled lists [8], [9].

2   Filtering and Verification Process

The filter and verification process worked in two main steps: gathering word frequency data from the Internet and applying this data to filter and verify the proper name list.

Word frequency data was collected by aggregating the total number of hits returned back by various popular search engines (a mixture of Google, Yahoo! and AltaVista) when presented with a query for every name in the list. The values were then averaged using a weighted function that assigned more importance to search engines that index more documents.

The resulting name-frequency list was then ranked by frequency and a modified version of the Levenstein string distance algorithm [10] used to obtain clusters containing similar names. The most frequently occurring names were clustered first based on the assumption that these would produce the most interesting clusters. Table 1 shows an example cluster obtained for the name "Angel" in the female name list.

Table 1. Example Cluster

Rank	Word	Frequency	Freq/Total
1	Angel	13500000	0.825285627
2	Ange	1840000	0.112483374
3	Andel	720000	0.044015233
4	Anel	164000	0.010025692
5	Aneel	37700	0.002304687
6	Aniel	27000	0.001650571
7	Agel	20800	0.001271551
8	Anjel	16500	0.001008682
9	Annel	9940	0.000607655
10	Angee	7620	0.000465828
11	Angal	2650	0.000162001
12	Augel	2280	0.000139382
13	Anngel	2230	0.000136325
14	Anzel	2090	0.000127766
15	Anyel	1390	8.49739E-05
16	Anxel	1300	7.94719E-05
17	Aggel	1240	7.5804E-05
18	Aungel	558	3.41118E-05
19	Aingel	471	2.87933E-05
20	Aegel	204	1.2471E-05
	Total	**16357973**	**1.00**

Two methods of verifying the proper names in every cluster were considered. The first method involved a simple selection process where the top words accounting for 99.99% of the frequency count were selected. For the example cluster shown in Table 1, all the words from ranks 1-17 inclusive will be selected. The top 17 names in the cluster are indeed all proper names in some language or another – while items 18-20 are not. A small random sample of the clusters shows that the top words accounting for 99.99% of the frequency count are generally true proper names.

The second method tried to use a less arbitrary method of selecting the threshold value by utilising the observation that most frequency distributions in the clusters exhibited a roughly exponential distribution. A set of exponential growth trend analyses were made, with a trend curve being fitted for items 1-20, 2-20, 3-20, ..., 19-20. Multiple exponential trends were computed to smooth out the errors in the trend values especially since some commonly occurring names have very high frequency counts that may skew the trend calculations.

For every curve, the values were extrapolated for the next item that would appear in the cluster – in the example case item 21. This was done to determine a lower bound value for the threshold value to be used for that particular cluster. Table 2 displays the resulting data series for the cluster shown in Table 1. The data series is displayed in a compact format with the data point for items 1-20 (79.97) appearing in the top left cell, continuing until the last data point for items 19-20 (88.36) at the bottom cell.

Table 2. Exponential Growth Trends for the example cluster in Table 1

79.97	112.06	141.73	179.09	207.14	210.05	213.61	221.10	236.48
249.29	272.34	247.63	219.22	196.98	183.22	150.88	125.73	137.86
88.36								

A visual check of the resulting data series for most of the clusters displayed the characteristics of a normal distribution. The Studentized range/standard deviation (also know as the w/s test) was performed to determine whether the data is normally distributed or not. For Table 2, the standard deviation is 56.41 and the mean 182.77, with a range of 192.368 giving a w/s ratio of 3.409. When interpreted correctly this means that the data series is normally distributed at the 0.005 level of significance [11].

The suggested threshold value is given by adding two standard deviations to the mean to give a Confidence Interval of more than 0.95 [12]. For the example cluster this gives a threshold value of 295.61. In this case items 1-19 would be chosen. The main advantage of this threshold value is that it is calculated entirely through sound statistical processes without involving any arbitrary or empirically-derived constants.

3   Conclusion

This short paper has presented part of a named entity recognition system developed at the University of Sheffield that bootstraps itself entirely from the Internet. The Internet-based verification and filter mechanism enables the system to automatically prune its own data set without any need for external help.

An interesting observation made possible by analysing the threshold data series produced for every cluster, is that at least 93% of the data clusters exhibited a normally distributed data series. This likely non-random result may suggest hitherto undiscovered patterns in the distribution of proper names on the Internet.

The established threshold values are useful in improving the performance of named entity recognisers by providing a simple verification mechanism whereby a new suspected named entity that is not mentioned enough times on the Internet is quickly ruled out. Speech recognition systems[1] can also benefit from these threshold values as it provides a possible means of determining which character patterns should be associated with particular names and which patterns are irrelevant.

Hopefully this work will contribute to more information extraction research in the area of automatic bootstrapping and data verification, enabling us to gain more information from the vast amounts of publicly available texts on the Internet.

References

1. Azzam, S., Humphreys, K. and Gaizauskas, R. 'Coreference resolution in a multilingual information extraction', *Proc. Workshop on Linguistic Coreference.* Granada, Spain, 1998.
2. Aone, C. and McKee, D. 'A language-independent anaphora resolution system for understanding multilingual texts', *Proc. 8th International Conference on Artificial Intelligence: Methodology, Systems, and Applications (AIMSA-98)*, 1-13. Sozopol, Bulgaria, Springer Lecture Notes in Artificial Intelligence, Vol. 1480, 1993.
3. Mitkov, Ruslan. Anaphora Resolution. London, Longman, 2002.
4. Harabagiu, S., Bunescu, R. and Maiorano, S. 'Text and knowledge mining for coreference resolution', *Proc. 2nd Meeting of the North American Chapter of the Association of Computational Linguistics (NAACL-2001)*, 55-62. Pittsburgh, PA, 2001.
5. Mitkov, R. 'Multilingual anaphora resolution', *Machine Translation*, 14 (3-4), 281-299, 1999.
6. Galicia-Haro, S.N., A. Gelbukh, and I.A. Bolshakov. 'Recognition of named entities in Spanish texts', *Mexican International Conference on Artificial Intelligence* (MICAI-2004). Lecture Notes in Artificial Intelligence, N 2972, Springer, 2004.
7. Calvo, H., and A. Gelbukh, 'Improving disambiguation of prepositional phrase attachments using the web as corpus', *CIARP'2003*. Lecture Notes in Computer Science, N 2905, Springer, 2003, pp. 604-610.
8. Muñoz, R., Montoyo, A., Llopis, F. and Suárez, A. 'Reconocimiento de entitades en el sistema EXIT', *Procesamiento del Lenguaje Natural*, 23, 47-53, 1998.
9. Stevenson, Mark and Gaizauskas, Robert. 'Using Corpus-derived Name Lists for Named Entity Recognition, *Proc. ANLP-2000*, Seattle, USA, 2000.
10. Levenstein, V.I. 'Binary codes capable of correcting insertions and reversals', *Sov. Phys. Dokl.*, 10 (707-10), 1966.
11. Sachs, L. Statistische Auswertung Methoden. 3rd ed. Berlin, Springer, 1972.
12. Kenney, J.F. and Keeping, E.S. 'Calculation of the Standard Deviation', *Mathematics of Statistics, Part 1*, 3rd ed. 77-80, Princeton, NJ, Van Nostrand, 1962.

[1] This work was partly funded by the EU FASiL project, which aims to produce a voice-controlled Virtual Personal Assistant (www.fasil.co.uk).

Boundary Correction of Protein Names Adapting Heuristic Rules

Tomohiro Mitsumori[1], Sevrani Fation[1], Masaki Murata[2], Kouichi Doi[1], and Hirohumi Doi[1]

[1] Graduate School of Information Science,
Nara Institute Science and Technology,
8916-5 Takayama-cho Ikoma 630-0101, Japan
{mitsumor, fation, doy}@is.aist-nara.ac.jp
doi@cl-sciences.co.jp
[2] Keihanna Human Info-Communication Research Center,
2-2-2 Hikaridai, Seika-cho, Soraku-gun, Kyoto, 619-0289, Japan
murata@crl.go.jp

Abstract. In this study, we made some heuristic rules related to the boundary of protein names for automated extraction of protein names from biomedical literatures. The automated extraction of protein names was carried out based on Support Vector Machine (SVM). From the analysis of the results, we found whether some words of modifier words set were included or not as part of protein names. It is critical whether the modifier words set is or not included in a protein name. Adapting some heuristic rules to the corpus, the F-score was improved about 1.3% (from 76.10% to 77.41%) compared with the case without adapting proposed rules.

1 Introduction

The goal of our study is the automated information extraction related to the protein-protein interactions from biomedical literature. In this study, we carry out the extraction of protein names using SVM.

Recently, some studies have been reported regarding this issue. One difficulty is to exactly recognize the boundary of protein names because some of protein names are represented as compound words. Yamamoto et al. [1] reported a 74.9% F-score in case of exact boundary matching, and 85.0% in case of partial matching. The partial matching means that a word obtained after learning matches some of the words of the real word. Based on hand written rules, Franzén et al. [2] reported a F-score of 67.1% in case of exact boundary matching, and 82.9% in partial matching. In this paper, we make use of some heuristic rules concerning the boundary of protein names to improve precision and/or recall.

2 Experimental Conditions

Some studies reported about the protein name recognition. Some are based on the machine learning[1][3] and the other are based on the hand written

A. Gelbukh (Ed.): CICLing 2004, LNCS 2945, pp. 172–175, 2004.
© Springer-Verlag Berlin Heidelberg 2004

rules [2][4]. We used the Support Vector Machine algorithm (SVM) since it has achieved a good performance in many classification tasks. We used YamCha[5] which is SVM-based chunker.

The parameters and features for SVM learning are shown in Table 1. We used a polynomial kernel of degree two. The direction of parsing was forward (left to right). In Figure 1, we show an example of a context window (large framed box). Tag *B,I,* and *O* mean *b*eginning, *i*nner of chunking and *o*ther term respectively. For classifying *B*, *I* and *O*, we need to use SVM which expands multi-class problem. In this example, $\boxed{\text{I}}$ is the estimated tag. We used the following features such as word, orthographic, part of speech (POS), prefix, suffix and preceding class. Details of method using YamCha are shown in Ref. [7].

In this experiment, we used the GENIA corpus Ver. 3.01[6] as training and test data. This corpus was a set of 2,000 MEDLINE abstracts. Some of the words are cascaded annotations such as: <DNA><protein>*GS-CSF*</protein> *promoter*</DNA>. We defined the protein name enclosed in frame in <protein> ... </protein> . The results of SVM learning are shown in Table 4. In this experiment, we used 1,600 abstracts as training data and 400 abstracts as test data. The presented results were calculated from 10-fold cross validations. The precision, recall and F-score were 78.09, 74.21 and 76.10 respectively.

Table 1. The parameters of YamCha and the features used in this experiments.

Parameter	Value	Feature	Value
kernel	polynomial	word	all words in training data
degree of kernel	2	orthographic	Capital, Symbol etc. (see [3])
direction of parsing	forward	prefix	From 1, 2 to 3 gram of prefix
window position	-2,-1,0,+1,+2	suffix	From 1, 2 to 3 gram of suffix
multi-class	pair-wise	part of speech	Brill tagger
		preceding class	-2, -1

	WORD	POS	ORTHOGRAPHIC	PREFIX	SUFFIX	TAG
POS:-3	such	JJ	Lowercase	s su suc	h ch uch	O
POS:-2	as	IN	Lowercase	a as –	s as –	O
POS:-1	NF-kappa	NNP	Greek	N NF NF-	a pa ppa	B
POS:0	B	NNP	SingleCap	B – –	B – –	I
POS:+1	that	IN	Lowercase	t th tha	t at hat	O
POS:+2	are	VBP	Lowercase	a ar are	e re are	O
POS:+3	constitutively	RB	Lowercase	c co con	y ly ely	O

Fig. 1. An example of context window. This is an example of sentence "... *such as NF-kappa B that are constitutively* ...".

3   Making Heuristic Rules

In above experiment, it is regarded as correct if the words obtained after learning exactly match the real words. There are three cases of error. First case is that words obtained after training were incorrect. Second case is that the word could not be extracted. Last case is that the words obtained after training partially matched the real word. From the analysis of the last case, we found whether the some of modifier words were included or not as a part of protein names. For example, *NF-kappa B* was obtained as a protein name where in fact it is *human NF-kappa B*. *human IL-2* was obtained as a protein name where in fact it is *IL-2*. *human IL-7R alpha* was obtained as a protein name where in fact it is *human IL-7R alpha*. In the above examples, it is critical whether *human* is or not regarded as a part of protein name. Another example is shown in Table 2. In Table 3, we show such a modifier word set found by analysis of the results. Based on the fact, we corrected the boundary of the protein names in the corpus adapting the following rules.

Left boundary rule: If one of modifier word set exist at left side of protein name in training data, the modifier is included in the boundary of protein names. We found the number of 95 modifier words set.

Right boundary rule: If one of modifier word set exist at right side of protein name in training data, the modifier is included in the boundary of protein names. We found the number of 29 modifier words set.

The reasons using the rules are that:

i) These modifier words set do not change the meaning of the proper protein name. But they introduce some additional information regarding the protein.

ii) Correcting the boundary of protein name and contribute to improvement of precision and/or recall.

Table 2. Example of modifier one word at boundary of protein names.

Left one word		Right one word	
System results	Real word	System results	Real word
NF-kappa B	human NF-kappa B	bcl-6	bcl-6 protein
human IL-2	IL-2	c-Fos protein	c-Fos
human IL-7R alpha	human IL-7R alpha	E1A protein	E1A protein

4   Adapting Rules

After learning, we corrected the training data based on the rules. About 1,000 protein names were corrected which was about 3% of the protein names included

Table 3. Example of the modifier word set found at left/right side of protein names.

	Example
left side word set	basic, constitutive, endogenous, eukaryotic, human, inducible, major, multiple, mutant, etc.
right side word set	antibody, complex, family, heterodimer, inhibitor, kinase, ligand, protein, receptor, subunit, etc.

Table 4. Precision, Recall and F-score using rules.

	Precision/Recall/F-score
Without adapting rule	78.09 / 74.21 / 76.10
Adapting rules (our method)	79.42 / 75.51 / 77.41

in the corpus. We carried out again SVM learning using corrected training data. The precision, recall and F-score was 79.42%, 75.51% and 77.41% respectively (see Table 4). The effect of the boundary rules improved 1.31% the F-score points compared with the results of the training data without adapting rules. We suggest that the reason of the improvement is due to correction of the modifier words set listed in Table 3 as a part of protein names in the training data.

5 Conclusions

In this paper, we proposed some rules regarding the protein names. We corrected the training corpus by making use of these rules. As a result, the F-score increased about 1.3 % compared with the results without adapting the proposed rules.

References

1. K. Yamamoto, T. Kudo, A. Konagaya and Y. Matsumoto, Proceedings of the ACL 2003 Workshop on NLP in Biomedicine (2003) 65–72.
2. K. Franzén, G. Eriksson, F. Olsson, L. Asker, P. Lidén, and J. Cöster, International Journal of Medical Informatics,67 (2002) 49–61.
3. K.Takeuchi and N. Collier, Proceedings of the ACL 2003 Workshop on NLP in Biomedicine (2003) 57–64.
4. K. Fukuda, A. Tamura, T. Tsunoda and T. Takagi, Proceedings of the Pacific Symposium on Biocomputing (1999) 705–716.
5. T. Kudo and Y. Matsumoto, North American Chapter of the Association for Computational Linguistics(NAACL) (2001) 192–199.
6. T. Ohta, Y. Tateisi, H. Mima and J. Tsujii, In the Proceedings of he Human Language Technology Conference (HLT 2002).
7. http://cl.aist-nara.ac.jp/ taku-ku/software/yamcha/

Word Sense Disambiguation
Based on Weight Distribution Model
with Multiword Expression

Hee-Cheol Seo, Young-Sook Hwang, and Hae-Chang Rim

Dept. of Computer Science and Engineering, Korea University
1, 5-ka, Anam-dong, Seongbuk-Gu, Seoul, 136-701, Korea
{hcseo, yshwang, rim}@nlp.korea.ac.kr

Abstract. This paper proposes a two-phase word sense disambiguation method, which filters only the relevant senses by utilizing the multiword expression and then disambiguates the senses based on Weight Distribution Model. Multiword expression usually constrains the possible senses of a polysemous word in a context. Weight Distribution Model is based on the hypotheses that every word surrounding a polysemous word in a context contributes to disambiguating the senses according to its discrimination power. The experiments on English data in SENSEVAL-1 and SENSEVAL-2 show that multiword expression is useful to filter out irrelevant senses of a polysemous word in a given context, and Weight Distribution Model is more effective than Decision Lists.

1 Introduction

Word sense disambiguation(WSD) is the task of selecting the correct sense of a word in a context. Many applications of natural language processing(NLP), such as machine translation, information extraction, and question answering, require a semantic analysis where WSD plays a crucial role. With its importance, WSD has been known as a very important field of NLP and studied steadily since the advent of NLP in the 1950s.

One of the most successful current lines of the research is the corpus-based supervised learning approach. Most of the approaches([2][3][4][5]) try to disambiguate the word senses by utilizing the words which co-occur with a polysemous word in a sense tagged corpus. The words that frequently co-occur with a particular sense of the polysemous word are regarded as useful features.

Based on the same observation, multiword expression(MWE) like an idiom or a phrasal verb is particularly valuable at WSD. That is to say, the sense of a polysemous word can be constrained by the multiword expression with the word. For example, given a MWE *every day*, we immediately realize what the word *day* means. Hence, we use the multiword expression including a polysemous word to determine the sense of the polysemous word in a context.

MWE can be used as a sense tagger or a sense filter. As a sense tagger, MWE selects just one sense for a polysemous word in a context. However, if a MWE

A. Gelbukh (Ed.): CICLing 2004, LNCS 2945, pp. 176–187, 2004.
© Springer-Verlag Berlin Heidelberg 2004

is related to various senses of the word, the MWE can not be used as a sense tagger, since it does not select one sense. Instead, the MWE is able to rule out all senses irrelevant to the MWE, and filter only the relevant senses.

We have devised Weight Distribution Model(WDM) to identify the proper sense of a polysemous word in a context by only using the frequency information between each feature and the polysemous word. Though various approaches have achieved good performances to determine the correct sense, some approaches require a great number of time and space to train for a polysemous word. These approaches seem not to be appropriate for WSD, since the number of the senses of polysemous words in WSD task is too large to have the approaches learn to identify the correct senses of all words. For example, there are about sixty-thousand senses and about ten-thousand polysemous words in nominal part of WordNet. Instead, machine learning techniques using only frequency information without training phase such as Decision Lists[6][7], Naïve Bayesian Model[3] and the proposed model, WDM, can be applied to WSD task efficiently.

In summary, this paper proposes a two-phase word sense disambiguation method: firstly filtering the relevant senses by using MWE, and secondly identifying the proper sense based on WDM.

2   Multiword Expression as a Sense Filter

In order for MWE to filter senses of a polysemous word, it is necessary to acquire MWE and then to map MWE onto some senses of a polysemous word.

2.1   Acquiring Multiword Expression

MWEs are acquired from WordNet, which contains compounds, phrasal verbs, collocations and idiomatic phrases as well as words[8]. In this paper, every unit except the words in WordNet is regarded as MWE. WordNet consists of four parts: nominal, verbal, adverbial, and adjective parts. MWEs are extracted from every part in WordNet, such as *state of the art, call for, every day*, and *out of fashion.*

2.2   Mapping Multiword Expression onto Senses

MWEs are automatically mapped onto the senses of polysemous words using the sense tagged corpus, and the mapping information is recorded in the MWE-sense mapping table. The mapping steps are as follows:

1. Detect a sentence including MWE of a polysemous word in the sense tagged corpus.
2. Record MWE and the sense of the polysemous word in the sentence into the MWE-sense mapping table.

In the first phase, the inflected word forms in the sentence are converted into the base forms using WordNet morphological processor *Morphy*[8]. For example, consider the following instance with MWE *art historian* of polysemous word *art*[1].

<instance id="art.40116">
<answer senseid= "art_historian%1:18:00::">
<context>
... is dear to scholars, historians, literary critics and <head>art</head>
historians, especially the concept of a clear chronological sequence ...
</context>
</instance>

The inflected word *historians* in the above instance is converted into *historian*, and MWE *art historian* is detected. Since *art* in the context is assigned to the sense *art_historian%1:18:00::*, the pair of the MWE *art historian* and the sense *art_historian%1:18:00::* is inserted into the MWE-sense mapping table. Table 1 shows examples of the MWE-sense mapping table. In the table, some MWEs (e.g. *call in* and *call for*) are related to more than one sense of a word(i.e. *call*). Since these MWEs cannot identify just one sense, they cannot be utilized for sense taggers, but for sense filters.

Table 1. MWEs of word *art* and *call* in MWE-sense mapping table

MWE	sense tag
art gallery	art_gallery%1:06:00::
art historian	art_historian%1:18:00::
call in	call%2:32:04::
call in	call%2:41:14::
call in	call_in%2:32:02::
call for	call_for%2:32:04::
call for	call_for%2:42:00::

2.3   Sense Filtering by Multiword Expression

In this paper, MWEs are used as a sense filter, and the sense filtering steps are done as follows:

1. Check whether a polysemous word in a new sentence is in a MWE.
2. If the polysemous word is in a MWE, filter only the senses related to MWE by looking up MWE-sense mapping table, otherwise select all senses.

---

[1] In SENSEVAL-2 data, a polysemous word in a context is surrounded by *<head>* and *</head>*.

For example, consider the following instance with MWE *call for* of the polyse-mous word *call*:

"Among other things, the bill <head>calls</head> for a reorganization of the Justice Department."

By looking up MWE-sense mapping table, only two senses *call_for%2:32:04::* and *call_for%2:42:00::* among 17 senses of the word *call* are filtered.

3 Word Sense Disambiguation Based on Weight Distribution Model

Weight Distribution Model(WDM) has been devised based on the following hy-potheses:

- Every feature in the context more or less contributes to the word sense disambiguation according to its discrimination ability.
- The feature that co-occurs with several senses has less discrimination ability than the feature that co-occurs with only one sense.
- If a feature co-occurs with more than one sense, the relative contribution of the feature to each sense must be reflected in a model.

WDM determines a proper sense of a polysemous word pw in a context C as follows:

$$Sense(pw|C) \overset{\text{def}}{=} \arg\max_{s_i} \sum_{f_j inC} Weight(f_j) \times D(f_j, s_i) \qquad (1)$$

where $Weight(f_j)$ is the weight(or discrimination ability) of j-th feature f_j and is calculated based on the entropy measure:

$$Weight(f_j) = \log_2 n - Entropy(f_j) \qquad (2)$$

$$Entropy(f_j) = -\sum \frac{P(f_j|s_i)}{\sum_{k=1}^{n} P(f_j|s_k)} \log_2 \frac{P(f_j|s_i)}{\sum_{k=1}^{n} P(f_j|s_k)} \qquad (3)$$

where n is the number of senses, $Entropy(f_j)$ is the entropy of j-th feature f_j, and $P(f_j|s_i)$ is the conditional probability of f_j given the i-th sense s_i. $\log_2 n$ is the maximum value of the entropy[2]. Thus, the weight is always greater than or equal to zero. By using the entropy measure, the above second hypothesis is considered in the WDM: the feature which co-occurs with several senses has larger entropy value than the feature which co-occurs with only one sense, hence the weight of the former feature is smaller than the weight of the latter feature.

In equation 1, $D(f_j, s_i)$ is the degree which f_j distributes its weight to s_i, and is computed by the normalized conditional probability of f_j conditioned on the sense:

$$D(f_j, s_i) = \frac{P(f_j|s_i)}{\sum_{k=1}^{n} P(f_j|s_k)} \qquad (4)$$

---

[2] The entropy of a feature becomes maximal when the distribution of the feature is uniform.

By the normalized conditional probability, the sum of weights that f_j distributes to each sense becomes the weight of f_j.

WDM is free from the data sparseness problem, since features with zero frequencies in the training corpus are not used in WDM.

4   Feature Space

Feature space consists of three contexts: local context, topical context, and collocation context. Local context consists of the features of the following templates for each word within its window:

- *word_position* : a word and its position
- *word_PoS* : a word and its part-of-speech
- *PoS_position* : the part-of-speech and the position of a word

A word is represented by the surface form, and can be either one of open-class words or closed-class words. The window size ranges from 3 to +3 words, which is determined empirically.

Topical context includes every open-class word within its window, which contains the sentence with a target word, the preceding sentence, and the following sentence.

Finally, collocation context consists of the following features for each word pair within its window:

- *(word$_i$; word$_j$)* : the i-th word and j-th word ($i > j$)
- *(word$_i$; PoS$_j$)* : the i-th word and j-th part-of-speech ($i > j$)
- *(PoS$_i$:word$_j$)* : the i-th part-of-speech and j-th word($i > j$)

Unlike the local context and the topical contexts with unigram information, collocation contexts are composed of the information of word pairs surrounding the target word. Thus, the collocation context is useful to handle the collocations which is directly related to the sense of the target word. The window size ranges from 2 to +2 words. Figure 1 represents the corresponding local, topical and collocation contexts for the noun *art* in a example sentence.

5   Experiment

The proposed method has been evaluated on SENSEVAL-1 English corpus[3] and on the corpus of SENSEVAL-2 English lexical sample task.

---

[3] The words in English corpus of SENSEVAL-1 are tagged with noun, verb, adjective, and indeterminates. Among them, the words assigned to the indeterminates were not used. The words without the training data(i.e. *disability(noun)*, *rabbit(noun)*, *steering(noun)*, *deaf(adj)*) are also not employed. Therefore, experiments are conducted on the 7 adjectives, 12 nouns, and 13 verbs.

Sentence :
    This/DT man/NN plays/VBZ in/IN a/DT performance/NN <head>art</head> band/NN

Local context :
    in_-3, a_-2, performance_-1, art_0, band_+1, in_IN, a_DT, performance_NN,
    art_NN, band_NN, IN_-3, DT_-2, NN_-1, NN_0, NN_+1

Topical context :
    man, plays, performance, art, band

Collocation context :
    (a performance), (performance art), (art band), (a NN), (DT performance), (performance NN),
    (NN art), (art NN), (NN band)

Fig. 1. Example of local context, topical context and collocation context

5.1 Multiword Expression

MWEs have been extracted from WordNet version 1.7. Table 2 represents the number of MWE, the number of polysemous words having MWE, and the number of polysemous words on the experimental data.

Table 2. MWE information (# of MWE - # of polysemous words having the MWE - # of polysemous words

	SENSEVAL-1	SENSEVAL-2
adjective	12-3-7	60-9-15
noun	29-7-12	128-24-29
verb	6-4-13	94-20-28
overall	47-14-32	282-53-72

Table 3 represents the average number of senses filtered by MWE. The average number of senses per polysemous word is in the bracket. In the table, it is observed that through MWE filter, many senses are ruled out, and a small number of senses are passed into the disambiguation step.

Table 3. Average number of senses filtered by MWE(Average number of senses per polysemous word)

	SENSEVAL-1	SENSEVAL-2
adjective	1.33(6.86)	1.13(7.40)
noun	1.41(8.25)	1.12(8.10)
verb	2.00(7.38)	1.90(15.62)
overall	1.47(7.59)	1.38(10.95)

5.2   Coverage and Recall of Multiword Expression

We have examined the coverage and the recall of MWE. The coverage of MWE is the ratio of the number of instances with MWE to the total number of the instances with MWE, and the recall of MWE is the ratio of the number of the instances that the correct sense is filtered(or tagged) by MWE to the total number of the instances with MWE. Table 4 and Table 5 show the coverage and the recall of MWE as a sense filter and as a sense tagger, respectively. In the tables, it is found that the number of instances with MWE at SENSEVAL-1 data is smaller than SENSEVAL-2 data, and that MWEs hardly contribute to WSD as sense taggers at SENSEVAL-1 data. In particular, compared Table 4 with Table 5, MWE as a sense filter is more useful than as a sense tagger for verbs in SENSEVAL-2 data.

Table 4. Coverage and Recall of MWE as sense filter

	SENSEVAL-1			SENSEVAL-2		
	# of instances	coverage	recall	# of instances	coverage	recall
adjective	1,284	0.62%	100%	768	7.81%	91.67%
noun	2,199	1.91%	76.19%	1754	7.70%	97.78%
verb	2,501	2.36%	84.75%	1806	10.41%	80.32%
overall	5,984	1.82%	82.75%	4328	8.85%	88.25%

Table 5. Coverage and Recall of MWE as sense tagger

	SENSEVAL-1		SENSEVAL-2	
	coverage	recall	coverage	recall
adjective	0.00%	0.00%	6.90%	90.57%
noun	0.55%	91.67%	5.87%	97.09%
verb	0.00%	0.00%	1.88%	52.94%
overall	0.20%	91.67%	4.39%	87.37%

5.3   Contribution of Multiword Expression to Word Sense Disambiguation

We try to figure out how much MWE contributes to WSD as a sense filter or as a sense tagger. After MWE filtering, we disambiguate the senses of target words. Table 6 shows the experimental results using MWE or without using MWE.

In the table, it is shown that MWE hardly contributes to WSD at SENSEVAL-1 data, as can be expected, because of the low coverage of MWE. On the other hand, at SENSEVAL-2 data, MWE plays an important role in

Table 6. Contribution of Multiword Expression to WSD

	SENSEVAL-1			SENSEVAL-2		
	Without using MWE	Using MWE as		Without using MWE	Using MWE as	
		sense filter	sense tagger		sense filter	sense tagger
adjective	75.08%	75.47%	75.08%	67.06%	68.49%	68.49%
noun	77.63%	77.63%	77.63%	66.99%	68.70%	68.53%
verb	70.69%	70.57%	70.69%	55.20%	56.31%	55.32%
overall	74.18%	74.21%	74.18%	62.08%	63.49%	63.01%

improving the performance. Moreover, MWE as a sense filter is a little more helpful to WSD than as a sense tagger.

This experiment is done by using local context, topical context and collocation context as a feature space. Considering the different performance between using MWE and without using MWE, MWE is not recognized as a significant feature in the collocation context, since MWE does not occur frequently in a training corpus. Hence, MWE has to be handled separate from the feature space at WSD field.

We have investigated the words whose tagging precisions using MWE as a sense filter are different from the tagging precisions without using MWE. Table 7 shows the words, in which the first number in the bracket is the number of correctly tagged instances without a sense filter and the second number is the number of correctly tagged instances with a sense filter. For all words except only two words, *bet-v* at SENSEVAL-1 and *drift* at SENSEVAL-2, the better results are obtained when MWE is used as a sense filter.

Table 7. Words with different tagging results when using MWE as a sense filter: (# of correctly tagged instances without a sense filter and # of correctly tagged instances with a sense filter.)

	SENSEVAL-1	SENSEVAL-2
adjective	wooden-a(184-189)	fine(33-34),free(44-50), green(77-79), natural(52-53)
noun		art(51-57), bar(91-95), child(45-46), church(44-46), circuit(59-63), detention(25-27),holiday(26-29), lady(36-39), nature(32-33), post(43-44), restraint(30-31), sense(28-30)
verb	bet-v(76-73)	call(26-28),carry(25-26),dress(38-41), drift(15-14), drive(20-22), find(17-19), live(38-39),pull(17-21), strike(21-22), turn(22-26), wash(9-10)

We have also examined the words whose tagging precisions using MWE as a sense tagger are different from the tagging precisions without using MWE. The words are in Table 8. There are no words at SENSEVAL-1 data whose tagging precisions are changed.

Table 8. Words with different tagging results when using MWE as a sense tagger at SENSEVAL-2 data: (# of correctly tagged instances without a sense tagger and # of correctly tagged instances with a sense tagger.)

Adj	fine(33-34), free(44-50), green(77-79), natural(52-53), vital(35-36)
Noun	art(51-57),bar(91-95),child(45-46), church(44-46),circuit(59-62), detention(25-27), holiday(26-29), restraint(30-31), sense(28-30)
Verb	carry(25-26), pull(17-18)

The table shows that MWE as a sense tagger always improves the performance of all words at SENSEVAL-2. However, the overall increasing rate of the performance is lower than that of MWE as a sense filter, as shown in Table 6, because of the low coverage of the sense tagger.

5.4   Performance of Weight Distribution Model: Compared with Decision Lists

WDM has been compared with Decision Lists[6], which is known as one of the state of art models at WSD task. Like WDM, Decision Lists determine the proper sense of a polysemous word in a context by only using the frequency information between each feature and the polysemous word. However, the main difference between WDM and Decision Lists is whether the model depends on several informative words(WDM) or on just one informative word(Decision Lists). In this paper, the weight of a feature at Decision Lists is calculated as follows[10]:

$$weight(s_i, f_j) = \log \frac{P(f_j|s_i)}{P(f_j| \sim s_i)} \tag{5}$$

In the experiments, we have used the additive smoothing[4][11] for the conditional probability with zero in order to alleviate the sparse data problems.

Table 9 shows the experimental results of WDM and Decision Lists on SENSEVAL-1 and SENSEVAL-2 data. After filtering the senses by using MWE, each model disambiguates the word senses on the given feature spaces. In the table, a character L means local context, T topical context, and C collocation

---

[4] For additive smoothing, following equation is employed:

$$P(f_j|s_i) = \frac{\delta + c(f_j, s_i)}{\delta|V| + \sum_{f_k} c(f_k, s_i)}$$

where $|V|$ is the number of features, and $c(f_j, s_i)$ is the frequency that f_j and s_i co-occur in the training corpus. δ is set to 0.000001, empirically.

context, and $C+T$ means that the feature space consists of the local context and the topical context, and so on. The best result for each PoS is printed in boldface.

Table 9. Experimental results of WDM and Decision Lists

		SENSEVAL-1		SENSEVAL-2	
feature space	word type	WDM(%)	DL(%)	WDM(%)	DL(%)
Local	Adjective	64.02	57.87	63.93	56.64
context	Noun	69.71	63.12	57.98	49.83
	Verb	62.26	52.58	49.00	41.14
	Overall	65.37	57.59	55.29	47.41
Topical	Adjective	66.12	39.25	67.45	44.40
context	Noun	59.48	45.07	62.43	41.56
	Verb	56.82	28.35	48.23	25.91
	Overall	59.79	36.83	57.39	35.54
Collocation	Adjective	64.10	59.50	60.29	55.60
context	Noun	75.13	70.76	58.89	52.45
	Verb	64.85	58.34	48.67	42.52
	Overall	68.47	63.15	54.88	48.87
L+T	Adjective	71.26	62.46	**70.83**	63.93
	Noun	69.90	64.80	67.73	59.29
	Verb	68.49	57.98	54.43	47.12
	Overall	69.60	61.45	62.73	55.04
L+C	Adjective	67.99	65.19	64.19	62.37
	Noun	75.67	72.58	60.66	57.35
	Verb	66.89	64.45	51.77	47.84
	Overall	70.35	67.60	57.58	54.27
T+C	Adjective	**75.62**	65.11	67.97	62.37
	Noun	76.85	72.71	**69.10**	60.66
	Verb	69.73	63.49	55.26	47.45
	Overall	73.61	67.23	63.12	55.45
L+T+C	Adjective	75.47	69.31	68.49	66.41
	Noun	**77.63**	74.22	68.70	63.11
	Verb	**70.57**	67.13	**56.31**	51.72
	Overall	**74.21**	70.20	**63.49**	58.94

According to the results shown in Table 9, we can claim that WDM is significantly better than Decision Lists both on SENSEVAL-1 data and SENSEVAL-2 data. In particular, WDM is more robust than Decision Lists referring to the results of the topical context. Among 32 words in SENSEVAL-1 data, WDM outperforms Decision Lists on 28 words with the feature space $L+T+B$, but on only two words, Decision Lists achieves better performance than WDM. Among 58 words at SENSEVAL-2 data, WDM outperforms Decision Lists on 36 words, but Decision Lists outperform WDM on 13 words on the feature space $L+T+B$.

It is also observed in the table that the model using the feature space composed of several contexts shows better performance, and that most of the best performances are achieved using three types of context together. Unlike the results reported by [3], even for nouns the local context is more reliable as an indicator of sense than the topical context, and for adjective words the topical context is better than the local context at SENSEVAL-1 data. The most difficult part-of-speech to disambiguate is the verb although the average sense number (8.25) of nouns is larger than the average sense number (7.38) of verbs at SENSEVAL-1 data.

6   Conclusion

In this paper, we have proposed a two-phase WSD method, which firstly filters the relevant senses with MWE and secondly disambiguates the senses based on WDM. The experimental results on SENSEVAL-1 data and on SENSEVAL-2 data showed: (1) MWE contributes to WSD as a sense tagger or as a sense filter, (2) MWE as a sense filter is more useful than as a sense tagger, (3) MWE is not recognized as a significant feature in the collocation context, thus it must be handled separate from the feature space at WSD field, and (4) the proposed model, WDM, is more effective for WSD than Decision Lists, which is known as one of the state of the art models at WSD task.

However, the contribution of MWE to WSD is not high, since the coverage of MWE is very low. In the future, we will try to expand the current sets of MWE by recognizing the collocations from the corpus. We will also attempt to compare WDM with other methods based on the statistics, such as Naïve Bayesian Classifier.

Acknowledgements. This work was supported by a Korea University Grant.

References

1. Ide, N., Veronis, J.: Introduction to the special issue on word sense disambiguation: The state of the art. Computational Linguistics **24** (1998) 1–40
2. Ng, H.T., Lee, H.B.: Integrating multiple knowledge sources to disambiguate word sense: An exemplar-based approach. In Joshi, A., Palmer, M., eds.: Proceedings of the Thirty-Fourth Annual Meeting of the Association for Computational Linguistics, San Francisco, Morgan Kaufmann Publishers (1996) 40–47
3. Leacock, C., Chodorow, M., , Miller, G.A.: Using corpus statistics and WordNet relations for sense identification. Computational Linguistics **24** (1998) 147–165
4. Yarowsky, D., Florian, R.: Evaluating sense disambiguation across diverse parameter spaces. Natural Language Engineering **8** (2002) 293–310
5. Mihalcea, R.F.: Word sense disambiguation with pattern learning and automatic feature selection. Natural Language Engineering **8** (2002) 343–358
6. Yarowsky, D.: Decision lists for lexical ambiguity resolution: Application to accent restoration in spanish and french. In: Proceedings of ACL-94. (1994) 88–95

7. Agirre, E., Martinez, D.: Exploring automatic word sense disambiguation with decision lists and the web. In: Proceedings of the Semantic Annotation And Intelligent Annotation Workshop organized by COLING, Luxembourg (2000) 11–19
8. Fellbaum, C.: An WordNet Electronic Lexical Database. The MIT Press (1998)
9. Lee, H., Rim, H.C., Seo, J.: Word sense disambiguation using the classification information model. Computers and the Humanities **34** (2000) 141–146
10. Yarowsky, D.: Hierarchical decision lists for word sense disambiguation. Computers and the Humanities **34** (2000) 179–186
11. Chen, S.F., Goodman, J.T.: An empirical study of smoothing techniques for language modeling. Technical Report TR-10-98, Computer Science Group, Harvard University (1998)

Combining EWN and Sense-Untagged Corpus for WSD

Iulia Nica[1,2], Mª. Antònia Martí[1], Andrés Montoyo[3], and Sonia Vázquez[3]

[1] CLiC-Department of General Linguistics
University of Barcelona, Spain
amarti@ub.edu
[2] University of Iasi, Romania
iulia@clic.fil.ub.es
[3] Department of Information Systems and Languages
University of Alicante, Spain
{montoyo, svazquez}@dlsi.ua.es

Abstract. In this paper we propose a mixed method for Word Sense Disambiguation, which combines lexical knowledge from EuroWordNet with corpora. The method tries to give a partial solution to the problem of the gap between lexicon and corpus by means of the approximation of the corpus to the lexicon. On the basis of the interaction that holds in natural language between the syntagmatic and the paradigmatic axes, we extract from corpus implicit information of paradigmatic type. On the information thus obtained we work with the information, also paradigmatic, contained in EWN. We evaluate the method and interpret the results.

Keywords: Word Sense Disambiguation, semantic annotation

1 Introduction

Word Sense Disambiguation (WSD) is an open problem for Natural Language Processing. The focus of interest in the area of WSD has been centred principally on the heuristics used and less on the linguistic aspects of the task. However, some recent experiments ([22], [32]) have revealed that the process is in a higher degree dependent on the information used than on the algorithms that exploit it.

On the basis of these results, the present paper investigates the intensive use of linguistic knowledge in the process of Word Sense Disambiguation. We analyse some essential questions for the task of WSD: the distance between the information in the lexicon and the one in the corpus, and the identification and the treatment of local context for an ambiguous occurrence.

Depending on the sense characterisation which is taken as reference in the WSD process, there took shape two principal approaches to the task: knowledge-driven methods, which use structured lexical sources (machine readable dictionaries, semantic nets, etc.) and corpus-based methods, which use sense-tagged examples. Between these two approaches there are the mixed systems, which combine two types of lexical sources.

A. Gelbukh (Ed.): CICLing 2004, LNCS 2945, pp. 188–200, 2004.
© Springer-Verlag Berlin Heidelberg 2004

Both the knowledge-driven and the corpus-based approaches to WSD have their limitations. By one hand, the knowledge-based systems use the information, principally a paradigmatic one, contained in the structured lexical sources. Thus they are affected by the problem of the gap between lexicon and corpus ([9]). The solution commonly adopted is to approximate the structured lexical sources to corpora by incorporating syntagmatic information ([27]). This approach is limited by the high cost of the extraction and representation process.

On the other hand, we have the corpus-based DSA systems, which do use syntagmatic information. These systems obtained better results in the two SENSEVAL competitions. Still, they are highly dependent on the availability of annotated examples with senses, since there is a direct proportion between the quantity of such examples and the quality of results. The manual acquisition of sense-tagged corpora is difficult and costly, so there are alternative proposals for their automatic obtaining ([6], [29], [31], [10], [15], etc.). The few evaluations of the automatically sense-tagged corpora are not very positive (for example, [1]).

In the present paper we propose a method for WSD which combines sense information contained in EuroWordNet ([28]) with the corpus. At the basis of our approach lies the interaction between the syntagmatic axis and the paradigmatic axis that holds in natural language. This allows us to extract and to exploit the implicit information, of paradigmatic type, present in the sense-untagged corpora and related to a word occurrence to be disambiguated. We combine then the paradigmatic information extracted from corpora with the one, also paradigmatic, contained in EWN, about the word and its senses. We achieve in this way the sense assignment for the ambiguous occurrence.

Our proposal assumes only a previous analysis of morphosyntactic type.[1] We have restricted ourselves to the analysis of Spanish nouns, but it can be equally adapted to the disambiguation of other parts of speech and extended to other languages.

After this introduction, in Section 2 we describe our approximation to WSD and in Section 3 the strategy of disambiguation we propose; in Section 4 we focus on the implementation of the method and in Section 5 we present its evaluation; finally, in Section 6, we formulate the conclusions and establish the directions for the future work.

2   Approach to WSD

Our approach to the lexical disambiguation is based on two issues we consider essential for the task of WSD: a) the identification and the treatment of the context of an ambiguous occurrence, and b) the distance between lexicon and corpus.

Identification and treatment of the context of an ambiguous occurrence. Context, in WSD, is usually divided into basic categories: local context and topical context. We have restricted our attention to local context. It has been frequently defined as a window, of previously established dimension, on both sides of the occurrence to be disambiguated.

---

[1] We used for Spanish the POS-tagger described in [3].

The exploitation of local context for the sense disambiguation task has been done basically following a "bag of words" approach, in which there are taken into account only the lexical content words and ignored the functional ones.

Another approach, more and more frequent, consists in using also the functional words that relate the ambiguous occurrence to the rest of lexical content units in the predefined context. From this perspective, context is treated as n-grams ([30], [21], [14], etc.) or as syntactic relations. In these cases, the syntactic information used for WSD has been generally limited, with some few exceptions (for example, [11], [26]), to verb-subject and verb-object relations ([18], [10], [5], [2], [13], etc.).

Some positive results ([32], [14], [7], etc.) have proven the utility of the contiguous functional words for disambiguating the ambiguous occurrence. Still, the use of grammatical content words in the WSD task has been performed especially within the example-based approach, and so it is dependent on a sense tagged corpus. If the syntactic relations are to be used, the corpus must be annotated also at the syntactic level.

Although local context is one of the subjects of interest in the WSD area, there is not a systematic analysis about how different types of information concerning local context contribute to WSD ([8]). Some recent attempts in this direction are [14], [23]. Lately, there is an increasing interest to use different contextual parameters for sense tagging, and to use algorithms for identifying the most informative parameter with respect to the sense ([14], [7], [32]). Still, both the delimitation and the treatment of context have been less investigated with linguistic criteria.

In our approach, local context of each ambiguous word must be specifically based on linguistic criteria. Our hypothesis is that, for nouns, strict local context of one word contains lexico-syntactic relations highly relevant for its disambiguation.

In order to allow a formal treatment of the local context for an ambiguous occurrence and to identify its lexico-syntactic relations there expressed, we introduce the concept of syntactic pattern.

We formally define a syntactic pattern as a triplet corresponding to a lexico-syntactic relation, made up by two units L1 and L2 of lexical content (nouns, adjectives, verbs, adverbs) and a lexico-syntactic pattern R expressing relations of dependency, coordination or simple adjacency:

$$L1 \quad - \quad R \quad - \quad L2.$$

This pattern includes the case of R with null value, as in simple adjacency or in noun-adjective relationship. Examples: *autoridad*-n *en_materia_de*-prep *fracasos*-n, *autoridad*-n *sanitaria*-adj.

Syntactic patterns include both treatments of local context: n-grams and syntactic relations.

From this perspective, a polysemous word and each of its senses can be characterised by means of the syntactic patterns in which it can participate.

Distance between lexicon and corpus. Contrary to the usual solution for filling the gap between lexicon and corpus by incorporating syntagmatic information in the lexical sources, we investigate the inverse possibility, bringing the corpus next to the lexicon.

We consider that the implicit information in corpora is exploitable by means of word grouping. As a basis for clustering, we took a fundamental property of natural language: the interaction between syntagmatic and paradigmatic axes. Words that follow one another in the oral or written string are situated on the syntagmatic axis, and establish local relationship that assure the coherence of the sentence. At the same time, a fixed element in a specific point of the syntagmatic axis can be substituted by other words, obtaining thus equally coherent sentences. The elements that substitute a certain element in a syntagmatic string belong to a paradigmatic axis, and establish paradigmatic relations. In this way, identical syntagmatic conditions delimit word sets of paradigmatic type: we assume that the different words which can appear in a position of a concrete syntactic pattern will have related senses, belonging to one or several common conceptual zones.[2]

Example:

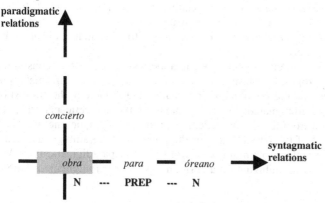

In the figure, the words *pieza* and *concierto* can substitute the noun *obra* in the syntactic pattern *obra para órgano*: *pieza para órgano* and *concierto para órgano* are perfectly possible in Spanish and indeed they appear in the CREA corpus[3]. The words *obra*, *concierto* and *pieza* are situated on a paradigmatic axis and establish syntagmatic relations between them.

The experiments of Miller and Charles ([16]) confirm that humans derive word semantic similarity from the similarity of the contexts they are used in.

Our approach is based, thus, on the local context and on the establishment of paradigmatic relations between elements mutually substitutable obtained starting from a syntactic pattern.

3   Strategy for WSD

The previous considerations lead us to a different approach to WSD: the occurrence to be disambiguated is considered not separately, but integrated into a syntactic pattern,

---

[2]   "Syntagmatic sense relations [...] are an expression of coherence constraints. Paradigmatic sense relations, on the other hand, operate within the sets of choices. Each such set represents the way the language articulates, or divides up, some conceptual area, and each displays a greater or lesser degree of systematic structuring. Paradigmatic relations are an expression of such structuring. [...] Paradigmatic and syntagmatic relations function in tandem, syntagmatic relations delimiting the space within which paradigmatic relations operate." ([4: 149])

[3]   The corpus of Real Academia Española, http://www.rae.es.

and its disambiguation is carried out in relation to this pattern. In this approach, the integration of a word occurrence into local syntactic patterns is a first approximation to its meaning in context.

This strategy is based on the hypothesis that the local syntactic patterns in which an ambiguous occurrence participates have decisive influence on its meaning and thus they are highly relevant for the sense identification. In other words, we assume that a word sense in context is delimited principally by the sum of restrictions that the local syntactic patterns operate on its meaning. With the purpose of facilitating the study and the formal treatment, we operate a reduction: we assume that every syntactic pattern has an independent influence on the meaning of the ambiguous word. In this way, we exploit separately each of the syntactic patterns for the sense disambiguation task, and then we confront these individual assignations for the final decision to be taken on the occurrence sense.

The integration of the ambiguous occurrence in a local syntactic pattern constitutes the key element of our proposal for bringing together the paradigmatic information in the lexicon (here EWN) and the syntagmatic information identifiable in the context of the occurrence to be disambiguated. On the grounds of the syntactic patterns, we carried out the transition from the syntagmatic axis to the paradigmatic one: we identify in the corpus the set of the possibilities for the position of the ambiguous occurrence into the syntactic pattern, obtaining so a word class of paradigmatic type. We apply then on this class a disambiguation algorithm based on paradigmatic relations from EWN.

4   Implementation

The word sense disambiguation process for an occurrence of a polysemous noun X will consist then, in our approach, of the following operations:

Step 1. We identify the syntactic patterns S_k in which the ambiguous occurrence X appears in the sentence (section 4.1).

Step 2. We exploit the previously identified syntactic patterns S_k for the sense assignment to the ambiguous occurrence X (section 4.2).

For every identified pattern S_k:

2a. We look, into the corpus, for the nouns p_j which can appear into the pattern S_k as substitutes of X. We obtain a paradigm P_{Sk} corresponding to this position of the pattern (section 4.2.1.).

2b. We apply the WSD heuristic on the paradigm P_{Sk}. We try in this way to identify lexico-semantic relations, from those in EWN, between the words in the paradigm previously delimited (section 4.2.2.).

Step 3. We establish the sense of the ambiguous occurrence X by confronting the individual proposals obtained for its sense in step 2°.

In the present article we treat only the first two steps. The last one needs a more detailed study, as the way to combine the proposals from the individual patterns for the final decision on the sense of the ambiguous occurrence is not trivial. The comparison of the results obtained here using each syntactic pattern will be very useful for this purpose. Due to the hypothesis of the autonomous influence of each syntactic pattern on the meaning of the ambiguous occurrence, the limitation to steps 1° and 2° is not very strong. In step 2°, which is fundamental for the strategy, we consider a unique pattern at once; with respect to this reduction, step 3° can be seen as a generalisation. Our principal objective in this work is to analyse the measure in which a local syntactic pattern containing an ambiguous occurrence, contributes to the identification of its sense, and so our interest focuses on step 2°.

We present below the operations implied in the two first steps.

4.1   Identification of the Local Syntactic Patterns

The delimitation of the syntactic patterns that contain the ambiguous occurrence is principally performed at the level of morphosyntactic categories, even if we also take into account the lemmas. To do this, the sentence is previously POS-tagged.

The sense assignation is very dependent on the quality of the pattern identification. In order to assure a proper extraction of syntactic patterns, we preferred to limit it in a first step to some few structural variants, although the variety of syntactic patterns in which a noun can appear is considerably large. Therefore, on the basis of the distributional and syntactic properties of nouns, we predefined two basic types of morphosyntactic patterns in which nouns take part:

N ADJ

N1 PREP N2.

In the patterns with two nouns, N1 PREP N2, we only considered the ones where the nominal occurrence to be disambiguated occupy the first position, N1.

Once we have found sequences corresponding to these morphosyntactic patterns, we consider them also at the lemma level, and it is with these patterns both of lemmas and morphosyntactic categories that we go on in the implementation of the strategy. For example, if we have found the sequence *canales-canal*-N *de-de*-PREP *televisión-televisión*-N, we consider the pattern as *canal*-N *de*-PREP *televisión*-N.

The patterns can have discontinuous realisations in texts. To cover these cases, we pre-established the following morphosyntactic schemes for the search into the corpus orientated to the identification of the considered syntactic pattern:

N ADJ1 (CONJ* ADJ2)

N1 (ADJ1) PREP* (DET) (ADJ2) N2,

where the units between brackets are optional and the asterisk indicates restrictions.

The sequences identified in the corpus starting from these schemes are to be split up into simple syntactic patterns. For example, the scheme:

N ADJ1 CONJ* ADJ2

splits up into two simple syntactic patterns: N ADJ1 and N ADJ1, meanwhile the scheme:

N1 ADJ PREP* N2,

splits into: N1 ADJ and N1 PREP* N2.

So, a particular sequence as:

> *autoridades-autoridad*-N *sanitarias-sanitaria*-ADJ *de-de*-PREP *muchos-mucho*-DET *países-país*-N,

should be finally divided into: *autoridad*-N *sanitaria*-ADJ and *autoridad*-N *de*-PREP *país*-N.

Since our purpose is to reach a high reliability in the extraction of syntactic patterns, we imposed restrictions on the functional elements. We took as reference point, in this action, an empirical study, for some few nouns, on the extraction of syntactic patterns exclusively on the basis of the mentioned structural criteria. We limited the conjunctions to the two most frequent ones: CONJ* = {*y*, *o*}. The selection of prepositions raised difficulties, due to its strong dependence on the noun to be disambiguated. Still, the empirical study revealed us that the dominating and also sufficiently reliable for a correct extraction of the syntactic patterns is the preposition *de*. We choose thus to consider only the preposition *de*. Obviously, taking into account uniquely the preposition *de* sensibly implicates to limit the coverage of the method, in quantitative and especially in qualitative terms. There are others the prepositions that characterise a noun in a more specific way and so can bring more information for its disambiguation.

4.2   A Heuristic for Sense Identification Using Local Syntactic Patterns

The use of syntactic patterns for sense assignment consists in two basic operations:

a) We look in the corpus for words that could feet into a given syntactic pattern on the position of the word to be disambiguated and we delimit in this way the corresponding paradigm to this position of the pattern.
b) We identify lexico-semantic relations (from those in EWN) between the words of the paradigm previously delimited, with the help of a WSD algorithm which exploits EWN. In this way we assign to these words one of the senses they have in EWN.

4.2.1   Extraction of the Associated Paradigm

Once we have identified the structure of the pattern S_{k0}: X_0-R_0-Y_0 in which the ambiguous occurrence X_0 is integrated, we maintain fixed the rest of the elements R_0 and Y_0 of the pattern (excepting the optional element DET and, for the X_0 PREP$_0$ N$_0$ pattern, also ADJ), in terms of lemmas and morphosyntactic categories, and let variable the position of the occurrence to be disambiguated X_0, within the same part of speech as the occurrence to be disambiguated (here noun). We look in the corpus for the possible nouns X to appear into the pattern, on the position of the ambiguous occurrence X_0.

The search into the corpus must be carried out in a similar way to the one done for the delimitation of the patterns, taking into account the discontinuous realisations of the pattern in the text. For example, if we have to disambiguate X_0 in the pattern:

$$X_0 \, PREP_0 \, N_0,$$

we maintain the elements $PREP_0$ and N_0 fixed at the lemma and morphosyntactic level and we look for the substitutes X of X_0 (with predetermined part of speech, the one of X_0, here N) in all the possible realisations of the pattern into the corpus:

$$X \, (ADJ) \, PREP_0 \, (DET) \, (ADJ) \, N_0.$$

We put into brackets the optional elements and marked with an 0 index the elements fixed at the lemma level; the elements without the 0 index can vary at the lemma level.

The possible elements X will be equally identified at the lemma level. The substitutes X of X_0 obtained in this way, together with X_0, form a set P_{Sk0} of paradigmatic type.

4.2.2   Disambiguation of the Elements in the Paradigm

We apply on the paradigmatic set P_{Sk0}, previously extracted, a WSD heuristic. We used, as WSD algorithm, the Specificity Mark ([17]). The intuitive base of this algorithm is the following: the more common information two concepts share the more related they will be. In EWN, the common information shared by two concepts corresponds to the father concept of both in the hierarchy, called Specificity Mark, SM, by the authors. The heuristic takes as input a noun set and looks for the SM in EuroWordNet with the bigger density of input words in its subtree[4]. It chooses as correct for every input word the sense situated in the sub-tree of the SM so identified, and it lets undisambiguated the words without senses in this subtree.

The application of the heuristic on the paradigm P_{Sk0} leads to the sense assignment, one or more, for X_0 and for the rest of the elements in $P_{Sk0.}$ In other words, the disambiguation for X_0 as for its substitutes X can be partial.

4.3   Example

We illustrate the strategy with an example from Senseval-2, the occurrences number 22 and 26 of the noun *corona*. We have to disambiguate *corona* in the following sentences:

22: *Hay también **coronas** de laurel, cuando la hoja del laurel va tomando el color de la ceniza o de arenas claras con un tinte beis.*

26: *Desde, todos los años, el día de los Caídos y el aniversario de la liberación de Palomares, las fuerzas vivas del pueblo y los chicos del Frente depositaban una simbólica **corona** de laurel sobre la tumba del mártir Gumersindo en el panteón familiar de los "Rameros", y, según*

---

[4] In its initial version, the algorithm of Specificity Marks was applied on the nouns contained in the sentence of the ambiguous occurrence, including the .

fue creciendo una nueva generación, las mozas quinceañeras se hacían cruces de que sus tías hubieran preferido quedarse solteronas antes que viudas de un héroe.

We first identify the local syntactic pattern. It is the same for both occurrences, as we work at the lemmas and morphosyntactic level:

CORONA *de laurel,*

and it corresponds to the structural pattern:

N1-PREP-N2.

In order to extract the paradigm associated to *corona* in this pattern, we fix the elements *de* and *laurel* and let variable the position of *corona* in the pattern. That is we look in the corpus for the nouns X, in terms of lemma, that can appear in the pattern:

X-N *de*-PREP *laurel*-N,

following the search schema:

X-N (ADJ) *de*-PREP (DET) (ADJ) *laurel*-N.

In this way, we found in the corpus the paradigm:

{*corona, friso, hoja, hojita, punta, rama, ramo, sombra, variedad*}.

By applying the ME algorithm on this paradigm, we assigned the following senses from EWN to *corona* and to the nouns that can substitute it in the pattern:

corona_3 (synset: 6987126), *hoja_3* (synset: 3574525), *rama_1* (synset: 14551953), *ramo_1* (synset: 645855), *sombra_1* (synset: 12655007), *friso_4* (synset: 6848840) and *friso_5* (synset: 6017013), *punta_5* (synset: 11396011) and *punta_9* (synset: 4671491), *variedad_1* (synset: 11137273) and *variedad_3* (synset: 1752450)[5].

The sense 3 in EWN obtained for *corona* in this pattern corresponds with the reference sense 1 in the golden corpus of Senseval-2 for both occurrences. We disambiguated thus simultaneously two occurrences of the same noun in different sentences.

5   Evaluation. Discussion

We carried out a preliminary control evaluation, with the purpose to verify the validity of our proposal. Specifically, we tested the practicability of two operations inside our strategy:

- disambiguation of an ambiguous occurrence by operating with paradigmatic information related to it, and

- acquisition of this information from untagged corpus at sense level, in an automatic way, starting from the local syntactic patterns of the ambiguous occurrence.

Thus the testing was projected as an orientating experimentation on these two aspects, being less of our interest the real quality of the disambiguation process.

---

[5] The diminutive *hojita* was not found in EWN, so it was not taken into consideration in the disambiguation process. On the other hand, the disambiguation was only partial for the nouns *friso, punta* and *variedad*.

In the preliminary test we present here we used LEXESP ([25]) as search corpus, with only five millions words, in order to speed up the testing. To achieve an estimation in objective terms, we implemented the method in the Senseval-2 conditions, on all seventeen words for Spanish. The obtained results are:

Precision	37 %
Recall	7 %
Coverage	16 %

The recall of 7% is low comparative to the level reached in the Spanish Senseval-2, between 45% and 66% for nouns ([24]). The precision, however, is of 37% on average, but it arrives to more than 50% in nine cases and to more than 60% in five cases on seventeen. The coverage, as we expected because of the little set of structural patterns we considered, is also low: 16%.

The modest level of the results is partially due to the use of a small corpus. Our method is highly dependent on the search into the corpus, equally in the delimitation of the local syntactic patterns (step 1), and in the extraction of the paradigm associated to the ambiguous occurrence integrated in a syntactic pattern (step 2a) and so, implicitly, in the quality of disambiguation (step 2b). Therefore this severe limitation had a negative impact on the disambiguation process, both in terms of coverage and of precision, thus of recall.

Furthermore, we have to stress that the evaluation has been performed along the case by case approach to WSD: it focuses only the starting ambiguous occurrences. It has not been taken into account the sense assignment to the other words in the paradigm extracted from the corpus for the position of the occurrence to be disambiguated in the syntactic pattern. Thus the evaluation does not estimate all the results obtained in the disambiguation, and the data for coverage and precision are partial.

Even if the results are low, we think that we did obtain positive evidence in favour of our proposal: we can do disambiguation with the help of paradigmatic information for the ambiguous occurrence, and we can obtain this information from untagged corpora at sense level, starting from syntactic patterns.

We also carried out an empirical study on some few nouns to verify the performance and the efficiency of the two steps in the disambiguation process. This study revealed us two principal limitations of the method: the heterogeneity of the paradigm extracted from the corpus, and the data sparseness, as the strategy largely depends on the search in the corpus.

6   Conclusions and Future Work

We present in this article a concrete method for using untagged corpora at sense level in Word Sense Disambiguation. The strategy proposed for sense tagging is based on the semantic interaction between the paradigmatic and syntagmatic axes which holds in natural language. This property allows us to identify in the corpus paradigmatic information related to the occurrence to be disambiguated, and on this one apply the information equally paradigmatic from the lexicon (EWN). We minimise thus the gap between lexicon and corpus that affects the process of WSD.

The method takes as unit to disambiguate an ambiguous occurrence integrated into a syntactic pattern. This integration confers to the process a large potential, as it allows the simultaneous disambiguation of different occurrences of a word in any text, when they appear in the same pattern.

An important characteristic of our proposal is the independence on a corpus tagged at sense or syntactic level. The method only needs a POS-tagger, for the analysis of the sentence in which occurs the token to be disambiguated and for the analysis of the search corpus.

We performed a preliminary testing of our method, on a limited corpus of five million words. The evaluation developed in the conditions of Senseval-2 indicates a low level of performance of our method, due partially to the limited corpus: 37% of precision, 7% of recall, 16% of coverage. The principal difficulties of the method are the heterogeneity of the paradigm corresponding to a position in a syntactic pattern and data sparseness.

Still, we obtained positive evidence in favour of our proposal: we can do disambiguation with the help of paradigmatic information for the ambiguous occurrence, and we can obtain this information from untagged corpora at sense level, starting from syntactic patterns.

As future work, we have to overcome the present limitations of the method with respect both to coverage and precision. We first have to repeat the test on a broader corpus, as EFE or on Internet, and re-evaluate the method. In order to enlarge the coverage, we will extend the structural patterns to be identified in the context of the ambiguous occurrence, always in parallel with a better filtering of them. Related to precision, we are currently developing different implementations of this procedure, which vary with respect to: the reference characterisation for senses; the algorithm to apply on the paradigm associated to a position in a syntactic pattern; and the modality to exploit the syntactic pattern.

At the same time, the dependence on corpus search which causes the problem of data sparseness has it good side: the flexibility of the method with respect to the corpus used allows it to constantly improve in parallel with the enlargement of the corpus.

If there is evidence that there can be obtained good sense assignments by using paradigmatic information, we believe that a next step is to study its combination with the syntagmatic information in the process of disambiguation.

Our proposal finds applications to the enrichment of knowledge associated to senses and to the obtaining of sense-tagged examples for corpora-based WSD systems.

At the same time, we are interested in the study of different aspects related to the contribution of local context, considered as syntactic patterns, on the word meaning, as well as the balance between the syntagmatic vs. the paradigmatic pressure on the word meaning. Thus, the proposal has theoretical implications, as it contributes to reveal the incidence of syntax on the word meaning and it could allow the study of objective criteria for sense discrimination.

References

1. Agirre, E. and D. Martinez, 2000. Exploring automatic WSD with decision lists and the Web. In: *Proceedings of the COLING Workshop on Semantic Annotation and Intelligent Content*, Saabrücken
2. Agirre, E. and D. Martínez, 2001. Learning class-to-class selectional preferences. In: *Proceedings of the ACL CONLL'2001 Workshop*, Tolouse
3. Civit, M., 2003. *Criterios de etiquetación y desambiguación morfosintáctica de corpus en español*, Ph.D.Thesis, University of Barcelona
4. Cruse, Alan, 2000. *Meaning in Language. An Introduction to Semantics and Pragmatics*, Oxford University Press
5. Federici, S., S. Montemagni and V. Pirelli, 2000. ROMANSEVAL: Results for Italian by SENSE, *Computers and the Humanities. Special Issue: Evaluating WSD Programs*, **34 (1-2)**
6. Gale, W.A., K.W. Church, and D. Yarowsky, 1992. "One sense per discourse". In: *Proceedings of DARPA speech and Natural Language Workshop*, Harriman, NY
7. Hoste, V., I. Hendrickx, W. Daelemans and A. van den Bosch, 2002. Parameter optimisation for machine-learning of WSD, *Natural Language Engineering, 8 (4)*
8. Ide, N. and J. Véronis, 1998. Introduction to the Special Issue on Word Sense Disambiguation. The State of the Art, *Computational Linguistics. Special Issue on Word Sense Disambiguation*, **24 (1)**
9. Kilgariff, A., 1998. Bridging the gap between lexicon and corpus: convergence of formalisms. In: *Proceedings of LREC'1998*, Granada
10. Leacock, C., M. Chodorow and G.A. Miller, 1998. Using Corpus Statistics and WordNet Relations for Sense Identification, *Computational Linguistics. Special Issue on Word Sense Disambiguation*, **24 (1)**
11. Lin, D., 1997. Using Syntactic Dependency as Local Context to Resolve Word Sense Ambiguity. In: *Proceedings of ACL and EACL'97*, Morgan Kaufman Publishers, San Francisco
12. Manning, C.D. and H. Schütze, 1999. *Foundations of Statistical Natural Language Processing*, 3rd printing, The MIT Press, Cambridge-London, cap. 7: *Word Sense Disambiguation*, 229-263
13. Martínez D., E. Agirre E. and L. Màrquez L, 2002. Syntactic Features for High Precision Word Sense Disambiguation. In: *Proceedings of the 19th International Conference on Computational Linguistics (COLING 2002)*, Taipei, Taiwan.
14. Mihalcea, R., 2002. WSD with pattern learning and feature selection, *Natural Language Engineering, 8(4)*, Cambridge University Press
15. Mihalcea, R. and D. Moldovan, 1999. An Automatic Method for Generating Sense Tagged Corpora. In: *Proceedings of AAAI '99*, Orlando
16. Miller, G. and W. Charles, 1991. Contextual correlates of semantic similarity, *Language and Cognitive Processes*, *6(1)*
17. Montoyo, A. and M. Palomar, 2000. Word Sense Disambiguation with Specification Marks in Unrestricted Texts. In: *Proceedings of the 11th International Workshop on DEXA*, Greenwich, London
18. Ng, H.T. and H.B. Lee, 1996. Integrating Multiple Knowledge Sources to Disambiguate Word Sense: An Exemplar-Based Approach. In: *Proceedings of the 34th Annual Meeting of the ACL*
19. Nica, I., M. A. Martí and A. Montoyo, 2003. Colaboración entre información paradigmática y sintagmática en la Desambiguación Semántica Automática, *XX Congreso de la SEPLN 2003*, Alcalá de Henares, Spain
20. Nica, I., M.A. Martí and A. Montoyo, 2003. Automatic sense (pre-)tagging by syntactic patterns. In: *Proceedings of International Conference on Recent Advances in Natural Language Processing (RANLP-03)*, Borovets, Bulgaria

21. Pedersen, T., 2001. A decision tree of bigrams is an accurate predictor of word sense. In: *Proceedings of NAACL 2001*, Pittsburg
22. Pedersen, T., 2002a. A Baseline Methodology for Word Sense Disambiguation. In: *Proceedings of the Third International Conference on Intelligent Text Processing and Computational Linguistics*, February, Mexico City
23. Pedersen, T., 2002b. Assessing System Agreement and Instance Difficulty in the Lexical Sample Tasks of SENSEVAL-2. In: *Proceedings of the Workshop on Word Sense Disambiguation: Recent Successes and Future Directions*, Philadelphia
24. Rigau, G., M. Taulé, A. Fernández and J. Gonzalo, 2001. Framework and results in the Spanish SENSEVAL. In: Preiss, J. and D. Yarowsky, 2001 (eds.), Proceedings of the SENSEVAL-2 Workshop. In conjunction with ACL'2001/EACL'2001, Toulouse
25. Sebastián, N., M.A. Martí, M. F. Carreiras and F. Cuetos Gómez, 2000. *Lexesp, léxico informatizado del español*, Edicions de la Universitat de Barcelona
26. Stetina, J., S. Kurohashi and M. Nagao, 1998. General WSD Method Based on a Full Sentential Context. In: *Proceedings of COLING-ACL Workshop*, Montreal
27. Véronis, J., 2001. Sense tagging: does it make sense?. Paper presented at the Corpus Linguistics'2001 Conference, Lancaster, U.K
28. Vossen, P., 1998 (ed.). *EUROWORDNET. A Multilingual Database with Lexical Semantic Networks*, Kluwer Academic Publishers, Dordrecht
29. Yarowsky, D., 1992. Word-Sense Disambiguation Using Statistical Models of Roget's Categories Trained on Large Corpora. In: *Proceedings of COLING-92*, Nantes, France
30. Yarowsky, D., 1993. One Sense per Collocation. In: *DARPA Workshop on Human Language Technology*, Princeton
31. Yarowsky, D., 1995. Unsupervised word sense disambiguation rivalising supervised methods. In: *Proceedings of ACL '95*, Dublin
32. Yarowsky, D. and R. Florian, 2002. Evaluating sense disambiguation across diverse parameter spaces, *Natural Language Engineering, 8(4),* Cambridge University Press

Feature Selection
for Chinese Character Sense Discrimination

Zheng-Yu Niu and Dong-Hong Ji

Institute for Infocomm Research
21 Heng Mui Keng Terrace, Singapore 119613, Republic of Singapore
{zniu, dhji}@i2r.a-star.edu.sg

Abstract. Word sense discrimination is to group occurrences of a word into clusters based on unsupervised classification method, where each cluster consists of occurrences having same meaning. Feature extraction method has been used to reduce the dimension of context vector in English word sense discrimination task. But if original dimension has a real meaning to users and relevant features exist in original dimensions, feature selection is a better choice for finding relevant features. In this paper we apply two unsupervised feature selection schemes to Chinese character sense discrimination, which are entropy based feature filter and Minimum Description Length based feature wrapper. Using precision evaluation and known ground-truth classification result, our preliminary experiment results demonstrate that feature selection method performs better than feature extraction method on Chinese character sense discrimination task.

1 Introduction

Word sense discrimination is to group occurrences of a word into clusters based on unsupervised learning method, where the occurrences in same cluster have same meaning [15]. In contrast with word sense disambiguation, word sense discrimination determines only which occurrences have the same meaning, but not what the meaning is. Compared with supervised word sense disambiguation, the burden to provide lexicon, hand tagged corpus or thesaurus can be avoided in word sense discrimination.

In [15] the author presents context group discrimination algorithm to solve word sense discrimination problem. Singular Value Decomposition (SVD) technique is used to reduce the dimension of context vectors. Principle Component Analysis (or Karhunen Loeve transformation, Singular Value Decomposition) is a well-established unsupervised feature extraction technique [3]. But if original dimension has a real meaning to users and relevant features exist in original dimensions, feature extraction technique is not appropriate for finding relevant features. The reason is that (1) the combination of original dimensions is difficult to interpret, and (2) the irrelevant original dimension are not clearly removed because they are required to determine the new dimension, and this will deteriorate the performance of clustering algorithm. In Chinese language, an ambiguous

A. Gelbukh (Ed.): CICLing 2004, LNCS 2945, pp. 201–208, 2004.
© Springer-Verlag Berlin Heidelberg 2004

character may have different meaning when it is part of different words. Some characters in the context of ambiguous character's occurrence can indicate semantic component of ambiguous characters. Important features are included in these characters. So feature selection should be more effective than feature extraction for Chinese character sense discrimination task.

Feature selection technique has a long history in the context of supervised learning, which can be categorized as filter approach and wrapper approach [7]. Supervised feature selection method has been applied to word sense disambiguation problem, which will use class label information to evaluate feature subset [10]. But in unsupervised learning, unsupervised learners have no access to class label in data set. Recently some researchers have explored to utilize the intrinsic property in data set or model selection criterion to help evaluate feature subsets for unsupervised feature selection [2,4,5,9,11,12,17]. In this paper, we investigate two unsupervised feature selection schemes for Chinese character sense discrimination: entropy based feature filter [2] and Minimum Description Length (MDL) based feature wrapper. Entropy based feature filter determines optimal feature subset via minimizing the entropy of data set in selected feature subspace. This method is based upon the assumption that a feature is irrelevant if the presence of it obscures the separability of data set. After feature filtering, a mixture model based clustering algorithm [1] is used to group data set in selected feature subspace and determine the correct number of clusters using MDL criterion. MDL-based feature wrapper finds optimal feature subset using MDL criterion. For every possible feature subset candidate, data set projected in feature subspace is clustered and clustering result is evaluated based on MDL criterion. The optimal feature subset and cluster number are determined via minimizing MDL criterion. Our preliminary results empirically demonstrate that feature selection algorithm can find relevant features and achieve better results than SVD technique on Chinese character sense discrimination problem.

We now give out the outline of this paper. In section 2 we will describe how to use feature selection algorithms to solve word sense discrimination problem. Section 3 will give out the experimental results of SVD technique, feature filter and feature wrapper on Chinese character sense disambiguation task. Then we will discuss some findings from these results. In section 4 we will conclude our work and suggest possible improvement.

2   Feature Selection for Word Sense Discrimination

In [15] the author presents context group discrimination algorithm for word sense discrimination. Next we will briefly formulate their data model for word sense discrimination.

Let D be context set of an ambiguous word's occurrences, then $D = \{d_n\}_{n=1}^{N}$, where d_n represents local context or global context of the n-th occurrence, and N is total number of this ambiguous word's occurrences.

W is used to denote all contextual words occurring in context set D, then $W = \{w_m\}_{m=1}^M$, where w_m denotes a contextual word occurring in D, and M is the total number of different contextual words.

Let V represent the second-order matrix, then $V = \{v(w_j)\}_{j=1}^M$, where $v(w_j)$ represents the word vector of contextual word w_j in second-order matrix.

H is the weight matrix of contextual words, then $H = \{h_{i,j}\}$, where $h_{i,j}$ represents the weight of word w_j in d_i, $1 \le i \le N$, and $1 \le j \le M$. In [15], they weight a word vector according to its discriminating potential. In our algorithm, we do not associate a weight with word vector when conducting feature selection because the importance of a word is unknown before finding the optimal feature subset. We set $h_{i,j}$ as one if the word w_j occurs in d_i, otherwise it is set as zero.

Let C^{T1} denote context matrix of context set D in feature space T, and c_i be the ith row of C^T. The j-th dimension in T corresponds to word w_j in W, $1 \le j \le M$. Then c_i may be written as

$$c_i = \sum_{j=1}^M (h_{i,j}v(w_j)), 1 \le i \le N. \tag{1}$$

Then N-by-M matrix C^T can be factored as $(C^T)' = U \times diag(\delta_1, ..., \delta_p) \times V'$, where $p = \min(M, N)$. Then dimensionality reduction can be completed by keeping only the first k columns (from left to right) in matrix V, which corresponds to the k dimensional transformed space. This is the feature extraction technique used in [15].

In this paper, we do not conduct any space transformation on matrix C^T. Instead we try to select some feature subset t to minimize the value of entropy measure or MDL criterion on context vector matrix C^t, where $t = \{w_{i_1}, w_{i_2}, ..., w_{i_k}\}$, $1 \le i_1 < i_2 < ... < i_k \le M$, $1 \le k \le M$. Before feature subset selection, stop words and low-frequency words are removed, then remaining words are ranked according to their frequency in context set D. Search in the ranked feature set will help improve the efficiency of feature selection algorithm. Next we will describe the feature subset selection algorithm for word sense discrimination.

First, we select first r high-frequency features from the ranked feature list to let the percent of contexts containing at least one feature be no less than a given threshold τ. This is based on the assumption that in most of contexts there is at least one feature that indicates contextual similarity. In this paper we set τ as 0.9.

Then we conduct feature subset selection in word set W. The feature subset selection in word set W can be formulated as:

$$\hat{T} = \arg\min_{t \in T}\{criterion(C^t)\}, \tag{2}$$

where $\hat{T}$ is the optimal feature subspace, and $criterion$ is the entropy measure or MDL criterion. In the search process, the percent of contexts containing at least one feature will be no less than the given threshold τ always.

---

[1] In this paper, C^T denotes the representation of C in space T. We use C' to denote the transpose of C.

The entropy measure for matrix C represented in space t is defined as [2]

$$E(C^t) = -\sum_{i=1}^{N}\sum_{j=1}^{N}(S_{i,j}\log S_{i,j} + (1 - S_{i,j})\log(1 - S_{i,j})),\qquad(3)$$

where $S_{i,j}$ is the similarity between c_i and c_j. Then this entropy measure can be used to evaluate the separability of data set C^t.

The MDL criterion is given by [1]:

$$MDL(t, K, \hat{\theta}(t, K)) = -\sum_{n=1}^{N}\log(\sum_{i=1}^{K}p(c_n|k, \theta_k)\pi_k) + \frac{1}{2}L\log(NM),\qquad(4)$$

$$L = K(1 + M + \frac{(M+1)M}{2}) - 1,\qquad(5)$$

where $\hat{\theta}(t, K)$ denotes model parameter estimated on data set C^t and K is the number of mixture components.

Our feature selection problem can be deemed as a search in feature space. Different search engines have been suggested to find optimal or near optimal feature subset [6,13,14,16]. In this paper we consider two search algorithms, which are greedy sequential forward floating search algorithm and best-first sequential forward floating search algorithm [7]. We set $l = 1$, $m = 1$, and $k = 10$, where l is plus step, m is take-away step, and k is expansion step with no improvement on objective function.

For data set with a large number of data points, our feature selection algorithm is still impractical. The time complexity of these algorithms is approximately exponential of $M * N$. In order to improve the efficiency of feature selection, we use random sampling technique on data set. We sample q times on data set and the number of samples in each sampling is k. In this paper, we set $q = 10$, and $k = \frac{N}{q}$. The score of feature selection criterion is the average of scores in q samplings.

3   Experiments and Results

For comparison of feature selection algorithm with SVD-based feature extraction algorithm, we evaluate them on sense discrimination of ambiguous character "chao2". Chinese character "chao2" has two pronunciation ("chao2" and "zhao1") and four main senses: $sense_1$, Part of the meaning [Korea] or [Korean]; $sense_2$, [dynasty]; $sense_3$, [toward] or [facing]; $sense_4$, [morning]. In our experiments, Chinese character sense discrimination is based on characters occurring in the context of ambiguous character. We take People Daily (Jan. 1991-Dec. 1995) and Xinhua News (Jan. 1994-Apr. 1996) as our corpus. A second order co-occurrence matrix for 6768 commonly used Chinese characters is constructed based on this corpus.

3.1   Data Set

We construct two Chinese text test sets: small test set and large test set (for downloading data sets or more details on the experiments, please refer to our technical report available at http://www.comp.nus.edu.sg/~niuzheng/ publication.html). The large test set consists of 3565 sentences containing ambiguous character "chao2". There are three senses of character "chao2" in large test set: $sense_1$ (1500 sentences), $sense_2$ (976 sentences), $sense_3$ (1089 sentences). In our experiments we consider local context strategy, which focuses on sentences containing ambiguous character and ignores the remaining corpus. We construct the large test set by selecting first 1500 sentences with occurrences (having the meaning $sense_1$) of Chinese word "chao2xian3" , all sentences with occurrences (having the meaning $sense_2$) of Chinese words "tang2chao2" (163 occurrences), "song4chao2" (64 occurrences), "yuan2chao2" (106 occurrences), "ming2chao2" (213 occurrences), "qing1chao2" (413 occurrences), "sui2chao2" (17 occurrences), and all sentences with occurrences (having the meaning $sense_3$) of Chinese word "chao2zhe5". Small test set consists of randomly selected sentences from large test set and there are 150 sentences: 50 sentences containing Chinese word "chao2xian3ban4dao3" (having the meaning $sense_1$), 50 sentences containing Chinese word "qing1chao2" (having the meaning $sense_2$), and 50 sentences containing Chinese word "chao2zhe5" (having the meaning $sense_3$).

3.2   Experiments

Our experiments are conducted under five varied conditions: 1) SVD technique vs. feature filter and feature wrapper; 2) Context window size: 1, 5, 15, 25; 3) Feature pre-selection criterion: χ^2 or $frequency$; 4) Search strategy: greedy forward floating search (GFFS) or best-first forward floating search (BFFS) 5) Clustering with ground-truth cluster number as input vs. automatic estimation of correct cluster number using MDL criterion. If the context window size is set as k, the neighbor is any character that occurs at a distance of at most k characters from the ambiguous character. Only neighbors of ambiguous character are considered as feature candidates.

Before feature pre-selection according to χ^2 or $frequency$ criterion, the stop characters and low-frequency characters are removed from both small data set and large data set. We select top 100 high frequency characters as stop characters, and characters whose frequency is less than 1000 as low-frequency characters. The frequency of all characters is counted in People Daily (Jan. 1991-Dec. 1995) and Xinhua News (Jan. 1994-Apr. 1996).

We conduct three experiments under different conditions:

Experiment (1): We select top 100 or 1000 characters in the ranked feature list as feature candidates in experiments on small test set or large test set, which are sorted based on χ^2 or $frequency$ criterion. SVD is used to reduce the dimension of context vectors to 1/10. After feature extraction, $Cluster$ [1] is used to group the occurrences in these two test sets into a predetermined number of clusters.

In this experiment we set the mixture component number as 3 for both small test set and large test set, which is equal to the ground-truth class number.

Experiment (2): We use entropy based feature filter to select important feature subset and use *Cluster* to classify the occurrences in two test sets. The feature candidates for filter are selected based on *frequency* pre-selection criterion. In the experiment on large test set, we limit search of feature space in only top 10% high-frequency contextual characters. For small test set, we search feature subset in the whole *frequency*-based feature candidate set. For comparison of the effect of condition (5) on clustering result, we conduct experiments under different setting: fixing cluster number or automatically estimating cluster number.

Experiment (3): The experimental setting of wrapper method is as same as that of filter method. Wrapper can determine both optimal feature subset and cluster number at the same time. We also conduct experiments under different setting of condition (5). It should be mentioned that the ground-truth cluster number is not an input to feature wrapper in two experiments. In the experiment with ground-truth cluster number as input, we use wrapper as a preprocessing step. After feature selection step, we conduct clustering on the two test sets with ground-truth cluster number as input.

In this paper we employ the method suggested in [8] for comparison between ground-truth classification and clustering result. If k data points in clustering result have as same labels as those in ground-truth classification under agreement-maximization permutation, the precision of this clustering result is defined as $\frac{k}{N}$, where N is the total number of data points. We use this measure as our evaluation criterion of clustering result.

3.3   Discussion

Figure 1 shows a comparison among SVD technique, filter method and wrapper method on two test sets. Under same experiment setting, feature selection methods can achieve higher precision than SVD technique on both small test set and large test set. In most of cases with same setting, filter performs better than wrapper. In the experiment using SVD based method, clustering based on *frequency* feature pre-selection criterion performs better than that based on χ^2 feature pre-selection criterion. It indicates that relevant features are included in local high-frequency characters. When the context window size varies from 1 to 25, the precision of filter and wrapper decreases on both test sets. This is due to that with the increment of context window size, more and more irrelevant features are included in feature candidate set. The information of ground-truth cluster number will affect the performance of filter and wrapper. With ground-truth cluster number as input, filter and wrapper can achieve better result. On small test set, MDL criterion can estimate the correct cluster number due to that the data has well-formed clusters. On large test set, the correct cluster number can not be inferred. Best-first algorithm usually finds a larger feature subset due to that best-first search is more thorough search. In our experiment result, we can find that better feature subset based on feature selection evaluation criterion

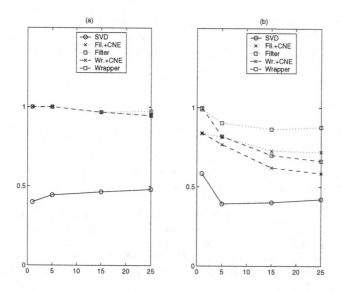

Fig. 1. This figure shows the average precision(axis Y) of SVD-based method, feature filter and feature wrapper versus different context window size(axis X) on (a) small test set and (b) large test set. *SVD* represents the average precision of SVD using χ^2 and *frequency*. *Fil. + CNE* is the average precision of filter with cluster number estimation using GFFS and BFFS. *Filter* indicates the average precision of filter with ground-truth cluster number as input using GFFS and BFFS. *Wr. + CNE* is the average precision of wrapper with cluster number estimation using GFFS and BFFS. *Wrapper* denotes average precision of wrapper with ground-truth cluster number as input using GFFS and BFFS.

yields better clustering result based on precision evaluation criterion in most of cases. It seems that increasing the search effort helps improve the clustering performance.

4   Conclusion

In this paper we apply two general unsupervised feature selection schemes to Chinese character sense discrimination: entropy based feature filter and MDL based feature wrapper. Using precision evaluation and known ground-truth classification, we empirically demonstrate that feature selection method yields better result than feature extraction method on Chinese character sense discrimination task. In contrast with feature exaction approach, feature selection method can provide better understanding of data set in selected feature subspace and remove irrelevant features clearly.

There are some possible improvements on this work. In our feature selection algorithm, the threshold τ is required to be set by users. In future work, we would like improve our algorithm to determine the threshold without user's intervention. In this paper we examine unsupervised feature selection algorithm on sense discrimination of only one ambiguous Chinese character. This work may be extended to more ambiguous Chinese characters and other languages including English.

References

1. Bouman, A. C., Shapiro, M., Cook, W. G., Atkins, B. C., & Cheng, H.: Cluster: An Unsupervsied Algorithm for Modeling Gaussian Mixtures. http://dynamo.ecn.purdue.edu/~bouman/software/cluster/. (1998)
2. Dash, M., Choi, K., Scheuermann, P., & Liu, H.: Feature Selection for Clustering – A Filter Solution. Proc. IEEE Int. Conf. on Data Mining, Maebashi City, Japan. (2002)
3. Deerwester, S. C., Dumais, S. T., Landauer, T. K., Furnas, G. W., & Harshman, R. A.: Indexing by Latent Semantic Analysis. Journal of the American Society of Information Science, 41:6, 391–407. (1990)
4. Devaney, M., & Ram, A.: Efficient Feature Selection in Conceptual Clustering. Proc. 14th Int. Conf. on Machine Learning(pp. 92–97), Morgan Kaufmann, San Francisco, CA. (1997)
5. Dy, J. G., & Brodley, C.E.: Feature Subset Selection and Order Identification for Unsupervised Learning. Proc. 17th Int. Conf. on Machine Learning (pp. 247–254), Morgan Kaufmann, San Francisco, CA. (2000)
6. Iannarilli, F. J., & Rubin, P.A.: Feature Selection for Multiclass Discrimination via Mixed-Integer Linear Programming. IEEE Transactions on Pattern Analysis and Machine Intelligence, 25:6, 779–783.(2003)
7. Kohavi, R., & John, G. H.: Wrappers for Feature Subset Selection. Artificial Intelligence Journal:Special Issue on Relevance (pp. 273–324).(1997)
8. Lange, T., Braun, M., Roth, V., & Buhmann, J. M.: Stability-Based Model Selection. Advances in Neural Information Processing Systems 15.(2002)
9. Law, M. H., Figueiredo, M., & Jain, A. K.: Feature Selection in Mixture-Based Clustering. Advances in Neural Information Processing Systems 15. (2002)
10. Mihalcea, R.: Instance Based Learning with Automatic Feature Selection Applied to Word Sense Disambiguation. Proceedings of the 19th International Conference on Computational Linguistics, Taiwan. (2002)
11. Mitra, P., Murthy, A. C., & Pal, K. S.: Unsupervised Feature Selection Using Feature Similarity. IEEE Transactions on Pattern Analysis and Machine Intelligence, 24:4, 301–312. (2002)
12. Modha, D. S., & Spangler, W. S.: Feature Weighting in k-Means Clustering. Machine Learning, 52:3, 217–237.(2003)
13. Narendra, P., & Fukunaga, K.: A Branch and Bound Algorithm for Feature Subset Selection. IEEE Transactions on Computers, 26:9, 917–922.(1977)
14. Pudil, P., Novovicova, J., & Kittler, J.: Floating search methods in feature selection. Pattern Recognigion Letters, Vol. 15, 1119-1125. (1994)
15. Schütze, H.: Automatic Word Sense Discrimination. Computational Linguistics, 24:1, 97–123. (1998)
16. Siedlecki, W., & Sklansky, J.: A note on genetic algorithms for large scale on feature selection. Pattern Recognition Letters, Vol. 10, 335-347. (1989)
17. Vaithyanathan, S., & Dom, B.: Generalized Model Selection For Unsupervised Learning in High Dimensions. Advances in Neural Information Processing Systems 12 (pp. 970-976). (1999)

The Role of Temporal Expressions in Word Sense Disambiguation*

Sonia Vázquez, Estela Saquete, Andrés Montoyo, Patricio Martínez-Barco, and
Rafael Muñoz

Grupo de investigación del Procesamiento del Lenguaje y Sistemas de Información.
Departamento de Lenguajes y Sistemas Informáticos. Universidad de Alicante.
{svazquez, stela, montoyo, patricio, rafael}@dlsi.ua.es

Abstract. This paper presents an exhaustive study about the Temporal
Expression (TE) influence in the task of Word Sense Disambiguation
(WSD). The hypothesis was that previous identification of some words
or word groups could improved the efficiency of WSD systems. In this
case, the experiments carried out show that the identification of temporal
expressions made up of one or more words (i.e. *today* or *the following day*)
improves around 10% precision of the Word Domain Disambiguation
Framework. The improvement of the WSD task is achieved by extracting
temporal expressions from the corpus which allows us to limit the spread
of a search across the EuroWordNet hierarchy. The corpus used to this
research was the Spanish lexical sample task from Senseval-2[1].

1 Introduction

This paper has been focused on how temporal expressions could help to the resolution of the lexical ambiguity. The main goal was to investigate the hypothesis
that getting out of the temporal expressions from the context of the sentence to
be disambiguated could improve the resolution of the lexical ambiguity.

Temporal Expressions. Temporal expressions are a kind of linguistic coreference. There are two types of temporal expressions, explicit temporal expressions and implicit temporal expressions. An explicit temporal expressions is a
complete date whereas an implicit temporal expression is an expression that
refers to a date named before in the text. Every temporal expression is identified
and tagged in the text. Thus, some examples of explicit and implicit temporal
expressions are listed below:

- *Explicit:*Complete Dates or dates of Events:"11/01/2002" (01/11/2002),
  "Navidad" (Christmas),...
- *Implicit:*Expressions that refer to the document date or another date: "ayer"
  (yesterday), "un día antes" (a day before),...

* This paper has been supported by the Spanish government, projects FIT-150500-
2002-244 and FIT-150500-2002-416 and the Valencia Government (OCyT) under
project number CTIDIB-2002-151.
[1] http://www.senseval.org/

© Springer-Verlag Berlin Heidelberg 2004

Word Sense Disambiguation. The specific task that resolves the lexical ambiguity is commonly referred to as Word Sense Disambiguation (WSD). The disambiguation of a word sense is an "intermediate task" and is necessary for resolving such problems in certain NLP applications. In general terms, WSD involves assigning a definition to a given word, in either a text or a discourse. This association of a word to one specific sense is achieved by acceding to two different information sources, known as "context" and "external knowledge sources". In [1], are described different approaches to word-sense disambiguation systems. The methods used in this paper, are based on strategic knowledge, i.e., the disambiguation of nouns by matching the context in which they appear with information from an external knowledge source (knowledge-driven WSD).

2   Description of TERSEO System

In Figure 1 the graphic representation of the system proposed for the recognition of TEs and for the resolution of its references is shown, according to the temporal model proposed. The texts are tagged with lexical and morphological information and this information is the input to the temporal parser. This temporal parser is implemented using an ascending technique (chart parser) and it is based on a temporal grammar. Once the parser recognizes the TEs in the text, these are introduced into the resolution unit, which will update the value of the reference according to the date it is referring and generate the XML tags for each expression. Finally, these tags are the input of a event ordering unit that gives back the ordered text.

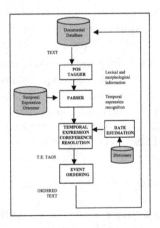

Fig. 1. Graphic representation of TERSEO

The parser uses a grammar based on two different kinds of rules. On one hand there are rules for the date and time recognition (Explicit dates 12/06/1975) and on the other hand there are rules for the temporal reference recognition (implicit dates TEs that need the location of another complete TE to be understood "two days before"). For the anaphoric relation resolution we use an inference engine that interprets every reference named before. In some cases the references are estimated using the newspaper's date (FechaP). Others refer to a date named before in the text that is being analyzed (FechaA). For these cases, a temporal model that allows to know over what date the dictionary operations are going to be done, is defined. For tagging temporal expressions, a set of XML tags is defined in order to standardize the different kinds of TEs. These tags show the following structure:

```
<DATE TIME(_REF) ID=''value'' TYPE=''value'' VALDATE1=''value''
VALTIME1=''value'' VALDATE2=''value'' VALTIME2=''value''
VALORDER=''value''>expression</DATE_TIME>
```

DATE_TIME is used for explicit TEs and DATE_TIME_REF is used for implicit TEs. Every expression has an numeric ID to identify it and VALDATE# and VALTIME# store the range of dates and times obtained from the inference engine.

The evaluation of the system uses Spanish newspapers on the Internet. The system was able to identify 204, but it only tagged 195 accurately. Thus, the recall was 82,28 % and the precision 95,55 % for this kind of expressions.

3   WSD Methods

In this section we present two WSD methods based on the knowledge-based methodological approach:

Specification Marks Method (SM). This method which uses WordNet as lexical knowledge base is developed in [2] and consists basically of the automatic sense-disambiguating of nouns that appear within the context of a sentence and whose different possible senses are quite related.

Domain Based Method (WDD). WDD is a Knowledge-driven method which uses a new resource "Relevant Domains" [3] as information source for disambiguating word senses into a text.

4   Evaluation and Discussion

The goal of this section is to show the influence of temporal expressions resolution in word sense disambiguation task. This study has been made using the corpus of Spanish lexical sample task from Senseval-2 with Specification Marks and Domain Based methods with/without temporal expressions. The results obtained are showed next:

Evaluation of the specification marks method. The results obtained by the Specification Marks Method with/without resolving temporal expressions for the Spanish lexical sample task from Senseval-2 are the same. Fine-grained scoring reported by Senseval-2 commitee are precision=0.566 and recall=0.435. This results are due to SM method uses the most specific concept that subsumes the full set of names in the WordNet taxonomy for establishing relations between names. In other words, in general terms temporal expressions (day, week, etc) do not share information with other words in texts.

Evaluation of the Domain-based method. The results obtained by the Domain-based method with/without temporal expressions identified for the Spanish lexical sample task from Senseval-2 are different. The scores obtained without identifying temporal expressions is precission=0.466 and recall=0.335. Nevertheless, the scores obtained with identifying temporal expressions are precission=0.507 and recall=0.335. The temporal expressions identification applied to domain-based method improves the WSD task. It is due to the use of domain labels instead of the WordNet taxonomy. For instance, domingo (Sunday) can belong to different domains: time period, religion, tourism and party. Because of that, context vectors will be different with/without temporal expressions and disambiguation will be different too.

5   Conclusions

In this paper, we focused on how temporal expressions could help to solve the lexical ambiguity. The corpus used for the evaluation of WSD task was the Spanish lexical sample task of Senseval-2. The main goal was to investigate the hypothesis that getting out of the temporal expressions from the sentence context to be disambiguated could improve the resolution of the lexical ambiguity. Thus, the experiments carried out show that the scores achieved using domain labels for WSD task were improved because of the extraction of temporal expressions limits the EWN hierarchy. However, the Specification Marks method was not improved using temporal expressions identification because this method uses Wordnet taxonomy and temporal expressions do not belong to the "Entity" top concept and they do not help for WSD resolution of most nouns on the Spanish lexical sample task from Senseval-2 that belong to the "Entity" top concept.

References

1. N. Ide and J. Véronis. Introduction to the Special Issue on Word Sense Disambiguation: The State of the Art. *Computational Linguistics*, 24(1):1–40, 1998.
2. Andrés Montoyo and Manuel Palomar. Word Sense Disambiguation with Specification Marks in Unrestricted Texts. In *Proceedings of 11th International Workshop on Database and Expert Systems Applications (DEXA 2000). 11th International Workshop on Database and Expert Systems Applications*, pages 103–107, Greenwich, London, UK, September 2000. IEEE Computer Society.
3. Andres Montoyo Sonia Vazquez and German Rigau. Método de desambiguación léxica basada en el recurso léxico Dominios Releventes. *Journal of Artificial Intelligence Research*, 9:247–293, 1998.

An Empirical Study on Pronoun Resolution in Chinese*

Houfeng Wang and Zheng Mei

Department of Computer Science and Technology
School of Electronic Engineering and Computer Science
Peking University, Beijing, 100871, China
{wanghf,kevinmei}@pku.edu.cn

Abstract. In this paper, we discuss how to identify three important features by our empirical observation — gender and number features of antecedent as well as grammatical role of personal pronoun, which have no overt mark in Chinese. Only a tagger with extended POS set and some special word-lists are used. Finally, We describe an implemented prototypical system to resolve personal pronouns. Evaluation shows that the result is satisfactory.

1 Introduction

Anaphora resolution is a very important task for NLP applications like Text summarization, Information Extraction, Multilingual Information Retrieval and so forth. In the past 10 years, researchers have made great advance in this field. Various approaches, such as linguistic knowledge based methods [5], Machine Learning methods [2][6] and robust methods with less language knowledge or even without parsing [1][3], were proposed. However, there are a number of issues remaining unsolved in anaphora resolution [4] and the precision and the recall are still low.

Unlike in some Euro-languages, the grammatical role of personal pronoun in Chinese, which is commonly thought as an important factor, has no overt mark; in addition, the gender and number features of potential antecedents are unclear. In this paper, we present an inexpensive approach to solving these problems and resolving personal pronoun based on our empirical observation.

Our approach makes use of a tagger with an extended set of POS, plus simple heuristic rules, and operates on basic agreements and preferences to resolve anaphora. The evaluation shows that our approach reaches a satisfactory result.

2 Approach

Personal pronoun resolution relies on the constraints between pronouns and antecedents. Among them, the grammatical roles, gender and number of pronouns and ante

---

* This work is funded by National Natural Science Foundation of Chinese (No. 60173005)

A. Gelbukh (Ed.): CICLing 2004, LNCS 2945, pp. 213–216, 2004.
© Springer-Verlag Berlin Heidelberg 2004

cedents are three most important features. In the following, we will discuss how to identify these features.

2.1 Grammatical Roles

We will only consider how to recognize the grammatical roles of personal pronouns in the limited space. It is the same with antecedents.

Table1 gives personal pronouns in Chinese. It is obvious that there is no different between the nominative form and the objective one for each pronoun. In our approach, we set the default role of a personal pronoun as subject. If one of the following three heuristic rules is successfully applied, the grammatical role will be re-set.

Hrule-1: Punctuation Mark Indicator

Let Pr be a personal pronoun, S-Set={。, ? , ! , , } a set of punctuation marks.

If Pr +punctuation Mark ∈ S-Set, **Then** *Pr is object*

Hrule-2: Verb Indicator

Let Vt be a transitive verb; Vr a reporting verb; Vo-s a verb followed by a pivot word (noun or pronoun) which is both an object of verb Vo-s and a subject of the following verb (see the following example Ex2-1); X a sequence of words (may be empty) in which no noun, pronoun or verb occurs.

Hrule-2-1 *If Vt + X + Pr,* **Then** *Pr is an object*

Hrule-2-2 *If Vr + X + Pr,* **Then** *Pr is a subject*

Hrule-2-3 *If Vo-s + X + Pr,* **Then** *Pr is a pivot case.*

Ex2-1 张三(Zhang San) 让(let) 他(him) 招待(treat) 李四(Li Si).

 Zhang San let him treat Li Si.

In Ex2-1, personal pronoun 他 (he/him) is a pivot word. It is an object of Vo-s 让(let) and a subject of verb 招待 (treat). This kind of sentence is controlled by the first verb Vo-s like 让.

Hrule-3: Preposition Indicator

Let Pt be a preposition followed by a noun (or pronoun) as object.

If Pt +X + Pr, **Then** *Pr is an object*

The above mentioned POSs (Pt, Pr, Vo-s, etc.) are tags of the extended set of POS.

Table1. Personal pronouns and their possessives[1] (Possessive-S is the possessive of singular pronouns and Possessive-P is the possessive of plural ones)

	Singular	Possessive-S	Plural	Possessive-P
1st person	我(I,me)	我+的(my, mine)	我们(we, us)	我们+的(our, ours)
2nd person	你(you)	你+的(your,yours)	你们(you)	你们+的(your, yours)
3rd person-1	他(he,him)	他+的(his)	他们(they, them)	他们+的(their, theirs)
3rd person-2	她(she,her)	她+的(her, hers)	她们(they, them)	她们+的(their,theirs)

For possessive pronouns in Chinese, they usually have the following pattern:

{ **Singular Pronoun | Plural Pronoun** } + 的

---

[1] Pronoun "它(it)' is not considered in this paper

However, a personal pronoun can sometimes act as possessive determiner itself without '的'. For instance, 他爸(his father). We give Hrule-4 to process this issue:

Hrule-4: *if* Pr + X + noun, **then** Pr is a possessive determiner.

Considering that a possessive determiner and a possessive pronoun share the same resolution strategy, it is unnecessary to distinguish between them.

2.2 Gender and Number

Personal noun is usually referred to using personal pronoun. By personal noun here we mean a noun whose referent is human being; for instance, teacher, boy and president etc. In our approach, we used the following strategies to identify its gender:

Strategy-1: gender Indicators

The last character of some words can be used to determine the gender. For example, the word with the last character "父"(father), such as {家父, 养父, 舅父, 姨夫, 岳父, 曾祖父,...} indicates that fact of being male. Also, there are some determiners such as "女/女子"(female) which precedes a noun phrase and indicates the fact of being female.

Strategy-2: gender negative words

Some words can be used to determine the gender of its preceding personal noun by setting the opposite sex of these words, for example, 校长的太太(president wife) means the gender of 校长 (president) is male. On the other hand, the gender of some gender negative words can be determined by the preceding or following personal noun, for example, 他的情人 (his lover) means the gender of 情人(lover) is female.

Strategr-3: gender information

For Some words with gender information that cannot be reduced to Strategy-1, we built a special word-list to identify them. For example, 护士(nurse).

Indeed, it is difficult to identify the gender of each personal noun since most of them have no gender information and indicator. We recognize them as unknown gender. So they will not be filtered with gender agreement.

The number features:

Plural: organization name, place name[2].

Singular-I: person name.

Singular-II: some special words such as title. For example, 总统(president).

Singular-III: some phrases have the following pattern:

(这(this)| 那(that) | 该(the) |某(some)| 一(one)) + [位 | 名] + X + **Personal noun**

The others will be thought as plural.

3 Implementation and Evaluation

The process of pronouns resolution is to collect initial antecedent candidates (personal noun, person name, organization name, place name or even personal pronoun) left to

---

[2] Organization name and place name are usually referred to by plural pronoun in Chinese.

the anaphor, filter candidates with constraints and select a final candidate with preference (grammatical role parallelism). The preference is often true in Chinese. The algorithm of pronouns resolution is informally outlined as follows:

1. Filter antecedent candidates that do not agree in gender and number feature with personal pronouns; and eliminate antecedents by mutual exclusion between subject and object, between pivot word and subject, also between pivot word and object in the same clause.
2. Select the closest candidate for a possessive pronoun.
3. For a subject pronoun, look backward for a candidate as subject sentence by sentence until one is found.
4. For an object pronoun, select a candidate as object in the preceding sentence; if not found, select the subject candidate in the same sentence and then determiner. In backward way, sentence by sentence, until one is found.

We implemented a prototypical system based on the above algorithm and tested this system by *People Daily* corpus, in which 276 "他" and 128 "他们" are contained. The results are manually checked and the correct numbers are given in Table 2. The results of a "Baseline most recent" are also shown in the table.

Table 2. A comparison with the "Baseline most recent"

	Our Approach	Baseline (most recent)
他	219 (or 79.3%)	178 (or 64.5%)
他们	96 (or 75.0%)	85 (66.4%)

The "Baseline (most recent)" was processed by human. It is not affected by pre-processing errors, such as the tagging errors and the errors of grammatical role identification for antecedents. However, many errors in our approach come from the two kinds of errors. Therefore, one of our future tasks is to reduce these errors.

References

1. Christopher Kennedy and Branimir Boguraev: Anaphora for everyone: pronominal anaphora resolution without a parser. In Proceedings of the 16th International Conference on Computational Linguistics (COLING'96),Copenhagen, Denmark.(1996) 113–118
2. Roland Stuckardt: Machine-learning-based vs. manually designed approaches to anaphor resolution: the best of two worlds. In: Proceedings of the 4th Discourse Anaphora and Anaphor Resolution Colloquium (2002) 211–216
3. Ruslan Mitkov: Robust Pronoun Resolution with limited knowledge. In Proceedings of the 17th COLING, Montreal, Canada (1998) 869–875
4. Ruslan Mitkov: Outstanding issues in anaphora resolution. In Al. Gelbukh, editor, Computational Linguistics and Intelligent Text Processing. Springer-Verlag(2001) 110–125
5. Shalom Lappin and Herbert Leass: An algorithm for pronominal anaphora resolution. Computational Linguistics, Vol.20 No.4(1994) 535–561
6. Wee Meng Soon, Hwee Tou Ng and Chung Yong Lim: A Machine Learning Approach to Coreference Resolution of Noun Phrases. Computational Linguistics (Special Issue on Computational Anaphora Resolution), Vol. 27, No 4(2001) 521–544

Language-Independent Methods for Compiling Monolingual Lexical Data

Christian Biemann[1], Stefan Bordag[1], Gerhard Heyer[1], Uwe Quasthoff[1], and Christian Wolff [2]

[1]Leipzig University
Computer Science Institute, NLP Dept.
Augustusplatz 10/11
04109 Leipzig, Germany
{biem, sbordag, heyer, quasthoff}@informatik.uni-leipzig.de
[2]University of Regensburg
PT 3.3.48
93040 Regensburg
christian.wolff@sprachlit.uni-regensburg.de

Abstract. In this paper we describe a flexible, portable and language-independent infrastructure for setting up large monolingual language corpora. The approach is based on collecting a large amount of monolingual text from various sources. The input data is processed on the basis of a sentence-based text segmentation algorithm. We describe the entry structure of the corpus database as well as various query types and tools for information extraction. Among them, the extraction and usage of sentence-based word collocations is discussed in detail. Finally we give an overview of different applications for this language resource. A WWW interface allows for public access to most of the data and information extraction tools (*http://wortschatz.uni-leipzig.de*).

1   Introduction

We describe an infrastructure for managing large monolingual language resources. Several language independent methods are used to detect semantic relations between the words of a language. These methods differ in productivity and precision for different languages, but there are highly productive and accurate methods for all languages tested. The process starts with the collection of monolingual text corpora from the Web. Next, we identify collocations, i.e. words that occur significantly often together. These collocations form a network that is analyzed further to identify semantic relations. Because semantic features are often reflected in morphosyntactic structures, we apply classifiers that use the sequence of its characters for classification. Moreover, we use context information and POS-information, if available.

While it is clear that the above mentioned methods can be used to find semantic relations or, can be used to verify the corresponding hypotheses, we want to present abstract methods, specific application and results for different languages.

A. Gelbukh (Ed.): CICLing 2004, LNCS 2945, pp. 217–228, 2004.
© Springer-Verlag Berlin Heidelberg 2004

Since 1995, we have accumulated a German text corpus of more than 500 Million words with approx. 9 Million different word forms in approx. 36 Million sentences. The Project - originally called "Deutscher Wortschatz" (*German Vocabulary*) - has been extended to include corpora of other European languages (Dutch, English, French, Italian). Recently, we incorporated the processing of Unicode, giving rise to a Korean Corpus as well, with more languages to follow in the near future (see table 1)

Table 1. Basic Characteristics of some of our corpora.

	German	English	Italian	Korean
Word tokens	500 Mill.	260 Mill.	140 Mill.	38 Mill.
Sentences	36 Mill.	13 Mill.	9 Mill.	2,3 Mill.
Word types	9 Mill.	1,2 Mill.	0,8 Mill.	3,8 Mill.

The corpus is available on the WWW (*http://www.wortschatz.uni-leipzig.de*) and may be used as a large online dictionary.

2   Methodological Approach

Our collection is comprehensive rather than error-free. In the long run we aim at representing a large portion of current-day word usage (see [Quasthoff et al. 2003]) for a discussion on daily fluctuation of word usage) available from various sources. While this does not prevent inclusion of errors (like typos in newspaper text), we are able to eliminate typical sources of erroneous information by statistical as well as intellectual optimization routines (see [Quasthoff 1998a] for details).

In addition, only a high data volume of the corpus allows for the extraction of information like sentence-based word collocations and information about low frequency terms. At the same time, the infrastructure should be open for the integration of various knowledge sources and tools: We strongly believe that there is no single linguistic or statistical approach for all operational needs (optimization tasks, information extraction etc.). Hence, we provide data for very different purposes.

3   Integrating Diverse Data Resources

3.1   Data Sources

The main (and in most cases only) source is text in the corresponding language taken from the web. The amount of text varies from 2 to 36 million sentences. The text is taken from web pages with the corresponding domain ending.

If available, we include information taken from electronic dictionaries. Multiword dictionary entries are especially of interest because they are needed as a seed to find more.

3.2   Text Processing

In this section we describe the construction of a text database for a given fixed language.

The preprocessing steps include format conversion, i.e. HTML-stripping, and sentence separation.

Sentence separation is done with the help of an abbreviation list. We assume the text being written in a single and previously known language. In this case we can prepare a list of abbreviations (only abbreviations ending in a period are relevant for sentence separation). If no such abbreviations are available, a preliminary list of common abbreviations that are found in multiple languages can be used.

The next step performs language verification. Here we can sort out sentences that are not in the language under consideration. The language detection module uses lists of about 1000 most frequent words of different languages. The language of a sentence is then identified comparing its words with those lists.

3.3   Indexing

Lexical analysis consists of the separation of words and multiwords and indexing of the whole text corpus. While word separation is usually simple, multiwords have to be supplied in advance to be recognized.

We maintain a complete full-text index for the whole corpus, making analysis of typical word usage a simple task.

3.4   Collocations

The occurrence of two or more words within a well-defined unit of information (sentence, document) is called a collocation.[1] For the selection of meaningful and significant collocations, an adequate collocation measure has to be defined: Our significance measure is based on a function comparable to the well-known statistical *G-Test* for Poisson distributions: Given two words A, B, each occurring a, b times in sentences, and k times together, we calculate the significance *sig(A, B)* of their occurrence in a sentence as follows:

$$sig(A, B) = x - k \log x + \log k!, \quad x = \frac{ab}{n},$$

where n is the number of sentences.

Two different types of collocations are generated: Collocation based on occurrence *within the same sentence* as well as *immediate left and right neighbors of each word*. Fig. 1 shows an example listing of the top 50 collocations for the term *Daewoo* taken from the English corpus, number in brackets indicate the relative strength of the collocation measure.

---

[1] Some authors use the term *collocation* in a different sense, referring to pairs of syntactically and semantically related words [Bolshakov 2004]. Though such pairs have a number of important applications, e.g. [Gelbukh *et al.* 2000], and can be inferred logically [Bolshakov & Gelbukh 2002], sophisticated syntactic analysis is required for their automatic acquisition [Gelbukh *et al.* 2004]. We use a more practical, statistical definition.

Significant sentence-based collocations for Daewoo:
Leading (272), Edge (253), Motor (132), Korean (108), Co (85), Telecom (83), Korea's (82), Hyundai (67), Mo-tors (66), Shipbuilding (66), Kia (62), Korea (52), South (49), Heavy (48), Corp (46), GM (46), Samsung (44), conglomerate (39), Group (38), Ltd (37), Kim (34), LeMans (31), owned (31), Edge's (29), Products (27), group (27), Fason (26), General (25), Machinery (25), PCs (25), bankruptcy (22), venture (21), Industries (20), Electronics (19), contract (19), joint (18), shipyard (18), Goldstar (17), Okpo (17), Seoul (17), workers (17), Woo (16), cars (15), subsidiary (15), Lucky-Goldstar (14), dealers (14), industrial (14), conglomerates (13), manufacturer (13), strike (13), supplier (13), Choong (12), auto (12), Agbay (11), Koje (11), Pontiac (11), Telecommunications (11), plant (11), 50-50 (10), Dae-woo's (10), Woo-choong (10), factory (10), Joong (9), joint-venture (9), Pupyong (8), giant (8), signed (8), vehicles (8), Inchon (7), Motor's (7), Precision (7), Yoon (7), agreement (7), car (7), chaebol (7), exports (7), logo (7), multibillion-dollar (7), sell (7), units (7)

Significant left neighbors of Daewoo:
Korea's (46), conglomerate (15), Korea-based (7), manufacturer (4)

Significant right neighbors of Daewoo:
Motor (124), Telecom (110), Shipbuilding (73), Group (44), Corp (34), Heavy (25), group (23), Telecommunications (21), Electronics (14), officials (8), Precision (7), Motors (5), Securities (5), Shipbuilding's (5), industrial (5)

Fig. 1. Collocation Sets for *Daewoo* (English corpus)

Although the calculation of collocations for a large set of terms is a computationally expensive procedure, we have developed efficient trie-based algorithms that allow for a collocation analysis of the complete corpus in feasible time.

For a given word, its collocation set very much reflects human associations. For this reason, collocation sets are used as input for some of the information extraction algorithms described in section 4.

3.5   POS-Tagging

If available, we use POS-tagging for the following tasks:

1. Disambiguation: If different meanings of a word differ by its POS-tag, we get different collocation sets according to the different POS-tags.

    Consider the following example in Figure 2, illustrating the disambiguation of *wish* as noun and as verb in two POS-tagged English sentences.

2. For several applications, one looks for collocations with a certain POS-tag. In example, when looking for synonyms the candidate set for a given word reduces to those candidates having the same POS-tag.

We use TNT, a freely available POS-Tagger based on Cascaded Markov Models (cf. [Brants 2000]).

For[IF] six[MC] months[NNT2] ,[YC] the[AT] young[JJ] family[NN1] physician[NN1] got[VVD] her[APPG] **wish[NN1]** ,[YC] developing[VVG] close[JJ] relationships[NN2] with[IW] her[APPG] mostly[RR] single[JJ] and[CC] minority[NN1] women[NN2] patients[NN2]

I[PPIS1] am[VBN] trying[VVG] to[TO] lead[VV0] a[AT1] different[JJ] life[NN1] now[RT] and[CC] I[PPIS1] just[RR] **wish[VV0]** all[DB] that[CST] stuff[NN1] hadn't[VVD] been[VBN] dredged[VVN*] up[RP] again[RT] ,[YC] said[VVD] the[AT] 52-year-old[NN1*]

Fig. 2. Disambiguation of *wish* with POS.tags.

3.6   Entry Structure

The basic structure of entries in the corpus database includes information on the absolute word frequency for each entry (i. e. each inflected word form or each identified phrase like the proper name *Helmut Kohl*). Additional frequency class is calculated based on a logarithmic scale relative to the most frequent word in the corpus. For the English corpus, the most frequent word, *the*, has frequency class 0, while an entry like *Acropolis* with an absolute frequency of 20 belongs to frequency class 18, as the occurs approx. 2^{18} times more often.

In addition to this basic statistical information, example sentences extracted from the texts most recently included in the corpus are given for each word.

4   Tools for Information Extraction

4.1   Morphology Related Similarity

Denoted with morphology related similarity are relations between words that can first be noticed due to its regularity in word formation. Especially we find

- inflection
- derivation
- compound formation

Secondly we can identify groups of words due to low-frequent n-grams of characters, which might be considered as a weaker form of morphology.

Those methods can be used to identify words to belong to some sublanguage. Examples are

- names of chemical substances
- highly technical terms in general
- proper names of regional origin, for instance, Italian surnames compared to English words.

For classifying words based on morphological similarity, we use a trie-like data structure, the *affix-compression trie* that is trained on the characters of a word read from the beginning or reversed.

For training, a pair wise list of words and their classes is needed. A toy example for base form reduction can be found in table 2:

Table 2. Training set for base form reduction. The semantics of the instruction: cut n characters (number) away and add the following text characters.

Word form	Reduction instruction
Price	0
Vice	0
Mice	3ouse
splice	0

Now we train a suffix compression trie on the reversed word forms. Nodes in the trie get all the reduction instructions assigned to them that can be found in the subnodes, together with their number of occurrences. The leaves of the trie correspond to one word form. Figure 3 shows the suffix compression trie for the training set of Table 2:

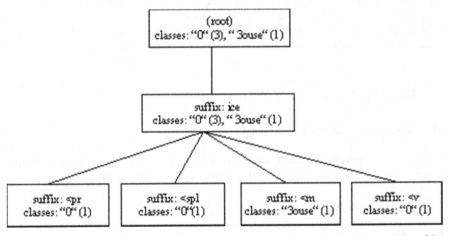

Fig. 3. Suffix compression trie. Note that the intermediate suffix node "ice" bears a bias of 3:1 for the reduction instruction "0". The start-of-word character is "<"

When classifying words with the suffix tree, the path through the trie is followed until no more node matches. In case of a word in the training set, the resulting node is a leaf, for unknown words the node is usually at intermediate position from root to the leaves. For nodes with multiple reduction instruction classes, the instruction having the highest number of occurrences is selected.

In the example, when classifying *voice*, the resulting node is "ice" with the winning instruction "0". The suffix path for *police* is "ice"-"<spl" (partial match) with the same reduction instruction, while *half-mice* is correctly reduced to *half-mouse*.

4.2   Splitting Subgraphs for Lexical Disambiguation

As the collocation analysis results in one large, connected graph with words as nodes and the collocation relationship as links between such nodes it is worth-while to have a closer look at the structure of this graph. First of all, standard measurements can be performed like the distribution of node degrees, the average shortest path length, clustering coefficient and others, see [Steyvers & Tenenbaum 2002] for a comprehensive work. Though from all these measurements it is possible to infer that the graph must have the small world property, described by [Strogatz 1998] and further developed by [Barabasi 2000], this knowledge can also be of practical use.

From the graph having the small world property it is possible to assume that the whole graph is structured into local clusters of words or 'communities' to borrow terminology from research on the Web as a graph [Kleinberg et al. 1999]. These clusters consist of words which belong together due to various semantic relations like cohyponymy, synonymy, antonomy and other as opposed to other words which are not in this cluster because there is no semantic relationship between most of the words from the cluster and the given other word.

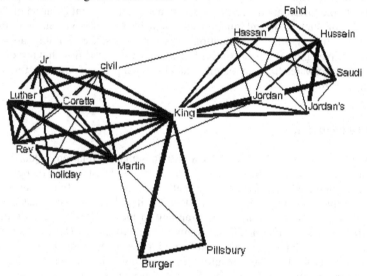

Fig. 4. Collocation graph for *King* (English Corpus)

Now it is obvious that if a word is ambiguous, it will occur in two or more such clusters at the same time, whereas there will be no other connections between those clusters as they otherwise denote different topics, see the visualized subgraph (simulated annealing, [Schmidt 1999]) example of the word *king* in Figure 4. It is then possible to formulate the two following assumptions:

- The whole graph consists of clusters
- There is no such triplet of words which is still ambiguous

There are only very rare exceptions to the second assumption like 'gold', 'silver' and 'bronze' where having three words still is ambiguous.

Sense Nr 1 : Car · Greyhound · Highway · Interstate · Mahoney · Patrol · Sgt. · Taxi · Trooper · accident · airbags · apparently · authorities · automatic · bags · belts · bomb · brake · brakes · bus · buses · cab · car · cars · chase · chased · collided · collision · crash · crashed · critically · crossing · crushed · dead · door · driven · driver's · drivers · driving · drove · drunk · drunken · engine · exploded [40 more]

Sense Nr 2 : 1-2-3 · 16-bit · 24-bit · 8-bit · 8514/A · ADI · ANSI · API · AUTOEXEC · Adapter · Adobe · Apple's · Apple-Talk · AutoCAD · Autodesk · BAT · BIOS · BallPoint · Ballpoint · BitBlt · Bus · CD-ROM · COM · CON · CONFIG · CTL · Chooser · DEVHLP · DEVICE · DEVICEHIGH · DEVLOD · DLL · DMA · DOS · DeskJet · DeskWriter · Device · Display · Drivers · EGA · EMM · EMS · EXE [200 more]

Fig. 5. Lexical disambiguation of *driver*.

Using these assumptions it was possible to formulate an algorithm, described in greater detail in [Bordag 2003], which can split the subgraph around a given word according to the different clusters, thus giving a semantic disambiguation of the word. The results of such a disambiguation can then be used for various purposes like information retrieval, other classification tasks and word sense disambiguation.

Figure 5 gives the fully unsupervised disambiguation of *driver*, having on the one hand the *conductor* reading, on the other hand being a piece of *software* for accessing connected hardware.

4.3   The Pendulum

For extending sets of words that bear a certain semantic relation, [Quasthoff et al. 2002] describes a method that extracts first names and last names of persons from indexed, unannotated text. Using fuzzy pattern rules on very flat features, like "if there is a capitalized word behind a first name, it is likely to be a last name", the algorithm is able to extract in a bootstrapping fashion several thousands of person names from a small start set (20-50 examples are sufficient). High accuracy (about 98%, depending on language, rules and features) is assured through the iteration of a search and a verification step, resulting in accepting a name candidate only if the fuzzy rules match at a certain rate for all occurrences of the name candidate.

The Pendulum algorithm is applicable to word sets whose elements show up in certain patterns and has been successfully applied to all kinds of Named Entity subclassification, i.e. company names (see [Biemann et al. 2003a]) or island names.

Through the flatness of the features used the method is language independent in a way that most patterns are reflected in several languages and names already learnt on other language sources can be used as start sets for an new language. Moreover, patterns do not have to be handcrafted, but can be inferred from small training texts. The principle bootstrapping by search and verification can not only be applied on text as data source – experiments on POS-filtered collocations determining related concepts for given word sets are very promising.

4.4 Collocation Set Disjunction

The calculation of collocations can be iterated to obtain collocations of higher order in the following way: while the first-order calculation operates on sentences, the second order calculation operates on the outcome of the first order calculation and so forth. Intuitively, second-order collocations happen to be strong if two words appear in the same context and can be roughly compared to de Saussure's paradigmatic relations (cf. [de Saussure 1916], [Rapp 2002]).

However, second- or higher order collocations are in general not restrictive enough to derive synonymy or cohyonomy directly from them. But they can serve as a data source where other methods build upon. In [Biemann et al. 2003b] we describe and evaluate a method that yields good candidates for extending hierarchical synset-based lexicons like WordNet [Miller 1990] by performing set disjunction on the collocation sets of several input words that are close together in the hierarchy.

Figure 6 shows a German example, performing disjunction on the third-order collocation sets of two words after applying a word class filter.

start set: [warm, kalt] *[warm, cold]*

result set: [heiß, wärmer, kälter, erwärmt, gut, heißer, hoch, höher, niedriger, schlecht, frei] *[hot, warmer, colder, warmed, good, hotter, high, higher, lower, bad, free]*

start set: [gelb, rot] *[yellow, red]*

result set: [blau, grün, schwarz, grau, bunt, leuchtend, rötlich, braun, dunkel, rotbraun, weiß] *[blue, green, black, grey, colorful, bright, reddish, brown, dark, red-brown, white]*

start set: [Mörder, Killer] *[murderer, killer]*

result set: [Täter, Straftäter, Verbrecher, Kriegsverbrecher, Räuber, Terroristen, Mann, Mitglieder, Männer, Attentäter] *[offender, delinquent, criminal, war criminal, robber, terrorists, man, members, men, assassin]*

Fig. 6. Disjunction of third-order collocations. The original language in the experiment was German, English translations are marked in *italics*.

The introduction of part-of-speech information additionally allows a more precise selection of collocation sets: Using the sets of immediate left and right neighbor collocations, it is possible to retrieve typical adjectives that appear to the left of a given noun or, verbs that appear to the right of a given noun.

5   Applications

One major advantage of the infrastructure developed for this project is its immediate portability for different languages, text domains, and application: The basic structure consisting of text processing tools, data model, and information extraction algorithms may be applied to any given corpus of textual data. This makes this approach applicable to a wide variety of basic language technology problems like

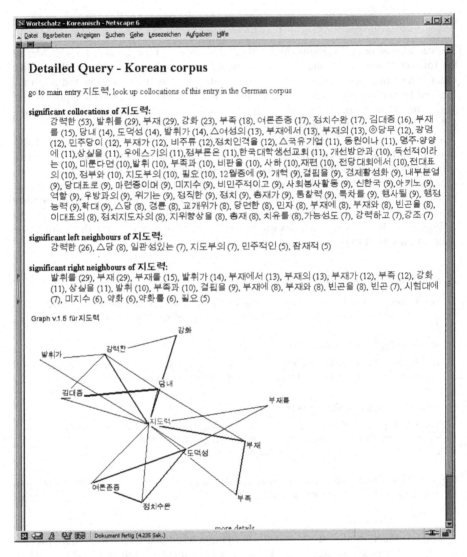

Fig. 7. Web-interface for Korean: Collocations of *(leadership)*

- text classification
- document management, or
- information retrieval

Beside the project's WWW interface and its usage as a general-purpose dictionary (basic statistical, syntactic and semantic information, typical usage examples) current applications include collocation-based query expansion in Web search engines. The latter shall be illustrated by an example: Typical usage of Web Search engines is characterized by very short queries and low retrieval effectiveness (cf. [Silverstein et al. 1999], [Jansen et al. 2000]). Possible remedies for this are query expansion techniques and collocation sets can be used for this.

While this application makes use of our "standard" data corpus, the infrastructure can be applied to different data sets or text collection without modification. Thus, further applications like comparing special purpose document collections with the general language corpus are possible. The difference in the statistical data can help identifying important concepts ant their relations. Applications of this analysis are

- Terminology extraction and
- Support of object oriented modeling of business processes.

6 Further Research

After five years of being online, we register now more than 170'000 monthly visits and 4,7 Mio. page hits at 50% of yearly growth. Due to increasing access counts, we are currently developing a clustered storage and access infrastructure that will not only provide higher throughput for Web access but also a structural separation of production and presentation databases.

After setting up a language classifier, we will set up corpora in different standard sizes for all major languages on the web. See Figure 7 for our web interface for Korean.

References

[Biemann et al. 2003a] Biemann, C., Quasthoff, U., Böhm, K., Wolff, C. (2003): Automatic discovery and Aggregation of Compound Names for the Use in Knowledge Representations, Journal of Universal Computer Science (JUCS), Volume 9, Number 6, Pp. 530-541, June 2003

[Biemann et al. 2003b] Biemann, C., Bordag, S., Quasthoff, U (2003): Lernen von paradigmatischen Relationen auf iterierten Kollokationen, Proceedings of GermeNet Workshop 2003, Tübingen, Germany

[Barabasi 2000] A.L. Barabasi et al . Scale-free characteristics of random networks: the topology of the World-wide web, Physica A (281)70-77, 2000

[Bolshakov 2004] Bolshakov, I. A.: Getting One's First Million... Collocations. In: A. Gelbukh (Ed.) *Computational Linguistics and Intelligent Text Processing*. Lecture Notes in Computer Science, N 2945, Springer-Verlag, 2004 (this volume), pp. 226–239.

[Bolshakov & Gelbukh 2002] Bolshakov, I.A., A. Gelbukh. Heuristics-based replenishment of collocation databases. In: Advances in Natural Language Processing (PorTAL-2002). Lecture Notes in Computer Science, N 2389, Springer-Verlag, 2002, p. 25-32.

[Bordag 2002] Bordag, S. (2003): Sentence Co-occurrences as Small-World Graphs: A solution to Automatic Lexical Disambiguation, A. Gelbukh (Ed.): CICLing 2003, LNCS 2588, pp. 329-332, Springer-Verlag Berlin Heidelberg.

[Brants 2000] Brants, T. (2000). TnT - A Statistical Part-of-Speech Tagger. In Proceedings of the Sixth Applied Natural Language Processing Conference ANLP-2000, Seattle, WA.

[Davidson & Harel 1006] Davidson, R., Harel, D. (1996): Drawing Graphs Nicely Using Simulated Annealing, ACM Transactions on Graphics 15(4), 301-331.

[Gelbukh *et al.* 2000] Gelbukh, A., G. Sidorov, and I. A. Bolshakov.: Dictionary-based Method for Coherence Maintenance in Man-Machine Dialogue with Indirect Antecedents and Ellipses. In: Text, Speech and Dialogue (TSD-2000). Lecture Notes in Artificial Intelligence, N 1902, Springer-Verlag, 2000, pp. 357-362.

[Gelbukh *et al.* 2004] Gelbukh, A., G. Sidorov, S.-Y. Han, E. Hernández-Rubio. *Automatic Enrichment of Very Large Dictionary of Word Combinations on the Basis of Dependency Formalism.* In: Proc. Mexican International Conference on Artificial Intelligence (MICAI-2004). Lecture Notes in Artificial Intelligence, N 2972, Springer-Verlag, 2004.

[Jansen et al. 2000] Jansen, B. J. et al. (2000), Real Life, Real Users, and Real Needs: A Study and Analysis of User Queries on the Web. In Information Processing & Management 36(2), 207-227.

[Kleinberg et al. 1999] Kleinberg, J., M., Kumar, R., Raghavan, P., Rajagopalan, S., Tomkins, A., S. (1999): The web as a graph: Measurements, models and methods. Lecture Notes in Computer Science, vol. 1627, pp.1-18.

[Läuter & Quasthoff 1999] Läuter, M., Quasthoff, U. (1999), Kollokationen und semantisches Clustering. In Gippert, J. (ed.) 1999. Multilinguale Corpora. Codierung, Strukturierung, Analyse. Proc. 11. GLDV-Jahrestagung. Prague: Enigma Corporation, 34-41.

[Miller 1990] Miller, G.A. (1990): Wordnet - an on-line lexical database, International Journal of Lexikography 3(4):235-312

[Quasthoff 1998a] Quasthoff, U. (1998): Tools for Automatic Lexicon Maintenance: Acquisition, Error Correction, and the Generation of Missing Values." In: Proc. First International Conference on Language Resources & Evaluation [LREC], Granada, May 1998, Vol. II, 853-856.

[Quasthoff 1998] Quasthoff, U. (1998): Projekt der deutsche Wortschatz. In Heyer, G., Wolff, Ch. (eds.). Linguistik und neue Medien. Wiesbaden: Dt. Universitätsverlag, 93-99.

[Quasthoff et al. 2002] Quasthoff, U., Biemann, C., Wolff, C. (2002): Named Entity Learning and Verification: EM in large Corpora, Proceedings of CoNNL-2002, Taipei, Taiwan

[Quasthoff et al. 2003] Quasthoff, U., Richter, M., Wolff, C., Medienalalyse und Visualisierung – Auswertung von Online-Pressetexten durch Text Mining, in Uta Seewald-Heeg (Ed.), Sprachtechnologie für die multilinguale Kommunikation, Proceedings of GLDV-03, Sankt Augustin

[Rapp 2002] Rapp, R. (2002): The Computation of Word Association: Comparing Syntagmatic and Paradigmatic Approaches, Proceedings of COLING-02, Taipei, Taiwan

[Saussure 1916] Saussure, F de. (1916): Cours de Linguistique Générale, Paris, Payot.

[Schmidt 1999] Schmidt, F. (1999): Automatische Ermittlung semantischer Zusammenhänge lexikalischer Einheiten und deren graphische Darstellung, Diplomarbeit, Universität Leipzig.

[Silverstein et al. 1999] Silverstein, C. et al. (1999): Analysis of a Very Large Web Search Engine Query Log. In SIGIR Forum 33(1), 6-12.

[Steyvers & Tenenbaum 2002] M. Steyvers, J. B. Tenenbaum. The large-scale structure of semantic networks: statistical analyses and a model of semantic growth. M. Steyvers, J. B. Tenenbaum, Cognitive Science, 2002

[Strogatz 1998] D. J. Watts, S.H. Strogatz. Collective dynamics of 'small-world' networks, Nature 393:440-442, 1998.

[Voorhees & Harman 1999] Voorhees, E.; Harman, D. (eds.) (1999): Overview of the Seventh Text REtrieval Conference (TREC-7). In Voorhees, E.; Harman, D. (eds.), Proc. TREC-7. The Seventh Text REtrieval Conference. Gaithersburg/MD: NIST [= NIST Special Publication 500-242].

Getting One's First Million... Collocations*

Igor A. Bolshakov

Center for Computing Research
National Polytechnic Institute, Mexico City, Mexico
igor@cic.ipn.mx

Abstract. Many-long-years-of experience in creating a very large database of Russian collocations is summarized. The *collocations* here described are syntactically connected and semantically compatible pairs of content components—single or multi-words. We begin from a synopsis of various applications of collocation databases (CDBs). Then we describe the main features of collocation components, syntactic types of collocations, and links of other nature between their components that amplify the applicability of the enclosing systems. All of the above-mentioned characterizes the CrossLexica system created for Russian but with a universal structure suited for other languages. The statistics of CrossLexica is given and discussed. It now contains more that a million collocations and more than a million WordNet-like links.

1 Introduction

The term *collocation* is widely used in both theoretical and computational linguistics but without a generally agreed definition. We define a *collocation* as a syntactically connected and semantically compatible pair of content words, like *full-length dress*, *well expressed*, *to briefly expose*, *to pick up the knife* or *to listen to the radio*, where the collocation components (hereafter *collocatives*) are underlined.

Syntactical connectedness is understood as in dependency grammars [21] and it is in no way merely a co-occurrence of the collocatives in a short span of a text [1, 27]. The head collocative syntactically governs the dependent collocative, being adjoined to it directly or through an auxiliary word (usually a preposition). Sequentially, the collocatives can be at any distance from each other in a sentence, but are nearby in the dependency tree.

The stability of a collocation can be determined as rather high mutual information of its collocatives quantitatively evaluated within a large text corpus [20; 17, 18].

The idiomaticity of collocations is an intuitively graduated measure as illustrated below with the English verb *see*. In the phrase *to see a jungle* both collocatives have their direct meaning; in *to see a doctor* 'to visit a doctor for consultations or treatment' *doctor* has its direct meaning, while the meaning of *see* is supplemented by other elements; in *to see the reason* 'to have or understand the reason' the direct meaning of *see* is not traced at all; the phrase *to see light at the end of the tunnel* 'to

---

* Work done under partial support of Micra Inc., USA (1993–1994), Soros Foundation, Russia (1995), and Mexican Government (CONACyT, SNI, CGPI–IPN) (since 1999). Thanks to Dr. Patrick Cassidy for his valuable suggestions.

A. Gelbukh (Ed.): CICLing 2004, LNCS 2945, pp. 229–242, 2004.
© Springer-Verlag Berlin Heidelberg 2004

renew a hope in a difficult situation' does not contain the meaning of either collocative. The first and the last examples—a free word combination with the meaning directly composed of the meanings of its collocatives, and a complete idiom—are not collocations in terms of [22]. Meanwhile, we consider as collocations word combinations of **any** stability and of **any** idiomaticity, including both of the above-mentioned extremes; cf. the discussion in Section 7.

For a long time collocations were studied in lexicography rather than in computational linguistics. The mainstream initiated by N. Chomsky usually treats collocations simply as Ngrams, i.e. a series of two or more words occurring together in a narrow window moving along a text [27].

The emergence of WordNet [15, 28] created an illusion that it can describe all conceivable semantic links between words of a given language, so that the only necessity is to discover new types of such links and to search around for corresponding examples. Then it was realized that WordNet includes semantic links only of the paradigmatic type whose related terms usually consist of semantically associated components and do not necessarily co-occur in close contexts.

Meanwhile lexicographers always considered collocations as semantic connections of syntagmatic type with the collocatives regularly co-occurring in texts. A rather limited but very useful part of English collocations were first gathered in BBI dictionary [2], and now students of English have available the much more comprehensive Oxford dictionary [23]. At the same time, the only theory that gave a consistent description of all types of word combinations proved to be the Meaning—Text Theory [21, 22]. However the MTT is usually ignored in computational linguistics when multiword expressions are studied [24].

To our knowledge, publicly available electronic databases of collocations did not exist until 1997, when the Advanced Reader's Collocation Searcher (ARCS) for English emerged [3]. However its deficiencies are too severe for indulgent criticism.

The only project in the recent decade of a very large collocation database (CDB) attainable for local use was dedicated to Russian. This is the topic of our paper, which summarizes the author's activities in 1990–2003 on the creation of an interactive system called **CrossLexica**. The core part of CrossLexica is a database of Russian collocations, with an auxiliary part containing something like a language-specific ingredient of EuroWordNet.

Ideologically, CrossLexica is based on the MTT, but it does not describe collocations in terms of lexical functions [21], and its syntactic types of collocations are not as fine-grained as the Superficial Syntactic Relations of the MTT.

For practical implementation, its unified interface, database management routines, and the first experiments were programmed by Alexander Gelbukh.

Though the main properties of CrossLexica and its possible applications were featured repeatedly, in Russian, Spanish, and English [5–13], some important issues, e.g., the diversified nature of the collocatives and peculiarities of the Russian collocation database, have not been described to date. This leaves room for this paper.

More specifically, our objectives are:

- To outline the most evident applications of the collocation databases;
- To describe possible options for the collocatives;
- To characterize the most important types of the collocations;
- To indicate other types of links between the collocatives in CrossLexica;

- To prove the interlingual universality of CrossLexica;
- To statistically characterize and to shortly discuss CrossLexica in its present state.

We use English examples for the illustrations except when English analogies fail.

2   Most Evident Applications

It seems instructive and motivating to start with the most evident and important applications of the CDBs, in order to see later how applicative demands could be satisfied.

Foreign language learning. The indispensability of collocations for learning foreign languages was made absolutely clear in the introduction to the popular manual [23], as well as in the theoretical study [22]. We have nothing to add.

Parsing. The modern non-lexicalized parsers usually produce numerous variants, i.e. different constituency trees for constituency grammars, and different dependency trees for dependency grammars. It is clear that dependency trees whose subtrees coincide with the collocations recorded in a CDB are more probable than others. In various languages, the coincidence is especially important for the correct attachment of prepositional phrases [25, 14]. E.g., the correct dependencies within the phrase *to boycott the election in protest against the tax* are revealed as soon as the collocation-based parser finds *to boycott the election, to boycott ... in protest,* and *protest against the tax* in its CDB, and does not find *election in protest* and *election against the tax*.

Word sense disambiguation. Taken out of context, a collocative can have different meanings, whereas any supplementary collocative can disambiguate its sense immediately. E.g., *bank* is for money in the CDB-proven context *reserve bank*, is by the river in *opposite bank*, and is for transfusion in *blood bank*, see, for example, [26; 19].

Malapropism detection & correction. Malapropism is the semantic error of replacing a real word by another real word, similar to the intended one in the sound and the syntactic function but quite different in the meaning, e.g., *travel around the <u>word</u>* (stands for *world*). To detect malapropisms, it was proposed in [12] to rely on semantic anomalies in texts arising from that the malapropisms usually destroy context collocation(s). E.g., the above phrase is syntactically correct but is not a collocation. The absence of such a combination in the CDB could signal a malapropism in the text under revision. To correct the error, it is necessary to search among real words for those similar to the offending one. If a candidate restores collocation(s) with other context words, it would be shown to the user to evaluate.

Automatic translation. Imagine a CDB with a foreign interface option. A user can introduce as a query a correct collocation in the predetermined foreign language. If the CDB contains, for each foreign collocative, an exhaustive list of its equivalents in the native language, all correct equivalents of the queried collocation will be output. Note that in the reverse direction a correct translation is generally unattainable.

Revealing text cohesion. The text *Mary ate quickly, the donuts were tasty* seems cohesive to us, since donuts are a food article; this makes clear just what Mary ate. An application can emulate the recognition of text cohesion if it finds the collocation *to eat the donuts* in its CDB [16].

Segmentation into paragraphs. In [9] a method was proposed for the automatic segmentation of texts into paragraphs. The cohesion at a current word is measured by the number of both purely semantic and intra-collocational links the word is within. A paragraph break is set near each rather deep local minimum for the cohesion measure.

Note that each application except that of language learning needs both idiomatic and free combinations [10]. In other words, the larger a CDB, the better performance is attainable in parsing, word sense disambiguation, malapropism detection & correction, etc. Since the total number of collocations (as we defined them) reaches several millions in any language, a CDB has no strict limits in its enlargement, but for each application there exists a minimal size allowing one to efficiently use the CDB.

3   Types and Features of Collocatives

The collocatives constitute a systemic dictionary of the corresponding CDB. They can be subdivided by several important features:

Parts of speech. The POS of a collocative is determined by its syntactical role in the corresponding collocations: it can be a noun, adjective, adverb or verb, i.e. any of the four principal POS. The adjectival role is inherent to both adjectives and participles. A prepositional phrase can play both an adjectival and adverbial role, e.g., the phrase *in substance* is adjectival in the collocation *unconstitutionality in substance* (≈ 'substantial') and is adverbial in *to verify in substance* (≈ 'substantially'). We consider such bi-functional collocatives homonymous, namely, of two different POS.

Grammemes. It was early proved that for the same Russian noun, the singular and plural number variants have their own sets of supplementing collocatives that intersect only partially. Printed dictionaries mark this feature as *mainly plur* or the like. So we split the morphoparadigm of each Russian noun to singular and plural, calling such subparadigms grammemes.

Verbs in European languages can play various syntactic roles: the participles are usually adjectivals, Russian and Spanish gerunds are adverbial, and personal forms are grammatical predicates. Based on the syntactic roles of the verbal collocatives in Russian, we divide their morphoparadigms into the grammemes of participles, gerunds, and personal forms plus infinitives.

Russian verbs have two aspects, perfect and imperfect, morphologically differing in their affixes, types of conjugation, and the way of tense formation. The aspects differ considerably in their combinability as well: the perfect tends to collocate with nouns in the singular, while the imperfect is indifferent to noun number; the perfect is usually modified with 'concentrated' adverbials like *suddenly, at once* or *straightway*, while the imperfect prefers 'spread' adverbials like *gradually, continuously* or *repeatedly*. So we additionally split Russian verbs into aspectual grammemes.

Homonyms. We consider various homonyms separately, just as in general-purpose dictionaries. Being combinatorially different, homonyms are especially useful for word sense disambiguation. The division into homonyms can be done in the CDBs on even more natural grounds than in common dictionaries. E.g., for the Russian noun *vremja* usually considered in only two senses, 'time' and 'tense', the first sense should be split in the CDBs at least to 'time$_1$ as measurable process' (*time elapsed*), 'time$_2$ as amount of time$_1$' (*considerable time*), and 'time$_3$ as a moment of time$_1$' (*arrival time*). The division into grammemes sometimes multiplies homonyms too. E.g., Rus. *banki* of plural has two senses: 'banks as financial institutions' and 'jars', whereas their singular forms are different: *bank* vs. *banka*.

Idioms. Idiomatic collocations like *point of* view taken as collocatives, since their meaning is not reducible to that of their heads and there always exists a difference in combinability between the idiom and its head. The use of idioms as collocatives does not contradict the additional inclusion of its components into the CDB as collocatives. Idiomatic composites with only one content word like *in no way* are collocatives too.

Multiword concepts. If a non-idiomatic multiword denotes a distinct concept expressible by single-word synonym, we treat it as a collocative. E.g., the Rus. term *puti soobščenija* 'routes of communications' has the synonym *kommunikacii*. A significant part of sci-tech terms are non-idiomatic but have a strict meaning by definition. Since they appear in common texts more and more frequently, we include them in the CDB. Though a multiword term conserves meanings of its components, its combinability usually differs from that of its head. Cf. the similar problem in EuroWordNet [4].

Absolute synonyms, abbreviations, morphologic variants. The concept of absolute synonyms is known in linguistics. They are replaceable in any context without alteration of the meaning (*sofa* = *settee*). Since all their collocations are the same, it is unreasonable to store them all. Absolute synonyms are very rare in any language, but rather frequent are various abbreviations (*United States of America* = *USA* = *United States*) and the so-called morphological variants (e.g., Rus. *nul'* = *nol'* 'zero' or *mučat'* = *mučit'* 'to torture'). We select one of these equivalents as a collocative and store collocations only for it, supplying the rest with the equivalence references to the preselected object. If a user demands collocations with an unselected equivalent, they are formed at runtime by corresponding replacement in the available collocation set.

Paste-ups. Many Russian noun-headed concepts are used in two equivalent forms: (1) a bigram consisting of a modifier with the stem S_1 plus its head noun with the stem S_2, or (2) a single noun containing the stems S_1 and S_2 or their initial parts or only S_1: *električeskij tok* 'electrical current' = *elektrotok*; *fizičeskij fakul'tet* 'physical faculty' = *fizfak*; *komičeskij akter* 'comical actor' = *komik*. The number of the paste-ups grows, especially in the newswire and everyday speech, but in dictionaries they are scarce. CrossLexica stores plenty of them in both forms. The paste-up is considered as a collocative, an absolute synonym of the bigram and a hyponym of its head, while the bigram is considered as a collocation.

Compound pairs. Russian has numerous stable pairs of nouns with dash between. The first noun has a fixed form (*press-centr* 'press center', *kakao-boby* 'cocoa beans') or, more frequently, is declinable, with the same grammatical case for the both nouns: *strana-učastnica* 'participant country', *letčik-ispytatel'* 'test pilot', *zavod-izgotovitel'* 'manufacturing plant'. A compound pair is also considered collocative, with the combinability different from that of its components.

Coordinated pairs. In all previous cases, the dependency links within multiword collocatives were of the subordinate type. However, a collocative can be a stable coordinated pair: *mother and father, safe and sound, sooner or later.* Some coordinated pairs have single-word synonym: *mother and father = parents, by and by = sometime.* We consider such pairs as both collocations (e.g., *sooner* and *later* are collocatives of the collocation *sooner or later*) and collocatives of the potential enclosing collocations. As an example of the recurrent decomposition, each bracketed item of the term [[[*probability*] [*theory*]] *and* [[*mathematical*] [*statistics*]]] is considered a collocative to be stored in the dictionary autonomously.

Synonyms, hyperonyms/hyponyms, antonyms. The links of synonymy, hyperonymy/hyponymy, and antonymy differ radically from those considered above. Yet we have involved, with the normal collocatives, single or multiwords linked to other collocatives in a purely semantic way—to enrich the CDB at runtime (see the section 5). Each of them should be an element of texts rather than a conceptual construct.

Proper names. We also consider as collocatives those proper names that constitute an inalienable part of our encyclopedic knowledge: geographic objects, countries, famous persons, large organizations, etc. All of them are linked to their hyperonyms: *country, mountains, island, writer, organization,* etc.

Semantic derivates. For any lexeme, its SDs are lexemes of any POS with meaning containing basically the same elements, cf. the section 5 on why we involve SDs. E.g., *to marry, marriage, bride, bridegroom,* and *matrimonial* are SDs of each other. In WordNet, such links between words of different POS are called XPOS [28]. Luckily, many SDs acquire their collocations in the process of replenishment of CDBs.

Idiomaticity in general. All complete idioms found were included as collocations. There was no problem in decomposition of syntactically bipartite idioms (*sest'* | *v galošu* 'to get | into a fix', lit. 'to sit | into a galosh'). In rarer cases of tripartite idioms the dichotomy was merely a practical step. E.g., in *byt'* | *bez carja v golove* 'to be stupid', lit. 'to be | without the tsar in one's head', we regard the right part as a modifier. Only two labels to characterize the idiomacity were taken: **idiom** and **possible idiom**. The latter concerns collocations with both figurative and direct senses, e.g., *sest' v lužu* means 'to get into a mess' or 'to sit down into a puddle'. We label not only complete idioms, but without a strict threshold of idiomaticity (cf. the section 1).

Usage marks. We take the following usage categories: (1) **neutral**: neither mark nor limitations on the use are needed; (2) **special, bookish or obsolete**: the use in writing is recommended if the meaning is clear to the speaker; (3) **colloquial**: the use in official writing is not recommended; (4) **vulgar**: both written and oral use are prohibited; and (5) **incorrect**: is encountered sometimes but is prohibited as contradicting language norms. If a usage mark labels a collocative, all its collocations are transitively labeled in the same way.

4 Types of Collocations

In many languages, collocations join collocatives of any POS among the principal four, the case of POS coincidence included. However the whole set of collocation types and the percentage of each type in the global set is specific for each language. The following are types of Russian collocations illustrated where possible by English examples. Each collocation is accessible through both its collocatives, so that the syntactic category of the collocative supplementing the queried one depends on direction of the access.

Modifiers. We combine in a single group all modifying and attributive collocatives irrespective of what POS has the head collocative: _great_ ← _country_; _man_ → _of letters_; _eat_ → _quickly_; _enormously_ ← _big_; _very_ ← _well_. Here the arrows give syntactic dependencies, and the modifiers are underlined. In response to a queried headword, the delivery category is HAS_MODIFIERS, in the inverse direction, IS_MODIFIER_OF.

Verbs with their subjects. The grammatical subject is a specific dependent of a predicate verb: _father_ ← _died_; _bus_ ← _arrives_. In response to a queried verb, the delivery category is HAS_SUBJECTS, in the inverse direction, IS_SUBJECT_OF. A specifically Russian type of the subject-to-predicate link concerns a predicate containing the standard copula _byt'_ 'to be' (omitted in present tense) and an adjectival in short form: _god_ ← _zaveršen_ (participle) 'the year is over'; _vek_ ← _korotok_ (adjective) 'the age is short'.

Verbs with their noun complements. We call noun complements of a verb all the nouns dependent on the verb as direct, indirect or prepositional object: _to read a book_; _to strive for peace_. We also consider as complements circumstantial phrases like _to travel by train_. A verb can have any number of complements; each its collocation picks up only one of them, while the omission of other obligatory complement(s) (if any) is marked in the delivery with the ellipsis: _to give ... to the boy_. In response to a queried verb, the delivery category is HAS_COMPLEMENTS, in the inverse direction, IS_COMPLEMENT_OF. Just the same categories are valid for all the following types of collocations with complements.

Nouns with their noun complements. In dependency grammars, all POS can have noun complements depending on the heads in similar ways as on verbs. E.g., the collocations _capital of the country_ and _struggle against poverty_ have noun heads.

Adjectivals with their noun complements. These are collocations like _blind with rage_, _mentioned by the observer_ or _going to the cinema_.

Verbs with their infinitive complements. These are collocations like _stop to talk_ or _permit to enter_.

Nouns with their infinitive complements. These are collocations like _permission to enter_ or _cream to protect_.

Adjectivals with their infinitive complements. These are collocations like _forced to return_ or _ready to appeal_.

Adverbials with their infinitive complements. These are purely Russian collocations: *xolodno idti* 'it is cold to go', lit. 'coldly to go'. They are possible only with
specific predicative adverbs. The same link exists for gerunds: *reshiv idti* 'after having decided to go'.

Adverbials with their noun complements. These are purely Russian collocations:
xolodno (adverb) *bez pal'to* 'it is cold without a coat', lit. 'coldly without a coat';
pobyvav (gerund) *v centre* 'after visiting the center'.

Verbs with their adjectival complements. These are collocations like *to remain
silent* or *to consider... stupid*.

Adjectivals with their adjectival complements. These are collocations like *remaining silent* or *considering ... stupid*.

Coordinated pairs. These are collocations like *mom and dad, safe and sound*, or
sooner or later, cf. [13] for detail.

5   Other Links between Collocatives

The first auxiliary group of links between collocatives comprises the following semantic links:

Synonyms. In distinction from WordNet synsets, our synonymy group has a dominant member and maybe member(s) marked as absolute synonym(s) of the dominant.
Our synonyms can be actually periphrastic multiwords or even short descriptive definitions: *to help* ≈ *to give help; fall* ≈ *quick descent; suffocation* ≈ *lack of fresh air*.
Non-absolute synonyms are used for heuristic inferences of new collocations from
those already available in the CDB [11]: if the collocative C_1 has the dominant D, and
D forms a collocation with the collocative C_2, then C_1 forms the collocation of the
same type with C_2 (Cf. the discussion of such inferences in the section 7).

Hyponyms *vs.* Hyperonyms. Hyponym-to-hyperonym links form a multihierarchy
on the collocative set. Hyperonyms are used for the inferences too [11]: if the collocative C_1 has the hyperonym H, and H forms a collocation with the collocative C_2,
then C_1 forms the collocation of the same type with C_2. If the hyperonym H of C_1 has
no relevant collocations, a hyperonym of H is tested for the same purpose, etc.

Antonyms. Together with antonyms in their standard definition (*good—bad, van-
guard—rearguard*), we consider opposite notions: *missiles—antimissiles*.

Meronyms *vs.* Holonyms. Meronym-to-holonym (part-to-the-whole) links like *finger—hand, motor—car* also form a multihierarchy on the collocative set.

Semantic derivates (SD). Following is a sample family with each member being
derivate of the rest: *Nouns: possession, property, possessor; Adjs: possessive, possessing, possessed; Verbs: possess, be possessed, appropriate; Advs: in possession*.
   There are several reasons of involving SDs. Firstly, only SD families connect parts
of the morphoparadigms split into grammemes. Secondly, SDs describe the same idea

from various aspects, thus compensating for the lack of glosses in CrossLexica. Some derivates give related information of an encyclopedic nature. For this purpose, in the families dedicated to countries, together with their names, the names of corresponding capitals, nationals, and currency units are included.

The second auxiliary block of links concerns the exterior similarity of words.

Literal paronyms. They are at the distance of few editing operations from each other. In the simplest case, the operation is single: a replacement of a letter with another letter, an omission of a letter, an insertion of a letter or a permutation of two adjacent letters. E.g., the literal paronyms of *sign* are *sigh, sin, sing*. The literal paronyms are useful to correct the malapropisms: the correcting program does not search candidates for replacement by tentative editing operations, but it immediately takes all previously collected literal paronyms of a suspicious word met in a text.

Morphemic paronyms. They are of the same POS and radix but have different prefixes and/or suffixes. E.g., *sens-ation-al, sens-ible, in-sens-ible, sens-itive, sens-less, sens-ual* are morphemic paronyms to each other, and if to convert them to the strings of morphemic symbols, the strings *sens-ible, sens-itive, sens-less, sens-ual* will be at the minimal distance 1 of each other. Foreigners' malapropisms can be just the replacements of one morphemic paronym by another. CrossLexica stores numerous families of morphemic paronyms to immediately propose candidates for correcting such errors. Linguistically, this is excursion to the word derivation.

The third auxiliary block is the bilingual dictionary 'Russian collocatives—all their English equivalents' and its inverse file. A user can compose a query in English only of those equivalents but finds all corresponding Russian collocations.

The fourth auxiliary block generates all morphological forms of a queried collocative. This excursion to the word formation completes CrossLexica as a morphologic, syntactic, and lexical 'reference book'.

6 Structural Universality

CrossLexica contains two main data structures: a dictionary of collocatives and a set of links between them. Each dictionary entry contains the list of morphological categories of a given collocative and a series of references to the substructures of links between this collocative and the rest. Hence the structure of the upper level does not depend on specific language.

On the lower level, the links between collocatives can be language specific. Let us outline grammatical peculiarities of Russian that influence these links, comparing them mainly with English.

Nouns declinable. Russian complements depend on their heads either directly, with a certain grammatical case (and thus the ending) of the dependent, or through a preposition determining the dependent's case. So a link between a head collocative and its complement codes the combination {preposition, case}. If a language does not have cases (as English), the link codes merely the ordinal number of the preposition.

Adjectivals declinable. Russian adjectivals have number, gender, case, and animacy agreeing with the head nouns. Each adjectival is stored in the dictionary in its standard form {singular, masculine, nominative case}, and the agreement in a collocation is reached at runtime. In English this problem does not exist.

Too few tenses. Russian verbs have three tenses. So the involving of all possible tenses met in texts does not inflate the CDB. English has many tenses. Were it proven that the supplementing collocative sets do not depend on tense, the CDB could store collocations with the most frequent tense, and the rest could be generated on the user's demand. However, some English verbs are not used in a continuous tense (*to see*), whereas some others occur predominantly in that form (*to be teething*). If a lexicographic study will confirm the combinatorial opposition 'continuous *vs.* non-continuous', the opposing tense groups should be considered separate grammemes.

No articles. Russian has no articles, whereas in the article-using languages the links to complements contain articles in definite, indefinite or empty form. Hence, for language learning, especially of Romance languages amalgamating articles with prepositions, it is important to know all possible articles in each collocation. A tentative solution is to include a special symbol instead of the article and to generate all its options at runtime on the user's demand. To represent only permitted options for each collocation, a laborious lexicographic study is needed.

No phrasal verbs. Only few Russian verbs significantly change their combinability after the adjunction of an auxiliary word, e.g. *vesti* 'to drive/lead' vs. *vesti sebja* 'to behave'. In English, the phrasal verbs are different in their combinability from the basic verbs. Treating phrasal verbs as multiword collocatives eliminates the problem.

Nouns cannot modify nouns. In Russian a noun set at anteposition to another noun to modify or attribute the latter is impossible, whereas in English the collocations like *mother board* are quite common. Many preceding nouns in English can have their own preceding nouns, while the preceding adjectives cannot be modified in such a way. Hence, to treat the preceding nouns as adjectivals is impossible and a specifically English attributive type should be introduced for such collocations.

The considerations above prove that the Cross-Lexica structure is linguistically universal. Indeed, the identified differences in the coding of links between the collocatives can be easily resolved while programming.

7   Statistics and Some Discussion

The dictionary of collocatives in CrossLexica now (November, 2003) totals to slightly more that 120,000 entries.

All collocations are divided into three classes: primary, secondary, and inferred.

The primary collocations are acquired by types from various sources, by hand or semi-automatically, and constitute large textual *I*-files. The latter are transformed into textual *M*-files where collocatives are automatically (unassisted by any side dictionary) supplied with relevant morphological features.

The secondary collocations result from morphological transformations of the primary *M*-files. For example, the *M*-files 'verbs with their noun complements' are transformed to the *M*-files 'adjectivals with their noun complements' (e.g., *to participate in the meeting* gives *participating in the meeting*). With enumeration of collocation types given in Table 1, the transformations are **1→2, 2→1, 3→5, 3→11.** All morphologically wrong results occurring during the transformations are discarded. The *M*-files are destined for the further conversion to the operational (runtime ready) form, with creation of the collocative dictionary and the set of links.

Table 1. Statistics of collocations

No.	Type of collocations	Primary	Secondary
1	Nouns/Verbs/Adjs/Advs with modifiers	*276,200	*99,300
2	Verbs with their subjects	*104,600	*27,300
3	Verbs with their noun complements	*201,400	
4	Nouns with their noun complements	*125,000	
5	Adjectivals with their noun complements	13,400	173,200
6	Verbs with their infinitive complements	11,600	
7	Nouns with their infinitive complements	5,700	
8	Verbs with their adjectival complements	6,600	
9	Adverbials with their infinitive complements	1,300	
10	Adjectivals with their infinitive complements	200	
11	Adverbials with their noun complements	100	148,800
12	Adjectivals with their adjectival complements	100	
13	Coordinated pairs	3,300	
	Totals	**749,500**	**448,600**

Table 1 gives statistics for the primary and secondary collocations. The asterisks show what classes are already converted to the operational form. Within the primary files, the operational form is completed now for only four types of 12, but this is 94% of the collocations of this type. Among the secondary collocations, the operational form covers now two classes of four, i.e. 28% of collocations. The numbers of primary and secondary collocations are 749,500 and 448,600 relatively, totally ca. 1.2 million. Since each collocation is accessible from both sides, the total of the unilateral links is ca. 2.4 millions.

The inferred collocations are formed at runtime, based on the primary collocations and the semantic links among collocatives (cf. the section 5). Besides synonymy and hyperonymy, the links between related grammemes are used for this purpose: 'plural *vs.* singular' for nouns and 'perfect *vs.* imperfect' for verbs. The links between grammemes are used if only one related grammeme in the pair has collocations of the relevant type, while the query contains the supplementing one.

All heuristic inferences are performed with some constraints [11], e.g., the source collocation cannot be an idiom, to avoid the inference like (*hot dog*)idiom & (*poodle* **IS_A** *dog*) → *(*hot poodle*). Nevertheless, correct collocations are mostly inferred for 'homogeneous' nouns like flowers, fruits, refreshing drinks, etc. CrossLexica takes their generic names and infers collocations for the species. In any language, these nouns are not so numerous. The remaining inferences can be questionable but provide useful raw material for off-line enrichment of the primary files.

The total of the inferred collocations never exceeded 6 to 8% of the primaries and has been declining, because the rare species are getting, one-by-one, a full description within the primaries. In Table 1, we did not take into account inferred collocations.

In Table 2, statistics of other links between collocatives is given. All links are considered unilateral, e.g., n antonyms pairs give $2n$ unilateral links, and a group of n synonyms gives $n(n-1)/2$ links. The groups **1** to **5** (91% of links) are already in the operational form. One can see that the total approaches to 1.2 million links.

Table 2. Statistics of semantic and other links

No.	Type of links	Amt. of links
1	Semantic derivates	821,200
2	Synonyms	212,200
3	Meronyms *vs.* holonyms	20,700
4	Hyponyms *vs.* hyperonyms	13,700
5	Antonyms	10,500
6	Morphemic paronyms	86,200
7	Literal paronyms	20,400
	Total	**1,184,900**

Statistics of collocational productivity of the collocatives proved to be very instructive. Dividing the number of the collocations 'verbs with their noun complements' by the number of the dependent nouns, we obtain the mean value 15.1, whereas its division by the number of the verbs gives 17.8. If we divide the number of the collocations 'nouns with their noun complements' by the number of the dependent nouns, the mean value is 13.4, whereas its division by the number of the heads gives 12.6. The average group of modifiers of the primary class numbers 12.7, etc. All mean values are in the interval 8 to 18 and became stable after gathering only a third part of the actual total of the primary files.

The amount of the involved word combinations is too large to consider such low mean values as a matter of chance. This means that no soaring inflation of the CDB occurred because of the involving of semantically free word combinations. Though English and Russian are different and the introduction of grammemes influenced the statistics, we can very roughly estimate this inflation—by comparing sizes of Oxford dictionary (150,000 collocations, cf. [19]) and ours (750,000)—at five. The evident explanation is that the very semantics of collocatives imposes constraints on the number of word combinations they can be in.

The mentioned stability seems to confirm our strategy for collocation acquisition. It can be defined as **intuitively conceived recurrence** in texts of each acquired word combination. Any use of intuition by a dictionary compiler can be debatable as subjective and even contradicting to 'strict' statistical methods, but no new dictionary was ever compiled without intuition.

Our approach does not mean that **each** word combination met it texts is accepted. We reject word combinations like *practitioner's dress* or *sperm of the president* from the story on the Clinton *vs.* Lewinsky scandal because the description of the next top-rank scandal will scarcely contain them. However both these combinations can be **inferred** from such a CDB and therefore be admitted as conceivable.

8 Conclusions and Further Work

We have developed a system consisting of a Russian collocation database (more than a million collocations) and a multitude of WordNet-like links between collocation components (more than a million unilateral links). Besides Russian language learning and interactive word processing, the system can be considered as a mighty tool for numerous computational applications: syntactic analysis; word sense disambiguation; semantic errors detection & correction; text translation, generation and segmentation; revealing text cohesion.

We anticipate the following directions of further research & development:

1. Conversion of collocations of all classes and types to their operational form;
2. An intensive proofreading of the database created by a single person—in orthographic, morphologic, homonymic, and idiomatic aspects;
3. Splitting a greater number of collocatives into homonyms, based on the already available sets of their collocations;
4. Progressive enlargement of the database, especially by use of the Internet;
5. Performing a large series of tests on what part of text of various genres is covered by the available collocation set, with filling any identified lacunas.
6. Carrying out pilot projects on the applications of the system at large.

References

1. Banerjee, Satanjeev, T. Pedersen. *The Design, Implementation and Use of Ngram Statistics Package*. In: A. Gelbukh (Ed.). *Computational Linguistics and Intelligent Text Processing*. Proc. Intern. Conf. CICLing-2003, Febrary 2003, Mexico. Lecture Notes in Computer Science 2588, Springer, 2003, p. 370-381.
2. Benson, M., E. Benson, R. Ilson. *The BBI Combinatory Dictionary of English*. John Benjamin Publ., 1986.
3. Bogatz, H. *The Advanced Reader's Collocation Searcher (ARCS)*. ISBN 09709341-4-9, http:www.asksam.com/web/bogatz, 1997.
4. Bentivogli, L., E. Pianta. *Detecting Hidden Multiwords in Bilingual Dictionaries*. Proc. 10th EURALEX Intern. Congress, Copenhagen, Denmark, August 2002, p. 14-17.
5. Bolshakov, I. A. *Thesaurus in word processing: What should it be?* International Forum on Information and Documentation. Vol. 16, No. 2, 1991, p. 3-10.
6. Bolshakov, I. A. *Multifunctional thesaurus for computerized preparation of Russian texts*. Automatic Documentation and Mathematical Linguistics. Allerton Press Inc. Vol. 28, No. 1, 1994, p. 13-28.
7. Bolshakov, I. A. *Multifunction thesaurus for Russian word processing*. Proc. 4th Conf. on Applied Natural language Processing, Stuttgart, October 1994, p. 200-202.
8. Bolshakov, I. A., A. Gelbukh. *A Very Large Database of Collocations and Semantic Links*. In: M. Bouzeghoub *et al.* (Eds.) *Natural Language Processing and Information Systems*. Proc. Intern. Conf. on Applications of Natural Language to Information Systems NLDB-2000. Lecture Notes in Computer Science 1959, Springer, 2001, p. 103-114.
9. Bolshakov, I. A., A. Gelbukh. *Text Segmentation to Paragraphs Based on Local Text Cohesion*. In: V. Matoušek *et al.* (Eds.) *Text, Speech and Dialogue*. Proc. 4th Intern. Conf. TSD-2001. Lecture Notes in Artificial Intelligence 2166, Springer, 2001, p. 158-166.
10. Bolshakov, I. A., A. Gelbukh. *Word Combinations as an Important Part of Modern Electronic Dictionaries*. Procesamiento del Lenguaje Natural, No. 29, 2002, p. 47-54.

11. Bolshakov, I. A., A. Gelbukh. *Heuristics-Based Replenishment of Collocation Databases.* In: E. Ranchhold, N. J. Mamede (Eds.) *Advances in Natural Language Processing.* Proc. Intern. Conf. PorTAL 2002, Faro, Portugal. Lecture Notes in Artificial Intelligence 2389, Springer, 2002, p. 25-32.

12. Bolshakov, I. A., A. Gelbukh. *On Detection of Malapropisms by Multistage Collocation Testing.* In: A. Düsterhöft, B. Talheim (Eds.) Proc. 8th Intern. Conf. on Applications of Natural Language to Information Systems NLDB-2003, Burg, Germany. GI-Edition, Lecture Notes in Informatics V. P-29, Bonn, 2003, p. 28-41.

13. Bolshakov, I. A., A. Gelbukh, S. N. Galicia-Haro. *Stable Coordinated Pairs in Text Processing.* In: V. Matoušek, P. Mautner (Eds.) *Text, Speech and Dialogue.* Proc. 6th Intern. Conf. TSD 2003. Lecture Notes in Artificial Intelligence 2807, Springer, 2003, p. 27-34.

14. Calvo, H., and A. Gelbukh. *Improving Disambiguation of Prepositional Phrase Attachments Using the Web as Corpus.* In: Progress in Pattern Recognition, Speech and Image Analysis (CIARP'2003), Lecture Notes in Computer Science 2905, Springer-Verlag, 2003, pp. 604-610.

15. Fellbaum, Ch. (Ed.) *WordNet: An Electronic Lexical Database.* MIT Press, 1998.

16. Gelbukh, A., G. Sidorov, I. A. Bolshakov. *Dictionary-based Method for Coherence Maintenance in Man-Machine Dialogue with Indirect Antecedents and Ellipses.* In: P. Sojka *et al.* (Eds.) *Text, Speech and Dialogue.* Proc. 3rd Intern. Conf. TSD-2000. Lecture Notes in Artificial Intelligence 1902, Springer, 2000, p. 357-352.

17. Gelbukh, A., G. Sidorov , S.-Y. Han, E. Hernández-Rubio. *Automatic Syntactic Analysis for Detection of Word Combinations.* Computational Linguistics and Intelligent Text Processing (CICLing-2004). Lecture Notes in Computer Science, N 2945, Springer-Verlag, 2004 (this volume), pp. 240–244.

18. Gelbukh, A., G. Sidorov , S.-Y. Han, E. Hernández-Rubio. *Automatic Enrichment of Very Large Dictionary of Word Combinations on the Basis of Dependency Formalism.* In: Proc. Mexican International Conference on Artificial Intelligence (MICAI-2004). Lecture Notes in Artificial Intelligence, N 2972, Springer-Verlag, 2004.

19. Ledo Mezquita, Y., G. Sidorov, A. Gelbukh. *Tool for Computer-Aided Spanish Word Sense Disambiguation.* In: Computational Linguistics and Intelligent Text Processing (CICLing-2003). Lecture Notes in Computer Science, N 2588, Springer-Verlag6 2003, pp. 277-280.

20. Manning, Ch. D., H. Schütze. *Foundations of Statistical Natural Language Processing.* MIT Press, 1999.

21. Mel'čuk, I. *Dependency Syntax: Theory and Practice.* SONY Press, NY, 1988.

22. Mel'čuk, I. *Phrasemes in Language and Phraseology in Linguistics.* In: M. Everaert *et al.* (Eds.) *Idioms: Structural and Psychological Perspectives.* Lawrence Erlbaum Associates Publ., Hillsdale, NJ / Hove, UK, 1995, p. 169-252.

23. *Oxford Collocations Dictionary for Students of English.* Oxford University Press. 2003.

24. Sag, I. A. *et al. Multiword Expressions: A Pain in the Neck for NLP.* In: A. Gelbukh (Ed.). *Computational Linguistics and Intelligent Text Processing.* Proc. Intern. Conf. CICLing-2002. Lecture Notes in Computer Science 2276, Springer, 2002, p. 1-15.

25. Satoshi Sekine *et al. Automatic Learning for Semantic Collocation.* Proc. 3rd Conf. on Applied Natural Language Processing ANLP, Trento, Italy, 1992, p. 104-110.

26. Sidorov, G., and A. Gelbukh. Word sense disambiguation in a Spanish explanatory dictionary. Proc. of TALN-2001 (Tratamiento automático de lenguaje natural), Tours, France, July 2–5, 2001, pp 398-402.

27. Smadja, F. *Retrieving Collocations from text: Xtract.* Computational Linguistics. Vol. 19, No. 1, 1990, p. 143-177.

28. Vossen, P. (Ed.). *EuroWordNet General Document.* Vers. 3 final. www.hum.uva.nl/~ewn. 2000.

Automatic Syntactic Analysis
for Detection of Word Combinations*

Alexander Gelbukh[1,2], Grigori Sidorov[1], Sang-Yong Han[2+], and
Erika Hernández-Rubio[1]

[1] Center for Computing Research, National Polytechnic Institute,
Av. Juan Dios Batiz s/n, Zacatenco 07738, Mexico City, Mexico
{gelbukh, sidorov}@cic.ipn.mx, www.gelbukh.com
[2] Department of Computer Science and Engineering, Chung-Ang University,
221 Huksuk-Dong, DongJak-Ku, Seoul, 156-756, Korea
hansy@cau.ac.kr

Abstract. The paper presents a method for automatic detection of "non-trivial" word combinations in the text. It is based on automatic syntactic analysis. The method shows better precision and recall than the baseline method (bigrams). It was tested on a text in Spanish. The method can be used for enrichment of very large dictionaries of word combinations.

1 Introduction

The concept of word combination is related to the possibility of different words to appear together in the text connected by a syntactic link. The task is not computationally trivial because syntactically connected words can be linearly far from each other, i.e., separated by other words.

There are different types of word combinations. Some word combinations are fixed, like idioms, e.g., *to kick the bucket* or lexical functions like *to pay attention* [14]. In case of idioms and lexical functions, the meaning of the whole cannot be deduced from the meaning of the constituent words. In idioms, usually all words loose theirs meanings. As far as lexical functions are concerned, only one word (in case of our example, *attention*) keeps its meaning, while the other word (*to pay*) expresses standard semantic relation between actants of the situation. Detailed description of lexical functions can be found, for example, in [14] or other works by Mel' uk. Since the meaning of the combinations is not a sum of the meanings of the words, there are severe restrictions for compatibility in lexical functions. Namely, if we want to express the given meaning and the words that conserves its meaning is known, then usually the choice of the other word is predetermined.

---

* Work done under partial support of Mexican Government (CONACyT, SNI), IPN (CGPI, COFAA, PIFI), Korean Government (KIPA Professorship for Visiting Faculty Positions in Korea), and ITRI of Chung-Ang University. First author is currently on Sabbatical leave at Chung-Ang University. We thank Prof. I. A. Bolshakov for useful discussion.
+ Corresponding author.

A. Gelbukh (Ed.): CICLing 2004, LNCS 2945, pp. 243–247, 2004.
© Springer-Verlag Berlin Heidelberg 2004

In free word combinations, the meaning of a whole is obtained by summing the meanings of the constituent words. Still, always there are semantic constraints for compatibility even in free word combinations. For example, for the verb *to eat*, it is expected that its dependent (direct object) will be certain kind of food, etc. Thus, some words have a broader compatibility than the other, for example, *to see* can be combined with practically any physical object, while *to read* only with something that contains written material (some metaphoric usages are possible also), etc.

For denoting some "important" word combinations, a term *collocation* is used. There is no commonly accepted definition of collocation. In a strict sense, only idioms and lexical functions are collocations because they contain the information that cannot be deduced. Nevertheless, this contradicts to common practice [1, 2, 15], when frequent word combinations are also considered collocations.

In NLP tasks, a dominating approach for defining collocations is based on the mutual information of words. We can see that some pairs of words have high conditional probability, i.e., if we encounter one word in the text, then the probability to encounter the other word is relatively high; while the conditional probabilities of the majority of randomly chosen word pairs are very low. It is called mutual information. This is purely statistic point of view that ignores the semantic properties of word combinations. In many works, collocations (in the sense of mutual information) are detected automatically [4, 9, 11, 12, 16, 18]. In [16], some syntactic heuristics are used additionally for filtering the obtained collocations. Nevertheless, these methods ignore the overwhelming majority of word combinations including lexical functions and idioms that do not have sufficiently high frequency.

Are idioms, lexical functions, and free word combinations useful in natural language processing? The answer for idioms and lexical functions is obviously positive. Free word combinations (even without sufficient mutual information) are also useful for many NLP tasks; see, for example, [3, 8, 13, 17]. This idea is supported by manual development of the dictionaries of word combinations [2, 5, 6, 7, 15].

In this paper, we propose a method of automatic detection of word combinations of different types based on the automatic syntactic analysis (parsing).

The proposed method can be used for semiautomatic enrichment of the dictionaries of collocations and free word combinations. For example, one of the largest dictionaries of this type is CrossLexica [5, 7, 8] that contains about 750,000 word combinations for Russian language. CrossLexica was compiled manually during about 14 years. We hope that our method can facilitate substantially the compilation process.

In the rest of the paper, we first describe the method of automatic detection of word combinations, evaluate its performance, and finally draw some conclusions.

2   Experimental Setting

We conducted our experiment for a randomly selected Spanish text available from Internet (*Cervantes Digital Library*). In our experiments, we used probabilistic parser and CF-grammar with unification for Spanish language described in [10].

In the experiment, we apply the program that performs syntactic analysis, obtains word combinations with corresponding relation between words, filters them, and stores them in a database.

For filtering, we use both syntactic and morphological features. Say, we filter out relations with pronouns and articles according to morphological filters. In addition, we apply syntactic filters, according to which only word combinations that have the following syntactic relations are left: verb-subject, verb-object (direct or indirect), noun-modifier (adjective or other noun), verb-modifier (adverb). The other syntactic relations are filtered out. The name of relation is stored as well.

Some special cases are: (1) coordinative relation (for example, *to read newspaper and magazine* should give two word combinations *to read newspaper* and *to read magazine*), so, we split the relation; (2) relation with preposition. In case of prepositions, we took the dependent word of the preposition and marked its relation with the head (master) word of the preposition. This is justified by the fact that prepositions usually express grammar relations (say, in some languages these relations can be expressed by grammar cases), so they are not important for lexical links. On the other hand, the choice of a preposition is important linguistic information. Therefore, in this case we store all three members.

We used as a baseline a method of gathering the word combinations that takes all word pairs that are immediate neighbors (bigrams). We incorporated certain intelligence into the baseline method. Namely, after the modification, it ignores the articles and takes into account the prepositions. Let us present an example of our analysis.

Mamá compró una torta pequeñita y un pastel con una bailarina en zapatillas de punta. (Mother bought a little bun and a cake with a dancer in ballet-shoes.)

The following syntactic dependency tree corresponds to this sentence. The dependent words are below the headword with the horizontal shift equal to the horizontal shift of the headword plus 1, e.g., the verb in the line 1 has dependents in the lines 2, 14, 15; the conjunction in the line 2 has dependents in the line 3 and in the line 6; etc.

Note that the words are normalizes morphologically. We used Spanish morphological analyzer described in [10].

We mark with bold the syntactic categories that are used in our grammar. They have natural interpretation: *V* stands for verb, *N* – for noun, *SG* – for singular, etc. For marking the name of syntactic relation, {} are used. Note that the name of relation is stored with the dependent word, because the head can have several dependents. In parenthesis (), there are the word and its lemma along with their translation into English, e.g. (*compró: comprar / bought : to buy*).

```
1  V(SG,3PRS,MEAN) ( compró: comprar / bought : to buy)
2     CONJ_C {obj} ( y: y / and : and)
3        N(SG,FEM) {coord_conj} ( torta: torta / bun : bun)
4           ADJ(SG,FEM) {mod} ( pequeñita: pequeñito / little : little)
5              ART(SG,FEM) {det} ( una: un / a : a)
6        N(SG,MASC) {coord_conj} ( pastel: pastel / cake : cake)
7           PR {prep} ( con: con / with : with)
8              N(SG,FEM) {prep} ( bailarina: bailarina / dancer : dancer)
9                 PR {prep} ( con: con / with : with)
10                   N(PL,FEM) {prep} ( zapatillas: zapatilla / shoes : shoe)
11                      PR {prep} ( de: de / of : of)
12                         N(SG,FEM) {prep} ( punta: punta / point : point)
13                            ART(SG,FEM) {det} ( una: un / a : a)
14    N(SG,FEM) {subj} ( mamá: mamá / mother : mother)
15    $PERIOD (.: .,)
```

The following word combinations were found in this sentence. Note that the word combinations 4 and 7 are filtered out due to the morphological filters.

1. *comprar* (obj) *torta*{Sg} (*buy* (obj) *bun*{Sg})
2. *comprar* (obj) *pastel* {Sg} (*buy* (obj) *cake* {Sg})
3. *torta* (mod) *pequeñito* (*bun* (mod) *little*)
4. *torta* (det) *un* (*bun* (det) *a*)
5. *pastel* (mod) [*con*] *bailarina* {Sg} (*cake* (mod) [*with*] *dancer* {Sg})
6. *bailarina* (mod) [*con*] *zapatilla* {Pl} (*dancer* (mod) [*with*] *shoe* {Pl})
7. *bailarina* (det) *un* (*dancer* (det) *a*)
8. *zapatilla* (mod) [*de*] *punta* {Sg} (*shoe* (mod) [*with*] *point* {Sg} //= *ballet shoe*)
9. *comprar* (subj) *mamá* {Sg} (*buy* (subj) *mother* {Sg})

We also store the information about morphological form of the dependent word in some cases (number for nouns; gerund/infinitive/finite for verbs) since this information may affect the compatibility. Note that the words are normalized anyway: e.g., we store *shoe* {Pl} instead of *shoes*. This can be necessary for further calculation of statistics with the possibility to take into account or ignore these morphological characteristics.

3 Experimental Results

The parsed text contains 741 words in 60 sentences. Average length of a sentence is 12.4 words. Apart, we marked syntactic relations in these sentences manually.

For the baseline, the total number of words is 588 because among 741 words there are 153 articles and prepositions in the sentences.

The following results were obtained. The total number of correct manually marked word combinations is 208. From these, 148 word combinations were found by our method. At the same time, the baseline method found correctly 111 word combinations. On the other hand, our method found only 63 incorrect word combinations, while the baseline method marked as word combinations 1175 pairs (588*2 − 1 = 1175), from which 1064 are wrong pairs (1175 − 111 = 1064).

These numbers give us the following values of precision and recall. Let us remind that precision is the relation of the correctly found to totally found, while recall is the relation of the correctly found to the total number that should have been found. For our method, precision is 148 / (148+63) = 0.70 and recall is 148 / 208 = 0.71. For the baseline method, precision is 111 / 1175 = 0.09 and recall is 111 / 208 = 0.53. It can be seen that recall of our method is better and precision is much better than those parameters of the baseline method.

The results of our method can be improved by developing better grammar for the Spanish language than the grammar that we use now.

4 Conclusions

We presented a method of automatic detection of word combinations of certain types. The method is based on the results of syntactic analysis. Syntactic and morphological filters are used to avoid the trivial word combinations.

The method was tested for Spanish and shows better precision and recall than the baseline bigram method that takes all word pairs that are immediate neighbors. In our case, the baseline method was improved by ignoring the articles and processing prepositions. The proposed method can be used for semiautomatic enrichment of dictionaries of word combinations and allows for making it much easier and faster.

References

1. Baddorf, D. S. and M. W. Evens. Finding phrases rather than discovering collocations: Searching corpora for dictionary phrases. In: *Proc. of the 9th Midwest Artificial Intelligence and Cognitive Science Conference (MAICS'98)*, Dayton, USA, 1998.
2. Bank of English. Collins. http://titania.cobuild.collins.co.uk/boe_info.html
3. Basili, R., M. T. Pazienza, and P. Velardi. Semi-automatic extraction of linguistic information for syntactic disambiguation. *Applied Artificial Intelligence*, 7:339-64, 1993.
4. Biemann, C., S. Bordag, G. Heyer, U. Quasthoff, C. Wolff. Language-independent methods for compiling monolingual lexical data. In: A. Gelbukh (Ed.) *Computational Linguistics and Intelligent Text Processing*. Lecture Notes in Computer Science, N 2945, Springer-Verlag, 2004 (this volume).
5. Bolshakov, I. A. Multifunction thesaurus for Russian word processing. In: *Proceedings of 4th Conference on Applied Natural language Processing*, Stuttgart, 1994, p. 200-202.
6. Bolshakov, I. A. Getting One's First Million... Collocations. In: A. Gelbukh (Ed.) *Computational Linguistics and Intelligent Text Processing*. Lecture Notes in Computer Science, N 2945, Springer-Verlag, 2004 (this volume).
7. Bolshakov, I. A., A. Gelbukh. A Very Large Database of Collocations and Semantic Links. In: Mokrane et al. (Eds.) *Natural Language Processing and Information* Systems *(NLDB-2000)*. Lecture Notes in Computer Science 1959, Springer, 2001, p. 103-114.
8. Bolshakov, I. A., A. Gelbukh. Word Combinations as an Important Part of Modern Electronic Dictionaries. *Procesamiento del Lenguaje Natural*, No. 29, 2002, p. 47-54.
9. Dagan, I., L. Lee, and F. Pereira. Similarity-based models of word cooccurrence probabilities. *Machine Learning*, 34(1), 1999.
10. Gelbukh, A., G. Sidorov, S. Galicia Haro, I. Bolshakov. Environment for Development of a Natural Language Syntactic Analyzer. *Acta Academia 2002*, Moldova, 2002, p. 206-213.
11. Kim, S., J. Yoon, and M. Song. Automatic extraction of collocations from Korean text. *Computers and the Humanities* 35 (3): 273-297, 2001, Kluwer Academic Publishers.
12. Kita, K., Y. Kato, T. Omoto, and Y. Yano. A comparative study of automatic extraction of collocations from corpora: Mutual information vs. cost criteria. *Journal of Natural Language Processing*, 1(1):21-33, 1994.
13. Koster, C.H.A. Head/Modifier Frames for Information Retrieval. In: A. Gelbukh (Ed.) *Computational Linguistics and Intelligent Text Processing*. Lecture Notes in Computer Science, N 2945, Springer-Verlag, 2004 (this volume).
14. Mel'čuk, I.Phrasemes in language and phraseology in linguistics. In: *Idioms: structural and psychological perspective*, pp. 167-232.
15. *Oxford collocation dictionary*, Oxford, 2003.
16. Smadja, F. Retrieving collocations from texts: Xtract. *Computational linguistics*, 19 (1):143-177, March 1993.
17. Strzalkowski, T. Evaluating natural language processing techniques in information retrieval. In: T. Strzalkowski (ed.) Natural language information retrieval. Kluwer, 1999.
18. Yu, J., Zh. Jin, and Zh. Wen. Automatic extraction of collocations. 2003.

A Small System Storing Spanish Collocations[*]

Igor A. Bolshakov and Sabino Miranda-Jiménez

Center for Computing Research
National Polytechnic Institute, Mexico City, Mexico
igor@cic.ipn.mx, sabino@correo.cic.ipn.mx

Abstract. Collocations are defined as syntactically connected and semantically compatible pairs of content components, like Spanish *prestar atención* 'give attention', *presidente del país* 'president of the country', *país grande* 'large country' or *muy bien* 'very well'. The collocation databases are important for numerous applications of computational linguistics. A small system storing Spanish collocations is reported. Each collocation is accessible from both its components while querying. As compared with its Russian prototype, its size is now spare and the collocation types are limited to a few most productive ones. However, the available relation of the hyponym/hyperonym type between the systemic dictionary entries permits to infer some additional collocations at runtime. The actual statistics of the system is given.

1 Introduction

We call collocation a syntactically connected and semantically compatible pair of content words,[1] like Spanish <u>abandonarse</u> *a la* <u>desesperación</u> 'to fall into despair', <u>vocero</u> *del* <u>gobierno</u> 'press secretary of the government', <u>trabajar</u> <u>fuertemente</u> 'to work hard' or <u>muy</u> <u>grande</u> 'very large', where the two principal components are underlined. Just as in [1, 2], we treat as collocations word combinations of any stability, including full idioms and free word combinations.

As it is extensively explained in [1], collocation databases (CDBs) in any language can be used in language learning and in numerous tasks of text processing, among them lexicalized parsing, word sense disambiguation, malapropism detection & correction, automatic translation, revealing text cohesion, and segmentation of texts to paragraphs. Thus the creation of CDBs is topical for any language. However, the situation with CDBs poorly corresponds to the needs mentioned. For example, there is an excellent English collocations dictionary [10] but no good English CDB, so that all applications of CDBs different from word learning are left unprovided. Among other European languages only Russian has now a large CDB [1, 2]. For Spanish, there are neither dictionaries nor CDBs.

This paper reports on a small system called **CrossLexica-Esp** whose principal part is just a Spanish collocation database. In distinction from common dictionaries, each

---

[*] Work done under partial support of Mexican Government (CONACyT, SNI) and CGPI-IPN.
[1] Unlike some other authors, who use this term to refer to mere co-occurrences, e.g., [3]

A. Gelbukh (Ed.): CICLing 2004, LNCS 2945, pp. 248–252, 2004.
© Springer-Verlag Berlin Heidelberg 2004

collocation in the CDB is accessible from both its components while querying. Our system also contains semantic relations of hyponymy/hyperonymy (sub-class/superclass) type that permit to generate at runtime a number of additional collo-cations not available in the CDB continuously.

As a prototype for the system under elaboration, the CrossLexica system [1, 2] was taken, which contains a very large database of Russian collocations and numerous WordNet-like semantic relations [9, 11] between collocation components. Because of the change of the basic language, CrossLexica-Esp contains some changes in storing links between collocation components. However, the structure of the system remained basically the same. As to the syntactic types of collocations, we took those most fre-quent in texts which are the same in Russian, Spanish and other European languages.

2   Collocation Types

CrossLexica-type system contains two main data structures: a dictionary of colloca-tion components and a set of links between them. At each moment, a fragment of the dictionary is demonstrated on the screen, and a user can select any its entry as a query or introduce a string in a special line. The information delivered on the screen is a categorized list of collocations the queried word is in (cf. also the section 4).

The collocation categories are types of syntactic links between their components.

We treat as **modifiers** any single or multiword depending on and modifying an-other word of any POS: *país* → *grande* 'large country'; *puerta* → *de madera* 'door of wood', *trabajar* → *mucho* 'to work much'; *enormemente* ← *largo* 'enormously long'; *muy* ← *bien* 'very well'. Here the arrows are syntactic dependencies, and the modifiers are underlined. In response to a queried headword, the delivery category is HAS_MODIFIERS, in the inverse direction, IS_MODIFIER_OF.

Grammatical **subjects** are specific dependents of predicative verbs: *autobús* ← *llegó* 'bus came'. In response to a queried verb, the delivery category is HAS_SUBJECTS, in the inverse direction, IS_SUBJECT_OF.

We call **noun complements of verb** its direct, indirect or prepositional objects: *leer* → *(un) libro* 'to read a book'; *dar* → *(al) niño* 'to give to the boy'; *traducir* → *(de) español* 'to tranlsate from Spanish'. We also consider as complements circum-stantial expressions like *ir* → *(tras el) bosque* 'to go through the forest'.

Nouns also have their own **noun complements**, e.g., *paz* → *(del) mundo* 'peace in the world'.

The system also stores **hyponym-to-hyperonym** links between some dictionary entries that are used for heuristic inferences of new collocations: if the entry C_1 has hyperonym H, and H forms a collocation with the entry C_2, then C_1 forms the colloca-tion of the same type with C_2.

3   Structural Peculiarities of CrossLexica-Esp

Any dictionary entry of a CDB contains the list of its morphological categories and a series of lists of links between this entry and others. Thus the upper level of the whole

CBD structure does not depend on a specific language. On the lower level, the links between collocation components can be language specific. Let us outline peculiarities of these links in CrossLexica-Esp in comparison to the Russian prototype.

In distinction from Russian, Spanish has grammatical cases for neither nouns nor adjectives. Hence, a link between a head collocation component and its complement stores only a preposition (if exists).

Russian verbs have only three tenses. Tenses in Spanish are numerous, so that we should select the most frequent among them for the deliveries. The rest are to be generated at runtime, at a user's demand. (This option will be implemented in the future.)

Russian does not comprise articles, whereas Spanish not only has them in definite, indefinite or empty form, but also amalgamates the prepositions *a* and *de* with the article *el*. Hence, it seems important, especially for language learning, to output all possible combinations of the preposition and articles for each collocation with complement. A tentative step is to include special symbol instead of article and to generate all its options at runtime on user's demand. In the actual state, CrossLexica-Esp stores only the most frequent combination 'preposition—article' for a collocation.

Russian puts modifiers of nouns in anteposition (these are mostly agreed adjectives) or in postposition (these are mostly non-agreed attributive phrases like Sp. *puerta de madera* 'door of wood'). Spanish operates with modifiers of the same groups, but agreed adjectives are usually to the right of the noun, and the attributive phrases are much more frequent than in Russian.

The considerations given above prove that the Cross-Lexica-Esp structure is very similar to that of its prototype. Indeed, the differences at links between the collocative components can be easily bypassed while programming.

4   Interface of CrossLexica-Esp

The interface of CrossLexica-Esp is shown in the Fig. 1. To the right of the menu bar, the keyword, i.e. the queried item of the dictionary is given, with all its morphological features: part of speech (POS), gender and number (for nouns).

The line below contains the query word once more. The user can introduce a query just to this line. There are two large windows under it, with a fragment of the dictionary to the left and with the delivery, i.e. relevant collocations and semantic links of the query word to the right. The user can select the next query making click at an item of the dictionary or the delivery list. Thus he navigates through the CDB.

In example given in Fig. 1, the noun *flores* 'flowers' has the following type of collocations it is in: TIENE_MODIFICADORES (HAS_MODIFIERS), ES_COMPLEMENTO_DE_VERBO (IS_COMPLEMENT_OF_VERB), and ES_COMPLE-MENTO_DE_SUSTANTIVO (IS_COMPLEMENT_OF_NOUN).

An innovative feature of the system is the inference of new collocations at runtime. For example, *flores* 'flowers' has *tulipanes* 'tulips' between its hyponyms (HIPÓNIMOS) and the collocations *flores aromáticas, flores exóticas...* 'aromatic flowers, exotic flowers...'. On this basis, for the query *tulipanes*, the system generates at runtime the collocations *tulipanes aromáticos, tulipanes exóticos,...* 'aromatic tulips, exotic tulips,...'.

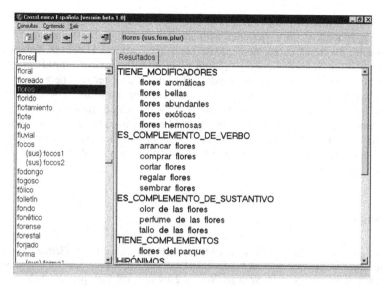

Fig. 1. Interface of CrossLexica-Esp

Some collocations are labeled as idioms or sci-tech terms in the system. This information is useful for learning new words and collocations, especially for foreigners.

5 Statistics of CrossLexica-Esp

The dictionary of collocation components numbers now (October, 2003) slightly more that 4,000 entries. The statistics of collocations is given in Table 1.

As compared with the Russian prototype, the size is now ca. 50 times less, however all 100% of the collocations are in the runtime ready form.

Table 1. Statistics of collocations

Type of collocations	Coll. Amt.
Nouns/Verbs/Adjs/Advs with modifiers	6,300
Verbs with their subjects	2,400
Verbs with their noun complements	3,200
Nouns with their noun complements	3,900
Total	15,800

6 Conclusions and Future Work

We have developed a system containing a small database of Spanish collocations and a limited semantic tool for generating a number of new collocations by analogy with those already available in the CDB.

So far, the limited size of our system does not permit its autonomous use for text processing. Indeed, as the experience with Russian analogue shows, the size should be increased by 50 times or so, to facilitate such applications. However, CrossLexica-Esp is ready for Spanish language learning, as well for further amplifications. The amplification could be much more modest, if to use the system cooperatively with an Internet search engine. Then the system could contain the most frequently occurred collocations, while more rare combinations could be tested through noisy and sluggish Internet [4]. The method described in [5, 6] can be used for automatic enrichment of CrossLexica-Esp through a very large corpus or Internet [8]. Another future linguistic improvement is integration into the system of the module for automatic morphological analysis of Spanish [7].

References

1. Bolshakov, I. A. Getting One's First Million... Collocations. In: A. Gelbukh (Ed.) *Computational Linguistics and Intelligent Text Processing* (CICLing-2004). Lecture Notes in Computer Science, N 2945, Springer-Verlag, 2004 (this volume), pp. 229–242.
2. Bolshakov, I. A. and A. Gelbukh. A Very Large Database of Collocations and Semantic Links. In: M. Bouzeghoub *et al.* (Eds.) *Natural Language Processing and Information Systems* (NLDB-2000). Lecture Notes in Computer Science 1959, Springer-Verlag, 2001, p. 103–114.
3. Biemann, C., S. Bordag, G. Heyer, U. Quasthoff, C. Wolff. Language-independent methods for compiling monolingual lexical data. In: A. Gelbukh (Ed.) *Computational Linguistics and Intelligent Text Processing*. Lecture Notes in Computer Science, N 2945, Springer-Verlag, 2004 (this volume), pp. 217–228.
4. Calvo, H., and A. Gelbukh. Improving Disambiguation of Prepositional Phrase Attachments Using the Web as Corpus. In: *Progress in Pattern Recognition, Speech and Image Analysis* (CIARP'2003), Lecture Notes in Computer Science, N 2905, Springer-Verlag, 2003, pp. 604-610.
5. Gelbukh, A., G. Sidorov, San-Yong Han, and E. Hernández-Rubio. Automatic Syntactic Analysis for Detection of Word Combinations. In: A. Gelbukh (Ed.) *Computational Linguistics and Intelligent Text Processing* (CICLing-2004). Lecture Notes in Computer Science, N 2945, Springer-Verlag, 2004 (this volume), pp. 243–247.
6. Gelbukh, A., G. Sidorov , S.-Y. Han, E. Hernández-Rubio. Automatic Enrichment of Very Large Dictionary of Word Combinations on the Basis of Dependency Formalism. In: *Proc. Mexican International Conference on Artificial Intelligence* (MICAI-2004). Lecture Notes in Artificial Intelligence, N 2972, Springer-Verlag, 2004.
7. Gelbukh, A. and G. Sidorov. Approach to construction of automatic morphological analysis systems for inflective languages with little effort. In: *Computational Linguistics and Intelligent Text Processing* (CICLing-2003). Lecture Notes in Computer Science, N 2588, Springer-Verlag, pp. 215–220.
8. Gelbukh, A., G. Sidorov, and L. Chanona-Hernandez. Compilation of a Spanish representative corpus. In: *Computational Linguistics and Intelligent Text Processing* (CICLing-2002). Lecture Notes in Computer Science, N 2276, Springer-Verlag, 2002, pp. 285-288.
9. Fellbaum, Ch. (Ed.) *WordNet: An Electronic Lexical Database*. MIT Press, 1998.
10. *Oxford Collocations Dictionary for Students of English*. Oxford University Press. 2003.
11. Vossen, P. (Ed.). *EuroWordNet General Document*. Vers. 3 final. www.hum.uva.nl/~ewn.

A Semi-automatic Tree Annotating Workbench
for Building a Korean Treebank

Joon-Ho Lim, So-Young Park, Yong-Jae Kwak, and Hae-Chang Rim

Department of Computer Science & Engineering Korea University
5-ka, Anam-dong, SEOUL, 136-701, KOREA
{jhlim, ssoya, yjkwak, rim}@nlp.korea.ac.kr

Abstract. In this paper, we propose a semi-automatic tree annotating workbench for building a Korean treebank. Generally, building a treebank requires an enormous effort by the annotator. In order to improve annotating efficiency, decrease the number of intervention required by the annotator, and help maintain consistent annotation in building a treebank, we have developed a semi-automatic tree annotating workbench consisting of following three stages: syntactic pattern extraction, syntactic pattern selection, and syntactic pattern application. The experiment was carried out with 27,966 tree tagged sentences as a training set and 3,108 sentences as a test set. As a result, the burden of manual annotation can be reduced by about 47% with the best selection of the feature set by using the proposed tree annotating workbench.

1 Introduction

A syntactically annotated treebank is a highly useful language resource which can represent syntactic information with the tree structures of the given sentences. However, in building a treebank, a vast amount of time and effort is required by the annotator. Furthermore, maintaining the consistency of the constructed treebank is difficult if the annotation is performed only manually ([4]). Therefore, we need a tree annotating workbench which can improve the annotating efficiency, decrease the number of annotator's intervention, and help maintain consistent annotation in constructing a treebank.

Some approaches to tree annotating workbench, such as [1] for PennTreeBank([4]), [2] for STEP2000([3]), and [8], have been previously developed. In [1] and [2], the heuristic rules written by annotators are used for deterministically attaching a partial syntactic structure. However, the workbenches are limited in terms of efficiency improvement and the manual work reduction. In [8], the limited part of speech tag sequences are extracted from the previously constructed treebank, and the extracted POS sequences are used in building a new treebank. However, this workbench does not allow the annotator to select the context size or the context information.

In this paper, we propose a semi-automatic tree annotating workbench for building a Korean treebank. It extracts various syntactic patterns from the previously constructed treebank based on the selected features, and It automatically applies the extracted syntactic patterns to the appropriate states.

A. Gelbukh (Ed.): CICLing 2004, LNCS 2945, pp. 253–257, 2004.
© Springer-Verlag Berlin Heidelberg 2004

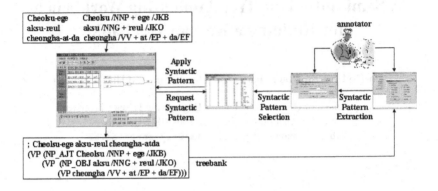

Fig. 1. Semi-Automatic Tree Annotating Workbench

2   Semi-automatic Tree Annotating Workbench

Figure1 represents the process of constructing a treebank by using the proposed workbench. As shown in figure 1, the workbench goes through the syntactic pattern extraction
stage, the syntactic pattern selection stage, and the syntactic pattern application stage in
constructing a treebank.

2.1   Syntactic Pattern Extraction

In using the tree annotating workbench, an annotator is allowed to select a set of features
which can represent useful syntactic information. Syntactic patterns are extracted from
the preciously constructed treebank based on the selected features [5]. The syntactic
patterns are composed of two parts: a condition part and an action part. The condition
part consists of selected features, and the action part can have a value : *shift* or *reduce*. For
example, the syntactic patterns represented in Figure2 would be extracted from the left-
side tree-tagged sentence if the annotator selects the features such as syntactic-functional
tags and the part-of-speech tags of the left and right phrases.

	action	left syn-func	left head POS	right syn-func	right head POS	Notes
	shift	NP_AJT	NNP + JKB	NP_OBJ	NNG + JKO	Cheolsu-ege aksu-reul
	reduce	NP_OBJ	NNG + JKO	VP	VV + EP + EF	aksu-reul cheongha-at-da
	reduce	NP_AJT	NNP + JBB	VP	VV + EP + EF	Cheolsu-ege cheongha-at-da

(VP (NP_AJT Cheolsu/NNP+ ege/JKB)
(VP (NP_OBJ aksu/NNG+ reul/JKO)
(VP cheongha/VV+ at/EP+ da/EF))) — shift reduce reduce

Fig. 2. A Tree-tagged Sentence, and Syntactic Patterns extracted from it

2.2   Syntactic Pattern Selection

Before all syntactic patterns extracted from the treebank are applied to the appropriate
occasions, only the reliable syntactic patterns are selected based on the confidence level.

Based on the assumption that the action part of the syntactic pattern is determined to be *reduce* or *shift* according to the accumulated binomial distribution, the confidence level - a statistical hypothesis testing - of the syntactic pattern is defined as *1 - risk rate* where *risk rate* indicates the rate of randomly selecting a syntactic pattern in the accumulated binomial distribution [6].

Therefore, confidence level is defined as follows:

$$confidence\ level = 1 - risk\ rate = 1 - P(X \geq r)$$
$$= 1 - \sum_{i=r}^{n} \frac{n!}{i!(n-i)!} \cdot p^i \cdot (1-p)^{n-i}$$

where n is the frequency of a syntactic pattern, and r is the frequency of the selected action (i.e. *reduce* or *shift*). At the moment, the value of p is fixed at 0.5 because the probability of randomly selecting *reduce* is the same as the probability of selecting *shift*.

2.3 Syntactic Pattern Application

At the syntactic pattern application stage, an annotator can build a parse tree with the help of the automatic application of operations. If the condition part of the selected syntactic pattern matches the context of the current state, the action part (*shift* or *reduce*) of the syntactic pattern is applied to the current state, and the result is visually displayed on the workbench. However, the annotator has to confirm the operation, and manually backtrack the operation if the automatic operation is incorrect.

3 Experiments

In this experiment, KAIST Language Resource[3] is transformed according to the tag set and the phrase structure proposed by SEJONG project [7]; 27,966 sentences(90%) are used for the training set and 3,108(10%) sentences are used for the test set. In this experiment, we try to evaluate the performance of the proposed workbench based on syntactic pattern precision, syntactic pattern recall, and the reduction rate of the manual annotation as follows :

$$pattern\ precision = \frac{\alpha}{\alpha+\beta}, \ pattern\ recall = \frac{\alpha}{\alpha+\gamma}, \ reduction\ rate = \frac{\alpha-\beta}{\alpha+\gamma} \quad (1)$$

where α is the number of correct decisions made by the syntactic patterns, β is the number of incorrect decisions made by the syntactic patterns, and γ is the number of decisions made by an annotator.

Table 1. Experimental Result with 95% confidence level Syntactic Patterns

Feature Set	pattern precision	pattern recall	reduction rate
1: synctactic-funcntional tag	55.4	70.7	14.0
2: 1 + POS-tag	73.4	74.8	47.8
3: 2 + the number of eojeols	74.6	56.3	37.2
4: 2 + word sequence of each head	99.1	3.9	3.9

In order to investigate the relationship between the set of features and the performance, we evaluated the performance with four different sets of features. Four sets of features and the experimental results are presented in Table 1.

According to the experimental result, each feature set is analyzed as follows. Feature set 1 is not enough to decide the operation correctly. Feature set 2 including the part-of-speech tag sequence can obtain better precision and the largest reduction rate. Feature set 3 includes the number of eojeols, but the performance is somewhat worse than feature set 2 in terms of the recall rate and reduction rate. Feature set 4 achieves the best precision, but it obtains the worst recall rate and reduction rate because of the data sparseness problem. We expect that the problem will be diminish as the size of the training treebank is grows.

4   Conclusion

This paper proposes a semi-automatic tree annotating workbench for building a Korean treebank which can utilize the various syntactic patterns. The desirable characteristics of the proposed workbench are as follows. First, the workbench can help an annotator maintain consistent annotation by providing an automatic mechanism of extracting and applying syntactic patterns. Second, the workbench can decrease the number of manual annotations by providing a means of extracting various syntactic patterns from the previously constructed treebank based on the selected features. Third, the workbench allows an annotator to select various features such as functional tags, POS tags, case information, and a word sequence in order to compose an appropriate syntactic pattern. In our future research, we will study the relationship between the features and the recall and precision rate of syntactic patterns. Furthermore, we will try to generalize syntactic patterns by using a machine learning technique.

Acknowledgements. This work was supported by Korea Research Foundation Grant(KRF-2002-042-D00485).

References

1. Hindle, Donald : Acquiring disambiguation rules from text. Proceeding. ACL, (1989) pp. 118–125
2. Byung-Gyu Chang, Kong Joo Lee, Gil Chang Kim : Design and Implementation of Tree Tagging Workbench to Build a Large Tree Tagged Corpus of Korean. Proc. of the 9th Conference of Hangul and Korean Information Processing, (1997) pp. 421–429
3. Kong Joo Lee, Byung-Gyu Chang, Gil Chang Kim : Bracketing Guidelines for Korean Syntactic Tree Tagged Corpus Version 1. Technical Report CS/TR-97-112, KAIST, Dept. of Computer Science (1997).
4. Mitchell P. Marcus, B. Santorini, and M. A. Marcinkiewicz : Building a large annotated corpus of English : the Penn Treebank. Computational Linguistics, Vol.19, No.2, (1993) pp. 313–330
5. So-Young Park, Yong-Jae Kwak, Hoo-Jung Chung, Young-Sook Hwang, Hae-Chang Rim : Learning Syntactic Constraints for Improving the Efficiency of Korean Parsing. Journal of Korean Information Science Society, vol. 29, No. 10(B), (2002) pp. 755–765

6. Tom M. Mitchell : Machine Learning. McGraw-Hill (1997)
7. Ui-su Kim, Beom-mo Kang : Principles, methods and some problems in compiling a Korean treebank. Proc. of the 14th Conference of Hangul and Korean Information Processing, (2002) pp.155–162
8. Yong-Jae Kwak, Young-Sook Hwang, Hoo-Jung Chung, So-Young Park and Hae-Chang Rim : FIDELITY: A Framework for Context-Sensitive Grammar Development. Proc. of the 2001 International Conference on Computer Processing of Oriental Languages, (2001) pp. 305–308

Extracting Semantic Categories of Nouns for Syntactic Disambiguation from Human-Oriented Explanatory Dictionaries*

Hiram Calvo [1] and Alexander Gelbukh [1,2]

[1] Center for Computing Research, National Polytechnic Institute,
Av. Juan de Dios Bátiz s/n, esq. Av. Mendizábal, México, D.F., 07738. México
hcalvo@sagitario.cic.ipn.mx, gelbukh@cic.ipn.mx; www.gelbukh.com
[2] Department of Computer Science and Engineering, Chung-Ang University,
221 Huksuk-Dong, DongJak-Ku, Seoul, 156-756, Korea

Abstract. Syntactic disambiguation frequently requires knowledge of the semantic categories of nouns, especially in languages with free word order. For example, in Spanish the phrases *pintó un cuadro un pintor* (lit. *painted a picture a painter*) and *pintó un pintor un cuadro* (lit. *painted a painter a picture*) mean the same: 'a painter painted a picture'. The only way to tell the subject from the object is by knowing that *pintor* 'painter' is a causal agent and *cuadro* is a thing. We present a method for extracting semantic information of this kind from existing machine-readable human-oriented explanatory dictionaries. Application of this procedure to two different human-oriented Spanish dictionaries gives additional information as compared with using solely Spanish EuroWordNet. In addition, we show the results of an experiment conducted to evaluate the similarity of word classifications using this method.

1 Introduction

Determining the function of a noun phrase in a sentence cannot rely solely on word order, particularly for languages that have a rather free order of constituents, such as Spanish. For example consider the following sentences: (1) *La señora llevó a la niña a la calle,* lit. 'The woman took to the girl to the street' and (2) *La señora llevó a la calle a la niña,* lit. 'The woman took to the street to the girl'. Both sentences convey the same meaning: 'The woman took the girl to the street'. In Spanish, a noun preceded by the preposition *a* 'to' has the role of direct object if it is animate, or indirect object or circumstantial complement if it is not animate. Without semantic information, a system is not able to determine the syntactic functions of *a la niña* and *a la calle* in a sentence. When information on the semantic categories of *niña* 'girl' (causal_agent) and *calle* 'street' (place) is considered, it is possible to determine automatically that *la señora* 'the woman' is the subject, *a la niña* is the direct object and *a la calle* is a circumstantial complement of place.

---

* Work done under partial support of Mexican Government (CONACyT, SNI, PIFI-IPN, CGEPI-IPN), Korean Government (KIPA Professorship for Visiting Faculty Positions in Korea), ITRI of Chung-Ang University, and RITOS-2. The second author is currently on Sabbatical leave at Chung-Ang University.

A. Gelbukh (Ed.): CICLing 2004, LNCS 2945, pp. 258–261, 2004.
© Springer-Verlag Berlin Heidelberg 2004

Existing sources providing semantic information of this kind in a formal way usable for automatic text processing are incomplete and/or difficult to find, especially for languages other than English. This paper presents a method for acquiring semantic categories of nouns from human-oriented explanatory dictionaries (hereafter, HOED).

The first work that pursued the construction of a taxonomy from a HOED was Amsler's [1]. He worked manually with the Merriam-Webster Pocket Dictionary. Subsequently, several studies were carried out on other dictionaries using automatic methods. Chodorow *et al.* [2] worked with Webster's New Collegiate Dictionary, whereas both Guthrie *et al.* [3] and Vossen [4] used the Longman Dictionary of Contemporary English (LDOCE) [5]. Ageno *et al.* [6] have created an environment facilitating extraction of semantic information from HOEDs. In this environment, the user has to select manually the correct hypernym sense amongst those proposed by the system. In other fields, there are works devoted to WordNet enrichment with semantic information extracted from HOEDs, e.g., Montoyo *et al.* [7] and Nastase *et al.* [8].

In general, the purpose of the work done on extracting semantic information from HOEDs differs from ours in that these works attempt to extract a whole taxonomy from a HOED, while our purpose is to determine the semantic category of a noun out of a set of predefined categories selected for the task of determining the function(s) of a noun phrase in a sentence. As we show in the next section, this task can be done in an automated manner.

2 Acquiring Semantic Categories from a Dictionary

In short, our method consists in following the is-a chain formed by the nouns in word definitions, until a word with a known (manually assigned) category is reached; the word in question inherits this category. For example, for the word *abeto* 'fir' we have:

$$abeto \xrightarrow{\text{is-a}} árbol \xrightarrow{\text{is-a}} planta \xrightarrow{\text{is-a}} ser \qquad \text{'fir} \xrightarrow{\text{is-a}} tree \xrightarrow{\text{is-a}} plant \xrightarrow{\text{is-a}} being',$$

where *ser* 'being' has the category *life_form* assigned to it manually (see Table 1), thus giving this same category for the initial word *abeto* 'fir'.

A complication of the process of building such chains is that sometimes they have cycles: a word is (indirectly) defined through another word that in its turn is defined through the first one. Cycles in the system of definitions are inevitable in any dictionary in which all words, even such general ones as *thing* or *something*, have definitions; to break the cyclic chains, some (few) words are to be chosen as top concepts, whose categories are assigned manually [10]. The algorithm does not try to generalize further these concepts, which ends the chain.

The set of categories we have chosen comprise the 25 unique beginners for Word-Net nouns described in [11]. Table 1 shows these categories along with the top concepts manually selected to which they have been assigned.

3 Experiment

In order to evaluate the quality of the categories of words found through our procedure, we considered two HOEDs: Lara [9] and Anaya. The first dictionary (Lara)

Table 1. Top concepts corresponding to the semantic categories of nouns

Category	Top concepts	Category	Top concepts
activity	*action, act, activity*	feeling	*feeling, emotion*
animal	*animal*	form	*figure, form, line*
life_form	*life, organism, being*	food	*food, comestible*
phenomenon	*phenomenon*	state	*state, condition*
thing	*instrument, object, thing*	grouping	*set, group, series*
causal_agent	*being, person, human*	substance	*substance, energy, liquid, fiber*
place	*space, place, distance*	attribute	*property, quality, color*
flora	*plant, fruit, flower*	time	*time, period*
cognition	*knowledge, abstraction*	part	*part, member, limb*
process	*process*	possession	*accumulation, assignation*
event	*event, happening*	motivation	*desire, incentive, cause*

Table 2. Pair-wise comparison of dictionaries.

f1c1	a	b	f1c1(a,b)	f1c1(b,a)	total classif.	%[2]
	la	an	3427	3427	36427	18.82%
	an	wn	7243	7243	69171	20.94%
	la	wn	2830	2830	47544	11.90%
					average:	17.22%
f1c0	**a**	**b**	**f1c0(a,b)**	**f1c0(b,a)**	**total classif.**	**%**
	la	an	2853	7172	36427	27.52%
	an	wn	13501	15332	69171	41.68%
	la	wn	3204	8686	47544	25.01%
					average:	31.40%
f0c0	**a**	**b**	**f0c0(a,b)**	**f0c0(b,a)**	**total classif.**	**%**
	la	an	1390	18428	36427	54.40%
	an	wn	8283	17569	69171	37.37%
	la	wn	1366	28628	47544	63.09%
					average:	51.62%

contains approximately 8,000 nouns. The second dictionary (Anaya) has nearly 33,000 nouns. We applied our method to both HOEDs and then we compared the categories found with those of Spanish EuroWordNet[1] (henceforth S-EWN). As in the case of HOEDs, in S-EWN the semantic categories of nouns were defined by the construction of is-a chains.

We measured three aspects of similarity of the categories yielded by the three dictionaries comparing pairs of dictionaries: **f1c1**(a,b): nouns found in both dictionaries (a and b) with matching classification; **f1c0**(a,b): nouns found in both dictionaries, but the classification in the first dictionary (a) doesn't match any of the second (b); and **f0c0**(a,b): nouns classified in the first dictionary (a) that are not found in the second dictionary (b). Table 3 shows the results of comparing each possible pair of dictionaries. **la** stands for Lara, **an** for Anaya, and **wn** for S-EWN. The **total classif.** column shows the sum of the number of nouns classified in dictionary (a) plus those of (b). This way results are normalized, compensating the difference among dictionary sizes.

---

[1] S-EWN was jointly developed by the University of Barcelona (UB), the National University of Distance Education (UNED), and the Polytechnic University of Catalonia (UPC), Spain.

[2] ([f1c1(a,b)+f1c1(b,a)] / total_clasif) x 100%

On average, **17.22%** of the nouns were classified equally amongst the three dictionaries, **31.40%** are found but their classification does not match, and **51.62%** are different nouns. If we consider only the nouns that are found amongst the three dictionaries (that is, 100% − 51.62% = **48.38%**), we find that **35.60%** are classified equally, and **64.91%** are classified differently. In other words, little more than a third part of the classifications matches in average amongst the three dictionaries.

4 Conclusions and Future Work

Using a HOED, semantic categories can be determined for nouns absent from Spanish EuroWordNet (S-EWN). However, the agreement of classifications among the three dictionaries studied, two of them HOEDs, and the other S-EWN, was lower than expected. An average of 35.60% of the total number of words classified by the three dictionaries agrees in classification. This is possibly due to the lack of a WSD module, as well as the different definition schemes adopted by the three dictionaries.

In the future, a WSD module can be added to the procedure of chain construction, and the heuristics used to extracting the hypernym for a word from its definition, including the words chosen as top concepts, should be revised.

Finally, an evaluation of syntactic analysis using the semantic categories provided by this method is convenient to determine the degree to which the semantic categories extracted from HOEDs enhance syntactic analysis disambiguation when the noun classifications among different dictionaries vary.

References

1. R. A. Amsler, *The structure of the Merriam-Webster Pocket Dictionary*. Ph.D. Dissertation, U. of Texas, 1980.
2. M. Chodorow, R. J. Byrd and G. E. Heidorn, Extracting Semantic Hierarchies from a Large On-Line Dictionary. In *Proc. of the 23rd Meeting of the* ACL, pp. 299-304, 1985.
3. L. Guthrie, B. Slator, Y. Wilks, and R. Bruce. Is there content in empty heads? In *Proc. of the 13th Intl. Conf. on Comp. Linguistics,* COLING90, 1990.
4. P. Vossen, The end of the chain: where does decomposition of lexical knowledge lead us eventually? ACQUILEX WP 010. English Department, U. of Amsterdam, 1990.
5. P. Proctor, (Ed.). *The Longman Dictionary of Contemporary English*. London, 1978
6. A. Ageno, I. Castellón, M. A. Martí, F. Ribas, G. Rigau, H. Rodríguez, M. Taulé, F. Verdejo. SEID: An environment for extraction of Semantic Information from on-line dictionaries. In *Proc. of 3th conf. on Applied NLP*. Trento, It., 1992.
7. A. Montoyo, M. Palomar and G. Rigau. WordNet Enrichment with Classification Systems, in *Proc. of NAACL 2001*, Pittsburgh, PA, USA, 2001.
8. V. Nastase and S. Szpakowicz, Augmenting WordNet's Structure Using LDOCE. In A. Gelbukh (ed): CICLing 2003, LNCS 2588: 281–294, Springer-Verlag, 2003.
9. L. F. Lara, *Diccionario del español usual en México*. Digital edition. Colegio de México, Center of Linguistic and Literary Studies, 1996.
10. A. Gelbukh and G. Sidorov. Selección automática del vocabulario definidor en un diccionario explicativo. *Procesamiento del Lenguaje Natural* 29: 55–62, 2002.
11. G. Miller. Nouns in WordNet: a Lexical Inheritance System, *International Journal of Lexicography*, Volume 3. num. 4, pp. 245-264, 1994.

Hierarchies Measuring Qualitative Variables

Serguei Levachkine and Adolfo Guzmán-Arenas

Centre for Computing Research (CIC) - National Polytechnic Institute (IPN)
UPALMZ, CIC Building, 07738, Mexico City, MEXICO
palych@cic.ipn.mx, a.guzman@acm.org

Abstract. Qualitative variables take symbolic values, such as *hot, shoe, Europe or France*. Sometimes, the values may be arranged in layers or levels of detail. For instance, the variable *place_of_origin* takes as level-1 values *European, African...* as level-2 values *French, German...* as level-3 values *Californian, Texan...* The paper describes a hierarchy, a mathematical construct among these variables. The confusion resulting when using a value instead of another is defined, as well as the closeness to which object *o* fulfills predicate *P*. Other operations among and properties of hierarchical values are derived. Hierarchies are compared with ontologies. Hierarchies find use in measuring linguistic relatedness or similarity. Hierarchical variables abound and are commonly used, often with suggestive string values, without fully realizing or exploiting its properties. We deal with arbitrary hierarchies. Examples are given.

1   Introduction

A datum is a relational entity. Nothing is a datum itself; i.e. a context[1] is required. This thesis is especially true for qualitative data. Notice that many works on qualitative data processing usually omit the problem under consideration context. In contrast, we use the hierarchies to measure similarity and dissimilarity between qualitative values, attempting to keep the context. To some extent, the notion of hierarchy provides an adequate tool for qualitative data analysis, processing and classification, because the hierarchies encapsulate the (sometimes ordered) relations between partitions of the dataset and therefore easily maintain the problem context.

What wearing apparel do we wear for rainy days? *Raincoat* is a correct answer; *umbrella* is a close miss; *belt* a fair error, and *typewriter* a gross error. What is closer

---

[1] The notion of context depends on particular environment (subject domain, representation space...) into which the data are embedded. In turn the relatedness between data elements depends on the context. For example, the *pale* and *beige* could be much closed (to indistinguishable) in one context while in another they should be far distanced. Subsequently this paper concerns not only with the problem to appropriately define the closeness of data elements but also to take into consideration the properties of the representation space. This can be observed as a context-oriented approach to qualitative data processing (see also §1.3).

A. Gelbukh (Ed.): CICLing 2004, LNCS 2945, pp. 262–274, 2004.
© Springer-Verlag Berlin Heidelberg 2004

to an *apple*, a *pear* or a *caterpillar?* Can we measure these errors and similarities? How related or close are these words? Some preliminary definitions follow.

Element set. A set[2] E whose elements are explicitly defined. $\blacklozenge$[3] *Example*: {*red, blue, white, black, pale*}.

Ordered set. An element set whose values are ordered by a < ("less than") relation.$\blacklozenge$ *Example*: {*very_cold, cold, warm, hot, very_hot*}.

Covering. K is a covering for set E if K is a set of subsets $s_i \subset E$, such that $\cup\, s_i = E.$$\blacklozenge$ Every element of E is in some subset $s_i \in K$. If K is not a covering of E, we can make it so by adding a new s_j to it, named "others", that contains all other elements of E that do not belong to any of the previous s_i.

Exclusive set. K is an exclusive set if $s_i \cap s_j = \varnothing$, for every s_i, $s_j \in K$. $\blacklozenge$ Its elements are mutually exclusive. If K is not an exclusive set, we can make it so by replacing every two overlapping s_i, $s_j \in K$ with three: $s_i - s_j$, $s_j - s_i$, and $s_i \cap s_j$.

Partition. P is a partition of set E if it is both a covering for E and an exclusive set.

Qualitative variable. A single-valued variable that takes symbolic values. $\blacklozenge$ Its value cannot be a set.[4] By symbolic we mean qualitative, as opposed to numeric, vector or quantitative variables.

A symbolic value v **represents** a set E, written v $\propto$ E, if v can be considered a name or a depiction of E. $\blacklozenge$ *Example*: *Pale* $\propto$ {*white, yellow, orange, beige*}.

1.1   Hierarchy

For an element set E, a **hierarchy** H of E is another element set where each element e_i is a symbolic value that represents either a single element of E or a partition, and $\cup_i$ $\{r_i \mid e_i \propto r_i\} = E$ (The union of all sets represented by the e_i is E). $\blacklozenge$ *Example* (Hierarchy H_1): for E = {*Canada, USA, Mexico, Cuba, Puerto_Rico, Jamaica, Guatemala, Honduras, Costa_Rica*}={a, b, c, d, e, f, g, h, i}, a hierarchy H_1 is {*North_America, Caribbean_Island, Central_America*}={H_1^1, H_1^2, H_1^3}, where *North_America* $\propto$ {*Canada, USA, Mexico*}; *Caribbean_Island* $\propto$ {*English_Speaking_Island, Spanish_Speaking_Island*}={H_1^{21}, H_1^{22}}; *English_Speaking_Island* $\propto$ {*Jamaica*}; *Spanish_Speaking_Island* $\propto$ {*Cuba, Puerto_Rico*}; *Central_America* $\propto$ {*Guatemala, Honduras, Costa_Rica*}.

Hierarchies make it easier to compare qualitative values belonging to the same hierarchy (§3), and even to different hierarchies (procedure sim in [17]).

---

[2] Perhaps infinite, perhaps empty.

[3] The symbol $\blacklozenge$ stands for the end of definition.

[4] Variable, attribute and property are used interchangeably. An object may have an attribute (Ex: weight) while others do not: the weight of blue *does not make sense*, as opposed to saying that the weight of blue *is unknown* or not given. A variable (*color, height*) describes an aspect of an object; its value (*blue, 2 Kg*) is such description or measurement.

A **hierarchical variable** is a qualitative variable whose values belong to a hierarchy (The data type of a hierarchical variable is hierarchy). ♦ *Example: place_of_origin* that takes values from H_1. Note: hierarchical variables are single-valued. Thus, a value for *place_of_origin* can be *North_America* or *Mexico*, but not {*Canada, USA, Mexico*}, although *North_America* ∝ {*Canada, USA, Mexico*}.

1.2 Notation

The sets represented by each element of a hierarchy form a tree under the relation subset. *Example*: for H_1, such tree is given in Figure 1.

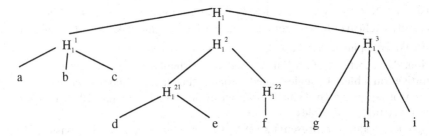

Fig. 1. The tree induced by hierarchy H_1.

We will also write a hierarchy such as H_1 thus: {*North_America* ∝ {*Canada USA Mexico*} *Caribbean Island* ∝ {*Spanish_Speaking_Island* ∝ {*Cuba Puerto_Rico*} *English_Speaking_Island* ∝ {*Jamaica*} } *Central_America* ∝ {*Guatemala Honduras Costa_Rica*} }.

father_of (v). In a tree representing a hierarchy (such as H_1), the father_of a node is the node from which it hangs. ♦ Similarly, the **sons_of** (v) are the values hanging from v. The nodes with the same father are **siblings**. ♦ Similarly, **grand_father_of, brothers_of, aunt, ascendants, descendants**... are defined, when they exist. ♦ The **root** is the node that has no father. ♦

1.3 Previous Related Work

CYC [12] was an early attempt to build the concept tree (an ontology) for common concepts. Clasitex [7] finds the themes of an article written in Spanish or English, performing a task equivalent to disambiguation of a word into its different senses. It uses the concept tree, and a word (words lie outside the context tree) *suggests the topic of* one or more concepts in the tree. A document that talks about Cervantes, horses and corruption will be classified (indexed) in these three nodes in the tree. In [8, 9], each agent possesses its own ontology of concepts, but must map these into natural language words for communication [17]. Thus LIA, a language for agent interaction [8], has an ontology comparator COM, that maps a concept from one ontology into the closest corresponding concept of another ontology. COM achieves communication without need of a common or *standard ontology;* it is used in sim of §3.4. Ontologies' relation to hierarchies will be further elaborated here.

The set of data items that we have to process is of course finite (Cf. footnote 1). First of all, we have to ask about the nature of the *representation space,* i.e., we need to know whether the data can be regarded as "*values*" of certain "*variables*" (Cf. §1), and whether these variables have certain properties: are we at liberty to embed the data into some "*space*", and to perform certain *operations* on them?

Traditionally [2, 19], the representation space is regarded as a metric space with some "exotic" or *ad hoc* distance (e.g., ultrametric distance to measure the proximity among members of a hierarchy; see §2). However, this requires a proof that such a distance meets the needs of the classification problem under consideration. Since, in general, the data of a problem consist at best of distances in the ordinary sense, the requirement is to obtain the "exotic distance" from an "ordinary distance." The intermediate data conversion often makes it difficult for any algorithms to define and exploit errors in using one data element instead of another; this is crucial for many domains involving qualitative variables (§3). Another problem with this conversion is its significant computational cost. A solution for these problems herein developed is to avoid the requirement of the measure to be a "distance" (even an "exotic" distance), defining so-called similarity or dissimilarity (confusion) functions on data elements of arbitrary nature in a manner similar to the human handling of these qualitative variables (it is hard to expect that they first define a distance to distinguish the *low_cost* and *high_cost* of goods). This is the main goal of the present paper, its novelty and its unique contribution (§3).

2   Theoretical Background

In this section we put forward some formal definitions previously developed and extensively commented in [10, 13, 14]. We should underline that the notion of *ultrametric distance* introduced in the following (§2.3) is accepted as "natural" measure of the hierarchical elements [2, 19] but is useless as well as any other *distance* within our context-oriented approach. Thus, it should be revised and replaced in §3.

2.1   Partitions of a Finite Set

Two elements x and y of E are **equivalent** in a partition P if they belong to the same class s_i; this is denoted by xPy. ◆

Let **P**(E) be the set of all partitions of E; an **order relation** among the members of **P**(E), denoted by <, can be defined thus: for any two partitions P and P', P<P' iff xPy→xP'y. Partition P is said to be **finer** than P'; it has more classes than P'. ◆

A **lattice** structure for **P**(E) can be based on the order relation. For every pair of partitions P and P' there is a least upper bound (l.u.b.) P∨P', and greatest lower bound (g.l.b.) P∧P'. ◆

Let us call P_k a partition of k classes where k is the level of P_k. A partition P' is said to **cover** a partition P if and only if P' results from combining *two* classes of P. A **chain** in the lattice is a sequence of partitions in order, e.g. $(P_1, P_2, ..., P_j)$ where $P_1 < P_2 < ... < P_j$; the term is understood in the sense of an elementary chain in graph theory.

2.2   Hierarchies

Let E be a set of n elements, $\wp(E)$ the set of all subsets of E and **P**(E) the **lattice** of the **partitions** defined by the **order relation** P < Q. Let CH be a complete **chain** in the lattice, i.e. a chain linking the **finest partition** P_n, of n elements, to the **coarsest partition** $P_1 = E$. Now we can give two equivalent definitions of a **hierarchy**.

   (1) A hierarchy is a set of partition classes constituting a complete chain, including in particular the set E itself and the n subsets formed by the elements of E. ◆

   The passage from level k to level k-1 on CH corresponds to combining two classes. However, several levels can be passed over. Let P and Q be two non-consecutive partitions on CH, so that the classes of Q are either those of P or combinations of two or more classes of P. This leads to another direct definition.

   (2) A hierarchy is a subset H of $\wp(E)$ such that (1) $E \in H$, (2) if x and y are elements of E, then $\{x\}, \{y\} \in H$, (3) if h and h' are elements of H, then either $h \cap h' = \varnothing$ or $h \cap h' \neq \varnothing$, in which case either $h \subset h'$ or $h' \subset h$. ◆ *Example:* See Figure 1.

2.3   Ultrametrics

A partial ordering of the elements of a hierarchy can be based on the inclusion relation and can be made a total ordering by the process of ascending a complete chain CH. In general, the same hierarchy can be defined by several different chains; thus if E={a,b,c,d,e,f}, then for the hierarchy H formed by the subsets {a}, {b}, {c}, {d}, {e}, {f} with $h_1 = E$, $h_2 = \{a,b,c,d\}$, $h_3 = \{e,f\}$ and $h_4 = \{a,b,c\}$, we can use three chains CH1, CH2 and CH3, with their nodes numbered 0,1,2,3,4 as follows:

CH1	*a,b,c,d,e,f*	*abc,d,e,f*	*abc,d,ef*	*abcd,ef*	*abcdef*
CH2	*a,b,c,d,e,f*	*abc,d,e,f*	*abcd,e,f*	*abcd,ef*	*abcdef*
CH3	*a,b,c,d,e,f*	*a,b,c,d,ef*	*abc,d,ef*	*abcd,ef*	*abcdef*
	0	**1**	**2**	**3**	**4**

Two elements of E occur in the same subset at a given node of CH, this being a partition of E. Given the chain, the node numbers characterize each pair of elements of E. We can now show how they can be used to define a special kind of distance.

2.3.1   Ultrametric Distance
If i, j and k are three elements of a set E, the **ultrametric distance** δ is d fined as a function of E×E in R^+ as follows: $\delta(i,i) = 0$, $\delta(i,j) = \delta(j,i)$, $\delta(i,j) \leq \max[\delta(i,k), \delta(j,k)]$. ◆

   So we might define a distance between elements of E by means of a chain of partitions, and it is clear that this is an ultrametric distance in the sense just defined. It is also clear that infinity of ultrametric distances can be defined so as to be consistent with the order imposed by the chain CH, and we must remember that the same hierarchy can be specified by several different such chains. Conversely, an **indexed hierarchy** can be considered, given an ultrametric distance.

3   Properties and Functions on Hierarchies

I ask for a *European car*, and I get a *German car*. Is there an error? Now, I ask for a *German car*, and a *European car* comes. Can we measure this error? Can we systematize or organize these values? Hierarchies of symbolic values allow measuring the similarity between these values, and the error when one is used instead of another.

3.1   Confusion in Using r Instead of s, for a Hierarchy H

If r, s ∈ H, then the **confusion** in using r instead of s, written conf(r, s), is: **(1)** conf (r, r) = conf (r, s) = 0, where s is any ascendant of r; **(2)** conf (r, s) = 1 + conf (r, father_of(s)) ♦ To measure conf, count the *descending* links from r to s, the replaced value. conf is not a *distance*, nor *ultradistance*. To differentiate, we prefer to use **confusion** instead of other linguistic terms like relatedness or closeness.

Example (Hierarchy H_2): conf(r, s) for H_2 of Figure 2 is given in Table 1:

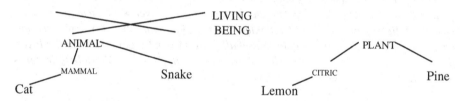

Fig. 2. A hierarchy H_2 of living beings.

The confusion thus introduced *resembles reality* and *catches the hierarchy semantics*. For example, conf (*animal, living_being*) = 0: if they ask you for a living being and you give them an animal, the error of using animal instead of living being is 0, since all animals are living beings. Giving a living being when asked for an animal has error 1; conf (*living_being, animal*) = 1. The confusion among two brothers (say, dog and cat) is 1; using a son instead of the father produces conf=0; using the father instead of the son makes conf = 1. conf is *not* a symmetric property. Using *general things* (see row 'living being') instead of *specific things* produces *high errors*. Using *specific things* (see row 'lemon') instead of *general things* produces *low errors*. The table's lower triangular half has *smaller errors* than its upper triangular half[5].

---

[5] These triangular parts would result to be equal for ultrametric distance. Thus, ultrametrics represents a context-looseness measure in this case.

Table 1. conf(r, s): Confusion in using r instead of s for the living beings of H_2.

Conf	Living b.	Animal	Plant	Mam.	Snake	Citric	Pine	Cat	Lemon
Living b.	0	1	1	2	2	2	2	3	3
Animal	0	0	1	1	1	2	2	2	3
Plant	0	1	0	2	2	1	1	3	2
Mam.	0	0	1	0	1	2	2	1	3
Snake	0	0	1	1	0	2	2	2	3
Citric	0	1	0	2	2	0	1	3	1
Pine	0	1	0	2	2	1	0	3	2
Cat	0	0	1	0	1	2	2	0	3
Lemon	0	1	0	2	2	0	1	3	0

3.1.1 Confusion in Using r Instead of s, for Hierarchies That Are Bags

Now consider a hierarchy H (of an element set E) but composed of bags (unordered collection where repetitions are allowed) instead of sets.

For bags, the **similarity** in using r instead of s, sim^b (r, s), is: **(1)** sim^b (r, r) = sim^b (r, any ascendant_of (r)) = 1; **(2)** if s = some son_of(r), sim^b (r, s) = number of elements of E $\cap$ r $\cap$ s / number of elements of E $\cap$ r = relative popularity of s in r^6; **(3)** sim^b (r, s) = sim^b (r, some son_of(r)) * sim^b (that son_of(r)), s). ♦

The **confusion** in using r instead of s, conf'(r, s), is 1 – sim^b (r, s). ♦

Example: If *baseball_player* = {*pitcher catcher base_player* ∝ {*baseman baseman baseman*} *field_player* ∝ {*fielder fielder fielder*} *shortstop*} then (a) conf' (*fielder, baseball_player*) = 1 – sim^b (*fielder, baseball_player*) = 0; (b) conf' (*baseball_player, fielder*) = 1 – 1/3 = 2/3; (c) conf' (*baseball_player, left_fielder*) = 8/9 (a *left_fielder* is one of those three fielders); (d) conf' (*base_player, fielder*) = 2/3.

3.1.2 Confusion in Using r Instead of s, for Hierarchies That Are Lists

For hierarchies that are lists (ordered sets, for instance Temp = {icy, cold, normal, warm, hot, burning}), the **confusion** in using r instead of s, conf'' (r, s), is defined as follows: **(1)** conf'' (r, r) = conf (r, any ascendant of r) = 0; **(2)** If r and s are distinct brothers, conf'' (r, s) = 1 if the father is not an ordered set; else, conf'' (r, s) = the relative distance from r to s = the number of steps needed to jump from r to s in the ordering, divided by the cardinality-1 of the father; **(3)** conf'' (r, s) = 1 + conf''(r, father_of(s)). ♦ This is like conf for *hierarchies formed by sets*, except that there the error between two brothers is 1, and here it is a number ≤ 1. *Example*: in the list Temp, conf'' (*icy, cold*) = 1/5, while conf'' (*icy, burning*) = 5/5.

The rest of the paper will derive results for conf; those for conf' and conf'' can be similarly derived.

---

[6] Number of elements of E that are in r and that also occur in s / number of elements of E that are also in r = relative popularity or percentage of s in r.

3.2   The Set of Values That Are Equal to Another, up to a Given Confusion

A **value u is equal to value v, within a given confusion ε**, written u $=_\varepsilon$ v, iff conf(u, v) $\leq$ ε (It means that value u can be used instead of v, within error ε). ♦ *Example*: If v = *lemon* (Figure 2), then (a) the set of values equal to v with confusion 0 is {*lemon*}; (b) the set of values equal to v with confusion 1 is {*citric lemon*}; (c) the set of values equal to v with confusion 2 is {*plant citric pine lemon*}. Notice that $=_\varepsilon$ is neither *symmetric* nor *transitive*.

3.2.1   Queries

Objects possessing several properties (or variables), some of them perhaps hierarchical variables, can best be stored as rows of a table in a relational database. We now extend the notion of queries to tables with hierarchical variables,[7] by defining the set S of objects that satisfy predicate P within a given confusion ε.

P holds for object o with confusion ε, or P holds for o within ε, iff (1) if P is formed by non-hierarchical variables, iff P is true for o; (2) for pr a hierarchical variable and P of the form (pr = c), iff for value v of property pr in object o, v $=_\varepsilon$ c (if the value v of the object can be used instead of c with confusion ε); (3) if P is of the form P1 $\vee$ P2, iff P1 holds for o within ε or P2 holds for o within ε; (4) if P is of the form P1 $\wedge$ P2, iff P1 holds for o within ε and P2 holds for o within ε; (5) if P is of the form $\neg$P1, iff P1 does not hold for o within ε. ♦

Example 1 (refer to hierarchies H_1 and H_2 above): Let the *predicates* be: P = (*lives_in* = *USA*) $\vee$ (*pet* = *cat*), Q = (*lives_in* = *USA*) $\wedge$ (*pet* = *cat*), R = $\neg$ (*lives_in* = *Spanish_Speaking_Island*); and the *objects* be (Ann (*lives_in USA*) (*pet snake*)), (Bill (*lives_in English_Speaking_Island*) (*pet citric*)), (Fred (*lives_in USA*) (*pet cat*)), (Tom (*lives_in Mexico*) (*pet cat*)), (Sam (*lives_in Cuba*) (*pet pine*)). Then we have the following results (Table 2):

Table 2. How the predicates P, Q and R of example 1 hold for several objects.

	P holds within ε for:	Q holds within ε for:	R holds within ε for:
ε = 0	Ann, Fred, Tom	Fred	Ann, Bill, Fred, Tom
ε = 1	Ann, Fred, Tom	Fred, Tom	Ann, Fred, Tom
ε = 2	Ann, Fred, Tom, Sam	Ann, Fred, Tom	Nobody

3.2.2   The Smallest ε for Which P(o) Is True

How close is Tom to be like Ann in Example 1? Ann lives in the USA and her pet is a snake, while Tom lives in Mexico and his pet is a cat. When we apply S = (*lives_in* = *USA*) $\wedge$ (*pet* = *snake*) to Tom, we see that S starts holding for ε=1. The answer to "How close is Tom to Ann?" is 1. Notice that this is not a *symmetric* property.

---

[7] For variables that are not hierarchical, a match in value means conf = 0; a mismatch means conf = ∞

Ann is close to Tom starting from $\varepsilon = 2$; that is, (*lives_in = Mexico*) $\wedge$ (*pet = cat*) does not hold for Ann at $\varepsilon=1$, but it starts holding for her at $\varepsilon=2$. This defines the "*closeness to*".

Object o ε-**fulfills** predicate P at threshold ε, if ε is the smallest number for which P holds for o within ε. ♦ Such smallest ε is the **closeness** of o to P. ♦ It is an integer number defined between an object and a predicate. The closer is ε to 0, the "tighter" P holds. Compare with the *membership function* for fuzzy sets.

3.3   Confusion between Variables (Not Values) That Form a Hierarchy

What could be the error in "Sue directed the thesis of Fred", if all we know is "Sue was in the examination committee of Fred"? Up to now, the *values* of a hierarchical variable form a hierarchy (Cf. §1.1). Now, consider the case where the *variables* (or relations) form a hierarchy. For instance, relative and brother, in a universe of kinship relations E = {*sister, aunt*...}. Consider *hierarchies H_3 and H_4*: (H_3) *relative* $\propto$ {*close_relative* $\propto$ {*father mother son daughter brother sister*} *mid_relative* $\propto$ {*aunt uncle niece cousin*} *far_relative* $\propto$ {*grandfather grandmother grandson grand-daughter grandaunt granduncle grandcousin grandniece*} }, (H_4) *player* $\propto$ {*socker_player* $\propto$ {*John Ed*} *basketball_player* $\propto$ {*Susan Fred*} }.

In hierarchy H_3, conf (*son, relative*) = 0; conf (*relative, son*) = 2. We know that, for object (Kim (*close_relative Ed*) (*pet cat*)), the predicate V = (*close_relative Ed*) holds with confusion 0. It is reasonable to assume that W = (*son Ed*) holds for Kim with confusion 1;[8] that X = (*relative Ed*) holds for Kim with confusion 0. Moreover, since Ed is a member of hierarchy H_4, it is reasonable to assume that for object (Carl (*close_relative socker_player*) (*pet pine*)) the predicate V holds with confusion 1, X holds with confusion 1 and W holds with confusion 1+1 = 2. Thus, we can extend the definition to variables that are members of a hierarchy, by adding another bullet to the definition of §3.2.1, thus:

If P is of the form (var = c), for var a variable member of a hierarchy, iff $\exists$ variable var_2 for which (var_2=c) holds for o within ε – conf (var, var_2), where var_2 also belongs to the hierarchy of var. ♦ The confusion of the variables *adds* to the confusion of the values. *Example*: For (Burt (*relative basketball_player*) (*pet cat*)), V holds with confusion 1+2=3, W with confusion 2+2=4, and X with confusion 0+2=2.

3.4   Similarity for Values in Different Hierarchies and in Different Ontologies

When v_1 belongs to a hierarchy H_1 and v_2 to another hierarchy H_2, both with the same element set E, it is best to construct an *ontology* O_U from E, and then to use it to measure the similarity sim'(v_1, v_2), as follows: sim' (c_U, d_U) for two concepts belonging to the *same ontology* O_U, is defined as the 1/(1 + length of the path going from c_U to d_U in the O_U tree). ♦ sim' is defined for *concepts*, not for symbolic values.

---

[8] We are looking for a person that is a son of Ed, and we find Kim, a close relative of Ed.

Also, for concepts c_A, d_B belonging to *different ontologies* O_A, O_B, we define: sim'' (c_A, d_B) when d_B is *not* the most similar concept in O_B to $c_A \in O_A$, is equal to $s_1 s_2$, where $s_1 = $ sim (c_A, O_A, O_B) [sim gives the similarity between c_A and its most similar concept c_B in O_B; sim also finds c_B], and $s_2 = $ sim' (c_B, d_B). ◆

3.5 Comments and Summing-up

It is worth pausing at this point to look again at ideas of similarity, dissimilarity (confusion) and distance as they apply to a set E. It is difficult in practice to set up a partial order if the number of elements x, y, z... of E is large, and if it is possible it is difficult to make this order without running the risk of generating contradictions. In fact, *the only practical way to establish a partial order is to define a numerical function of similarity or dissimilarity (confusion)* that can be computed in terms of the attributes of every element of E: the **similarity** $\mu(x,y)$ will be greater the more closely x resembles y; the **dissimilarity (confusion)** $\lambda(x,y)$ will be smaller the more closely x resembles y. The same partial order can be generated by any of an unlimited number such functions. Some dissimilarity functions, however, may not be distances (Cf. §§3.1-3.4). However, we can make simple transformations of $\lambda(x,y)$ without affecting the corresponding partial ordering [2, 19] and loss the context. Our point is that it is *not necessary* to be done (more arguments in [13]).

Summing-up the analysis presented in previous sections, we can emphasize:

1   Attempting to define a distance on hierarchies of symbolic values to measure closeness between hierarchical elements and hold its partial (total) order, we can lose the *context* of a problem under consideration (§3.1, Table 1).

2   When the context (semantics) of a problem is considered, by expressing the similarity function in terms of the data attributes, we can overcome it (§3.1 and [10, 13]).

3   Such approach finds the set of values that are equal to another up to a given confusion (§3.2) as well as the closeness of an object to the predicate. Similarity functions for values in different hierarchies (or ontologies) can be defined (§3.4 and [13]).

4   Hierarchies are simpler than ontologies, although very useful. They are easier to understand, and the extensions to searches, queries and imperfect answers are straightforward (§3.2-3.3 and [13]). Ontologies promise longer mileage, although they are more complex to understand, to implement, and to apply. For instance, BiblioDigital is a recent development that uses for document classification and indexing a rich taxonomy, like an ontology, but with *confusion* properties, like a hierarchy [11].

4   Some Applications to Linguistic Analysis[9]

Quasihierarchies and recursive structures have been used in [1] for linguistic analysis of Russian and English texts, verses translation, and computer program comments (fogware). Clasitex [7] is a program that tells us the themes of an article written in Spanish or English. It uses the concept tree, and a word (not in the tree) *suggests the topic of* one or more concepts in the tree. Other potential applications of the quasi-synonymic relation introduced by our method go far beyond agent communication in electronic commerce, covering ontology-based natural language interfaces [21], information retrieval [15, 16], text segmentation and coherence evaluation [3], collocation inference [4], etc., to mention only a few.

Recent computational linguistics researches can be linked to our topic as follows.

Information in mostly used WordNet is organized around logical groupings called synsets. Each synset consists of a list of synonymous words or collocations (e.g., "fountain pen", "take in"), and pointers that describe the relations between this synset and other synsets. A word or collocation may appear in more than one synset, and in more than one part of speech. The words in a synset are logically grouped such that they are interchangeable in some *context*. Two kinds of relations are represented by pointers: lexical and semantic. Lexical relations hold between word forms; semantic relations hold between word meanings. These relations include (but are not limited to) hypernymy/hyponymy, antonymy, entailment, and meronymy/holonymy. Nouns and verbs are organized into *hierarchies* based on the hypernymy/hyponymy relation between synsets. Additional pointers are used to indicate other relations [20].

Five different proposed measures of similarity or semantic distance in WordNet were experimentally compared by examining their performance in a real-word spelling correction system [5]. It was found that Jiang and Conrath's measure gave the best results overall. That of Hirst-St-Onge seriously over-related, that of Resnik seriously under-related [18], and those of Lin and of Leacock-Chodorow fell in between.

Note that all the measures except of Hirst and St-Onge are *similarity* (not relatedness) measures considering only *the hyponymy hierarchy* of WordNet.

Thus, the measures herein proposed can be compared for at least that hierarchy (§3). Moreover, we shall attempt to compare Hirst-St-Onge's measure and the measure of §3.4 on overall WordNet structure, maybe, by using the same methodology as in [5]. Other issue that can be addressed by our approach is the possibility provided by the definitions of §3.2 for another evaluation method besides those in [5]. Yet other issue is a search for explanation of difference in performance of the "looking arithmetically identical" Jiang-Conrath's and Lin's measures [5]. The prompt is that both measures should be seriously embedded into WordNet context by the interaction procedure of [17]. Our future research will be concerned with these issues. These issues will also be addressed in the now-developing project "Precision-controlled retrieval of qualitative information." We also invite the CL community to test our measures in existing linguistic data bases thus providing some sort of validation.

---

[9] We limited these to WordNet due to the page limit. More applications and examples in NLP and several other areas of AI can be found in [7] [9] [15].

5 Conclusion

The notions of hierarchy and hierarchical variable make it possible to measure the *confusion* when a value is used instead of another. This makes a natural generalization for predicates and queries. The notions were introduced and developed for arbitrary hierarchies formed by sets, but they can be extended to bags and lists too.

The concepts given herein have practical applications, since they mimic the manner in which people process qualitative values and disambiguate senses (an interesting procedure is [6]). Some examples are given.

References

1. Alexandrov, V., Arsentieva, A.: *Dialogue Structure (Dialogue – Is It an Art or Science?)*. Leningrad Inst. for Informatics and Aut. of the USSR Acad. of Sciences (1984).
2. Alexandrov, V.: *Developing Systems in Science, Technique, Society and Culture.* Nauka, Saint Petersburg (2002)
3. Bolshakov, I. A., A. Gelbukh. Text segmentation into paragraphs based on local text cohesion. In: Text, Speech and Dialogue (TSD-2001). Lecture Notes in Artificial Intelligence, N 2166, Springer-Verlag, pp. 158–166.
4. Bolshakov, I. A., A. Gelbukh. Heuristics-based replenishment of collocation databases. In: E. Ranchhold, N. J. Mamede (Eds.) Advances in Natural Language Processing (PorTAL-2002). Lecture Notes in Computer Science, N 2389, Springer-Verlag, p. 25–32.
5. Budanitsky, A., Hirst, G.: Semantic Distance in WordNet: An Experimental, Application-oriented Evaluation of Five Measures. Workshop on WordNet and Other Lexical Resources, in the *North American Chapter of the Association for Computational Linguistics* (NAACL-2000), Pittsburgh, PA, June 2001
6. Gelbukh, A. Using a semantic network for lexical and syntactical disambiguation. Proc. CIC-97, *Simposium Internacional de Computación,* 12-14, 1997, CIC, IPN, Mexico City, Mexico, 352–366. www.gelbukh.com/CV/Publications/1997/CIC-97-Sem-Net.htm
7. Guzman, A.: Finding the Main Themes in a Spanish Document. *Journal Expert Systems with Applications,* Vol. **14**, No. 1/2 (1998) 139-148
8. Guzman, A., Olivares, J., Demetrio, D., Dominguez, C.: Interaction of Purposeful Agents that use Different Ontologies. *Lecture Notes in Artificial Intelligence*, Vol. **1793**. Springer-Verlag, Berlin Heidelberg New York (2000) 557-573
9. Guzman, A., Dominguez, C., Olivares, J.: Reacting to Unexpected Events and Communicating in spite of Mixed Ontologies. *Lecture Notes in Artificial Intelligence*, Vol. **2313**. Springer-Verlag, Berlin Heidelberg New York (2002) 377-386
10. Guzman, A., Levachkine, S.: Graduate Errors in Approximation Queries using Hierarchies and Ordered Sets. Submitted to *MICAI 2004.*
11. de Gyves, V., Guzman, A.: *BiblioDigital.* © SoftwarePro International (work in progress)
12. Lenat, D.B., Guha, R.V.: *Building Large Knowledge-Based Systems.* Addison-Wesley (1989)
13. Levachkine, S., Guzman, A.: Hierarchies as a New Data Type for Qualitative Variables. Submitted to the *Journal of Data Knowledge Engineering,* Elsevier (2002)
14. Levachkine, S., Guzmaan, A.: Confusion between hierarchies partitioned by a Percentage rule. Submitted to *MICAI 04.*

15. Montes-y-Gómez, M., A. López-López, and A. Gelbukh. Information Retrieval with Conceptual Graph Matching. In: Database and Expert Systems Applications (DEXA-2000). Lecture Notes in Computer Science, N 1873, Springer-Verlag, pp. 312–321.

16. Montes-y-Gómez, M., A. Gelbukh, A. López-López, R. Baeza-Yates. Flexible Comparison of Conceptual Graphs. In: Mayr, H.C., Lazansky, J., Quirchmayr, G., Vogel, P. (Eds.), In: Database and Expert Systems Applications (DEXA-2001). Lecture Notes in Computer Science, N 2113, Springer-Verlag, pp. 102–111.

17. Olivares, J., Guzman, A.: Measuring the Comprehension or Understanding between two Agents (to appear)

18. Resnik, P.: Disambiguating Noun Groupings with respect to WordNet Senses. In: Armstrong, S. et al. (eds.): *Natural Language Processing Using Very Large Corpora*. Kluwer Academic Publishing, Dordrecht (1995) 77-98

19. Simon, J.-C.: *Patterns and Operators. The Foundations of Data Representation.* McGraw-Hill (1984)

20. WordNet: A Lexical Database for the English Language, www.cogsci.princeton.edu/~wn/

21. Zárate, A., R. Pazos, A. Gelbukh, I. Padrón. A portable natural language interface for diverse databases using ontologies. In: Computational Linguistics and Intelligent Text Processing (CICLing-2003). Lecture Notes in Computer Science, N 2588, Springer-Verlag, pp. 494–505.

Substring Alignment Using Suffix Trees

Martin Kay

Stanford University

Abstract. Alignment of the sentences of an original text and a translation is considerably better understood than alignment of smaller units such as words and phrases. This paper makes some preliminary proposals for solving the problem of aligning substrings that should be treated as basic translation unites even though they may not begin and end at word boundaries. The proposals make crucial use of suffix trees as a way of identifying repeated substrings of the texts that occur significantly often.

It is fitting that one should take advantage of the few occasions on which one is invited to address an important and prestigious professional meeting like this to depart from the standard practice of reporting results and instead to seek adherents to a new enterprise, even if it is one the details of which one can only partially discern. In this case, I intend to take that opportunity to propose a new direction for a line of work that I first became involved in in the early 1990's [3]. It had to do with the automatic alignment of the sentences of a text with those in its translation into another language. The problem is nontrivial because translators frequently translate one sentence with two, or two with one. Sometimes the departure from the expected one-to-one alignment is even greater. We undertook this work not so much because we thought it was of great importance but because it seemed to us rather audacious to attempt to establish these alignments on the basis of no *a priori* assumptions about the languages involved or about correspondences between pairs of words.

As often happens, it turned out that what we thought of as new and audacious was already "in the air" and, while we a were at work, Gale and Church [2] published a solution to the problem that was arguably somewhat less accurate than ours, but was altogether simpler, computationally less complex, and entirely adequate for practical purposes. Whereas their approach was based on nothing more than the lengths of the sentences, in terms either of characters or words, ours made hypotheses about word alignments on the basis of which it circumscribed the space of possible sentence alignments. It then refined the initial set of word alignments, and proceeded back and forth in this manner until no further refinements were possible. Fortunately the process converged fast.

In the relatively short time since this work was done, sentence alignment has come to be seen as a central tool in work on machine translation. During this time the perception has grown that the rules that direct the operation of a machine-translation system should be derived automatically from existing translations rather than being composed one by one by linguists and system designers. The first step in just about any such learning procedure is to set the sentences in correspondence with one another because sentences continue to be seen as providing the framework within which translation is done.

A. Gelbukh (Ed.): CICLing 2004, LNCS 2945, pp. 275–282, 2004.
© Springer-Verlag Berlin Heidelberg 2004

The natural second step is to attempt an alignment of the parts of an aligned pair of sentences as a prelude to proposing some kind of translation rule. A great many approaches to this problem have been proposed, but they fall naturally into two classes depending on whether the aligned sentence sequences that they work on are analysed in some way, perhaps by associating a syntactic structure with them, or whether the work continues to be done entirely on the basis of strings. The former approach has the drawback that disambiguation of the output of a syntactic parser is still expensive, unreliable, or both. On the other hand, it suggests a much broader set of finer tools for alignment below the sentence level than are available for working simply on strings. Suppose that it has been established beyond reasonable doubt that a pair of nouns should be aligned with one another, and that each is modified by a single adjective which may not, however, occur next to it in the string. Clearly, this constitutes stronger evidence for the alignment of the adjectives than would be possible purely on the basis of the strings. More simply put, the hypothesis that phrases translate phrases is not only a strong and appealing one, but it in fact underlies a great deal of the work that has been done on machine translation.

It goes without saying that natural languages provide innumerable examples of translation units that almost certainly could not be reliably identified without recourse to the syntactic structure of the sentences in which they occurred. Discontinuities are perhaps the most obvious example. English *take ... into consideration* presumably often constitutes a unit for translation, but only when the gap is filled with a noun phrase. Separable verbs in German and their analogues present a similar problem, as do their analogues in English, namely verbs involving particles. Some less severe problems might be made less severe by working with a string of lemmas or with tagged text. In many languages, a sequence that should be treated as a translation unit, like French *carte orange* ('subway pass'; literally 'orange card') supports changes in the middle of the string. Thus, the plural of *carte orange* is *cartes oranges*. This problem is exacerbated in other languages, such as German, where various different changes are possible, depending not only on number, but also on gender.

While phrases clearly do often translate phrases, it is equally clearly the case that substrings of a sentence that do not constitute phrases can also function as units for translation. The English preposition *as* often corresponds to *au four et à mesure* in French, but this is at best a compound preposition and no phrase. The words *one and the same* might be called fixed phrase in everyday parlance, but they do not constitute a phrase in linguistic terms. The French word *connaître* translates into English in many ways, including *know* and *get to know*, the second of which could hardly be regarded as phrase. The question of how to identify sequences like these quickly and easily, especially during the early phases of working on a new language, is one that is surely worthy of attention.

The question of how to identify translation units that consist of several words is one side of a coin whose other side concerns translation units that are smaller than a word or whose end points are not marked by word boundaries. The most obvious examples of these are the components of compound nouns in a language like German in which these components are not separated by spaces. In a language in which word boundaries are not routinely represented in text, the problem becomes acute.

The approach to these problems that is advocated, though only partially worked out, in this paper, is to place word boundaries on an equal footing with all other characters. In particular, it gives to no special status to translation units whose boundaries correspond to word boundaries.

If translation units are not to be sought between word boundaries, the first question that arises is, what substrings are considered as candidates for this status? The possibility of giving all substrings equal status can presumably be excluded on the grounds that there are simply too many of them. A text consisting of n characters contains $n(n + 1)$ substrings. If the strings are confined within sentences and a string contains m sentences of k characters each, then there are mk $(k + 1)$ substrings. This is more manageable. A 50-character sentence contains 1275 substrings, and a-200 character sentence 20,100 and a 500-character sentence 125,250. But the number of substrings that actually needs to be considered is a great deal less.

The substrings that need to be considered as candidates as translation units should surely have at least two properties. The first is that they should occur enough times in the text to make them interesting. The second is that, if some set of the substrings are distributionally indistinguishable, then they should be treated as the same.

The first of these properties is fairly straightforward and uncontroversial. The second can be made clear with one or two examples. Consider the substrings "uncontroversia" and "uncontroversial" of the first sentence of this paragraph. The first is clearly found wherever the second is because it is a prefix of the second. But the second will probably be found, in just about any text of English, wherever the first is, because there is, I suppose, no word of English containing the letters "uncontroversia" in which they are not followed by "l". The distributions of the two strings will therefore be the same and each will therefore be equivalent to the other from the point of view of an investigation which, like the present one, gives not special status to word boundaries. Notice that, simply by engaging in a brief discussion of these example, we have made the present text an exception to the supposed rule. In particular, this text contains to instances of the sequence "uncontroversia" followed, not by "l", but by quotation marks. Another member of this equivalence class, at least in most texts, will likely be the string "ncontroversial" because, at least outside this sentence, it will almost always follow the letter "u". Other members of the class are "unconversi", and "uncontrovers", but not, of course "controversial".

A fact that is not immediately obvious is that the number of equivalence classes exemplified in a text of n characters, even if sentence boundaries are ignored, can be no more than $2n - 1$. This, as we shall see, is direct consequence of the fact that there are n terminal nodes, and at most $n - 1$ branching nonterminal nodes in a *suffix tree* constructed from a string of n characters.

Suffix trees constitute a well understood, extremely elegant, but regrettably poorly appreciated data structure with potentially many applications in language processing. For a gentle introduction, see [4]. We shall have space here only for the briefest of introductions, which we begin by considering a related but somewhat simpler structure called a *suffix trie*. A *trie* [1] is a very well-known data structure often used for storing words so that they can be looked up easily. It is a deterministic finite-state automaton whose transition diagram has the shape of a tree and in which the symbols encountered on a path from its initial state to a final state spell out a word. A suffix trie is a trie built, not from words in the usual lexicographic sense, but from the strings that are the suffixes of some text. If the entire text consists of the word "mississippi", the corresponding suffix tree is the one depicted in Figure 1. In this diagram, the labels on every path from the start state at the root of the tree, on the left of the diagram, to a terminal node on the right spells out some suffix of the text. Since every substring of the text is a prefix of some suffix, it follows that every substring is spelled out by the characters on the path from the root to some node, terminal or nonterminal. An extra character ($), know not to occur otherwise in the text, is added to the end for technical reasons.

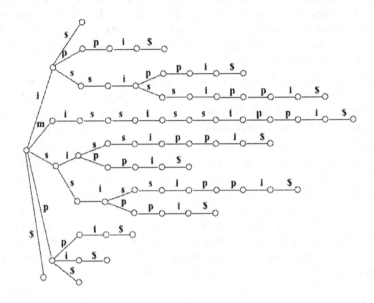

Fig. 1. A Suffix Trie

Before moving from suffix tries to suffix trees, let us pause to verify that the tries already have one of the properties of "interesting" substrings of a text. A branching nonterminal node is one out of which there is more than one transition. Any substring that ends at such a node can be continued in more than one way, that is, by at least two different characters, thus meeting one of the requirements of an "interesting" substring. It follows that there can be no more "interesting" substrings of the text than there are branching nodes in the suffix tree constructed from it. As we shall see in a moment, the corresponding constraint can be verified at the left hand end of the string just as readily.

The branching nodes in the suffix trie have a special interest for us and it is worth noting that there must be strictly less of these than there are suffixes. This follows immediately from the following pair of observations. First, when the initial suffix is placed in the tree, no branching nodes are created. Secondly, the entry into the trie of each succeeding suffix can give rise to at most one new branching node.

The trouble with suffix trees is that they are totally impractical for large texts because of their sheer size and the time it takes to build them. However, these things are suddenly brought under control in the passage from tries to trees. This is accomplished by replacing every sequence of transitions and nonbranching nodes by a single transition labelled with the corresponding sequence of characters. This sequence, however, is represented, not by the characters themselves, but by a pair of integers giving the end points of an occurrence of the string in the text. Nothing is lost by representing the tree in this way, because points represented by erased nodes can be reconstructed trivially, and pairs of integers constructed to represent the nodes in and out of them. The results of performing this operation on the trie in Figure 1 are shown in Figure 2.

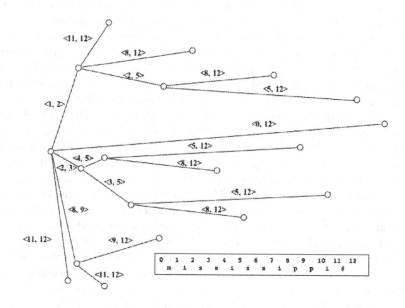

Fig. 2. A Suffix Tree

The importance of this transformation cannot be overstated. The upper bound on the number of transitions in the original trie was $k(k + 1)$ for a text of k characters. This has been reduced to $k - 1$, and the size of the label on a transition remains constant. The size of the tree is therefore linear in the size of the text. A somewhat surprising fact that we shall not be able to go into here is that methods also exist for constructing these trees in linear time ([5] and [6]).

A few words are in order on the question of how to read substrings out of the suffix tree represented in this particular way. It is generally necessary, when tracing a path from the root to a particular other node in the tree, to keep track of the length of the string traversed. This is simply a matter of adding the difference between each pair of text pointers encountered to a running count. The starting point of the string ending in a particular transition is the second of the numbers labelling that transition minus the current count. The various occurrences of the substring ending at a particular node, whether branching, and therefore "actual" or non branching, and therefore "virtual", can be enumerated straightforwardly and in a time that depends on the number of them that there are in the text and not on the actual length of the text. The method of doing this depends on the following observation: Just as the beginning of the substring corresponding to a sequence of arcs starting at the root can be determined by keeping track of the lengths of the segments covered by each transition, so the end points of the various occurrence of the substring represented by a particular node can be determined by keeping track of the lengths of the segments from the node to the various terminal nodes reachable from it.

Consider the string "si" which traces out a path through the tree shown in Figure 2 over the edges $< 2, 3 >$ and $< 4, 5 >$. The string is of length 2 and its first occurrence in the text is at position $5 - (5 - 4 + 3 - 2) = 3$. The complete set of its occurrences are found by continuing the search to all possible—in this case 2—terminal nodes. The lengths of the suffixes of the text covered in tracing out these two paths, including the substring itself are $(3 - 2) + (5 - 4) + (12 - 5) = 9$ and $(3 - 2) + (5 - 4) + (12 - 8) = 6$. These are the lengths of the suffixes of the text that begin with the string "si" so that their locations in the text are $12 - 9 = 3$ and $12 - 6 = 6$. Now suppose that the substring of interest is "s", reachable from the root over the single transition $< 2, 3 >$ and with paths to terminal nodes of lengths $(3 - 2) + (5 - 4) + (5 - 12) = 9$, $(3 - 2) + (5 - 4) + (12 - 8) = 4$, $(3 - 2) + (5 - 3) + (12 - 5) = 10$ and $(3 - 2) + (5 - 3) + (12 - 8) = 7$. This shows that it has four locations in the text at positions $12 - 9 = 3$, $12 - 4 = 8$, $12 - 10 = 2$ and $12 - 7 = 5$. Notice that, if a substring occurs in k locations, finding them in this way involves visiting no more than $2k - 1$ nodes, once the first occurrence has been located.

Since it is computationally inexpensive to locate all the instances of a string in a text using a suffix tree, it is also inexpensive to determine whether these instances are all preceded by the same character, thus making the "uninteresting" for present purposes. In fact let us assume that the process of building a suffix tree for those purposes includes a step in which a bit is associated with every node to show whether the corresponding substring of the text has this property. We are now in a strong position to locate, in linear time, all substrings of an arbitrary text which, for given integers L and R,

1. consist of at least L characters,
2. are repeated at least R times,
3. are not always preceded by the same character,
4. are not always followed by the same character, and
5. that do not cross a sentence boundary.

These will be our initial candidate translation units.

If we were to abandon all further concern for computational complexity at this point, the plan for completing at least the first version of the project would be fairly straightforward. It would consist in aligning the sentences of a text and its translation in another language, locating "interesting" substrings of the two text and then evaluating the similarity of pairs "interesting" strings in terms of the overlap in the sets of aligned sentences in which they occur. Let A be the set of sentences in which one of the strings occurs, and B the set in which the other string occurs. A reasonable measure of similarity might by $|A \cap B|/|A \cup B|$ which has values v in the range $0 \le v \le 1$, the value 1 representing identity, and 0 representing disjointness. The only problem with the plan, at least in this simple form, lies in the fact that its time complexity is $O(mn)$, if m and

n are the lengths of the two texts. Unfortunately, this represents not simply the cost of an extreme worst case. It is also a reasonable estimate of the average situation, in the absence of any *a priori* knowledge of which pairs of strings are likely to align well.

While we have no proposal reducing the worst-case complexity, there is some hope of substantially reducing the constants involved in determining the computational cost. With this in mind, we propose to increase the amount of information carried by a node in the suffix tree. We will add a new pointer from each node to its parent in the tree and a field, which we call the *count* field, capable of accommodating an integer. We will also construct an index with an entry for every (aligned) sentence, containing pointers to the terminal nodes of the suffix tree corresponding to suffixes of the text that begin in a given sentence. Using this index, and the parent pointers, we can quickly visit all the substrings of the text that occur in a given sentence. In particular, given a particular set of sentences, we can cheaply populate the counter fields of the nodes to show how many of them the corresponding string occurs in. Crucially, we can do this while visiting only nodes for strings that occur in at least one of the sentences. Notice that, if this procedure assigns to non-zero value to the count at a given node, it will also assign a non-zero value, and indeed at least as high a value, to all nodes on paths from the root to that node. Once the values have been assigned, it will therefore be possible to traverse the tree, visiting only nodes for strings that occur in the current set of sentences.

With these mechanisms in place, we are in a position to proceed as follows. Conduct traversal of the suffix tree of the first text to locate "interesting" strings and obtain for each of these, the list of the sentences in which it occurs. Using the sentence index and the parent pointers of the other tree, assign value to the count fields of the strings that occur in the corresponding sentences of the other language. We now conduct a search for "interesting" strings in the suffix tree for the second text, limiting the search to nodes whose count fields contain non-zero values. Not surprisingly, this limitation is very significant if the string in the first language is indeed "interesting". The techniques are manifestly still in need of considerable refinement. Experiments are still in a very early stage so that it would be fruitless to give statistics. But there is some good news, both for engineers who want results, and scientists who want more problems to solve. Much of the bad news can be ascribed to the fact that the only texts that have been involved in the experiments consist of some 600 sentences from a single automobile maintenance manual and its French and German translations.

A consequence of working with too little data is that strings are allowed to qualify as "interesting" when they are in fact too long. This is because, in this particular text, for example, all instances of the word *warning* are followed by *light* and there are no instances of *warn* in any but the present-participle form. But light remains "interesting" because it is not always preceded by *warning*. The English *warning* was set in correspondence with the German *Kontroll* in the compound *Kontrolleuchte*. Indeed there was an encouraging measure of success in properly aligning the parts of German compounds. When words are chosen as "interesting" substrings, they generally have an initial space attached. Whether they also have a final space depends of whether they have been observed at the end of a sentence, or otherwise before a punctuation mark. The word *coolant* is not "interesting" because it occurs only in *coolant in the engine* which is aligned with the French string *du liquide de refroidissment dans le moteur*. The inclusion of the initial *du* is an artifact of the very small number of contexts in which the string was found.

When the parameters were set so as to allow very short words to count as "interesting", correspondences were recognized even among function words and inflexions. The English suffixes "ic", and "ly" (with the trailing space) were aligned with French "ique" and "ment". The French sequence "les" (with spaces on both ends) was aligned with English "s" (with a trailing space). This last alignment presumable reflects that fact the French grammar requires more frequent use of the definite article than English does so that "les" more readily contracts an alignment with the plural ending of the noun. It may also have something to do with the fact that *les* occurred nowhere in this text as an object clitic.

Encouraging though these preliminary results are, they also reveal important short-comings of the technique and challenges for the future. The most important of these will almost certainly involve additional procedures with unappealing complexity properties. As usual with ordinary language, ambiguity, or at least *relative ambiguity*, is at the heart of the severest of the problems.

A string in one language is ambiguous relative to another language if it is routinely translated differently in that other language, depending on the context. Simplifying somewhat, we can say that French *haut* translates into English as either or *high* or *tall*. If one of these adjectives were somehow replaced by the other in a English text before the alignment process began, there would be good reason to hope that a strong alignment with French *haut* would be recognized. But there appears to be no basis to make any such conflation of words, especially within a system in which the very notion of a word is so carefully deemphasized. The general problem is to be able to recognize situations in which a distribution that is abundantly endowed with "interesting" properties, aligns with the (disjoint) union of two or more distributions in the other language.

Another way to think about this problem involves abandoning the notion of similarity, which is inherently symmetrical, in favor of a notion of inclusion of one distribution in another. Continuing the above simplified example, this would allow an alignment to be established between French *haut* and English *high* on the grounds that the distribution of *haut* largely contains that of the English *high*. Suppose this were successful, it might then be possible to seek other alignments for just those instances *haut* that did not participate in the first alignment.

References

[1] Fredkin, E. Trie memory. Informal Memorandum. *Communications of the ACM*, 3,(9), 490–500 (1960).
[2] William A. Gale and Kenneth W.Church A program for Aligning Sentences in Bilingual Corpora. *Computational Linguistics* 19 (1) pp. 61–74, 1993
[3] M. Kay & M. Röscheisen. Text-Translation Alignment, *Computational Linguistics* 19:1, 1995
[4] Nelson, Mark. Fast String Searching With Suffix Trees, *Dr. Dobb's Journal* August, 1996.
[5] McCreight, E.M. A space-economical suffix tree construction algorithm. *Journal of the ACM*, 23:262-272, 1976.
[6] Ukkonen, E. On-line construction of suffix trees. Algorithmica, 14(3):249–260, September 1995.

Exploiting Hidden Meanings: Using Bilingual Text for Monolingual Annotation

Philip Resnik

Department of Linguistics
and Institute for Advanced Computer Studies
University of Maryland
College Park, Maryland 20742 USA
resnik@umd.edu

Abstract. The last decade has taught computational linguists that high performance on broad-coverage natural language processing tasks is best obtained using supervised learning techniques, which require annotation of large quantities of training data. But annotated text is hard to obtain. Some have emphasized making the most out of limited amounts of annotation. Others have argued that we should focus on simpler learning algorithms and find ways to exploit much larger quantities of text, though those efforts have tended to focus on linguistically shallow problems. In this paper, I describe my efforts to exploit larger quantities of data while still focusing on linguistically deeper problems such as parsing and word sense disambiguation. The trick, I argue, is to take advantage of the shared meaning hidden between the lines of sentences in parallel translation.

1 The Problem of Resources

1.1 Knowledge versus Data

Success in natural language processing depends crucially on good resources. In the early days, knowledge-based approaches depended heavily on good knowledge resources — grammars, lexicons, and the like. Consider LUNAR [1], which permitted users to ask questions about moon rocks using natural language sentences. As an early question answering system, LUNAR was successful not just because of a clever formalism, but also largely because of the human effort that went into a detailed characterization of linguistic alternatives, expressed as an augmented transition network grammar and lexical entries associated with that grammar.

In the late 1980s, natural language processing began to change dramatically as the result of an influsion of ideas and techniques from the speech recognition, information retrieval, and machine learning communities. Ten years ago, the "balancing act" between symbolic and statistical methods was an exciting topic for a computational linguistics workshop [2]; today it's an apt description of the

A. Gelbukh (Ed.): CICLing 2004, LNCS 2945, pp. 283–299, 2004.
© Springer-Verlag Berlin Heidelberg 2004

entire field. Over the course of this transition, resources have remained essential, but these days what matters most is not good *knowledge* resources but rather good *data* resources. As an example, the Collins parser [3,4] is successful not just because of a clever model, but also because of the human effort that went into annotating the Penn Treebank [5], implicitly characterizing distributions over linguistic alternatives by creating explicit linguistic representations for a large sample of text.

The impact of this shift from knowledge resources to data resources cannot be overstated. Even as the pendulum begins to swing back in the other direction, with increased attention to the potential advantages of exploiting deeper linguistic representations, the lessons of statistical methods are not being forgotten. For example, Gildea and Jurafsky [6] take a significant step toward automatic semantic interpretation by introducing a system that identifies the semantic roles, such as agent or patient, that are filled by the constituents of a sentence. They accomplish this by treating the problem as one of statistical classification, relying on a large number of sentences manually annotated with semantic role representations [7].

Annotating linguistic data with linguistic representations is undoubtedly easier than, say, writing grammars. As Sapir [8] points out, "All grammars leak" — that is, it is never possible to come up with a grammar that accurately characterizes all the data. In contrast, linguistic annotation need not be one hundred percent perfect, nor is there an expectation that it will be: instead, quality is measured by comparing the representations assigned by independent annotators to the same data, and measuring inter-annotator agreement. Variability is a given, and accurate measurement of quality given observed data is understood by all to be a part of the process. Statistics is, after all, a science of measuring uncertainty [9]. The most common use of these linguistic annotations is in probabilistic models: rather than writing rules, we estimate parameters, and by definition an estimate admits of uncertainty.

The shift from knowledge acquisition to data acquisition is not, however, free of cost. One problem that comes up again and again is the sensitivity of statistical techniques to the data on which they are trained. Good part-of-speech taggers boast accuracies within a few percent of perfect, but the published results are almost always based on experiments in which a single data set is split into training material and test material, enforcing the constraint that the training data be statistically representative of the data on which the system will be tested. In the real world, of course, this constraint can only be assumed, not enforced, and often it is not valid — taggers trained on the Wall Street Journal perform less well on data from other newswire sources, and still less well if the input text comes from another genre entirely. (To be fair, knowledge-rich approaches never did particularly well at domain-independent performance either.) This problem is gaining wider attention, and solutions are likely to come from the speech community, where automatic *adaptation* is an important topic of current research.

1.2   Acquiring Annotated Data

But of course adaptation to new kinds of data requires... data. And this is the fundamental cost in corpus-based techniques, because the techniques that perform best are all hungry for high quality annotated data. Consider parsing. Over the period from 1989 to 1992, the Penn Treebank project created skeletal parse trees for some 2.8 million words of English text, with productivity estimates (including quality control) based on annotators producing syntactic representations at an average rate of 750 words per hour [5]. The state of the art for parsing English is something on the order of 90% F-measure (harmonic mean of precision and recall) for unlabeled syntactic dependencies — and most parsers capable of producing such numbers are evaluated using the Wall Street Journal subset of the Penn Treebank, enforcing, as usual, that the training and test data are sampled from the same source. The Penn Chinese Treebank project started in the summer of 1998, and two years years later had produced an order of magnitude less data (about 100,000 words from a single newswire source), with the best parsers achieving an F-measure of 75-80%. Training good statistical parsers on the recent Chinese Treebank 3.0 release, which has 250,000 words, yields performance comparable to English (Dan Jurafsky, personal communication); but this release came out in 2003, five years after the start of the project.

If state of the art performance requires this level of annotation effort and time spent for English and Chinese, what of languages that typically receive less effort, or no effort, but suddenly become important? (For an example, see Oard et al. [10].) How can one ever hope to build annotated resources for more than a handful of the world's languages?

An interesting point of comparison is the problem of Bible translation. Here, too, is an effort to manually construct data in a large number of the world's languages, with a size that is reasonably comparable to the sizes of today's treebanks (about 800,000 words for the most-translated 66 book set, which includes both Old and New Testaments). One could argue that high quality translation is on the same order of magnitude of difficulty as detailed linguistic annotation — turnaround times for professional translation services, based on an informal survey of several Web sites, suggest a productivity estimate of around 200-300 words per hour for experienced translators. Despite a huge surge in Bible translation effort over the last century or two, and particularly in the last fifty years, today there are only approximately 400 languages for which there exist complete Bibles, and around 1000 languages for which there are New Testament translations (a difference that reflects the Bible translation community's priorities).[1] If this is the rate of progress for a task given a zealous, world-wide effort, the prospect for manual annotation of linguistic representations across hundreds of languages seems bleak indeed.[2]

---

[1] For current statistics, see http://www.wycliffe.org/wbt-usa/trangoal.htm. See Resnik, Olsen, and Diab [11] for a detailed discussion of the Bible as a resource for computational linguistics.

[2] Of course, Bible translation is not the same as translation in general, so this comparison must be treated with great caution. Wycliffe, a major organization in worldwide

A number of clever algorithmic solutions to the annotated data acquisition bottleneck have been and are currently being explored. One approach, active learning, pursues the idea that annotation should be done in partnership with the learning algorithm: by focusing annotation effort where it will help the learning algorithm most, rather than sampling randomly, less annotation will need to be done (see Tong [12] and references therein). Active learning is sometimes categorized as a "weakly supervised" learning approach, i.e. one in which a smaller amount of annotation data is used in combination with a large quantity unannotated data; additional avenues of research in weakly supervised learning include other general techniques such as co-training, where each of multiple learners automatically generates training examples for other learners in the set [13,14], as well as task-specific forms of bootstrapping from small annotated subsets, e.g. in word sense disambiguation [15].

1.3   Avoiding Expensive Data Annotation

Another influential line of research, advocated recently by Eric Brill and colleagues [16,17], suggests that instead of focusing on developing learning algorithms that make clever use of what data are available, we focus on using simpler algorithms, and obtaining a lot more data from which they can learn. This idea makes the most sense for tasks like the one explored by Banko and Brill [16], tasks for which "annotated data is essentially free" — they demonstrate that the quantity of data matters much more than the particular cleverness of the learning algorithm when disambiguating confusable word pairs such as *too* versus *to* versus *two*. (In some ways, their general point is related to Church and Mercer's [18] argument that it is better to simply collect very large quantities of corpus data than to devote effort to curating "balanced" corpora.)

For tasks such as word sense disambiguation, where the labels are not free, other novel strategies for avoiding expensive data annotation have proven useful. For example, Mihalcea and colleagues [19,20] have explored novel ways of obtaining annotated data by taking advantage of the Web. These include both the automatic identification of new training exemplars and the elicitation of human judgments via a Web interface.

In the remainder of this paper, I will discuss another approach to the annotated data acquisition bottleneck. It is not quite the same as doing without annotated data altogether, nor the same as restricting one's attention to shallow tasks where the data are completely free; but it is also not quite the same as performing annotation in the conventional, expensive, labor-intensive way. In

Bible translation, notes that translation of a New Testament can often take ten to twenty years, depending on level of participation, health of the translator (!), and other factors [http://www.wycliffe.org/wbt-usa/faq.htm]. On the other hand, Wycliffe alone has over 5100 career and short-term members, which is orders of magnitude greater than the number of people one would ever expect to find doing linguistic annotation. Readers interested in Bible translation and multilingual computing more generally should also be aware of the Summer Institute of Linguistics (SIL), which has a long history of working with lesser-known languages [http://www.sil.org].

Section 2, I discuss supervised versus unsupervised learning and highlight a central characteristic of the supervised paradigm. In Section 3, I argue that text in parallel translation offers this desirable property. Section 4 fleshes out the story by showing how this intuition can be applied in solving monolingual problems. Finally, Section 5 wraps up with some conclusions and discussion of work in progress.

2 Supervised Learning and Multiple Observables

I will begin the discussion with something obvious: for natural language processing tasks where both have been tried, supervised techniques generally work immensely better than unsupervised techniques. That is why there is such a demand for annotated data.

But why do supervised techniques work so much better? One answer is that by learning from annotated data, the search space over possible models is drastically reduced, in comparison to learning from unannotated data. Consider estimating the probabilities associated with a stochastic context-free grammar. Learning the parameters of the grammar — the probabilities associated with the rules — can be viewed as a search over the (very large) space of possible parameter combinations. In both the supervised case and the unsupervised case, the set of parameters is defined by the context-free structure.[3] But in the supervised case, the annotations can be viewed as providing an additional set of constraints: among sets of possible parameter values, a learning algorithm should be favoring the ones that are consistent with the observed structural annotations of the training sentences. The unsupervised learner (e.g., the Inside-Outside algorithm [21]), lacking those structural analyses, is free to find solutions that are consistent with the observed data but which are likely not to be consistent with the desired annotations. As Pereira and Schabes [22] put it, "although SCFGs provide a hierarchical model of the language, that structure is undetermined by raw text and only by chance will the inferred grammar agree with qualitative linguistic judgments of sentence structure."[4]

Another way of looking at this is in terms of what the learning algorithm gets to observe. For unsupervised algorithms, there is a set of data with representations that are observable to the algorithm, and the task is to characterize those

---

[3] As an aside, to repeat a point I still see too little emphasized in many discussions of statistical techniques, this is an illustration of why there is no such thing as a "purely statistical" model or method. Regardless of where the numeric parameters (the probabilities) come from, in any method, supervised or unsupervised, there is always an algebraic structure underlying the probability model; that's part of what it means for something to be a probabilistic model. Even n-gram models, which are about as "purely statistical" as one can get, embody a Markov assumption, which is equivalent to saying that their underlying algebraic structure is equivalent to a finite-state automaton.

[4] In their paper, Pereira and Schabes demonstrate that by adding *partial* structural annotation — constituent bracketing, but without the constituent labels — the search space can still be restricted significantly, even in the absence of full parse trees.

data within the bounds imposed by an underlying model. In supervised learning paradigms, however, one finds that there are always *two* observables: a representation of the input data, and the desired output representation. Probabilistic generative models for speech recognition illustrate this. The speech stream O provides one observable, and the transcribed sequence of word tokens W is the second observable. The learning problem is to *relate* those two observables, and typically this is done by estimating a model of their joint probability $\Pr(W, O)$, given samples of the two observables paired together. In practice, speech recognition systems model the relationship by decomposing the problem into a language model $\Pr(W)$ that knows about what sorts of sequences of words get uttered and a channel model $\Pr(O|W)$ that knows how word sequences get turned into sounds.

Standard supervised classification is another illustration. Commonly the data are represented as feature vectors x_i, and the learning algorithm gets to observe a sample of these paired with the classes y_i to which they belong. Imagine, for example, that x_i are collections of features that describe people, such as age, height, weight, sex, blood pressure, etc., and that y_i can be either *yes* or *no* depending on whether or not the person is considered high risk for a heart attack. Again, supervised learning can be seen as *relating* the two kinds of representations. Many methods do this by learning a separating function (e.g. a hyperplane in the feature space) that separates the x_i according to the classes to which they belong — a dividing line, so to speak, between members of the classes. Other methods, such as naive Bayes classification or maximum entropy, are better thought of as estimating the conditional probability distribution $\Pr(Y|X)$ or the joint distribution $\Pr(X, Y)$.

This characterization of supervised learning in terms of representations is really the same as the first answer, in that the "two observables" idea describes the way in which knowledge of the desired outcomes provides a second constraint on learning, over and above the pre-determined structure of the model (stochastic CFG, noisy channel model, separating hyperplane, etc.). However, thinking in terms of observables leads to the following interesting line of thought. Supervised algorithms work well because they take advantage of two observables. Linguistic annotations, on the other hand, are unobservable representations — the standard annotation process seeks to make them observable by brute force, writing them down. Instead of giving up and summing over all the possible observables (unsupervised learning), or finding ways to perform this expensive operation on a smaller set of data (active learning), might it be possible to turn the unobservable into something that *can* be observed?

I argue that text in parallel translation provides a unique opportunity to do just that.

3   Parallel Translations and Multiple Observables

Begin with a sentence e in a single language, say, English. In addition to the observable sentence itself, we as linguists believe that there is an unobservable representation m_e of the sentence's meaning. Just characterizing a representational framework in which to express m_e is an enormously difficult problem that keeps semanticists and philosophers very busy, and it seems fair to say that actually constructing instantiations of m_e reliably for real sentences is a long way off; indeed, it's one of those problems that annotation is supposed to help us solve (e.g. [6,7,23]). For practical purposes, m_e is a hidden meaning.

Now consider a sentence, f, that is a translation of e. It seems safe to assume that f, too, has a hidden meaning, m_f. Let us assume, moreover, that all languages are capable of expressing the same set of meanings and use the same representational framework.[5] Then, given that e and f are translations, they express the same meaning, and $m_e = m_f$.

This fact presents an interesting opportunity. Looking monolingually, we have two observable/unobservable pairs $\langle e, m_e \rangle$ and $\langle f, m_f \rangle$. But the fact that e and f are translations of each other means that this collection of information really gives us *two observables*. The fact that they share the hidden meaning $m_e = m_f$ makes this possible, but it also means that we don't need to care about the details of that meaning representation, which is a good thing for everyone except semanticists and philosophers.

The fact that there are two observables suggests that we may be able to get some of the same advantage from parallel translations, monolingually, that can be obtained in monolingual settings where we have a single language plus its annotations: the better learning associated with supervised systems. One language can be thought of as providing constraints on the search space for models of the other language.

This is an idea that has been explored before in a modeling setting: it is the essence of stochastic bilingual grammar formalisms. For example, Alshawi et al. [24] show that one can obtain dependency analyses for unannotated parallel text by modeling word-level alignments and syntactic dependencies together, and Wu [25] presents a bilingual grammar model that permits simultaneous learning and parsing. These approaches go part of the way toward exploiting bilingual text to perform monolingual annotation, but still suffer from a propensity to

---

[5] This assumption is potentially controversial, since there are certainly meanings that can be concisely expressed in one language that are difficult — some might even say impossible — to express in another. The concept of *Schadenfreude* is one commonly mentioned example. Another of my favorites is the American phrase *doggie bag*, which denotes an idea that can only really make sense if a meal in a restaurant is interpreted as transferring ownership of an entity rather than providing an experience. (I discovered this in France, where it appeared that the concept of bringing the dog to a restaurant meal was acceptable but the converse was not.) These objections are obviously a challenge, but at the same time, they tend to apply primarily to claims about *lexicalized concepts* in one language being translatable as lexicalized concepts in the other. Whether or not some nuances are truly untranslatable, I would argue that most of what we say to each other can be translated, if not efficiently. The concise phrase *doggie bag* can be expressed in another language as a longer noun phrase, e.g. *a package of left-over food that you bring home to eat later, or more likely put in the refrigerator and then throw away when it becomes moldy.*

allow solutions that are justified by the data but inconsistent with linguistic intuitions — for example, Alshawi's model is perfectly comfortable identifying *collect* rather than *call* as a direct dependent of the verb in the sentence *I want to make a collect call.*[6] If the goal to is to facilitate annotating a new language with linguistically intuitive representations we hope to be able to obtain automatically, still further constraints are needed.

The further constraints come from one more assumption that tends to be true in the real world: quite frequently the language of *e* can be English, for which the investment in annotation has already been made, and for which, therefore, we have high accuracy algorithms for automatic annotation. The way to take full advantage of parallel text to solve monolingual problems is by using it to gain maximal leverage from the resources that have already been built.[7]

4   Using Parallel Text to Solve Monolingual Problems

4.1   Parsing

Since parsing has been a focus thus far, I begin with a discussion of my lab's experiments in automatically obtaining syntactic annotations for new languages by taking advantage of parallel text [26].

We have argued that the following assumption appears at least implicitly in almost all stochastic models that attempt to characterize the relationship between syntactic representations in two languages:[8]

> **Direct Correspondence Assumption (DCA)**: Given a pair of sentences E and F that are (literal) translations of each other with syntactic structures $Tree_E$ and $Tree_F$, if nodes x_E and y_E of $Tree_E$ are aligned with nodes x_F and y_F of $Tree_F$, respectively, and if syntactic relationship $R(x_E, y_E)$ holds in $Tree_E$, then $R(x_F, y_F)$ holds in $Tree_F$.

As an example, consider this English-Basque sentence pair:

(1)   a. I got a gift for my brother

---

[6] Wu [25] shows that his algorithm can be modified to take advantage of monolingual parse trees to "[facilitate] a kind of transfer of grammatical expertise in one language toward bootstrapping grammar acquisition in another", which is precisely my goal in Section 4.1. However, I am not aware of results obtained using his algorithm. In addition, what I describe is a modular approach rather than an attempt to capture everything within a single probabilistic model; see discussion in Section 5.

[7] Naturally the approach can be used in any language pair where high quality annotation exists for one of the two languages. If the approach I describe here is successful, that set will grow quickly; the greater limitation then becomes the availability of parallel text in relevant language pairs.

[8] A very recent exception is work by Jason Eisner [27] on a synchronous stochastic grammar model that permits non-isomorphic mappings between dependency trees in two languages. His model has not yet, however, been fully implemented and tested.

Table 1. Correspondences preserved in an English-Basque sentence pair

R	x_{Eng}	y_{Eng}	x_{Bsq}	y_{Bsq}
verb-subj	got	I	erosi	nik
verb-obj	got	gift	erosi	opari
noun-det	gift	a	opari	bat
noun-mod	brother	my	anaiari	nire

   b. Nik (I) nire (MY) anaiari (BROTHER-DAT) opari (GIFT) bat (A) erosi (BUY) nion (PAST)

Table 1 shows the syntactic correspondences that are preserved under a valid word alignment between the two sentences. The correspondence is not perfect — in particular, the goal of the action is expressed as a prepositional phrase in English and via dative noun-phrase marking in Basque — but the degree of correspondence is striking, especially given that Basque and English are typologically quite distinct.

At the same time, the Direct Correspondence Assumption is just that, an assumption, and although this example is encouraging (and other encouraging examples are easy to find), it is too strong to rely upon. The distinction between a preposition and dative-marking to mark the goal phrase is but one of many examples that prove problematic. Another widespread category is the lexical expression of items in a second language that are implicit in English, such as the aspectual markers in Chinese. Since these do not appear in English there is nothing to which they can directly correspond.

One approach to this problem is to attempt to explicitly model the divergences between English and the second language [28,29] (see also the syntactic noisy channel model proposed by Yamada and Knight [30]). Another, which I sketch here, is to accept that the correspondence may not be exactly correct, but still use the English analysis as the starting point for the second language analysis, correcting the results on the second language side. (See [26] for details.)

The algorithm for projection of syntactic dependency annotations operationalizes the DCA as directly as possible: if there is a syntactic relationship between two English words, it attempts to ensure that the same syntactic relationship also exists between their corresponding words in the second language.

Algorithm. Given word-aligned sentence pair (E, F), together with a dependency analysis of E, introduce dependencies for F according to the following cases of word-level alignment.

– **One-to-one.** If $h_E \in E$ is aligned with a unique $h_F \in F$ and m_E is aligned with a unique $m_F \in F$, then if $R(h_E, m_E)$, conclude $R(h_F, m_F)$.

– **Unaligned (E).** If $w_E \in E$ is not aligned with any word in F, then create a new empty word $n_F \in F$ such that for any x_E aligned with a unique x_F, $R(x_E, w_E) \Rightarrow R(x_F, n_F)$ and $R(w_E, x_E) \Rightarrow R(n_F, x_F)$.

Table 2. Quality of projected dependency analyses for Chinese, using clean English parses and correct alignments (%)

Method	Precision	Recall	F-measure
Direct	34.5	42.5	38.1
Head-initial	59.4	59.4	59.4
Other rules	68.0	66.6	67.3

- **One-to-many.** If $w_E \in E$ is aligned with $w_{1_F}, \ldots, w_{n_F}$, then create a new empty word $m_F \in F$ such that m_F is the parent of $w_{1_F}, \ldots, w_{n_F}$ and set w_E to align to m_F instead.
- **Many-to-one.** If $w_{1_E}, \ldots, w_{n_E} \in E$ are all uniquely aligned to $w_F \in F$, then delete all alignments between $w_{i_E} (1 \leq i \leq n)$ and w_F except for the head of $w_{1_E}, \ldots, w_{n_E}$.
- **Many-to-many.** First perform the one-to-many step, then many-to-one.
- **Unaligned (F).** Unaligned words in the second language are left out of the projected tree.

In a set of in-principle experiments on English paired with Chinese, using manually corrected parses and manually created word-level alignments, we found that direct projection of English dependencies led to poor accuracy of Chinese analyses, as measured using the precision and recall of unlabeled syntactic dependencies for a test set. However, analysis of the errors made it clear that a great many of the problems could be solved with automatic post-projection tranformations of the Chinese trees — moreover, we found that these transformations could be formulated in principled ways, taking advantage of general linguistic properties of the language, and using only a very small amount of lexically-specific information such as the identification of words in a small number of closed class categories. For example, promoting the initial word in a multi-word constituent to be the head, making the remaining words its dependents, had a dramatic effect on accuracy, understandably, because Chinese is for the most part a head-initial language. Other refinements included modifying the head-promotion rule to pay attention to parts of speech (like English, the Chinese nominal system is head-final) and additional operations such as attaching an aspectual marker to the preceding verb. Within two or three person-days of language-specific effort, the quality of the projected trees, based on ideal parses and alignments, had improved dramatically, as illustrated in Table 2.

These results demonstrated that, in principle, reasonably high quality trees for Chinese could be obtained via projection of English analyses followed by post-projection transformations. (Recall that automatic statistical parsers trained on the Penn Chinese Treebank, after two years of manually intensive treebank construction, typically obtained an F-measure of only 75-80%.) We hoped that by trading off somewhat reduced quality for quantity — creating a treebank via projection with an order of magnitude more Chinese sentences — it would be

Table 3. Quality of parser performance for Spanish, training on a treebank that was obtained *fully automatically* via projection of annotations from English followed by a small set of post-projection transformations (%)

Method	Training corpus	Sentence pairs	Parser accuracy
Baseline	-		34
Statistical parser	UN/FBIS/Bible	98,000	67
Statistical parser	UN/FBIS/Bible (filtered)	20,000	72
Commercial parser	-	-	69

possible to make up for the fact that, even with ideal English parses and idea word alignments, the projected trees are fairly noisy.

However, it turned out that English-Chinese projection did not work as well using automatically obtained parses and word alignments. On further analysis, varying the quality of both the parser and the word alignments, it became apparent that the barrier to high quality automatic projection is not the automatic parsing on the English side, but rather the quality that could be obtained in automatic word alignment between English and Chinese.

In order to confirm that this was indeed the case, we followed up our English-Chinese experiment with an experiment in automatic projected treebanking using English-Spanish as a language pair, since English and Spanish are much easier to automatically align. We followed precisely the same paradigm, including a several person-day effort to develop Spanish-specific post-projection transformations. Table 3 shows the results.

The table provides a comparison against a simple baseline in which every word is considered a dependent of the previous word. It also shows the benefit of automatically filtering the projected trees in order to remove cases that are likely to hurt rather than help in parser training. Filtering criteria included, for example, English-Spanish alignments in which too many words were unaligned, alignments in which there was an n-to-1 alignment for too large an n, and cases where the projected tree contains too many crossing dependencies. (All thresholds, etc., were manually tuned on development data prior to test, of course.) The key result here is the performance of the statistical parser in comparison to a state-of-the-art, rule-based commercial parser for Spanish. Without manual annotation of any Spanish training data, and with only a few days of linguistically informed effort (compared to months or years of grammar writing), this approach yields a Spanish parser with state of the art performance.

4.2 Word Sense Disambiguation

As is the case for parsing, there is a dramatic difference in the performance of supervised versus unsupervised learners in word sense disambiguation (WSD). Unlike parsing, the state of the art even for supervised annotation of word senses is not high enough to inspire confidence that the sense tags should be projected to a second language. The question arises, therefore, as to whether the information present in parallel texts can be used to help improve *English* word sense tagging — and secondarily, perhaps, to bootstrap WSD in the second language, as well. Mona Diab explored this question in her doctoral dissertation [44]; here I sketch the approach and results reported by Diab and Resnik [31].

It has long been observed that translation into distinct foreign language words often makes a sense distinction evident [32,33,34,35,36,37,38,39]. The oft-cited financial and riverbank senses of *bank*, for example, are realized in French as *banque* and *rive*, showing how the two meanings, hidden behind the same word, can be made observable by noting a lexical correspondence with another language. If the word *bank* occurs in an English sentence, and it corresponds to *banque* in the French translation, then clearly the financial sense is intended.

In considering how parallel translation might provide a useful set of constraints for learning to disambigate word senses, it is interesting to observe that the converse also holds: when two distinct English words can be translated as the *same* word in a second language, it often indicates that the two are being used in senses that share some element of meaning. For example, *bank* may be ambiguous, as just noted, and so might the word *shore* (it can refer both to a shoreline and to a piece of wood used as a brace or support). But both *bank* and *shore* can be translated into French as *rive*, and this fact suggests that the two senses corresponding to that translation have something in common — some semantic quality we might call *rive*-ness, so to speak.

To the extent that it is reliable, this additional information available from the second language translation can be exploited in order to narrow in on English word senses, even in the absence of sense-tagged English training data. Algorithmically, the process requires treating a second-language word like *rive* as an anchor point that delineates a set of putatively-related English words. For example, analysis of a word-aligned parallel corpus might produce the information that French *rive* shows up with the set of English words *bank*, *shore*, and *shoreline*.

This information can be used to establish preferences among senses in an English sense inventory, so long as that sense inventory provides some way to measure the similarity of (or distance between) word senses. Intuitively, in those cases where *bank* is translated as *rive*, one can assume as a working hypothesis that it is being used in the sense that is most similar to the senses of *shore* and *shoreline* when *they* can be translated as *rive*. Operationally, it is straightforward to design an algorithm that takes a set of related words such as {*bank*, *shore*, *shoreline*}, and reinforces the words' different senses differentially depending on their similarity to the senses of other words in the set [40].

One of the problems with using this idea for sense disambiguation is evaluation: there are many parallel corpora, and there are a number of relatively standard WSD test sets, but it is virtually impossible to find a test set that exists in parallel translation with a second language, in order to evaluate the extent to which the second language could help in disambiguation. Rather than manually sense-annotating a parallel corpus, which would have been quite expensive, we instead opted to use a carefully sense-tagged test set for English and to use machine translation to produce a pseudo-parallel corpus.

Across a range of conditions (varying the languages, the machine translation system used to provide pseudo-parallel text, and experimenting with combining information across languages), the approach performed consistently well on the SENSEVAL-2 test data, achieving precision in the vicinity of 60% and with recall around 54% for disambiguation of nouns in the "All Words" task. (See Diab [44] for details and additional performance improvements, as well as for experiments using human-translated data and other extensions.) This compares quite favorably with the performance of the other unsupervised SENSEVAL-2 systems, and in fact it places this approach on par with a number of the supervised systems.

Interestingly, these results were obtained not only without any manually sense tagged training data, but also without taking advantage of any monolingual context whatsoever. There is, therefore, good reason to believe that further improvements can be obtained by combining the cross-language approach with the better unsupervised methods for sense classification.

5 Conclusions

Supervised techniques have revolutionized natural language processing; as a result, data annotation is its greatest bottleneck. In this paper I have suggested a strategy that complements other approaches to reducing the annotation burden: using the constraints provided by parallel translation to create noisy annotations of large quantities of text, rather than focusing on high quality annotation for smaller data sets. Because the constraints implicit in parallel translation are still not a guarantee that the resulting annotations will look like what is needed, the strategy gains leverage from the existence of high quality broad-coverage annotation tools for English.

The research described here is intimately connected with the work of David Yarowsky and students [41,42,43]. Their ground-breaking work on the projection of shallower representations across parallel text in order to bootstrap language analyzers (including part of speech taggers, morphological analyzers, noun phrase bracketers, and named entity taggers) is complemented by the work I have described here, which focuses on linguistically deeper representations such as syntactic dependencies and word senses. These are two facets of a joint research project focused both on improving statistical machine translation with richer linguistic features and on rapidly bootstrapping monolingual analyzers for new languages. We refer to the process of creating analyzers via projection of representations from English as the annotation-projection-training approach, or just as "annotation projection."

I have already briefly discussed several similarly motivated lines of work that attempt to account for both rich monolingual representations and cross-language relationships in a single model, e.g. Alshawi et al. [24], Eisner [27], and Wu [25]. Such approaches certainly are capable of taking advantage of constraints from high quality English annotations in their modeling. I have tended to avoid this style of modeling in favor of actually projecting explicit representations, however, for a number of reasons. One is that the barriers to entry are much lower when it is possible to work with modular software components; one need not implement an end-to-end probabilistic framework from scratch, with all that entails, particularly the complexities of parameter estimation and search. As a closely related issue, adopting a modular architecture rather than a unified model makes it easy to swap in and out components such as English analyzers, word alignment methods, and supervised learning algorithms.[9] Finally, and most important, I am a great believer in taking advantage of independently motivated development activity, in this case the rapid progress being made in supervised learning methods for natural language processing.

I am currently pursuing several continuations of the current research. In parsing, I am exploring the possibility that post-projection linguistic transformations can be made unnecessary. The key observation is that, given a small treebank in a language of interest, it is possible to train a parser that captures some of the most important language-specific phenomena (e.g. aspectual marker attachment in Chinese), even if its training data are too sparse for it to take advantage of, for example, lexical conditioning of syntactic rules. At the same time, the annotation projection approach can produce large numbers of trees that capture a great deal of valid knowledge carried over from English, but which leave a parser ignorant of language-specific constraints. Students and I are exploring an iterative approach to expanding the small, high quality monolingual treebank using parallel text. Given a large parallel corpus of sentence pairs $\langle e, f \rangle$, the idea at iteration i is to parse a new sentence f with the currently trained small-treebank-parser π_i, producing n-best "monolingually informed" trees, $\{T_\pi^1, T_\pi^2, \ldots, T_\pi^n\}$. Simultaneously, we project syntactic annotations from e to produce m-best "English-informed" projected trees for f, $\{T_E^1, T_E^2, \ldots, T_E^m\}$. By combining knowledge from the English-informed and monolingually-informed tree sets for f, it should be possible to select the "best" of the automatically obtained T_π trees for addition to the training set at iteration $i+1$, as judged not only on its monolingual confidence score (a variant of self-training), but also on the extent to which the relationships it encodes are consistent with the English analysis. It should also be possible to create a "consensus" analysis that combines the most confidently assigned dependencies from the T_π and T_E analyses. For example, in the English-Chinese case, the T_E trees may be able to confidently identify the verb-subject and verb-object relations, and the T_π trees may be able to provide confident attachment points for aspectual markers.

In word sense disambiguation, I am exploring a similar combination of unsupervised and supervised methods in order to identify larger numbers of training samples. In this case, a large parallel sample will be used as the basis for bilingual unsupervised sense tagging (in the style of Diab [31,44]). A small portion of

---

[9] Recent developments by Jason Eisner may affect these considerations; his Dyna programming language is designed to facilitate exploration of alternative models by automating many of the implementation details. See
http://www.cs.jhu.edu/~jason/dyna/.

held-out annotated data will be used to develop a classifier for confidence estimation, in order to identify automatically sense tagged items above a confidence threshold. These high-confidence items will be added to the training sample, and the process will continue iteratively.

Ultimately, the goals of this work are three-fold. First, as has been emphasized in this paper, it is to be hoped that by gaining leverage from parallel translation, it will be possible to develop linguistically deeper monolingual analyzers for a wider range of the world's languages. Second, there is, of course, a close connection between this work and the development of more sophisticated statistical models for machine translation — it is widely agreed among statistical MT researchers that many of the shortcomings of current technology have their source in a less than adequate treatment of syntactic behavior, which is leading to increased exploration of a syntactically more sophisticated set of statistical models. And finally, there is a goal that is connected with these technological goals only indirectly: it is to be hoped that by exploring the way different languages express the same hidden meaning, facilitated by the tools and models of statistical NLP, we may come closer to understanding the nature of language itself.

Acknowledgments. Work described in this paper was done in collaboration with Mona Diab, Rebecca Hwa, Okan Kolak, and Amy Weinberg; please see works cited for details. The author gratefully acknowledges the support of Department of Defense contract RD-02-5700, DARPA/ITO Cooperative Agreement N660010028910, and ONR MURI Contract FCPO.810548265. This paper was written while the author was on sabbatical at Johns Hopkins University; discussion of this research with colleagues and students there was much appreciated. Any errors are solely the responsibility of the author or the author's dog.

References

1. Woods, W.A., Kaplan, R.: The lunar sciences natural language information system. Technical Report 2265, Bolt, Beranek, and Newman, Cambridge, MA (1971)
2. Klavans, J., Resnik, P., eds.: The Balancing Act: Combining Symbolic and Statistical Approaches to Language. MIT Press (1996) http://mitpress.mit.edu/book-home.tcl?isbn=0262611228.
3. Collins, M.: Three generative, lexicalised models for statistical parsing. In: Proceedings of the 35th Annual Meeting of the ACL, Madrid (1997)
4. Collins, M.: Head-driven statistical models for natural language parsing. Computational Linguistics (to appear)
5. Marcus, M.P., Santorini, B., Marcinkiewicz, M.: Building a large annotated corpus of English: the Penn Treebank. Computational Linguistics **19** (1993) 313–330
6. Gildea, D., Jurafsky, D.: Automatic labeling of semantic roles. Computational Linguistics **28** (2002) 245–288
7. Fillmore, C.J., Johnson, C.R., Petruck, M.R.: Background to FrameNet. International Journal of Lexicography **16** (2003) 235–250
8. Sapir, E.: Language: An Introduction to the Study of Speech. New York: Harcourt, Brace (1921) www.bartleby.com/186/.

9. Stigler, S.M.: The History of Statistics. Harvard University Press (1986)
10. Oard, D.W., Doermann, D., Dorr, B., He, D., Resnik, P., Weinberg, A., Byrne, W., Khudanpur, S., Yarowsky, D., Leuski, A., Koehn, P., Knight, K.: Desperately seeking Cebuano. In: Proceedings of the HLT-NAACL Conference. (2003) 76–78 Late Breaking Results.
11. Resnik, P., Olsen, M.B., Diab, M.: The Bible as a parallel corpus: Annotating the 'Book of 2000 Tongues'. Computers and the Humanities **33** (1999) 129–153
12. Tong, S.: Active Learning: Theory and Applications. PhD thesis, Stanford University (2001) http://www.robotics.stanford.edu/~stong/papers/tong_thesis.ps.gz.
13. Blum, A., Mitchell, T.: Combining labeled and unlabeled data with co-training. In: COLT: Proceedings of the Workshop on Computational Learning Theory, Morgan Kaufmann Publishers. (1998)
14. Sarkar, A.: Applying cotraining methods to statistical parsing. In: Proceedings of the Second North American Conference on Computational Linguistics (NAACL 2001). (2001)
15. Yarowsky, D.: Unsupervised word sense disambiguation rivaling supervised methods. In: Proceedings of the 33rd Annual Meeting of the Association for Computational Linguistics, Cambridge, MA, Association for Computational Linguistics (1995) 189–196
16. Banko, M., Brill, E.: Mitigating the paucity-of-data problem: Exploring the effect of training corpus size on classifier performance for natural language processing. In: Human Language Technology Conference (HLT). (2001)
17. Brill, E., Lin, J., Banko, M., Dumais, S., Ng, A.: Data-intensive question answering. In: Proceedings of TREC 2001. (2001)
18. Church, K.W., Mercer, R.: Introduction to the special issue on computational linguistics using large corpora. Computational Linguistics **19** (1993) 1–24
19. Chklovski, T., Mihalcea, R.: Building a sense tagged corpus with open mind word expert. In: Proceedings of the ACL 2002 Workshop on 'Word Sense Disambiguation: Recent Successes and Future Directions'. (2002)
20. Mihalcea, R.: Bootstrapping large sense tagged corpora. In: Proceedings of the 3rd International Conference on Languages Resources and Evaluations (LREC 2002). (2002)
21. Baker, J.: Trainable grammars for speech recognition. In: Proceedings of the Spring Conference of the Acoustical Society of America, Boston, MA (1979) 547–550
22. Pereira, F., Schabes, Y.: Inside-outside reestimation from partially bracketed corpora. Proceedings of the February 1992 DARPA Speech and Natural Language Workshop (1992) 122–127
23. Kingsbury, P., Palmer, M., Marcus, M.: Adding semantic annotation to the Penn TreeBank. In: Proceedings of the Human Language Technology Conference (HLT'02). (2002)
24. Alshawi, H., Srinivas, B., Douglas, S.: Learning dependency translation models as collections of finite state head transducers. Computational Linguistics **26** (2000)
25. Wu, D.: Stochastic inversion transduction grammars and bilingual parsing of parallel corpora. Computational Linguistics (**23**) 377–403
26. Hwa, R., Resnik, P., Weinberg, A., Kolak, O.: Evaluating translational correspondence using annotation projection. In: 40th Anniversary Meeting of the Association for Computational Linguistics (ACL-02), Philadelphia (2002)
27. Eisner, J.: Learning non-isomorphic tree mappings for machine translation. In: Proceedings of the 41st Meeting of the Association for Computational Linguistics (companion volume). (2003)

28. Dorr, B.J., Pearl, L., Hwa, R., Habash, N.: DUSTer: A method for unraveling cross-language divergences for statistical word-level alignment. In: AMTA. (2002) 31–43
29. Drabek, E., Yarowsky, D.: personal communication.
30. Yamada, K., Knight, K.: A syntax-based statistical translation model. (In: Proceedings of the 39th Meeting of the Association for Computational Linguistics (ACL 2001)) 523–530
31. Diab, M., Resnik, P.: An unsupervised method for word sense tagging using parallel corpora. In: 40th Anniversary Meeting of the Association for Computational Linguistics (ACL-02), Philadelphia (2002)
32. Brown, P.F., Della Pietra, S.A., Della Pietra, V.J., Mercer, R.L.: A statistical approach to sense disambiguation in machine translation. In: Proc. of the Speech and Natural Language Workshop, Pacific Grove, CA (1991) 146–151
33. Dagan, I.: Lexical disambiguation: sources of information and their statistical realization. In: Proceedings of the 29th Annual Meeting of the Association for Computational Linguistics. (1991) Berkeley, California.
34. Dagan, I., Itai, A.: Word sense disambiguation using a second language monolingual corpus (1994)
35. Dyvik, H.: Translations as semantic mirrors. In: Proceedings of Workshop W13: Multilinguality in the lexicon II, Brighton, UK, The 13th biennial European Conference on Artificial Intelligence ECAI 98 (1998) 24–44
36. Ide, N.: Cross-lingual sense determination: Can it work? Computers and the Humanities: Special issue on SENSEVAL 34 (2000) 223–234
37. Ide, N., Erjavec, T., Tufis, D.: Automatic sense tagging using parallel corpora. In: Proceedings of the Sixth Natural Language Processing Pacific Rim Symposium. (2001) 83–89
38. Ide, N., Erjavec, T., Tufis, D.: Sense discrimination with parallel corpora. In: Proceedings of ACL'02 Workshop on Word Sense Disambiguation: Recent Successes and Future Directions. (2002) 54–60
39. Resnik, P., Yarowsky, D.: Distinguishing systems and distinguishing senses: New evaluation methods for word sense disambiguation. Natural Language Engineering 5 (1999) 113–133
40. Resnik, P.: Semantic similarity in a taxonomy: An information-based measure and its application to problems of ambiguity in natural language. Journal of Artificial Intelligence Research (JAIR) 11 (1999) 95–130
41. Yarowsky, D., Ngai, G.: Inducing multilingual pos taggers and np bracketers via robust projection across aligned corpora. In: Proceedings of NAACL-2001. (2001) 200–207
42. Yarowsky, D., Wicentowski, R.: Minimally supervised morphological analysis by multimodal alignment. In: Proceedings of ACL-2000. (2000) 207–216
43. Yarowsky, D., Ngai, G., Wicentowski, R.: Inducing multilingual text analysis tools via robust projection across aligned corpora. (In: Proceedings of the First International Conference on Human Language Technology Research (HLT 2001),)
44. Diab, M.: Word Sense Disambiguation within a Multilingual Framework. PhD thesis, University of Maryland (2003)

Acquisition of Word Translations Using Local Focus-Based Learning in Ainu-Japanese Parallel Corpora

Hiroshi Echizen-ya[1], Kenji Araki[2], Yoshio Momouchi[3], and Koji Tochinai[4]

[1] Dept. of Electronics and Information, Hokkai-Gakuen University, S26-Jo,
W11-Chome, Chuo-ku Sapporo, 064-0926 Japan
echi@eli.hokkai-s-u.ac.jp,
TEL: +81-11-841-1161(ext.7863), FAX: +81-11-551-2951
[2] Division of Electronics and Information, Hokkaido University, N13-Jo, W8-Chome,
Kita-ku Sapporo, 060-8628 Japan
araki@media.eng.hokudai.ac.jp,
TEL: +81-11-706-6534, FAX: +81-11-706-6534
[3] Dept. of Electronics and Information, Hokkai-Gakuen University, S26-Jo,
W11-Chome, Chuo-ku Sapporo, 064-0926 Japan
momouchi@eli.hokkai-s-u.ac.jp,
TEL: +81-11-841-1161(ext.7864), FAX: +81-11-551-2951
[4] Division of Business Administration, Hokkai-Gakuen University, 4-Chome,
Asahi-machi, Toyohira-ku Sapporo, 060-8790 Japan
tochinai@econ.hokkai-s-u.ac.jp,
TEL: +81-11-841-1161(ext.2753), FAX: +81-11-824-7729

Abstract. This paper describes a new learning method for acquisition of word translations from small parallel corpora. Our proposed method, **Local Focus-based Learning (LFL)**, efficiently acquires word translations and collocation templates by focusing on parts of sentences, not on entire sentences. Collocation templates have collocation information to acquire word translations from each sentence pair. This method is useful even when frequency of appearances of word translations is very low in sentence pairs. The LFL system described in this paper extracts Ainu-Japanese word translations from small Ainu-Japanese parallel corpora. The Ainu language is spoken by the Ainu ethnic group residing in northern Japan and Sakhalin. An evaluation experiment indicated that the recall was 57.4% and the precision was 72.0% to 546 kinds of nouns and verbs in 287 Ainu-Japanese sentence pairs even though the average frequency of appearances of the 546 kinds of nouns and verbs was 1.98.

1 Introduction

In recent years, many studies have addressed methods for building bilingual dictionaries from bilingual corpora [1,2,3,4]. Using bilingual corpora, such methods can obtain natural equivalents. However, these methods require large parallel corpora to acquire many word translations that are corresponding words of source

A. Gelbukh (Ed.): CICLing 2004, LNCS 2945, pp. 300–304, 2004.
© Springer-Verlag Berlin Heidelberg 2004

language words and target language words because they cannot acquire many word translations when the frequency of appearances of word translations is low. In an earlier study, we proposed a learning method that acquires bilingual knowledge to solve such problems [5]. A system described in our past work acquires bilingual knowledge using no large parallel corpus. However, the sentences in parallel corpora are very simple. Moreover, many similar sentence pairs are needed in the system based on translation patterns [6]. This fact renders that system inefficient. Sentence pairs are pairs of source language sentences and target language sentences.

This paper proposes a new learning method for acquisition of word translations from small parallel corpora containing many long sentences. We call this method Local Focus-based Learning (LFL). This LFL system efficiently acquires word translations and collocation templates by focusing on parts of sentences, not on the entire sentences. Collocation templates have collocation information to acquire word translations from each sentence pair. This method is useful even when frequency of appearances of word translations is very low in sentence pairs. We used Ainu-Japanese parallel corpora to confirm the effectiveness of our method. In that case, it is difficult to obtain large Ainu-Japanese parallel corpora. However, it is important to acquire word translations from Ainu-Japanese parallel corpora because we can get natural equivalents. Our method is effective to acquire word translations from such small parallel corpora. Ainu language is spoken by the Ainu ethnic group residing in northern Japan and Sakhalin. Although typologically similar in some respects to Japanese, Ainu is a language isolate: it has no known relation to other languages. Evaluation experiment results show that this LFL system acquired many Ainu-Japanese word translations without using large parallel corpora. In 287 Ainu-Japanese sentence pairs, there were 546 kinds of nouns and verbs. We obtained a recall rate of 57.4% with precision of 72.0% even though the average frequency of appearance of the 546 kinds of nouns and verbs is 1.98. From these results, we confirmed that LFL is very effective to acquire word translations.

2   Acquisition of Word Translations Using LFL

This LFL system acquires Ainu-Japanese noun and verb word translations from a few Ainu-Japanese sentence pairs. In Japanese sentences of sentence pairs, part-of-speech information serves as static linguistic knowledge because this LFL system obtains the basic vocabulary item for verbs and each morpheme in Japanese. In addition, a heuristic for position information, based on the similarity of collocation between Ainu and Japanese, is used to prevent the acquisition of erroneous Ainu-Japanese word translations. Japanese is an agglutinative language. Ainu is expressed as a non-agglutinative language even though no formal orthography exists for writing Ainu. Latin-based scripts devised by linguists, as well as the Japanese katakana syllabary, are used variously.

Our LFL is a very simple method. Figure 1 shows an example of acquisition of word translations using LFL. This LFL system focuses on sentence parts by

Process 1: Focusing of sentence parts using two sentence pairs

Sentence pair No.1

(ku= kor totto poro su <u>ani</u> **sayo** <u>kar</u>. ;母/が/大鍋/<u>で</u>/**お/粥**/<u>を</u>/作り/ます。

[*haha ga onabe <u>de</u> **okayu** <u>o tsukuri</u> masu.*])

English: My mother would make a big pot of porridge.

Sentence pair No.2

(k= onaha anakne sipe kap <u>ani</u> **ker** <u>kar</u>.

;父/は/サケ/の/皮/<u>で</u>/**靴**/<u>を</u>/作り/ました。

[*chichi wa sake no kawa <u>de</u> **kutsu** <u>o tsukuri</u> mashi ta.*])

English: My father used to make boots out of salmon skin.

Collocation templates

(@ kar; @/を/作り

[@ o tsukuri])

(ani @ ;で/@ [de @])

Noun word translations (sayo;お/粥 [*okayu*]) English: porridge, (ker;靴 [*kutsu*]) English: boots

Process 2: Focusing of sentence parts using acquired collocation template

Acquired collocation template   (<u>ani</u> @ ;<u>で</u>/@ [*de @*])

Sentence pair No.3

(ku= tekehe piro hi ta ku= kor totto noya ham uk wa tekkotoro <u>ani</u> **nuyanuya**.

;私/が/手/に/けが/を/し/た/時/は/、/母/は/ヨモギ/の/葉/を/採っ/て/手のひら/<u>で</u>/**揉み**/ました。

[*watashi ga te ni kega o shi ta toki wa , haha wa yomogi no ha o totte tenohira <u>de</u> **momi** mashi ta.*])

English: Whenever I hurt my hand, my mother would pick some mugwort and rub it between the palms of her hands.

Verb word translation   (nuyanuya;揉む [*momu*]) English: rub

Fig. 1. Acquisition of word translations using LFL

two processes. The first process focuses on sentence parts using two sentence pairs, as shown in process 1 of Fig. 1. In process 1, this LFL system acquires word translations and collocation templates. Collocation templates express collocation information to acquire word translations efficiently from various sentence pairs. This LFL system acquires new word translations through the use of these collocation templates. Details of this process are the following:

(1) This LFL system selects two sentence pairs that have two common parts. In process 1, "ani", "kar" and "で [*de*][1]", "を/作り[2] [*o tsukuri*]" are common parts in sentence pair Nos. 1 and 2.

(2) This LFL system extracts parts between two common parts from Ainu sentences and Japanese sentences; it then obtains word translations by combining them. In process 1, "sayo" and "ker" are extracted from Ainu sentences, and "お/粥 [*okayu*]" and "靴 [*kutsu*]" are extracted from Japanese sentences. As a result, (sayo; お/粥 [*okayu*]) and (ker; 靴 [*kutsu*]) are obtained as noun word translations. The "sayo" and "お/粥 [*okayu*]" mean "porridge" in English, whereas "ker" and "靴 [*kutsu*]" mean "boots" in English.

(3) This LFL system replaces extracted parts with variables "@", and acquires collocation templates by separating variables "@" and their adjoining common parts from sentence pairs. In process 1, (@ kar;@/を [*@ o*]) and (ani @; で/@ [*@ de*]) are acquired as collocation templates.

---

[1] Italics express pronunciation in Japanese

[2] "/" in Japanese sentences are inserted after each morpheme.

The second process focuses on sentence parts using acquired collocation templates, as shown in process 2 of Fig. 1. Details of this process are the following:

(1) This LFL system selects collocation templates in which Ainu parts, aside from variables, have identical character strings to those parts in Ainu sentences, and in which Japanese parts, aside from variables, have the same character strings as parts in the Japanese sentences. In process 2, (ani @; で/@ [@ de]) is selected because "ani" and "で [de]" have the same character strings as parts in sentence pair No. 3.

(2) This LFL system extracts words that correspond to variables from Ainu sentences and Japanese sentences. In that case, this LFL system extracts one word from Ainu sentences, and extracts one noun word, one verb word, or one noun phrase, one verb phrase from Japanese sentences. This LFL system obtains word translation by combining them. In process 2, "nuyanuya" and "揉む [momu]" are extracted from sentence pair No. 3. Consequently, (nuyanuya; 揉む [momu]) is obtained as verb word translation. The "nuyanuya" and "揉む [momu]" mean "rub" in English.

This LFL system can acquire various word translations by these processes. In process 1, $n{:}m$ lexical translations are also acquired, and $1{:}n$ lexical translations are acquired in process 2.

3 Experiments and Discussion

Evaluation experiment used 287 Ainu and Japanese sentence pairs as experimental data. These sentence pairs were taken from two books [7,8]. The average number of words in Ainu sentences of all sentence pairs was 11.8. Among these 287 sentence pairs, 546 kinds of nouns and verbs existed. Their average frequency of appearance was 1.98. All sentence pairs were processed by the method described Section 2. In that case, the dictionary was initially empty.

Evaluation experiment showed a 57.4% recall rate with 72.0% precision. The recall rate indicates the rate of acquired correct word translations among the 546 kinds of nouns and verbs. The precision is the rate of acquired correct word translations among the acquired word translations to the 546 kinds of nouns and verbs. In the 546 kinds of nouns and verbs, there were 356 (65.2%) kinds of nouns and verbs for which the frequency of appearance was only. This means that this LFL system can acquire noun and verb word translations which the frequency of appearances is very low.

References

1. Smadja, F., K. R. McKeown and V. Hatzivassiloglou. 1996. Translating Collocations for Bilingual Lexicons: A Statistical Approach. *Computational Linguistics*, vol.22, no.1, pp. 1–38.
2. Haruno, M., S. Ikehara and T. Yamazaki. 1996. Learning Bilingual Collocations by Word-Level Sorting. In *Proceedings of Coling '96*.

3. Melamed, I.D. 1997. A Word-to-Word Model of Translation Equivalence. In *Proceedings of ACL '97*.

4. Sato, K. and H. Saito 2002. Extracting Word Sequence Correspondences with Support Vector Machines. In *Proceedings of Coling '02*.

5. Echizen-ya, H., K. Araki, Y. Momouchi, and K. Tochinai. 2002. Study of Practical Effectiveness for Machine Translation Using Recursive Chain-link-type Learning. In *Proceedings of Coling '02*.

6. McTait, K. 2001. Linguistic Knowledge and Complexity in an EBMT System Based on Translation Patterns. In *Proceedings Workshop on EBMT, MT Summit VIII*.

7. Nakamoto, M. and T. Katayama. 1999. The wisdom of the Ainu: UPASKUMA 1. Shin Nippon Kyouiku Tosho.

8. Nakamoto, M. and T. Katayama. 2001. The wisdom of the Ainu: UPASKUMA 2. Shin Nippon Kyouiku Tosho.

Sentence Alignment for Spanish-Basque Bitexts: Word Correspondences vs. Markup Similarity

Arantza Casillas[1], Idoia Fernández[1], and Raquel Martínez[2]

[1] Dpt. de Electricidad y Electrónica, Facultad de C. y Tecnología
Universidad del País Vasco
arantza@we.lc.ehu.es webfeani@lc.ehu.es
[2] Escuela Superior de CC. Experimentales y Tecnología
Universidad Rey Juan Carlos
r.martinez@escet.urjc.es

Abstract. In this paper, we present an evaluation of two different sentence alignment techniques. One is the well-known SIMR algorithm based on word correspondences on both sides of a bitext. The other one is the ALINOR algorithm, which is based on the similarity of the markup on both sides of a bitext. Both algorithms are accurate in 1-1 alignment, but ALINOR works slightly better in the case of N-M alignment.

1 Introduction

Corpora containing bilingual versions of the same text entity (bitext) are a very useful source of data. The bitext increases its value by obtaining aligned pairs of source and target language sentences. These aligned sentences are immensely valuable for different Natural Language Processing applications, such as example and memory based machine translation, multilingual information retrieval, and bilingual terminology extraction.

On the one hand, manual alignment is a very expensive process. On the other hand, automatic alignment can be obtained given limited time and resources. Several automatic techniques have been presented in the relevant literature: length-based statistical approach, pattern recognition, lexical approach, and combinations of the foregoing are the main ones. The ideal sentence alignment algorithm should be accurate and independent of the language pair.

In this work, we compare our sentence alignment algorithm ALINOR (presented in [Martinez 1998a] and [Martinez 1998b]) with the well-known Smooth Injective Map Recognizer (SIMR) algorithm of I. Dan Melamed ([Melamed 1996], [Melamed 1997]). ALINOR is based on evaluating the similarity of the linguistic and extra-linguistic markup on both sides of a bitext. It is quite language independent and obtains good accuracy rates without extra bilingual knowledge. SIMR generates word correspondences relying on cognates and, in addition, it can use a translation lexicon. If sentence boundary information is provided to the algorithm, the output corresponds to sentence alignment.

In this paper, we present the results of the evaluation of the two algorithms running on a Spanish-Basque parallel corpus. Section 2 briefly describes the

A. Gelbukh (Ed.): CICLing 2004, LNCS 2945, pp. 305–308, 2004.
© Springer-Verlag Berlin Heidelberg 2004

SIMR and ALINOR algorithms; Section 3 presents the experiment and its results; finally, Section 4 summaries the conclusions drawn from this work.

2   SIMR and ALINOR Algorithms Description

The SIMR algorithm ([Melamed 1996], [Melamed 1997]) is a generic pattern recognition algorithm well-suited to mapping bitexts. SIMR generates candidate points of correspondence in the search space using one of its matching predicates (heuristics for deciding whether a given pair of tokens are likely to be mutual translations). The matching predicates usually rely on cognates and translation lexicons. Each chain of the bitext map is found in two steps: generation and recognition. In the generation step, the algorithm generates all the points of correspondence that satisfy the matching predicate supplied. In the recognition step, SIMR uses the chain recognition heuristic to find suitable chains among the points generated.

The ALINOR algorithm is an improved version of the algorithm presented in [Martinez 1998a]. ALINOR is based on formalizing alignment as a matching problem in a bipartite graph. The two disjoint sets of vertices correspond to the sentences in the two languages, and the edges represent candidate matchings quantified by the similarity metric of Dice's coefficient. In order to establish the candidate matchings, there are constraints that take into account the order in which sentences in both the source and target texts have been written. These constraints capture the prevailing fact that translators tend to maintain the order of the original text in their translations. ALINOR works in two steps. First, it obtains a similarity matrix from Dice's coefficients corresponding to the candidate alignment options. Next, the algorithm solves an assignment problem. Its main peculiarity is the fact that it uses the mark-up (SGML, XML) as the sole foundation for determining the similarity between sentences. In this way, the alignment is not disrupted by differences in word order, and it does not have a strong dependence on cognates or other bilingual resources.

3   Experiments

For the experiments we tried a parallel corpus in Spanish and Basque in the administrative domain. There are many cognates (proper nouns, words derived from the same root, etc.) in the corpus, but there are some sentences that do not contain cognates. The bitexts were created at the Basque administration; examples of these publication are: edicts, regulations, announcements, etc. The corpus contains over 192,000 words in both languages, consisting of 692 documents (346 in each language). There are 7,538 sentences (3,748 in Spanish and 3,790 in Basque) distributed in 6,671 paragraphs (3,326 in Spanish and 3,345 in Basque).

This parallel corpus was hand-aligned at the sentence level. Both algorithms were evaluated on these hand-aligned bitexts in Spanish-Basque. Each side of the bitext was automatically marked-up in a separate way with SGML tags. The tagged elements belong to general encoding (paragraph, sentence, quoted text, dates, numbers, abbreviations, etc.). This tagged bitext was the input data for the ALINOR algorithm.

In order to compare ALINOR and SIMR, we provided Melamed's algorithm with the documents segmented into sentences, in such a way that the segment boundaries correspond to sentence boundaries. We did not provide any translation lexicon or SGML tags to the SIMR algorithm, so it used only cognate information.

In order to determine the similarity between sentences, ALINOR used the tags of the following SGML elements: abbreviations, quotations, proper nouns, numbers, dates, punctuation marks, and enumerations. We considered all tags as having the same weight.

The results of sentence alignment with the two algorithms can be seen in Table 1. They obtained similar, high accuracy rates for 1-1 alignment. In the N-M alignment, ALINOR obtained slightly better accuracy rates than SIMR.

Table 1. Results of SIMR and ALINOR sentence alignment algorithms

Cases	%Corpus	SIMR % Accuracy	ALINOR % Accuracy
1 - 1	94.06%	99.44%	99.53%
N - M	5.94%	93.89%	99.02%

The slightly better accuracy of our approach is due to the absence of cognates in some sentences. Table 2 shows an example without cognates in the two sentences. In this example, the positions of the sentences on the two sides of the bitext are reversed: sentence 1 in Spanish corresponds to sentence 2 in Basque, and sentence 2 in Spanish corresponds to sentence 1 in Basque. In addition, Table 2 shows how SIMR and ALINOR solve this sentence alignment. The results of the two algorithms are different; in this case the alignment produced by ALINOR is correct.

Table 2. Example of sentences with no cognates and their alignment with SIMR and ALINOR

Spanish Sentences	Basque Sentences
1 Se ha reunido el Presidente de la Comisión con el Secretario de Asuntos Exteriores. 2 El Presidente ha decidido que no habrá reunión con los partidos políticos.	1 Lehendakariak alderdi politikoekin bilerarik izango ez dela erabaki du. 2 Batzordeko Lehendakaria bildu da Kanpo Harremanetarako Idazkariarekin.
SIMR alignment	ALINOR alignment
1$\Longrightarrow$1 2$\Longrightarrow$2	1$\Longrightarrow$2 2$\Longrightarrow$1

These experiments were performed on a Pentium IV at 2.4 GHz with 512 MB of RAM. Although we have not taken time as our main comparison point, it is remarkable that ALINOR took 3 minutes and 57 seconds to align 692 documents, whereas SIMR took 65 minutes and 29 seconds to align the same group of documents.

4   Conclusions

We have compared two sentence alignment approaches: SIMR and ALINOR. These algorithms were evaluated on hand-aligned Spanish-Basque bitexts.

On the one hand, SIMR used cognates as its sole source of information for aligning. On the other hand, ALINOR used the SGML tags of the texts as its sole source of information. The experiment shows that both algorithms work better for 1-1 alignment than for N-M alignment. In the 1-1 alignment SIMR and ALINOR obtain accuracy rates close to 99.5%. ALINOR obtains slightly better accuracy rates than SIMR in N-M alignment.

Although between Spanish and Basque administrative texts there are many cognates, there are some sentences without cognates which cannot be dealt with by SIMR without a translation lexicon. The main advantage of our approach is that ALINOR can align sentences which have no cognates without the need of a translation lexicon or additional resources, but with some SGML or XML annotations. Nowadays, more and more texts have some type of mark-up (XML, SGML, HTML), so this approach may be a very sensible and efficient method of exploiting parallel corpora when annotations exist.

Acknowledgments. This research is being supported by the University and Government of the Basque Country, Project UE02/B02, and by the Madrid Research Agency, Project 07T/0030/2003.

References

[Martinez 1998a] Martínez R., Abaitua J., Casillas A. "Bitext Correspondences through Rich Mark-up". *Proceedings of the 17th International Conference on Computational Linguistics (COLING'98) and 36th Annual Meeting of the Association for Computational Linguistics (ACL'98)*, (1998).

[Martinez 1998b] Martínez R., Abaitua J., Casillas A. "Aligning tagged bitext". *Proceedings of the Sixth Workshop on Very Large Corpora*, (1998).

[Melamed 1996] Melamed I. Dan. "A Geometric Approach to Mapping Bitext Correspondence". *Proceedings of the Conference on Empirical Methods in Natural Language Processing*, 1–12, (1996).

[Melamed 1997] Melamed I. Dan. "A Portable Algorithm for Mapping Bitext Correspondence". *35th Conference of the Association for Computational Linguistics (ACL'97)*, (1997).

Two-Level Alignment by Words and Phrases Based on Syntactic Information

Seonho Kim[1], Juntae Yoon[2], and Dong-Yul Ra[3]

[1] Institute of Language and Information Studies,
Yonsei University, Seoul, Korea
shkim@lex.yonsei.ac.kr
[2] NLP Lab., Daumsoft, Seoul, Korea
jtyoon@daumsoft.com
[3] Dept. of Computer Science, Yonsei University, Korea
dyra@magics.yonsei.ac.kr

Abstract. As a part of work on alignment of the English and Korean parallel corpus, this paper presents a statistical translation model incorporating linguistic knowledge of syntactic and phrasal information for better translations. For this, we propose three models: First, we incorporate syntactic information such as part of speech into the word-based lexical alignment. Based on this model, we propose the second model which finds phrasal correspondence in the parallel corpus. Phrasal mapping through chunk-based shallow parsing enables to settle mismatch of meaningful units in the two languages. Lastly, we develop a two-level alignment model by combining these two models in order to construct both the word and phrase-based translation model. Model parameters are automatically estimated from a set of bilingual sentence pairs by applying the EM algorithm. Experiments show that the structural relationship helps construct a better translation model for structurally different languages like Korean and English.

1 Statistical Translation Model

Pairs of sentences aligned with words or phrases can be exploited as a valuable resource for work on bilingual systems such as machine translation, cross languages information retrieval, bilingual lexicography, and bilingual parsing. As large scale bilingual corpora are available, a lot of statistical approaches have been proposed for finding sets of corresponding word tokens [2,5], phrases [3,6, 11,12,14], and syntactic structures [10,13,15] from a bitext.

Many of those works have been initiated with statistical machine translation (SMT) model pioneered by Brown et al. (See [2]), which estimates, directly from bilingual corpora, parameters for a word-to-word alignment model. In this framework, Korean-to-English machine translation is assumed that each source language ($\mathbf{k}$) is transformed to its target language ($\mathbf{e}$) by means of a stochastic process. Typically, the stochastic process is represented by $P(\mathbf{e}|\mathbf{k}) = P(\mathbf{e})P(\mathbf{k}|\mathbf{e})$, where $P(\mathbf{e})$ is called a language model (LM), and $P(\mathbf{k}|\mathbf{e})$ is referred to as a

A. Gelbukh (Ed.): CICLing 2004, LNCS 2945, pp. 309–320, 2004.
© Springer-Verlag Berlin Heidelberg 2004

translation model (TM). In this paper, the TM, which reasons about how English **e** is turned into Korean **k**, is a matter of main concern.

Brown et al. [2] have modeled the translation process by operations of duplication and deletion (fertility), NULL insertion, reordering (distortion), and translation (lexical modeling), which turns out to be successfully applied to similar language pairs. However, the translation process has some limitations: (1) limited coverage of the word-to-word alignment that a source word is not often aligned with two or more target words, (2) the over-fitting problem, and (3) the weak model structure which fails to capture complicated word correspondence in the absence of structural representation of alignment parameters. In particular, the problems can be more serious in a syntactically different language pair such as Korean and English.

As an alternative, alignment models considering syntactic information such as phrase or structure, have been discussed. For example, alignment of bags of words [3,12], syntax-based TM [6,11,14], bilingual parsing [13], parse-to-parse mapping [15], and structural alignment [10] have been performed and various input formats like a sequence of words [2,3], a sequence of phrases, templates [11], and syntactic tree [14] have been used. Moreover, some studies automatically infer phrases (or chunks) in EM training setting without external resources [12] or extract phrases from alignment results generated by the IBM models with appropriate measures [9].

These methods, however, also have some difficulties. The bags of words approaches are restrictive in lengths of word sequences since considering all substrings of a sentence is too arbitrary. Also, as real bitexts generally do not exhibit parse tree isomorphism, the parsing-based approaches such as tree-to-tree or tree-to-string alignment model often confront structural mismatching between two languages in addition to the parsing quality problem. Besides, it is hard to describe the transformation between parse trees across two languages, since it is conducted on complex and hierarchical syntactic structures.

In order to cope with those problems, this paper suggests a two-level alignment model, where words and phrases are aligned simultaneously in one framework. In this paper, phrase is defined as an extended concept of chunking, and chunks are identified using external resources. In contrast to parsing, chunking is relatively easy to be implemented, and the accuracy is quite good as well.

Besides, to consider the structural relation between two languages, we incorporate syntactic class of a word and a phrase into the model . That is, the syntactic class of a word is represented by a part-of-speech (POS) tag, the surface syntactic information (class) of a phrase by a POS tag sequence. It turns out that the use of explicit syntactic information by POS provides more improved translation results as well as alleviating the data sparseness.

2   Problems of Phrasal Restriction of IBM Model

Basically, in the IBM Models, a target word can be aligned to only a single source word. IBM Model 4 and 5 partially treat the tendency of phrases to move around as units using the distortion parameter. The generative scenario of IBM Model 4 is as follows: First, choose the number of words, ϕ_i to generate (or delete) for each source word with the fertility probability (n). Next, generate extraneous NULL words, ϕ_0 and translate generated words with the translation (lexical) probability (t). Finally, reorder the translated words with the distortion probability (d). The process can be summarized as the following equation.

$$p(\mathbf{k},|\mathbf{e}) \equiv \sum_{a_1=0}^{l} \sum_{a_m=0}^{l} \binom{m - \phi_0}{\phi_0} p_0^{m-2\phi_0} p_1^{\phi_0} \prod_{i=1}^{l} \phi_i! n(\phi_i|e_i) \times$$

$$\prod_{j=1}^{m} t(k_j|e_{a_j}) d_1(j - \odot_{i-1}|\mathcal{A}(e_{[i-1]}), \mathcal{B}(k_j))(d_{>1}(j(\pi_{[i]k}) - \pi_{[i]k-1}|\mathcal{B}(k_j))$$

In here, the distortion probability is computed by two sets of parameters: d_1 is for a head word and $d_{>1}$ is for a non-head word. In addition, $\mathcal{A}$ and $\mathcal{B}$ are class functions. The notation of $\odot_{i-1}$ means the center of the positions in Korean string of the words from the tablet of the $i - 1^{th}$ English word and $\pi_{[i]k-1}$ is the position of a previous target word generated from the same i^{th} English source word. However, the fertility probability for word deletion and the NULL insertion probability are weak description for translation modeling. Also, even though IBM model 4 (and 5) parameterizes phrasal constraints using the distortion probability, the result of IBM model 4 does not sufficiently capture locality for phrasal movement, as shown in the following example.

input	$geugeos_1$ eun_2 $daegyumo_3$ ui_4 $boan_5$ $sang_6$ ui_7 $jalmos_8$ i_9 $eoss_{10}$ $seunida_{11}$
model 4	NULL(9 10 11) it(1 2) was ( ) massive (3) security(5) lapse (4 6 7 8)
reference 1	NULL() it(1 2) was (9 10 11) massive (3 4) [security lapse] (5 6 7 8)
reference 2	NULL(2 11) it(1) was (9 10) massive (3 4) [security lapse] (5 6 7 8)

Therefore, we suggest an alternative chunk-to-chunk alignment model for a syntactically different language pair such as Korean and English. In our model, the fertility probability and the NULL insertion probability are replaced by the chunk-mapping probability.

3   Translation Models

In this section, we describe the two-level alignment model by word and phrase. In order to derive the model, we first present a word-based alignment model where part of speech information is used to improve the translation process. On the basis of the framework, we propose a phrase-based alignment model, where sequences of POS tags are used to reduce the parameter space. Lastly, the two models are combined to yield a better translation.

3.1   Model 1

Linguistic information inherent in the languages is ignored in the IBM models, since word alignments in the models are mainly dependent on the surface structure. It is a main reason that the models do not often work well for alignment of linguistically different languages. Our first model is enhanced by incorporating linguistic information such as part of speech. The model proposed is actually the same as IBM model 1 except that class (POS) mapping information is used instead of the reordering process.

This model is motivated the fact that parts of speech tend to be preserved in mutual translation [7], although they do not appear in the surface strings. For instance, in many cases, a noun in Korean is translated to a noun or a noun preceded by an article in English. To identify POS of words, we conduct morphological analysis for Korean and POS tagging for both languages. Thus, a Korean word '*hagsaengi*(student/SUBJ)' is analyzed as '*hagsaeng*(student)+*i*(SUBJ marker)'. In particular, short words in Korean often have lexical ambiguities (homograph), which are easily discriminated by the POS information.

As mentioned before, the main goal of this work is to construct a translation model, namely estimating translation probabilities of the source language to the target language. However, we cannot assess translation probabilities directly from a parallel corpus. Instead, we can only get the expectation which is represented with summation of each alignment, as follows:

$$P(\mathbf{k}|\mathbf{e}) = \sum_{\mathbf{a}} P(\mathbf{k}, \mathbf{a}|\mathbf{e}) \tag{1}$$

There are many ways to represent the conditional probability on the right-hand side of Equation (1). An alignment model, written in terms of the conditional probability, can be constructed by setting up appropriate parameters for translation modeling. In our model, given an English sentence, we assume that a linguistic class of each word, i.e. part of speech, is inherently assigned. Therefore, the alignment model is represented as the following formula.

$$P(\mathbf{k}, \mathbf{a}|\mathbf{e}) \equiv P(\mathbf{k}, \mathcal{T}(\mathbf{k}), \mathbf{a}|\mathbf{e}, \mathcal{T}(\mathbf{e})) \tag{2}$$

In this formula, $\mathcal{T}$ is a class function that returns a POS tag for a word and a POS tag sequence for a list of words. Since direct use of Equation (2) is not possible, we make independence assumptions to reduce the parameters. First, it is assumed that every word-POS pair is generated independently each other. The word alignment model is to independently translate each word by multiple single words and to determine the POS of each translated word. Then, the alignment model on the right-hand side of Equation (1) can be represented as follows:

$$P(\mathbf{k}, \mathbf{a}|\mathbf{e}) = \prod_{j=1}^{m} P(k_j, \mathcal{T}(k_j)|e_{a_j}, \mathcal{T}(e_{a_j}))$$

$$= \prod_{j=1}^{m} t(k_j|e_{a_j}) \times p(\mathcal{T}(k_j)|\mathcal{T}(e_{a_j})) \tag{3}$$

Here, k_j and e_{a_j} is a Korean word in the jth position and an English word aligned with the jth Korean word, respectively. In addition, the parameters, t and p, are the lexical translation probability and the POS correspondence probability. According to the equation, the model considers not only words but also POS tags inherent in the languages when generating a Korean string with a specific alignment from an English string. Figure 1 shows an example of the translation process by Model 1.

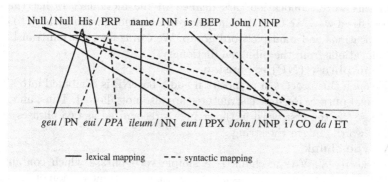

Fig. 1. Translation process by Model 1

3.2   Model 2

The word-to-word translation model often fails to make mapping of syntactic or meaningful units between English and Korean. For instance, a noun phrase (NP) in Korean can correspond to a prepositional phrase (PP) in English. A preposition, the head of PP, is a word in English, but a postposition, the correspondent of it, is not regarded as a word in Korean. Actually, it is treated like affix morphologically. As a result, many prepositions are connected to NULL or incorrectly in the word-based model. The multiple word group is another example which brings about this type of mismatch. For example, an English phrasal verb such as 'make use of' is translated into a Korean word '*iyongha-da*'. Also, collocation generally represents one concept consisting of multiple words and the meaning is not decomposed into word-to-word translation. Furthermore, the single-word based TM does not provide contextual information for translation. For example, an English word "*natural*" is translated into a Korean adjective "*jayeonsreo-un*" in "*natural voice*", whereas it is translated into a noun "*jayeon*" in "*natural language*". Therefore, phrase-based translation is crucial for conveying the meaning of a source language.

In Model 2, we describe the phrase-based TM, which can learn translations for phrases. To identify the phrasal units in a sentence, we utilize shallow-level syntactic analysis which is an extended version of chunking. For this purpose, POS tagging and NP chunking are conducted for each sentence in English and

Korean. The POS tagger and chunker presented by [1] and [8] are used for English text analysis, and those presented by [16] are used for Korean text analysis.

Chunking is a process to partition a sentence into non-overlapping and non-recursive phrases. However, we still have mismatch at the conceptual level, as the chunking process exclude structures containing recursion, e.g. preposition phrase and collocation, so we extend a chunking process for recognizing them. The program consists of several processes as follows:

1. **Collocation recognition**
   In this work, collocations are defined in the dictionary rather than in a statistical way. We used the machine readable bilingual dictionary to extract collocations and multiple word group. We can collect mutual translation of collocations from the bilingual dictionary.
2. **Noun phrase (NP) expansion**
   Through this process, a preposition and a baseNP is combined into a prepositional phrase. Recursive structures are also not allowed. Thus, an example phrase 'by the first word in the string' is recognized as two phrases, 'by the first word' and 'in the string'.
3. **V-type chunk**
   Unlike in [8], V-type chunk is a simple verb phrase which contains only auxiliary verbs and a verb as a head. Since the current version of the English chunker does not produce V-type chunks, we added a finite-state transducer for V-type chunk.
4. **Single word chunk**
   We regard the remaining words as single word chunks.

We also use syntactic information in this model. In fact, data sparseness due to huge parameter space is a very critical issue in the lexical-level phrase alignment. In fact, syntactic information helps to alleviate the data sparseness problem.

In general, many researchers have used syntactic categories obtained by parsing for exploiting structural information. However, since these approaches are based on context-free backbone, they cannot reflect the property of the constituents inside. For instance, the constituents inside corresponding NPs can be different. In order to use syntactic information in flat structures (chunks), we propose a method that represent the syntactic category using a sequence of POS tags. Namely, a POS sequence is treated as phrasal tag. For instance, the syntactic category of a phrase 'the student' is 'DT[1]+NN', which can be mapped into a tag sequence 'NN[2]+PPS' or 'NN+PPO' in Korean. But the tag sequence 'DT+NN' would rarely be mapped to 'ADJ+NN+NN'. By this method, we can avoid mapping of too abstract level of syntactic information and simplify the model as much as Model 1.

---

[1] We adapt the Penn Treebank POS tagset for English.

[2] Korean POS tags in this paper are as follows: NN:noun, PN:pronoun, VB:verb, ADJ:adjective, DT:determiner, PPS:subjective postposition, PPO:objective postposition, PPA:adnominal postposition, PPD:adverbial postposition, PPX:auxiliary postposition, PE:tense marker preceding ending, ET:ending

Consequently, this model is the same as Model 1 except that the translation unit of the model is not a word but a phrase. Model 2 considers the correspondences of words and POS tags between Korean and English phrases (chunks). That is, a Korean sentence is represented with a series of phrases $\bar{k}_1, \ldots, \bar{k}_n$ which of each has POS tag sequences $\mathcal{T}(\bar{k}_1), \ldots, \mathcal{T}(\bar{k}_n)$. An English sentence is represented by $\bar{k}_1, \ldots, \bar{k}_n$ and $\mathcal{T}(\bar{k}_1), \ldots, \mathcal{T}(\bar{k}_n)$. Then, the alignment model can be modeled as follows:

$$P(\mathbf{k}, \mathbf{a}|\mathbf{e}) \equiv \prod_{j=1}^{n} P(\bar{k}_j, \mathcal{T}(\bar{k}_j)|\bar{e}_{a_j}, \mathcal{T}(\bar{e}_{a_j}))$$

$$= \prod_{j=1}^{n} \bar{t}(\bar{k}_j|\bar{e}_{a_j}) \times \bar{p}(\mathcal{T}(\bar{k}_j)|\mathcal{T}(\bar{e}_{a_j})) \tag{4}$$

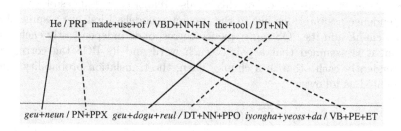

Fig. 2. Translation process by Model 2

In the above Equation, $\bar{k}_j$ and $\bar{e}_{a_j}$ is a Korean chunk in the jth position and an English chunk aligned with the jth Korean chunk, respectively. In addition, the parameters $\bar{t}$ and $\bar{p}$ denote the phrase-level lexical translation probability and the correspondence probability of POS tag sequences, respectively. Figure 2 shows an example of the translation process by Model 2.

3.3   Model 3

Until now, we have described the word-based model (Model 1) and the phrase-based model (Model 2). In this section, We describe a method for incorporating the two models.

Model 2 has an advantage in that it provides translation between meaningful units of the source and target language. It, however, has a deficiency that it considers only phrase translation but not word translation, thus fails to translate words inside a phrase. In order to solve this problem, we propose Model 3 which allows the word-based and phrase-based translation simultaneously.

The basic idea underlying Model 3 is the following: Given an English sentence with a series of phrases each of which consists of several words, a Korean sentence is generated by determining a Korean phrase for each English phrase and then generating Korean words as translation for words in the corresponding English phrase. In this model, an English sentence consists of a series of chunks which of each is composed of a sequence of words. This is applied to Korean sentences in the same way.

$$\mathbf{e} = \bar{e}_1, \bar{e}_2 \ldots \bar{e}_q,$$
$$= (e_{11}, e_{12} \ldots e_{1l_1})(e_{21}, e_{22} \ldots e_{2l_2}) \ldots (e_{q1}, e_{q2} \ldots e_{ql_q})$$
$$\mathbf{k} = \bar{k}_1, \bar{k}_2 \ldots \bar{k}_q,$$
$$= (k_{11}, k_{12} \ldots k_{1m_1})(k_{21}, k_{22} \ldots k_{2m_2}) \ldots (k_{q1}, k_{q2} \ldots k_{qm_q})$$

Then, the alignment model is represented by Equation (5):

$$P(\mathbf{k}, \mathbf{a}|\mathbf{e}) \equiv P(\mathbf{k}, \mathcal{T}(\mathbf{k}), \mathbf{a}, \bar{\mathbf{k}}, \mathcal{T}(\bar{\mathbf{k}}), \bar{\mathbf{a}}|\mathbf{e}, \mathcal{T}(\mathbf{e}), \bar{\mathbf{e}}, \mathcal{T}(\bar{\mathbf{e}})) \tag{5}$$

Since direct computation of this is also realistically impossible, we make independence assumptions like in the previous models. First, we assume that a pair of chunk and its POS tag sequence corresponds independently each other. Second, it is assumed that a pair of each word and its POS tag corresponds independently each other in a chunk. Then, the translation probability can be represented as follows:

$$P(\mathbf{k}|\mathbf{e}) = \sum_{\mathbf{a}} P(\mathbf{k}, \mathbf{a}|\mathbf{e})$$
$$= \sum_{\mathbf{a}} \prod_{i=1}^{q} \bar{t}(\bar{k}_i|\bar{e}_i)\bar{p}(\mathcal{T}(\bar{k}_i)|\mathcal{T}(\bar{e}_i)) \times$$
$$\prod_{j=1}^{|k_i|} t(k_{ij}|e_{h_i a_j})p(\mathcal{T}(k_{ij})|\mathcal{T}(e_{h_i a_j})) \tag{6}$$

In this Equation, q denotes the number of chunks, and h_i, the position of the English chunk corresponding to the ith Korean chunk. In addition, $|k_i|$ means the number of words in the ith chunk. According to this Equation, given an English sentence segmented by chunk, the corresponding Korean chunks are generated first. Then, each English word in an English chunk is translated to a Korean word in a Korean chunk.

However, there is no efficient way to avoid the explicit summation over all alignment even though the formula is much simplified by our assumption. In order to reduce this computational complexity, Brown et al. [2] considered a subset of promising alignments, which is obtained from a neighborhood $\mathcal{N}(\mathbf{a})$ for the most likely alignment $\mathbf{a}$ which is computed by the simpler model. In this work, we used a modified version of the Inside-Outside algorithm as presented in Yamada and Knight [14] for training.

Figure 3 shows the result of phrase alignment obtained by Model 3. In addition, Figure 4 represents an example of word alignment inside chunks aligned.

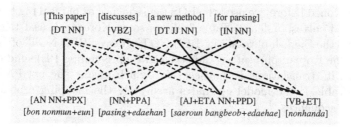

Fig. 3. Phrase mapping in Model 3 (The solid line is the correct mapping). The number of possible chunk alignments is 4!

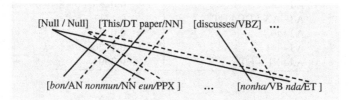

Fig. 4. Word mapping in Model 3 (Part of Figure 3)

4   Experiments

The alignment models are trained and tested on pairs of English-Korean bilingual sentences, which are extracted from the web site of 'Korea Times'. The corpus was split into two parts: 27,916 (13,958 sentence pairs) for training and 200 sentence pairs for testing. For simplicity, the corpus was composed of sentence pairs with less than 12 words on the basis of the length of English words. We evaluate our alignment models in terms of agreement with human-aligned alignments between the sentence pairs. Also, to compare the quality of our system to the IBM models, we trained GIZA on our corpus.

Figure 5 shows some results of the Viterbi alignment of our Model 1–3. In the figure, '+' in Korean words denotes multi-morphemic words.

English	(1) certainly/RB the/DT numbers/NNS are/BEP very/RB small/JJ
	(2) [certainly/RB] [the/DT numbers/NNS] [are/BEP small/JJ] very/RB
Korean	(1) *hwagsilhi*/AD *geu*/AN *susja*/NN *neun*/PPX *maeu*/AD *jeog*/AJ *seubnida*/ET
	(2) [*hwagsilhi*/AD] [*geu*/AN *susja*/NN *neun*/PPX] c [*maeu*/AD] [*jeog*/AJ *seubnida*/ET]
Model 1	*hwagsilhi*-certainly *geu*-the *susja*-numbers *neun*-the *maeu*-very *jeog*-small *seubnida*-NULL
Model 2	[*hwagsilhi*]-[certainly] [*geu susja+neun*]-[the numbers] [*maeu*]-[very] [*jeog+seubnida*]-[small]
Model 3	[*hwagsilhi*]-[certainly]:*hwagsilhi*-certainly
	[*geu susja+neun*]-[the numbers]:*geu*-the *susja*-numbers *neun*-NULL
	[*maeu*]-[very]:*maeu*-very
	[*jeog+seubnida*]-[small]:*jeog*-small *seubnida*-are

Fig. 5. Examples of input and output of Model 1–3

As mentioned before, we used the POS tag sequence as phrasal tag to capture syntax-based correspondence. Table 1 shows some Korean phrasal tags corresponding to the English phrasal tag 'BED NOT'. It says 'BED NOT' often corresponds to the Korean phrasal tag, adjective(AJ)+pre-ending(PE)+ending(ET), and one of its translations is "*ani-eoss-da*" which means "be not-PAST". As shown in Table 1, the model estimates accurately the mapping probability of phrasal tag sequences.

Table 1. Example of Korean phrasal tags corresponding to 'BED NOT' in English

Korean POS tag sequences	mapping probability
AJ	0.0285
AJ+AX+PE+ET	0.1711
AJ+EC	0.0571
AJ+ET	0.1126
AJ+PE+ET	0.3994

Table 2 shows the number of parameters. The number of alignments for each model is different from each other since the translation units are different. As shown in Table 2, the number of phrasal tags to appear in the parallel corpus is 1,345, which is much less than the number of lexical phrases - actually less than the number of single words. It means that our method using POS tag sequences as well as POS tags can remarkably reduce the parameter space.

Table 2. Number of parameters

	English	Korean
vocabulary size	8,759	8,765
# of POS	45	39
# of lexical phrase	19,105	22,598
# of phrasal tag	1,006	1,345
	# of correspondences between phrasal tags	# of meaningful correspondences between phrasal tags
	27,744	8,739

For the comparison of alignment quality, we use alignment error rate (AER) of Och and Ney(2000), which is represented with two parameters, A and R. A is the set of translation pairs aligned by system and R is the reference set aligned by human.

$$AER(A, R) = 1 - \frac{2|A \cap R|}{|A| + |R|} \qquad (7)$$

Table 3 shows the alignment error rate for each model. We compared our model with IBM Model 4 which considers phrasal movement. As shown in the table, Model 1-3 outperforms the IBM model. It means that syntactic information has an effect on alignment of a bilingual corpus in syntactically different languages such as Korean and English.

Table 3. Alignment error rate

model	AER
IBM model 4	0.40
Model 1	0.33
Model 2	0.24
Model 3	0.21

The phrasal units in the statistical machine translation framework have been implemented by cluster-to-string [11] , tree-to-string [14], string-to-string [12] translation modeling. Our chunk-to-chunk model is better both in complexity and alignment error than structure-to-string, string-to-string models, and it could be significant advantage in practice. In addition, the number of chunks for source and target is not needed to be equal in our model.

In particular, it turns out that the alignment precision of Model 2 is pretty high, even though the phrase-level alignment generally is expected to have the serious problem with data sparseness. Such good results indicate that the POS tag sequences is effective for identifying the syntactic feature of a phrase.

However, mismatch of translation still happens despite of the phrase-based mapping. It is caused by rhetorical difference between English and Korean, which should be studied in the future. For instance, literal translation of a Korean phrase 'gyesogha-eseo jikyeobol-geos-ida' is 'will watch continuously', but its correct translation, which actually appears in the corpus, is 'will continue to watch'.

5 Conclusion

In this paper, we assumed that lexical alignments can be established not only at the word level, but at the phrase level as well. We restricted the lexical dependencies by incorporating structural aspects of the language like POS tag and chunk information, and presented three translation models, Model 1–3. We first proposed Model 1 in order to alleviate data sparseness due to linguistic difference of English and Korean. This model is simple but could effectively make the word-to-word alignment by introducing linguistic information such as POS tags. Second, we developed Model 2 in order to solve the mismatch of the translation unit in text alignment. In our model, the phrase was set to an extended version of chunk, and we could get alignment of meaningful units based on this idea. Lastly, by combining the two models, we constructed two-level alignment Model 3, where both the word-based and phrase-based alignment is possible.

Experiments have shown that Model 3 produces pretty good results in lexical alignment for the parallel corpus. Furthermore, it turns out that the linguistic features such as POS and structural information helps develop a better translation model.

References

1. Brill, Eric. Transformation-based error-driven learning and natural language processing: A case study in part-of-speech tagging. *Computational Linguistics*, 21(4):543-565, 1995.
2. Brown, Peter F., Stephen A. Della Pietra, Vincent J. Della Pietra, and Robert L. Mercer. The mathematics of statistical machine translation: parameter estimation. *Computational Linguistics*, 19(2):263-311, 1993.
3. Marcu, Daniel and William Wong. 2002. A phrase-based, joint probability model for statistical machine translation. In *Proceedings of EMNLP 2002*.
4. Dempster, A. P., N. M. Laird and D. B. Rubin. Maximum likelihood from incomplete data via the EM algorithm. *The Royal Statistics Society*, 39(B) 205-237, 1976.
5. Melamed, I. Dan. A word-to-word model of translation equivalence. In *Proceedings of ACL 35/EACL 8*, 16-23, 1997.
6. Och, Franz Josef and Hermann Ney. Improved statistical alignment models. In *Proceedings of ACL*, 2000.
7. Papageorgiou, H., L. Cranias and S. Piperidis. Automatic alignment in parallel corpora. In *Proceedings of ACL 32 (Student Session)*, 1994.
8. Ramshaw, Lance and Mitch Marcus. Text chunking using transformation-based learning. In *Proceedings of the 4th Workshop on Very Large Corpora*, 82-94, 1995.
9. Venugopal, Ashish, Vogel, Stephan, and Waibel, Alex. Effective Phrase Translation Exctraction from Alignment Models. In *Proceedings of ACL 2003*.
10. Wang, Wei, Ming Zhou, Jin-Xia Huang, and Chang-Ning Huang. Structure Alignment Using Bilingual Chunking. In *Proceedings of COLING 2002*.
11. Wang, Ye-Yi and Alex Waibel. Modeling with structures in machine translation. In *Proceedings of ACL 36/COLING*.
12. Watanabe,Taro, Sumita, Eiichiro, and Okuno, G. Hiroshi Chunk-based Statistical Translation In *Proceedings of ACL 2003*.
13. Wu, Dekai. Stochastic Inversion Transduction Grammar and Bilingual Parsing of Parallel Corpora. *Computational Linguistics*, 23(3):377-403.
14. Yamada, Kenji and Kevin Knight. A Syntax-based statistical translation model. In *Proceedings of ACL 2001*.
15. Yamamoto, Kaoru and Yuji Matsumoto. Acquisition of Phrase-level Bilingual Correspondence using Dependency Structure. In *Proceedings of COLING 2000*.
16. Yoon, Juntae, Key-Sun Choi and Mansuk Song. Three Types of Chunking in Korean and Dependency Analysis Based on Lexical Association. In *Proceedings of International Conference on Computer Processing of Oriental Languages*, 1999.

Exploiting a Mono-bilingual Dictionary for English-Korean Translation Selection and Sense Disambiguation

Hyun Ah Lee[1], Juntae Yoon[2], and Gil Chang Kim[1]

[1] Dept. of EECS, Korea Advanced Institute of Science and Technology (KAIST),
373-1 GusongDong, YusongGu, Daejon, 305-701, Republic of Korea
halee@csone.kaist.ac.kr, gckim@cs.kaist.ac.kr
[2] Daumsoft Inc., 946-12 DaechiDong, GangnamGu, Seoul, 135-280, Republic of Korea
jtyoon@daumsoft.com

Abstract. A mono-bilingual dictionary is a combined dictionary of a monolingual and bilingual dictionary, which contains rich information for translation. In this paper, we propose to exploit a mono-bilingual dictionary for sense disambiguation and translation selection. Based on the 'word-to-sense and sense-to-word' relationship, our method selects translation through two steps – sense disambiguation of a source word and selection of a target word. Each step requires various information including clue words for sense disambiguation, sense-to-word mapping and syntactic relation mapping information, and we extract them from a mono-bilingual dictionary. Evaluation results showed that our method selects more appropriate target words.

1 Introduction

Translation selection is a process to select, from a set of target language words corresponding to a source language word, one that conveys the correct sense of a source word and makes more fluent target language sentences. Translation selection is a key problem in machine translation (MT) since the quality of translation varies significantly according to results of translation selection.

The difficulty of translation selection and machine translation is that they link two different languages thus requiring more complex knowledge than other problems concerning only one language. So, the following has become important issues – what kind of knowledge to be used for translation, how to acquire and use the knowledge. Among them, knowledge acquisition is a critical problem for many MT systems and translation selection methods.

A bilingual dictionary is a good knowledge source for MT and translation selection. An entry in a bilingual dictionary generally contains translation definitions, and example sentences in source and target languages. On the other hand, an entry in a common monolingual dictionary includes sense definitions and monolingual example sentences. A mono-bilingual dictionary is a combination of a monolingual and a bilingual dictionary, in which a word entry has sense definitions in a source language, translation definitions, and pairs of example sentences in both languages as shown in Fig. 1.

A. Gelbukh (Ed.): CICLing 2004, LNCS 2945, pp. 321–333, 2004.
© Springer-Verlag Berlin Heidelberg 2004

catch [kætʃ] *v.* (**caught** [kɔːt]) *vt.* 1 (P6.13) take and hold; capture. …을 (붙)잡다; 붙들다 (opp. lose). ¶ ~ *a thief* 도둑을 잡다 / ~ *a rat in a trap* 덫으로 쥐를 잡다 / ~ *a lion alive* 사자를 사로잡다 / ~ *someone by the arm [sleeve]* 아무의 팔을[소매를] 잡다 2 (P6) get hold of (something moving, flying, etc.); receive and hold. (움직이는 것)을 잡다; 받다 ¶ ~ *a ball* 볼을 잡다[받다] 3 (P6,7,13) grasp with the senses or mind; see; hear; understand. …을 알아채다; 알아듣다; 이해하다. ¶ ~ *the meaning* 뜻을 이해하다 / ~ *someone's words* 아무의 말을 알아듣다 4 (P6) be in time for [to take]; come to or catch up with. (열차·배 따위)에 시간을 대어 타다; …을 따라잡다 ¶ ~ *the 8:00 limited express,* 8시발 특급을 타다 5 (P6) become infected with (a disease); form (habits) ; contract; incur. (병)에 걸리다; 감염하다; (습관)에 물들다; (바람직하지 않은 일 등)을 당하다; 초래하다. ¶ ~ *(a) cold* 감기에 걸리다 / *catch (the) measles* 홍역에 걸리다 / ~ *hatred [danger]* 증오를[위험을] 초래하다 / ~ *his manner* 그의 태도에 물들다. 6 ....

Fig. 1. A part of an English-English Korean mono-bilingual dictionary [10]

In this paper, we propose to exploit a mono-bilingual dictionary to extract knowledge for English-Korean translation selection and sense disambiguation. To select a target word, we disambiguate the sense of a source word and select the most appropriate one among various target words that correspond to the resolved sense. By dividing translation selection into two sub-problems, we can select translation using automatically obtained knowledge. Knowledge for sense disambiguation and word selection is extracted from a mono-bilingual dictionary and target language monolingual corpora. From a dictionary, we extract clue words for sense disambiguation, frequency information for senses, sense-to-word mapping and syntactic relation mapping information. From target language corpora, we extract statistics of target word co-occurrence.

The rest of the paper is organized as follows. Related works are reviewed in Sect. 2. In Sect. 3, we show our method for translation selection. The knowledge extraction method is described in Sect. 4, and the computing model of the translation preference is explained in Sect. 5. The results of evaluation are shown in Sect. 6, and we conclude in Sect. 7.

2   Previous Work

For translation selection, classical systems with a transfer-based method have generally relied on hand-crafted rules, lexicons or knowledge bases [1]. Although those rule-based methods are intuitive and reliable, they have difficulty in acquiring rules or knowledge. To overcome the difficulty of knowledge acquisition, some studies have attempted to extract rules or knowledge automatically from existing resources such as a machine readable dictionary (MRD) [2,3]. However, those methods did not show practical results since they were concerned with limited types of words or applicable only when extra knowledge sources including a multilingual large knowledge base or a bilingual corpus already exist.

As masses of language resources have become available, a lot of statistical methods have been attempted for translation selection. Approaches based on statistical machine translation [4] exploit a bilingual corpus, however, as Koehn and Knight [7] pointed out, a bilingual corpus is hard to acquire in itself and even it does not provide sufficient information for translation.

Dagan and Itai [5] have proposed a new method for sense disambiguation and translation selection that uses word co-occurrence in a target language corpus. Based on this method, some latest approaches proposed advanced probabilistic models that exploit monolingual corpora [6,7].

Those target language based methods could relieve the knowledge acquisition problem since they need only a monolingual corpus and simple mapping information between a source word and its target words. However, they are apt to select an incorrect translation because of ambiguity of target word senses for individual source words. For example, in an English phrase 'have a car', 'car' is translated into a Korean word '*cha*', which has two different meanings – car and tea. The word 'have' has many senses, for example possess, eat, and drink, which are mapped into '*gaji-da*', '*meok-da*' and '*masi-da*' respectively. From these examples, we get three possible translations '*cha-reul gaji-da*', '*cha-reul meok-da*' and '*cha-reul masi-da*', among which the first one is correct translation. However, a target language based method chooses incorrect translation '*cha-reul masi-da*' (meaning 'drink a tea') because the co-occurring frequency of '*cha*' and '*masi-da*' is dominant in a corpus over that of all other translations.

Another flaw of previous target language based methods is that they are not concerned about difference between source and target languages. Consider the translation of an English phrase 'catch a disease', in which a noun 'disease' is an object to a verb 'catch'. However, in its correct Korean translation '*byeong-e geollida*', '*byeong*' (disease) is not an object to a verb '*geolli-da*' (catch). Previous target language based methods generally use a syntactic relation in a source language to compute translation probability. Therefore, in translation of 'catch a disease', those methods generate an incorrect translation '*byeong-eul jab-da*' (meaning 'grip a bottle') because '*byeong*' has both senses of bottle and disease and, in a Korean corpus, '*byeong*' hardly appears as an object of '*geolli-da*' but often appears as an object of '*jab-da*'.

3   Translation Selection through Sense Disambiguation and Word Selection

In this paper, we select a translation word based on the method of Lee and Kim [8]. They proposed to select a target word through disambiguation of a source word sense and selection of a target word based on the 'word-to-sense and sense-to-word' relationship, which means a word in a source language has multiple senses and each sense can be mapped into multiple target words. Based on the relationship, their method selects correct translation for 'have a car' though it also uses target word co-occurrence. For translation selection through sense disambiguation and word selection, they introduce three measures: the sense preference (spf), the sense probability (sp) and the word probability (wp). The sense preference and the sense probability are measures for sense disambiguation, and the word probability is a measure for word selection.

The sense preference is calculated with clues for sense disambiguation in a dictionary. As shown in the dictionary of Fig. 1, example sentences of the capture

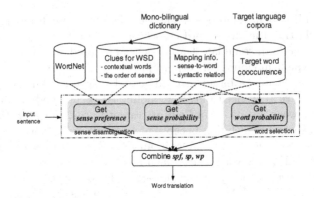

Fig. 2. Our process of translation selection

sense of 'catch' have words like 'thief' and 'rat', and those of the infected sense have 'measles' and 'cold'. Those words are semantic and syntactic contexts for each sense of 'catch', thus they can work as good indicators for senses. The sense preference of each sense of a word is computed by estimating similarity between words in an input sentence and words in example and definition sentences. In addition to those semantic and syntactic contexts, they also utilize the order of each sense in a dictionary as sense frequency information.

The sense probability is calculated by using target word co-occurrence and mapping information between source and target languages. In a bilingual dictionary, each sense division of a source word is mapped into a set of target words. Words in an individual set have the same sense or similar usage, so they can be replaced with each other in a translated sentence. For example, we can extract a set of target words {'jap-da', 'butdeul-da'} for the capture sense of 'catch' from Fig. 1, and both of 'doduk-eul jap-da' and 'doduk-eul butdeul-da' are correct translations of a phrase 'catch a thief'. Using those sets of target words that correspond to each sense division in a dictionary, we calculate the sense probability.

The word probability is the measure for word selection, which represents how likely a target word is selected from the set of words in the same sense division. As the level of naturalness of a phrase can be captured by word co-occurrence, we use target word co-occurrence to get the word probability.

Figure 2 shows the process for selecting translation and knowledge extraction. In the next section, our knowledge extraction method is explained.

4   Knowledge Extraction from a Dictionary and Corpora

For translation selection, our method uses knowledge for sense disambiguation, mapping information between source and target languages, and target word co-occurrence as shown in Fig. 2. They are extracted from a mono-bilingual dictionary and target language monolingual corpora.

4.1   Knowledge Extraction from a Mono-bilingual Dictionary

From a mono-bilingual dictionary, we extract knowledge for sense disambiguation and mapping information between source and target languages. As knowledge for sense disambiguation, the order of sense and contextual words in definition sentences and example sentences are extracted. As mapping information, we extract a set of target words for each sense of a source word (sense-to-word mapping) and mapping of syntactic relations.

Knowledge for Sense Disambiguation. Sense definitions and example sentences in a dictionary provide good information for resolving each sense of a word [9]. We extract content words in definition and example sentences as clues for sense disambiguation. For a source word s, let us denote the f-th sense of s as s^f, the set of content words in sense definitions of s^f as DEF_{s^f} and the set of content words in examples as EX_{s^f}. Figure 3 shows clue words for sense disambiguation extracted from the dictionary of Fig. 1. The order of the sense f is also extracted as knowledge for sense disambiguation.

Sense	DEF_{catch^f}	EX_{catch^f}
$catch^1$ (capture)	take hold capture	thief rat lion someone
$catch^3$ (understand)	grasp sense mind see hear undertand	meaning someone word
$catch^5$ (infected)	become infect disease form habit ...	cold measles hatred danger ...

Fig. 3. Clues for sense disambiguation extracted from Fig. 1

Sense-to-Word Mapping. Each sense of a source word might be mapped into a set of target words. Let us suppose that the set of translations of a sense s^f is $T(s^f)$ and an element of $T(s^f)$ is t_q^f. From translation definitions in a bilingual dictionary, we extract the mapping from s^f to $\{t_1^f, \cdots, t_n^f\}$, i.e. sense-to-word mapping.

To extract translations, we divide a translation definition into a set of phrases by delimiters, and obtain refined definitions by deleting special characters and expanding expressions in brackets. Figure 4 shows some examples of extracted translations. For example, from a translation definition of the first sense of engross ($engross^1$) 'eyoljung [moldu] ha ke ha-da', 'eyoljungha-ke ha-da' and 'molduha-ke ha-da' are expanded as refined definitions.

Sense	Translation definition	Refined definition	Extracted target word
$engross^1$	열중 [몰두] 하게 하다 (eyoljung [moldu] ha ke ha-da)	열중하게 하다 (eyoljungha-ke ha-da) 몰두하게 하다 (molduha-ke ha-da)	열중하다 (eyoljungha-da) 몰두하다 (molduha-da)
$arrange^3$	...의 준비를 하다 ; (...ui junbi-lul ha-da) 계획을 짜다; (kyeheok-ul jja-da)	준비를 하다 (junbi-lul ha-da) 계획을 짜다 (kyeheok-ul jja-da) 조처하다 (jocheoha-da)	준비하다 (junbiha-da) 계획짜다 (kyeheo-jja-da) 짜다 (jja-da)

Fig. 4. Extraction of sense-to-word mapping from translation definitions

To calculate the sense probability and the word probability, one word should be extracted as translation. To get one-word translations, we analyze a translation definition morphologically and, if it is composed of more than one word, extract a headword. For instance, the phrase 'yeoljungha-ke ha-da' is shortened to 'yeoljungha-da' because '-ke ha-' is an auxiliary verb phrase.

Although a headword of a translation definition generally has a representative meaning of an entry word, some headwords do not have meaningful senses. For instance, while 'ha-da' that is a light verb meaning do is the syntactic head of 'junbi-reul ha-da' (meaning make preparation), it has no effect on the sense of 'arrange'. To get more appropriate translation, we remove meaningless words from translation definitions, and rearrange the remaining words. For this purpose, we made a list of meaningless words and rearranging heuristics, which includes 'X-reul ha-da (meaning do X) → Xha-da' and 'X-han sangtae (meaning X state) → X'. Using them, 'junbi-reul ha-da' is reduced to one word 'junbiha-da' (meaning prepare).

Furthermore, we use example sentences, in that source and target sentences are aligned, to extract sense-to-word mapping that does not appear in translation definitions. To extract translations of an entry word from its example sentences, we use simple heuristics that utilizes part of speech (POS) tags and translation words extracted from translation definitions, as follows:

Step 1) Find Korean translations of each word in an English example sentence using sense-to-word mapping extracted from translation definitions.

Step 2) If an aligned Korean example sentence has a Korean translation that is identified in Step 1 as a translation of an entry word, choose it as a translation.

Step 3) If there exist Korean words that are not matched by translation definitions and only one of them has a POS that is compatible with the POS of an entry word, choose it as a translation word.

For example, the third sense of arrange ($arrange^3$) has four example sentences in a dictionary and the sentence (1) below is one of them. In the sentence, 'maryeonha-da' is extracted as a translation of 'catch' in Step 3, which does not appears in translation definitions of $arrange^3$ in Fig. 4.

(1) "arrange a marriage for someone"
   amu-ui   honsa-ruel   maryeonha-da.
   someone-POSSESS   marriage-OBJECT   arrange-DECLARATIVE

Knowledge for Syntactic Relation Mapping. In some cases, a syntactic relation between words is changed in the process of translation. In the sentence (2), the relation between words 'catch' and 'disease' in an English sentence is V-OBJ, which corresponds to V-CMP in a Korean sentence with a postposition 'e'.

(2) "His son <u>catches a disease</u>."
   keu-ui   adeul-i   byeong-e   geolli-da.
   he-POSSESS   son-SUBJECT   disease-COMPLEMENT   catch-DECLARATIVE

As shown in Fig. 1, a mono-bilingual dictionary provides aligned example sentences in a source language and a target language. From them we extract information for syntactic relation mapping for all predicates (verbs and adjectives) by the following step.

Step 1) Find dependents of a predicate in an English example sentence.
Step 2) Look up all translations of each dependent from sense-to-word mapping.
Step 3) If an aligned Korean example sentence contains only one translation of a dependent, choose its postposition as a mapping relation.

From the sentence (2), the syntatic relation between 'catch' and its object in English is mapped into a Korean postposition 'e', since 'disease' is an object of 'catch' and '*byeong*' is a translation of 'disease'.

4.2   Extraction of Word Co-occurrence from Target Language Corpora

To compute the sense probability and the word probability, we use target word co-occurrence with its syntactic relation. Figure 5 shows some co-occurrences extracted from Korean corpora. Given two target words t_i and t_j, $f(t_i, t_j, c)$ denotes the frequency of co-occurring t_i and t_j with a syntactic relation c. For example, $f(jap\text{-}da, byeong, e)$ is 4 in Fig. 5.

We extract syntactic tuples from raw corpora based on the method proposed by Yoon [13]. He extracted co-occurrences with a rule-based partial parser and acquired meaningful co-occurrences based on *z-score*.

head	dependent	relation	freq.
butdeul-da (붙들다, capture) /V	*somae* (소매, sleeve) /N	*reul* (V-OBJ)	4
jap-da (잡다, capture) /V	*byeong*(병, bottle) /N	*reul* (V-OBJ)	6
geolli-da (걸리다, infected) /V	*byeong*(병, disease) /N	*e* (V-CMP)	429
wijungha-da (위중하다, serious) /J	*byeong*(병, disease) /N	*ga* (J-SBJ)	4
geolli-da (걸리다, infected) /V	*gamgi*(감기, cold)/N	*e* (V-CMP)	169
yebang (예방, prevention)/N	*gamgi*(감기, cold)/N	φ (N-modN)	1

Fig. 5. Extraction of word co-occurrence from a Korean corpus

5   Calculation of Translation Preference

Using knowledge extracted from a dictionary and target language corpora, we calculate the translation preference for each target word by combining the sense preference, the sense probability and the word probability.

5.1 Sense Preference

The sense preference is obtained by calculating similarity between words in an input sentence and clues for sense disambiguation. Let us suppose that the i-th word in an input sentence is s_i and the k-th sense of s_i is s_i^k. Given s_i and s_i^k, we calculate the sense preference $spf(s_i^k)$ by (1). In the equation, SNT is a set of all content words except s_i in an input sentence. $DEF_{s_i^k}$ and $EX_{s_i^k}$ are the sets of words in sense definitions and examples respectively as defined in the previous section. $|EX_{s_i^k}|$ is the number of elements in $EX_{s_i^k}$. For all words in an input sentence ($w_j \in SNT$), we sum up the maximum similarity between w_i and all clue words (i.e. w_d and w_e).

$$spf(s_i^k) = \sum_{w_j \in SNT} \left(\frac{\max\limits_{w_d \in DEF_{s_i^k}} sim(w_j, w_d)}{|DEF_{s_i^k}|} + \frac{\max\limits_{w_e \in EX_{s_i^k}} sim(w_j, w_e)}{|EX_{s_i^k}|} \right) . \quad (1)$$

As senses in a dictionary are ordered by significance in most cases, the order of senses generally reflects the frequency of each sense. To reflect distribution of senses in real text, we use a weight factor $\phi(s_i^k)$ that is inversely proportional to the order of a sense s_i^k in a dictionary. Then we normalize the sense preference.

$$spf_w(s_i^k) = \phi(s_i^k) \cdot \frac{spf(s_i^k)}{\sum_x spf(s_i^x)} . \qquad spf_{norm}(s_i^k) = \frac{spf_w(s_i^k)}{\sum_x spf_w(s_i^x)} . \quad (2)$$

5.2 Sense Probability

The sense probability represents how likely target words with the same sense co-occur with translations of other words in an input sentence. Given an input word s_i and its sense s_i^k, the sense probability $sp(s_i^k)$ is computed as follows:

$$n(t_{iq}^k) = \sum_{(s_j, m, c) \in \Theta(s_i)} \sum_{p=1}^{m} \frac{f(t_{iq}^k, t_{jp}, c)}{f(t_{iq}^k) + f(t_{jp})} . \qquad sp(s_i^k) = \frac{\sum_q n(t_{iq}^k)}{\sum_x \sum_y n(t_{iy}^x)} . \quad (3)$$

In the equation, $\Theta(s_i)$ signifies a set of co-occurrences of a word s_i on a syntactic relation. In an element (s_j, m, c) of $\Theta(s_i)$, s_j is a word that co-occurs with s_i in an input sentence, c is a syntactic relation between s_i and s_j, and m is the number of translations of s_j. Given the set of translation of a sense s_i^k is $T(s_i^k)$ and a member of $T(s_i^k)$ is t_{iq}^k, the frequency of co-occurring t_{iq}^k and t_{jp} with a syntactic relation c is denoted as $f(t_{iq}^k, t_{jp}, c)$. In (3), $n(t_{iq}^k)$ represents how frequently t_{iq}^k co-occurs with translations of s_j. By summing up $n(t_{iq}^k)$ for all target words in $T(s_i^k)$, we obtain the sense probability of a sense s_i^k.

5.3 Word Probability

The word probability represents how frequently a target word in a sense division co-occurs, in a corpus, with translations of other words of an input sentence. We denote the word probability by $wp(t_{iq}^k)$ that is a probability of selecting t_{iq}^k from $T(s_i^k)$. Using $n(t_{iq}^k)$ in (3), we calculate the word probability as follows:

$$wp(t_{iq}^k) = \frac{n(t_{iq}^k)}{\sum_x n(t_{ix}^k)} \ . \tag{4}$$

5.4 Translation Preference

To select a target word among all translations of a source word, we compute preference for each translation by merging the sense preference, the sense probability and the word probability. In (5), δ is a weighting factor for the sense preference and $\eta(T_i^k)$ is a normalizing factor for $wp(t_{iq}^k)$. We select a target word with the highest tpf as a translation.

$$tpf(t_{iq}^k) = (\delta \cdot spf_{norm}(s_i^k) + (1-\delta) \cdot sp(s_i^k)) \cdot \ wp(t_{iq}^k)/\eta(T_i^k) \ . \tag{5}$$

6 Evaluation

6.1 Environment

The EssEEKD [10] was used as a mono-bilingual dictionary. We converted it into a machine-readable form, which has about 43,000 entries. From the MRD, we extracted knowledge for sense disambiguation and mapping information between English and Korean. Co-occurrence data in Korean were extracted from the Yonsei Corpus, the KAIST Corpus and the Sejong Corpus. We used only reliable co-occurrences with high confidence among the extracted co-occurrences. As a result, the number of co-occurrences used is about 600,000.

We used Brill's tagger to analyze English sentences. When calculating the sense probability and the word probability, we used syntactic relations between words. Syntactic relations in English sentences were deduced from the results of Memory-Based Shallow Parser [11].

We evaluated our method for five English verbs – reach, enter, answer, catch and win. We used the same evaluation method with Lee and Kim [8], which extracts an evaluation set from aligned sentences by utilizing a bilingual lexicon to exclude any kind of human intervention during evaluation. From sentences in an English-Korean aligned corpus that include one of the five verbs and satisfy the condition for the evaluation set, 101 sentences were randomly chosen as an evaluation set for sense disambiguation and translation selection.

6.2 Results

We evaluated the results of our method for knowledge extraction, sense disambiguation and translation selection.

Extraction of Sense-to-Word Mapping. As we explained in Sect. 4, we extracted target words that correspond to each sense of a source word from translation definitions and aligned example sentences in a mono-bilingual dictionary. To evaluate the accuracy of sense-to-word mapping extraction, we randomly chose 200 translation definitions and example sentences and tested whether correct translation words are extracted from each of them.

In extraction of words from translation definitions, our method scores the precision of 90.3%. Most errors occur from translation definitions with more than one word. The percentage of extracting meaningless or irrelevant words is 8.21%. The percentage of extracting wrong translation is 1.49% that is mainly caused by mistake in expanding bracket expressions or POS tagging. The total error rate is about 10% and, as extracted translations were used for translation selection without modification, those errors influenced the accuracy of translation selection.

In extraction of translation words from aligned example sentences, 54,401 Korean words are extracted from 60,833 example sentences, thus our method scores the coverage 89.43%. Among them, 51.6% are extracted using translation definitions and 37.83% are extracted by heuristics. The precision of extraction using translation definitions is 100%, and the recall is 97.95%. The precision of translation extraction using heuristics is 81.90% and the recall is 86.87%. Although simple heuristics is used to extract target words from aligned sentences, we gain high precision and recall by utilizing translation definitions properly. Furthermore, word alignment is much easier in example sentences than sentences in a bilingual corpus since example sentences in a dictionary are simple and short, which seems to serve for heightening precision.

To evaluate usefulness of extracted sense-to-word mapping, we made a test of aligning words in an English-Korean bilingual corpus. Among 177,753 English content words in a bilingual corpus, 50.56% were matched by translation words extracted from translation definitions. When we used translations from both translation definitions and example sentences, the percentage increased to 54.36%. Unmatched are mainly caused by 1:n, n:1 or n:m word mapping, idiomatic expressions and shortage of translations in a dictionary.

Sense Disambiguation. For sense disambiguation, we used two measures: sense preference (spf) and sense probability (sp). The accuracy of each measure was evaluated by testing whether any target word of the sense that scores the highest value is identified as translation of its source word in an aligned target sentence. The result of sense disambiguation with the sense preference is similar to Lee and Kim [8], so results with clue words in example sentences and with the order of sense score the best precision 67.33%.

The accuracy of the sense probability is shown in Table 1. In the equation (3) for the sense probability, we used word co-occurrences that are syntactically related in an input sentence. In the table, the results in the column named case cooc word were obtained by using words on a syntactic relation in English, and those named target case word were obtained by using words on a syntactic relation in Korean, which are switched by altering a syntactic relation c in the equation (3). The results in the row with without translations from examples were obtained by using translation words extracted from translation definitions, and those with with translations from examples were obtained by using translation words extracted from both translation definitions and aligned example sentences.

The results show that use of syntactic relations in Korean absolutely increases the accuracy of sense disambiguation. However, translation words extracted from example sentences decrease accuracy because some incorrect translation words from example sentences work as noise in computing the sense probability and the word probability.

Table 1. Accuracy of the sense probability (sp)

	case cooc word	target case word
without translations from examples	40.59%	57.43%
with translations from examples	27.72%	46.53%

Translation selection. Table 2 shows the result of translation selection. The experiment was conducted with altering the combination of the sense preference, the sense probability and the word probability. When calculating each measure, we used the best combination of clues (without translations from examples for the sense probability and the word probability). The $sp \times wp$ column is the result from combining the sense probability and the word probability by assigning 0 to δ in the equation (5), and the $spf \times wp$ column is the result from combining the sense preference and the word probability. The $(spf+sp) \times wp$ column is the result from combining all measures, which is obtained by assigning 0.7 to δ. The wp column is the result using only the word probability, which is obtained by assuming all translations of a source word have the same sense. The results in the row with case cooc word were obtain by using words on a syntactic relation in English, and those with target case word were obtain by using words on a syntactic relation in Korean. As baseline results, we set two types : BASE-I is a result of random selection and BASE-II is a result of selecting most frequent translation.

Table 2. Accuracy of translation selection

	BASE-I	BASE-II	wp	$sp \times wp$	$spf \times wp$	$(spf+sp) \times wp$
case cooc word	2.74%	23.76%	19.80%	20.79%	40.59%	22.77%
target case word			39.60%	40.59%	60.40%	41.58%

For all cases, the results using syntactic relations in a target language are superior to the results using syntactic relations in a source language. In the experiment, the combination of the sense preference and the word probability (*spf*× *wp* column) gets higher accuracy than the result only using the word probability (*wp* column) and the combination with the sense probability (*sp*× *wp* and (*spf*+ *sp*)× *wp* columns). This shows that our sense disambiguation method based on knowledge from a mono-bilingual dictionary works better than that based on target word co-occurrence. For the best case, the accuracy of our method for verbs is 60.40%, thus we increase the precision 52.53% by combining the sense preference and the word probability, and 48.8% by using syntactic relations in a target language.

The results in Table 2 are measured by an automatic evaluation method, in which a selected translation is treated as incorrect if it is not exactly the same as a word in an aligned target language sentence. When measured manually, the accuracy of our result with *spf*× *wp* and target case word is about 79%. In manual evaluation, translation is evaluated as correct if it satisfies both fidelity and intelligibility (i.e. reflects the precise meaning of an input word and composes a fluent target sentence), so a selected word is exactly replaceable with its correspondence in an aligned target sentence.

7   Conclusion

In this paper, we proposed to extract knowledge from a mono-bilingual dictionary for a 'word-to-sense and sense-to-word' translation selection method. We extracted clues for sense disambiguation and syntactic relation mapping between source and target languages, and by utilizing them, our method increases the accuracies of sense disambiguation and translation selection.

Although example sentences in a dictionary seems to be good sources for extracting sense-to-word mapping, they increase the coverage of word alignment slightly and even decrease the accuracies of sense disambiguation and translation selection. We expect to refine our knowledge extraction method and expand it to *n*:*m* word mapping by utilizing other information in a dictionary.

References

1. W. John Hutchins and Harold L. Somers, "An Introduction to Machine Translation", Academic Press, 1992
2. Ann Copestake, Ted Briscoe, Piek Vossen, Alicia Ageno, Irene Casteloon, Grancesc Ribas, German Rigau, Horacio Rodrìguez and Anna Samiotou, "Acquisition of lexical translation relations from MRDs", *Machine Translation*, Vol.9, No.3, 1995
3. Judith Klavans and Evelyne Tzoukermann, "Combining corpus and machine-readable dictionary data for building bilingual lexicons", *Machine Translation*, Vol.10, No.3, 1996
4. Peter F. Brown, John Cocke, Vincent Della Pietra, Stephen Della Pietra, Frederick Jelinek, John D. Lafferty, Robert L. Mercer and Paul S. Roossin, "A Statistical Approach to Machine Translation", *Computational Linguistics*, Vol.16, No.2, 1990
5. Ido Dagan and Alon Itai, "Word Sense Disambiguation Using a Second Language Monoligual Corpus", *Computational Linguistics*, Vol.20, No.4, 1994

6. Detlef Prescher, Stefan Riezler and Mats Rooth, "Using a Probabilistic Class-Based Lexicon for Lexical Ambiguity Resolution", In *Proceedings of the 18th International Conference on Computational Linguistics (COLING)*, 2000

7. Philipp Koehn and Kevin Knight, "Knowledge Sources for Word-Level Translation Models", In *Proceedings of Empirical Methods in Natural Language Processing conference (EMNLP)*, 2001

8. Hyun Ah Lee and Gil Chang Kim, "Translation Selection through Source Word Sense Disambiguation and Target Word Selection", In *Proceedings of the 19th International Conference on Computational Linguistics (COLING)*, 2002

9. Susan W. McRoy, "Using Multiple Knowledge Sources for Word Sense Discrimination", *Computational Linguistics*, Vol.18, No.1, 1992

10. EssEEKD, "Essence English-English Korean Dictionary", MinJung SeoRim, 1995

11. Walter Daelemans, Sabine Buchholz and Jorn Veenstra, "Memory-Based Shallow Parsing", In *Proceedings of the 3rd International Workshop on Computational Natural Language Learning (CoNLL)*, 1999

12. Jae-Hoon Kim and Gil Chang Kim, "Fuzzy Network Model for Part-of-Speech Tagging under Small Training Data", *Natural Language Engineering*, Vol.2, No.2, 1996

13. Juntae Yoon, "Efficient Dependency Analysis for Korean Sentences Based on Lexical Association and Multi-layered Chunking", *Literary and Linguistic Computing*, Vol.16, No.3, 2001

Source Language Effect
on Translating Korean Honorifics

Kyonghee Paik[1], Kiyonori Ohtake[1], Francis Bond[2], and Kazuhide Yamamoto[1,3]

[1] ATR Spoken Language Translation Research Laboratories
2-2-2 Hikaridai "Keihanna Science City", Kyoto 619-0288 JAPAN
{kyonghee.paik, kiyonori.ohtake}@atr.co.jp
[2] Nippon Telegraph and Telephone Corporation
2-4 Hikaridai, "Keihanna Science City", Kyoto 619-0237 JAPAN
bond@cslab.kecl.ntt.co.jp
[3] Nagaoka University of Technology
1603-1 Kamitomioka, Nagaoka City, Niigata 940-2188 JAPAN
yamamoto@fw.ipsj.or.jp

Abstract. This paper investigates honorific phenomena on two variants of Korean translation corpus, based on translations from Japanese and English. One surprising result is how different the corpora were, even after normalizing orthographic differences. Translations are dependent not just meaning, but also on the structure of the source text.

1 Introduction

This paper investigates the effect of source language on honorifics in translations using two variants of a Korean translation corpus. The original corpus was compiled from Japanese-English parallel sentences collected from phrase books for Japanese traveling abroad. The corpora used for this research consist of 324,616 Korean sentences. Half of the Korean sentences (162,308 sentences: henceforth, K_J) were translated from Japanese and the other half (henceforth, K_E) have been translated from English sentences which match the Japanese.

Although the two Korean corpora are generally equivalent in meaning, they have different characteristics, since they were translated from such different languages as English and Japanese. We show that the differences between English and Japanese lead to different results in the Korean translation, even though the original source texts were matching Japanese-English translation pairs.

Our ultimate goal is to find the differences in translations by comparing two variants with different source texts in order to improve the quality of machine translation. So far such comparison has not been extensively studied.

2 Honorifics in Japanese and Korean

Korean is an honorific language with an extremely systematic grammaticalization. A sentence cannot be uttered without the speaker's knowledge of their

A. Gelbukh (Ed.): CICLing 2004, LNCS 2945, pp. 334–337, 2004.
© Springer-Verlag Berlin Heidelberg 2004

social relationship to the addressee and referent considering social status, age, kinship, familiarity and so on. Otherwise, the utterance may sound rude, inappropriate, or even awkward (Sohn 1999, p.16).

Japanese honorifics are also expressed by various forms according to the degree of honor or respect, addressee, or situation. Like Korean, Japanese can make nouns and verbs honorific using different lexical items or adding prefixes and suffixes. For verbal constructions, Japanese uses *o/go- V ni naru* "do" (subject honorific) and *o/go -V suru* "do" (addressee honorific (humble)) as well as two different speech levels of verb endings: *da* (plain) *desu* (polite) (Kaiser et al 2001). Korean uses verbal suffixes *-si* to make subject honorifics and *-sup* to make addressee honorifics, along with six different speech levels.

There are many mismatches between the two systems from Japanese to Korean. For example, Japanese beautifies nouns *o-* or *go-* before nouns like *o-saifu* "wallet", *o-sio* "salt", *go-tsugo* "convenience". However, Korean does not have a corresponding system to this. As for verb honorifics at speech levels, Korean has six different levels whereas Japanese has only two levels. This will cause mistakes in machine translation between the two languages.

3   Analysis of Our Corpora

We compared sentences using the perl module `String::Similarity` (Lehman 2000). It returns a similarity score based on the edit distance (the number of characters that need to be deleted, added or substituted to change one string into another), normalized to give a score between 0 and 1 (see Meyers (1986) for a fuller description). Two completely different strings have a score of zero, while two identical strings have a score of one. There were 136,529 sentences. Their distribution is given in Table 1. As there were many identical sentences in each corpus, we give the distribution over both all sentences and unique sentences. Less than 2% of the sentences were the same in both corpora. Most sentences were reasonably similar (0.4–0.8). Very few sentences were identical (less than 4%) and even fewer were totally dissimilar (less than 0.1%). There were some minor orthographic differences. When they were resolved, only 8.3% of the sentences were identical. To put this in perspective, Culy and Riehemann (2003) discuss the fact that there is considerable variation in translations from exactly the same source text. It is impossible to explicitly compare their results for two reasons: (1) they are looking at more literary texts, where the translators certainly were aware of the previous translations and trying to differentiate their own; (2) they do not quantify the differences using the same measure as us.

We took one percent of the unique sentences for each of 9 similarity bands from 0.1–0.2 to 0.9–1.0 for more detailed evaluation. The sample size was proportional to the number of sentences in each band — so the samples are small at each extreme and large in the center. We evaluated 1,360 randomly chosen sample sentences and all 58 sentences of the least similar band (0.0–0.1).

Since our corpora deals with the topics related to various travel situations, there are numerous sentences inquiring and trying to get information which are

Table 1. Distribution of the sentences by similarity score

	Similarity Score										
	0-0.1	0.1-0.2	0.2-0.3	0.3-0.4	0.4-0.5	0.5-0.6	0.6-0.7	0.7-0.8	0.8-0.9	0.9-1.0	Total
S_{all}	100	1,910	11,006	23,126	33,755	34,888	28,083	17,400	7,693	4,347	162,308
S_{uniq}	58	1,243	7,876	19,351	29,053	30,149	24,382	14,946	6,434	3,037	136,529

uttered using polite or deferential forms of interrogatives in most cases. The different use of adjectives, adverbs, or their phrases are also found all through different similarity scores. These phenomena form a useful source for learning lexical paraphrasing rules for example-based paraphrasing.

We found strikingly different distributions in K_J and K_E with regard to honorifics, which are shown in Table 2 and discussed below.

Table 2. Honorific differences between K_J and K_E

		Similarity Score									
		0.0-0.1	0.1-0.2	0.2-0.3	0.3-0.4	0.4-0.5	0.5-0.6	0.6-0.7	0.7-0.8	0.8-0.9	0.9-1.0
Samples		58	12	78	192	290	300	243	149	64	30
Honorific	(K_J)	4	1	10	16	82	101	76	32	11	2
Honorific	(K_E)	2	0	8	15	20	32	31	9	2	0
Loan word	(K_J)	0	0	5	16	14	15	7	6	0	0
Loan word	(K_E)	0	0	0	7	11	9	11	3	0	0

The differences shown in Table 2 mainly arise from the fact that K_J tends to use more deferential honorifics whereas the K_E tends to use more polite honorifics, although this distinction is not made in either English or Japanese. Even so, the source language affects the degree or level of honorifics. For example, K_E tend to use polite speech levels like – 요 –(B -yo where as K_J tend to use deferential forms like – 습니까 – (B -(su)pnika for asking questions. This systematic difference makes these two corpora a suitable source for the automatic acquisition of paraphrasing rules. The difference in honorific use is strongly shown in the bands from 0.4 to 0.9. In general, K_J used more honorifics than K_E overall, and the effect was to make it a more natural collection of travel phrases.

As we have seen, the source language has a large effect on the translation, although we have focused on honorifics in this paper. This suggests that the optimal translation strategy may be different between language pairs. In particular, a system translating between Japanese and Korean needs to put less effort into lexical and syntactic choice, and more into the use of honorifics. A system going between English and Korean has a much harder task, and must consider lexical and syntactic choice, zero pronoun resolution in addition to the use of honorifics.

Differences in honorific usage appeared to be fairly predictable between the two corpora, and lead to the hope that a paraphrasing module can be used to fix the honorific levels after translation itself occurs, along the lines suggested by Ohtake and Yamamoto (2001).

Another interesting difference was in the distribution of borrowed words or foreign words from languages other than Chinese. We expected that more loan words would be used in K_E because most loan words come from English. However, according to Table 2 the result is the opposite. Further, the loan words translated from Japanese, were in general more natural (73%) than those translated from English (50%). After examining the source corpora of K_J, we found that many "Katakana" loan words are used in the Japanese corpus. Almost all of the Katakana words are translated into loan words in Korean. In contrast, all the English words are equally foreign, so for any word, there is little pressure for it to be translated into a loan word, rather than into native Korean. When English words were translated as loan words, they tended to be poor literal translations.

4 Conclusion and Further Work

We investigated two variants of a Korean translation corpus, based on translations from Japanese and English. We have shown that the source language text has a large influence on the target text. One surprising result is how different the corpora were, even after normalizing orthographic differences. In practice, translations are dependent not just on meaning, but also on the structure of the source text. We find that the expressions on honorifics which were examined using similarity scores are reliable resources for paraphrasing.

Based on these findings, we intend to examine whether we can automatically extract grammatical, semantic and lexical paraphrases by comparing corpora using similarity scores.

Acknowledgement. This research was supported in part by the Telecommunications Advancement Organization of Japan.

References

Culy, C. & S. Z. Riehemann: 2003, "The limits of N-gram translation evaluation metrics", in *Proceedings of MT Summit IX*, New Orleans.

Kaiser, Stefan, Y. Ichikawa, N. Kobayashi & H. Yamamoto: 2001, *Japanese: A Comprehensive Grammar*, Routledge.

Lehmann, Marc: 2000, "String::Similarity", Perl Module (cpan.org), (v0.02).

Myers, Eugene: 1986, "An O(ND) difference algorithm and its variations", *Algorithmica*, **1**(2): 251–266.

Ohtake, Kiyonori & Kazuhide Yamamoto: 2001, "Paraphrasing honorifics", in *NLPRS-2001*, Tokyo, pp. 13–20.

Sohn, Ho-Min: 1999, *The Korean Language*, Cambridge Language Surveys, Cambridge University Press.

An Algorithm for Determining DingYu Structural Particle Using Grammar Knowledge and Statistical Information

Fuji Ren

Faculty of Engineering, Tokushima University
Tokushima, 770-8506 Japan
ren@is.tokushima-u.ac.jp

Abstract. In a machine translation system from one language to Chinese, it is difficult to decide whether there is a structural particle "DE" between the "DingYu" and the "ZhongXinCi". The DingYu is a term in Chinese grammar which resembles the modifier and the attributive words or phrases in English or Japanese, but not the same. The ZhongXinCi is refered to the word modified by DingYu. Nowadays a practical Japanese-Chinese machine translation system based on translation rules has been implemented. However, the current system lacks the ability for resolving the problem mentioned above. To resolve this problem, this paper presents an algorithm for determining DingYu structural particle using the grammar knowledge and statidtical information. We first collect a large number of grammar items from Chinese grammar books, and obtain some elementary judgment rules by classifying and inducing the collected grammar items. Then we put these judgment rules into use in actual Chinese language, and modify the rules by checking their results instantly. Lastly we check and modify the rules by using the statistical information from a actual corpus. An experiment system based on the proposed algorithm has been constructed and an experiment is carried out. The result shows the effectiveness of the presented method.

1 Introduction

The machine translation for practical use has been developed rapidly these days[2,3]. The Japanese-Chinese and English-Chinese translations using machines are also being studied actively for the last several years[6,8,9,10,11]. However, there are many unsolved problems that need to be further explored for Chinese processing. We are studying and developing of Japanese-Chinese machine translation based on the linguistic characteristics of the languages. This paper discusses a problem which will occur in case of machine translation for Chinese language, presents an algorithm for determining Chinese "DingYu"[1]

---

[1] In this paper, Roman alphabet is used to indicate the Chinese character. For example, *ji* indicates a Chinese character, and *ji suan ji* indicate three Chinese characters (meaning "computer"). Notice that the first *ji* and the last *ji* are written in different Chinese characters, although they are written same in the Roman alphabets.

A. Gelbukh (Ed.): CICLing 2004, LNCS 2945, pp. 338–349, 2004.
© Springer-Verlag Berlin Heidelberg 2004

structural particle "DE" and, shows the results of experiments based on the proposed algorithm.

Incidentally, "DingYu" is a Chinese grammatical term. Since it is similar to attributive word or adjunct in English or Japanese language, but not the same, in this paper the Chinese grammatical term "DingYu" is adopted. In the simplest explanation, DingYu can qualify ZhongXinCi[2] in various ways, however, the semantic relations between DingYu and ZhongXinCi are very complicated if we examine them closely. A structural particle "DE" often comes after DingYu but we cannot say that it always does. Whether "DE" comes after the DingYu or not depends on the relation between the characteristics of the words which are used as a DingYu and the grammatical meaning of DingYu.

There are two structural forms as follows in DingYu. Here, DY indicates DingYu and ZXC indicates the ZhongXinCi.

$$DY + ZXC \tag{1}$$

$$DY + "DE" + ZXC \tag{2}$$

According to our research, no perfect solution to the issue has found yet and, at present most of the practical systems are asking their users to edit later. To solve this problem we used the semantic structural technique for "Y no X" which is suggested for the analysis of Japanese language[7] and tried to apply it to the Japanese-Chinese machine translation system, however, it did not turn out successfully. The usage of "DE" is considered to be formed by the linguistic custom. So, we decided to separate this issue from the original language and deal with it on the side of the object language. This approach might be useful for the multilingual machine translation.

Theoretically, the method proposed in the paper is language independent, however, for the comparative explanation, the issue is discussed related with Japanese language in many parts of the paper.

We picked out 248 phrases with DY and ZXC from 120,000 sentences obtained through the Japanese-Chinese machine translation and also 255 phrases from a corpus of 200,000 sentences originally written in Chinese. These phrases were used for the experiments to analyze the usage of "DE". As the result the 93% correct answers were obtained and proved the efficiency of the method.

In the following, Section 2 introduces the function and the grammatical meaning of the Chinese DingYu. Section 3 describes the structural features of DingYu and shows the differences between adjective modifiers in Japanese and in Chinese. Section 4 presents the algorithm for determining Chinese structural particle DE. Section 5 explains the methods used for the experiments and their evaluations.

---

[2] ZhongXinCi is a grammatical term in Chinese language, In this paper it means a word which is qualified by the DingYu.

2   Function and Grammatical Meaning of DingYu

DingYu of the Chinese language, which is one of the qualifiers, is used to qualify the noun. DingYu also qualifies the subject and the object of the sentence. Different from Japanese language[5,4], the adjective modifier in Chinese language also qualifies the verbs and the adjectives which become the subjects or the objects of the sentences. Like the Japanese modifier, DingYu always comes in front of the ZhongXinCi except when there is a specific rhetorical command.

DingYu can qualify ZhongXinCi from the various aspects. The grammatical meanings of DingYu, or in other words, the semantic relations between DingYu and ZhongXinCi can be very complicated, however, at least they can be basically categorized into two: the attributive and the descriptive. In the following, we will discuss these two meanings of DingYu which take important roles in dealing with DingYu .

2.1   The Attributive DingYu

The attributive DingYu explains ZhongXinCi from the aspects of quantity, time, location, belonging, dimension, etc. The following examples are to see the characteristics of the attributive DingYu.

(1) Aquantity
   Ex.1: hen duo xue sheng zai cao chang shang duan lian shen ti.
   /Many students are training on the athletic field.
   In the above sentence "hen duo /many" is DingYu qualifying ZhongXinCi "xue sheng /students" . In the examples in the paper, the underlined words indicate DingYu and the meshed words indicate ZhongXinCi.

(2) Time
   Ex.2: ta gei wo jiang le yi bian guo qu de qing kuang.
   /He told me the previous situations.

(3) Location
   Ex3: shu bao li de shu shi wo cong tu shu guan jie lai de.
   /The book in the bag is the one I borrowed from the library.

(4) Belonging
   Ex4: zhe shi ling mu de ge ren ji suan ji.
   /This is Mr. Suzuki's personal computer.

(5) Dimension
   Ex.5: ta men zhong jian de duo shu hui jue wu guo lai.
   /Many of them will wake up.

2.2   The Descriptive DingYu

The descriptive DingYu explains ZhongXinCi from the aspects of nature, situation, characteristic, application, material, profession, etc.

(1) Nature /Situation

Ex.6: zhe shi yi ge fei chang zhong yao de hui yi.

/This is a very important | meeting |.

(2) Characteristic

Ex.7: ta shi yi ge lei li feng xing de ren.

/He is a | person | of stern and prompt action.

(3) Application

Ex.8: wo mai yi zhi hua hua yong de qian bi.

/I want to buy a | pencil | to draw a picture.

(4) Material

Ex.9: zhi xiang zi li zhuang man le shu.

/There are full of books in the cardboard | box |.

(5) Profession

Ex.10: ling mu de fu qin shi han yu lao shi.

/Mr. Suzuki's father is a Chinese language | teacher |.

A【Japanese】	+	ZXC【Japanese】	(a)
N【Japanese】	+	ZXC【Japanese】	(b)
N【Japanese】	+ no +	ZXC【Japanese】	(c)
V【Japanese】	+	ZXC【Japanese】	(d)

Fig. 1. Structure of Japanese Modifier

3   Structural Features

Generally the structures of the Japanese modifier and the Chinese DingYu can be indicated as Figure1 and 2 respectively. In the figures, "A" is adjective, "N" is noun, "V" is verb, "D" is adverb, "O" is onomatopoeia, "P_{phr}" is phrase of preposition and ZXC indicates ZhongXinCi.

In Chinese language the basic sentence structure consists of SVO. When there are other elements between the verb and the ZhongXinCi, the extra treatments will be required. In such a case, the verb function will be shown as $V(\alpha)$.

Chinese language often accompanies a structural particle "DE" after DingYu and whether the "DE" is necessary or not depends on the characteristics of the words /phrases that consist of DingYu and also the grammatical meanings of DingYu. We finalized the rules by referring to Chinese grammar books and research materials and also by using a corpus.

Section 3 examined the features of both Chinese DingYu and Japanese modifiers. Especially the usage of structural particle of the Chinese language "DE" was studied about its application system from the documents, and generative rules were induced. As the result, conclusions are obtained as follows:

(1) The information of semantic classification can not be judged correctly the necessity of the Chinese structural particle "DE". As a matter of fact it is also very difficult to obtain the semantic classification.
(2) It is difficult to judge whether "DE" is necessary or not simply from the structure of the modifiers of both languages.
(3) It seems more effective to judge the necessity of "DE" from the Japanese text than from the Chinese text.
(4) The corpus derived some of the judging rules for the necessity of "DE". Section 4 refers to the judging algorism for the necessity of "DE".

```
A 【Chinese】   +  ZXC 【Chinese】          (1)
A 【Chinese】   +  ZXC 【Chinese】          (2)
N 【Chinese】   +  ZXC 【Chinese】          (3)
N 【Chinese】 + de + ZXC 【Chinese】        (4)
V(α) 【Chinese】   +  ZXC 【Chinese】       (5)
V(α) 【Chinese】 + de + ZXC 【Chinese】     (6)
D 【Chinese】 + de + ZXC 【Chinese】        (7)
O 【Chinese】 + de + ZXC 【Chinese】        (8)
P_phr 【Chinese】 + de + ZXC 【Chinese】    (9)
```

Fig. 2. Structure of Chinese Dingyu

4   Judging Method of the Structural Particle "DE"

4.1   Gist of the Judging Method

The gist of the judgment for the necessity of the structural particle "DE" in the Chinese DingYu is as follows:

(1) Prepare the judging rules for the necessity of "DE" in advance.
(2) Extract DingYu and ZhongXinCi.
(3) Search the feature of DingYu.
(4) Collate the feature of DingYu with the judging rule obtained in (1).
(5) If required, search the attribute of the ZhongXinCi.
(6) If required, confirm the additional condition introduced in (1).
(7) Decide the necessity of the structural particle "DE".

Table 1 shows the judging rule which is made on the purpose of explanation, the information needs to be coded through the inductive joint for the effective use when the information is installed in the system.

The next explains the points to judge the necessity of the structural particle "DE".

Table 1. Rules for Determining Structural Particle DE

No.	Class	Kind of Modifier	Attribution of ZhonXinCi	Additional Condition Use of DE
0	Default			
1	Quantifier	Borrowed Measure Word		Definitive Function
2	Quantifier	Quantifier		Descriptive Function
3	Quantifier	"man" meaning "full"		Descriptive Function
4	Quantifier	Particle		
5	Quantifier	Repeated Pharases of Quantifier with Numeral "one" and Measure Word		
6	Quantifier			Descriptie Function
7	Quantifier			Definitive Function
8	Quantifier	Quantifier Pharase, Numeral and Measure Word		Definitive Function
9	Quantifier	Repeated Measure Word		
10	Quantifier	Special Part of Speech such as "some" or "many"		
11	Pronoun	Pronoun "bie"		
12	Pronoun	Pronoun "shui"		Belong Relation
13	Pronoun	Pronoun		Descriptive Function
14	Pronoun	Demonstrative Pronoun		Definitive Function
15	Pronoun	Interrogative Pronoun		Definitive Function
16	Pronoun	Phrase with 13,14 and Quantifier		Definitive Function
17	Pronoun	Personal Pronoun		Belong Relation
18	Pronoun	Personal Pronoun	Name for Person	
19	Pronoun	Personal Pronoun	Name for Group /Organization	
20	Pronoun	Personal Pronoun	Direction Word	
21	Noun	Noun		Belong Relation
22	Noun	Noun	Direction Word	
23	Noun	Noun		Descriptive Function
24	Noun	Noun indicating Material		Descriptive Function
25	Noun	Noun indicating Profession		Descriptive Function
26	Noun	Noun + Sex		
27	Adjective	Adjective(Mono syllable)		Attribute Relation
28	Adjective	Adjective(Poly syllable)		
29	Adjective	Adjective		Situation /Emphasis Function
30	Adjective	Adjctive		Descriptive Function
31	Adjective	Fixed Phrasal Adjective		
32	Adjective	Adjective with Conjunction		
33	Adjective	Adjective(AABB,ABB,BB Type)		
34	Adjective	"henduo", "hao", "bu"		
35	Verb	Subject-Predicate Phrase		
36	Syntactic	Preposition Phrase		
37	Syntactic	Four Character Idiom		
38	Syntactic	Phrase with Complex Sentence		
39	Syntactic	Adverb		
40	Syntactic	HE, JI		
41	Syntactic	Special Part of Speech such as..., SHI, SHANG, JIAN		

4.2   Obtain the Feature of DingYu

The feature of DingYu can be explained from the following three aspects:

(1) Dictionary

The information such as a borrowed measure word or a personal pronoun should be registered in the Chinese dictionary beforehand.

(2) Form

DingYu can be judged from its form: a repeated quantifier phrase with a numeral "one" and a quantifier such as "one X one X", AABB type adjectives or ABB type adjectives. Especially, AABB type and ABB type are the vital expression form of the adjectives, so they have certain usages.

(3) Analysis

For example, in order to judge if the phrase is a subject-predicate phrase or a preposition phrase the analysis of the syntax structure should be conducted.

At the present stage, since the perfect analysis system has not been fully completed yet, the analysis is limited. For example, as for a preposition phrase, in first refers to the preposition table, pick out the preposition, then skips a set of noun phrase and puts "DE" in front of the following noun (ZhongXinCi).

4.3   Judgment of the Definitive/Descriptive DingYu

A semantic relation between DingYu and ZhongXinCi becomes one of the condition to judge if the structural particle "DE" is necessary or not. It means that the judgment if DingYu has definitive or descriptive feature should be required. This judgment has to rely on a semantic analysis and there are still many problems to be solved. At present we are making the judgment as follows:

(1) Definitive DingYu

The definitive DingYu has a recognizing function to identify one thing from other things. In other words, the definitive adjective modifier specifies which the thing is. Generally, DingYu indicating time, place or belongings can be categorized as a definitive adjective modifier. A subject-predicate phrase containing a verb without any adjunct components can be also categorized as a definitive DingYu.

(2) Descriptive DingYu

A descriptive DingYu describes something. When a speaker uses a descriptive DingYu, the speaker is mainly focusing on the thing to be described and does not concern the other same kind of things. In other words a descriptive DingYu describes how the thing is. Generally an adjective or a subject-predicate phrase containing an adjective is categorized as a descriptive DingYu.

Figure 3 provides the algorism to judge whether DingYu is definitive or descriptive.

In the figure, Time_Type(input) shows a process in order to decide whether the input letter string is a noun indicating time(T) or whether it has a feature of time. In like wise, Space_Type(input) shows a process in order to judge whether DingYu is a noun indicating location, Belong_Type(input) shows a process to judge belonging, Subject_Predicate_Type(input) shows a process to judge a subject-object phrase, Adjective_Type(input) shows a process to judge an adjective and Material_Type(Input) shows a process to judge an adjective phrase. The details of each process are not dealt in this paper.

```
Modifier_Type()
{
 Initialization;
  Input = modification string;
   if((Time_Type(Input)) or
      (Space_Type(Input)) or
      (Belong_Type(Input)) or
      (Subject_Predicate_Type(Input)) )
      {/* definitive modifier */
          put definitive sign; }
    else
     if( (Adjective_Type(Input)) or
        (Material_Type(Input)) or
        (Adjective_Phrase_Type(Input)) )
        {/* descriptive modifier */
            put descriptive modifier; }
      else
          { Default_Processing; }
      return the sign;
}
```

Fig. 3. The Modifier_Type Algorithm

4.4 Priority of the Judging Rules

The rules to judge the necessity of the structural particle "DE" are made by statistic and inductive methods. They are not completely exclusive and they might not even exist. They are neither independent nor irrelevant. Therefore the priority of the judgments should be set up. The principle to set the priority was to give priority to the rule with detailed conditions. Because several cases allow both with "DE" or without "DE", we decided the priority according to our preferenc when the rules have the conditions of the same level.

5 Experiment and Consideration

The following part of this paper is to discuss the experiment which was conducted to confirm the efficiency of the methods to judge the necessity of a structural particle "DE".

This experiment basically does not deal with the whole sentence but the phrase with DingYu and ZhongXinCi. That is, this experiment did not analyze the sentence but attempted to judge the necessity of "DE" using the related elements with DingYu and ZhongXinCi.

5.1 Method Used for the Experiment

In Chinese language sometimes "DE" is used between DingYu (DY) and ZhongX-inCi(ZXC) and sometimes no "DE" in between. Therefore it is very difficult to extract DY and ZXC without analyzing sentence structures in the documents written in Chinese. On the other hands, since one of our purposes of the experiment is to apply the result to generate Chinese sentences by machine translation, the following Data A and Data B are used for this experiment.

(1) Data A

Data A are collected automatically through the Japanese-Chinese machine translation system created by our group, which extracted PSA patterns in the Japanese texts[6].

Firstly, we picked out 2319 phrases with PSA patterns from the documents indicated and translated them into the corresponding Chinese phrases.

Then we excluded the analysis-errors and wrong translations, and got a collection of Chinese translations.

Finally, we extracted 248 phrases at random from the collection and made them Data A for the experiment. Data A have "DE" in between DY and ZXC.

(2) Data B

We extracted 255 phrases with DingYu and ZhongXinCi from the original Chinese texts.

(3) Tagging

Replace all "DE" in Data A by "@". As for Data B, when there is "DE", replace all "DE" by "@". When there is no "DE", put "@" in between DingYu and ZhongXinCi.

(4) Dictionary

We used a Chinese dictionary compiled by Dalian University of Science and Technology. The capacity of the dictionary was 45,000 words. Some information of the words were added or modified by us.

5.2   Evaluation

How to evaluate the results obtained by the method should be explained. Let us start with the signs as follows:

1. pr_de: Frequency of appearing a structural particle "DE" in DY@ZXC
2. pr_wu: Frequency of disappearing a structural particle "DE" in DY@ZXC
3. pr_both: Frequency of the case in which both with "DE" and without "DE" is acceptable
4. pp_detode: Frequency of the case in which @ is "DE" and the judgment is also "DE"
5. pp_wutowu: Frequency of the case in which @ is "kong" and the judgment is also "kong".
6. pp_botode: Frequency of the case in which both with "DE" and without "DE" are acceptable and the judgment is with "DE".
7. pp_botowu: Frequency of the case in which both with "DE" and without "DE" are acceptable and the judgment is without "DE"
8. pp_detowu: Frequency of the case in which @ is "DE" but the judgment is "kong".

9. pp_wutode: Frequency of the case in which @ is "kong" but the judgment is "DE"

Consequently, the correct rate of the judgment (CP) will be calculated by the following formula (3):

$$CP = \frac{pp\_detode + pp\_wutowu + pp\_botode + pp\_botowu}{\Sigma @}$$

$$(3)$$

The Error rate of the judgment (EP), the "dede" rate of the judgment(DDP) and the "kongkong" rate of the judgment(WWP) will be calculated by the following formulas:

$$\text{Error Rate of the Judgment (EP)} = \frac{pp\_detowu + pp\_wutode}{\Sigma @} \quad (4)$$

$$\text{"dede" Rate of the Judgment (DDP)} = \frac{pp\_detode}{pr\_de} \quad (5)$$

$$\text{"kongkong" Rate of the Judgment (WWP)} = \frac{pp\_wutowu}{pr\_wu}$$

5.3   Result of the Experiment

Table 2 shows the result of the experiment. The correct rate of our judging method was 93.0%.

Table 2. Results of the experiment

Term	A Type Data	B Type Data	Total
pr_de	186	127	313
pr_wu	47	109	156
pr_both	15	19	34
pp_detode	183	123	306
pp_wutowu	32	96	128
pp_botode	14	15	29
pp_detowu	3	4	7
pp_wutode	15	13	28
CP	92.7%	93.3%	93.0%
EP	7.3%	6.7%	7.0%
DDP	98.4%	98.7%	98.6%
WWP	68.1%	88.1%	82.1%

In this paper we proposed a method to judge the necessity of a structural particle based on an actual linguistic phenomenon. As the result of the experiment, the "dede" rate of the judgment was 98.6%, the "kong kon" rate of the judgment was 82.1% and the correct rate of the judgment was 93.0%. As seen in the results the judgments to decide the necessity of "DE" were made effectively, and proved the efficiency of the judging method we proposed in the paper.

6   Conclusion

This paper proposed a method to judge the necessity of a structural particle "DE" for DingYu in Chinese language. The judging rules were finalized based on an investigation of large numbers of Chinese grammar books and the actual Chinese linguistic expressions, and the rules were used to judge the necessity of "DE". The point of the rules was that the characteristics of DingYu and ZhongXinCi were utilized skillfully. Especially the particular parts of speech recognized from a corpus were found out to play an important role in our methods.

As the result of the experiment with DingYu and ZhongXinCi, the correct rate of the judgment was 93.0%, which confirmed the efficiency of the methods.

In future, we would like to extend these methods in order to deal with the multiple DingYu, establish more precise and standardized rule system including semantic analysis, and also install them in practical systems.

Acknowledgements. We would like to thank all our colleagues participating in this project. This work has been supported by the Education Ministry of Japan under Grant-in-Aid for Scientific Research B (No.14380166) and the Outstanding Overseas Chinese Scholars Fund of Chinese Academy of Sciences (No.2003-1-1).

References

1. Y. Matsumoto, S. Kurohashi, Y. Nyoki, H. Shinho, M. Nagao, User's Guide for the JUMAN System, a User-Extensible Morphological Analyzer for Japanese(1995).
2. Makoto Nagao, Natural Language Processing for the next Generation Machine Translation, Journal of the Japanese Society for Artificial Intelligence, Vol.11, No.4,(1996)
3. Makoto Nagao (Ed.), Natural Language Processing, Iwanami, (1996)
4. Yuehua Liu, Wenyu Pan, Wei Gu, Modern Chinese Grammar, Kurosio, (1988)
5. Yoichi Tomiura, Teigo Nakamura, Toru Hitaka, Semantic Structure of Japanese Noun Phrases 'NP no NP', Transactions of Information Processing Society Of Japan, Vol.36, No.6,(1995),1441-1448.
6. Fuji Ren, Lixin Fan, Miyanaga Y., Tochinai K.: On Reservable Structural Ambiguities in Japanese Chinese Machine Translation, Transactions of Information Processing Society Of Japan, Vol.34, No.8,(1993),1682-1691.

7. Ruri Yanada, The attribute modifier of Chinese and Japanese, Stusy and Research Japanese, Vol.83, No. 4 (1995), pp.19-24,

8. Fuji Ren, Jiannyun Nie, The Concept of Sensitive Word in Chinese - Survey in a Machine-Readable Dictionary,Journal of Natural Language Processing, Vol. 6 No.1(1999),59-78.

9. Lixin Fan, Fuji Ren, Miyanaga Y., Tochinai K.: Automatic Composition of Chinese Compound Words for Chinese-Japanese Machine Translation, Transactions of Information Processing Society Of Japan, Vol.33,No.9,(1992),1103-1113.

10. Fuji Ren, Shingo Kuroiwa: New Advances on Multi-Lingual Multi-Function Multi-Media Intelligent System, International Journal of Information Technology and Decision Making, Vol.1, No.1, (2002), 83-92.

11. Fuji Ren, Lixin Fan: Translation Rule and Empirical Knowledge in Machine Translation, International Journal of INFORMATION, Vol.5, No.1, (2002), 81-91.

Generating Natural Word Orders in a Semi–free Word Order Language: Treebank-Based Linearization Preferences for German

Gerard Kempen[1] and Karin Harbusch[2]

[1] Dept. of Psychology, Leiden Univ. and MPI for Psycholinguistics, Nijmegen
kempen@fsw.leidenuniv.nl
[2] Computer Science Dept., Univ. of Koblenz–Landau
harbusch@informatik.uni-koblenz.de

Abstract. We outline an algorithm capable of generating varied but natural sounding sequences of argument NPs in subordinate clauses of German, a semi-free word order language. In order to attain the right level of output flexibility, the algorithm considers (1) the relevant lexical properties of the head verb (not only transitivity type but also reflexivity, thematic relations expressed by the NPs, etc.), and (2) the animacy and definiteness values of the arguments, and their length. The relevant statistical data were extracted from the NEGRA–II treebank and from hand-coded features for animacy and definiteness. The algorithm maps the relevant properties onto "primary" versus "secondary" placement options in the generator. The algorithm is restricted in that it does not take into account linear order determinants related to the sentence's information structure and its discourse context (e.g. contrastiveness). These factors may modulate the above preferences or license "tertiary" linear orders beyond the primary and secondary options considered here.

1 Introduction

Computational sentence generators should be able to order constituents in agreement with linearization preferences and habits of native speakers/writers. This knowledge can be attained by exploiting text corpora (cf. [1]). In the following we concentrate on extracting appropriate word order rules for German, a (semi-)free word order language.

Target languages with strict word order rules do not present much of a problem here although the grammaticality contrast between examples such as *Pat picked a book up* and *?Pat picked a very large mint–green hardcover book up* [2, p. 7] shows that, even in English, knowledge of linear order preferences comes in handy. In the case of (semi–)free word order languages, the problem of how to select natural sounding permutations of constituents from among those licensed by the grammar is much more widespread. Sentence generators striving for natural and varied output, e.g., in question–answering systems or computer–supported language training environments, should neither select the same permutation at all times, nor produce the various grammatical permutations at random.

A. Gelbukh (Ed.): CICLing 2004, LNCS 2945, pp. 350–354, 2004.
© Springer-Verlag Berlin Heidelberg 2004

The naturalness of a particular ordering of constituents often depends on subtle conceptual or pragmatic factors that grammars of the target language fail to capture. A well–known case in point is German, whose grammar does not impose hard constraints on the linear order of Subject (SB), Indirect Object (IO) and Direct Object (DO) in finite subordinate clauses. (For an overview of the relevant linguistic literature, see [3].) All six possible orders are acceptable, although with varying degrees of grammaticality [4]. Given this flexibility, which factors control the actual linearization preferences of speakers/writers of German? In this paper, we explore the feasibility of extracting relevant linear order constraints from a treebank, *in casu* the NEGRA II corpus of German [5].

Students of constituent order in German have proposed linear precedence rules such as (1) SB $\prec$ IO/DO, (2) pronominal NPs $\prec$ full NPs, and (3) IO $\prec$ DO (where the symbol "$\prec$" means "precedes"; cf. [6], [7], [3]). However, these rules are not very helpful in designing a sentence generator: As will become clear hereafter, there are systematic exceptions to each of them, and important argument ordering preferences are linked to lexical properties of the head verb. Other studies have explored the impact of conceptual factors, e.g. whether the argument NP is definite or indefinite [8], and whether it refers to an animate or inanimate entity [9]). Another factor likely to play a role is length (cf. "heavy NP shift"; [10], [2]).

In this paper we take the following determinants into consideration:

- Grammatical function: SB, IO, DO
- Form: pronominal (consisting of a personal or reflexive pronoun) or full (otherwise)
- NP length: number of terminal nodes dominated by the NP (as determined by the TIGERSearch tool [12])
- Animacy: referring to a human or animal, or a collective of humans/animals (hand–coded[1])
- Definiteness: definite vs. indefinite reference (hand–coded according to Tables 1 and 2 in [11]).

We study the influence of these factors and some their interactions in *subordinate clauses introduced by a subordinating conjunction* (for example, *daß/dass* 'that', *ob* 'whether', *weil* 'because', *obwohl* 'although', *wenn* 'when, if'). The main reason for this restriction is a strategic one: The linear ordering patterns in these subordinate clauses are simpler than those in other clause types (e.g., no obligatory fronting of Wh-constituents).

2 Method

Recently, the NEGRA–II corpus has become available, a German treebank containing about 20,000 newspaper sentences annotated in full syntactic detail. Us-

---

[1] In case of doubt, we counted a referent as animate. Reflexive pronouns received the same animacy value as their antecedents. (There were no *reciprocal* pronouns fulfilling SB, IO or DO function.)

ing version 2.1 of TIGERSearch, we extracted all clauses introduced by a subordinating conjunction and containing an (SB,IO) and/or and (SB,DO) pair, possibly with an additional (IO,DO) pair (with the members of a pair occurring in any order). For details of the clause selection method, see [9]. As for terminology, clauses containing only an (SB,IO) pair are called *intransitive*. We distinguish two types of *transitive* clauses: those including only an (SB,DO) pair are termed *monotransitive*; clauses containing three pairs — (SB,DO), (SB,IO) as well as (IO,DO) — are *ditransitive*. We found 907 monotransitive, 99 intransitive, and 54 ditransitive clauses meeting our criteria. Every argument NP in these clauses was assigned a value on each of the five properties listed above.

As noted in an earlier paper [13], the observed constituent order frequencies can be accounted for in terms of the rather rigid rule schema in Fig. 1, which assigns to individual constituents a standard ("primary") position before or after their clausemates. Full NPs have an alternative ("secondary") placement option indicated by the labeled arrows. Animacy is one of the factors determining whether or not the secondary placement option is taken [9]: In transitive clauses, full Subject NPs ("SBful") are more likely to precede pronominal DO NPs ("DOpro") if they are animate than if they are inanimate; in intransitive clauses, animate IOful NPs precede SBful significantly more often than inanimate ones do. (For the inversion of DOful and IOful, see below.)

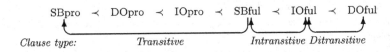

Fig. 1. Rule schema representing the linearization options observed in the treebank in clauses headed by a mono–, di–, or intransitive head verb.

3   Results

We now present new results regarding factors determining the choice between primary or secondary placement options licensed by the rule schema, as well as on some of their interactions.

Monotransitive clauses. Of 179 clauses with an (SBful,DOpro) pair, 143 have a reflexive head verb. In these clauses, *sich* 'him–, her–, itself; themselves' is the obligatory reflexive pronoun. As this pronoun is coreferential with the Subject, the members of a pair are either both animate or both inanimate. Of 65 inanimate pairs, SBful takes the secondary placement option (i.e., before DOpro) in 9 cases (14%); in the remaining 78 instances of animate pairs, SBful precedes DOpro 38 times (49%). In the remaining 36 *non–reflexive* clauses, the latter fifty–fifty pattern holds uniformly for all four possible pairings of an animate and/or an inanimate NP. Early SBs tend to be shorter than late SBs in reflexive as well as non-reflexive clauses (mean lengths 2.62 vs. 4.03 words). In the 179 clauses considered here, definiteness of SBful has no influence on its being placed early or late: In the SBful NPs that precede the DOpro NPs, the proportion of definites is the same as in the SBful NPs that follow DOpro (65% in both cases).

Intransitive clauses. Here we distinguish three types of IOful NPs based on the thematic role they express:

- recipient: in passive clauses headed by a ditransitive verb (e.g., *übertragen werden* 'to be transferred'; IOful first: 9 clauses, SBful first: 12)
- patient (or "co–agent"): in active clauses headed by verbs such as *helfen* 'help', *folgen* 'follow', *beitreten* 'join' (IOful first: 0 clauses, SBful first: 17)
- experiencer: in active clauses headed by verbs like *gefallen* 'please', *gehören* 'belong', *entsprechen* 'correspond' (IOful first: 11 clauses, SBful first: 13).

Patient–IOful NPs (*helfen*–type) never precede the SBful NP. Experiencer–IOs (*gefallen*–type) and recipient–IOs (*übertragen werden*) all adhere to the rule "animate $\prec$ inanimate". Neither length of the NPs nor their (in)definiteness seem to play a prominent role here. Where the animacy rule does not apply, the recipient–IOs select the primary or secondary position more or less at random, whereas the experiencer–IOs invariably choose the primary position.

Ditransitive clauses. The NP orderings agree with the primary positions depicted in Fig. 1, with two exceptions. Animate SBful NPs (length ≤ 2) precede pronominal arguments with proportions roughly comparable to those in monotransitive clauses. Three clauses instantiate the inverted DOful $\prec$ IOful sequence. They contain verbs where this order is standard (e.g., $etwas_{DO}$ $etwas_{IO}$ *angleichen* 'assimilate something$_{DO}$ to something$_{IO}$').

Definiteness, animacy, and length. The observed tendency for animate arguments to precede inanimate ones cannot be attributed to definiteness of the NPs because animacy and definiteness turn out to be uncorrelated. This preference cannot be attributed to length either despite that, on average, animate NPs are shorter than inanimate ones, and short NPs also prefer early positions. The stronger leftward tendency of animate in comparison with inanimate NPs remains clearly visible if one only looks at NPs of equal length (length = 1, length = 2, or length > 2).

4 Conclusion

An algorithm capable of generating varied but natural sounding sequences of argument NPs in subordinate clauses of German can take the primary positions in the rule schema of Fig. 1 as starting point. In order to attain output flexibility, it should consider (1) the relevant lexical properties of the head verb (not only transitivity type but also reflexivity, thematic relation expressed by IO, etc.), and (2) the animacy values of the arguments. Probabilistic functions embodying the statistical regularities sketched above are needed to map these features onto primary versus secondary placement options. Length and definiteness may add some further refinements. A generator incorporating such an algorithm is currently under development at our institutes.

354   G. Kempen and K. Harbusch

Finally, we should point out that the approach taken here cannot uncover linear order determinants related to the sentence's information structure and its discourse context (e.g. contrastiveness). Such factors may modulate the above preferences or license "tertiary" linear orders beyond the primary and secondary options considered here.

References

1. Langkilde, I., Knight, K.: Generation that exploits corpus–based statistical knowledge. In: Proceedings of the 36th ACL & 17th COLING, Montreal (1998)
2. Wasow, T.: Postverbal behavior. CSLI Publications, Stanford CA (2002)
3. Müller, G.: Optimality, markedness, and word order in German. Linguistics **37** (1999) 777–815
4. Keller, F.: Gradience in grammar: Experimental and computational aspects of degrees of grammaticality. Unpublished Ph.D. thesis, Univ. of Edinburgh (2000)
5. Skut, W., Krenn, B., Brants, T., Uszkoreit, H.: An annotation scheme for free word order languages. In: Proceedings of the Fifth ANLP, Washington D.C. (1997)
6. Uszkoreit, H.: Word Order and Constituent Structure in German. CSLI Publication, Stanford CA (1987)
7. Pechmann, T., Uszkoreit, H., Engelkamp, J., Zerbst, D.: Wortstellung im deutschen Mittelfeld. Linguistische Theorie und psycholinguistische Evidenz. In: Perspektiven der Kognitiven Linguistik. Westdeutscher Verlag, Wiesbaden (1996)
8. Kurz, D.: A statistical account on word order variation in German. In Abeillé, A., Brants, T., Uszkoreit, H., eds.: Proceedings of the COLING Workshop on Linguistically Interpreted Corpora, Luxembourg (2000)
9. Kempen, G., Harbusch, K.: A corpus study into word order variation in German subordinate clauses: Animacy affects linearization independently of grammatical function assignment. In Pechmann, T., Habel, C., eds.: Multidisciplinary approaches to language production. Mouton De Gruyter, Berlin (in press)
10. Hawkins, J.A.: A performance theory of order and constituency. Cambridge University Press, Cambridge (1994)
11. Abbott, B.: Definiteness and indefiniteness. In Horn, L.R., Ward, G., eds.: Handbook of Pragmatics. Blackwell, Oxford (in press)
12. König, E., Lezius, W.: A description language for syntactically annotated corpora. In: Proceedings of the 18th COLING, Saarbrücken (2000)
13. Kempen, G., Harbusch, K.: How flexible is constituent order in the midfield of German subordinate clauses? A corpus study revealing unexpected rigidity. In: Proceedings of the International Conference on Linguistic Evidence, Tübingen (2004)

Guideline for Developing a Software Life Cycle Process in Natural Language Generation Projects

Mª del Socorro Bernardos

Departamento de Sistemas Informáticos y Programación, Facultad de Informática,
Universidad Complutense de Madrid. C/ Juan del Rosal, 8, 28040, Madrid, Spain
sbernardos@sip.ucm.es

Abstract. This paper is an attempt to provide a general framework that helps develop a natural language generation (NLG) project from the conception of the need to the retirement of the product. This framework consists of a set of systematic activities that can be carried out in order to build or modify an NLG system. Assuming that a NLG system is software, we take IEEE Std. 1074-1997 –a standard for developing a software life cycle process– as a general framework and adapt it for NLG projects. We focus especially on activities related to domain information, requirements, design, knowledge elicitation and reuse.

1   Introduction

Natural Language Generation (NLG) is a Natural Language Processing (NLP) area concerned with the production of human languages. It is a relatively new field that has only been treated as a matter of its own since 1980's [11]. One of the characteristics of young disciplines is their lack of standards and/or commonly accepted practices, and NLG is no exception. As a consequence, one of the first problems people involved in an NLG project have to face is that they do not have an NLG-specific framework that guides them along the project. This issue is especially important in real-world projects, where the solutions must not only perform as required, but also conform to externally-specified criteria, typically related to time, personnel and equipment. In this paper we suggest a way to solve this problem, by providing a set of systematic activities that involve all the work related to NLG projects.

IEEE [6] defines software as 'computer programs, procedures, and possibly associated data pertaining to the operation of a computer system'. According to this, the product of an NLG project can be considered as software. Thus, NLG systems can be built or modified using one of the existing standards for developing a software life cycle process (SLCP). The main problem to apply this approach derives from the fact that those standards have been mostly used within the software engineering (SE) field, and NLG is a knowledge-intensive process [5], therefore, requiring of knowledge engineering (KE) solutions too [10]. That is why those SLCP standards need some adaptation to be really useful for an NLG project.

A. Gelbukh (Ed.): CICLing 2004, LNCS 2945, pp. 355–359, 2004.
© Springer-Verlag Berlin Heidelberg 2004

One of the mostly accepted standards that have been applied to the development of an SLCP is IEEE 1074, whose last revision dates from 1997 [7]. This standard also takes into account the harmonization with other well-known standards, e.g. IEEE/EIA 12207-1996 [8]. That is why we have chosen IEEE1074-1997 as the basis of our proposal.

2   Overview of the IEEE Std. 1074-1997

IEEE Std. 1074-1997 is a standard for the generation of the process that governs a software project. This standard applies to all aspects of the software life cycle from concept exploration to retirement and its contents can be summarized as follows:

A.1 Project Management Activity Groups. These groups *initiate* a software project; *plan* all the project management; and *monitor and control* the project throughout its life cycle. Especial consideration is given to the *management of risk*.

A.2 Pre-Development Activity Groups. These groups take place before software development can begin. They are used to *explore concepts* and *allocate system requirements*. The activities related to *software importation* are also part of the pre-development activity groups.

A.3 Development Activity Groups. These groups are carried out during the development of a software product. They include *software requirements*, *design* and *implementation*.

A.4 Post-Development Activity Groups. These groups are performed to *install*, *maintain* and *retire* a software product.

A.5 Integral Activity Groups. These groups are needed to successfully complete the project activities. They include the *evaluation* of the products and processes that are used to develop the product, the *software configuration management*, the *documentation development*, and the *training* of people.

The order in which the activities will be performed will depend on the project.

3   Our Adaptation of IEEE 1074-1997 to NLG

Table 1 shows the guideline proposed here. The activities that differ from the standard are written in *cursive*; those activities that belonged to the standard but are not part of our guideline are crossed out. The activities are identified by an "A" followed by three numbers: section; activity group; and activity. The activities that are equal to the standard ones keep the same reference. New activity groups have a consecutive number to the existing groups in the corresponding section. New activities in existing groups have an apostrophe in order to distinguish them from the standard ones that have the same numbering -original activities are on the right side of the new ones proposed here-. Our experience so far has also allowed us to point out some useful tips for other activities (marked by a #) and to develop some methods for the new ones (marked by an *). The main differences from the standard are the use of a corpus [3, 11] to specify the functional requirements and the need of a knowledge elicitation activity. As the standard, our guideline takes into account reuse, but instead of considering it as a pre-development activity, it has been included within the integral ones. Only the reuse of the domain information source is left in the pre-development section. Space constraints do not let us discuss them here; you can get detailed information in [4].

Table 1. IEEE 1074-1997 adapted to NLG

A.1 Project Management Activities Groups
  A.1.1 Project Initiation Activities
    A.1.1.1 Create SLCP #
    A.1.1.2 Perform Estimations #
    A.1.1.3 Allocate Project Resources
    A.1.1.4 Define Metrics
  A.1.2 Project Planning Activities
    A.1.2.1 Plan Evaluations
    A.1.2.2 Plan Configuration Management
    A.1.2.3 Plan System Transition (If app.)
    A.1.2.4 Plan Installation
    A.1.2.5 Plan Documentation
    A.1.2.6 Plan Training
    A.1.2.7 Plan Project Management
    A.1.2.8 Plan Integration
  A.1.3 Project Monitoring and Control Activities
    A.1.3.1 Manage Risks
    A.1.3.2 Manage the Project
    A.1.3.3 Identify SLCP Improvement Needs
    A.1.3.4 Retain Records
    A.1.3.5 Collect and Analyze Metric Data
A.2 Pre-development Activity Groups
  A.2.1 Concept Exploration Activities
    A.2.1.1 Identify Ideas on Needs
    A.2.1.2 Formulate Potential Approaches #
    A.2.1.3 Conduct Feasibility Studies #
    A.2.1.4 Refine and Finalize the Idea or Need
  ~~A.2.2 System Allocation Activities~~
    ~~A.2.2.1 Analyze Functions~~
    ~~A.2.2.2 Develop System Architecture~~
    ~~A.2.2.3 Decompose System Requirements~~
  ~~A.2.3 Software Importation Activities~~
    ~~A.2.3.1 Identify Imported Software Requirements~~
    ~~A.2.3.2 Evaluate Software Import Sources (If app.)~~
    ~~A.2.3.3 Define Software Import Method (If app.)~~
    ~~A.2.3.4 Import Software (If app.)~~
  A.2.4 *Domain Information Access Activities*
    A.2.4.1 *Identify Domain Information Requirements*
    A.2.4.2 *Evaluate Domain Information Sources (If app.)*
    A.2.4.3 *Select the Domain Information Source*
    A.2.4.4 *Import the Domain Information Source*
A.3 Development Activity Group
  A.3.1 Requirements Activities
    A.3.1.1' *Define General Objectives*   ~~A.3.1.1 Define and Develop Software Requirements~~
    A.3.1.2' *Define Specific Functional Requirements**   ~~A.3.1.2 Define Interface Requirements~~
    A.3.1.3' *Define Interface Requirements*   ~~A.3.1.3 Prioritize and Integrate Software Requirements~~
  A.3.4 *Knowledge Elicitation Activities*
    A.3.4.1 *Perform Linguistic Knowledge Elicitation **

A.3.2 Design Activities
  A.3.2.1 Perform Architectural Design
  A.3.2.2' *Perform Resource Detailed Design**   ~~A.3.2.2 Design Data Base (If app.)~~
  A.3.2.3' *Perform Module Detailed Design**   ~~A.3.2.3 Design Interfaces~~
  A.3.2.4' *Perform Interface Detailed Design*   ~~A.3.2.4 Perform Detailed Design~~
  A.3.3 Implementation Activities
    A.3.3.1 Create Executable Code
    A.3.3.2 Create Operating Documentation
    A.3.3.3 Perform Integration
A.4 Post-Development Activity Groups
  A.4.1 Installation Activities
    A.4.1.1 Distribute Software
    A.4.1.2 Install Software
    A.4.1.3 Accept Software in Operational Environment
  A.4.2 Operation and Support Activities
    A.4.2.1 Operate the System
    A.4.2.2 Provide Technical Assistance and Consulting
    A.4.2.3 Maintain Support Request Log
  A.4.3 Maintenance Activities
    A.4.3.1 Identify software Improvement Needs
    A.4.3.2 Implement Problem Reporting Method
    A.4.3.3 Reapply SLC
  A.4.4 Retirement Activities
    A.4.4.1 Notify User
    A.4.4.2 Conduct Parallel Operations (If app.)
    A.4.4.3 Retire System
A.5 Integral Activities Groups
  A.5.1 Evaluation Activities
    A.5.1.1 Conduct Reviews
    A.5.1.2 Create Traceability Matrix
    A.5.1.3 Conduct Audits
    A.5.1.4 Develop Test Procedures #
    A.5.1.5 Create Test Data
    A.5.1.6 Execute Tests
    A.5.1.7 Report Evaluation Results
  A.5.2 Software Configuration Management Activities
    A.5.2.1 Develop Configuration Identification
    A.5.2.2 Perform Configuration Control
    A.5.2.3 Perform Status Accounting
  A.5.3 Documentation Development Activities
    A.5.3.1 Implement Documentation
    A.5.3.2 Produce and Distribute Documentation
  A.5.4 Training Activities
    A.5.4.1 Develop Training Materials
    A.5.4.2 Validate the Training Program
    A.5.4.3 Implement the Training Program
  A.5.5 *Reuse Activities*
    A.5.5.1 *Identify Possible Reusable Components*
    A.5.5.2 *Evaluate Reusable Components (If app.)*
    A.5.5.3 *Select Reusable Components (If app.)*
    A.5.5.4 *Import Selected Reusable Components (If app.)*

In order to validate our guideline, we decided to apply it in a new NLG project. This project, called GENPLANMED, consists in the construction of a query system about medical plants. The approach we followed was to compare the software life cycle process associated to this project –a project which used our set of systematic activities– to the one corresponding to a similar NLG project, called ONTOGENERATION [1] –a project which did not used it. We verified that the guideline lets the team define what has to be done relatively soon –planning and estimation issues–, enabling the members of the team have at any moment a clear idea of what has been done so far and what remains to be done. All this helps the team people to control and manage the project –monitoring, traceability and visibility issues–, and makes systematic tests of the products delivered along the life cycle process easier – evaluation issues–. The guideline is useful to incorporate external components into the project as well –reuse issues. These circumstances contribute to prevent the team from carrying out things that become useless in the end and from not doing things that would facilitate the process –performance issues–. Since our guideline was not tailored to GENPLANMED, we do not think that it is unreasonable to think that it can be useful for more NLG projects –independence issues–.

4   Conclusions and Future Work

The guideline proposed in this paper provides for all the activities that have to be taken into account in an NLG project, since the conception of the system to its retirement. Currently, there are methods and techniques to solve specific NLG problems (see, e.g. [9], [11]), but we do not know of any that explicitly involves the whole life cycle process associated to an NLG project. The suggested set of activities is an adaptation of IEEE Std. 1074-1997 to NLG peculiarities. The application of our set of activities to a NLG project has proved that it can be useful, al least it has been for GENPLANMED.

This work is only a first step. In order to refine andconsolidate it within the NLG community it needs to be applied to more projects. That way, reports of its use could be obtained that could help us to improve it, not only the guideline as a whole, but also each single activity. The guideline could also be applied to other NLP areas. We do not know of an equivalent guideline in other NLP fields and our knowledge and experience do not allow us to guess to what extent our work can be valid for them. However, they share some characteristics with NLG – e.g. they are typically knowledge-intensive areas- that make us think that it could be useful.

References

1. Aguado, G., Bañón, A., Bateman, J., Bernardos, S., Fernández, M., Gómez, A., Nieto, E., Olalla, A., Plaza, R., Sánchez, A.: Ontogeneration: Reusing domain and linguistic ontologies for Spanish text generation. Workshop on Applications of Ontologies and Problem Solving Methods, ECAI'98. Brighton (1998)
2. Bateman, J.: Automated discourse generation. In Encyclopedia of Library and Information Science, suplement 25. Marcel Dekker, Inc, New York (1998) 62:1-54

3. Bernardos, S. and Aguado, G.: A new approach in building a corpus for natural language generation systems. In Proceedings of the 2nd International Conference on Intelligent Text Processing and Computational Linguistics (CICLING- 2001), México D. F. (Mexico). Lecture Notes in Computer Science, Vol. 2004. Springer-Verlag, Berlin Heidelberg New York (2001) 216-225

4. Bernardos, S.: Marco metodológico para la construcción de sistemas de generación de lenguaje natural. PhD. thesis. Facultad de Informática, Universidad Politécnica de Madrid (2003)

5. de Smedt, K., Horacek, H., and Zock, M.: Architectures for natural language generation: problems and perspectives. In G. Ardoni y M. Zock (eds.) Trends in natural language generation: an artificial intelligence perspective. Springer-Verlag, Berlin, Heidelberg, New York (1996) 17-46

6. IEEE Standard Glossary of Software Engineering Terminology (1990)

7. IEEE Std. 1074-1997. IEEE Standard for developing Software Life Cycle Processes (1997)

8. IEEE/EIA 12207.0-1996. Software life cycle processes (1998)

9. RAGS team. Towards a reference architecture for natural language generation systems. RAGS Technical Report. Information Technology Research Institute, University of Brighton (2000). Last revision: The RAGS reference manual, (2002)

10. Reiter, E., Robertson, R., and Osman, L.: Knowledge acquisition for natural language generation. In Proceedings of the 1st International Conference on Natural Language Generation (INLG 2000), Mitzpe Ramon (Israel), (2000) 217-224

11. Reiter, E. and Dale, R.: Building natural language generation systems. Cambridge University Press, Cambridge (2000)

A Plug and Play Spoken Dialogue Interface for Smart Environments

Germán Montoro, Xavier Alamán, and Pablo A. Haya

Universidad Autónoma de Madrid
Departamento de Ingeniería Informática
Ctra. de Colmenar Km. 15. Madrid 28049 Spain
{German.Montoro, Xavier.Alaman, Pablo.Haya}@ii.uam.es

Abstract. In this paper we present a plug and play dialogue system for smart environments. The environment description and its state are stored on a domain ontology. This ontology is formed by entities that represent real world contextual information and abstract concepts. This information is complemented with linguistic parts that allow to automatically create a spoken interface for the environment. The spoken interface is based on multiple dialogues, related to every ontology entity with linguistic information. Firstly, the dialogue system creates appropriate grammars for the dialogues. Secondly, it creates the dialogue parts, employing a tree structure. Grammars support the recognition process and the dialogue tree supports the interpretation and generation processes. The system is being tested with a prototype formed by a living room. Users may interact with and modify the physical state of this living room environment by means of the spoken dialogue interface.

1 Introduction

In the last years, computational services have abandoned a centralized structure, based on the desktop metaphor, to be omnipresent in our environments. Following these changes, interfaces are transforming very fast to adapt to the new user necessities [1]. Leaving behind some old command line and graphical interfaces, systems have changed to provide new user-friendly approaches. The new interfaces have to adapt to the users, so that users may communicate with the system as naturally as possible.

Among these interfaces, spoken dialogue systems offer a wide range of possibilities, but also new challenges [2]. Dialogue interfaces (spoken or not) are frequently tied to a specific domain and, even more, are specially designed for the tasks they have to deal with. They are usually based on hand crafted dialogue designs. On the one hand, this makes harder to build a dialogue interface, increasing considerably its cost, on the other hand, changes in the system may necessarily imply modifications in the interface.

An approach to solve this problem is the automatic dialogue generation, based on ontological domain knowledge [3]. These systems provide plug and play spoken interfaces, avoiding the necessity of creating them from scratch and making them more easily reconfigurable.

A. Gelbukh (Ed.): CICLing 2004, LNCS 2945, pp. 360–370, 2004.
© Springer-Verlag Berlin Heidelberg 2004

This solution becomes much more effective in the case of smart environments. The configuration of these environments is highly dynamic and it may change considerably from one to another. New entities may be added, removed or temporally stopped, and the spoken interface should be aware of these changes.

In this paper we present a plug and play dialogue system for smart environments. Our system automatically creates and manages the dialogues, being based on the information stored on the environment ontology.

Section two presents a description of our system, section three describes the ontology; section four shows how the plug and play spoken dialogues are created; section five describes the implementation and evaluation of the system; and; finally, in section six we discuss the conclusions and future work.

2 System Description

Our work is related to the research area known as smart environments. Smart environments are based on the concept of ubiquitous computing, originally defined by [4].

Ubiquitous computing systems provide access to computational services but make the computational devices invisible to the users. Users should not be aware of their presence and therefore the system should have a similar behavior to a human being [2]. Users are not in charge of finding the interface, but the system has the responsibility of serving the users [5].

Following the ideas of ubiquitous computing, a smart environment is a "highly embedded, interactive space that brings computation into the real, physical world". It allows computers "to participate in activities that have never previously involved computation" and people "to interact with computational systems the way they would with other people: via gesture, voice, movement, and context" [6].

Different and highly heterogeneous technologies may be found inside a smart environment, from hardware devices, such as sensors, switches, appliances, web cams, etc. to legacy software, such as voice recognizers, multimedia streaming servers, mail agents, etc. On the one hand, all of these entities have to be seamlessly integrated and controlled using the same user interface. For instance, users have to be able to start a broadcasting music server as easily as to turn off the lights. On the other hand, user interaction has to be kept as flexible as possible. It should be based on multiple and distinct modalities, such as web, voice, touch... so that user preferences and capabilities can be considered.

Bearing in mind these conditions we have developed a working prototype based on a real environment. This prototype includes an ontology, which provides a simple mechanism to represent the environment and communicate its state, and two different plug and play user interfaces (a web-based user interface and a spoken dialogue user interface), which interact with and control the elements of a real environment. These interfaces are automatically created and managed, being based on the information extracted from the ontology.

This real environment consists of a laboratory furnished as a living room, with several devices. There are two kinds of devices: control and multimedia. Control devices are lighting controls, a door opening mechanism, a presence detector, smart-cards, etc. Multimedia devices, such as speakers, microphones, a TV and an IP video-camera are accessible through a backbone IP. Control devices are connected to an EIB (EIBA) network and a gateway joins the two networks. The blackboard that accesses to the physical layer is harmonized through a SMNP (Simple Management Network Protocol) layer [7].

3   Environment Ontology

The ontology is implemented in a middleware layer, which is the glue between the user interface and the environment. The interaction between them is based on an event-driven protocol. The environment layout and its state are stored on a common repository, called blackboard [8].

This blackboard holds a representation of multiple characteristics of the environment. These include the distribution of the environment (buildings and rooms), the environment active entities, their location, their state, the possible relationships between them and the flows of information. The nature of an entity can range from a physical device to an abstract concept, such as the number of persons in a room or the list of persons allowed to get into it.

The ontological environment representation is written in an XML document. This document is parsed to obtain a repository, the blackboard, which is used as a proxy information server. Interfaces and applications may ask the blackboard to obtain information about the state of any entity or to change it. Entity descriptions can be added or removed to the blackboard in run-time, and the new information can be reused by the rest of applications. Applications and interfaces do not interact directly with the physical world or between them, but they only have access to the blackboard layer (see figure 1).

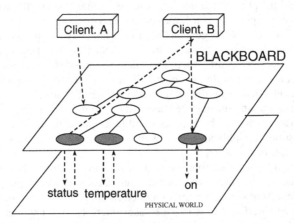

Fig. 1. Blackboard interaction

All the entities of the same type share a set of common properties that describe universal accepted features of the entity. Specific properties represent custom application information. In order to automatically create dialogues associated to the entities, common linguistic information is attached to the entities. This linguistic information comprises most of the possible ways a user may employ to interact with the entity. Basically it is formed by a verb part (the actions that can be taken with the entity), an object part (the name it can be given), a modifier part (the kind of object entity), a location part (where it is in the environment) and an additional information part (additional information about the entity). These linguistic parts permit the use of synonyms, to allow a more natural interaction with the system. Additionally, entities store the name of the action method that has to be called after its linguistic information is completed and the name of its associated template grammar. Figure 2 shows a simplified example of the linguistic information presented on an entity.

```
<entity name="Lamp_1" id="1" type="0">
  <property name="Status">
    <paramSet name="jeoffrey" id="2"> ... </paramSet>
    <paramSet name="Odisea" id="3">
      <paramSet name="sentence" id="4" action="EncenderApagarLuz">
        <param name="verbPart">encender dar</param>
        <param name="objectPart">luz</param>
        <param name="modifierPart"></param>
        <param name="locationPart">techo arriba</param>
        <param name="aditionalInformationPart"></param>
      </paramSet>
      <paramSet name="sentence" id="5"> ... </paramSet>
  </property>
</entity>
```

Fig. 2. Ontology dialogue information

The employ of these common linguistic properties makes that, in most cases, when a user defines a new entity its spoken dialogue interface will automatically come attached to it. Only in a few cases, some changes have to be done to adapt the location part for a particular entity or, eventually, to refine other parts.

4   Dialogue Creation

As it was said above, the system employs the linguistic information presented on the ontology to automatically create the spoken dialogue interface.

At startup, the dialogue system reads every entity from the ontology. When an entity has associated dialogue information, the system adds the linguistic information to the appropriate grammar and adds a new dialogue part to the spoken dialogue interface.

4.1 Grammar Creation

Most of the spoken dialogue systems employ specialized grammars to increase the recognition accuracy. Grammars support the recognition process by specifying the possible sentences that may be uttered by the users, limiting the number of possible inputs expected by the recognizer [9].

Our spoken dialogue system creates a grammar for every different type of entity and modifies it according to the linguistic information attached to the entity. As an example, an entity of type *light*, that represents a light presented in a room, has associated an action grammar. This action grammar allows to utter a wide range of sentences oriented to access to and control general environment devices.

In addition to the entity dialogues, the system may create new dialogues that do not depend on any entity. That is the case, for instance, of a *politeness dialogue*, which user and system may employ to thank, say hello, good bye, etc. This dialogue has associated a plain grammar. Plain grammars do not have any verb, questioning or location parts.

At the dialogue creation process the system reads all the entities from the ontology. For every entity the system checks if it has associated linguistic information. If so, it gets the name of its corresponding grammar template and checks if a previous grammar was already created by an entity of that type (as it was said above, all the entities of the same type share the same grammar). If that type of entity does not have a grammar yet, the system creates a new grammar based on the entity grammar template. For this grammar (or for a previous grammar created by other entity of the same type) it adds each linguistic part to the corresponding position in the grammar.

All the grammar templates have the same rules. They only differ on the possible sentences that are supported. The interface is based on Spanish, and therefore the nouns, adjectives and articles have number and gender. For instance, for the object part they all have the <singular female noun>, <singular male noun>, <plural female noun>, <plural male noun> and <invariant common noun> rules. Some of these rules will be filled in by different entities of the same type and some others will be left empty.

Given that the linguistic parts of an entity come in one form of the word (infinitive for verbs or singular male for nouns) we employ a tagged lexicon and a syntactic parser [10] to obtain the most appropriate rule and the rest of the forms of the words for that rule.

The new linguistic parts append new words to the rules, preserving the words previously added for other entities of the same type. If a rule already contained that word, the new word is not added again.

As an example of this process we may consider the entities fluorescent, lamp (both of type light) and front door (of type door) and a system dialogue for yes and no. The three entities have associated an action grammar and the system dialogue has associated a plain grammar. The fluorescent entity will create a new grammar based on the action grammar template and will add its parts to this grammar. Given that the lamp entity is of the same type as the fluorescent entity (type light) it will employ the grammar already created by the fluorescent entity to append its linguistic parts. The front door entity will create a new grammar (since there is not a previous entity of the type door) also based on the action grammar template and it will append its linguistic parts. Finally the yes/no system dialogue will create a new grammar based on the plain grammar template. The grammar set will be formed by three grammars, two of them based on the action grammar template and the last one based on the plain grammar template.

Once the grammars are created, the system may employ them for recognition, and activate and deactivate them at its convenience.

4.2 Dialogue Part Creation

Besides the grammar creation process, for each entity the system creates the dialogue parts that will be employed later to provide interpretation and generation capabilities.

Dialogue parts are added as dialogue nodes to a tree structure. This structure establishes a new linguistic ontology that will carry on the process of interaction with the user.

At the beginning of the process the dialogue tree is formed by an empty root node. For each entity with linguistic information, the system adds new nodes or provides new information to existing nodes, according to the linguistic parts associated to the entity. Nodes are formed by a word and a list of the entities that contained that word.

To add a new part the system always starts from the root. The first linguistic part added to the tree is the verb part. If the root node does not have any child node containing the verb word, the system will create a new node containing the word and the entity where it belonged. If the root node already had a child node containing the verb word, the system adds the name of the entity to the list of entities of that node. The system follows the same process for all the verb synonyms. After the verb part addition is concluded it will continue with the object part. The object part nodes will be children of all the verb part nodes (all the verb synonyms) previously created. If the dialogue part did not have a verb part, the object part would hang from the root. This means that parts of the same type may have different depth in the tree. After the object part is added to the tree, this is completed with the modifier, location and additional information parts.

Let us see an example taken from our real smart environment (here simplified to improve its comprehension). The room has a fluorescent light and a radio. The fluorescent entity is called light_1 and the radio entity is called radio_1. The light_1 entity has associated the following linguistic information:

("encender dar", "luz", "", "techo arriba", "")
("apagar", "luz", "", "techo arriba", "")
("encender", "fluorescente", "", "", "")
("apagar", "fluorescente", "", "", "")

The first column corresponds with the verb part, the second column with the object part, the third one with the modifier part, the forth one with the location part and the last one with the additional information part. These sentence skeletons establish all the possible ways to interact with and control this fluorescent light. As it was said above, the use of grammars will transform these four skeleton sentences in multiple sentences that will provide a natural and intuitive way to interact with the system. Notice that some parts are empty and that other parts contain more than one word (what denotes the use of synonyms).

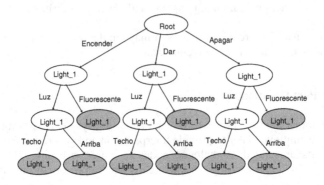

Fig. 3. Partial linguistic tree

Figure 3 shows the linguistic tree that is created with the linguistic information specified above. Shadowed nodes correspond with action nodes. Every time the dialogue system reaches one of these nodes it executes the action associated to the entity specified in the node. In this case, it would execute the action associated to the entity light_1, what would turn the fluorescent on or off, depending on the node.

Following with the creation of the linguistic tree, the radio entity has the next linguistic information (to simplify, we only show the turn off information, not considering the linguistic information to select a specific radio station or change the radio station or the volume, which is present on the real scenario):

$$(\text{"apagar", "radio", "", "", ""})$$

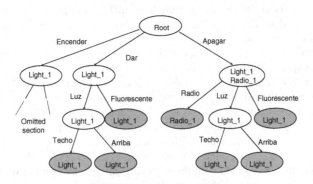

Fig. 4. New linguistic tree

Figure 4 shows how the tree is completed with this new linguistic information, adding new nodes and modifying some of the already existing ones. In this case, if the dialogue system reaches the shadowed node named radio_1, it would turn off the radio (or answer back to the user if the radio was already off), as it is set in the action method associated to the radio_1 entity. Notice that the node under the arrow "apagar" contains two entities. This means that there are two entities in the environment that may be turned off ("apagar"). This node information will be used later at the interpretation and generation processes.

4.3 Interpretation and Generation

Once the linguistic tree is created, the system is ready to interact with the user by means of the spoken dialogue interface. This interaction will be based on the information presented on the linguistic tree. Although the generation and interpretation processes are quite complex and therefore they are out of the scope of this paper, we will give a brief overview of them for a better understanding of the tree generation process.

After a user utterance the system will go down the tree to interpret the sentence. If it reaches an action node, it executes the associated action method. Its execution usually implies some change in the environment, although it may also initiate a system question or answer utterance. If it does not reach an action node, the system will try to find out if it may take some action, being based on the environment current state and the nodes under the node where it stopped. In any case, the system will either take an action or prompt the user for more information by generating a sentence based on the information gathered from the environment and the tree.

To go down through the tree the system will take into consideration if a dialogue was completed in the last interaction (if an action was executed), if it is in the middle of a dialogue, the exact sentence uttered by the user and the environment state.

As an example, based on the tree described above, let us suppose that the user utters the sentence *I would like to turn off* ..., where ... corresponds with noise. The system starts on the root node, goes down the arrow "apagar" and stops there. Once there it may take several actions. The system checks the nodes under the node where it stopped and realizes that there are two entities that may be turned off: "radio" and "luz techo" (notice that the system recognizes that "luz arriba" and "fluorescent" refer to the same entity as "luz techo" so it only considers the first linguistic information encountered). Next, it gets the state of the fluorescent and the radio. If only one of them is on, it may turn it off. If they are both on, it will generate a sentence asking which one of them the user wants to turn off. If they are both off, the system will inform the user in this respect.

As it can be seen in this example, the dialogue interpretation and generation processes are related to the domain ontology and the linguistic information presented on the tree. Not only the dialogue creation process varies depending on the environment but the interpretation and generation do not follow a fixed script and they also adapt to the environment circumstances.

5 Evaluation

The system has been implemented and tested employing the real environment already mentioned. This environment consists of a laboratory furnished as a living room. It is equipped with a television, a DVD player, a radio tuner, an IP Web cam, a flat screen, an electrical door lock, an alphanumeric screen, personalized smart cards, two fluorescent lights, two halogen floor lights, two hi-fi speakers and one wireless microphone (see figure 5).

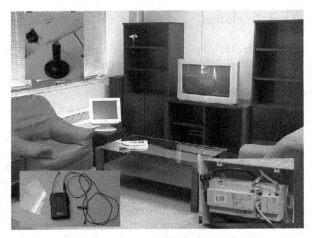

Fig. 5. Snapshot of the living room

Test dialogues interfaces have been created employing different room elements in each test. Combinations of elements of the same and different types were made so that we could check the correctness and accuracy of the grammar and dialogue tree creation processes. In any case the grammar and dialogue tree construction were fully satisfactory.

Let us explain one simple developed test to show the system performance. A spoken dialogue interface was automatically created for a room with a fluorescent light, two floor lights (each with a dimmable and a reading light), a radio tuner and a door lock. This interface has to support dialogues that allow to turn on and off the fluorescent or any of the two reading lights, dim up or down any of the two dimmable lights, open the door, turn on or off the radio and change the radio station. An additional *politeness dialogue* allows users and system to thank, say hello, good bye, etc. In this case the system created a new grammar (based on the action template grammar) for the fluorescent light, adding the information required to turn on, turn off and refer to a fluorescent light. After that it continued with the first floor lamp, composed by a reading and a dimmable light. It appended the information needed to refer to a reading light (the information employed to turn on or turn off a reading light was not added, since it was exactly the same as the fluorescent light information). After that it added the information necessary to dim up or down a dimmable light, to refer to it and, given that there is more than one floor light, it also added the location information employed to distinguish between both lights. Next, the system processed the second floor light. In this case it only had to append the location information for the new light, given that the rest of the linguistic information was shared with the first floor light. This concluded with the creation of the lighting grammar. Other three grammars were also constructed for the radio and door control and the *politeness* capabilities. Concurrently with the grammars creation, the system built the linguistic tree. The final tree was formed by dozens of nodes (many of them shared by several entities) and numerous action nodes. The automatic linguistic tree generation is not described in detail because it would imply a long explanation, but it followed the steps illustrated in section 4.2. These two processes completed the spoken dialogue interface creation. After that, the grammar and dialogue trees were examined to make sure that they were properly created and that they supported all the possible known dialogues. Finally, we tested the system with real users to check the accuracy, efficiency and naturalness of the interface (this final evaluation test corresponds with the interpretation and generation processes).

In every case we found that the system created desired and accurate interfaces for the proposed environments and that the interface construction efficiently adapted to the different environment domains. Interfaces were always produced being based on real elements of our smart environment. As a result we got interfaces that could be employed by users to interact with real devices and rooms, making easier to evaluate their creation process and final performance.

6 Conclusions and Future Work

In this paper we have presented a dialogue system that automatically creates a spoken dialogue interface for a smart environment.

Smart environments are resulting in an increasing interest in the research and industry fields. They provide an *augmented* space that offers new services and ways of interaction [11]. These services have lots of applications for homes, working environments, elderly people, etc. improving considerably the quality of life of their inhabitants. Nevertheless, it is absolutely necessary to provide them with easy-to-use and intuitive interfaces.

To get this, the interface must be created with the minimum effort, making possible the fast development and implantation of these environments. According with these ideas we have developed a real smart environment. Users may interact with it thanks to a plug and play, automatically created, spoken interface. The environment is placed in a laboratory where it is being tested with trained and untrained people of different skills, in order to get performance results and improve its functioning.

Currently we keep working to improve and add new functionalities to the dialogue system.

The linguistic ontology will contain a new part, the question part, which will allow users to make questions about the environment. Current dialogue interpretation and generation processes will have to suffer some changes to support questions, but the dialogue creation process will remain as explained, except by the fact that the linguistic parts will be added to the tree in different order.

We are also trying to integrate the spoken modal interface with other modal interfaces. For instance, in some situations the system may require information to the user by uttering a sentence or by showing the information on a screen. The user may answer either by speaking or by clicking on the selected choice.

Dialogues are added to the system when entities with linguistic information are inserted in the domain ontology. Nevertheless they are not efficiently removed from the tree or stopped when the entity is eliminated from the ontology or stopped.

This plug and play spoken dialogue interface is the result of the continuous process of evaluation tests carried out during its development and current state. New tests, with more and bigger rooms, will also refine the automatic creation methods so that we can test its performance in large scale environments.

Acknowledgments. This paper has been sponsored by the Spanish Ministry of Science and Technology, project number TIC2000-0464.

References

1. Weiser, M. "The world is not a desktop". ACM Interactions, 1, 1, 7-8, 1994.
2. Yankelovich, N. "How do users know what to say?" ACM Interactions, 3, 6, December, 1996.
3. Milward, D. and Beveridge, M. "Ontology-based dialogue systems". IJCAI WS on Knowledge and reasoning in practical dialogue systems, Acapulco, Mexico, August 10, 2003.
4. Weiser, M. "The computer of the 21st century". Scientific American, 265, 3, 66-75, 1991.
5. Abowd, G.D. "Software design issues for ubiquitous computing". IEEE CS Annual Workshop on VLSI: System Level Design (IWV '98), Orlando, FL, April 16-17, 1998.
6. Coen, M.H. "Design Principles for Intelligent Environments". Proceedings of the AAAI Spring Symposium on Intelligent Environments (AAAI98). Stanford University in Palo Alto, California, 1998.
7. Martínez, A.E., Cabello, R., Gómez, F. J. and Martínez, J. "INTERACT-DM. A Solution For The Integration Of Domestic Devices On Network Management Platforms". IFIP/IEEE International Symposium on Integrated Network Management. Colorado Springs, Colorado, USA, 2003.
8. Engelmore, R. And Mogan, T. Blackboard Systems. Addison-Wesley, 1988.
9. Dahlbäck, N. and Jönsson, A. "An empirically based computationally tractable dialogue model". Proceedings of the 14th Annual Conference of the Cognitive Science Society (COGSCI'92), July 1992.
10. Carmona, J.; Cervell, S.; Atserias, J.; Cervell S.; Márquez, L.; Martí, M.A.; Padró, L.; Placer, R.; Rodríguez, H.; Taulé, M. and Turmo, J. "An Environment for Morphosyntactic Processing of Unrestricted Spanish Text". Proceedings of 1st International Conferenceon Language Resources and Evaluation (LREC'98), Granada, Spain, 1998.
11. Wellner, P. "Interacting with paper on the digital desk". Communications of the ACM, 36, 7, 86-96, 1993.

Evaluation of Japanese Dialogue Processing Method Based on Similarity Measure Using $tf \cdot AoI$

Yasutomo Kimura[1], Kenji Araki[1], and Koji Tochinai[2]

[1] Graduate School of Engineering, Hokkaido University,
Kita 13 Nishi 8, Kita-ku, Sapporo-shi, 060-8628 Japan
{kimu,araki}@media.eng.hokudai.ac.jp
[2] Graduate School of Business Administration, Hokkai-Gakuen Universi ty,
Asahi-machi 4-1-40, Toyohira-ku, Sapporo-shi, 062-8625 Japan
tochinai@econ.hokkai-s-u.ac.jp

Abstract. In this paper, we propose a Japanese dialogue processin g method based on a similarity measure using $tf \cdot AoI(term frequency \times Amount of Information)$. Keywords are specially used in a spoken dia - logue system because a user utterance includes an erroneous recognition , filler and a noise. However, when a system uses keywords for robustness , it is difficult to realize detailed differences. Therefore, our method calcu - lates similarity between two sentences without deleting any word from an input sentence, and we use a weight which multiplies term frequenc y and amount of information($tf \cdot AoI$). We use 173 open data sets which are collected from 12,095 sentences in SLDB. The experimental result us - ing our method has a correct response rate of 67.1%. We confirmed tha t correct response rate of our method was 11.6 points higher than that o f the matching rate measure between an input sentence and a comparison sentence. Furthermore that of our method was 7.0 points higher than that of $tf \cdot iaf$.

1 Introduction

Recently, Information Extraction, Information Retrieval and Summariza tion at-tract attention in NLP. In these researches, sentences or words are classifi ed into information types by a similarity measure. Similarity measures are used n ot only for classification problems but also for comparison of documents. Theref ore it is applicable also to a dialogue processing system. From such a backgroun d, simi-larity measures are recognized to be indispensable technology in the ap plicable field of NLP.

A similarity measure is used as a criterion for comparing either w ords or sentences. When we calculate similarity between two sentences, the sam e sen-tences which consist of perfect matching become the highest similarity. H owever, two sentences which have high matching rate are not necessarily simila r. Each domain should select an expression of a similarity measure. In Informat ion Re-trieval, some similarity measure expressions have been proposed such as B oolean

A. Gelbukh (Ed.): CICLing 2004, LNCS 2945, pp. 371–382, 2004.
© Springer-Verlag Berlin Heidelberg 2004

model, Vector Space model and so on. Although a Boolean model expresses a search question by the logic formula, it almost becomes the same as a matching comparison. In vector space model, a similarity measure is calculated using the Euclidean distance, a cosine, a Dice coefficient and so on. A similarity measure has been multiplied term frequency and another weight just like *iaf* in order to make the characteristic of an input sentence reflect.

By the way a dialogue processing system has used keywords since 1960s[1]. Especially keywords have been used in a spoken dialogue processing[2][3][4] because a spoken dialogue includes a speech recognition error, an interjection, and noise. However, the sentence that does not include any keyword often has an important meaning.

In information retrieval, $tf \cdot iaf$ is used widely[5]. $tf \cdot iaf$ means multiplying term frequency and inverse document frequency. The value of $tf \cdot iaf$ becomes higher when the term does not exist in other document very much. However, it does not give suitable weight when there is only a little difference of iaf.

In this paper, we propose Euclidean distance based on $tf \cdot AoI$ in order to measure similarity of two sentences which do not have many words. AoI which is short for Amount of Information shows as follows:

$$AoI = -log_2 P(x) = -log_2 \frac{f(x)}{N} \quad \cdots (1)$$

N means number of running words, and $f(x)$ means frequency which the word x exists. In our method, high frequency interjection and unpredictable noise can become small weight because noise and interjection tend to repeat. Therefore we give a weight of $tf \cdot AoI$. In a vector space model, a setup of the feature amount has big influence on results. Most of vector models delete stop words. However stop words are sometimes necessarily. Our method calculates weights for all words of input sentence. In this paper, we describe how to calculate a weight, and try to increase correct response number by changing parameter. Furthermore we describe how to apply to dialogue processing.

First we explain $tf \cdot iaf$ in Chapter 2, and Chapter 3 describes this technique of our method. In Chapter 4 and Chapter 5, we describe the result of the evaluation experiment by the dialogue processing based on our method. Finally, we describe the effectiveness of our method and a future subject.

2 $tf \cdot idf$

In information retrieval, $tf \cdot iaf$ ($term frequency \times inverse document frequency$) is used for calculating the weight of each word. Table.1 shows how to calculate $tf \cdot idf$. Each line represents one document, each row represents an indexing word. d_1 line includes each term frequency within the document d_1. The t_1 column shows the term frequency in each document. iaf means the following formula

$$iaf(t) = log \frac{N}{af(t)} + 1 \quad \cdots (2)$$

Table 1. Example of tf, af, iaf.

	t_1	t_2	t_3	t_4
d_1	1	2	0	2
d_2	0	3	2	0
d_3	2	1	1	0
af	2	3	2	1
	\multicolumn{4}{c}{$log_2\frac{D}{df}+1$}			
iaf	2.58	1.00	1.58	2.58

Table 2. Example of $tf \cdot iaf$.

	t_1	t_2	t_3	t_4
d_1	2.58	1.00	0.00	5.16
d_2	0.00	3.00	3.16	0.00
d_3	5.16	1.00	1.58	0.00
af	2	3	2	1
iaf	2.58	1.00	1.58	2.58

At this point, "+1" means a smoothing for taking account of $log\frac{N}{af(t)}$=0. Each term weight is calculated by $tf \times iaf$. Table 2 shows the result of each weight of a term. For example, if indexing words could be t_1 and t_2, each document would then be as follows:

d_1 2.58 + 1.00 = 3.58
d_2 0.00 + 3.00 = 3.00
d_3 5.16 + 1.00 = 6.16

Next paragraph, we explain our method with the difference from $tf \cdot iaf$.

3   Similarity of Euclidean Distance Using $tf \cdot AoI$

3.1   Basic Idea

Our method calculates similarity between two sentences. Although the comparison using matching rate measure does not deal with the difference between an important word and an unimportant word, our method calculates the weight of each word. We deal with spoken dialogue examples which include interjections and length expression. Since these expressions usually depend on a person, it is difficult to make stop word list. In this paper, we try to resolve this problem by using calculating a word weight. The word weight is multiplied term frequency and amount of information. Furthermore spoken dialogue examples often include inverted sentences. We try to resolve this problem by using a vector space model which has robustness.

By the way, a spoken dialogue system needs some basic research such as a parser and semantic analysis. However, it is difficult to clarify a problem of an erroneous response when a dialogue system uses many techniques. In this paper, we clarify the problem of our method by simplifying a problem. We prepare a data which consists of pairs between a question and an answer. And when our system finds the highest similarity pair between an input sentence and a question of the data, the answer of the selected pair is replied.

3.2   Similarity

We use Euclidean distance for our similarity measure. When there are (α, β) and (γ, δ) in the vector space model, Euclidean distance becomes $\sqrt{(\alpha - \gamma)^2 + (\beta - \delta)^2}$. Each element of the feature is calculated by multiplication between term frequency and amount of information. We call this weight $tf \cdot AoI$. Table 3 shows examples of calculating the similarity. First, a criteria sentence is divided into by the morphological tool[6]. We call an input sentence the criteria sentence. Here, our system does not use a domestic knowledge which depends on specific language because we consider that our system applies to spoken dialogue system and other languages. When "number of difference words" of the criteria sentence is "n", our system calculates by n dimensions. Sentence A's $tf (term frequency)$ is the word frequency of each word in the document. When different words are $(t_1, t_2, \cdots, t_n)$, features of tf become $tf(tf_1, tf_2, \cdots, tf_n)$ As the features are only the appearance words, tf of the criteria sentence occurs more than once. According to each weight of features, $tf \cdot AoI$ becomes $(tf_1 \cdot AoI(t_1), tf_2 \cdot AoI(t_2), \cdots, tf_n \cdot AoI(t_n))$. We assume that a sentence A is a comparison sentence for comparing with the criteria sentence. The tf of the comparison sentence A becomes $(tf_{a1}, tf_{a2}, \cdots, tf_{an})$. Euclidean Distance between the criteria sentence and the comparison sentence is calculated by $tf \cdot AoI$. The formula is as follows:

$$D = \sqrt{\sum_{i=1}^{n} (tf_i \cdot AoI(t_i) - tf_{ai} \cdot AoI(t_{ai}))^2} \quad \cdots (3)$$

$$Similarity = \frac{1}{D + 1} \quad \cdots (4)$$

When there are not the difference between a criteria sentence and a comparison sentence, Euclidean distance becomes " 0 " . Therefore the highest similarity is " 1 " .

4   Experiment

4.1   Purpose of Experiment

The purpose of this experiment is to compare our method with other methods, and we clarify effectiveness of our method. First the compared method is the

Table 3. How to calculate a similarity.

criteria sentence	$(t_1$	$, t_2$	$, \cdots ,$	t_n $)$
tf	$(tf_1$	$, tf_2$	$, \cdots ,$	tf_n $)$
AoI	$(-log_2 \frac{tf_1}{N}$	$, -log_2 \frac{tf_2}{N}$	$, \cdots ,$	$-log_2 \frac{tf_n}{N}$ $)$
$tf \cdot AoI$	$(tf_1 \cdot AoI(t_1)$	$, tf_2 \cdot AoI(t_2)$	$, \cdots ,$	$tf_n \cdot AoI(t_n))$
Comparison sentence A	$(t_{a1}$	$, t_{a2}$	$, \cdots ,$	t_{an} $)$
tf_a	$(tf_a1$	$, tf_a2$	$, \cdots ,$	$tf_a n$ $)$
$AoI(t_a)$	$(-log_2 \frac{tf_{a1}}{N}$	$, -log_2 \frac{tf_{a2}}{N}$	$, \cdots ,$	$-log_2 \frac{tf_{an}}{N}$ $)$
$tf_a \cdot AoI(t_a)$	$(tf_{a1} \cdot AoI(t_{a1})$	$, tf_{a2} \cdot AoI(t_{a2})$	$, \cdots ,$	$tf_n \cdot AoI(t_{an}))$
Euclidean Distance	$\sqrt{\sum_{i=1}^{n} (tf_i \cdot AoI(t_i) - tf_{ai} \cdot AoI(t_{ai}))^2}$			
Similarity	$\frac{1}{Euclidean Distance + 1}$			

Euclidean Distance by adding weight of $tf \cdot iaf$. Second the compared method is the matching rate between a criteria sentence and a comparison sentence.

A2 sentence is same as AN sentence .

Fig. 1. How to collect data.

How to collect experiment data We would like to collect data which consist of two different questions of the same meaning and one answer for two questions. Therefore, we searched for the training data and the test data from SLDB[7] which includes 12,095 sentences. Figure.1 shows how to get the experiment data. In order to collect the experiment data, we use the following procedure:

Step1 Find the same sentences in SLDB, such as A2 and AN in Figure 1.

Step2 Determine the difference between the sentences communicated prior to the matching sentences such as Step1.

Step3 Having less than four different previous sentences because the meanings between previous sentences tend to become different in many same sentences.

Step4 Collect a set which consists of two different sentences that generated the same response by human observation.

Figure 2 shows examples of the collected data. Here, Question 1 and Answer are the training data, and Question 2 is the test data. These Questions does not necessarily become interrogative sentences in terms of the collected procedure. We could collect 173 sets from 12,095 sentences. However, They are not many set because there are many cases which have different meaning between previous sentences. 173 sets are regarded as the training data and the test data. The number of difference words is 745 and the number of running words is 5,190.

Question 1	先ほどチェックインしました百七号室の鈴木和子です。 (I'm Kazuko Suzuki . I've just checked in your room one o seven .)
Question 2	先ほどチェックインしました一〇七号室の鈴木和子と申しますが。 (My name is Kazuko Suzuki . I've just checked in to room one o seven .)
Answer	はい、鈴木様、どういった御用件でしょうか。 (Yes , Miss Suzuki , how can I help you ?)
Question 1	かしこまりました。そう致します。鈴木様、明朝のモーニングコールは差し上げましょうか。(Yes , of course , we'll certainly do so . And uh will you be requiring a wake-up call , Miss Suzuki ?)
Question 2	はい、えーではどなたかお見えになったら、お電話差し上げます。はい、えー明朝のモーニングコールはいかがなさいますか。 (Yes , I'll call you if someone should come to visit . Shall I give you a wake-up call tomorrow morning ?)
Answer	ええ、七時にお願いします。(Yes , at seven o'clock , please .)

Fig. 2. Examples of the collected data.

4.2   Experiment Procedure

Figure 3 shows how to reply using our similarity measure which calculates Euclidean Distance using $tf \cdot AoI$. Here, the training data consists of 173 pairs between a question and an answer. In the foregoing paragraph, we collected such a open data. When our system calculates the Euclidean Distance between a question of the test data and an input sentence of training data, the system replies the answer of high similarity which is the nearest distance in the training data. If the system could find a suitable answer for each question, we evaluate the correct answer. If not, it becomes an erroneous answer. The comparison experiment is conducted by the three following method.

- Similarity of Euclidean Distance using $tf \cdot AoI$
- Similarity of Euclidean Distance using $tf \cdot iaf$
- Matching rate between an input sentence and a comparison sentence.

Similarity of Euclidean Distance using $tf \cdot AoI$ is our method. Here, an input sentence is treated as a criteria sentence. Similarity of Euclidean Distance using $tf \cdot iaf$ is different in terms of the weight. Matching rate measure is selected by high matching rate.

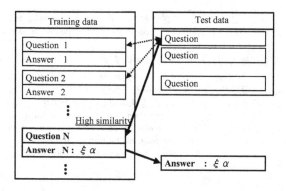

Fig. 3. Dialogue processing.

4.3 Experiment Result

Table 4 shows the experiment results. Here, a correct answer is defined as the correct response which has the only best value since the system has to choose the best answer when there are two or more responses which have the best same value. Our method performed the correct selection of 112 answers for 173 questions The correct response rate of our method had 64.7%, and we confirmed 9.2 points higher than that of the matching rate measure which has 55.5%. Furthermore the correct response rate of our method was 4.6 points higher than that of the similarity which uses Euclidean Distance using $tf \cdot iaf$. In the matching rate measure, there are 3 correct responses which our method cannot select correctly. In the similarity which uses Euclidean Distance using $tf \cdot iaf$, there are 3 correct responses which our method cannot select correctly. We consider that our system's ability includes other method's merit because there are not almost the correct responses which our system could not select in the correct responses of other systems.

Table 4. Experiment result

	Our method	$tf \cdot iaf$	Matching rate measure
Correct response number	112/173	104/173	96/173
Correct response rates	64.7%	60.1%	55.5%
Correct response number which excludes our correct responses	-	3	3

Input	はい、三人部屋でしたらございますが、あしかしえ一お子様の年齢はおいくつですか。(Well Yes we do have rooms ah for three people. However , um how old is your child?)																					
Sentence A	え **お子様 は お** 幾つ で いらっしゃい **ます か** 。(And how old is your child ?)																					
Sentence B	<u>はい</u>、そう<u>します</u> と、うん「のぞみ九号」博多行きという<u>の が</u> 有り<u>ます</u> ね。こちらの 電車<u>です</u> と、東京を九時五十六分に出まして、京都に<u>は</u> 十二時十一分に着き<u>ます</u> 。 お 値段<u>の 方は</u> 乗車券と特急券を併せて、<u>お</u> <u>一人</u> 一万三千九百二十円<u>です</u> ね。(I see , then , we have a Nozomi number nine that's bound for Hakata. This one leaves Tokyo at nine fifty-six and arrives at Kyoto at twelve eleven. The price will be thirteen thousand nine hundred and twenty yen per person , which includes both the boarding ticket and the limited express ticket.)																					
Words	はい	、	三	人	部屋	でし	たら	ござい	ます	が	あ	しかし	えー	お子様	の	年齢	は	お	いくつ	です	か	。
f(x)	87	262	42	13	2	4	9	101	221	71	9	0	14	1	140	0	83	62	0	156	118	530
tf_input	1	2	1	1	1	1	1	1	1	1	1	1	1	1	1	1	1	1	1	1	1	1
tf_A	0	0	0	0	0	0	0	0	1	0	0	0	0	1	0	0	1	1	0	0	1	1
tf_B	1	5	1	1	0	0	0	0	3	1	0	0	0	0	3	0	2	2	0	2	0	3

Fig. 4. Different example of a response selection.

4.4   Consideration

Figure 4 shows the difference between the matching rate measure and our similarity. The example of input sentence means "Well yes we do have room ah for three persons. However , um how old is your child?". This sentence becomes the criteria sentence, and includes filler such as 「**あ** しか**しえ一**」 .[3] Our method selected Sentence A which means "And how old is your child?", and this sentence is correct answer. The matching rate measure selected *SentenceB* which means "I see , then , we have a Nozomi number nine that's bound for Hakata. This one leaves Tokyo at nine fifty-six and arrives at Kyoto at twelve eleven. The price will be thirteen thousand nine hundred and twenty yen per person , which includes both the boarding ticket and the limited express ticket." Here, a denominator of the matching rate is words number of the criteria sentence. Notice that the maximum word number of the denominator depends on the criteria sentence. For example, although 22 words of *SentenceB* are matching for the criteria's words of Figure 4, the matching words become 12 words. Therefore the matching rate of *SentenceA* is $\frac{6}{23} = 26.1\%$, and that of $Sent_B$ is $\frac{12}{23} = 52.2\%$. Here, we explain about calculation of our method. The criteria ' s frequency of " はい (Yes) " is "1", and *SentenceA* 's frequency of it is "0". AoI of " はい (Yes) " is $-log_2 \frac{87}{5190}$ because the number of running words is 5,190 and frequency of " はい (Yes) " is 87. The calculation expression is as follows:

$$\sqrt{((1-0) \cdot -log_2 \tfrac{87}{5190})^2 + ((2-0) \cdot -log_2 \tfrac{262}{5190})^2 + \cdots}$$

---

[3] The underline means filler.

The calculation expression for $Sent_B$ is as follows:

$$\sqrt{((1-1)\cdot -log_2\tfrac{87}{5190})^2 + ((1-5)\cdot -log_2\tfrac{262}{5190})^2 + \cdots}$$

In our method, the similarity for $Sent_A$ was 0.0271(35.9), the similarity for $Sent_B$ was 0.0240(40.6). Here, our method could select correctly using "$tf\cdot AoI$". Although there were many same values in the calculation of the matching rate measure, our system could calculate difference for each sentence.

There were 47 questions which three systems could not select correctly. We collected 173 sets according to processing of 4.1. Therefore it is an example as follows Figure 5.

Here, Question 1 and Response became the training data, Question 2 be-

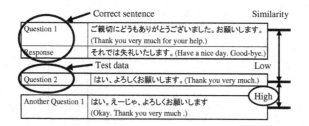

Fig. 5. The reason of erroneous responses.

came the test data. The similarity between Question 1 and Question 2 was 0.0777(11.87). However there were the sentences which have very similarity for Question 2. In other words, their sentences were almost the same as Question 2. For example, there was " はい。えーじゃ、よろしくお願いします。 ". This sentence is almost same as Question2. Most of erroneous results included this reason. In this experiment, we collected the experiment data fairly. Therefore we consider this erroneous reason shows fairness of the experiment data.

The following paragraph explains the parameter setting in order to improve our method.

5   Parameter Evaluation Experiment

5.1   Purpose of Experiment

The calculation result using our method changes by setting up a criteria sentence and adding a parameter. In this experiment, we try to improve correct response rate by changing them. First, There are two Euclidean distances by the criteria sentence. Two distances are as follows:

D_1 A criteria sentence is an input sentence.
D_2 A criteria sentence is each sentence in the training data.

In the case of D_1, feature number becomes the number of difference words in a input sentence, On the other hand, feature number of D_2 change by each sentence in the training data. For example, we assume that Ex.1 is "I am a boy" and Ex.2 is "I am Sam". Feature number becomes four when Ex.1 is set to the criteria sentence. It becomes three when Ex.2 is set to the criteria sentence. Thus, a similarity is difference between D_1 and D_2. Therefore we reflect two distances as follows:

$$D_1 + \alpha \times D_2$$

In this experiment, we find the best value of the coefficient α.

Table 5. Experiment results.

	D_1	D_2	$D_1 + D_2$
Correct response number	112/173	28/173	83/173
Correct response rates	64.7%	16.2%	48.0%
Correct response number which exlude our correct responses	-	7	8

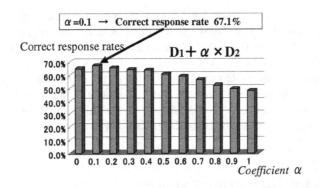

Fig. 6. Evaluation experiment of α .

5.2 Experiment Results and Consideration

Table 5 shows the comparison result by changing the criteria sentence. We added the result of $D_1 + 1 \times D_2$ in Table 5. The correct response rate of D_1 was the highest in three calculation method. That of D_1 was the worst of three, and correct response number became 28 responses. However, there were 7 correct

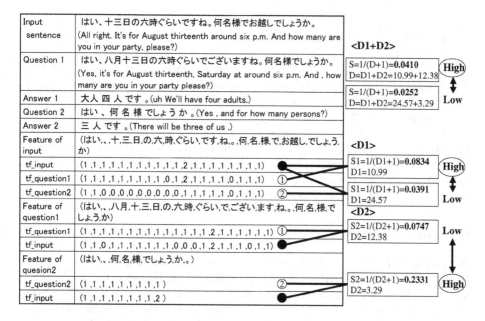

Fig. 7. Example of a calculation.

responses which does not include correct responses of D_1. We can confirm there were the different selection between D_1 and D_2.

Here, we explain three methods in Figure 7. We assume that an input sentence is "はい、十三日の六時ぐらいですね。何名様でお越しでしょうか". When the input sentence is the criteria sentence, feature becomes (はい,、, ,十,三,日,の,六,時, ぐらい,です,ね,。,何,名,様,で,お越し,でしょ,う,か). Therefore, the vector is expressed like (1 ,1 ,1 ,1 ,1 ,1 ,1 ,1 ,1 ,1 ,1 ,2 ,1 ,1 ,1 ,1 ,1 ,1 ,1 ,1). The vector of Question 1 is (1 ,1 ,1 ,1 ,1 ,1 ,1 ,1 ,1 ,0 ,1 ,2 ,1 ,1 ,1 ,1 ,0 ,1 ,1 ,1) because the Question 1 is "はい、八月十三日の六時ぐらいでございますね。何名様でしょ うか。" However, when Question 1 is the criteria sentence, features become (は い,、, ,八月,十,三,日,の,六,時,ぐらい,で,ござい,ます,ね,。,何,名,様,でしょ, う,か). The vector of Question 1 is expressed like (1 ,1 ,1 ,1 ,1 ,1 ,1 ,1 ,1 ,1 ,1 ,1 ,1 ,1 ,2 ,1 ,1 ,1 ,1 ,1 ,1). The vector of the input sentence is expressed like (1 ,1 ,0 ,1 ,1 ,1 ,1 ,1 ,1 ,1 ,0 ,0 ,0 ,1 ,2 ,1 ,1 ,1 ,0 ,1 ,1). In the case of D_1, Question1 was higher than Question 2 because the similarity between Question1 and the input sentence became 0.0834(10.99)[4], the similarity between Question2 and the input sentence became 0.0391(24.57). In the case of D_2, Question2 was higher than Question 1 because the similarity between Question1 and the input sentence became 0.0747(12.38), the similarity between Question2 and the input sentence became 0.2331(3.29). In the case of " $D_1 + D_2$ ", Question1 was higher than

---

[4] A value in the parenthesis is the Euclidean distance.

Question 2 because the similarity between Question1 and the input sentence became 0.0410(23.37), the similarity between Question2 and the input sentence became 0.0347(27.86). Although the selection of D_1 is same as that of $D_1 + D_2$ in this example, we confirmed the correct response rates fall by the result of D_2. The results of D_2 tend to become high similarity when Question 2 is shorter than Question 1. From this result, it is possible to improve correct response rate by changing the coefficient.

We find the best coefficient value of $D_1 + \alpha \times D_2$. We changed the coefficient from 0 to 1. Figure 6 shows the experiment result. The best correct response rate was 67.1% when α was 0.1. We confirmed that correct response rate of our method was 11.6 points higher than that of the matching rate between an input sentence and a comparison sentence.

6   Conclusion

We proposed Euclidean Distance using $tf \cdot AoI$ for similarity of dialogue processing. We compared with "Similarity of Euclidean Distance using $tf \cdot iaf$" and "Matching rate". As a result, the correct response rate of our method had 64.7%, and we confirmed 9.2 points higher than that of the matching rate measure which has 55.5%. Furthermore we improved our method. The best correct response rate was 67.1% when α was 0.1. We confirmed that correct response rate of our method was 11.6 points higher than that of the matching rate between an input sentence and a comparison sentence.

References

1. J. Weizenbaum, "ELIZA - A Computer Program for the Study of Natural Language Comunication Between Man And Machine," Communications of the Association for Computing Machinery,vol.9,no.1,pp.36-45,1966.
2. Takebayashi, Y., H. Tsuboi, H. Kanazawa, Y. Sadamoto, H. Hashimoto, and H. Shinichi. 1993. A real-time speech dialog system using spontaneous speech understanding. IEICE Trans. Inf. and Syst. E-76D(1)(Jan).
3. Victor Zue, Stephanie Seneff, James Glass, Joseph Polifroni, Christine Pao, Timothy J. Hazen and Lee Hetherington, "JUPITER: A telephone-based conversational interface for weather information," IEEE Transactions on Speech and Audio Processing, Vol. 8 , No. 1, January 2000.
4. Diane Litman, Shimei Pan and Marilyn Walker, "Evaluating Response Strategies in a Web-Based Spoken Dialogue Agent." In Proceedings of ACL/COLING 98 , 1998.
5. A. Aizawa, "The Feature Quantity: An Information Theoretic Perspective of Tfidf-like Measures," proc. of ACM SIGIR 2000, pp.104–111,2000.
6. Japanese Morphological Analysis System ChaSen version 2.2.1" ,Yuji Matsumoto, Akira Kitauchi, Tatsuo Yamashita, Yoshitaka Hirano, Hiroshi Matsuda, Kazuma Takaoka, Masayuki Asahara, Dec, 2000.
7. T. Morimoto, N. Uratani, T. Takezawa, O. Furuse, Y. Sobashima, H. Iida, A. Nakamura, Y. Sagisaka, N. Higuchi and Y. Yamazaki, "A speech and language database for speech translation research," Proc. ICSLP'94, pp.1791–1794, 1994.

Towards Programming in Everyday Language: A Case for Email Management

Toru Sugimoto, Noriko Ito, Shino Iwashita, and Michio Sugeno

RIKEN Brain Science Institute
2-1 Hirosawa, Wako, Saitama, 351-0198 Japan
{sugimoto, itoh, iwas, msgn}@brain.riken.jp

Abstract. In order to extend the application domain of natural language interfaces to more realistic tasks without the decrease of user's performance, it is desirable for users to be able to specify their requests as coherent texts consisting of more than one sentence, in other words, to write a program in everyday language. In this paper, we present a processing model of a natural language interface that accepts such an input text. It consists of the text understanding process using a systemic functional linguistic resource called the Semiotic Base, and the mapping process from the structure of the input text to the structure of an output computer program. The algorithms explained in this paper have been fully implemented in our everyday language programming system that deals with personal email management tasks.

1 Introduction

Recent developments in natural language interfaces enable a wider range of people to access computing systems easily and friendly. Some systems only accept words or single sentences (i.e., commands) as inputs to the natural language interface, and other systems allow the users to converse with them interactively in either system/user initiative mode [1][3]. However, most of the existing systems interpret and process each sentence in the user inputs one by one.

In order to extend the application domain of natural language interfaces to more realistic and complex tasks without the decrease of user's performance, users should be allowed to specify their complex requests and conditions as coherent texts consisting of more than one sentence, which are processed by the system in a unified way. Figure 1 shows an example of such an input text in a personal email management domain. It consists of three conditionals, which jointly specify a procedure for handling the user's incoming emails. If we assume that *"the lab"* referred to in the second sentence is a part of *"RIKEN"*[1], and that *"lab"* and *"RIKEN"* are the names of separate mail folders, then naive interpretations of the first two sentences give us inconsistent requests for handling emails from people in the lab. So we need to modify naive interpretations to understand the user's intention behind the input text as a whole. In general,

---

[1] "RIKEN" is the name of a research institute in Japan to which the authors belong.

A. Gelbukh (Ed.): CICLing 2004, LNCS 2945, pp. 383–394, 2004.
© Springer-Verlag Berlin Heidelberg 2004

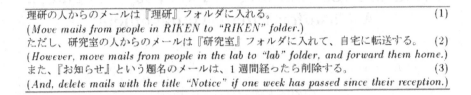

理研の人からのメールは『理研』フォルダに入れる。   (1)
(*Move mails from people in RIKEN to "RIKEN" folder.*)
ただし、研究室の人からのメールは『研究室』フォルダに入れて、自宅に転送する。   (2)
(*However, move mails from people in the lab to "lab" folder, and forward them home.*)
また、『お知らせ』という題名のメールは、1週間経ったら削除する。   (3)
(*And, delete mails with the title "Notice" if one week has passed since their reception.*)

Fig. 1. Example of an everyday language program

sentences in a text may have various kinds of logical and temporal dependency, and supplement each other. Understanding of these relationships and mapping of them to computing procedures are essential.

In this paper, we present a processing model of natural language interface that accepts user's coherent input texts consisting of more than one sentence. An input of this interface is a text written in *everyday language*, that is, language that people use in their daily life. An output of this interface is a script program written in an ordinary programming language. Using an analogy of high level programming languages compiled into machine languages, we call an input text an *everyday language program*, and regard the process of generating an output program as the understanding and *compilation* of it. In order to understand everyday language texts, we take a systemic functional linguistic approach, and use a linguistic resource called the *Semiotic Base*. Then, domain knowledge and compilation rules are used to supplement the understanding result and to compile the program into the target language.

We take the email management domain as an example, and provide an illustration of our processing model. We think that our approach is valid for many other scripting domain, such as file management, scheduling, and control of one or several application programs.

The structure of this paper is as follows: Section 2 discusses the characteristics of the structures of everyday language texts and computer programs. Section 3 presents our processing model of everyday language programs. Section 4 discusses problems in the previous work and compares them with our model. Section 5 presents our conclusion.

2   Text Structures and Program Structures

When people express their requests and conditions in everyday language, they do not necessarily express them in a clear and logically sound way. Pane et al. [13] studied the linguistic structure of complex computing task specifications written by non-programmers, and gave a number of observations, some of which we list below:

– Explicit specification of an iteration was rarely used. Instead, people often used set expressions and plurals to specify operations on multiple objects.

- Complex conditionals such as nestings of "if-then-else" were avoided. Explicit negations were used in few cases.
- People used connectives such as "and" and "or" in various ways. For example, the word "and" was used to mean either boolean conjunction or sequencing.
- Task specifications written by non-programmers were often incomplete, and sometimes incorrect.

These observations show that the correspondence between everyday language texts and computer programs are not so simple that deterministic one-to-one mapping rules can be provided. In order to develop a mapping method, it is necessary to study theories of the structures of both everyday language texts and computer programs, as well as constraints on the correspondence between them.

Structure of texts can be considered from two aspects, that is, semantic *coherence* and syntactic *cohesion* [5]. Coherence of a text can be modeled by *rhetorical structure theory* [9], where the structure of a text is viewed as a tree structure consisting of text segments tied together by various types of rhetorical relations. Rhetorical relations are often indicated by *discourse markers*, e.g., conjunctions. Identification of the rhetorical relation types between segments in a given text is important to understand the user's intention, and thus important to determine the structure of the target program. On the other hand, cohesion of a text includes referring expressions, ellipses, repetitions, and so on. In order to understand cohesion of a text, we need to model the syntactic instance structure of the text.

Structure of computer programs can also be considered from various viewpoints. At a macro level, we can consider structure of software components and design patterns. At a micro level, which is more relevant to our current purpose, we can consider data structures and control structures. Traditional control structures are constructed by operations of sequencing, conditioning, iteration and recursion. In order to understand or write computer programs, we need to examine carefully the scope and the ordering of these constructs.

3 Processing Model

3.1 Overview

The processing model of everyday language programs is illustrated in Fig. 2. A user writes an everyday language program, i.e., a natural coherent text that specifies his/her requests and conditions on computing tasks, and inputs it to the system. The program is analyzed using a systemic functional linguistic resource called Semiotic Base, as well as domain knowledge and status information about the current linguistic and task contexts. The result of the analysis is a linguistic (i.e., graphological, lexicogrammatical, semantic and conceptual) instance structure that corresponds to the input text. The form and the content of everyday language programs are generally not suited to be mapped directly

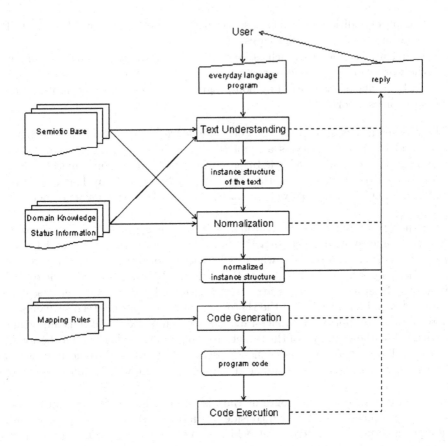

Fig. 2. Overview of the processing model

to computer programs, and thus we normalize the instance structure by supplementing missing information and changing the level of abstraction, referring to domain knowledge and the current status information again. Finally, applying the recursive mapping rules, we generate a program code, and execute it.

Since initial input programs do not necessarily contain enough information to confidently generate and execute computer programs, the system is likely to be helpful and robust if it gives feedback to the user. In our current implementation, a user can confirm the processing result before the execution of the generated code, by examining the reply text which is automatically generated from the normalized instance structure and shown on the screen. If the user finds misunderstandings of his/her program, s/he can re-enter the program with more or other words. It may also be helpful if other types of reply can be triggered in each stage and the user can converse with the system interactively (dotted lines in the figure).

Table 1. Structure and Contents of the Semiotic Base

Components in Semiotic Base		General/ Situation-specific	metafunctional diversification of language		
			ideational	interpersonal	textual
Context Base	Situation Base	General	situation type		
			field	tenor	mode
	Stage Base	Situation-specific	generic structure, stage, move		
	Concept Repository	Situation-specific	class concept, instance concept		
Meaning Base		General	figure, element, sequence	speech function	rhetorical structure, lexical chain
Wording Base		General	transitivity, phase	mood, modality, tense	theme, conjunction
Expression Base		General	punctuation		
Machine Readable Dictionary	General Dictionary	General	general word dictionary, collocation dictionary, verb pattern dictionary, concept dictionary		
	Situation-specific Dictionary	Situation-specific	situation-specific word dictionary		
Corpus Base		Situation-specific	discourse sample, discourse log		

3.2 Semiotic Base

As a basic linguistic theory to deal with everyday language, we adopt *Systemic Functional Linguistics* (SFL) [4], which models language and its use in social contexts. SFL introduces multiple dimensions of linguistic organization, including global dimensions such as stratification, instantiation and metafunction, and local dimensions such as rank and axis, so that we can locate most of linguistic phenomena somewhere in this multiple dimension space. For example, static linguistic knowledge such as grammar and dictionary is located at one end of the instantiation axis ("potential"), while dynamic status information about the current context is located at the other end of the axis ("instance"). Individualization is also considered, which is helpful when we deal with a user's characteristics of everyday language use.

We are developing the *Semiotic Base* [6][15], a systemic functional linguistic resource that can be used to understand and generate natural language texts. Table 1 shows the structure and the summary of the contents of the Semiotic Base. Corresponding to the stratificational organization of a language stressed in SFL, the Semiotic Base has four main components: Context Base, Meaning Base, Wording Base, and Expression Base. Each of these bases stores knowledge about each stratum of language in the form of a *system network*. A system network represents taxonomy and interrelation of linguistic features. Figure 3

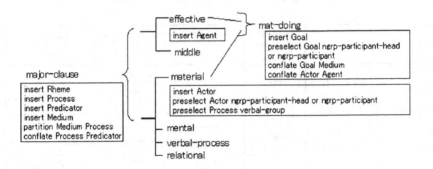

Fig. 3. Fragment of a system network and associated realization statements

shows an example of a system network extracted from Wording Base. Some features in the network are associated with *realization statements* (shown inside the boxes under the feature names), which are used to specify instance structures containing these features.

Besides the system network of situational features (i.e., Situation Base), Context Base stores knowledge about generic structure of dialogues (Stage Base), and frame-like conceptual knowledge (Concept Repository). Moreover, machine readable dictionaries (situation-independent General Dictionary, and Situation-Specific Dictionary) and corpora are included in the Semiotic Base. Each entry in Concept Repository and machine readable dictionaries is associated with relevant features in Meaning Base and Wording Base.

3.3   Text Understanding Algorithm

A user's input text is analyzed using the Semiotic Base. Figure 4 shows the flow of the text understanding process. In this section, we briefly explain the algorithm using an example text shown in Fig. 1. For more detailed explanations of the text understanding algorithm, see [6].

The first half of the text understanding process (the upper half of the diagram) is the preprocessing phase, which prepares the inputs to the later phases where SFL analyses are conducted using main components of the Semiotic Base. First, the morphological and the dependency structure analyses of a text are performed using ChaSen and CaboCha [8]. Then, the dictionary lookup is performed referring to General Dictionary together with the EDR Japanese dictionary [7]. The result contains SFL features and EDR concept identifiers corresponding to words in the text, and they are input to the later processing phases.

The lexicogrammatical and the semantic analyses are performed to construct the instance structures of the text at corresponding strata. The system networks and the realization statements in Wording Base and Meaning Base are used,

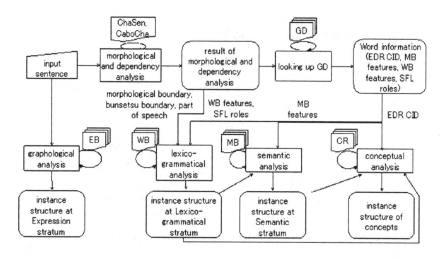

Fig. 4. Overview of the text understanding process

but from a viewpoint of efficiency, they are precompiled into *partial-structures* [12], which specify possible patterns of features appearing in tree-like instance structures. The construction of an instance structure proceeds from the morpheme/element rank to the clause/figure (, move, or rhetorical unit mentioned later) rank, using a bottom-up chart parsing method. This algorithm is based on O'Donnell's idea realized in his WAG systemic parser [12], but significantly extended to incorporate various types of preprocessing results and the forward chaining mechanism to infer additional features.

Finally, the conceptual analysis is conducted to create an instance concept frame representing the conceptual content of the input text. Slots of the instance concept are filled recursively by other concepts, which correspond to child segments of the text. Type constraints on slot fillers are checked according to both the class hierarchy of Concept Repository and the EDR concept classification hierarchy that has richer contents for general concepts. Figure 5 shows the resulting instance concept frame that corresponds to Sentence (1) in Fig. 1.

As a part of Meaning Base, we have textual semantic features and realization statements that correspond to the contents of the rhetorical structure theory. Figure 6 shows a fragment of the system network representing taxonomy of paratactic rhetorical relations, and realization statements representing constraints on features of the nucleus units. Using them, we can construct the inter-sentential instance structure of the text in Fig. 1, which we show partly in Fig. 7. Each box in Fig. 7 represents a semantic unit with a selection path of semantic features. Only inter-sentential units are drawn in the figure, and instance structures within sentences are omitted because of the space limitations. Rhetorical structures are identified using constraints on the relationship between

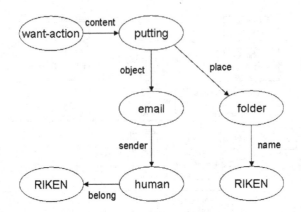

Fig. 5. Conceptual instance structure for Sentence (1)

rhetorical relations and lexicogrammatical features, which are represented as realization statements. Currently we only consider features about conjunctions and thematicality to identify rhetorical structures. Incorporation of other factors such as cohesion, sentence mood and positions is left for the future work.

3.4   Normalization of Programs

After constructing an instance structure that corresponds to a user's input text, we attempt to normalize it by supplementing information missing in the input text, and changing the abstraction level of segments of the structure. Examples of the former case are resolution of ambiguities at various levels, identification of the referents of expressions, and ellipsis resolution. In our scenario, the object of the latter half of Sentence (2) is omitted in Japanese (while it appears as pronoun "*them*" in English). We supplement missing information by referring mainly to the status information about the current linguistic and task contexts.

People often use abstract expressions that cannot be mapped directly to computer commands, and thus we need to convert such fragments of an instance structure to more concrete executable form. The following is an example of such a conversion:

"a mail from a person in RIKEN" →
"a mail whose sender address ends with '.riken.jp' ".

In the current implementation, conversions of this type are realized using procedural transformation rules at the conceptual level.

3.5   Code Generation

We have developed a Perl library for manipulating Microsoft Outlook, and a set of procedural mapping rules from fragments of instance structures to Perl

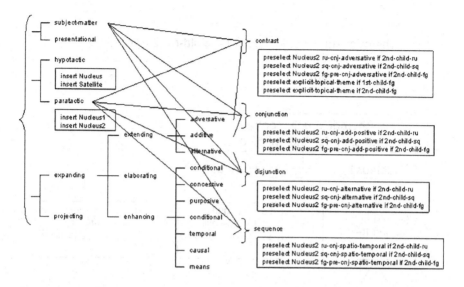

Fig. 6. Fragment of a rhetorical system network and associated realization statements

program codes. The target code is generated by applying mapping rules recursively corresponding to the instance structure constructed in previous phases. Within a sentence, conceptual structure is used to specify the mapping. Roughly speaking, nominal concepts corresponding to groups and phrases are mapped to values (including variables) with constraints, and verbal concepts corresponding to clauses are mapped to statements.

An inter-sentential semantic instance structure (i.e., rhetorical structure) is used to combine program codes generated from conceptual structures corresponding to sentences in a text. The combination procedure consists of the following tasks:

- unification of variables that refer to the same objects,
- determination of the ordering among fragments considering their dependencies, and
- restructuring of control constructs such as moving loops outside and composition of conditional statements.

In doing the second and the third tasks, rhetorical relation types in the instance structure are considered. In our example text, Sentence (1) is *contrasted* with Sentence (2), and thus depends on the result of the processing for Sentence (2). Therefore, we put the program code corresponding to Sentence (1) after the code for Sentence (2). On the other hand, Sentence (3) is in a *conjunction* relation to the rest of the text, and there is no constraint on the ordering between them. Figure 8 shows the final result of code generation.

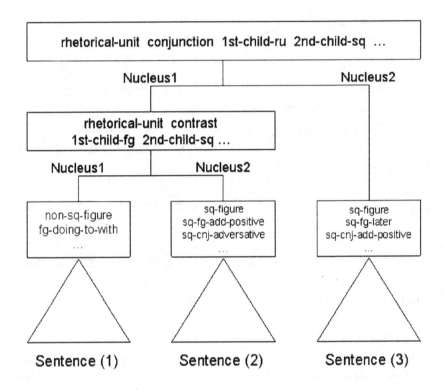

Fig. 7. Semantic instance structure for the example program

4   Discussion

From 80's, there are a number of experimental studies on automatic generation of program codes from specifications written in natural language [2][14][16]. Nevertheless, the technology for processing natural language programs is still under the practical level. We think there are several reasons for this. First, most of previous works placed more importance on the structure and contents of the generated program codes such as correctness and generality than the structure of the input texts. As Pane et al.'s study [13] shows, the structure of natural language programs reflects the human style of everyday thinking, and it is not suited to be mapped directly to the structure of computer programs. Instead, we attempt to model everyday language texts properly in the framework of SFL, where various linguistic features such as lexicogrammatical features, rhetorical relations, and contextual settings are dealt with in a uniform way. We use constraints on structures of both texts and computer programs to limit possible correspondence between input and output.

```perl
require 'mail-lib.pl';

@mails = &mail::get_items;
foreach $mail (@mails) {
    if ($mail::sender_address{$mail} eq 'sugimoto@brain.riken.jp' ||
        $mail::sender_address{$mail} eq 'itoh@brain.riken.jp' ||
        $mail::sender_address{$mail} eq 'iwas@brain.riken.jp' ||
                    (omitted)
        $mail::sender_address{$mail} eq 'msgn@brain.riken.jp') {
        &mail::forward($mail, 'sugimoto@home.address');
        &mail::move($mail, '研究室');
    } elsif (index($mail::sender_address{$mail}, 'riken.jp') >= 0) {
        &mail::move($mail, '理研');
    }
    if ($mail::subject{$mail} eq 'お知らせ' &&
        &time - $mail::received_time{$mail} >= 7 * 24 * 60 * 60) {
        &mail::delete($mail);
    }
}
```

Fig. 8. Generated program code for the example program

Second, the technology of natural language processing in general is not so matured that texts with complex semantic contents can be analyzed accurately enough. Third, task specifications written in natural language are often incomplete and important conditions are left implicit. These two facts indicate that users should be given chances to restate and supplement their previous input programs. Our system gives such chances to the user by providing him/her with the text understanding result in the form of a paraphrased everyday language text. It will be certainly more helpful if the system can converse with a user interactively with the ability of inferring the user's intentions behind the text. We are planning to enhance our system to incorporate this feature.

5   Conclusion

We have discussed the need to extend natural language interfaces so that they can accept complex multi-sentential task specifications written in everyday language. We have presented the processing model for such an interface, which consists of the text understanding with the Semiotic Base and the code generation using the normalization and mapping rules.

The algorithms explained in this paper have been implemented in our everyday language programming system that deals with personal email management tasks. The overall system and the Semiotic Base have been implemented in Java, and the system can generate Perl programs that manipulate Microsoft Outlook.

The current version of the Semiotic Base has approximately 1600 features and 1100 realization statements. We are currently developing the resource so that more variations of texts can be processed and examined in this system.

References

1. Allen, J. F., Byron, D. K., Dzikovska, M., Ferguson, G., Galescu, L. and Stent, A.: Towards Conversational Human-Computer Interaction. AI Magazine, Vol. 22, No. 4 (2001) 27–38
2. Biermann, A., Ballard, B. and Sigmon, A.: An Experimental Study of Natural Language Programming. International Journal of Man-Machine Studies, Vol. 18 (1983) 71–87
3. Chu-Carroll, J.: MIMIC: An Adaptive Mixed Initiative Spoken Dialogue System for Information Queries. Proceedings of the 6th ACL Conference on Applied Natural Language Processing (2000) 97–104
4. Halliday, M. A. K.: An Introduction to Functional Grammar (2nd ed.). London, Edward Arnold (1994)
5. Halliday, M. A. K. and Hasan, R.: Cohesion in English. Longman (1976)
6. Ito, N., Sugimoto, T. and Sugeno, M.: A Systemic-Functional Approach to Japanese Text Understanding. Proceedings of CICLing-2004 (2004)
7. Japan Electronic Dictionary Research Institute Ltd.: EDR Dictionary (Version 2.0). Tokyo, Japan (2001)
8. Kudo, T. and Matsumoto, Y.: Japanese Dependency Analysis using Cascaded Chunking. Proceedings of the 6th Conference on Natural Language Learning (2002) 63–69
9. Mann, W. C., Matthiessen, C. M. I. M., and Thompson, S. A.: Rhetorical Structure Theory and Text Analysis. Mann. W. C. and Thompson, S. A. eds., Discourse Description: Diverse Linguistic Analyses of a Fund-Raising Text. Amsterdam: John Benjamins (1992)
10. Marcu, D.: The Theory and Practice of Discourse Parsing and Summarizations. MIT Press (2000)
11. Matthiessen, C. M. I. M. and Bateman, J. A.: Text Generation and Systemic-Functional Linguistics: Experiences from English and Japanese. London, Pinter (1991)
12. O'Donnell, M.: Sentence Analysis and Generation: A Systemic Perspective. Ph.D. Dissertation, University of Sydney (1994)
13. Pane, J. F., Ratanamahatana, C. A., and Myers, B. A.: Studying the Language and Structure in Non-Programmers' Solutions to Programming Problems. International Journal of Human-Computer Studies, Vol.54, No.2 (2001) 237–264
14. Price, D., Riloff, E., Zachary, J. and Harvey, B.: Natural Java: A Natural Language Interface for Programming in Java. Proceedings of the 2000 International Conference on Intelligent User Interfaces (2000) 207–211
15. Sugimoto, T., Ito, N., Fujishiro, H. and Sugeno, M.: Dialogue Management with the Semiotic Base: A Systemic Functional Linguistic Approach. Proceedings of SCIS & ISIS 2002, Tsukuba, Japan (2002)
16. Sugiyama, K., Kameda, M., Akiyama, K. and Makinouchi, A.: Understanding of Japanese in an Interactive Programming System. Proceeding of 10th International Conference on Computational Linguistics (1984) 385–388

Specifying Affect and Emotion for Expressive Speech Synthesis

Nick Campbell

ATR Human Information Science Laboratories, Kyoto, Japan.
nick@atr.co.jp

Abstract. Speech synthesis is not necessarily synonymous with text-to-speech. This paper describes a prototype talking machine that produces synthesised speech from a combination of speaker, language, speaking-style, and content information, using icon-based input. The paper addresses the problems of specifying the text-content and output realisation of a conversational utterance from a combination of conceptual icons, in conjunction with language and speaker information. It concludes that in order to specify the speech content (i.e., both text details and speaking-style) adequately, selection options for speaker-commitment and speaker-listener relations will be required. The paper closes with a description of a constraint-based method for selection of affect-marked speech samples for concatenative speech synthesis.

1 Introduction

For unrestricted text-to-speech conversion, the problems of text anomaly resolution and given/new or focus determination can be profound. They can require a level of world-knowledge and discourse modelling that is still beyond the capability of most text-to-speech synthesis systems. One implication of this is that the prosody component of the speech synthesiser can only be provided with a default specification of the intentions of the speaker or of the underlying discourse-related meanings and intentions of the utterance, resulting in a flat rendering of the text into speech. This is not a problem for the majority of synthesis applications, such as news-reading or information announcement services, but if the synthesiser is to be used in place of a human voice for interactive spoken dialogue, or conversation, then the speech will be perceived as lacking in illocutionary force, or worse, it will give the listener a false impression of the intentions of the utterance and of the speaker-listener relationships, leading to potentially severe misunderstandings.

When a synthesiser is to be used in place of a human voice in conversational situations, such as in a communication aid for the vocally impaired, in speech translation systems, or in call-centre operations, then there is a clear need for the vocal expression of more than just the semantic and syntactic linguistic content of the utterance. Paralinguistic information related to dialogue turns, and speaker interest is signalled along with the syntactic structure of the speech by means of prosody and voice quality [1].

A. Gelbukh (Ed.): CICLing 2004, LNCS 2945, pp. 395–406, 2004.
© Springer-Verlag Berlin Heidelberg 2004

Since the information signalled in human speech includes linguistic, para-linguistic, and extra-linguistic layers, the listener presumably parses all three sources to gain access to the intended meaning of each utterance. Just as stereo-scopic vision yields more than the simple sum of input from the two eyes alone, so paralinguistic speech understanding gives us more than just the sum of the text and its prosody alone [2]. For example, the lexical item 'yes' doesn't always function to mean *yes* in conversation; when spoken slowly and with a rise-fall-rise intonation, it can instead be interpreted as meaning 'no', or as signalling hesitation (i.e., that the premise is understood but not ncessarily agreed to), thus paralinguistically qualifying the interpretation of the lexical content and signalling both speaker-affect and discourse-related functions to the listener. Someone speaking with 'an authoritative tone of voice' is more likely to be listened to! Similarly, if it is clear from the speaking style that a speaker is in-toxicated (for example) then the listener may be likely to interpret the content of that speech with more caution. If it is apparent that this style of speaking is under conscious control, then the words can take on yet another meaning. Such speaking-style information is not yet freely controlled by the current generation of speech synthesisers.

Paralinguistic information, signalled by tone-of-voice, prosody, and speak-ing style selection, becomes more important as the conversation becomes more personal. Newsreaders and announcers can distance themselves from the con-tent of their utterances by use of an impersonal 'reporting' style of speaking, but customer-care personnel may want to do the opposite, in order to calm a client who is complaining, or to reassure one who is uncertain. When speaking with friends, for example, we use a different speaking style and tone-of-voice than when addressing a stranger or a wider audience. Voice quality is controlled (though probably not consciously) for politeness, for interlocutor, and for differ-ent types of speech act [1]. Speech synthesis must become capable of expressing such differences if it is to be of use in personal or conversational applications.

2   Expressive Speech

As part of the JST (Japan Science & Technology Agency) CREST (Core Re-search for Evolutional Science and Technology) ESP (Expressive Speech Process-ing) Project [3,4], we are collecting 1000 hours of interactive daily-conversational speech, and are building an interface for a CHATR-type synthesiser [5,6] to al-low synthesis of speech from the resulting corpus that will be capable of full expressive variation for paralinguistic effect.

Volunteers wear head-mounted close-talking studio-quality microphones and record their daily spoken interactions to Minidisc devices in blocks of 160 minutes each [7,8]. We now have more than two-years worth of such daily-conversational speech data from a small number of subjects. These samples are transcribed manually and segmentally aligned automatically from the transcriptions. A large part of the research effort is concerned with the choice of appropriate features for describing the salient points of this interactive speech, and with the development of algorithms and tools for the automatic detection and labelling of equivalent features in the acoustic signal [9,10].

Part of this project includes the development of a communication aid [11, 12] and, in particular, an interface for the speedy input of target utterances (the subject of the first part of this paper). We are not concerned with text-to-speech processing in this project, and require instead a fully annotated input that is rich enough to specify not just the lexical content of the desired utterance, but also the speaking style (including the paralinguistic and extralinguistic features) so that the synthesised speech will match the discourse context and enable the 'speaker' to convey all aspects of the intended meaning.

We have been testing our prototypes with disabled users, including muscular-dystrophy or ALS patients, who need a speech synthesiser for essential daily communication with friends, family, and care providers [13], but we also envisage business and other uses of such a system in situations where overt speech may be difficult. For example, a busy executive may want to telephone home to inform her partner that she will be returning later than usual because of an unexpectedly lengthy business meeting. She might prefer to use a synthesiser to speak on her behalf, in order not to disturb the meeting. She may also want to convey information regarding the progress of the business deal at the same time. In such a case, the words 'I'll be late tonight' could be spoken (synthesised) with a happy voice to indicate that positive progress is being made. However, if the same message were intended as warning or as an apology, then a happy voice would be quite inappropriate. As noted above, human listeners read as much from the tone of voice and speaking style in such cases as they do from the linguistic message. [1]

The JST/CREST ESP project aims at producing synthesised speech that is able to express paralinguistic as well as linguistic information, and from our analysis of the data collected so far (about 250 hours of transcribed speech, with the same amount yet to be transcribed for this collection paradigm) we observe that as the interactions become more personal, so the paralinguistic component takes on a greater role in the speech. Utterances become shorter, more common knowledge is assumed, and prosody and voice-quality carry a larger proportion of the information in the message; i.e., the speech becomes more expressive. This is in contrast to most of the corpora used for speech synthesis, where a trained or professional speaker ususally reads from prepared texts in order to produce a balanced corpus with the least amount of effort [14]. We were surprised to find that more than half of the speech, in terms of the number of utterances transcribed, consisted of non-lexical items or 'grunts', for which no dictionary entry exists, and which can only be interpreted in terms of discourse control and expression of speaker affect by their prosody and phonation characteristics. These may turn out to be the most difficult speech items to synthesise, because they are textually ambiguous and require paralinguistic descriptors for their specification.

---

[1] Animals, on the other hand, and soon robots too, may actually read more from the tone of voice than from the content of the speech.

Fig. 1. A sample screen-dump of the GUI interface for use from a web page or personal assistant (left), and a Java-based (i-mode) interface downloaded to a cell-phone (right)

3   Icons and Utterances

In the case of the business user described above, the use of a keyboard for inputting the text would be highly intrusive into the social situation of a business meeting. Annotating that text for paralinguistic and speaking-style information would also be a tedious and time-consuming process. For such situations, we have designed a front-end interface to the synthesiser, for use with a personal assistant or cell phone, so that the speaking style and message can be selected quickly from a menu by toggling buttons to choose between iconic specifiers for the selection parameters. Figure 1 shows a sample screen-dump of the GUI interface, programmed in Flash with a socket-based perl interface to CHATR, for use from a web page or personal assistant (left), and the equivalent Java-based i-mode interface, downloaded to a cellular phone (right).

3.1   Speech Content Specification

Because this device is intended not for the synthesis of unrestricted text-to-speech, but primarily for the generation of interactive daily-conversational utterances, we take advantage of the repetitive and simple nature of this speaking style. Most of the utterances in daily conversation are heavily stylised and repetitive, and the conversations are made up of novel combinations of these basic forms. However, while these building-blocks of conversation may be textually simple and limited in number (many of them are backchannel utterances, laughs, grunts, and fillers), their prosodic realisation can be complex and varied.

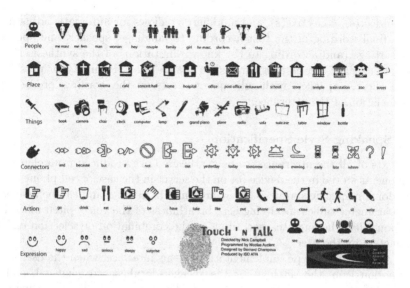

Fig. 2. A chart of the icons currently being tested for use in text selection - objects, operators, and connectives are included, but the list is not intended to be exhaustive at this early stage

We therefore designed this prototype synthesiser to enable the rapid generation of text strings with facilities for the user to easily specify the affectual flavourings and discoursal function of each utterance.

The buttons on the right of the display in figure 1 are used for selecting speaker, speaking-style, and language respectively. They toggle to show the owner of the voice (male, female, asiatic, caucasian, young,old, etc.), the emotion desired for the utterance (currently happy, sad, angry, and 'normal'), and a flag indicating the language (currently only Japanese and English [19,20] though dialectal variants of each are available). The equivalent functions on the cell-phone are bound to the numeral keys 1, 2, and 3 on the dial pad. The icons mapped to the text buttons (left of the main display in figure 1) are illustrated in Figure 2 in the form of a table. Utterance-content icons are represented by their equivalent text on the cell-phone screen. These are bound to the numeral keys 7, 8, and 9 on the cell-phone. 0 is mapped to the 'enter' function to activate the synthesiser. The synthesised speech can be sent directly to the user's device, or redirected to a distant phone. The text icons are grouped into five functional classes: 'people', 'places', 'things', 'actions', and 'connectors'.

By selecting a combination of these icons, the text to be synthesised can be specified. A simplified version of the text, indicating key words alone, appears for confirmation in the central display window (the sand-box) and can be edited if required. A separate window can be popped up for the entry of additional items from a customisable user-specified word list, e.g., for proper names or personalised slot-fillers. This minimal iconic specification of the utterance (subject, verb, object(s), conective(s), and modifier(s)) allows for automatic adjustments to the final wording of the text according to language, speaker, and speaking-style settings (and according to the known limitations of the synthesiser). The choice of speaker can be programmed to change voice, formality, or personality of the selected speaker, with subsequent effects on the wording, prosody, and pronunciation of the utterance.

3.2   Speaking Style Specification

The texts of all the utterances to be synthesised are produced from elementary components stored in the device (or on the server in the case of cell-phone access) as in domain-specific synthesis. They are finite in number and can be associated with parameter tables specifying e.g., breathiness of the voice, pitch inflections, durational lengthening etc., according to the combination or selection of other parameters by the user.

In the first prototype implementation of this interface, when the user selects an emotion icon, the settings for the speaker-database are changed, and the speech is synthesised using separate source databases, each characterising a different emotion. Work is in progress both to merge these individual 'emotionally-marked' databases for each speaker, to enable selection using higher-level descriptors of the speech-style characteristics, and to replace the hard-wired database-switching with an improved expressive unit-selection procedure using the large conversational-speech corpora, as detailed below.

The final text generation is hard-coded using a series of conditional and branching operations. All combinations of frequently-used components are exhaustively listed in the source code, and the appropriate prosodic and speaking-style annotations are then added manually. This step is both inelegant and labour-intensive, and we are considering methods of automating the creation of the dictionary component from an analysis of the transcriptions in the ESP corpus to take advantage of the repetitive nature of conversational speech. However, because the text, the translation, the prosody, the voice characteristics, and the speaking style can be all pre-programmed, and do not need to be computed by the synthesiser at run-time, a higher quality of synthesised speech can be guaranteed. The problems of the text-processing and prosody-prediction components have been eliminated from the synthesis process and the brunt of the responsibility now rests on the unit-selection procedures. Furthermore, the inflections of the text can be adjusted to produce an utterance that is fitting to the selection of speaker and style.

3.3   Emotion and Style

Experience with testing the above interface has revealed several aspects of the design that need further consideration. In addition to the database merging and dictionary automation mentioned above, we must also consider changes to the 'emotion' (speaking-style) selector. The interface was prepared before we had started analysing any speech from the conversational corpus, and was designed primarily to facilitate the expression of emotion in synthesised speech. However, analysis of the conversational-speech corpus in terms of emotion, using the broad-class labels 'happy', 'sad', 'angry', and 'normal' has proved extremely difficult, for several reasons.

Firstly, the definition of 'normal' appears to be highly context-dependent, as the speaking style varies according to both familiarity with the interlocutor, and type of conversation. By far the majority of the speech falls under this cat-egory, and there are remarkably few angry or sad tokens in the corpus (which now contains more than two-years of speech). Normal seems to be 'moderately happy', but rather than expressing pure emotion (which is perhaps just an extra-linguistic aspect of the speech, irrelevant to the discourse), 'speaker involvment' and 'discourse intention' appear to be the main dimensions of paralinguistic vari-ation. Many of the extracts that we examined (often just one side of a phone conversation with a friend or relative) were textually very repetitive, but prosod-ically extremely rich, and varied considerably in their expressivity and functional meaning. Much of the 'language' consisted of grunts and fillers, often monosyl-labic, or repeating the same syllable many times. There is no facility for such back-channelling in the current interface, nor any way of specifying the 'flavour of the grunt' if there were.

Secondly, the 'emotion' labels have proved to be over-simplistic. It is not at all easy to classify a given utterance into one of the above basic classes without first making clear whether we are referring to the speaker's subjective emotional states (both short-term, and long-term) or to the emotional colouring of the ut-terance itself (and whether intended or not). A dimension of 'control' is needed in addition to the switch for emotion, so that we can distinguish between re-vealed and intended variants. For example, a schoolteacher might not in fact be angry when speaking (as part of the job) in an angry manner to control unruly students in the class. Conversely, the person might be feeling extremely angry (for unrelated personal reasons), but manages for social reasons not to reveal it in the speech. Both of these variants are marked with respect to speaking style.

For the labelling of paralinguistic characteristics in the speech database, each utterance must be evaluated separately in terms of such features as the relation-ships between speaker and hearer (age, sex, familiarity, rank, politeness, etc.), the degree of commitment to the content of the utterance (citing, recalling, reveal-ing, acting, informing, insisting, etc.), the long-term and short-term emotional and attitudinal states of the speaker, the pragmatic force of the speech act, the voice-quality of the utterance (breathy, relaxed, pressed, forced), and so on. The list is not complete. The simplistic notion of a single switch for 'emotion' in an expressive speech synthesiser would appear to need considerable rethinking. The reduction of such complex features to a simple descriptor continues as the core of our work.

3.4 Future Work

In place of an over-simplistic 'emotion button' on the synthesiser interface, we are now considering a combination of three 'buttons', or feature dimensions, for determining the paralinguistic information that governs the speaking style of an utterance; one for 'self', one for 'other', and one for 'act'. The 'self' button might be toggled between four states, to select between two levels (high and low) of interest and mood. The 'other' button similarly with two levels (high and low) of 'friend' and 'friendly' relationship to the listener (this will be the first time that a difference in the listener will be considered as a factor in speech synthesis output control). The 'act' (or illocutionary-force) button will be used to specify directionality of the utterance (whether offering or eliciting) and its intention (conveying primarily either affect or information).

It is clear from our observations of the ESP conversational speech corpus that, rather than a single 'emotion' factor, at least these three dimensions of speaking-style control are required. The speaker's degree of involvement in the utterance is of prime concern — the amount of interest in the topic of the conversation, the quality of personal experience underlying the expression of the current utterance, and the degree of belief in the premise of the utterance, as well as factors such as the speaker's current mood and state of health. For simplicity we have reduced these parameters to two levels, high or low, of interest and mood.

Relationship with the listener appears to be the second most important determinant of speaking style. Whether talking to a friend or a stranger, a businesss acquaintance or a family member, and whether the context of the discourse allows a more or less friendly or intimate speaking style. Simply knowing the relationship with the listener is not enough; it is also important to know the circunmstances in which the discourse is taking place. For example, the speaking style adopted when answering a question by a family member may depend on whether that question is asked at the dining table or in a conference hall.

Thirdly, the intentions underlying the utterance, the pragmatics of the speech event, play an important part in determining how it is to be realised. There are many sections of a conversation where the content (and intent) could be fully specified by a simple transcription of the words alone, and where prosody plays only a small part. We denote these as 'information'. And there are almost as many sections where the words themselves play a smaller part than the way in which they are said — we denote these as 'affect'. For simplicity, we choose to consider for our next implementation only the directionality and type of each utterance — whether the speech event functions primarily to express (or to request the expression of) affect or information. It must remain as future work to determine how the combination of each is realised in a single utterance.

4   Unit Selection for Expressive Speech Synthesis

This section describes a method by which the synthesis of spontaneous-sounding conversational speech can be generated using a small speech synthesiser as a driver for concatenative unit selection from a large spontaneous speech database. The driver is used to generate acoustic targets, which are then used for pre-selection of acoustic waveforms for the synthesis units, with the final candidates filtered according to further acoustic constraints to ensure the selection of units having appropriate voice and speaking style characteristics.

Mokhtari & Campbell [15] have described a method whereby acoustic syllables can be automatically demarcated in running speech and used as targets for the selection of units of natural speech from a large database for concatenative synthesis. Here, we show how those targets can be used as the basis of spontaneous or expressive speech synthesis, further selecting from among the candidates thus obtained by use of voice-quality, speaking-rate, and pitch-range for a finer control of speaking styles.

There are now several very large corpora of spontaneous speech that could be used as resources for producing spontaneous-sounding speech synthesis (e.g., [16,17,18]) but the task of segmentally labelling them is considerable, and many of the problems related to modelling the acoustic characteristics of spontaneous speech have yet to be resolved. Until recently, detailed phonemic labelling has been a prerequisite for the use of a database in concatenative speech synthesis. However, previous work on the synthesis of multilingual speech [19,20] resulted in a procedure for using the voice of a speaker of the target language to generate a sequence of acoustic vectors that can then be used for the selection of units from the native-language database of a non-native speaker of the target language. This work was carried out in the framework of multilingual synthesis for speech translation and resulted in more natural pronunciation of the target 'foreign language' speech, but can be applied as well to the synthesis of spontaneous or conversational speech. i.e., we can use a subset of well-labelled speech, in the voice of a given speaker, as targets for the selection of units from a larger database of spontaneous speech from the same speaker.

4.1   Corpus-Based Expressive Speech Synthesis

As noted above, by far the majority of databases that have been used for speech synthesis research have been purpose-designed and carefully read, usually by professional announcers, under studio conditions. They are not representative of 'speech in action', nor do they include the variety of natural speaking styles and situations that are encountered in everyday spoken conversations. Such studio recordings of speech can illustrate many of the formal linguistic aspects of spoken language, but few of the functional social or interactive aspects of spoken communication. Many attempts at producing corpora of spontaneous speech for synthesis research have failed, due to the acoustic and psychological difficulties of capturing natural samples of ordinary speech in everyday interactive situations. The "Observer's Paradox" (after Labov [21]) is well known to researchers in the social sciences, who have observed that when people are confronted with a microphone, their speech undergoes subtle changes and may no longer be representative of that used in their normal daily-life interactive situations. Several ways have recently been proposed to overcome this problem.

For the Corpus of Spontaneous Japanese [16] the researchers have chosen to collect a subset of spontaneous speech limited to those situations where a microphone is a common and predictable accessory, such as public lectures and

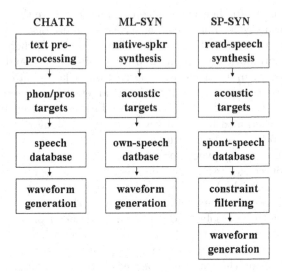

Fig. 3. Comparing the three methods of synthesis. The left column is common to all three systems, and is standard for CHATR. The middle column shows the flow for multi-language synthesis (ML), taking input (top box) from the output of the left column (bottom box) to use a native-speaker's voice as target. The right column shows the proposed system, similar to ML, but with the added filtering necessary to reduce the diversity of candidates found in the spontaneous speech database.

broadcasting environments. The resulting speech is spontaneous but formal, i.e., the speakers show a public rather than a personal face. The JST/CREST ESP corpus is another example, where the speakers and their interlocutors become accustomed to the presence of a microphone by having it worn on the body for extended periods of time. Both the above projects have produced speech data that is illustrative of the type that will be used in future corpus-based speech synthesis, but these corpora raise many problems that were not encountered in traditional concatenative speech synthesis.

The biggest problem, perhaps, lies in the amount of manual work that has been required for the processing of a speech database in order to produce a set of units suitable for concatenation. As corpora become larger, this must be automated or reduced. Consequently, we have proposed a method for using acoustic vectors as targets for the unit-selection [9,10,15]. The acoustic parameters obtained by concatenative synthesis from a relatively restricted (typically read-speech) database of the source speaker, are used as targets for selecting from among the loosely-matching candidates in the much larger non-read (spontaneous) speech database of the same speaker. This method relies upon the fact that the spectral representation of speech varies less than the possible prosodic representations of an equivalent utterance. We can select all acoustic waveforms having the same phonemic segmental content as the target utterance and then further select from amongst them acording to the desired prosodic and voice-quality characteristics.

This paralinguistic speaking-style-based constraint on the unit-selection procedure requires a third stage of unit-selection to filter the candidates according to stylistic attributes that are more varied in the spontaneous speech corpus than in the read speech corpus (see Figure 3). The acoustic targets which correlate with the phonetically-motivated vocal-tract configurations (such as formants) are weighted more heavily as initial selection criteria than those which correlate with the prosodic aspects of the speech (such as spectral tilt). The prosodic constraints (e.g., 'high breathiness', 'low fundamental frequency', 'slow speech') are then used as filters in an intermediate stage to reduce the number of candidates to only those having the appropriate speaking-style characteristics for the desired 'spontaneous' speech utterance. The final selection stage is further constrained by 'join-cost' concatenation criteria to ensure a smooth and continuous sequence of units for signal generation.

5 Conclusion

For conversational speech synthesis, the text of an utterance alone is inadequate as a specification of the style in which it is to be rendered, which depends largely upon interacting factors such as speaker-state, purpose, involvement, and relations with the listener.

This paper has presented techniques for the synthesis of conversational speech, expressing paralinguistic information by means of pre-stored annotations on texts. Variants are selected by a combination of choices that define the basic components of each utterance, such as voice, language, and speaking style. The prototype is still rudimentary, but experience with this interface is allowing us to consider better ways of simply specifying the attributes of speech to be synthesised.

The paper has also presented a novel method for the synthesis of spontaneous-sounding speech, using a smaller read-speech database from the same speaker as a bootstrap for producing intermediate acoustic targets. The best-matching candidates are selected from the spontaneous-speech database and filtered by prosodic constraints so that only those having the appropriate speaking-style characteristics will be made available to the waveform-concatenation module.

Acknowledgements. This chapter is an extended and updated version of work first presented at the Acoustical Society of Japan and the 2001 IEEE Speech Synthesis workshop, with contributions from P. Mokhtari and researchers and staff of the ESP project, N. Auclerc, B. Champoux, and students of the Department of Applied Linguistics at NAIST. This work is supported partly by a grant from the Japan Science & Technology Agency under CREST Project #131, and partly by aid from the Telecommunications Advancement Organisation of Japan.

References

1. Campbell, N & Mokhtari, P., "Voice Quality; the 4th prosodic parameter", in Proc 15th ICPhS, Barcelona, Spain, 2003.
2. Antoine Auchlin, Linguistics, Geneva, personal communication, 2003.
3. JST/CREST Expressive Speech Processing project, introductory web pages at: http://feast.his.atr.co.jp/
4. Campbell, W.N., "Databases of Emotional Speech", in Proc ISCA (International Speech Communication Association) ITRW on Speech and Emotion, pp. 34–38, 2000.
5. Campbell, W. N. and Black, A. W. "CHATR a multi-lingual speech re-sequencing synthesis system". Technical Report of IEICE SP96-7, 45–52, 1996.
6. Campbell, W. N. "Processing a Speech Corpus for CHATR Synthesis". Proceedings of The International Conference on Speech Processing pp. 183–186, 1997.
7. Campbell, W. N., "The Recording of Emotional speech; JST/CREST database research", in Proc LREC 2002.
8. Campbell, N & Mokhtari, P., "DAT vs. Minidisc — Is MD recording quality good enough for prosodic analysis?", Proc ASJ Spring Meeting 2002, 1-P-27.
9. Campbell, W. N., Marumoto, T., "Automatic labelling of voice-quality in speech databases for synthesis", in Proceedings of 6th ICSLP 2000, pp. 468–471, 2000.
10. Mokhtari, P, & Campbell, W. N., "Automatic detection of acoustic centres of reliability for tagging paralinguistic information in expressive speech.", in Proc LREC 2002.
11. Iida, A., Iga, S., Higuchi, F., Campbell, N., Yasumura, M., "A speech synthesis system with emotion for assisting communication", ISCA (International Speech Communication and Assosiation) ITRW on Speech and Emotion, pp. 167–172, 2000.
12. Iida, A., Campbell, N. and Yasumura, M. "Design and Evaluation of Synthesised Speech with Emotion". Journal of Information Processing Society of Japan Vol. 40, 1998.
13. Iida, A., Sakurada,Y., Campbell, N., Yasumura,M., "Communication aid for non-vocal people using corpus-based concatenative speech synthesis", Eurospeech 2001.
14. Campbell, W. N., "Recording Techniques for capturing natural everyday speech", in Proc Language Resources and Evaluation Conference (LREC-2002), Las Palmas, Spain, 2002.
15. Mokhtari, P. and Campbell, N. "Automatic measurement of pressed/breathy phonation at acoustic centres of reliability in continuous speech", in Special Issue on Speech Information Processing of the IEICE Transactions on Information and Systems, The Institute of Electronics, Information and Communication Engineers, Japan, Vol. E-86-D, No. 3 (March), pp. 574–582, 2003
16. Maekawa, K., Koiso, H., Furui, S., & Isahara, H., "Spontaneous Speech Corpus of Japanese", pp. 94-7-952, Proc LREC 2000, Athens, Greece, 2000.
17. Switchboard telephone-speech database: www.ldc.upenn.edu.
18. CALLFRIEND: a telephone-speech database, LDC Catalog, 2001.
19. Campbell, W. N., "Foreign-Language Speech Synthesis", Proceedings ESCA/CO-COSDA 3rd Speech Synthesis Workshop, Jenolan Caves, Australia 1998/11/26.
20. Campbell, W. N., "Multi-Lingual Concatenative Speech Synthesis", pp. 2835–2838 in Proc ICSLP'98 (5th International Conference on Spoken Language Processing), Sydney Australia 1998.
21. Labov, W., Yeager, M., & Steiner, R., "Quantitative study of sound change in progress", Philadelphia PA: U.S. Regional Survey, 1972.

Overcoming the Sparseness Problem
of Spoken Language Corpora Using Other
Large Corpora of Distinct Characteristics

Sehyeong Cho[1], SangHun Kim[2], Jun Park[2], and YoungJik Lee[2]

[1] MyongJi University, Department of Computer Science
San 38-2 Yong In, KyungGi, Korea
shcho@mju.ac.kr
[2] Electronics and Telecommunication Research Institute,
Yusong, Daejon, Korea

Abstract. This paper proposes a method of combining two n-gram language
models, one constructed from a very small corpus of the right domain of interest, the other constructed from a large but less adequate corpus, resulting in a
significantly enhanced language model. This method is based on the observation that a small corpus from the right domain has high quality n-grams but has
serious sparseness problem, while a large corpus from a different domain has
more n-gram statistics but inadequately biased. Two n-gram models are combined by extending the idea of Katz's *backoff*. We ran experiments with 3-gram
language models constructed from newspaper corpora of several million to tens
of million words together with models from smaller broadcast news corpora.
The target domain was broadcast news. We obtained significant improvement
(30%) by incorporating a small corpus around one thirtieth size of the newspaper corpus.

1 Introduction

Language modeling is an attempt to capture the regularities and make predictions, and
is an essential component of automatic speech recognition. Statistical language models are constructed from large text, or corpus. However, it is not easy to collect
enough spoken language text. Other corpora are readily available, but the difference
in spoken and written language leads to a poor quality.

This granted, what we need is a way of making use of existing information to help
lower the perplexity of the language model. However, simply merging two corpora
will not help much, as we shall see later in the next section.

2 Related Work

Linear combination is probably the simplest way of combining two language models:
$P_{combined}(w \mid h) = \sum_{k=1..n} \lambda_k P_k(w \mid h)$. Linear interpolation has the advantage of extreme
simplicity. It is easy to implement, easy to compute. Linear combination is consistent
as far as n-gram models are concerned.

A. Gelbukh (Ed.): CICLing 2004, LNCS 2945, pp. 407–411, 2004.
© Springer-Verlag Berlin Heidelberg 2004

Maximum entropy method [1] can be used to incorporate two information sources. For instance, suppose we had an *n*-gram model probability and a trigger pair model probability: $P(bank \mid in, the)$ and $P(bank \mid loan \in history)$. When the two conditions are both satisfied, then maximum entropy method can find a solution without sacrificing the consistency by imposing that the constraints are satisfied *on average*.

However, if we had the same event space, then Maximum entropy method will result in trouble, because

$$\underset{h \text{ ends in 'in the'}}{E}[P_{combined}(bank \mid h)] = P_1(bank \mid in, the),$$

$$\underset{h \text{ ends in 'in the'}}{E}[P_{combined}(bank \mid h)] = P_2(bank \mid in, the)$$

should both be true. However they contradict each other because $P_1(bank \mid in, the) \neq P_2(bank \mid in, the)$.

Akiba [6] proposed using selective backoff. Their approach is similar to ours in that they use backoff with two different models. One of the models is probabilistic model and the other is a grammar network. The aim of their combination is to delete probabilities of all unnecessary *n*-grams, that is, those that are not possible word sequences according to the simpler grammar-based transition network.

Adaptation ([7], for example) is a dynamic switching of language models based on the present situation. While adaptation focuses on dynamically detecting the shift among domains or topics, our problems deals with constructing a language model *per se* by using information from two models.

3   Proposed Approach

Define a *primary corpus* as a corpus from a domain of interest. A *secondary corpus* is a (relatively larger) corpus, from another domain. A *primary language model*, then, is a language model constructed from a primary corpus. A *secondary language model* is a language model constructed from a secondary corpus. C_1 is the primary corpus, and C_2 is the secondary corpus. P_1 denotes the probability obtained by maximum likelihood estimation from the primary corpus. $\overline{P}_1$ denotes a discounted primary probability. P_2 and $\overline{P}_2$ are likewise defined.

We measured the perplexity [9] of spoken language models and written language models against broadcast script. With the same 3-gram hit ratio, the perplexity of the latter is almost twice higher (e.g., 17.5% / 560 / 970). Conversely, with similar perplexity, hit ratio of the primary model is lower. In other words, a small primary model has quality 30gram statistics, while a large, secondary model has simply more 3-grams. Then it would be nice if we had a way of combining the two.

Therefore given appropriate sizes, we may be able to take advantage of *n*-gram probabilities in both models. We assumed that the secondary corpus is at least one order of magnitude larger than the primary corpus. We also assumed primary 3-gram statistics best reflect the actual probability. Next are 3-gram (secondary) , 2-gram (primary), 2-gram(secondary), 1-gram(primary), and 1-gram (secondary), in order.

The basic idea is this: the probability of a trigram x,y,z is calculated from primary 3-gram, if any. If it doesn't exist, use probability of a trigram x,y, z from secondary 3-grams, then primary 2-gram, and so on. In order to be consistent (i.e., sum of probabilities equal to 1), we do as follows, based on Katz's idea [2].

We first discount[3] the MLE probabilities of the non-zerotons. Let $\beta = 1 - \sum_{xyz \in C_1} \overline{P_1}(z \mid x, y)$. Then we redistribute the mass to zeroton 3-grams (i.e., the 3-

gram xyz's, such that $xyz \notin C_1$), in proportion to either secondary 3-gram probability or primary 2-gram. Assuming that the secondary corpus is larger by at least one order of magnitude,

$$\overline{P}(z \mid xy) = \begin{cases} \overline{P_1}(z \mid xy) & \text{if } xyz \in C_1 \\ \alpha_{xy}\overline{P_2}(z \mid xy) & \text{if } xyz \notin C_1, xyz \in C_2 \\ \alpha_{xy}\overline{P}(z \mid y) & \text{otherwise} \end{cases} \tag{1}$$

In the above formula, α_{xy} is a normalizing constant, calculated as equation 5.

$$\alpha_{xy} = \frac{\beta}{\sum_{\substack{xyz \notin C_1 \\ xyz \in C_2}} \overline{P_2}(z \mid xy) + \sum_{\substack{xyz \notin C_1 \\ xyz \in C_2}} \overline{P}(z \mid y)} . \tag{2}$$

Unlike Katz's coefficients, there is no simple computation procedure for α_{xy}, and thus repeated summation is required, which took hours in a machine with two Xeon 2GHz processors. Fortunately, the calculation needs to be done only once and it need not be calculated in real-time.

The 2-gram probability $\overline{P}(z \mid y)$ and 1-gram probability are defined similarly.

$$\overline{P}(z \mid y) = \begin{cases} \overline{P_1}(z \mid y) & \text{if } yz \in C_1 \\ \alpha_y \overline{P_2}(z \mid y) & \text{if } yz \notin C_1, yz \in C_2 \\ \alpha_y \overline{P}(z) & \text{otherwise} \end{cases} \tag{3}$$

$$\overline{P}(z) = \begin{cases} \overline{P_1}(z) & \text{if } z \in C_1 \\ \alpha_0 \overline{P_2}(z) & \text{if } z \notin C_1, z \in C_2 \\ \alpha'_0 & \text{otherwise} \end{cases} \tag{4}$$

4 Concluding Remarks

We used CMU-Cambridge toolkit to construct secondary models in ARPA-format from a newspaper corpus (Dong A Ilbo news) from 4 million to 8 million words. We also constructed 4 primary models from SBS broadcast news (100K to 400K words). Test corpus was a separate SBS broadcast news text of 10K size.

By simply mixing up primary and secondary models, we obtained 10 to 17 percent decrease in perplexity. With optimal mixing ratio by linear interpolation, additional 5 to 6 % decrease is seen [10]. The result of the dual-source experiment showed around 30% decrease in perplexity. Considering that 20% decrease in perplexity shows notable increase in the accuracy of the speech recognizer, this can be regarded a meaningful result.

Table 1. Resulting Perplexity of interpolated model and dual-source backoff model

Size(1-ary/2ndary)	Linear Interpolation (1:1)	dual-source backoff
100K/4M	377	242
200K/5M	359	244
300K/6M	333	230
400K/8M	300	206

The experiment clearly showed that there is improvement. However, it is not certain if this is indeed the optimal. As we discussed earlier the relative quality of the primary and the secondary n-grams depend on the corpora sizes. For instance, if the size of the primary corpus is very small compared to the secondary model, the secondary 2-gram probability may prove to be more reliable than the primary 3-gram. Lastly, the algorithm needs to be generalized to n-gram models of arbitrary n values. Theoretically, it is a straightforward generalization of equation 4 into equation 5:

$$\overline{P}(w_m \mid w_{1..n-1}) = \begin{cases} \overline{P}_1(w_m \mid w_{1..n-1}) & \text{if } w_{1..n} \in C_1 \\ \alpha_{w_{1..n-1}} \overline{P}_2(w_m \mid w_{1..n-1}) & \text{if } w_{1..n} \notin C_1, w_{1..n} \in C_2 \\ \alpha_{w_{1..n-1}} \overline{P}(w_m \mid w_{2..n-1}) & \text{otherwise} \end{cases} \quad (5)$$

However, the real problem is in determining the order of applications. This is not merely a theoretical a problem, but a practical one, since it may well depend on the sizes of the corpora – relative or absolute – and also on the similarity among primary, secondary, and the test corpora.

Acknowledgement. This research was supported by Center for Speech and Language Research in ETRI.

References

[1]   Rosenfeld, R. Adaptive Statistical Language Modeling: A Maximum Entropy Approach, Ph.D. dissertation, April 1994, Carnegie-Mellon University

[2]   Katz, S.M. "Estimation of Probabilities from Sparse Data for the Language Model Component of a Speech Recognizer," IEEE Transactions on Acoustics, Speech and signal Processing, vol. ASSP-35, pp 400-401, March 1987

[3]   Good, I.J. "The Population frequencies of species and the Estimation of Population parameters," Biometrica, vol.40, parts3,4 pp.237-264

[4]   Goodman, J.T. "A Bit of Progress in Language Modeling," Computer Speech and Language vol 15, pp.403-434, 2001

[5]   Bahl, L., Brown, P. , deSouza, P. and Mercer, R. "A tree-based Statistical Language Model for natural Language Speech Recognition," IEEE Tr. On Acoustics, Speech, and Signal Processing, 37, pp.1001-1008, 1989

[6]   Akiba, T., Itou, K., Fujii, A. and Ishikawa, T. "Selective Backoff smoothing for incorporating grammatical constraints into the n-gram language model," in Proc. International Conference on Spoken Language Processing, pp. 881-884, Sept. 2002

[7]   Chen, S. F. et al, "Topic Adaptation for Language Modeling Using Unnormalized Exponential Models," in Proc. ICASSP'98, Vol. 2, pp. 681-684, May 12-15, 1998

[8]   Jurafsky, D. and Martin, J.H., Speech and Language Processing, Prentice-Hall, 2000

[9]   Jelinek, F. et al, "Perplexity – A Measure of the difficulty of speech recognition tasks," Journal of the Acoustics Society of America, 62, S63. Supplement 1, 1977

[10] Sehyeong Cho, http://nlp.mju.ac.kr/dualsource/

A Syllabification Algorithm for Spanish

Heriberto Cuayáhuitl

Universidad Autónoma de Tlaxcala,
Department of Engineering and Technology,
Intelligent Systems Research Group,
Apartado Postal #140, Apizaco, Tlaxcala, Mexico, 90300.
hcuayahu@ingenieria.uatx.mx

Abstract. This paper presents an algorithm for dividing Spanish words into syllables. This algorithm is based on grammatical rules which were translated into a simple algorithm, easy to implement and with low computational cost. Experimental results in an evaluation text corpus show an overall error rate of 1.6%. Most of the error is attributed to words with diphthongs and to confusion in the use of prefixes where grammatical rules are not always absolute. Syllabification is an essential component of many speech and language processing systems, and this algorithm might be very useful to researchers working with the Spanish language.

1 Introduction

Currently, the development of speech synthesizers and speech recognizers, frequently requires working with subword units such as syllables [1-3]. For instance, robust speech recognition often makes use of word spotters based on syllables for detecting Out-of-Vocabulary (OOV) speech [2] and for modeling unknown words in spontaneous speech [3]. Today, every new system being developed requires the implementation of a new algorithm for dividing words into syllables, due to the fact that a formal algorithm shared among the linguistic community does not exist, at least for Spanish. In the linguistic literature, we can find grammatical rules or attempts to explain the division of words into syllables step-by-step, but nothing beyond that. In the past, syllabification algorithms have been proposed for different languages, including English and German, among others [4], implemented as a weighted finite state transducer, but this is not the case for Spanish, where few research efforts have been documented. Thus, the purpose of this work is to formulate an algorithm for dividing Spanish words into syllables, and to share this algorithm so that other researchers in the area of speech and language processing will not have to duplicate the work.

In this research, is proposed an algorithm to divide Spanish words into syllables. Our experiments are based on a text corpus containing representative words for each grammatical rule. Results are given in terms of a simple division of correctly syllabified words by the total number of words. In the remainder of this paper we first provide an overview of Spanish syllabification in section 2. In section 3 we describe the syllabification algorithm itself. In section 4 we present experimental results. Finally, we provide some conclusions and future directions.

A. Gelbukh (Ed.): CICLing 2004, LNCS 2945, pp. 412–415, 2004.
© Springer-Verlag Berlin Heidelberg 2004

2   Syllabification in Spanish

Spanish letters are either vowels (a,e,i,o,u) or consonants ($b,c,d,f,g,h,j,k,l,ll,m,ñ,$ n,p,q,r,rr,s,t,v,w,x,y,z), and vowels are either weak (i,u) or strong (a,e,o). Letters *ch*, *ll*, and *rr* are considered as single consonants. In order to illustrate the syllabification process [5], the following steps were considered for creating the algorithm:

1. Scan the word from left to right
2. If the word begins with a prefix, divide between the word and the prefix
3. Ignore one or two consonants if they begin a word
4. Skip over vowels
5. When you come to a consonant, see how many consonants are between vowels
   a) If there is only one, divide to the left of it;
   b) If there are two, divide to the left of the second one, but if the second one is *l* or *r*, divide to the left of the first one;
   c) If there are three, divide to the left of the third one, but if the third one is *l* or *r*, divide to the left of the second one;
   d) If there are four, the fourth one will always be *l* or *r*, so divide before the third consonant.
6. If the consonant ends the word, ignore it
7. Scan the word a second time to see if two or more vowels are together
   a) If two vowels together are both weak, ignore them;
   b) If one of the vowels is weak, ignore it, but if the *u* or *i* has an accent mark, divide between the two vowels;
   c) If only one of the vowels is weak, and there is an accent mark which is not on the *u* or *i*, ignore them;
   d) If both vowels are strong, divide between the vowels;
   e) If there are three vowels together, ignore them if two of them are weak even if there is an accent mark; if two of the three vowels are strong, separate the two strong vowels if they are side by side.

3   The Syllabification Algorithm

The syllabification algorithm (figure 1) basically follows the steps provided above and is written with a neutral notation so that it can be implemented in virtually any programming language. For implementing a syllabifier, following the algorithm should be easier and faster than following the textual description provided in section 2, because coding is straightforward. The complexity of this algorithm is $O(n+m)$, where n is the number of entries in the prefix list, and m is the number of characters in the string. Prefixes played an important role in the algorithm due to the fact that we had to keep these subword units together. Here is the list of prefixes used in our experiments: *circun, cuadri, cuadru, cuatri, quinqu, archi, arqui, citer, cuasi, infra, inter, intra, multi, radio, retro, satis, sobre, super, supra, trans, ulter, ultra, yuxta, ante, anti, cata, deci, ecto, endo, hemi, hipo, meta, omni, pali, para, peri, post, radi, tras, vice, cons, abs, ana, apo, arz, bis, biz, cis, com, con, des, dia, dis, dis, epi, exo, met, pen, pos, pre, pro, pro, tri, uni, viz, ins, nos.*

algorithm **Syllabifier**(String S) **return (N+T)**

$P = \{x \mid x \text{ is a } prefix\}$, $V = \{x \mid x \text{ is a } vowel\}$, $C = \{x \mid x \text{ is a } consonant\}$
$V_s = \{x \mid x \text{ is a } strong\ vowel\}$, $V_w = \{x \mid x \text{ is a } weak\ vowel\}$
$V_{wa} = \{x \mid x \text{ is a } weak\ accented\ vowel\}$, $N = T = ""$, $i = 0$

for $x = 0, \ldots, \mid P \mid$-1 **do**
  if $(P_x \in S)$ **then**
    $N \leftarrow P_x + " - "$
    $i \leftarrow \mid P_x \mid$
    break
  end if
end for

for $i = i, \ldots, \mid S \mid$-1 **do**
  if $(((S_{i-1} \in V_s) \vee (S_{i-1} \in V_{wa})) \wedge (S_i \in V_s)) \vee ((S_{i-1} \in V) \wedge (S_i \in V_{wa}))$ **then**
    $N \leftarrow N + " - "$
    $T \leftarrow S_i$
    continue
  end if

  if $((S_i \in C) \wedge (S_{i+1} \in V)) \vee ((S_{i+1} \in V_a) \wedge (T \neq \emptyset))$ **then**
    if $(S_i \in \{l, r\}) \wedge (S_{i-1} \in C)$ **then**
      if $(i > 1)$ **then**
        $T \leftarrow T_k, \forall\ 0 \leq k \leq (\mid T \mid -1)$
        $N \leftarrow N + T + " - "$
        $T \leftarrow S_{i-1} + S_i$
      else
        $T \leftarrow T + S_i$
      end if
    else
      $N \leftarrow N + T + " - "$
      $T \leftarrow S_i$
    end if
  else
    $T \leftarrow T + S_i$
  end if
end for

Fig. 1. The Syllabification Algorithm. Sample output given the same text without divisions (words in bold font were incorrectly divided): *Cier-to hom-bre, que ha-bí-a com-pra-do u-na va-ca mag-ní-fi-ca, so-ñó la mis-ma no-che que cre-cí-an a-las sobre la es-pal-da del a-ni-mal, y que és-te se mar-cha-ba vo-lan-do. Con-si-de-ran-do es-to un pre-sa-gio de in-for-tu-nio in-mi-nen-te, lle-vó la va-ca al mer-ca-do nue-va-men-te, y la ven-dió con gran pér-di-da. En-vol-vien-do en un pa-ño la pla-ta que re-ci-bió, la e-chó sobre su es-pal-da, y a mi-tad del ca-mi-no a su ca-sa, vio a un hal-cón co-mien-do par-te de u-na lie-bre. A-cer-cán-do-se al a-ve, des-cu-brió que e-ra bas-tan-te man-sa, de ma-ne-ra que le a-tó u-na pa-ta a u-na de las es-qui-nas con pa-ño en que es-ta-ba su di-ne-ro. El hal-cón **a-le-te-a-ba** mu-cho, tra-tan-do de es-ca-par, y tras un ra-to, al a-flo-jar-se **mo-men-tá-ne-a-men-te** la ma-no del hom-bre, vo-ló con to-do y el tra-po y el di-ne-ro. "Fue el des-ti-no", di-jo el hom-bre ca-da vez que con-tó la his-to-ria; ig-no-ran-te de que, pri-me-ro, no de-be te-ner-se fe en los sue-ños; y, se-gun-do, de que la gen-te no de-be re-co-ger co-sas que ve al la-do del ca-mi-no. Los cua-drú-pe-dos ge-ne-ral-men-te no vue-lan.*

4   Experiments and Results

For detecting errors in the preliminary version we used representative words for each rule provided by [5]. The evaluation text corpus consisted of 316 words ranging from one to six syllables, extracted from [6-8]. Part of this evaluation corpus is shown in figure 1. The evaluation was performed with a simple division between the number of correctly syllabified words and the total number of words. Our results show a 98.4% of accuracy where most of the error can be attributed to words with diphthongs and to confusion in the application of prefixes, so we could see that grammatical rules are not absolute. For instance, one of the grammatical rules says that "prefixes should remain intact", but although there is a prefix *extra*, the word *extraer* should be syllabified as *ex-tra-er*.

5   Conclusions and Future Work

In this paper is presented an algorithm for dividing Spanish words into syllables. The algorithm is based on grammatical rules proposed by [5] and does not require high computational cost. Because of its simplicity, the implementation of this algorithm into several programming languages should be feasible with minimal effort. we recommend this simple, easy to implement, and accurate algorithm to the community interested in the area of speech and language processing for Spanish. An immediate future work consist in resolving current problems of this algorithm in order to provide an accurate algorithm to the linguistic community. Perhaps, the Porter Stemming Algorithm [9], used to find root words, may help to detect if a word has a prefix. Also we plan the incorporation of this algorithm to the generation of a robust speech recognizer for dealing with OOV speech.

References

[1] Black, A. and Lenzo, K.: Optimal Data Selection for Unit Selection Synthesis. In proceedings of the 4th Speech Synthesis Workshop, Scotland (2001)

[2] Cuayáhuitl, H. and Serridge, B.: Out-Of-Vocabulary Word Modeling and Rejection for Spanish Keyword Spotting Systems. In proceedings of the MICAI, Springer-Verlag, LNAI 2313, Merida, Mexico (2002) 158-167

[3] Kemp, T. and Jusek, A.: Modeling Unknown Words in Spontaneous Speech. In Proceedings of ICASSP, Atlanta, GA (1996) 530-533

[4] Kiraz, G. A. and Mobius, B.: Multilingual syllabification using weighted finite-state transducers. In Proceedings of the Third ESCA Workshop on Speech Synthesis, Jenolan Caves, Australia (1998)

[5] Glenn Humphries: Syllabification: The Division of Words into Syllables. http://glenn.humphries.com/Notebook/toc.htm

[6] Uzcanga, A. M.: La Ortografía es fácil. EDAMEX, ISBN 968-409-914-2 (2000)

[7] Mungia, I., Mungia, M. E., and Rocha, G.: Gramática de Lengua Española - Reglas y Ejercicios. LAROUSSE, ISBN 970-22-0058-X (2000)

[8] Maqueo, A. M.: Ortografia. LIMUSA, ISBN 968-18-1547-5 (2002)

[9] Jurafsky, D. and Martin, J.H.: Speech and Language Processing. An Introduction to Natural Language Processing, Computational Linguistics, and Speech Recognition. Prentice Hall, Upper Saddle River, 2000.

Experiments on the Construction of
a Phonetically Balanced Corpus from the Web

Luis Villaseñor-Pineda[1], Manuel Montes-y-Gómez[1], Dominique Vaufreydaz[2],
and Jean-François Serignat[2]

[1] Laboratorio de Tecnologías del Lenguaje, INAOE, México
{villasen, mmontesg}@inaoep.mx
[2] Laboratoire CLIPS/IMAG, France
{Dominique.Vaufreydaz, Jean-Francois.Serignat}@imag.fr

Abstract. The construction of a speech recognition system requires a recorded set of phrases to compute the pertinent acoustic models. This set of phrases must be phonetically rich and balanced in order to obtain a robust recognizer. By tradition, this set is defined manually implicating a great human effort. In this paper we propose an automated method for assembling a phonetically balanced corpus (set of phrases) from the Web. The proposed method was used to construct a phonetically balanced corpus for the Mexican Spanish language.

1   Introduction

The construction of a speech recognition system requires a set of recordings to obtain the pertinent acoustic models. These recordings must consider several aspects in order to produce a robust recognizer. For instance, (i) the spoken corpus must be *rich*, i.e., it must contain all the phonemes of the language, and (ii) it must be *balanced*, i.e., it must preserve the phonetic distribution of the language.

The construction of a phonetically rich and balanced corpus is based on the selection of a set of *phrases* that will be recorded. Traditionally, this selection involves a great human effort. First, it is necessary to select a set of words phonetically rich, and join them to form the desired phrases. Later on, it is necessary to verify the phonetic distribution of the constructed phrases, and if required, add and delete some phrases. Certainly, these changes affect the overall phonetic distribution, and thus, the process must be repeated until an adequate distribution is reached.

In this paper, we propose a straightforward method for selecting a set of phrases to be recorded. This method is entirely different from the traditional process. It is supported on the hypothesis that the Web, for its huge size, is already a phonetically rich and balanced source, and thus, taking a subset of it is enough to assemble a phonetically rich and balanced corpus.

The following sections describe the proposed method, and illustrate the construction of a phonetically rich and balanced corpus for the *Mexican Spanish language*.

A. Gelbukh (Ed.): CICLing 2004, LNCS 2945, pp. 416–419, 2004.
© Springer-Verlag Berlin Heidelberg 2004

2   Collecting Documents from the Web

In order to assemble the desired corpus, we first need to collect a set of documents from the web (a broad exposition on this problem was presented in [2, 3]). For this purpose, we used the CLIPS-Index web robot [1]. This robot starts from an initial set of URLs, and gathers all their web pages (in simple HTML format) and text documents. This robot also allows filtering the web pages in accordance with a domain of interest. In our case, we downloaded only the pages from the Mexican domains.

Additionally, we deleted all the tags, headers and other metadata from the downloaded web pages and documents. After this process, we obtained a text corpus, presumably in Mexican Spanish, of 1.2 Gbytes, with a total of 244,251,605 words and 15,081,123 lines.

3   Selecting a Set of Phrases for Recording

The text corpus collected from the web was our raw material. From this corpus we selected the phrases containing only Spanish words (a lexicon was used for this task) and having more than 30 words.

Initially, we used a lexicon of 177,290 lexical forms obtained from two Spanish dictionaries and several Mexican newspapers and magazines. Using this lexicon we selected a primary set of phrases called Corpus170.

Because we considered that the initial lexicon was not bigger enough for the task at hand, we performed another experiment with an enlarged lexicon of 235,891 lexical forms. This new lexicon was constructed as follows. First, based on the initial lexicon, we extracted the unknown words from the text corpus (refer to the section 2). Then, using Google, we looked for the Spanish web pages containing the unknown words. Finally, we counted the occurrences for each word in the returned pages, and aggregated to the initial lexicon those having an occurrence greater than some given threshold. Using this enriched lexicon we obtained a new set of phrases called Corpus230.

The table 1 shows the main characteristics of both sets of phrases, the Corpus170 and the Corpus230.

Table 1. The collections Corpus170 and Corpus230

	Lexicon Size	Number of phrases	Number of words	Number of words per phrase
Corpus170	177,290	339,833	14,511,061	42.7
Corpus230	235,891	344,619	14,766,638	42.8

3.1 Phonetic Distribution

In order to evaluate the quality (i.e., richness and balance) of the selected set of phrases, we compared its phonetic distribution[1] with the phonetic distribution of the Spanish language reported in the literature. The figure 1 shows the phonetic distribution of our corpora as well as the Spanish phonetic distribution in accordance with a Latin-american [5] and Iberian [6] studies. From this figure we get the following conclusions:

1. *Our initial hypothesis is correct*; the phonetic distribution of the corpora obtained from the web is very close to those reported for the Spanish language. For instance, the correlation coefficient between the Corpus230 and the Latin-american and Iberian studies were 0.994 and 0.942 respectively.

2. *The size of the lexicon and the corpus is not a fundamental element.* For instance, the Corpus170 presents a notable correspondence to the Corpus230 (with a correlation coefficient of 0.99), even when they were built using lexicons with more than 60 thousand different lexical forms.

Figure 1 also shows that the generated corpora are phonetically more similar to the Latin-american Spanish than to the Iberian. The occurrence proportion of the phonemes /a/ and /e/ are good examples of this circumstance.

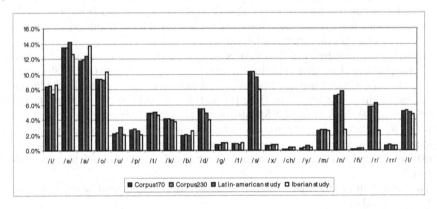

Fig. 1. Phonetic distribution of the generated corpora

3.2 Corpus Reduction

Approximately, only 6000 phrases are required in order to construct a 10 hours of recorded corpus. An automatic method to select the best phrases from the generated corpora consists in computing the perplexity of each phrase in accordance with a language model, and keeping those phrases having the lower perplexity. We constructed the language model from a collection of written conversations among several individuals. This collection is of 4.8Mb and has 864,166 words, and 20893 lexical forms. Using this language model we obtain a set of 6082 phrases with a

---

[1] We transformed the words of the corpora to their corresponding phonemes using a tool developed in the DIME project [4].

perplexity less than 7.25. The table 2 shows the main characteristics of this set of phrases.

It is important to mention that the phonetic distribution of the reduced corpus maintains a strong correlation with the Latin-american Spanish phonetic distribution (0.994) and with the Corpus 230 distribution (0.997).

Table 2. Corpus reduction

	Lexicon Size	Number of Phrases	Number of words	Number of words per phrase
Reduced Corpus	235,891	6082	220,776	36.3

4   Future Work

Before recording the corpus, it will be necessary to manually ensure its content. Basically, we plan to delete the phrases with vulgar or funny content as well as those having rare words. These actions will prevent future complications during the recording process, and consequently, will impact in the quality of the final recorded corpus.

Acknowledgements. This work has been partly supported by the project "Man-Machine Spoken Interaction" (LAFMI). We also want to express our gratitude to Esmeralda Uraga, Andrés González and Alberto López for their valuable help.

References

1. D. Vaufreydaz, C. Bergamini, J.F. Serignat, L. Besacier, M. Akbar, A New Methodology for Speech Corpora Definition from Internet Documents, *LREC'2000 Language Resources & Evaluation international Conference*, Athens, Greece, 2000.
2. S. Galicia-Haro. Procesamiento de Textos Electrónicos para la Construcción de un Corpus. *CORE-2003*, México, D.F. 2003.
3. Gelbukh, A., G. Sidorov and L. Chanona. Compilation of a Spanish Representative Corpus. *International Conference on Computational Linguistics and Intelligent Text Processing CICLing02*, LNCS 2276, Springer. 2002.
4. E. Uraga and L. Pineda. Automatic generation of pronunciation lexicons for Spanish. *International Conference on Computational Linguistics and Intelligent Text Processing CICLing 2002*. LNCS 2276, Springer, 2002.
5. H. E. Pérez. Frecuencia de fonemas. *Revista Electrónica de la Red Temática en Tecnologías del Habla*, Número 1, Marzo, 2003.
6. E. Alarcos-Llorach. *Fonología española*. Madrid, Gredos. 1965.

Head/Modifier Frames for Information Retrieval

Cornelis H.A. Koster

Computing Science Institute,
University of Nijmegen,
The Netherlands,
kees@cs.kun.nl

Abstract. We describe a principled method for representing documents
by phrases abstracted into Head/Modifier pairs. First the notion of
aboutness and the characterization of full-text documents by HM pairs
is didcussed. Based on linguistic arguments, a taxonomy of HM pairs
is derived. We briefly describe the EP4IR parser/transducer of English
and present some statistics of the distribution of HM pairs in newspaper
text.

Based on the HM pairs generated, a new technique to measure the accuracy of a parser is introduced, and applied to the EP4IR grammar of
English. Finally we discuss the merits of HM pairs and HM trees as a
document representation.

1 Introduction

The Information Retrieval community has for a long time held high hopes concerning the value of linguistic techniques. However, the improvements in precision and/or recall expected from the use of phrases in retrieval and in text
categorization have repeatedly been found disappointing [22].

Although the use of simple noun phrases as indexing terms is now commonly accepted, practical Information Retrieval systems using phrases like the
CLARIT system [7] do not appear to perform consistently better than those
based on keywords. There is a growing conviction that the value of Natural Language Processing to IR is dubious, even among people who tried hard to make
linguistically-based IR work [15,20]. The predominant feeling, as voiced in [18],
is that only 'shallow' linguistic techniques like the use of stop lists and lemmatization are of any use to IR, the rest is a question of using the right statistical
techniques.

In spite of these negative experiences, we are trying to improve the accuracy of automatic document classification techniques by using (abstractions
of) phrases as terms. In this paper we shall first discuss the notion of *aboutness*, which plays a central role in Information Retrieval. We then introduce
Head/Modifier (HM) pairs as an abstraction of phrases preserving their aboutness, and give a taxonomy of HM pairs based on the intra-sentence relations
they represent. We describe the EP4IR grammar, in which the transduction of
English text to HM pairs is realized, and which is now available in the public
domain.

A. Gelbukh (Ed.): CICLing 2004, LNCS 2945, pp. 420–432, 2004.
© Springer-Verlag Berlin Heidelberg 2004

We introduce a new technique to measure the accuracy of a parser/transducer, based on the HM pairs generated, and apply it to the EP4IR grammar. We give some experimental results about the distribution of HM pairs, and report our experiences in using HM pairs as indexing terms in Text Categorization. Finally we discuss the strengths and limitations of the HM pair representation.

2   Aboutness

The notion of *aboutness* is highly central to Information Retrieval: the user of a retrieval system expects the system, in response to a query, to supply a list of documents which are *about* that query. Practical retrieval systems using words as terms are based on an extremely simpleminded notion of aboutness:

If the word x occurs in the document then the document is *about x*.

This notion can be refined by introducing a measure for the *similarity* between the query and the document. For phrases, aboutness can be defined in the same way:

If the phrase x occurs in the document then the document is *about x*.

Although intuitively it seems likely that phrases provide a more informative document representation than keywords, the above formulation is not helpful in deciding what phrases to choose, which parts to eliminate and how to represent them. Certainly, taking literal phrases as terms may lead to very low Recall, because of the human preference for morphological, syntactical and semantical variation in formulating texts [1]. Furthermore, it considers a phrase as a monolithic term, disregarding the elements out of which it is composed. A model-theoretic basis for the notion of aboutness was described in [2]:

An information carrier i will be said to be *about* information carrier j if the information borne by j holds in i

The rather abstract sounding notion of "information carrier" can denote a single term, but also a composition of terms into a structured query or a document.

In other retrieval models (Boolean, vector space, logic-based or probabilistic) the notion of aboutness can be defined analoguously (see [3]). *The problem with all these definitions is that they are not concrete enough to use them in reasoning about document representations.*

Our treatment of phrases as indexing terms is based on the following premises:

- The representation of a phrase as an indexing term is composed of words extracted from the phrase occurring in a linguistically meaningful relation
- words that have no classificatory value as keywords (by themselves) can be omitted.

These thoughts are elaborated further in the following sections.

3   Linguistic Phrases as Indexing Terms

The use of Linguistically Motivated Indexing terms (some abstraction of linguistically derived phrases) has always fascinated researchers in IR (for an overview see [19]). Even our particular choice of abstraction, using HM pairs as indexing terms is not new: it has been made previously by many researchers like [8,21] and recently [9]. In particular the Noun Phrase enjoys popularity as an indexing term, because on the one hand it obviously carries a lot of information, and on the other hand it is relatively easy to extract.

3.1   Noun Phrases as Indexing Terms

According to [23], a Noun Phrase is to be considered as a *reference to, or description of a complicated concept*. It is interesting to note that the preferred form of informative titles of articles in the exact sciences appears to be a (complicated) noun phrase. As a query, a noun phrase is definitely more precise than the bag of its constituent words.

The use of simple NP's as indexing terms is now common practice in many Information Retrieval systems. NP's can be extracted from a text using a chunker or shallow parser (e.g. [6,10]) which is easier to construct than a full-blown grammar-based parser.

3.2   Verb Phrases as Indexing Terms

The verb phrase comprizes a verb group together with its complements. Semantically, a Verb Phrase can be seen as the *description of a fact, event or process*. It describes something dynamic, in contrast to the noun phrase which describes something static. For the aboutness of the phrase, only the main verb is of importance, because the auxiliaries serve to indicate time, modality, emotion. They will be elided during the transduction. The relations between the main verb and its complements however, including the subject, are essential for the aboutness of the phrase.

3.3   Phrase Normalization

Phrases used as terms are very precise, much more precise than single words. The reason why it is hard to gain by using them, is the very fact that they are so precise: the probability for a specific phrase to (re)occur in a document is much smaller than for a specific word. Thus, the term space for phrases is much more sparse than that of words. Using phrases instead of keywords, we may gain Precision but we loose Recall.

In writing a text, people prefer to avoid literal repetition, they will go out of their way to choose another word, another turn of phrase, using anaphora, synonymy, hypernymy, periphrasis, metaphor and hyperbole in order to avoid the literal repetition of something they have already said or written before. From a literary standpoint this is wonderful, but it gives complications in IR: we have to compensate for this human penchant for variety. Essentially, we must try to conflate all semantically equivalent forms of a phrase, for instance by mapping them onto one same form.

Rather than using literal phrases taken from the text as terms, we shall therefore reduce them to a normal form which expresses only the bare bones of their aboutness. We must eliminate all dispensable ornaments and undo all morphological, syntactic and semantic variation we can. In this way, we strive to regain Recall while surrendering little Precision.

4 HM Trees and HM Pairs

In the context of document classification, we shall represent each document by a bag of terms, where the terms are *Head/Modifier pairs*, derived from the phrases in the document by a *transduction* process. Each phrase is first transduced to a HM tree and then *unnested* to one or more HM pairs.

4.1 HM Trees

A Head/Modifier tree or HM tree is a form of (binary) dependency tree, denoted as a recursive structure over pairs of the form

    [head, modifier]

where both the head and the modifier consist of a sequence of zero or more words and (nested) HM trees. As an example, the HM tree

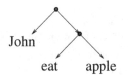

is denoted by [John, [eat, apple]].

4.2 HM Pairs

A pair [head, modifier] corresponds to a flat HM tree in which both the head and the modifier are not nested, i.e. consist only of zero or more words. A HM tree will be unnested to the set of HM pairs which are contained in it and we shall use a bag-of-HM pairs representation for documents.

The intuition behind using HM pairs as terms is that the modifier is joined to the head in order to make it more precise, i.e. to distinguish the pair from another pair with the same head, in particular to distinguish between different meanings of a polysemous head. Thus, there are many forms of engineering, but we may focus on [engineering, software].

It may be asked why we do not simply use *collocations* as terms, frequent multi-word combinations, such as software engineering. Apart from the necessity for conflation of equivalent terms, for which HM pairs give more scope, it should be pointed out that there is more information in the above HM pair than in the collocation: in expressing the relevance of a term to a class c we can use $P(c|head, modifier)$ in both cases, but $P(c|head, \overline{modifier})$ only for the HM pair – in this case the information that the document is about *another* form of engineering.

4.3   Unnesting

As produced by the transduction, trees may be nested, i.e. contain embedded trees.

```
[[mower, lawn], large]
[operation, [consuming, time]]
```

We want to use pairs without nesting as terms, possibly in combination with single words. A nested tree F may be unnested into a set of pairs S by repeatedly taking some embedded tree without nesting from F while replacing it by its head, and adding the corresponding pair to the set S, until F is empty. Some (artificial) examples:

```
[a, b] ==> [a, b]
[a, [b, c]] ==> [b, c][a, b]
[[a, b], c] ==> [a, b][a, c]
```

In the unnesting process, the head of a tree serves as an abstraction for that tree: a lawn mower is a (some kind of) mower, a large mower is a mower, etc.

```
[[mower, lawn], large] ==> [mower, lawn][mower, large]
```

```
[operation, [consuming,time]]
    ==> [operation,consuming][consuming,time]
```

We also allow the |-sign as an or-operator:

```
[a, b | c ] ==> [a, b][a, c]
[a | b, c ] ==> [a, c][b, c]
```

A tree with an empty head, typically occurring nested in another one, obtains an empty abstraction, e.g.

```
[I,[see,man [,[you,[give,book|to man]]]]]
    ==> [I,see][see,man][you,give][give,book][give,to man]
```

is transduced from the sentence I saw the man to whom you gave a book.

5   A Taxonomy of HM Pairs

Head/Modifier pairs should not be arbitrary combinations of words from the text, but they should represent some *linguistically meaningful relation* between components (words and collocations) extracted from the text. This is the basis for the following taxonomy.

5.1   Word Types

It is to be expected that the words (and collocations) occurring in the HM pairs should include the words that as keywords serve best to characterize the document; the pairs only add precision. Traditionally, nouns are considered the most important keywords, and function words are eliminated by the stop list. In [1] the relative contribution of words with different parts of speech to the accuracy in automatic document classification was investigated. It was found that eliminating all terms except nouns, adjectives and verbs gives no loss (sometimes a small gain) in classification accuracy. These words appear to carry all of the aboutness to be found in single keywords.

Our HM pairs will therefore be composed primarily out of nouns, adjectives and verbs. Furthermore we shall include prepositions forming part of a preposition phrase (PP). Lastly, we include the pronouns, not because they are by themselves very informative, but because they often appear as place holders. All other words like adverbs, auxiliaries, quantifiers, determiners etc will be elided.

5.2   Word Relations

The set of all possible pairwise combinations of the four word types can be analysed as follows (see Fig. 1):

head	modifier				
	V	N	P	A	PP
V	–	object relation		–	yes
N, P	subject relation	predicative/attributive relation			yes
A	–	–	–	–	yes

Fig. 1. Relations realized by HM pairs

1. verb in modifier position
   A pair of the form [N:, V:] or [P:, V:] represents the *subject relation*. The type [A:, V:] cannot occur, since an adjective in that position would be promoted to a noun ([N:A:, V:]).
2. verb in head position
   a pair of the form [V:, N:] or [V:, P:] where the verb should be transitive represents the *object relation*. The type [V:, A:] will not be generated: In a sentence like his nose turned red the verb does not provide any additional information beyond [N:nose, A:red].
3. no verb
   a) noun as head
      A noun can be modified by another noun [N:, N:], an adjective [N:, A:] or a (possessive) pronoun [N:, P:], all expressing the *attributive* relation (software engineering, the red car, my car). The same pairs arize

from the *predicative* relation (the car is a lemon, the car is red, the car is mine).

b) adjective as head

Will not occur, since an adjective can only be modified by an adverb, which is elided.

c) a pronoun in head position is treated like a noun.

4. verbs in both positions

Although a sentence like I like to walk might suggest a pair [V:like,V:walk], this sentence has the same aboutness as I walk. Similarly, he decided to leave the country can be argued to have the same aboutness as he left the country. But this is a moot point, since we have no good notion of aboutness.

To complicate matters, we have also to represent indirect objects, preposition complements and other adjuncts. For that purpose, we allow a verb, noun or adjective to have a modifier consisting of a preposition followed by a noun or pronoun which stands as the abstraction of an NP, for example

I give you a knife [P:I,[V:give,knife|to P:you]]

a cry for freedom [N:cry,for N:freedom]

open to suspicion [A:open,to N:suspicion]

Our HM trees include the *index expressions* of [4] as a subset, but they are richer because we also express the main verbs.

Other relationships (negation, quantification, auxiliary verbs, adverbial modifiers) are not expressed in the transduction, even though they are recognized by the grammar, because there is some evidence that they are not important for the intended application in text categorization [1].

Notice that the *order* of the constituents in a pair is important for all the relations described above. We shall exploit the *polarity* in the pairs to distinguish a pair [a, b] from a pair [b, a]. Thus, we shall not consider [air, pollution] as equivalent to [pollution, air].

Expressed in the framework of HM trees, the structure of a simple sentence will be:

[subject, [verb, object|other complement]]

where some of the elements may be missing. By unnesting, this structure yields the atomic HM pairs

[subject, verb], [verb, object] and [verb, other complement]

5.3 Morphological Normalization

All words or collocations occurring in the pairs will be morphologically normalized by lemmatization. The goal is to map all different forms of the same lemma onto one representative form. The lemmatization process is aided by the word type supplied in the transduction.

As an example, the pair [N:man, A:V:sneezing] may be obtained from both the attributive the sneezing man and the predicative the man is sneezing. It will be normalized to [man, sneeze]. The nested tree [N:man, [V:sneezed,]] obtained from this man sneezed has the same result, just like all its variants in time and modality.

All pronouns are mapped onto it, which can be seen as a place holder element, in particular for anaphora resolution (not yet implemented).

5.4 Syntactic Normalization

As indicated above, all elements which are deemed not to contribute to the aboutness will be elided during transduction: articles, quantifiers, adverbs, connectors - which is much like applying a stop list. We shall have to determine experimentally which elements may be elided and what information should be expressed in the pairs (e.g, time and modality). In our classification context, it is quite feasible to investigate for any specific feature whether its inclusion or exclusion would measurably influence the classification result. At a later time we will also investigate the use of HM trees rather than HM pairs, by dispensing with the unnesting.

For each construct described by the grammar, its transduction is described wholly by the grammar (as part of the syntax rule for the construct). Thus, the transductions of complicated constructs are expressed compositionally in terms of those of their components. In the process, elements are elided or re-ordered and additional symbols injected (like the [, , and]) in order to express uniformly the four relations described above.

The syntactic normalizations implemented in this way include *de-passivation*:
the train was driven by a clockwork engine
is, by unnesting and morphological normalization, turned into
[N:engine,N:clockwork] [N:engine,V:drive] [V:drive,N:train]

6 Extracting HM Pairs

In this section discuss the resources presently available for obtaining HM pairs from English text. We briefly describe the EP4IR grammar, introduce a technique for measuring the accuracy of a grammar in terms of the HM pairs produced, and apply it to the EP4IR grammar. We give some experimental results concerning the distribution of HM phrases in full text, and discuss the limitations of the HM pair approach.

6.1 The EP4IR Grammar

The 'English Phrases for IR' (EP4IR) grammar of English was developed for investigations into the effective use of phrasal document representations in Information Retrieval applications like document classification, filtering and routing. It is available in the public domain, together with its lexicon and the AGFL parser generator system [13].

The grammar is written in the AGFL formalism for the syntactic description of natural languages. An Affix Grammar over a Finite Lattice (AGFL) can be seen as a CF grammar extended with set-valued features (called affixes or attributes), where the features express finite syntactic and semantic categories like number, person, time, subcategorization, etc.

Since the grammar is not the subject of this paper, we will only sketch its main properties. It gives a robust description of the structure of the Noun Phrase and the Verb Phrase, including their transduction to Head/Modifier trees. It has an extensive lexicon (309007 entries including collocations) and uses various techniques to resolve ambiguity (subcategorization, penalties).

6.2 Some Statistics

In order to get an impression of the distribution of the various HM pair types, we have parsed the EPO1A corpus [14,12], using a parser/transducer generated from the EP4IR grammar and lexicon. The corpus contains 16000 abstracts of patent applications from the European Patent Office (2 Million words, totalling 12.4 Mbytes). This corpus yielded 727363 HM pairs (excluding adverbs, quantities etc).

Fig. 2 shows the relative distribution of the various types of HM pairs in the EPO1A corpus, which should be roughly similar for other corpora. As a rule of thumb, one HM pair is produced for every 2-3 words.

head	modifier				
	V	N	P	A	PP
V	12998	112557	2098	10263	58325
N	91648	150332	4000	152995	95484
P	30627	718	18	1735	1163
A					2368

Fig. 2. HM pairs in EPO1A

6.3 Measuring Grammar Accuracy

In developing a grammar, an objective measure is needed for the accuracy of the grammar, in order to do regression testing after each major modification to the grammar, and to assess the suitability of the parsers resulting from it for their intended purpose.

We can not use the ubiquitous Bracket Crossing (BC) measure [17]. To begin with, it has a large number of weakness and shortcomings [5]: it is not suited for partial parses, only useful for constituency based parsers, not fine grained enough for some specific syntactic phenomena, and there is no clear agreement on the granularity of bracketing. According to [16], in BC a mis-attachment can be punished more than once, so that a shallow parse with less syntactic information scores better than a "richer" analysis. Furthermore, the bracket-crossing approach needs an extensive syntactically analyzed corpus, which causes a chicken-and-egg problem, and it is very much oriented to parse trees, whereas we are interested in HM pairs.

The HM pairs generated from a text represent precisely the relations that we are interested in, and closely reflect the dependency relations in the text. If we can extract the right HM pairs from a sentence, we can also derive the complete sentence structure. Therefore we propose to express the accuracy of the grammar/transucer in terms of the HM pairs produced by it when applied to a reference corpus for which the HM pairs are known.

This HMP-annotated reference corpus is based on a collection of sentences which is representative for the intended application domain and for the syntactic constructions occurring in it. This collection need not be very big (in comparison with a modern treebank) but it must be expected to generate enough HM pairs to allow a measurement at the required granularity - say two thousand HM pairs if we want 3 decimals of accuracy, just a few hundred sentences.

The manual annotation of the reference corpus with the correct HM pairs is tedious and errorprone, but it can be performed in interaction with the parser to be tested, presenting the sentences in larger or smaller fragments and verifying the results by inspection. By skillfully exploiting the compositional character of grammar, this can be done in an efficient and reliable way.

Two persons may mark the same corpus and discuss the points of difference in order to guarantee the correctness of the reference corpus. The measurement procedure is as follows:

1. generate a parser/transducer from the grammar and its lexicon
2. collect the reference corpus
3. manually derive the HM pairs to be generated from it
4. let the parser generate HM pairs from it
5. compare these, computing precision and recall in the usual way.

6.4   The Accuracy of EP4IR

In order to get an indication of the accuracy (Precision and Recall) of EP4IR, we have constructed a small reference corpus, consisting of 26 sentences from the OHSUMED collection and 113 sentences from the EPO1A corpus, totalling 3458 words. By semi-automatic analysis, 1529 HM pairs were found in the test set.

We also analyzed the same test set automatically. As can be seen from Fig. 3, the overall Precision and Recall were 66.6% and 64.5%, giving an F1-value of 0.65. The traditional NN and NA combinations have the highest accuracy. The letter Z in this table stands for a PP.

The breakdown of Precision and Recall per type of HM pair allows us to focus on areas of improvement. There are some dubious combinations, like VV (also in the test set). PP attachment and the assignation of subject and object must be improved. The EP4IR grammar is not yet very accurate and there are still some inconsistensies in the transduction. The grammar should be made probabilistic, so that it becomes better at finding the most likely analysis. Furthermore, it is

HM pair	present	found	correct	recall	precision
AZ	2	3	0	0.000	0.000
NA	293	291	219	0.747	0.753
NN	379	376	254	0.670	0.676
NP	15	18	15	1.000	0.833
NV	190	174	107	0.563	0.615
NZ	147	174	83	0.565	0.477
PA	4	2	2	0.500	1.000
PN	1	4	0	0.000	0.000
PV	88	70	58	0.659	0.829
PZ	1	0	0	0.000	0.000
VA	8	15	1	0.125	0.067
VN	262	222	154	0.588	0.694
VP	4	5	2	0.500	0.400
VV	0	19	0	0.000	0.000
VZ	135	105	60	0.444	0.571
total	1529	1478	986	0.645	0.666

Fig. 3. HM pairs in mixed test set

weak in its treatment of coordination and some special constructs. But in the mean time it is available to the IR community.

6.5   Limitations of HM Pairs

The choice of HM pairs as a realizations of phrases has its limitations from a linguistic point of view:

- the many pairs involving a personal pronoun (PV and VP) show the need for anaphora resolution
- it is hard to normalize pairs representing periphrastic constructions (make a comparison between . . . and . . . for compare . . . with . . . , a number of cars vs many cars), especially when they border on idiom (a gaggle of geese)
- specialized lexical resources are needed for e.g. HM pair synonymy
- ternary (and higher) collocations are not expressible as a pair (software engineering conference; transverse collating bin)
- similar problem with composed words, especially in languages like German and Dutch (but also in English, e.g. well known, well-known and wellknown).

In fact, the problems with collocations and composed words can be solved by dealing with HM trees of order higher than one without unnesting But there is at present no theory of language modeling based on pairs, let alone based on trees. Both practically and theoretically, much remains to be done.

7 Conclusion

We have introduced HM trees and their unnesting to HM pairs, describing their use for document representation. We have introduced a linguistically motivated taxonomy of HM pairs allowing to capture the aboutness (as opposed to the constituency structure) of both the verb phrase and the noun phrase while rigorously eliminating non-informative elements.

We have introduced an accuracy measure for grammars transducing to HM pairs and used it to measure the Precision and Recall achieved by the EP4IR parser/transducer on a small test corpus. There is obviously room for improvement of the grammar, and we are working on it.

For experimental results using HM pairs in Text Categorization, the reader is referred to [12], which is concerned with the classification of the EPO1A corpus of patent abstracts. The results are (still) disappointing but it is argued that HM pairs may be better suited for query-based retrieval and Question Answering than for categorization, due to the strongly statistical character of the latter.

Further research on HM pairs is needed:

- to determine experimentally which elements of a sentence contribute most to the aboutness of a document
- to investigate theoretically how to make optimal use of structured terms such as HM pairs in text categorization
- to investigate anaphora resolution for HM pairs, selective clustering of terms and fuzzy semantic matching
- to investigate the possibility to dispense with unnesting, using arbitrarily complicated HM trees as terms.

Many improvements in theory, techniques and resources are still needed to reach a situation where phrases make an important improvement to Information Retrieval.

Acknowledgements. My sincere thanks go out to all participants in the DORO and PEKING projects, and in particular to T. Verhoeven who elaborated the HM pair-based grammar evaluation technique.

References

1. A. Arampatzis, Th.P. van der Weide, C.H.A. Koster, P. van Bommel (2000), An Evaluation of Linguistically-motivated Indexing Schemes. Proceedings BCS-IRSG 2000 Colloquium on IR Research, Cambridge, England.
2. P. Bruza and T.W.C. Huibers, (1994), Investigating Aboutness Axioms using Information Fields. Proceedings SIGIR 94, pp. 112–121.
3. P. Bruza and T.W.C. Huibers, (1996), A Study of Aboutness in Information Retrieval. *Artificial Intelligence Review*, 10, p 1–27.
4. Peter Bruza and Theo P. van der Weide (1991), The Modelling and Retrieval of Documents Using Index Expressions, SIGIR Forum vol 25 no 2, pp. 91–103.

5. J. Carroll, M. Guido and E. Briscoe (1999) Corpus Annotation for Parser Evaluation. *Proceedings of the EACL workshop on Linguistically Interpreted Corpora (LINC)*, 1999.

6. W. Daelemans, S. Buchholz and J. Veenstra (1999), Memory-based shallow parsing, proceedings CoNLL, Bergen, Norway.

7. D.A. Evans, R.G. Lefferts, G. Grefenstette, S.H. Handerson, W.R. Hersch and A.A. Archbold (1993), CLARIT TREC design, experiments and results. TREC-1 proceedings, pp. 251–286.

8. J.L. Fagan (1988), *Experiments in automatic phrase indexing for document retrieval: a comparison of syntactic and non-syntactic methods*, PhD Thesis, Cornell University.

9. A. Gelbukh, G. Sidorov , S.-Y. Han, E. Hernández-Rubio (2004), Automatic Syntactic Analysis for Detection of Word Combinations. In: A. Gelbukh (Ed.) Computational Linguistics and Intelligent Text Processing (CICLing-2004). Springer LNCS 2945 (this volume), p. 240–244.

10. G. Grefenstette (1996), Light parsing as finite state filtering. Workshop on Extended finite state models of language, Budapest, ECAI'96.

11. C.H.A. Koster, Affix Grammars for Natural Languages. In: H. Alblas and B. Melichar (Eds.), *Attribute Grammars, applications and systems*. SLNCS 545, Heidelberg, 1991, p. 469–484.

12. C.H.A. Koster and M. Seutter (2002), Taming Wild Phrases, Proceedings 25th European Conference on IR Research (ECIR 2003), Springer LNCS 2633, pp. 161–176.

13. C.H.A. Koster and E. Verbruggen, The AGFL Grammar Work Lab, Proceedings of the FREENIX/Usenix conference 2002, pp. 13–18.

14. M. Krier and F. Zaccà (2002), Automatic Categorisation Applications at the European Patent Office, World Patent Information 24, pp. 187–196, Elsevier Science Ltd.

15. D. D. Lewis (1992), *Representation and Learning in Information Retrieval*. PhD thesis, Department of Computer Science; Univ. of Massachusetts; Amherst, MA 01003.

16. D. Lin (1995), A dependency-based method for evaluating broad-coverage parsers. *Proceedings IJCAI-95*, pp. 1420–1425.

17. M. Marcus, B. Santorini and M. Marcinkiewicz (1994), Building a Large Annotated Corpus of English: The Penn Treebank. In: *Computational Linguistics*, 19(2):313–330, 1994.

18. K. Sparck Jones (1998), Information retrieval: how far will *really* simple methods take you? In: Proceedings TWTL 14, Twente University, the Netherlands, pp. 71–78.

19. K. Sparck Jones (1999), The role of NLP in Text Retrieval. In: [22] pp. 1–24.

20. A.F. Smeaton (1997), Using NLP and NLP resources for Information Retrieval Tasks. In: T. Strzalkowski (Ed.), *Natural Language Information Retrieval*, Kluwer Academic Publishers.

21. T. Strzalkowski (1995), Natural Language Information Retrieval, *Information Processing and Management*, 31 (3), pp. 397–417.

22. T. Strzalkowski, editor (1999), *Natural Language Information Retrieval*, Kluwer Academic Publishers, ISBN 0-7923-5685-3.

23. T. Winograd (1983), *Language as a Cognitive Process: Volume I: Syntax*, Reading MA, Addison-Wesley, 650 pp.

Performance Analysis of Semantic Indexing in Text Retrieval

Bo-Yeong Kang, Hae-Jung Kim, and Sang-Jo Lee

Department of Computer Engineering, Kyungpook National University,
Sangyuk-dong, Puk-gu, Daegu, 702-701, KOREA
comeng99@hotmail.com

Abstract. We developed a new indexing formalism that considers not only the terms in a document, but also the concepts to represent the semantic content of a document. In this approach, concept clusters are defined and a concept vector space model is proposed to represent the semantic importance of words and concepts within a document. Through experiments on the TREC-2 collection, we show that the proposed method outperforms an indexing method based on term frequency.

1 Introduction

To intelligently retrieve information, many indexing methods such as term frequency (TF), inverse document frequency (IDF), the product of TF and IDF have been proposed and tested [1]. Most of TF-based methods have difficulties in extracting semantically exact indexes that express the topics of a document. Consider the sample text below, the important terms that could be topics of the text are *anesthetic* and *machine(device)*. However, the TF weight of the word *machine* is 1, which is the same as that of semantically unimportant words such as *rate* and *blood*. Thus, the TF approach fails to discriminate the degree of semantic importance of each word within the text.

"Dr. Kenny has invented an anesthetic machine. This device controls the rate at which an anesthetic is pumped into the blood."

Linguistic phenomenon such as *lexical chain*[2], which links related words in a text, have been used to enhance the indexing performance[3]. In the sample text, we obtain two representative chains, *anesthetic − anesthetic* and *machine − device*, which correctly indicates that the focus words of the text are *anesthetic* and *machine/device*. In the present study, we propose a new semantic approach based on lexical chains for extracting words from a text and assigning them importance degrees, and analyze the performance of the proposed semantic indexing.

2 Semantic Indexing

Documents generally contain various concepts, and we must determine those concepts if we are to comprehend the aboutness of a document. In accordance

A. Gelbukh (Ed.): CICLing 2004, LNCS 2945, pp. 433–436, 2004.
© Springer-Verlag Berlin Heidelberg 2004

with the accepted view in the linguistics literature that lexical chains provide a good representation of discourse structures and topicality of segments [2], here we take each lexical chain to represent a concept that expresses one aspect of the meaning of a document. We define each lexical chain derived from a document as a concept cluster that captures one of the concepts of the document.

The proposed method first extracts concept clusters that represent the semantic content of the text and assigns scores to the extracted concept clusters and words in the clusters for representing semantic importance degree. Then, each scored concept is mapped onto the vector space, and the overall text vector is made up of those concept vectors. The semantic importance of concepts and words is then computed according to the overall text vector magnitude, which is used to extract the semantic indexes.

Concept Clustering. To compose of the concept cluster by related words, we use five relations (R) – identity, synonymy, hypernymy, hyponymy, meronymy – where the relation weight is in the order listed. The score of each concept cluster and the nouns in the cluster are defined as follows:

$$Score\ of\ noun\ W_i = \sum_{k \in R} number\ of\ relation\ k \times weight\ of\ relation\ k \quad (1)$$

$$Score\ of\ cluster\ C_x = \sum_{W_i \in C_x} score\ of\ noun\ W_i \quad (2)$$

For example, consider the system in Figure 1, in which the identity relation weight is set to 0.7 and the synonym relation weight is set to 0.5. The scores of noun W_1 and cluster C_1 are calculated as:

$$Score\ of\ noun\ W_1 = 1 \times 0.7 + 2 \times 0.5 = 1.7$$

$$Score\ of\ cluster\ C_1 = \sum_{i=1}^{4} Score\ of\ noun\ W_i = 3.4$$

From the scored concept clusters, we discriminate representative concept, since we cannot deal with all the concepts of a document. A concept C_j will be considered a representative concept if it satisfies the following criterion.

$$Representative\ concept\ cluster\ C_j \geq average\ score\ of\ concept\ clusters \quad (3)$$

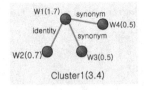

Fig. 1. Score of a sample cluster

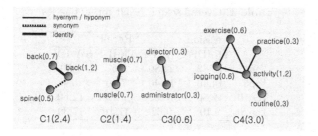

Fig. 2. Semantic importance of word

Semantic Importance Estimation. We can now discern which concepts are important and which are not using Eqs. 1–3. However, we cannot exactly calculate the semantic importance degree of each word. For example, Figure 2 shows four representative concept clusters for the below sample text.

"This exercise routine, developed by Steve, director of rehabilitation at the Center for Spine, and administrator of the Health Association, focuses on the right spots: It strengthens your back muscles, abdominals, and obliques (the ab muscles that run from front to back along your lower ribs) and stretches your legs and hips. Combine this practice with three 30-minute sessions of cardiovascular activity such as jogging, and you should be on your way to a healthier back."

The words *practice* and *director* both have scores of 0.3. However, we see that *practice* is semantically more important than *director*, because the cluster C_4 containing *practice* is a semantically more important than the C_3 containing *director*. Therefore, we assume that the semantic importance degree of a word is affected by the strength of the concept cluster in which it resides.

To recompute the importance degrees of words taking into consideration the concept cluster importance, a vector model is employed for the concept vector space model. Concept vector space is an n-dimensional space composed of n independent concept axes. The semantic importance of each concept and word can be derived from the properties of this concept vector space. For example, suppose that a text is composed of two concepts, C_1 and C_2. If the magnitudes of vectors $\boldsymbol{C_1}$ and $\boldsymbol{C_2}$ are $|C_1|$ and $|C_2|$, respectively, the overall text vector magnitude, $|\boldsymbol{T}|$, is $\sqrt{|C_1|^2 + |C_2|^2}$. Thus, the part that concept C_1 contributes to $\boldsymbol{T}$ is $|C_1|^2/\sqrt{|C_1|^2 + |C_2|^2}$, and the part that concept C_2 contributes is $|C_2|^2/\sqrt{|C_1|^2 + |C_2|^2}$. By generalizing this vector space property, the importance degree of a word W_j, Ω_{W_j}, in a cluster C_i can be estimated as Eq. 4 [4].

$$\Omega_{W_j} = |W_j| \frac{|C_i|}{\sqrt{\sum_k |C_k|^2}} \tag{4}$$

where k is the number of the representative concept clusters. After computing the importance degree of each word within an overall text, we extract words that are beyond the average importance degree of total words as semantic indexes.

Table 1. Overall search result for 40 queries

	Precision		Recall	
	TF·IDF	SW·IDF	TF·IDF	SW·IDF
Top1	12.82	22.80	0.57	1.50
Top5	14.40	18.46	7.40	9.50
Top10	12.56	13.08	9.79	12.60
Top20	9.10	9.62	17.10	17.30

3   Experiments and Conclusion

We discuss document retrieval experiments in which the proposed method and TF-based methods were applied to the TREC-2 collection of 1990 Wall Street Journal documents containing 21,705 documents. We incorporated IDF into both weighting schemes, and used 40 queries from the built-in query set. The relevance degree between query and document was calculated using the vector model.

The index term dimension is the number of index terms that are used to represent a document. When a document is indexed based on the TF, all the terms in the document are used as indexes, and hence the index term dimension simply equals the number of words in the document. However, when we index a document using the proposed indexing scheme, we first extract representative concepts from the document and then extract index terms from those concepts. This is clearly demonstrated in the present experiments on the 1990 WSJ documents, for which the average index term dimension was 89.55 using the TF method but 17.8 using the proposed method. We see that the proposed scheme reduces the index term dimension by about 80% compared to the TF method.

Table 1 shows the overall search results, average precision and recall for the top 1, top 5, top 10, and top 20 documents. The search results show that the proposed system outperforms the TF·IDF weighting method in all categories, especially for documents ranked in the top 5 or less. The precision of the proposed system for the top-ranked document is 10% higher than that of the TF·IDF system, and the precision of the proposed system for the top 5 documents is 4.06% higher.

Experiments in which the proposed approach was compared with the traditional TF method highlighted the superior performance of the proposed scheme, especially in regard to top few documents ranked as most relevant.

References

1. G. Salton and C. Buckley, Term-weighting approaches in automatic text retrieval, IP&M 24 (5), 1988, 513–523.
2. J. Morris and G. Hirst, Lexical cohesion computed by thesaural relations as an indicator of the structure of text, Computational Linguistics 17 (1), 1991, 21–43.
3. R. Kazmand, R. Al-Halimi, W. Hunt and M. Mantei, Four paradigms for indexing video conferences, IEEE Multimedia 3 (1), 1996, 63–73.
4. The full text is available from http://dragon.kaist.ac.kr/cicling2004.pdf

A Model for Extracting Keywords of Document Using Term Frequency and Distribution

Jae-Woo Lee and Doo-Kwon Baik

Software System Lab., Dept. of Computer Science & Engineering,
Korea University,
1, 5-ka, Anam-dong, SungBuk-ku, 136-701, Seoul, Korea
It21c@Korea.ac.kr, Baik@Swsys2.korea.ac.kr

Abstract. In information retrieval systems, it is very important that indexing is defined very well by appropriate terms about documents. In this paper, we propose a simple retrieval model based on terms distribution characteristics besides term frequency in documents. We define the keywords distribution characteristics using a statistics, standard deviation. We can extract document keywords that term frequency is great and standard deviation is great. And if term frequency is great and standard deviation is small, the terms can be defined as paragraph keywords. Applying our proposed retrieval model we can search many documents or knowledge using the document keywords and paragraph keywords.

1 Introduction

Information retrieval is one of the most important technologies at present. We can always get many information in the Internet or distributed computing systems using various information retrieval models. For searching proper information that we need, it is necessary to extract keywords of documents helping many web clients' requests. These information retrieval models specify how representations of text documents and information needs should be compared in order to estimate the likelihood that a document will be judged relevant. The estimates of the relevance of documents to a given query are the basis for the document rankings that are now a familiar part of information retrieval systems. Many models, including the probabilistic or Bayes classifier, have been proposed and are being used [1,2,3].

In information retrieval systems, it is very important that indexing is defined very well by appropriate terms about documents. In this paper, we propose a simple retrieval model based on terms distribution characteristics besides term frequency in documents. We define the keywords distribution characteristics using a statistics, standard deviation. By the standard deviation we define meaningful terms as document keywords or paragraph keywords, and the terms are selected by using stemming, filtering stop-lists, synonym for search meaningful terms in a document including TF-IDF(Term Frequency - Inverse Document Frequency). And then we can search many documents or knowledge using the keywords [2,4,5,6,7].

A. Gelbukh (Ed.): CICLing 2004, LNCS 2945, pp. 437–440, 2004.
© Springer-Verlag Berlin Heidelberg 2004

2   Keywords Extraction Model Using Distribution Characteristics

Keywords of a document appear here and there in the document. In our proposed information retrieval model, we use keywords distribution characteristics by a statistics, standard deviation. First, we extract important terms in documents or web pages and select meaningful terms applying TF-IDF. Next, we examine distribution characteristics of those keywords. And then we can extract document keywords and paragraph keywords. Our proposed extracting keywords model is summarized as following.

1. Extract worth terms in documents using stemming, filtering stop-lists, synonym, etc. This processing is scanning a document for searching meaningful terms(t_i).

2. When extract the meaningful terms applying TF-IDF, compute terms frequency(f_i), location of document(l_{ij}) respectively. After extract the meaningful terms, some terms can be eliminated by criterion of frequency(D).

3. Create profile about each terms frequency. And compute standard deviation(s_i) of the term in each location of document.

As shown in table 2.1, there are extracted terms and frequency, location, keywords distribution characteristics, standard deviation.

Table 2.1 Term's Frequency and Standard Deviation in Document

Extracted keywords	Frequency in document	Relative location in document(l_{ij})					Distribution (s_i)
t_1	f_1	l_1	$l_4\ l_5\ l_6$		l_9		s_1
t_2	f_2	l_2		l_8			s_2
t_3	f_3	l_3					s_3
...	...	...					...
t_i	f_i				l_{ij}		s_i
		...					
t_n	f_n					l_m	s_n

Keywords distribution characteristics, standard deviation of terms(t_i) is computed as

$$s_i^2 = \frac{1}{(f_i - 1)}\sum_j (l_{ij} - m_j)^2 \qquad \text{where } m_j \text{ is mean of relative location j.}$$

Using table 2.1, we can extract document keywords that term frequency is great and standard deviation is great, that is, wide distribution. And if term frequency is great and standard deviation is small, the terms can be defined as paragraph keywords. Because document keywords are widely distributed in a document and paragraph keywords are partly distributed in a document. In some cases, some keywords maybe appear just a little in a document. Our proposed retrieval model is very proper in that keywords appear many times in a document. Otherwise some terms cannot be extracted despite of very important keywords about document.

3   Keywords Extraction and Document Profile

We explain example of a document for extracting keywords. We use a document about "information retrieval" as shown in table 3.1. We assume a location of terms as 1 sentence, criterion(D) of term frequency is 2.

Table 3.1 A Sample Document about Information Retrieval

Location	Title of Document : Information Retrieval
1	Written as well as spoken text is a very important means of communicating human thoughts and knowledge.
2	In our current information society, we are overwhelmed with electronic textual documents.
3	Document collections are constantly growing and their content is constantly evolving.
4	Information retrieval and selection systems are becoming of increasing importance.
5	They must help us to find documents or information relevant to our needs.
6	Written text is considered as an intricate cognitive phenomenon.
7	The cognitive process of creating and understanding natural language text is complex and not yet completely understood.
8	However, it is clear that besides coding and decoding linguistic signs, it involves additional cognitive processes.
9	Communication through natural language text is basically ostensive and inferential.
10	The creator ostensively signals his or her communicative goals.
11	The inferential character of understanding natural language is one of the factors that makes an automated understanding of text a difficult operation.
12	The inferences refer to knowledge that is shared by the text's creator and user and that is not made explicit in the text.
13	The inferences also refer to the individual cognitive state of the user and allow determining the meaning of a text to the individual user.

Table 3.2 A Document Profile of the Sample Document

Terms	Frequency ($D \geq 2$)	Relative location in document(l_{ij})													
		1	2	3	4	5	6	7	8	9	10	11	12	13	(s_i)
text	7	1					1	1		1		1	1	1	4.1576
knowledge	2	1											1		7.7782
information	3		1		1	1									1.5275
document	3		1	1		1									1.5275
process	2						1	1							0.7071
language	3							1		1		1			2.0000
inference	2												1	1	0.7071

As shown in table 3.2, when the term frequency, 'text', is great and standard deviation is also great, the term can be document keywords because of widely distributed in a document. But the terms, like 'information' and 'document', partly distributed in sentence 2,3,4,5, term frequency is 3 and distribution value is 1.5275 so the terms can be defined as paragraph keywords. Using our proposed model we can easily extract document keywords and paragraph keywords than any other information retrieval model that term frequency is only applied. We can also meaningful paragraph in a document about a certain term.

4 Conclusion

In the Internet or distributed computing systems, it is necessary to construct efficient information retrieval systems helping many web clients' requests for searching proper information that they need. For searching proper information that we need, it is necessary to extract keywords of documents helping many web clients' requests. In this paper, we propose a simple retrieval model based on terms distribution characteristics besides term frequency in documents. We define the keywords distribution characteristics using a statistics, standard deviation. We can extract document keywords that term frequency is great and standard deviation is great. And if term frequency is great and standard deviation is small, the terms can be defined as paragraph keywords. Applying our proposed retrieval model we can search many documents or knowledge using the document keywords and paragraph keywords.

In the future, we will further research to represent various term distributions and extract various types of keywords for information retrieval systems. It will be very important that we define structure of document in detail and term distribution characteristics for information retrieval systems.

References

1. G. Salton and M. J. McGill, Introduction to Modern Information Retrieval, McGraw-Hill, 1983
2. William B. Frakes and Ricardo Baeza-Yates, Information Retrieval : Data Structures & Algorithms, Prentice Hall, 1992
3. Bookstein, A. and D. R. Swanson, "Probabilistic Models for Automatic Indexing," Journal of the American Society for Information Science, 25(5):312–318, 1974
4. Salton, G. and C. S. Yang, "On the Specification of Term Values in Automatic Indexing," Journal of Documentation, 29(4):351–372, 1973
5. Aho, A., and M. Corasick, "Efficient String Matching : An Aid to Bibliographic Search," Communication of the ACM, 18(6):333–340, 1975
6. Fox, C., "A Stop List for General Text," SIGIR Forum, 24(1-2):19–35, 1990
7. Harman, D., "How Effective is Suffixing?," Journal of the American Society for Information Science, 42(1):7–15, 1991

A Combining Approach to Automatic Keyphrases Indexing for Chinese News Documents*

Houfeng Wang, Sujian Li, Shiwen Yu, and Byeong Kwu Kang

Department of Computer Science and Technology
School of Electronic Engineering and Computer Science
Peking University, Beijing, 100871, China
{wanghf,yusw,lisujian,kbg43}@pku.edu.cn

Abstract. In this paper, we present a combinational approach to automatically supplying keyphrases for a Chinese news documen. In particular, we discuss some factors that have an effect on forming an initial set of keyphrase candidates and filtering unimportant candidates out from the initial set, as well as selecting the best items from the set of the remaining candidates. Experiments show that the approach reaches a satisfactory result.

1 Introduction

In this paper, we present a combinational approach to automatically supplying keyphrases for Chinese news documents.

Our approach is not the same as a pure keyphrase extractor. An extractor only extracts keyphrases from a source document. Supervised machine learning methods [2][4][5] and string-frequency method [1][3] are frequently used in extractors. However, the machine learning methods require a large amount of training documents with known keyphrases. Furthermore, for Chinese texts, in which there is no boundary between words except punctuation, words and phrases need to be recognized before the machine learning methods are availably applied. This is still considered as a difficult question in Chinese Processing. String-frequency method tries to avoid Chinese word segmentation. However, the method is not able to extract a valid phrase that does not occur sufficiently frequently and a resultant string as keyphrase even cannot be ensured as a clear meaning unit. One way of solving the problems is to select keyphrases from a controlled thesaurus. Fortunately, *People Daily* News Agency in China provided us with this thesaurus. We thus can gain some keyphrases by transforming extracted candidates into canonical terms according to this thesaurus, an abbreviation dictionary and a synonymous term dictionary.

Our approach is different from pure assignment tools as well, because our approach will directly extract some keyphrases from an article as long as they are thought as important based on our score strategies.

---

* This work is partially funded by National Natural Science Foundation of Chinese (grant No. 60173005).

A. Gelbukh (Ed.): CICLing 2004, LNCS 2945, pp. 441–444, 2004.
© Springer-Verlag Berlin Heidelberg 2004

2 Approach

The approach works as follows, extracts all Chinese character strings from a source article as initial keyphrase candidates which have more than one character and whose occurrence frequency is more than one time, eliminates meaningless candidates, transforms some candidates into canonical terms, scores each remaining candidate and selects the highest ones as keyphrases.

2.1 Elimination

E-Rule1, Meaningless unit filter: If a candidate cannot be segmented into a sequence of words successfully, it is meaningless and will be filtered out.

E-Rule2, POS filter: If the head of a candidate is not noun, it will be eliminated.

Some simple heuristics will be used to parse the head of a candidate. However, an individual word will not be affected by the rule.

E-Rule3, Non-subject word filter: If a candidate is a single word and the word does not belong to subject thesaurus, it will be filtered out.

E-Rule2 and E-Rule3 complement each other to filter out candidates.

Our subject thesaurus consists of 3721 terms (keyphrases) that are ordered in a hierarchical structure. It has been built by *People Daily* agency.

2.2 Transformation

Some terms will be transformed according to the following special word lists.

Abbreviations and Synonymous Terms

An abbreviation dictionary is built in order to transform them into their expansions. Similarly, a synonymous term dictionary is also built to transform synonymous terms into canonical terms that are collected in thesaurus.

Special Phrase Reconstruction

Some special words or phrases often cause ambiguities if they are extracted as keyphrases independently. They should be recombined with other word(s) into new phrases. For example, "钱伟长在上海喜度九十华诞" (Qian Weichang happily celebrating his 90th birthday in Shanghai). In the example, "钱伟长华诞" will be reconstructed as a keyphrase instead of independent "钱伟长" and "华诞". We have presented some recombination patterns for special words or phrases.

2.3 Selection

We present some indicators to score the candidates by our empirical observation. These factors play a decisive role in picking out keyphrases from the candidate set.

Position

Formula (1) gives a score to each candidate term based on its position in a document. The title and the section headings are commonly thought as condensed descriptions of a news document. Therefore, the candidate occurring in the title or the section headings is given the highest score. Also, the candidates in the first and the last paragraph are also given higher scores because they are much likely the keyphrase.

$$score(position(term)) = \begin{cases} w_{t-h} = 5 & position \ is \ Title \ or \ heading \\ w_{f-p} = 3 & position \ is \ the \ first \ paragraph \\ w_{l-p} = 2 & position \ is \ the \ last \ paragraph \\ 1 & others \end{cases} \quad (1)$$

Special Punctuation

$$punctuation(term) = \begin{cases} 1, \ if \ the \ term \ with \ special \ punctuation \\ 0, \ others \end{cases} \quad (2)$$

Some special punctuation marks such as '( )', ' " " ', can strengthen the importance of a candidate. The score of a candidate that is bracketed or leaded by them will be added as follows:

$$score(occurrence(term)) = score(position(term)) + punctuation(term) \quad (3)$$

Length

$$w_{len} = 1 + \lg \frac{1 \, 1}{|(length(phrase) - 7.1)| + 1} \quad (4)$$

The length of Chinese keyphrases which are manually given is from two characters to eleven ones and the average length of keyphrases is usually 7.1.

Named Entity

Person name, place name and organization name are very important in news documents. We will give a preference to them as follows:

$$w_{Ne-cp} = \begin{cases} 1.5 & if \ the \ phrase \ is \ named \ entity; \\ 1 & others \end{cases} \quad (5)$$

Frequency

It is assumed that a frequent term in an article is more important than an infrequent term. Therefore, it is an important factor and is reflected in formula (6).

Total Weigth

A term could occur in different position of an article and thus have different scores. We select the maximal one as Maxscore(term) to compute its total score as follows:

$$Total - score(term) = w_{len} * w_{Ne-cp} * Maxscore(term) * frequency(term) \quad (6)$$

3   Results

We select 60 articles from *People Daily* with manually assigned keyphrases to test our system. We classify these articles according to the number of the manually assigned keyphrases. Class-1 has three manual keyphrases, Class-2 has four, ... We do not select those articles that have two manually designed keyphrases or more than seven ones due to their small proportion.

Table1 gives the number of correct keyphrases that are indexed by our system for each rank in each class. An indexed keyphrase is defined as correct if it belongs to the set of manual keyphrases. The order of manual keyphrases is not considered in our evaluation. Rank indicates a sort order in descent based on total-score.

We simply calculated the correctness ratio for each class (Ratio-C) and the whole correctness ratio (Ratio-W) of all selected articles by formula (7).

$$Correctness - ratio = \frac{the\ number\ of\ keyphrases\ that\ are\ correctly\ indexed}{the\ number\ of\ manual\ keyphrases} \quad (7)$$

Table 1. Evluation of results: the number of correct keyphrases and the correctness ratio

Rank	Class-1	Class-2	Class-3	Class-4	Class-5
1	8	18	14	8	3
2	8	11	9	8	2
3	1	8	10	5	2
4		12	6	5	0
5			8	4	1
6				2	3
7					3
Total Articles	10	21	17	9	3
Ratio-C	56.6 %	58.3 %	67.1 %	57.4 %	66.7 %
Ratio-W	61.3 %				

Ratio-W indicates that the results are satisfactory. Also that the correct ratio Ratio-C for each class is nearly identical with Ratio-W shows that our approach is appropriate for both long news documents and short ones.

References

1. Chien, L. F.: PAT-Tree-based keyword Extraction for Chinese Information Retrieval, Proceedings of the ACM SIGIR International Conference on Information Retrieval (1997) 50–59
2. Frank, E., Paynter, G.W., Witten, I.H., Gutwin, C., and Nevill-Manning, C.G.: Domain-specific keyphrase extraction. Proceedings of the Sixteenth International Joint Conference on Artificial Intelligence (IJCAI-99). California: Morgan Kaufmann. (1999) 668–673
3. Ong T. and Chen H. : Updateable PAT-Tree Approach to Chinese Key Phrase Extraction using Mutual Information: A Linguistic Foundation for Knowledge Management. Proceedings of 2nd Asian Digital Labrary Conference. Taipei, Taiwan, Nov.8-9 (1999) 63–84
4. Turney, P.D.: Learning algorithms for keyphrase extraction. Information Retrieval, 2, (2000) 303–336
5. Witten, I.H., Paynter, G.W., Frank, E., Gutwin, C., and Nevill-Manning, C.G.: KEA: Practical automatic keyphrase extraction. Proceedings of Digital Libraries 99 (DL'99), ACM press (1999) 254–256

Challenges in the Interaction of Information Retrieval and Natural Language Processing*

Ricardo Baeza-Yates

Center for Web Research
Dept. of Computer Science, University of Chile
Blanco Encalada 2120, Santiago, Chile
rbaeza@dcc.uchile.cl

Abstract. In this paper we explore the challenges to effectively use natural language processing (NLP) for information retrieval. First, we briefly cover current NLP uses and research areas in the intersection of both fields, namely summarization, information extraction, and question answering. Second, we motivate other possible challenging uses of NLP for information retrieval such as determining context, semantic search, and supporting the Semantic Web. We end with a particular use of NLP for a new problem, searching the future, that poses additional NLP challenges.

1 Introduction

The interaction of Information Retrieval (IR) and Natural Language Processing (NLP) has two sides. The focus of this paper is NLP for IR. On the other hand, IR has always been a useful tool for NLP and will continue to be so. A short account of NLP research is given by Sparck-Jones in [43], but she also analyzes the accomplishments until 1994 and proposes summarization as the next step ahead [43]. The state of the art in natural language processing is covered in [6, 11,18,31].

The interaction, the role, the evaluation, and the progress of NLP for IR is covered in [44,42,45,37], respectively. Regarding the evaluation of the results, several authors point out that the improvements of using sophisticated NLP techniques are too small to justify their cost compared with statistical IR techniques [51,24,41]. Even the use of NLP resources such as thesauri coupled with IR techniques was discouraging [41]. Two issues are described and analyzed in [24]: (1) whether more refined natural language indexing is wanted, and, (2) whether controlled language indexing is really needed. Both imply non-trivial NLP research, such as indexing multiword expressions and finding semantic relations.

---

* Partially funded by Fondecyt Grant 1020803 of CONICYT Chile. This paper was written while visiting the Dept. of Computer Science and Software Engineering of the University of Melbourne, Australia.

A. Gelbukh (Ed.): CICLing 2004, LNCS 2945, pp. 445–456, 2004.
© Springer-Verlag Berlin Heidelberg 2004

They also make the distinction of data, text (or document), and knowledge retrieval, where the later is equivalent, for them, to question-answering. On the other hand, IR can be viewed as a great success story for simple NLP [51].

In [51], Voorhees claims that the factors that affect NLP compared to current IR techniques are: (1) the forgiving nature but broad coverage of a typical retrieval task; (2) the lack of good weighting techniques for compound terms; and (3) the implicit linguistic processing inherent in IR techniques. Hence, as long as NLP works very well and term weighting is not disturbed, the performance of the IR system can degrade significantly. Moreover, she claims that there is no evidence that detailed meaning structures are necessary to rank documents. As a corollary, [51] she points out that NLP techniques may be more important for related tasks such as question answering or document summarization. In some sense we reinforce that view in the sequel.

This article starts by briefly surveying the basic uses of NLP for IR as well as common areas of research. Then we propose several problems that poses interesting challenges to NLP for IR. Next, we introduce a new problem that needs good NLP as well as good IR: searching the future. The bibliography used is by no means exhaustive. On the contrary, it has been selected as the most relevant and novel for people interested in tackling the proposed challenges. Most of the referenced results of NLP applied to IR refer to symbolic NLP, rather than statistical NLP, which is newer (see [1] for a discussion on this topic). More bibliography about NLP can be found in the ACL anthology [2].

2   Current Uses of NLP for IR

2.1   Basic Uses

Information retrieval has always used basic natural language processing techniques [7,4]. The main techniques used are tokenization, stopword removal, stemming, and other text normalization tasks, which support the approach of viewing every document as "a bag of words."

Tokenization splits the text into a sequence of tokens, where each token is considered as a word. This removes punctuation and other special characters, and may or may not include numbers. In some languages finding the tokens can be non-trivial, as in German or worse, in Chinese. The result can be considered the most pure version of what is called *full text*. Subsequent processing produces document surrogates that can range from full text to just a list of keywords [7].

Stopwords are words that reflect little content or are so common that do not distinguish any subset of documents. They depend on the specific knowledge domain, but usually are functional words or acronyms. In the past most IR systems removed stopwords because the index size was reduced by half. However, stopwords are problematic for queries like *"to be or not to be"* and many studies have shown that there is no real impact of effectiveness for large document bases such as the Web. Hence, most modern IR systems, including Web search engines, do index stopwords, unless the documents are from restricted domains.

Stemming is used in IR to conflate morphological variants, obtaining the morphological root of every word. This may include plurals to singulars, verbal forms to infinitives, etc. The first problem with stemming is that is language dependent. For example, a rule based stemmer works well in English but fails in Spanish, where dictionary based stemmers have to be used. Moreover, in some languages, e.g. German or Arabic, stemming is quite difficult. Stemming also poses retrieval problems: it fails because is not context-dependent, conflates too much or misses some conflations, generates stems that are prefixes and not complete words, or does not allow queries that do care about number or tense. We can also have genuine ambiguity and hence, more than one possible stem.

Finally, text normalization may also include synonym translation, detecting multiword expressions such as *state of the art*, acronym consistency, etc. Two interesting normalizations that are not used too much are number and date conversion to standard forms. Both numbers and dates can be written in words or in different formats, being common in legal or commercial documents. Some NL based IR systems also discard *hapax legomena*, that is, words that appear just once. This may eliminate foreign or misspelled words, but can also remove a relevant term.

More complex processing such as phrase identification, finding named entities, concept extraction, anaphora resolution, or word sense disambiguation, depends on the application domain. Some of them are particularly useful in research areas that are in the intersection of IR & NLP as shown in the next section. However, in many cases if the NLP result is not perfect, more complex processing is useless (in addition it is usually expensive). For example, no technique or person can disambiguate an isolated ambiguous word, while statistical IR can disambiguate a word in the context of a document as well as NLP, but much faster. It is possible to apply statistical NLP to disambiguate words, but this technique may still fail if the correct sense is not the most common one [28, chapter 7].

2.2   Common Research Areas

There are several areas where the interaction of IR and NLP have been fruitful. They include summarization, information extraction, and question answering. In fact, the inclusion of some of these areas in the TREC conferences has helped to develop them as well as to show that NLP can be done efficiently in a larger scale [47].

Summarization tries to identify the essence of a document [27,46]. This is important to provide efficient access to large document bases, or to show extracts of documents as answers. Summarization involves the use of sophisticated NLP techniques and is one of the most actives areas of research of both the IR and NLP communities[1]. The next step in summarization is to define different types

---

[1] Summarization like machine translation and spoken language dialog systems, needs the three parts of a complete NLP system: understanding NL input, representing knowledge, and generating NL as output.

of summarization and evaluation measures (i.e. which summary is the most coherent and informative?), and create summaries that are not pieces of the original text (i.e. abstracts and not extracts).

Information extraction (IE) is related to summarization. The main goal of IE is to select and normalize pieces of text that can be used later in relational databases or ontologies (e.g. names of entities and its relationships). IE can be used for novelty detection and text mining, but still needs further research to improve its accuracy, detect better generic and ambiguous references as well as events and relations [34,35].

Question answering moves the focus from document retrieval to answer retrieval [36,52,46]. For many queries people want direct, brief answers. That is, starting from simple facts to what is called passage retrieval. This includes data mining from multiple sources, but not necessarily complex reasoning or taking actions. In this case NLP helps identifying the type of the answer, e.g. a number, a name, a date, etc., disambiguating the question or finding temporal restrictions.

There are two other related research areas that we should mention: cross language information retrieval (CLIR) [30,21] and text mining [22,48,49]. The goal of CLIR is to support queries in languages different from the languages in the document collection. Recent results have shown that the accuracy that can be achieved is almost the same as in monolingual IR. Text mining is to extract information from the text that was previously unknown, in particular because the query was not known. One important case, that not only includes text, is Web mining [16,17].

3   Future Challenges

Why has NLP failed for plain document retrieval? There are many reasons. In fact, statistical IR has "picked some of the easy fruit off the tree" [24] and what is left is much harder. Let's analyze the main problems are with current IR systems to explore if NLP can be useful. Figure 1 shows the complete typical retrieval process, which is interactive and iterative.

The main weaknesses are how the information need is transformed to a query, and the missing relevant documents. The first part depends on the person querying and depends a lot on knowledge and experience (and most users do not have it [24]). Using NL to pose the query does not help very much as the query *"Santiago"* is not too different from *"I want information about Santiago"*. Even for the best query, which should have more explicit context than our example, what makes a difference is the implicit context in it. In fact, if the IR system knows that the person has family in Chile, is Catholic, will travel to Cuba, lives in Argentina, is located in Santo Domingo, is an architect, loves Spanish movies, or is a baseball fan, the most probable relevant answers will be quite different[2]. So determining the context is crucial to improve effectiveness of IR systems and NLP can help finding part of it. In fact, the context is the clue for disambiguation.

---

[2] For the curious reader, the most probable answers are given just before the references

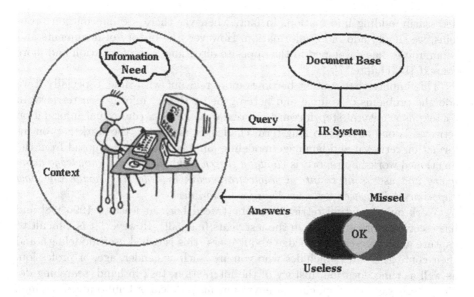

Fig. 1. The retrieval process.

The second problem is the documents missed because they do not match the query, the concept is expressed in another media, not text (e.g. an image), or they are in another language, among several other possible explanations. The latter case is the field of CLIR, while the two first require a semantic search. The simplest semantic search requires mapping terms to a common ontology. If we want more, we need to understand the text, certainly a NLP task. A possible way to alleviate the problem is improving the indexing of the document base, for example, assigning topics to each document, or adding semantic information, to build specific domain document bases. A side-effect of solving this problem is to partially reduce the number of useless documents.

In the following sections we explore in more detail the challenges described above. There are more problems, in particular the fact that information retrieval evolves during the interaction [23,29] and that current user interfaces could be much better [32].

3.1   Determining the Context

The word "context" comes from the Latin roots "cum" (with) and "texere" (to weave), suggesting an intertwining process. In fact, context shapes the content of a document, and vice versa, content implies a context. Notice that the root "texere" is also the origin of the words "text" (obviously) and "technology".

The design of a document interweaves the clues to read it. There is no information without context, but writers and designers always have the challenge of what context and what content must be omitted. Frequently, the fascination for content and its form, biased this balancing act to the information side, without necessarily adding information. In fact, whenever there are information problems, we should add more information. However, the history of documents and communities has developed in the opposite direction: less information and more context [14, chapter 7].

This implies that context becomes more relevant with time, especially if we add the problems of volume and heterogeneity. Hence, information retrieval in context is a natural step forward for research. In fact, contextual information retrieval is one of the two long-term challenges defined in the workshop on information retrieval and language modeling [3]. The exact goal, quoted from the mentioned workshop report, is *combine search technologies and knowledge about query and user context into a single framework in order to provide the most "appropriate" answer for a user's information needs.*

Work on contextual retrieval can be traced back at least to 1996 [38] and has received more attention in the last years (e.g [53]). However, it is difficult to capture and represent knowledge about users (this is called user modeling), and their context. Context includes who you are, such as gender, age, or profession, as well as time, location, history of the interaction, task in hand, searching device, speed and direction, current environment, physical or temporal constraints, relevance judgments, other information resources being used, etc.

We believe that many people do not want to give much information about their context, not only for privacy issues, but also because of the hassle of it. Context then must be obtained from personal Web pages, CVs, usage logs, IP addresses, browser information, etc. In many of these sources, NLP could help to extract the correct information regarding the context without being intrusive. One traditional way to include context is by performing query expansion through blind feedback done by the IR system [51], however user relevance feedback is be more effective [7].

3.2   Semantic Search

Why do we need semantics? Smeaton [41] says "we cannot handle cases of different words being used to represent the same meaning or concepts within documents or within queries, and we cannot handle polysemous words where single words have multiple meanings." Further, Voorhees [51] mentions three causes: different senses of a noun chosen for documents and queries when only one was intended; inability to select any sense due to the lack of context in the query; and adjective and a verb that share a common root and conflate to different nouns. Most of these cases could be blamed on bad sense disambiguation, a very limited kind of semantics, and hence term normalization might be beneficial. In fact, Sanderson found that disambiguation of at least 90% accuracy was required just to avoid degrading retrieval effectiveness [39].

Current text understanding effectiveness is poor, with the exception of some restricted knowledge domains. In the past, several people tried to do semantic search using knowledge bases such as WordNet without too much success [51, 41], although others may say the opposite. Part of the problem might be in the intrinsic incompleteness of such NL resources at that time. Perhaps the results would be different today using WordNet 2.0. Other authors believe that the final solution will always need human interaction, that is, semi-automatic techniques [46].

Thesauri work well in specific domains but not so well for domain-independent tasks. One line of research is to use NLP to bootstrap those kinds of resources. For example, to use document collections to create or improve thesauri and ontologies which can be then used to do better IR. An example of this for Web pages is OntoBuilder [33]. Other sources that can be used for the same purposes are usage logs, in particular the relations between users, queries, and answers selected by them. Techniques such as content filtering, topic detection and tracking [5], and message routing can be helpful.

One particularly important case for semantic search is the Semantic Web, which we cover separately, next.

3.3 Helping the Semantic Web

The Web has become the largest readily available repository of data. Hence, is natural to extract information from it and Web search engines have become one of the most widely used tools in Internet. However, the exponential growth and the fast pace of change of the Web, makes it really hard to retrieve all relevant information. Online topic detection would make it possible to build specific Web collections much faster [8]. In addition, there is the unwritten assumption that a physical file is a logical document, which is not always true [9]. Here NLP can help doing story boundary detection.

The two main problems with semantic information are standards for metadata that describe the semantic, and the quality or degree of trust of an information source. The first is being carried out by the WWW Consortium while the second needs hierarchical certification schemes that must be developed in the future. The main challenges of the Semantic Web itself are covered in [12, 25,50,9].

Dini [19] analyzes how NLP can help the Semantic Web (SW) in the acquisition side (building it) and in the retrieval side (accessing it). To build the SW we need very accurate tagging algorithms (see also [15,40]). To query the Semantic Web, NLP could help transforming semantic resources with simple but smart search interfaces. Another problem is to retrieve Web Services, not documents, which can be seen as an information extraction task followed by a best match search. This search will be done by programs, not persons. Another difference in the Web, is that not always the person will have an information need. Broder [13] reports that about half of current searches are navigational (the person is looking for a site) or transactional (the person wants to do a transaction). Dini also points out that if the SW succeeds, that will make NLP on the Web much easier. Hence, NLP has the opportunity of become an integral part of this new paradigm (see also [26]).

4   Searching the Future

Humans has always wanted to know their future, resorting from religious texts, astrology, or fortune tellers. Although we cannot know the future, a lot can be guessed about it because many things are planned several years in advance. The main sources for knowledge about future events is news. In fact, just looking at future years in Google News,[3] it is possible to find more than 50 thousand articles, with more than 10% having the year in the headline, and with references up to year 2050. For example, in 30 more years (2034) we can find the following:

1. The license of nuclear electric plants in Arkansas and Michigan will end.
2. The ownership of Dolphin Square in London must revert to an insurance company.
3. Voyager 2 should run out of fuel.
4. Long-term care facilities may have to house 2.1 million people in the USA.
5. A human base in the moon would be in operation.

So, when searching for *energy or health* in the future, we would like to retrieve 1 and 4, classified by year. If Searching for *2034 and space*, we would want to obtain 3 and 5. We call this new retrieval problem, *future retrieval* (FR), extending in some sense the concept of temporal databases to the field of IR (although temporal databases worry about the past, not the future). An FR system has the following components [10]:

- An NLP module that recognizes temporal expressions as times, dates, and durations (a particular kind of named entity recognition) and quantifies the likelihood of the future event (for example, news 1 and 2 will most probably happen, while 3 to 5 might have lower probability of happening).
- An IR system that indexes articles together with time segments and allows text queries, and optionally a time segment, such as the second query posed before. Any IR ranking can be extended in the time dimension, projected to a time segment, and sorted according to ranking or time.
- A text mining system that given a time query (a time segment for example), finds the most important topics associated with that segment. For example, *space travel* or *NASA* for 2034.

Here we have three different NLP challenges: (1) temporal expression recognition, that can be done fairly well in at least 90% of the cases (dates are more important than times or durations in our case); (2) finding the tense and mood of the main verb, which is a harder problem, but a first approach could be just to distinguish *will* and *must* from *should, could* and *would*; and (3) news topic extraction, a particular case of information extraction.

In [10] we present a proof of concept that at least the first two modules are feasible and that the results could be used in commercial or political decision systems. We are currently evaluating different ranking techniques for our system by using larger news collections, where we can use a first part as news base,

---

[3] http://news.google.com/.

and a second part to evaluate whether things happened or not (another NLP problem). The text mining module needs collaborative research from the NLP side.

5   Concluding Remarks

In this paper we have attempted to show the relevant possible future interactions of NLP and IR (see also [20]). Recently, use of NLP in IR research is blooming, due to new areas of interaction, meeting venues such as the Human Language Technology Research, or specific sessions [4] and invited articles in NLP conferences. The goal is not to use NLP for traditional IR, but to use NLP to build new IR systems, such as the future retrieval system outlined in the previous section.

In future standard document retrieval systems, NLP can help mainly in two cases: word-sense disambiguation for short queries and documents, as well as answer summarization when normal answers are too long or spread over multiple documents (see Figure 2). In addition, we have all the other research problems and challenges mentioned in this article. Finally, it may happen that near future NLP developments allow another intent to improve standard document retrieval.

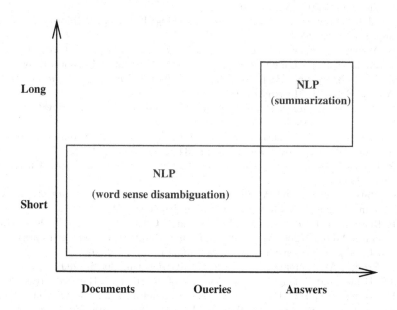

Fig. 2. Effective uses of NLP for standard document retrieval.

---

[4] For example, natural language technology in mobile IR and text processing user interface, a thematic session of the First Int. Joint Conference on NLP to be held in Sanjay City, Hainan, China in March of 2004.

Acknowledgements. We are grateful to the excellent comments and helpful pointers provided by Steven Bird, Trevor Cohn, and the invitation to write this paper from Alexander Gelbukh.

Note

The answers for the contextual example given are Santiago de Chile, Santiago de Compostela, Santiago de Cuba, Santiago del Estero, Santiago de los Caballeros, Santiago Calatrava, Santiago Segura, and Santiago Benito.

References

1. S. Abney, Statistical Methods and Linguistics, in Judith L. Klavans and Philip Resnik, editors, The Balancing Act: Combining Symbolic and Statistical Approaches to Language, 1–26, MIT Press, Cambridge, MA, 1996.
2. ACL Anthology. URL: acl.ldc.upenn.edu.
3. J. Allan and B. Croft, editors. Challenges in Information Retrieval and Language Modeling, CIIR, UMass, Amherst, MA, 2003.
4. J. Allan. NLP for IR, Slides of tutorial presented at Joint Language Technology Conference, Seattle, WA, 2000.
5. J. Allan, editor. Topic Detection and Tracking: Event-based Information Organization, Kluwer, 2002.
6. S. Armstrong, K.W. Church, P. Isabelle, S. Manzi, E. Tzoukermann, and D. Yarowsky. Natural Language Processing using Very Large Corpora, Kluwer, 1999.
7. R. Baeza-Yates and B. Ribeiro-Neto, *Modern Information Retrieval*, Addison-Wesley, England, 513 pages, 1999.
8. R. Baeza-Yates and J. Piquer. Agents, Crawlers, and Web Retrieval. CIA 2002, LNAI, Springer, Madrid, Spain, 2002, 1–9.
9. R. Baeza-Yates. Information Retrieval in the Web: beyond current search engines, Int. Journal of Approximate Reasoning 34 (2–3), 97–104, 2003.
10. R. Baeza-Yates. Searching the Future, Technical Report, CS Dept., University of Chile, 2003.
11. G. Battista Varile and A. Zampolli, editors. Survey of the State of the Art in Human Language Technology, Cambridge University Press, 1997.
12. R. Benjamins, J. Contreras, O. Corcho, and A. Gomez-Perez. Six Challenges for the Semantic Web, KR2002 Workshop on Formal Ontology, Knowledge Representation and Intelligent Systems for the Web, Toulouse, France, 2002.
13. A. Broder. A taxonomy of Web search, SIGIR Forum 36 (2), 2002.
14. J.S. Brown and P. Duguid, The social life of information, Harvard Press, 2000.
15. P. Buitelaar, and T. Declerck. Linguistic Annotation for the Semantic Web, in Annotation for the Semantic Web, S. Handschuch & S. Staab, editors, IOS Press, 2003.
16. S. Chakrabarti. Mining the Web: Discovering knowledge from hypertext data, Morgan Kaufmann, 2003.
17. R. Cooley, B. Mobasher, and J. Srivastava. Web Mining: Information and Pattern discovery on the World Wide Web, ICTAI 1997, 558–567.
18. R. Dale, H. Moisl, and H. Somers, editors. Handbook of Natural Language Processing, Marcel Dekker, NY, 2000.

19. L. Dini. NLP Technologies and the Semantic Web: Risks, Opportunities and Challenges, 8th Conference of the AI*IA, Pisa, Italy, 2003.
20. S. Feldman. NLP Meets the Jabberwocky: Natural Language Processing in Information Retrieval, ONLINE, May 1999.
21. G. Grefenstette, editor. Cross-Language Information Retrieval, Kluwer, 1998.
22. M. Hearst. Untangling Text Data Mining. In Proceedings of ACL'99: the 37th Annual Meeting of the Association for Computational Linguistics, Univ. of Maryland, June 20–26, 1999.
23. P. Ingwersen. Information Retrieval Interaction, Taylor Graham, 1992.
24. D. Lewis and K. Sparck-Jones. Natural Language Processing for Information Retrieval, Communications of the ACM 39(1), 92–101, 1996.
25. S. Lu, M. Dong, and F. Fotouhi. The Semantic Web: opportunities and challenges for next-generation Web applications. Information Research 7(4), 2002.
26. K. Mahesh, editor. Natural Language Processing for the World Wide Web, AAAI Press, 2002.
27. I. Mani. Automatic Summarization, John Benjamins, Amsterdam/Philadelphia, 2001.
28. C. Manning and H. Schütze. Foundations of Statistical Natural Language Processing, MIT Press, 1999.
29. G. Marchionini, Information Seeking in Electronic Environments, Cambridge University Press, 1992.
30. I.D. Melamed. Empirical Methods for Exploiting Parallel Texts, MIT Press, Cambridge, MA, 2001.
31. R. Mitkow, editor. The Oxford Handbook of Computational Linguistics, Oxford University Press, 2003.
32. J. Moore. Desiderata for an Every Citizen Interface to the National Information Structure: Challenges for NLP, in Natural Language Processing for the World Wide Web, K. Mahesh, editor, AAAI Press, 2002.
33. OntoBuilder. URL: http://ie.technion.ac.il/OntoBuilder/.
34. M.T. Pazienza, J.G. Carbonell, and J. Siekmann, editors. Information Extraction: Towards Scalable, Adaptable Systems, LNAI, Springer, 1999.
35. M.T. Pazienza, editor. Information Extraction in the Web Era: Natural Language Communication for Knowledge Acquisition and Intelligent Information Agents, LNAI 1714, Springer, 2003.
36. M. Pasca. Open-Domain Question Answering from Large Text Collections, CSLI, Stanford, CA, 2003.
37. J. Perez-Carballo and T. Strzalkowski. Natural Language Information Retrieval: Progress Report, Information Processing and Management 36(1), 155–178, 2000.
38. I. Ruthven and C.J. van Rijsbergen. Context Generation in Information Retrieval, Florida Artificial Intelligence Research Symposium, Key West, FA, 20–22, 1996.
39. M. Sanderson. Word sense disambiguation and information retrieval, Proc. of the 17th SIGIR Conference, 142–151, 1994.
40. SIG5-OntoWeb Project. URL: http://ontoweb-lt.dfki.de/
41. A. Smeaton. Using NLP or NLP Resources for Information Retrieval Tasks, in Natural Language Information Retrieval, T. Strzalkowski, editor, Kluwer, 1999.
42. K. Sparck-Jones. What is the role of NLP in text retrieval?, in Natural Language Information Retrieval, T. Strzalkowski, editor, Kluwer, 1999.
43. K. Sparck-Jones. Natural Language Processing: she needs something old and something new (maybe something borrowed and something blue, too), Presidential address, Association for Computational Linguistics, 1994.

44. T. Strzalkowski, editor. Natural Language Information Retrieval, Kluwer, 1999.

45. T. Strzalkowski, F. Lin, J. Wang, and J. Perez-Carballo, Evaluating NLP Techniques in IR, in Natural Language Information Retrieval, T. Strzalkowski, editor, Kluwer, 1999.

46. T. Strzalkowski, G. Stein, G.B. Wise, and A. Bagga. Towards the Next Generation Information Retrieval, in RIAO 2000, Paris, 2000.

47. T. Strzalkowski, J. Perez-Carballo, J. Karlgren, A. Hulth, P. Tapanainen, and T. Lahtinen. Natural Language Information Retrieval: TREC-8 Report, TREC Proceedings, 1999.

48. D. Sullivan. Document Warehousing and Text Mining, Wiley Computer Publishing, New York, 2001.

49. A-H. Tan. Text Mining: the State of the Art and the Challenges, in Proceedings of PAKDD'99 Workshop on Knowledge discovery from Advanced Databases, Beijing, 71–76, 1999.

50. F. van Harmelen. How the Semantic Web will change KR: challenges and opportunities for a new research agenda, The Knowledge Engineering Review 17(1), 2002.

51. E. Voorhees. Natural Language Processing and Information Retrieval, in Information Extraction: Towards Scalable, Adaptable Systems, M.T. Pazienza, editor, Lecture Notes in AI 1714, Springer, Berlin, 1999.

52. E. Voorhees. Evaluating the Evaluation: A Case Study using the TREC 2002 Question Answering Track, Proc. of HLT-NAAL 2003, Edmonton, Canada, 181–188, 2003.

53. R.W. White, J.M. Jose, and I. Ruthven. Using implicit contextual modelling to help users in information seeking (poster), Proceedings of Building Bridges: Interdisciplinary context-sensitive computing, Glasgow, 2002.

The Challenge of Creative Information Retrieval

Tony Veale

Department of Computer Science,
University College Dublin, Belfield, Dublin 6, Ireland.
Tony.veale@UCD.ie

Abstract. Information retrieval (IR) is an effective mechanism for text management that has received widespread adoption in the world at large. But it is not a particularly creative mechanism, in the sense of creating new conceptual structures or reorganizing existing ones to pull in documents that describe, in novel and inventive ways, a user's information needs. Since language is a dynamic and highly creative medium of expression, the concepts that one seeks will therefore represent a moving target for IR systems. We argue that only by thinking creatively can an IR system effectively retrieve documents that express themselves creatively.

1 Introduction

Most retrieval of textual information is literal in the sense that any retrieved document will literally match the keywords of the user's initial query. The query, whether a simple bag of conjoined keywords or a complex Boolean filter, essentially specifies the indices that should be examined to find matching documents. The set of matching documents is thus circumscribed by the keywords chosen by the user, making retrieval vulnerable to the *word mismatch problem* [2] if the authors of the most relevant documents have chosen to lexicalize their ideas in a different way. Of course, statistical and knowledge-based techniques (e.g., [3, 4, 5]) can be used to expand a query with highly correlated terms to permit the retrieval of additional relevant documents that do not literally contain any of the initial query terms. However, even these techniques still operate on the literal plane of meaning, by focusing on the conventional meaning of the keywords used (e.g., by using their synonyms, hypernyms and hyponyms).

This literal mindset in information retrieval (IR) ignores the fact that language is a creatively dynamic medium, one that is always striving to find new ways to communicate the same old ideas, often with an additional connotation or a different spin [6]. So while users of IR may be relentlessly literal in their choice of search terms, the authors of the documents they are hoping to retrieve will frequently be far more creative in their choice of words. To successfully retrieve these documents, it will be necessary for IR systems to demonstrate an equal level of creativity, to predict the innovative ways in which a relevant document might speak to the information needs of the user. These predictive techniques should be creative in the sense that they are capable of reorganizing an existing conceptual worldview (modeled using a taxonomy like WordNet [1], say) to look at a concept in new and interesting ways.

A. Gelbukh (Ed.): CICLing 2004, LNCS 2945, pp. 457–467, 2004.
© Springer-Verlag Berlin Heidelberg 2004

They may also need to be creative in the most obvious sense of the word, by exhibiting a capability to hypothesize and create new concepts that lead to insightful documents being retrieved.

This is the challenge of creative information retrieval: to imbue an IR engine with the conceptual tools and representations needed to express itself creatively, so it can predict the creative ways in which a user's search concept might be communicated. The need for creative IR is most keenly felt by search engines that manage a relatively small corpus of documents with little or no redundancy, such as on-line product catalogs. In such situations, a user must anticipate the ways in which a product may be marketed by its creators and choose an appropriate query to retrieve for that product. For example, it is now intellectually fashionable to refer to certain *comic books* as *graphic novels*. In a similar fashion, *suntan lotion* is variously marketed as *suntan oil, suntan ointment, suntan gel, suntan cream, suntan milk* and even *suntan butter*. Some of these variations are predictable from literal knowledge of the lotion/remedy domain, but others are clear uses of a food metaphor in which cream-as-lotion is perhaps the most entrenched instance. Product marketers strive for originality, so a statistical approach may not always learn such associations. However, in this paper we demonstrate how a creative system with basic metaphor capabilities can generate these variations from first principles, using a lexical knowledge-base like WordNet [1, 7].

2   Query Expansion

The search terms chosen by a user reflect the information needs of the user, but do not necessarily reflect the best set of indices with which to retrieve that information. Rather than use these terms as a query directly, intelligent search engines use them instead as merely a basis for constructing a query. This construction process, conventionally called query expansion, attempts to construct a rich query from the keywords offered by the user, in the hope that they will lead to greater document recall at equivalent levels of precision. Expansion of a user query can be performed using a variety of techniques, some of which are straightforward and mundane, but only some of which deserve to be labeled creative.

Statistical techniques can, in many cases, recognize domain correlations between terms, so that a query can be expanded with additional search terms that retrieve documents relevant to the same topic. For instance, corpus analysis reveals a strong co-occurrence probability for the word pairings *doctor* and *nurse, hospital* and *healthcare, Jaguar* and *sportscar*, etc. Relevance feedback techniques expand a query using terms extracted from the documents that a user has already marked as relevant to a query. The goal is to construct a query that returns more documents that are similar to those in which the user has expressed an interest, and dissimilar to those the user has deliberately avoided. Removing the need for user interaction, local context analysis (LCA) exploits the terms provided by the user as a first-cut query to retrieve an initial set of documents, the best of which are then statistically analysed to suggest additional search terms (both words and phrases) for an expanded query that will retrieve even more documents [3]. Statistical techniques typically require no domain knowledge to operate, and most can adapt to word-usage trends automatically if they are continually trained as new documents enter the IR index.

In contrast, knowledge-based approaches use a domain model to recognize the concepts denoted by the user's search terms, which enables their associated definitions to be exploited. This domain model may be provided by a general purpose lexical ontology like WordNet, a broad-coverage structured lexicon for the English language. By pin-pointing particular entries in such an ontology, the expansion process can exploit existing knowledge about synonyms (e.g., WordNet considers one sense of *cream* to be a synonym for *ointment*), hypernyms and hyponyms (e.g., WordNet considers *holy oil* to be a hyponym of *ointment*, which suggests that *oil* might be a useful alternate for *ointment* in a query), as well as partonyms and holonyms (e.g., WordNet describes one sense of *gondola* as being part of an *airship*).

These techniques tend, by their nature, to derive a literal perspective on a query and its conceptual content. Few large-scale ontologies contain explicit knowledge about metaphors and the schematic structures that permit them to be comprehended. Additionally, since novelty is a driving force in creative thinking, statistical techniques will not find sufficient data from which to derive the associations needed to understand creative metaphors (though we acknowledge that there has been some success in statistically recognizing established conventional metaphors).

3 Concept Creation

One test of a creative system is its ability to hypothesize and create new concepts to suit a given situation. This test discriminates those systems that mimic creative behaviour through the use of pre-coded rules and look-up tables from those that exhibit genuine innovation. For instance, a system might display an understanding of metaphoric language if it is given a sufficiently rich lexicon with appropriate cross-domain mappings, but one could not call such a system creative, as it limited to consider only those concepts that are defined by its knowledge-base. In contrast, a system that constructs such mappings on the fly (e.g., [8]), and which is thus not a priori limited, is creative in the sense of actually creating new knowledge.

Consider a simple case of knowledge-based query expansion for the user query *Jewish bread*. WordNet defines a range of hyponyms for {bread, breadstuff}, such as {muffin}, {wafer}, {biscuit} and {loaf}, that can all be used as expansion terms for *bread*. Additionally, WordNet specifies *Hebrew* as a synonym for *Jew*, so after some basic morphological analysis, we arrive at the following expansion:

Q1:   (Jewish *or* Hebrew) *near* (bread *or* loaf *or* biscuit *or* muffin)

WordNet defines a variety of specific bread types as hyponyms of {bread, breadstuff}, and two of these actually contain the word *Jewish* in their gloss. The first, {Challah}, is unambiguous and makes an excellent stand-alone query expansion. The second, {Jewish-Rye}, literally contains the query term in its lexical form, but still contributes to the expansion in a non-trivial way as follows:

Q2:   Challah *or* ((Jewish *or* Hebrew) *near* (bread *or* loaf *or* biscuit *or* rye *or* ...))

This use of hyponyms enriches the original query in a very effective way, but not all the relevant hyponyms in WordNet are recruited. For instance, the concept {matzo, matzoh, matzah, unleavened_bread} is also very relevant, but its gloss is tersely specified simply as *eaten at Passover*. However, WordNet defines the gloss for {Passover, Pesah, Pesach} as:

"a Jewish festival [...] celebrating the exodus of the Israelites from Egypt"

This may lead a creative system to construct a new concept, {Passover-bread}, to capture the implicit relationship between *Jewish* and *Matzo* and to unlock a range of productive expansion terms for our query as follows:

Q3:   Matzo *or* Matzoh *or* Matzah *or* Challah
        or   ((Jewish *or* Hebrew or unleavened *or* Passover *or* Pesah *or* ...)
        near (bread *or* loaf *or* biscuit *or* muffin *or* rye))

Further hypotheses might be inductively created on the basis of this concept [12]. For instance, since Passover is defined as a kind of {religious-holiday} in WordNet, a creative system might hypothesize a more general concept, {Jewish-Holiday-Bread}, in the expectation that other Jewish holidays may be associated with a particular kind of bread even in the absence of explicit WordNet examples. For instance, it happens that Hanukkah is associated with a traditional honey bread made with figs, a fact unknown to both WordNet and the authors of this paper until revealed by the creative information retrieval system described in this paper.

4 Lexical Analogies

Analogical expressions use terms from one domain of discourse to allude to terms in another, systematically parallel domain of discourse [13]. Analogy is thus useful when one knows of, or suspects, the existence of a given concept but does not know how it is lexicalized. For instance, a user may know that Islam is based on a particular sacred text but not know what it called or how it is spelled. In this case, an analogy like *the bible of Islam* can be used to allude to it indirectly. In a knowledge-based IR system, a lexical ontology like WordNet can be used to resolve this analogy prior to query expansion. The query that is then generated is simply:

Q4:   Koran *or* Quran *or* (Islam *near* bible)

Lexical analogies do not need to generate a one-to-one mapping of concepts, but can involve an indeterminacy that may usefully increase recall in an information retrieval setting. For instance, there is no particular book that one can definitively term the *Hindu bible*. However, WordNet defines {bible, scripture} as a hypernym of {sacred-text, sacred-writing}, and there are several other hyponyms of this parent whose gloss mentions *Hindu*, such as {Brahmana}, {Veda}, {Samhita} and {Mahabharata}. This leads to the following query expansion:

Q5:   Brahmana *or* Veda *or* Samhita *or* Mahabharata *or* "Hindu bible"

Such analogies are not difficult to generate using a lexical knowledge-base like WordNet, so this creative ability can be readily harnessed in an IR setting. Before explaining how, we must first consider some basic terminology. We define the *pivot* of a concept as the lowest hypernym that can be lexicalized as a single atomic term. The pivot of {Mars} is therefore {deity, god}, and not its immediate hypernym {Roman-deity}, which can only be lexicalized as a compound term. The intuition here is that compound terms are likely to represent a domain specialization of a concept, but good analogies should search outside this home domain to find a counterpart in a different part of the ontology. Additionally, we define the *discrimination set* of a concept as the set of words in its gloss that have been used in other WordNet compound terms as modifiers. For example, the gloss for {Mars} is shown below:

{Mars}   "(Roman mythology) god of <u>war</u> and agriculture"

The discrimination set of {Mars} is *{war, agriculture}*, since *war* is used in WordNet to differentiate {crime, law-breaking} into {war-crime} and *agriculture* is used to differentiate {department, section} into {agriculture-section}. These lexical precedents suggest that *war* and *agriculture* might also be useful in discriminating the {deity, god} category since they are used to define {Mars} and may help us find a similar deity. We do not place *Roman* in this set because it is explicitly tied to the home domain of {Mars} via {Roman-deity} and thus has no analogical potential.

We use a combination of the pivot and the discrimination set to gather a set of candidate source concepts for the target. The candidate set is defined as the collection of all concepts that are hyponyms of the pivot (a similarity constraint), and which reside at the same depth of the ontology as the target (a specificity constraint), and whose gloss contains at least one of the terms in the discrimination set of the target (a relevance constraint). The following concepts are therefore considered plausible candidate sources for the analogical target concept {Mars}:

{Durga}	"[Hindu] goddess of <u>war</u>"
{Ares}	"(Greek mythology) god of <u>war</u>"
{Morrigan}	"(Irish) <u>war</u> goddess"
{Skanda}	"[Hindu] god of <u>war</u>"
{Ishtar, Mylitta}	"(Babylonian and Assyrian) goddess of love [...] and <u>war</u>"
{Tiu}	"[Anglo-Saxon] god of <u>war</u> and sky"
{Tyr, Tyrr}	"god of <u>war</u> and strife and son of Odin"
{Hachiman}	"[Japanese] Shinto god of <u>war</u>"
{Nabu, Nebo}	"(Babylonian) god of wisdom and <u>agriculture</u> ..."
{Brigit}	"(Irish) goddess of fire and fertility and <u>agriculture</u> ..."
{Dagan}	"(Mesopotamia) god of <u>agriculture</u> and earth"
{Dagon}	"(Phoenician and Philistine) god of <u>agriculture</u> and the earth"

From these candidates an analogical query expansion can be created as follows:

Q6: Roman *and* (Durga *or* Ares *or* Morrigan *or* Skanda *or* Ishtar *or* Tiu *or* Tyr
          or Hachiman *or* Nabu *or* Nebo *or* Brigit *or* Dagan *or* Dagon)

Although fishing for poetic references, this query does succeed in finding documents that allude to {Mars} without actually mentioning *Mars*. For example, book VII of the Sibylline Oracles contains the following quotation:

> *But to them afterwards*
> *Shall Roman Ares flash from many a spear;*

Though this example is whimsical, lexical analogies can run the gamut from the poetic to the technical. For a consideration of the IR potential of analogy, see [13, 14].

5 Lexical Metaphors and Polysemy

Metaphor is a highly-generative conceptual phenomenon that can be used to create a wide range of linguistic expressions that refer to the same concept [6]. If we wish to retrieve documents that allude to a search concept figuratively rather than literally, it will be necessary to use an understanding of the metaphor process to expand the search query with plausible figurative lexicalizations of this concept. Consider the user query *Microsoft Monopoly*. There are three senses of *Monopoly* in WordNet:

{monopoly}:   a hyponym of {dominance, control, ascendance}
  "exclusive control or possession of something"

{monopoly}:   a hyponym of {market, market-place}
  "(Economics) A market in which there are many buyers but only one seller"

{monopoly}:   a hyponym of {board-game}
  "(Trademark) A board-game in which players attempt to gain a monopoly ..."

Clearly the first two senses are semantically related. Indeed, the second sense can be seen as a semantic bleaching of the first, in which the notion of exclusivity is abstracted out of the realm of economics and allowed to apply to any domain at all. We can exploit this polysemy to reformulate the idea of a monopoly as *a state of dominance in a market-place*, which in turn yields the expansion of Q7 below:

Q7:   Microsoft *and* (monopoly *or* (market *near* (control *or* dominance)))

This reformulation offers a more coherently unified view of the concept Monopoly than any single sense stored in WordNet. This should not be too surprising, since polysemy is often an artificial side-effect of the violence a sense-differentiating lexicon like WordNet must do to a concept in order to fit it into a branching taxonomic structure. Distinct word senses in WordNet thus capture just a sliver of the relational structure of the psychological concept, and it requires some creative thinking to reconstitute the conceptual whole from its various sense fragments. The reformulation in Q7 is a purely literal one, but it is also a more explanatory one from the perspective of IR, as expansion Q7 will now tend to retrieve documents that actually explain the hypothesis that Microsoft has a monopoly, by referring to dominance in particular markets, and should give more weight to those documents than to those that simply echo the hypothesis without additional insight.

By opening up a concept into a conjunction of other concepts, polysemy exposes the inner components of conceptual meaning to greater scrutiny, so that if applied recursively, it allows us to reformulate a metaphoric definition of the concept. For instance, the concept {dominance, control, ascendance} has other hyponyms besides {monopoly}, such as {mastery, supremacy}, {predominance, predomination}, {rule, domination} and, most interestingly, {tyranny, despotism}. This enables the following metaphoric expansion:

Q8:   Microsoft *and* (monopoly *or* (market *near* (dominance *or* rule *or* mastery
                          or tyranny *or* despotism *or* ascendance *or* supremacy))

In turn, *despotism* has two related senses in WordNet, the sense in Q8 which is a hyponym of {dominance, control} and another, more intense sense from the political domain: {despotism, totalitarianism, Stalinism, authoritarianism, dictatorship}. This sense leads to a highly-charged metaphoric expansion that should retrieve documents conveying the more extremist perspectives on Microsoft's market position.

Note how the concept {market, market-place} is not figuratively extended in Q8. The key to using polysemy for metaphoric query expansion is that only one component of a polysemous sense pair should be extended, while the other is left unchanged to serve as a domain anchor for the expansion, ensuring that the query remains on topic. Thus in Q7 and Q8, colorful terms like *tyranny* are constrained to occur in the proximity of the anchor term *market*, ensuring that the query never strays from its original focus. Conversely, if {market, market-place} is extended, to provide the term *shelf* say, {dominance, control, ascendance} should not.

These expansion strategies assume that instances of polysemy can be recognized in WordNet and differentiated from instances of homonymy, another form of lexical ambiguity in which the senses of a word are not psychologically related. However, the distinction between each kind of ambiguity is not explicitly marked in WordNet.

5.1 Detecting Polysemy in WordNet

Nonetheless, polysemous relationships can be recognized using a variety of automatic approaches. In the top down approach, *cousin relations* [7, 9] are manually established between concepts in the upper-ontology to explain the systematicity of polysemy at lower levels. For instance, once a connection between {animal} and {food} is established, it can be instantiated by words with both an animal and a food sense, such as *chicken* and *lamb*. This approach is limited by the number of high-level connections that are manually added, and by the need to list often copious exceptions to the pattern (e.g., *mate* the animal partner, and *mate* the berry drink, are merely homonyms; the latter is not derived from the former). Conversely, in the bottom-up approach, systematic patterns are first recognized in the lower ontology and then generalized to establish higher-level connections [10, 11]. For instance, several words have senses that denote both a kind of music and a kind of dance (e.g., *waltz, tango, conga*), which suggests a polysemous link between {music} and {dance}.

Both of these approaches treat polysemy as a systematic phenomenon best described at the level of word families. However, while such a treatment reveals interesting macro-tendencies in the lexicon, it does little to dispel the possibility that homonymy might still operate on the micro-level of individual words (as demonstrated by the size of the exception list needed for the first approach). We prefer instead to use an evidential case-by-case approach to detecting polysemy, connecting a pair of senses only when explicit local taxonomic evidence can be found to motivate a connection. This evidence can take many forms, so a patchwork of heuristic detectors is required. We describe here the three most interesting of these heuristics.

Explicit Ontological Bridging: a sense pair $<\omega_1, \omega_2>$ for a word ω can be linked if ω_1 has a hypernym that can be lexicalized as M-H and ω_2 has a hypernym that can be lexicalized as M, the rationale being that ω_2 is the M of ω_1 and ω_1 is the H of ω_2. E.g., the word *olive* has a sense with a hypernym {fruit-tree}, and another with the hypernym {fruit}, therefore M = fruit and H = tree. *(Coverage: 12%, Accuracy: 94%).*

Hierarchical Reinforcement: if $<\alpha_1, \alpha_2>$ and $<\beta_1, \beta_2>$ are sense pairs for two words α and β where α_1 is a hypernym of β_1 and α_2 is a hypernym of β_2, then $<\alpha_1, \alpha_2>$ reinforces the belief that $<\beta_1, \beta_2>$ is polysemous, and vice versa. For example, the word *herb* denotes both a plant and a foodstuff in WordNet, and each of these senses has a hyponym that can be lexicalized as *sage*. *(Coverage: 7%, Accuracy: 12%).*

Cross-Reference: if $<\omega_1, \omega_2>$ is a sense pair for a word ω and the WordNet gloss for ω_2 explicitly mentions a hypernym of ω_1, then ω_2 can be seen as a conceptual extension of ω_1. For instance, the railway-compartment sense of *diner* mentions *restaurant* in its gloss, while another sense actually specifies {restaurant} as a hypernym. This suggests that the railway sense is an extension of the restaurant sense that uses the later as a ground for its definition. *(Coverage: 62%, Accuracy: 85%).*

The coverage of each heuristic is estimated relative to that achieved by the *cousins* collection of 105 regular polysemy noun-sense groupings that are hand-coded in WordNet [7, 9]. Over-generation is estimated relative to the overlap with the cousins exception list [7], which permits us to also estimate the accuracy of each heuristic.

6   Concept Combination

User keyword-combinations run the gamut from existing WordNet compounds like *drug addict* to novel extensions of these compounds. The former are trivial to handle, and even the latter are straightforward if they can be shown to taxonomically extend an existing compound. In the case of *Prozac addiction*, the WordNet entry {drug-addiction} can be used as a guide to interpretation, since WordNet already defines {Prozac} as a kind of {drug}. Knowing how a novel compound fits into the WordNet taxonomy is extremely valuable for query expansion purposes. For instance, WordNet defines other hyponyms of {drug-addiction}, such as {heroin-addiction}, {cocaine-addiction} and {alcohol-addiction}, that also follow the same instantiation pattern since *heroin, cocaine* and *alcohol* all denote a hyponym of {drug}. These hyponyms point to other concepts that, by virtue of being lexicalized as modifiers of *addiction*, serve as prototypical addictive drugs. This allows us to generate a query composed of similes in which addiction is implicit:

Q9:   Prozac *near* like *near* (cocaine *or* heroin *or* opium *or* nicotine *or* alcohol)

These prototypes also point to other concepts that are strongly suggestive of addiction. For instance, in addition to the {drug-addiction}/{heroin-addiction} instantiation pattern, WordNet also instantiates {drug-addict, junky, junkie} with {heroin-addict} and {drug-abuse, habit} with {alcohol-abuse}. This leads us to consider other topics that are strongly related to the search query such as *Prozac addict* and *Prozac abuse*. Additionally, these compounds suggest useful synonyms in which the notion of addiction is implicit, such as *habit, junky* and *junkie*, but which do not arise from a consideration of the concept {addiction, dependency} in isolation.

Expansions such as these are a product of metonymy, a conceptual mechanism whereby a concept is used as a referential proxy for another, strongly associated concept. The textual glosses in WordNet are a fruitful basis for exploiting metonymy between concepts. For instance, from {drug-addict} one can infer a metonymic link to {withdrawal-symptom}, since the gloss for the latter contains the phrase *drug addict*. This metonymy suggests that *Prozac withdrawal symptom* is a relevant topic to include in the overall expansion, as follows:

Q10: Prozac *near* ((like *near* (cocaine *or* heroin *or* opium *or* nicotine *or* alcohol))
            or (addict *or* addiction *or* dependency *or* habit *or* abuse
            or "withdrawal symptom"))

It is generally safe to expand compound terms in this way, because these are far less ambiguous in WordNet than atomic terms, with most having just a single sense.

7   Some Concluding Remarks on Creative Reasoning in IR

Statistical approaches to generating conceptual associations have the considerable advantage of being dynamically attuned to the changing trends of language use, whereas knowledge-bases often need to be maintained by ontological engineers. However, when it comes to chaining together successive associations to generate a truly creative leap of the imagination, we believe that only a knowledge-based approach can sufficiently ensure the logical coherence of the resulting expansion.

Consider the initial user query *Italian recipes*. Statistical techniques will no doubt detect a strong co-occurrence between uses of the word *Italian* and *mozzarella, pizza*, and *antipasto*, as well as *Rome, mafia* and *soccer*. Additionally, there will be a strongly observed statistical association between recipes and *mozzarella, pizza* and *antipasto*. Using the associations common to both, we can generate a query like the following:

Q11:   (Italian *or* Mozzarella *or* pizza *or* antipasto) *near* recipes

Knowledge-based techniques can generate a similar query using WordNet as a base. But now consider how different associations can be chained together to yield a more creative expansion. WordNet 1.6 provides a strangely food-neutral definition of {recipe, formula} as *directions for making something*, and the only concept in which *recipe* appears as a gloss term is {cookbook, cookery-book}: *a book of recipes and cooking directions*. This suggests that *cookery-book* is actually a very effective metonym of *recipes*, so we can reformulate our query as:

Q12:   (Italian *or* Mozzarella *or*...) *near* ("cookery book" *or* cookbook *or* recipes)

Some linguistic word-play allows us to go from *Italian cookery-book* to *Italian-cookery book* without loss of information. However, the latter proves to be a much more fruitful organization of the query. WordNet defines {cookery, cooking, cuisine, culinary-art} as *the practice or manner of preparing food or the food so prepared* and only one of these gloss words, *food*, denotes a concept with hyponyms whose glosses contain *Italian*. Among those hyponyms of {food, nutrient} whose glosses mention *Italian* are {pizza}, {antipasto}, {Mozzarella}, {Ricotta} and {Frittata}. This reorganization thus suggests the following expansion:

Q13:   ((Italian *and* (cookery *or* food)) *or* pizza *or* antipasto *or* Mozzarella *or*...)
        near (book *or* cookbook *or* recipes))

Now, in searching the conceptual vicinity of {cookery-book, cookbook} for potential metaphors, we recognize an interesting example of WordNet polysemy in the word *bible*, which can denote either an authoritative handbook or a sacred text. This polysemy suggests that at least one sense of *bible* is metaphoric, which in turn suggests that *bible* may be a good metaphor for a cookery book, especially since both {cookery-book} and {bible} share a very specific common hypernym in {reference-book}. This leads us to produce the following figurative expansion:

Q14:   ((Italian *and* (cookery *or* food)) *or* pizza *or* antipasto *or* Mozzarella *or*...)
        near (book *or* cookbook *or* recipes *or* bible))

This final query is capable of matching creative allusions in text, such as *The Antipasto Bible*, that are strongly suggestive of the search concept *Italian recipes*. But note how this suggestion is an emergent one, arising out of a delicate interaction of connotations from the words *Antipasto* and *Bible*, the latter contributing *Italian* and *food*, the former contributing *book*, with the suggestion of *recipes* only arising out of the combination of both these connotations in *food + book*. It simply would not be coherent to leap from *recipes* to *bible* directly, or even to go via *cookery-book*, without first discharging the query's responsibility to somehow capture the implicit *food* theme of the original request.

To conclude: the challenge of creative IR is to be able to explore and stretch the boundaries of linguistic expression while keeping a query firmly on-topic. We believe that a knowledge-based approach, in which metaphor is represented and reasoned with as an explicit conceptual phenomenon, rather than as an epiphenomenon of word distribution, is best suited to meet this challenge.

References

1. Miller, G. A. WordNet: A Lexical Database for English. Communications of the ACM, Vol. 38 No. 11 (1995)
2. Furnas, G. W., Landauer, T. K., Gomez, L. M., Dumais, S. T. The vocabulary problem in human-system communication. Communications of the ACM, vol. 30, number 11. (1987)
3. Xu, J., Croft, W. B. Improving the Effectiveness of Information Retrieval using Local Context Analysis. ACM Transactions on Information Systems, vol . 18, number 1. (2000)
4. Qiu, Y., Frei, H. P. Concept-based Query Expansion. In the proceedings of the ACM SIGIR Int. Conference on Research and Development in Information Retrieval. (1993)
5. Navigli, R., Velardi, P. An Analysis of Ontology-Based Query Expansion Strategies. In the proceedings of the Int. Workshop on Adaptive Text Extraction and Mining at the 14th European Conference on Machine Learning. Dubrovnik, Croatia. (2003)
6. Lakoff, G, Johnson, M. Metaphors We Live By. Uni. of Chicago Press: Chicago (1980)
7. WordNet documentation. www.princeton.edu/~wn/ (2003)
8. M. Montes-y-Gómez, A. Gelbukh, A. López-López, R. Baeza-Yates. Flexible Comparison of Conceptual Graphs. In: Mayr, H.C., et al. (Eds.), Database and Expert Systems Applications (DEXA-2001). Lecture Notes in Computer Science, N 2113, Springer-Verlag, pp. 102–111 (2001)
9. Peters, W., Peters, I., Vossen, P. Automatic sense clustering in EuroWordNet. In the proceedings of the 1st international conference on Language Resources and Evaluation. Spain (1998)
10. Peters, I., Peters, P. Extracting Regular Polysemy Patterns in WordNet. Technical Report, University of Sheffield, UK. (2000)
11. Peters, W., Peters, I. Lexicalized Systematic Polysemy in WordNet. In the proceedings of the 2nd international conference on Language Resources and Evaluation. Athens. (2000)
12. Colton, S. Creative Logic Programming. In the proceedings of the 3rd Workshop on Creative Systems, held as part of the 18th International Joint Conference on Artificial Intelligence, IJCAI'03, Acapulco, Mexico (2003)
13. Tony Veale. The Analogical Thesaurus: An Emerging Application at the Juncture of Lexical Metaphor and Information Retrieval. In the proceedings of IAAI 2003, the 2003 International Conference on Innovative Applications of Artificial Intelligence. Acapulco, Mexico (2003)
14. Tony Veale. Dynamic Type Creation in Metaphor Interpretation and Analogical Reasoning: A Case-Study with WordNet. In the proceedings of ICCS2003, the 2003 International Conference on Conceptual Structures, Dresden, Germany (2003)

Using T-Ret System to Improve Incident Report Retrieval

Joe Carthy, David C. Wilson, Ruichao Wang,
John Dunnion, and Anne Drummond

Computer Science Department, University College Dublin, Dublin, Ireland
{Joe.Carthy,David.Wilson, Rachel,John.Dunnion,Anne.Drummond}@ucd.ie
http://www.cs.ucd.ie/contents.htm

Abstract. This papers describes novel research involving the development of Textual CBR techniques and applying them to the problem of Incident Report Retrieval. Incident Report Retrieval is a relatively new research area in the domain of Accident Reporting and Analysis. We describe T-Ret, an Incident Report Retrieval system that incorporates textual CBR techniques and outline preliminary evaluation results.

1 Introduction

In this paper we describe the the incorporation of Textual CBR techniques into the design of an Incident Report Retrieval system called T-Ret. Textual CBR involves the combining of text similarity metrics with CBR metrics. The Textual CBR approach we use is based on research carried out by Wilson [10]. The paper is structured as follows: Section 2 describes Textual CBR; Section 3 introduces the domain of Incident Reporting in more detail; Section 4 outlines the T-Ret system; Section 5 outlines our preliminary results; Section 6 describes future work and presents our conclusions.

2 Textual CBR

Much of current textual CBR (TCBR) research focuses on transforming or augmenting knowledge-poor textual documents such as legal decisions (e.g., [1,2,4]) or hotline support documentation (e.g., [3]), in order to generate hybrid structured representations that can be used by traditional knowledge-based CBR methods. Such support for textual CBR is especially important when the raw case information is composed entirely of free-form text.

We are investigating how techniques from information retrieval, which have been widely used to support document-as-case TCBR, can be applied in situations where textual information represents only a small, but useful part of the overall reasoning context. This has led us to view textual CBR along a continuum from "weakly-textual", where textual information offers limited reasoning support but does not require sophisticated processing, to "strongly-textual", where textual information is the focus of reasoning but requires much more specialized

A. Gelbukh (Ed.): CICLing 2004, LNCS 2945, pp. 468–471, 2004.
© Springer-Verlag Berlin Heidelberg 2004

treatment. For weakly-textual contexts, we propose that relatively simple and general information retrieval techniques can be used to provide a measure of textual distance that, although relatively weak in itself, is strong enough to enhance reasoning within a larger knowledge-based context. Such measures provide standard similarity metrics, such as nearest-neighbour methods, with support for "textual features", providing they are used with appropriate contextual support.

3   Incident Reporting

Incident Reporting and Analysis is a sub-area of the field of Accident Analysis, and it provides an important defence against future failures in many safety-critical industries. An *incident* may be roughly defined as an event that may potentially lead to an accident, and there is an empirical relationship of one accident to every 300 incidents. The relative frequency of incidents as opposed to the relative infrequency of accidents, helps to ensure that there is a focus on safety issues [9]. While incident reporting systems are of vital importance, they often attract little or no attention until a serious accident occurs such as a plane crash, rail crash, or the death of a patient undergoing minor surgery.

4   T-Ret System

The T-Ret system has been developed as part of our investigations into building intelligent incident management systems. We have previously reported promising results from the InRet system [5] which was based on straightforward CBR techniques. Johnson has also reported positive results from applying CBR techniques to accident analysis [8]. The InRet system only used the well-defined features of an incident such as aircraft manufacturer, pilot experience, engine type, and ignored the textual descriptions that are present in incident reports. The T-Ret system comprises of three individual components which employ different approaches to the similarity assessment and subsequent ranking of the incidents described by the incident reports contained in the corpus. Using the Cosine Similarity metric [6] as the base for our comparisons, it was decided to utilise a "full-document" approach as well as a "segmented-document" approach to evaluate the merits and potential of both strategies in the task of similarity ranking.

The first of these approaches is that of full-document retrieval. Using the cosine similarity measure of each report to all other reports in the corpus, it is possible to obtain a similarity ranking based on standard term-matching techniques utilised in classic Information Retrieval (*IR*). Using the Vector Space Model [7], each incident is stored as a vector of terms. The similarity between vectors is calculated and a score is returned and sorted to reveal the most textually similar reports for each report in the corpus. This approach is problematic in that, in terms of Incident Retrieval, incidents will be reported using vocabulary which is common to all incidents but may mask the key elements required for contextual similarity. Hence, in order to combat this problem, another approach was devised, based on CBR methodologies.

Instead of using the entire report for the comparison, each incident report may be segmented into three different sections; those of Causes, Witness Reports and Safety Recommendations. By analysing these individually, it was hoped to provide increased precision in the similarity calculations. Though the similarity of each section to its corresponding section in the other reports is carried out independently, the results obtained had to be combined in order to allow a representation of the report as a whole. For each report, the determined cause C, the safety recommendations SR and the witness account WA are compared. Once the similarity scores have been obtained, two ranking metrics are employed to provide a similarity score for the report as a whole. These are:

$$T - Ret_1 = Sim(C_1, C_2) * Sim(SR_1, SR_2) * Sim(WA_1, WA_2) \tag{1}$$

$$T - Ret_2 = (Sim(C_1, C_2) + Sim(SR_1, SR_2) + Sim(WA_1, WA_2))/3 \tag{2}$$

Also, in order to test the effectiveness of the standard IR approach against the feature-based CBR model, the non-textual features of each report were compared to evaluate the similarity of all reports to each other.

5   Results

The goal of these experiments was to explore whether or not the Textual CBR metrics devised could outperform the standard CBR and IR approaches in evaluating similarity between Incident Reports. An evaluator similarity ranking was obtained for a section of the corpus prior to our experimentation. For each report, the evaluator was presented with five additional reports and was asked to rank them according to their similarity to the original. The experiments were designed to retrieve the rank order of these five documents when all documents in the corpus were compared to the initial report. It was hoped that by analysing the report sections independently and combining the returned scores according to our two ranking metrics, $T - Ret_1$ and $T - Ret_2$, we would see an improvement in performance. Given Incident 46, the evaluator ranked Incidents 37, 47, 55, 15 and 16.

As can be seen from Table 1, the $T - Ret_1$ comparison corresponds most closely with the manual evaluations. Interestingly, the most similar incident according to the user, Incident 37 is assigned the highest similarity rating by

Table 1. All System Rankings

Rank	Evaluator	Full-Document	Feature-Selection	$T - Ret_1$	$T - Ret_2$
1	37	47	47	37	37
2	47	37	55	55	47
3	55	15	37	47	15
4	15	16	16	16	16
5	16	55	15	15	55

$T - Ret_1$ and $T - Ret_2$, the second highest rating by the full-document comparison and the third highest rating by the Feature selection approach. Based on these results, the "segmented-document" approach appears to perform relatively better. We are continuing to refine these experiments and also to enhance our evaluation process to take account of Precision and Recall metrics.

6   Future Work and Conclusions

The current evaluation is based on a small corpus of aviation reports. It will be necessary to apply our system to a larger corpus to assess the validity of the research.

This paper presented the preliminary results of the T-Ret Incident Management System. This is a novel system based on the use of Textual CBR techniques. We are optimistic that the initial results can be improved by taking account of the non-textual features in combination with the textual features.

References

1. Stefanie Brüninghaus and Kevin D. Ashley. Using machine learning to assign indices to legal cases. In Proceedings of the Second International Conference on Case-Based Reasoning, pages 303–314, Berlin, 1997. Springer-Verlag.
2. Jody J. Daniels and Edwina Rissland. What you saw is what you want: Using cases to seed information retrieval. In Proceedings of the Second International Conference on Case-Based Reasoning, Berlin, 1997. Springer-Verlag.
3. Mario Lenz. Defining knowledge layers for textual case-based reasoning. In P. Cunningham, B. Smyth, and M. Keane, editors, Advances in Case-Based Reasoning: Proceedings of EWCBR-98, number 1488 in Lecture Notes in Artificial Intelligence, Berlin, 1998. Springer-Verlag.
4. Rosina Weber, Alejandro Martins, and Ricardo M. Barcia. On legal texts and cases. In Mario Lenz and Kevin Ashley, editors, Proceedings of the AAAI-98 Workshop on Textual Case-Based Reasoning, pages 40–50, Menlo Park, CA, 1998. AAAI Press.
5. Carthy, J., InRet: An Intelligent Incident Management System, European Colloquium on Case-based Reasoning (ECCBR, 2002), Sept. 4–8th 2002
6. Gerard Salton and M. J. McGill. The SMART and SIRE Experimental Retrieval Systems. McGraw-Hill, New York, 1983.
7. G. Salton, A. Wong, and C. S. Yang. A vector space model for automatic indexing. Communications of the ACM, 18(11):613–620, 1971.
8. Johnson, C., Using Case based Reasoning to Support the Indexing and Retrieval of Incident Reports, In Proceedings of the 19th European Annual Conference Human Decision Making and Manual Control", pages 127–134, 1999.
9. Reason, J., Managing the Risks of Organisational Accidents, Ashgate, Aldershot, 1998.
10. Wilson, David C. and Bradshaw, Shannon. (1999). "CBR Textuality." Proceedings of the Fourth UK Case-Based Reasoning Workshop. pp. 67–80. AI-CBR, University of Salford.

Spanish Question Answering Evaluation

Anselmo Peñas, Felisa Verdejo, and Jesús Herrera

Dpto. Lenguajes y Sistemas Informáticos, UNED
{anselmo,felisa,jesus.herrera}@lsi.uned.es

Abstract. This paper reports the most significant issues related to the launching of a Monolingual Spanish Question Answering evaluation track at the Cross Language Evaluation Forum (CLEF 2003). It introduces some questions about multilingualism and describes the methodology for test suite production, task, judgment of answers as well as the results obtained by the participant systems.

1 Introduction

Evaluation forums as the Text REtrieval Conference (TREC[1]), NTCIR project[2] or the Cross-Language Evaluation Forum (CLEF[3]) have shown their capability to stimulate research, to establish shared working lines, and to serve as a meeting point for their respective communities. These forums permit the comparison of different systems evaluated under the same conditions. Thus, some evidences about which are better approaches can be extracted. In this kind of evaluation, test suites must be produced to serve as the common evaluation exercises for every system under competition. Test suites generation requires a considerable effort that is justified in such evaluation forums. At the end, these test suites remain as a very valuable resource for future systems evaluation.

Question Answering (QA) research has been promoted and evaluated in such way since TREC-8 in 1999. Now, the Cross-Language Evaluation Forum (CLEF 2003) has brought new challenges: to consider different languages than English and to perform translingual QA [3]. The UNED NLP Group (Spanish Distance Learning University), as Spanish member of the CLEF consortium, is responsible for the Spanish test suite generation in all the QA tasks that involve Spanish, and is also responsible for the results assessments when Spanish take part as target language. We report here the most significant issues related the Monolingual Spanish evaluation task which has been launched in CLEF 2003.

Sections 2 and 3 describe the usual methodology for a QA evaluation based on systems comparison and introduce the challenge of multilingualism. Sections 4 and 5 describe the production of the Spanish test suite. The task, the assessment process and the results for the first monolingual Spanish QA evaluation are described in sections 6, 7 and 8 respectively.

---

[1] http://trec.nist.gov
[2] http://research.nii.ac.jp/ntcir/index-en.html
[3] http://www.clef-campaign.org

A. Gelbukh (Ed.): CICLing 2004, LNCS 2945, pp. 472–483, 2004.
© Springer-Verlag Berlin Heidelberg 2004

2 Evaluation Methodology

Since a QA system must answer a question in natural language, the evaluation methodology has been the following:

1. *Test suite production.* Mainly, the compilation of the document collection and the formulation of some hundreds of questions over that collection.
2. *Participant systems answering.* All the systems must answer the questions and return their responses in a limited time.
3. *Judgment of answers by human assessors.* Systems answers are judged as correct, incorrect, non-exact, not supported by a document, etc.
4. *Measuring of systems behaviour.* Mainly, the percentage of questions correctly answered, the percentage of questions without answer correctly detected, and some measures such the Mean Reciprocal Rank (MRR) [6] or the Confidence-Weighted Score [8] aimed to give more value to the systems with more precise and confident answers.
5. *Results comparison.*

This methodology permits systems comparison but introduces some restrictions that must be considered in the tasks definition:

1. *Quantitative evaluation constrains the type of questions.* Answers must be valuable in terms of correctness, completeness and exactness in order to measure and compare systems behaviour. Thus, it is not possible to ask any kind of questions.
2. *Human resources* available for the test suite generation and the assessment of answers. Usually, this is an unfunded work that requires some volunteers, which determine not only the possible kind of questions we can evaluate, but also the number of questions and the number of answers per question we can allow.
3. *Collection.* Unfortunately, most of the times the use of a collection is determined by its availability. However, the collection determines the searching domain and so the systems behaviour. Looking for answers in a news collection is a different problem than looking for them in a patents collection. Also processing is different in specific domains or in unrestricted domains. Finally, the comparison between systems working over different languages requires, at least, the availability of comparable multilingual collections.
4. *Roadmap versus state of the art.* There is a good idea of what systems should do in future [1]. However, its necessary to determine when is possible to incorporate new features. Thus, the definition of the evaluation task become a compromise between what is desirable and what is realistic to expect from QA systems. Are systems already able to adjust their confidence in answer, to use encyclopaedic knowledge, to make inferences, to answer temporary questions, to evaluate consistency between different answers, to consider different sources and languages, etc.?
5. *Research direction.* There are some issues related to future system behaviour that are affected by the evaluation tasks definition. For example, systems are tuned according the evaluation measures in order to get better results. In this way, evaluation measures have evolved to give more value to the systems with desirable features (e.g. better answer validation). Another example that shows how the evaluation task definition affects systems behaviour is the decision of permitting or not the use of external resources as the web, which could serve to improve systems results without improving their own processing skills.

These considerations are present in the evaluation task definition. Since 1999, QA at TREC has evolved increasing the collection size, the number, types and difficulty of questions, and restricting the number and exactness of answers. Systems have been able to adapt to these challenges and get better results in each participation. Now, CLEF 2003 has launched a new challenge: multilingualism.

3   The Challenge of Multilingualism

Multilingualism is one of the *research directions* that can be promoted according to the current state of the art in Question Answering. The definition of new evaluation tasks with multilingual features supposes a new challenge that must be accompanied by an appropriate methodology. From the evaluation point of view, multilingualism introduces new questions that affect the evaluation methodology:

- How to ensure that fully multilingual systems receive the best evaluation?
- What multilingual tasks can be proposed with the current state of the art?
- What is the possible roadmap to achieve fully multilingual systems?
- Which resources are needed for the evaluation purposes?

These questions are very interrelated and we must give answers carefully (although they will evolve during the next years). For example, to ensure that fully multilingual systems receive the best evaluation, we could have considered a proposal in the following way:

1. Build a unique multilingual collection, with documents in all the languages under evaluation.
2. Build a unique set of questions in different languages. For example, if we have 250 questions and 5 languages we can formulate 50 questions in each language.
3. Ensure answers in just one of the target languages. Otherwise, if all the questions are formulated in all the languages and they have answers in all the languages, then a monolingual system can achieve the same results as a fully multilingual system. For example, if we have 250 questions and 5 languages, we can ensure that 10 questions in language A would have answer only in documents of language B, for all the 25 combinations of two languages A, B.
4. Run a unique evaluation task for all the systems and compare their results. Those that work with more languages would be able to get more answers and better results.

This methodology introduces some important difficulties:

- How to ensure answers in only one language? If we use comparable multilingual collections then a very hard pre-assessment is needed. If we use collections with different domains for each language then results could be biased. We would have to find some criteria based on things like dates or locality of events.
- How to find and appropriated balance among all languages and the type and difficulty of questions? The evaluation could reward systems centred in one of the languages if it is easier to find more answers in one language than in the others.

- The human assessment of correctness and exactness of answers must be performed by native speakers. Since systems would give an answer in any language, the human assessment process needs additional coordination to send each answer to the appropriate human assessor.

However, with the current state of the art systems it is not realistic to plan an evaluation like this in a very short term: Are systems able to answer a question in any language? Are systems able to find answers in sources of any language? A naive approach consists in the translation of questions by means of an automatic Machine Translation system and then use a monolingual QA system. So, we can expect systems to process questions in several languages and find answers in a different one, but very few systems will deal with more than one target language in order to find answers in more than one different collection.

In this way, to perform a separate evaluation for each target language seems to be more realistic in the very short term, and avoids the mentioned difficulties. This has been the option followed by CLEF 2003, in which the central issue has been to develop a methodology for the production of questions in several languages. However, we must follow closely the systems evolution in order to introduce global measures rewarding systems that consider as many languages as possible.

4 Spanish Test Suite

4.1 Spanish Document Collection

The collection used in the Monolingual Spanish QA task 2003 corresponds to the Spanish collection of CLEF 2002 campaign. This document set contains more than 200.000 international news from EFE Press Agency during the year 1994 (about 500 Mb). News cover a wide range of topics (sports, society, politics, etc.) so it is considered an unrestricted domain collection.

4.2 Spanish Questions Set

The questions set has been produced in coordination with the Italian ITC-IRST, UNED (Spanish Distance Learning University) and the University of Amsterdam. As a result of this coordinated work, the DISEQuA[4] corpus [2] has been created with 450 questions and answers translated into English, Spanish, Italian and Dutch.

Before starting the generation of questions, the TREC 2002 set of questions was studied with the aim to determine their style and the difficulties to find the answers. 73 questions were translated into Spanish and their answers were searched in the Spanish collection. We found that the Spanish document collection was large enough to find most of the answers. Since the TREC 2002 questions were public for potential participants, these Spanish translations were not used for CLEF 2003 edition.

The questions set production has followed a methodology in five steps:

1. *Production of 200 candidate questions in Spanish.* Candidate questions were formulated taking as starting point the topics produced in past editions of

---

[4] This corpus is available at http://clef-qa.itc.it and http://nlp.uned.es/QA

CLEF (Cross-Language Information Retrieval tasks at CLEF 2000, 2001 and 2002). In this way, candidate questions were produced without exploring the document collection, trying to avoid any influence in the questions formulation and wording. The type of questions corresponds to short and fact-based answers. Four people were involved in this work in order to include different styles in questions formulation.

2. *Selection of 147 questions with answer.* The answers for the 200 candidate questions were searched in the collection. A question has an answer in the collection if there is a document that contains and supports the correct answer without any inference implying knowledge outside the document. Finally, 147 questions with an answer in the document collection were selected and translated into English in order to share them with the Italian and Dutch QA coordinators.

3. *Processing of questions produced in Italian and Dutch.* A parallel process was followed in both Italian and Dutch languages, producing near 300 more questions translated into English. These 300 questions were translated into Spanish and, again, an answer for each one was searched in the collection. At this point, almost 450 different questions had been produced and translated into English, Spanish, Italian and Dutch. All of them have an answer in at least one collection of CLEF 2002 (except English). This is the corpus that we have called DISEQuA.

4. *Selection of 180 questions with known answer.* From the DISEQuA corpus, 180 questions with answers in the three collections were selected. The respective translation of these 180 questions were used in each of the three Monolingual QA tasks.

5. *Selection of the final 200 questions.* The final 200 Spanish questions set is composed by the 180 questions (in the Spanish version), and 20 more questions without known answer in the Spanish collection. These 20 questions have been used to evaluate systems capabilities to detect questions without answer. These final 200 questions are referred to facts (dates, quantities, persons, organizations, etc.)

4.3 Preliminary Assessment

Dates and numbers change across different news for the same event. Sometimes, the first information is incomplete or not well known yet. Sometimes, there is a changing process or an increasing count along several days. For example, the number of died people in one accident. In these cases, there is more than one answer supported by different documents. Assessors must evaluate an answer without any inference or use of information not contained in the supporting document. For example, some preliminary questions asked for events in 1994, but being the year of the news collection, this year doesn't appear explicitly in the document text and it had to be removed from the questions for the final version.

5 Dealing with Multilingualism in Questions Set Production

The production and translation of questions have some difficulties that we comment in the following subsections.

5.1 Several Spellings

Sometimes there are several possible spellings for an entity during the question translation process. One case corresponds to old or new writing styles. For example, the term "Malasia" corresponds to old style in Spanish, while the term "Malaisia" corresponds to the modern one. In these cases, when both expressions appear in the collection, the modern style has been chosen for production and translation of questions. Another case, are entities with two different *sounds* and both appear in the collection. For example, Oryx and Órice are both used in Spanish, but the Spanish-like sound corresponds to the second one. In these cases, the Spanish-like sound is chosen. When not further criteria are found, the most frequent translation in the collection is chosen.

5.2 Acronyms Translation

Some acronyms change across different languages. For example NATO and OTAN correspond to the English and Spanish versions respectively. In these cases, the acronym is translated. In some cases, there are frequent acronyms in English that correspond to entities that are not referred with acronyms in Spanish. For example, BSE (*Bovine Spongiform Encephalopathy*) is a frequent acronym in English, while in Spanish is more frequent the entire expression *Encefalopatía Espongiforme Bovina*, being not frequent their acronyms (either BSE or EEB). However, instead of using the most frequent expression, in these cases where the source question has an acronym, the translation into Spanish maintain the acronym but in the Spanish version.

5.3 Second Translations

Some final questions have been the result of two translations: one from the source language into English, and a second from English into the target language. English has been chosen as intermediate language for two reasons: First, to build a richer resource for ulterior multilingual QA evaluation, and second, to simplify the translation process between pairs of languages. However, each translation may modify slightly the original question and, finally, introduce some variation in meaning. This problem doesn't affect the monolingual task evaluation, but affects the quality of the question set as a resource for further multilingual QA evaluation. To avoid this problem, translators have considered both, the original question and the English version.

6 Monolingual Spanish Task

The guidelines[5] for the participants in CLEF 2003 were the same in all Monolingual Question Answering tasks (Spanish, Italian and Dutch). Systems could participate in one or both of the following subtasks: exact answer or 50 bytes long string answer. In the exact answer subtask the answer-string must contain exclusively a correct answer for the question. In the 50 bytes long string subtask, the correct answer must be a part of a 50 bytes-sized string, possibly containing irrelevant information. For example, for the question 'What is the capital of France?', either *paris* or *Paris* are always considered as correct answers (whenever the document supports the answer), while answers like:

- Paris is a very large city where
- 100 years ago, Paris was an

are consider correct only in the 50-bytes string subtask (whenever the document supports the answer).

Participants are provided with 200 questions intending to return short and fact-based answers. Then, they have to produce up to two runs without any kind of human intervention to obtain up to three answers per question and run. That means that each run contains one, two or three answers per question.

All the answers produced by participant systems are submitted into one file for each run, that responds to the following structure:

1. Each line of the file contains one single answer, then for each question will be one, two or three associate lines.
2. Each line is conformed by the following fields (in the same order that we quote them and separated by any amount of white space):

Field	Description
quid	Question number, provided by the organizers.
system run-tag	Unique identifier for a system and a run.
answer rank	Shows that the answers are ordered by confidence, and that the system places the surest response in the first position.
score	Integer or real number showing the system confidence in the answer. This field is not compulsory.
docid	Identifier of the supporting document, or the string 'NIL' to affirm that there is not answer in the colletion.
answer-string	Exact answer, or a string containing the answer (in 50-byte answer string task). If the field docid is 'NIL', this column is empty.

---

5 Available at http://clef-qa.itc.it

For example, this is part of one response file for the Monolingual Spanish QA task:

```
0013 alicex031ms 1 3003 EFE19940525-14752 1990
0013 alicex031ms 2 2003 EFE19941003-00830 lunes
0013 alicex031ms 3 2003 EFE19940520-11914 1993
0014 alicex031ms 1 2008 EFE19940901-00341 23 millones
0014 alicex031ms 2 2008 EFE19940330-18839 24.854
0014 alicex031ms 3 2007 EFE19941228-14902 8.815.000
0015 alicex031ms 1 2019 EFE19940103-00540 Ejército Republicano Irlandés
0015 alicex031ms 2 2002 EFE19940428-16985 Sociedad Romana Construcciones Mecánicas
0016 alicex031ms 1 0 NIL
```

7 Assessment Process

Human assessors have evaluated the runs produced by the systems, in order to qualify each given answer by assigning them one of the following judgements:

Judgement	Description
Incorrect	The answer-string does not contain a correct answer or the answer is not responsive.
Unsupported	The answer-string contains a correct answer but the document returned does not support that answer.
Non-exact	The answer-string contains a correct answer and the document supports that answer, but the answer contains more than just the answer. (Just for the exact answer runs).
Correct	The answer string consists of exactly a correct answer (or contains the correct answer within the 50 bytes long string) and that answer is supported by the document returned.

A sample of judgements is shown in the following figure:

Question / Answer	Judgement	Comment
M SPA 0002 ¿Qué país invadió Kuwait en 1990? 0002 alicex032ms 2 4010 EFE19940825-12206 **ONU**	Incorrect	
M SPA 0049 ¿Dónde explotó la primera bomba atómica? 0049 alicex032ms 2 3012 EFE19941203-01729 **Hiroshima**	Unsupported	Is not possible to infer from the doc. if the given answer is correct
M SPA 0036 ¿En qué año cayó el muro de Berlín? 0036 alicex032ms 1 2010 EFE19940107-02719 **noviembre de 1989**	Non-exact	The sub string 'noviembre de' exceeds but '1989' is correct
M SPA 0001 ¿Cuál es la capital de Croacia? 0001 alicex032ms 1 2050 EFE19940127-14481 **Zagreb**	Correct	

The following subsections discuss some criteria, problems and findings during the assessment process.

7.1 Correct and Exact Answers

Correctness and exactness of answers are in the opinion of human assessors. A numerical answer is considered more responsive if it includes the unit of measure, but depending on the measure it can be considered as correct or not; for example, '13 euros' and '13' would be positively considered. In case of dates of specific events that ended in the past, both day and year are normally required except if the question refers only to the year; or assessors consider that the year is sufficient. When the system answer contains some misspelling, the supporting documents are explored and if they are the source of that misspelling, the answer is considered as correct.

7.2 NIL Answers

According to the response format, there is no way for systems to explicitly indicate that they don't know or can't find the answer for a question. A NIL answer means that the system *decides* there isn't an answer for that question in the collection. For this reason, a NIL answer is correct if neither human assessors nor systems have found any answer before or after the assessment process. If there is an answer in the collection, NIL is evaluated as incorrect.

7.3 Not Exact, Not Responsive, and Not Supported Answers

The assessment process doesn't contemplate to give two qualifications for one answer. When the answer for a question presents simultaneously non-exact and not supported characteristics, it is necessary to choose a unique label. For example, to the question 'Where did the first atomic bomb explode?' one system gave the answer pair '*EFE19941020-11470 Hiroshima Nagasaki*'. This is not exact because the string exceeds the exact answer, and simultaneously, the answer is not supported by the indicated document, since it does not specify nor it is possible to be inferred that Hiroshima is the city where exploded the first atomic bomb. In these cases, we have to distinguish whether the system participates in the exact answer-string or in the 50-byte answer-string subtask. In the exact answer-string subtask, not exact answers must be evaluated as incorrect. In the 50-byte answer-string subtask the unsupported label is chosen for this case.

Analogously, if the answer is not supported and non-responsive it is qualified as incorrect. For example, to the same question above, one system gave the answer pair '*EFE19940613-07857 Japón*' which is not completely responsive. Simultaneously, the indicated document does not specify nor it is possible to be inferred that Japan is the country where exploded the first atomic bomb. If the assessor decides that the answer is not responsive, it must be tagged as incorrect. Otherwise, if the assessor considers that the answer is responsive, it must be tagged as unsupported.

7.4 Assessors Discrepancies

Two different human assessors have searched the answers for each question. The first assessment was performed before systems response, in order to select a set of evaluation questions with a known answer. The second one was performed after systems response, during the assessment process of their answers. Assessors for both tasks may change and may have different criteria to decide whether a question has a supported answer or not. For example, the first assessor may consider that is not possible to answer one question without considering inferences and knowledge outside the supporting documents and then the question is tagged with NIL answer. The second assessor may find that a system gives a correct answer instead of NIL for that question. In this case, the initial NIL tag must change in order to consider correctly the system answer. Another more problematic example of discrepancy is the opposite, when the first assessor found a possible answer, a system gave NIL and the second assessor agrees that is not possible to answer the question without considering further inferences and knowledge outside the supporting documents. In this case, the two assessors must discuss it in common and agree (even with a third opinion) whether initial tag must be changed or not.

7.5 Errors in Questions

During the assessment process we detected that one of the questions had a translation mistake. The word 'minister' in question 84 was translated as 'president'. The question was originally 'Who is the Italian minister of Foreign Affairs?', but the Spanish version was '¿Quién es el presidente italiano de Asuntos Exteriores?'. This failure may confuse the participant systems and we had to decide whether to discard the question or not. About errors in questions we can find some experience in past editions of QA at TREC. In TREC QA 2001 [7] eight questions were removed from the evaluation, mostly due to spelling mistakes in the question. However, in TREC 2002 [8] another criterion was taken and they decided to evaluate all the answers despite the remaining errors, arguing that it is difficult to know when to call something an error and it is assumed that systems have to cope with certain user errors. Despite the translation mistake, the meaning of the question remains clear enough, so we decided to follow TREC QA 2002 criterion in this case, understanding that systems must be robust in certain degree. We also studied to count NIL as a correct answer since, strictly, there isn't an answer for this question. However, no systems gave NIL answer for this question and assessment remained as usual.

8   Results of the Monolingual Spanish Task

Although up to four groups expressed their intention of participation, the University of Alicante (UA, Spain) [4] is the unique team that has taken part in the monolingual Spanish QA task of this year. UA has submitted two runs for the exact answer subtask. The first run contains 547 answers and the second 546. The following table summarizes the assessment statistics for both runs:

UA System	First Run				Second Run			
Ranking	1st	2nd	3rd	Total	1st	2nd	3rd	Total
Correct	49	16	26	91	51	15	13	79
Unsupported	0	2	7	9	2	3	4	9
Non-exact	6	1	3	10	6	1	3	10
Incorrect	145	157	135	437	141	156	151	448
Total	200	176	171	547	200	175	171	546

Responses per question are shown in the following table. UA systems were able to give correct answers for the 40% and 35% of questions respectively.

UA System	First Run	Second Run
Queries with no correct answer	120 (60%)	130 (65%)
Queries with correct answer	80 (40%)	70 (35%)
Mean Reciprocal Rank	0.31	0.30

With regard to the NIL answers, the following table shows that NIL was returned 21 times, being correct 5 of them and incorrect the other 16. From the 20 questions without known answer (before and after the assessment process) 15 of them didn't receive the NIL answer, i.e. NIL was not detected and systems gave wrong answers instead of NIL.

UA System	First Run	Second Run
NIL returned as a response	21	21
NIL correctly detected	5	5
NIL incorrectly responded	16	16
NIL not detected	15	15

9   Conclusions

Question Answering in Spanish is right now an emerging area of interest [5]. The first evaluation of Spanish QA systems has been reported in this paper. This first experience shows the effort put in the generation of useful resources for future multilingual QA evaluation. It also permitted to establish a methodology and some criteria for both, the test suite production and the assessment process. Unfortunately, only one group could adjust their systems on time to take part in the competition. We hope that the results and the resources developed in this first experience will encourage groups to continue their work in order to participate in future editions. Useful resources for Spanish Question Answering are publicly available at http://nlp.uned.es/QA as, for example, the questions and answers in CLEF 2003.

Next edition of the Multilingual Question Answering at CLEF will extend the multilingual tasks to any combination pairs between Spanish, Italian, Dutch, and possibly it will include also English, French and German. Exact answers will be required and the type of questions will include definitions. The three monolingual tasks will continue, and so, the Spanish Question Answering evaluation task.

Acknowledgements. We would like to thank the people that made possible this work: Bernardo Magnini, Alessandro Vallin, Maarten de Rijke, Carol Peters, Donna Harman, Julio Gonzalo and José Luis Vicedo.

This work has been supported by the Spanish government (MCyT, TIC-2002-10597-E).

References

1. Burger, J. et al. Issues, Tasks and Program Structures to Roadmap Research in Question & Answering. NIST. 2002.
2. Magnini, B. et al. Creating the DISEQuA corpus: a test set for Multilingual Question Answering. Evaluation of Cross-Language Information Systems, CLEF 2003. Lecture Notes in Computer Science. Springer-Verlag; 2004a.
3. Magnini, B. et al. The multiple language Question Answering Track at CLEF 2003. Evaluation of Cross-Language Information Systems, CLEF 2003. Lecture Notes in Computer Science. Springer-Verlag; 2004b.
4. Vicedo, J. L. SEMQA: A semantic model applied to Question Answering: Thesis, University of Alicante, Spain; 2002.
5. Vicedo, J. L. Rodríguez H. Peñas A. and Massot M. Los Sistemas de Búsqueda de Respuestas desde una perspectiva actual. Revista De La Sociedad Española Para El Procesamiento Del Lenguaje Natural. 2003; 31:351–367.
6. Voorhees, E. M. Overview of the TREC-8 Question Answering Track. Proceedings of Text Retrieval Conference 8. 2000.
7. Voorhees, E. M. Overview of the TREC 2001 Question Answering Track. Proceedings of Text Retrieval Conference 10. 2002.
8. Voorhees, E. M. Overview of the TREC 2002 Question Answering Track. Proceedings of Text Retrieval Conference 11. 2003.

Comparative Analysis of Term Distributions in a Sentence and in a Document for Sentence Retrieval

Kyoung-Soo Han and Hae-Chang Rim

Dept. of Computer Science and Engineering, Korea University
1, 5-ga, Anam-dong, Seoul 136-701, Korea
{kshan, rim}@nlp.korea.ac.kr
http://nlp.korea.ac.kr/~kshan/publications/cicling2004/

Abstract. Most of previous works of finding relevant sentences applied document retrieval models to sentence retrieval. However, the performance was very poor. This paper analyzes the reason of this poor performance by comparing term statistics in a document with those in a sentence. The analysis shows that the distribution of within-document and within-sentence term frequency is not similar, and the distribution of document frequency is similar to that of sentence frequency. Considering the discrepancy between the term statistics, it is not appropriate that document retrieval models, as they stand, are applied to sentence retrieval.

1 Introduction

It is necessary to find relevant information for many text processing systems including information retrieval, text summarization, and question answering. Recently, TREC 2002 novelty track defined the related task consisting of two phases[1]. The first phase was to first filter out all non-relevant information, defined in the track to be sentences, from a ranked list of documents. In the second phase, a system threw away any redundant information, defined also to be sentences, from the list of relevant sentences. The relevant information not containing any redundancy was called novel information. In this paper, we focus on the first phase, relevant sentence retrieval.

Most of systems participating in the TREC novelty track applied traditional document retrieval models to relevant sentence retrieval. However, their performance of finding relevant sentences was very poor, which were negative effect on the second phase.

To improve the sentence retrieval performance, Allan tried various techniques with traditional document retrieval models such as vector space model and language model[2]. While the pseudo-relevance feedback was useful to improve performance, almost all his trial was unsuccessful.

In this paper, we analyze the characteristics of sentence retrieval and examine the reason why the traditional document retrieval models suffered from the poor performance in sentence retrieval.

A. Gelbukh (Ed.): CICLing 2004, LNCS 2945, pp. 484–487, 2004.
© Springer-Verlag Berlin Heidelberg 2004

2   Analysis of Term Distributions

Most of traditional document retrieval models use term statistics such as term frequency within a document (tf) and the number of document within which a term occurs (df), and rank documents with $tf * idf$ term weighting.

When the document retrieval models are used for sentence retrieval, a sentence is considered as a document. Therefore, the tendency similarity of the term statistics in documents and those in sentences is essential for good performance of document retrieval model in the sentence retrieval environment.

We believe that the poor performance in TREC novelty track was caused by the discrepancy between the term statistics in document collection and those in sentence collection.

To prove this hypothesis empirically, we compare and analyze the term statistics in document and sentence collection. We use the test data used in TREC 2002 novelty track. For all our analysis, all sentences were stopped and stemmed with Porter stemmer. Table 1 shows the collection statistics.

Table 1. Statistics of the test data used in TREC 2002 novelty track

# of docs	1093
# of sents	56737
# of unique terms	25921
avg. # of unique terms per doc	239.20
avg. # of unique terms per sent	8.85

2.1   Term Frequency within a Document and within a Sentence

The tf is used for measuring how well the term describes the document contents. Similarly, we can borrow stf(term frequency within a sentence) for measuring how well the term describes the sentence contents. When document retrieval model is applied to sentence retrieval, this function of stf is assumed. Figure 1 shows that the assumption may not be true. The terminology used is as follows:

$$TermRatio(i) = \frac{|T_i|}{\sum_i |T_i|}$$

$$TokenRatio(i) = \frac{|O_i|}{\sum_i |O_i|}$$

where T_i is a set of terms whose tf is i, O_i is a bag of terms whose tf is i, $|T_i|$ is the number of terms whose tf is i, and $|O_i|$ is the number of occurrences of terms whose tf is i.

As the figure shows, most terms in a sentence occur only once; 95.68% terms and 90.77% tokens have stf of 1. As to tf value, 69.26% terms and 34.20 tokens have 1. To examine the weighting effect of terms, we used the $tf/\max tf$

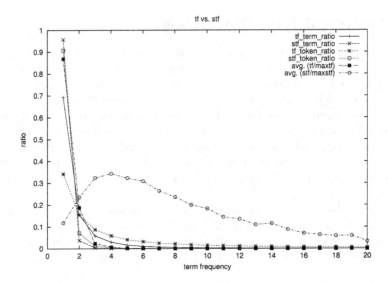

Fig. 1. Discrepancy between term frequency within a document and within a sentence

weighting. The $\max tf$ is the maximum value of tf in the document the term occurred. We calculated the weighting value in each document or sentence, and then the weighting value is averaged according to tf.

$$AvgWeight(i) = \frac{\sum_{w_j \in T_i} Weight(w_j)}{|T_i|}$$

The average weight in a document is widely distributed with term frequencies. However, in a sentence, the terms occurring only once control the weighting. As a result tf factor in the various weighting schemes of document retrieval models has little effect on retrieval result. Table 2 is a sentence retrieval result of vector space model with various weighting schemes. Although *dnultn* model did not use the tf factor, the performance is good especially with P5, P10, and P15.

Table 2. Retrieval results of vector space model with various weighting schemes

Model	Avg Prec	R-Prec	P5	P10	P15
dnultn	0.1468	0.1620	0.2204	0.2020	0.1986
Lnultn	0.1480	0.1727	0.2204	0.1980	0.1959
lnultn	0.1457	0.1750	0.2367	0.2000	0.1878
nnultn	0.1431	0.1738	0.2041	0.1939	0.1806
anultn	0.1389	0.1610	0.1389	0.1878	0.1864

2.2   Document Frequency and Sentence Frequency

Table 3 shows the number of documents (df) and that of sentences (sf) within which the term occurred. We can notice that these statistics are very similar.

Table 3. Document Frequency and Sentence Frequency

df or sf	df TermRatio	sf TermRatio	df or sf	df TermRatio	sf TermRatio
1	0.4967	0.3665	11	0.0084	0.0112
2	0.1333	0.1475	12	0.0080	0.0093
3	0.0686	0.0788	13	0.0069	0.0084
4	0.0413	0.0549	14	0.0066	0.0077
5	0.0298	0.0377	15	0.0060	0.0071
6	0.0230	0.0301	16	0.0052	0.0062
7	0.0187	0.0239	17	0.0042	0.0046
8	0.0144	0.0201	18	0.0036	0.0059
9	0.0108	0.0154	19	0.0039	0.0046
10	0.0093	0.0133	20	0.0030	0.0051

3   Conclusions

We analyzed the characteristics of the sentence retrieval environment comparing with the document retrieval. The analysis shows that the distribution of within-document term frequency is not similar to that of within-sentence term frequency. Therefore, it is not appropriate that document retrieval models, as they stand, are applied to sentence retrieval. Because most of terms in a sentence occur only once, term weighting in a sentence is very difficult. Term expansion rather than term weighting may be proper method for improving performance.

References

1. Harman, D.: Overview of the TREC 2002 novelty track. In: Proceedings of the 11th Text Retrieval Conference (TREC-2002). (2002) 17–28
2. James Allan, Courtney Wade, Alvaro Bolivar: Retrieval and novelty detection at the sentence level. In: Proceedings of the 26th Annual International ACM SIGIR Conference on Research and Development in Information Retrieval (SIGIR-2003). (2003) 314–321

Contextual Exploration of Text Collections

Manuel Montes-y-Gómez, Manuel Pérez-Coutiño,
Luis Villaseñor-Pineda, and Aurelio López-López

Laboratorio de Tecnologías del Lenguaje, INAOE, Mexico.
{mmontesg,mapco,villasen,allopez}@inaoep.mx

Abstract. Nowadays there is a large amount of digital texts available for every purpose. New flexible and robust approaches are necessary for their access and analysis. This paper proposes a text exploration scheme based on hypertext, which incorporates some elements from information retrieval and text mining in order to transform the blind navigation of the hypertext into a step-by-step informed exploration. The proposed scheme is of relevance since it integrates three basic exploration functionalities, i.e. access, navigation and analysis. The paper also presents some preliminary results on the generation of hypertext from two text collections in an implementation of the scheme.

Keywords: automatic text processing, information retrieval, hypertext, text mining, metadata, and information visualization.

1 Introduction

Nowadays there is a large amount of digital texts accessible from private collections as well as from the web. However, without the proper methods for its access and analysis, all this textual data is practically useless. In order to solve this dilemma several text-exploration approaches have emerged. Three popular examples are: information retrieval, hypertext and text mining.

Information retrieval [1] addresses the problems associated with retrieval of documents from a collection in response to a user query. The goal of an information retrieval system is to search a text collection and return as result a subset of documents ordered by decreasing likelihood of being relevant to the given query.

Hypertext [10] is a general manual medium for textual exploration. Its navigational interface, browsing facility, and its graph structure allow users to handle information easily. In a hypertext system, a user explores a text collection following the links among the documents, reading their content and extracting the desired information.

Text mining [7] is concerned with the automatic discovery of interesting patterns, such as clusters, associations and deviations, from text collections. Text mining is intended for analysis tasks rather than to facilitate access. However, some of its techniques can be used as a complement for accessing large text collections.

These three text-exploration approaches are different but complementary. On one hand, information retrieval is a robust and fast approach for *information access*. However, its results are non-explicitly inter-connected and thus they can only be explored sequentially. On the other hand, hypertexts are specifically designed for non-

A. Gelbukh (Ed.): CICLing 2004, LNCS 2945, pp. 488–497, 2004.
© Springer-Verlag Berlin Heidelberg 2004

sequential *navigation of texts collections*, but this navigation is blind (there is no precise information about the link nature or information about the document relevance to the user information need) and the user frequently gets lost in the hyperspace. Finally, text mining techniques, in particular document clustering and association discovery [2,3], support a pattern-based browsing of the text collections. Although these techniques allow the *content analysis* of the text collections, they are difficult to incorporate on exploration situations where the processing of information is done on the fly.

This paper proposes a new approach for text exploration. This approach, named *contextual exploration*, is primarily based on hypertext, but incorporates some elements from information retrieval and text mining in order to transform the blind navigation of the hypertext in a step-by-step informed exploration. In this way, contextual exploration is a *powerful and complete* text-exploration approach that integrates the three basic functionalities for this purpose: access, navigation and analysis.

The rest of the paper is organized as follows. Section 2 introduces the concept of contextual exploration. Section 3 presents the exploration scheme, and describes their main components. Section 4 discusses some experimental results on the hypertext generation and information visualization. Finally, Section 5 exposes our conclusions and future work.

2   Contextual Exploration

Hypertext is one of the most popular approaches for exploring text collections. Its graph structure (where the nodes represent documents and the edges indicate some relationships among them) allows users to handle information easily. This approach models the exploration of a text collection as a *graph traversing procedure*. Therefore, in order to explore a text collection, a user must take a document as starting point, follow the links among the documents, assess their content, and hopefully extract the desired information.

Hypertext, as defined above, seems to be a general, flexible and easy-way to explore text collections. However, navigating through hypertext frequently leads to the problem of *getting lost in the hyperspace*, i.e. knowing where you are in the hypergraph and knowing how to get to the place you are actually looking for [8]. In order to ameliorate this problem we introduce the idea of contextual exploration.

The *contextual exploration* is a hypertext navigational scheme that includes complementary information for each document (node) that allows evaluating the relevance of its content against the entire collection, as well as, the content of their associated (linked) documents. Basically, it considers the following three *contexts* of information (see Figure 1):

1. *Self context*, that includes some metadata from the document currently being displayed (for instance, date, author, and main topics) in addition to the actual document.
2. *Near context*, consisting of a set of related documents with their corresponding metadata. Its purpose is as an aid to understand the nature of each relation and the relevance of each related document to the user information need.

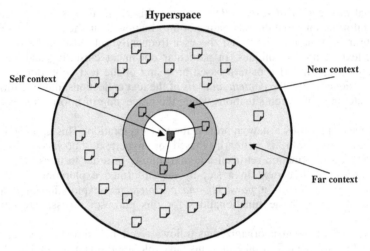

Fig. 1. Three information contexts about the current document

3. *Far context*, represented by a set of pertinent topic associations (i.e., global co-occurrence relations among the topics of the current document). Its aim is to provide a general mechanism to estimate the importance of the content of the current document in the whole collection.

Figure 3 in Section 4 shows a snapshot of the interface of our system for contextual navigation of text collections. This snapshot clarifies the way in which the three kinds of contextual information are integrated.

3 Scheme Description

This section describes the proposed scheme from two different perspectives. The subsection 3.1 briefly describes the *functionality* of the scheme, while the rest of the subsection discusses the applied *methods* for each one of the components.

3.1 Functional Overview

The system performs two kinds of processes: off-line and on-line. The goal of the *off-line processes* is to generate a set of intermediate document representations containing information from different context levels from a given text collection (as explained in section 2). On the other hand, the *on-line processes* use these representations for two different purposes. First, to filter the information that satisfies the user query, and second, to provide the user the search results in the form of a hypertext.

The *hypertext* assembled as an answer to the user query, not only considers the content of the documents found, but also some descriptive information in the form of metadata about them (i.e., self context information) as well as a list of related documents for each one of them (near context information). Additionally, it includes information about some topic associations (far context information), which are pertinent (directly related) to the document at hand.

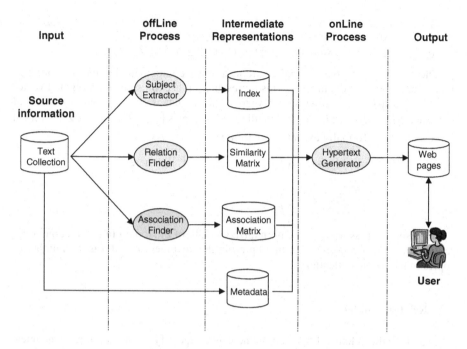

Fig. 2. Scheme overview

Figure 2 illustrates both on-line and off-line processes of the system. The components in the scheme can be extended in order to get information from more contexts. The subsequent subsections describe the goals and functionality of the four main components: the subject extractor, the relation finder, the association finder and the hypertext generator.

3.2 Subject Extractor

This component has two main tasks: to identify the candidate topics for each document of a given collection, and to build a representation of their content.

In order to identify the set of topics of a document, this extractor uses a method similar to that proposed by Gay and Croft [5], where the topics are related to noun strings. Basically, this component applies a set of heuristic rules specific for Spanish, based on the proximity of words that allows identifying and extracting key phrases. These rules are driven by the occurrence of articles and the preposition *de* ('of') along with nouns or proper names [4]. Some morphological inflection patterns (typical endings of nouns and verbs) are also taken into account [6]. For instance, given the paragraph below, the subject extractor component selects the underlined words as candidate topics:

"*Góngora Pimentel* aseguró que estas *demandas* se resolverán en un *plazo* no mayor de 30 días y que sin duda la *demanda interpuesta* por el *PRD* ante la *Suprema Corte de Justicia* se anexará a la que presentó el *Partido Acción Nacional*".[1]

Then, based on the candidate topics, this component builds an enriched representation of the documents. This representation is expressed as a weighted vector of topics in a given *n*-dimensional vector space. That is, for a given collection of documents $D = \{d_i\}$, with a corresponding set of topics $\{t_1, \ldots, t_n\}$, the new document representation is formally expressed as follows:

$$d_i \rightarrow \bar{d}_i = (w_i(t_1), w_i(t_2), \ldots, w_i(t_n)), \text{ where}:$$

$$w_i(t_j) = \frac{f_{ij}}{\sum\limits_{k=1}^{n} f_{ik}}$$

In these formulas, $w_i(t_j)$ is the normalized weight of the topic j in the document i; f_{ij} is the number of occurrences of the topic j in the document i; and n is the number of topics in the whole collection.

3.3 Relation Finder

The goal of the relation finder component is to identify the most significant inter-document relations. Basically, this component finds the set of thematically related documents for each item of the given source collection.

In order to accomplish its goal, the relation finder component computes the similarity for every pair of documents in the source collection, and then determines the most important connections.

The similarity measure used is based on the Dice coefficient [9]:

$$s(d_i, d_j) = s_{ij} = \frac{1}{2} \sum_{\forall t \in d_i \cap d_j} w_i(t) + w_j(t)$$

Here, the topic $t \in d_i \cap d_j$ is a common topic of both documents d_i and d_j, and $w_k(t)$ indicates the weight of the topic t in the document d_k.

The criteria used to determine the set of related items associated to the document d_i, after computing all the similarities, is the following:

$$R_i = \{d_j \mid s_{ij} \geq s_\mu, j \neq i\} \text{ where}:$$

$$s_\mu = \frac{2}{N(N-1)} \sum_{i=1}^{N} \sum_{\substack{j=i+1 \\ s_{ij}>0}}^{N} s_{ij}$$

Here, R_i is the set of thematically related documents for the document d_i, s_{ij} is the similarity measure of documents d_i and d_j, and N is the number of documents in the whole collection. Basing this criterion on the average similarity among documents

---

[1] *Góngora Pimentel* confirmed that these *demands* will be satisfied in a *period* not longer than 30 days and that without any doubt the *demand introduced* by the *PRD* to the *Justice Supreme Court* will be added to that presented by the *National Action Party*.'

allows producing an associated set of items, independently of how homogeneous is the collection. That is, even in highly heterogeneous collection (a very diverse set of topics), we can obtain existing relations.

3.4 Association Finder

This component focuses on the discovery of interesting topic associations between pairs of documents in a given text collection. We define a topic association as an expression $t_i \Rightarrow t_j$, where t_i and t_j are two different topics from the collection. This kind of associations indicates that the documents that contain the topic t_i tend to contain also the topic t_j.

Each topic association $t_i \Rightarrow t_j$ has a confidence value. This value is calculated as follows:

$$c_{ij} = \frac{|Q_{ij}|}{|Q_i|}, \text{ where}:$$

$$Q_{ij} = \left\{ d_k \middle| t_i, t_j \in d_k \right\}$$

$$Q_i = \left\{ d_k \middle| t_i \in d_k \right\}$$

Here, c_{ij} denotes the confidence value of the association $t_i \Rightarrow t_j$, and Q_{ij} and Q_i the sets of documents containing the topics t_i and t_j, and the topic t_i respectively.

The criterion used to determine the set of pertinent associations to the document d_k, is the following:

$$A_k = \left\{ \left(t_i \Rightarrow t_j, c_{ij} \right) \middle| c_{ij} \geq u, t_i \vee t_j \in d_k \right\}$$

This criterion selects as the set of pertinent associations for the document d_k, those having a confidence value greater than a predefined threshold u, and that include a topic of the document d_k.

3.5 Hypertext Generator

The output of the system is a hypertext document that unifies the information from the three context levels (self, near and far) in a single interface. For the case of the far-context information, i.e., the topic associations, the interface only displays those associations with a confidence value greater than a user-specified threshold u and related to the content of the current document (see Section 3.4).

The proposed interface is based on a template that fulfills the standard XHTML 1.0 proposed by the World Wide Web Consortium (W3C), and includes the following set of metadata: title, creator, publisher, date, subject and relation. It also contains the source document and a pointer to the document metadata representation that could be later accessed by software agents.

The output corresponding to the example text is shown in Figure 3.

4 Experimental Results

4.1 The Test Collections

In order to prove the functionality of the proposed system, we analyzed two document collections: *News94 and ExcelNews*. These collections are in raw text format (i.e. ASCII). They differ in their topics and in the document average size. Following, we describe the main characteristics of these collections. More details are in Table 1.

Collection News94

News94 is a set of 94 news documents. The average size per document is 3.44 Kb, and the biggest document size is 18 Kb. This collection is a subset of the ExcelNews data set.

Collection ExcelNews

This collection consists of 1,357 documents. These documents contain national and international news from 1998 to 2000 as well as cultural notes about literature, science and technology. The document average size is 3.52 Kb, and the biggest document size is 28 Kb.

An important characteristic of the ExcelNews collection is the variety of writing styles and lexical forms of its documents, causing a large distribution of terms in the vocabulary.

Table 1. Main data of test collections

Collection	Size (Mb)	Number of documents	Average document size	Number of pages	Number of lexical forms	Number of terms
News94	0.372	94	3.44 Kb	124	11,562	29,611
ExcelNews	4.81	1357	3.52 Kb	1,642	41,717	391,003

4.2 Results

Table 2 summarizes the results obtained from the preprocessing of the test collections (offline processes). These results consider three main aspects: (1) the topic distribution of the test collections, (2) the required time for their analysis, and (3) the connectivity level of the resulting hypertext document sets. In addition, Table 3 shows some topic associations and their confidence values.

Figure 3 shows a sample page of hypertext gathered from the given input collection (in this case, from News94). This interface has three regions. The *content region* shows the complete document content (self-context information). The *metadata region* considers descriptive data from the current document as well as the links to its related documents (self- and near-context information). Finally, the *detail region* provides additional details about the content of the current document, or the metadata of related documents, or even the set of pertinent topic associations (near- and far-context information). The second row of Figure 3 illustrates two of these different uses.

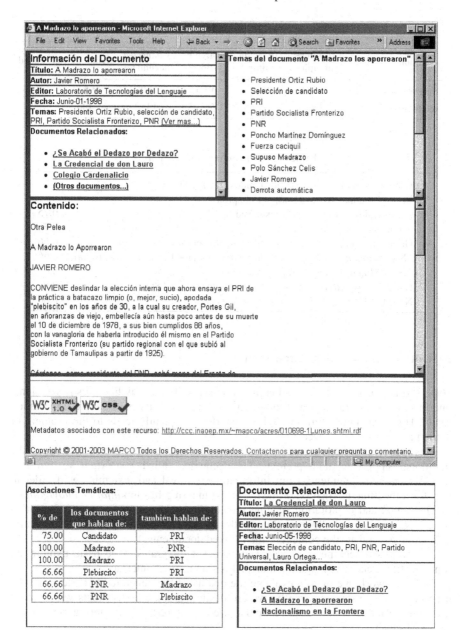

Fig. 3. A sample page of hypertext generated, and two different uses of the detail region

Table 2. Main results from the collection analysis

Collection	Topics	Instances of topics	Indexing time	Searching time	Connected documents	Relations	Average of related documents
News94	2,571	4,874	0''.26	0''.55	90	459	5
ExcelNews	24,298	72,983	3''.56	3'50''.59	1350	47,486	35

Table 3. Sample of topic associations

Recesión (*recession*)→ Estados Unidos (*United States*)	1
Banco Mundial (*World Bank*)→ Fobaproa	1
Neoliberal (*neoliberal*)→ Ernesto Zedillo	0.75
Amor (*love*)→ Novela (*novel*)	0.75
Oriente Medio (*middle east*)→ Estado de Israel (*State of Israel*)	0.66
PNR (*acronim of National Revolutionary Party*)→ Plebiscito (*plebiscite*)	0.66
Tercer Mundo (*Third World*)→ Aliado (*ally*)	0.66
Narcotráfico (*narcotraffic*)→ Estados Unidos (*United States*)	0.66
Naciones Unidas (*United Nations*)→ Guerra (*war*)	0.66

5   Conclusions and Future Work

Hypertext is a medium for textual exploration typically built by hand. Its navigational interface, browsing facility, and its graph structure allow users to handle information easily. However, navigating through a hypertext frequently leads to the problem of getting lost in the hyperspace.

This paper proposed a new scheme for textual exploration that extents the traditional approach of hypertext. This scheme, called *contextual exploration*, incorporates some elements from information retrieval and text mining in order to transform the blind navigation of the hypertext in a step-by-step *informed navigation*.

The contextual exploration scheme includes complementary context information for each document that allows evaluating the relevance of its content against the entire collection, as well as, the content of their linked documents.

The proposed scheme is of relevance since it integrates three basic exploration functionalities: access, navigation and analysis; in a single interface.

As future work, we plan to evaluate the quality of the generated hypertext and the usability of the system. Currently, we are designing some experiments with several users and different contexts (in particular, we are interested in exploring news about natural disasters).

Acknowledgements. This work has been partly supported by the CONACYT through project grant U39957-Y and scholarship for the second author, and by the Language Technologies Laboratory of INAOE.

References

1. Baeza-Yates and Ribeiro-Neto. *Modern Information Retrieval*, Addison-Wesley, 1999.
2. Cutting, Karger, Pedersen, and Tukey. Scatter/Gather: A Cluster-based Approach to Browsing Large Document Collections, *Proceedings of the 15th Annual International ACM/SIGIR Conference*, 1992.
3. Feldman, Klösgen, Yehuda, Kedar and Reznikov. Pattern Based Browsing in Document Collections, *Proc. of the 1st Conference on Principles of Knowledge Discovery and Data Mining (PKDD'97)*, 1997.
4. Galicia-Haro, S. N., A. Gelbukh, I. A. Bolshakov. Recognition of Named Entities in Spanish Texts. In: Mexican International Conference on Artificial Intelligence (MICAI-2004). Lecture Notes in Artificial Intelligence, N 2972, Springer-Verlag, 2004.
5. Gay and Croft. Interpreting Nominal Compounds for Information Retrieval. *Information Processing and Management* 26(1): 21–38, 1990.
6. Gelbukh, A., and G. Sidorov. Approach to construction of automatic morphological analysis systems for inflective languages with little effort. In: Computational Linguistics and Intelligent Text Processing (CICLing-2003). Lecture Notes in Computer Science, N 2588, Springer-Verlag, 2003, pp. 215–220.
7. Hearst. Untangling Text Data Mining, *Proc. of ACL'99: The 37th Annual Meeting of the Association for Computational Linguistics*, 1999.
8. Levene and Loizou. Navigation in hypertext is easy only sometimes. *SIAM Journal on Computing*, 29(3):728–760, 1999.
9. Lin. An Information-Theoretic Definition of Similarity, *Proc. of the International Conference on Machine Learning*, 1998.
10. Shneiderman and Kearsley. *Hipertext Hands On!*, Addison Wesley, 1989.

Automatic Classification and Skimming of Articles in a News Video Using Korean Closed-Caption

Jung-Won Cho[1], Seung-Do Jeong[1], and Byung-Uk Choi[2]

[1] Multimedia Laboratory, Department of Electrical and Computer Engineering,
Hanyang University, 17 Haengdang-dong, Sungdong-gu, Seoul, 133-791 Korea
[2] Division of Information and Communications,
Hanyang University, 17 Haengdang-dong, Sungdong-gu, Seoul, 133-791 Korea
{bigcho,kain,buchoi}@mlab.hanyang.ac.kr

Abstract. We are able to analyze the meaning in the news video by using various data, such as a moving picture, an audio, a caption, and so on. In order to browse the news video effectively, classification and skimming of the news articles are very essential. In this paper, we propose both the automatic classification and skimming methods of the news articles using the closed-caption. The automatic classification method uses tags in the closed-caption for the purpose of distinction of speakers. The skimming method extracts the part of the article introduced by an anchor in the closed-caption as a representative sentence, and also extracts the representative frames consisted of the anchor frame, open-caption frames, and frames synchronized with the frequently appeared terms.

1 Introduction

In order to obtain the precise retrieval results of queries, we have investigated indexing, storing, querying, and showing methods of the retrieval result [1][2]. The first thing we have to consider here is to analyze the user's demand and reflect it on indexing. The indexed news article is then able to be effectively retrieved by using knowledge-based query. This paper analyzes the meaning of the news article by using useful information extracted from the closed-caption. Also, we present automatic classification and skimming methods of news articles using the closed-caption.

2 Automatic Classification of Articles

For effective browsing of the news articles, classification according to a category of the article is required. In this paper, for the automatic classification, we extract the reporter's name in the closed-caption and match the name with the records in the database having information of reporter's affiliation [3]. Consequently, the articles can be classified into 7 categories, i.e., politics, economy, society, unification, information science, culture, and international affairs. Fig. 1 shows a schematic diagram of the proposed automatic classification system.

A. Gelbukh (Ed.): CICLing 2004, LNCS 2945, pp. 498–501, 2004.
© Springer-Verlag Berlin Heidelberg 2004

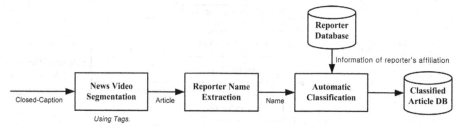

Fig. 1. Schematic diagram of automatic classification method

We make the reporter's affiliation table - the lists of reporters in Munhwa Broadcasting Corporation (MBC) of Korea on Feb. 2003. Note that the classification categories used here are chosen to be the same as those in the MBC homepage. The news article consists of the anchor, reporter, and interview part. The position in the closed-caption, where the reporter's name appears, is fixed. For example, the reporter's name appears two times in the following article:

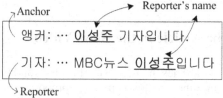

As above, the anchor introduces the article briefly, and calls the reporter's name. The reporter usually ends the article with referring his or her name. This is a general composition of news articles in Korea. Using this combination, we extract the reporter's name and query the reporter database. The search result of the query contains information of reporter's affiliation, which indicates the category of the article. Fig. 2 is a flow-chart of the automatic classification method using the reporter's name that is extracted from the closed-caption of the article.

In Fig. 2, the reporter's name is discovered at two different parts of the article. This name is used for querying the reporter database. The result will be the name of the reporter's affiliation. If the name discovered in the anchor part of the article is different from that in the reporter part of the article by any reason, we prefer the reporter's name that is extracted from the anchor part of the article. Since ambient

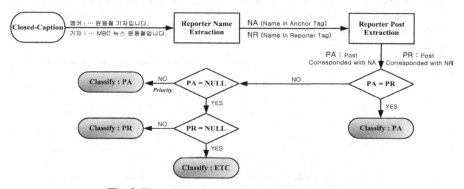

Fig. 2. Flow-chart of automatic classification method

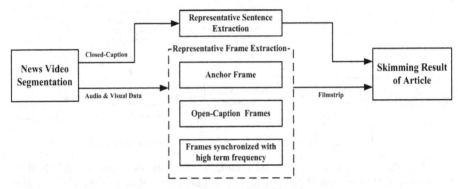

Fig. 3. Schematic diagram of the skimming system

noise does not exist in most of the broadcasting studios, the anchor part should be less vulnerable to the stenographic system's error comparing to the reporter part.

3   Skimming of the Article in the News Video

Playing with all the news articles in order to confirm the validity of the retrieval result is definitely a waste of time. In this paper, we propose a skimming method that summarizes the article with minimum loss of information. The result of the proposed skimming system consists of the representative sentences and the filmstrip having the anchor frame, the open-caption frames, and so on. At the same time, since the summarized result of the skimming system contains a filmstrip and text information, the distortion of the meaning can be minimized. Fig. 3 illustrates the proposed skimming method of a news article.

The representative frames provided to the user in this paper consists of the anchor frame, the open-caption frames containing the main contents of the article, and frames synchronized with the frequently appeared terms [3].

For the effective browsing, both the sentence which represents the article and the filmstrip which consists of representative frames are provided. The best suitable representative sentence is the part of the article introduced by the anchor. As shown in Fig. 4, we confirm that the anchor part conveys the abbreviated contents of the article. Fig. 5 shows the skimming result consisted of representative frames and representative sentence. We are able to browse the news articles successfully by using the skimming result as illustrated in Fig. 5.

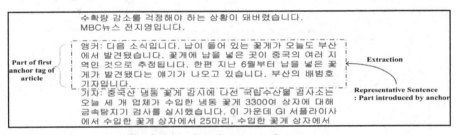

Fig. 4. Extraction of representative sentence

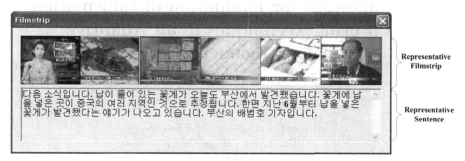

Fig. 5. Example of skimming result

4   Conclusion

In this paper, as an effective browsing technique, we have proposed the automatic classification and skimming methods of the articles in the news video by making use of the closed-caption. It is shown that the proposed methods overcome quite effectively the drawbacks in which the conventional techniques could hardly convey the meaning in the content-based retrieval based on the features, such as color, shape, texture, and so on. Moreover, since the processing mechanism in this paper is easy and runs fast, it is believed that the result can be employed in on-line applications.

Acknowledgment. This work was supported by HY-SDR Research Center at Hanyang University, Seoul, Korea, under the ITRC Program of IITA, Korea.

References

1. Howard D.W., Takeo K., Michael A.S., Scott M.S.: Intelligent Access to Digital Video: Informedia Project, IEEE Computer (Digital Library Initiative special), Vol. 29, No.5, (1996) 46–52
2. Alexander G.H., Michael J.W.: Informedia: News-on-Demand Multimedia Information Acquisition and Retrieval, Intelligent Multimedia Information Retrieval, AAAI Press/The MITPress, (1997) 215–240
3. http://vrs.hanyang.ac.kr/cicling/acas.pdf (References internet site where more detailed info on this work)

A Framework for Evaluation of Information Filtering Techniques in an Adaptive Recommender System

John O'Donovan and John Dunnion

Department of Computer Science,
University College Dublin,
Ireland.
{john.odonovan,john.dunnion}@ucd.ie

Abstract. This paper proposes that there is a substantial relative difference in the performance of information-filtering algorithms as they are applied to different datasets, and that these performance differences can be leveraged to form the basis of an Adaptive Information Filtering System. We classify five different datasets based on metrics such as sparsity, user-item ratio etc, and develop a regression function over these metrics in order to predict suitability of a particular recommendation algorithm to a new dataset, using only the aforementioned metrics. Our results show that the predicted best algorithm does perform better for the new dataset.

1 Introduction

Collaborative Filtering (CF) is a broad term for the process of recommending items to users based on similarities in user taste [10,3]. An increasing number of online stores provide collaborative recommender systems on their sites, e.g. E-Bay, Amazon.com etc. CF techniques tend to have the following advantages over others: They do not require items to be machine-analysable (as explained in [6]), they can arrive at serendipitous recommendations [12]. They also require little knowledge-engineering overhead. CF techniques are also subject to two serious restrictions. Sparsity Restriction: In any given case, it is unlikely that two users have co-rated many of the items in the system. Accurate similarity measurements depend on rich user profiles with high overlap. Latency Restriction: This affects new or unique items. These items will not be recommended by a system until they are included in a sufficient number of user profiles, as outlined in [12]. Similarity can be computed for CF by several well-known techniques, auch as Cosine Similarity, Spearman's or Pearson's Correlation [8]. For all of our similarity calculations we employ Pearson's, as it is the most widely used and allows for better comparison with other systems.

Different implementations of collaborative filtering will be affected to varying degrees by the problems mentioned above. Their performance will change based on the dataset that they operate on, and the information they harness to compile

A. Gelbukh (Ed.): CICLing 2004, LNCS 2945, pp. 502–506, 2004.
© Springer-Verlag Berlin Heidelberg 2004

a similarity model. For example, for a situation where the set of items to be recommended is relatively small and static, and there are a large number of users, it would be advisable to employ an item-based approach [11,5] to CF, since the similarity model is built up over the large number of user profiles. In this case a user-based filtering approach as in [1] would not perform as well since there would be insufficient items in each profile to provide the level of overlap required for a reliable similarity model.

2   Adaptive Information Filtering Using Regression

To achieve this adaptability in our system, we make the assumption that our datasets can be adequately classified (for CF purposes) by a set of their salient features. These include user-item ratio, sparsity and data type. We tested our three collaborative recommendation algorithms (User-Based; Item-Based; and Rule-Based CF) on four different experimental datasets (EachMovie; PTV; Jester and MovieLens), and noted the relative performance differences of each method with respect to the classification metrics above. From this information it was possible to develop a regression function for algorithm prediction based on the classification metrics alone. We test the performance of this function by introducing another dataset, (SmartRadio, a music ratings set [4]). This set is classified according to the required metrics, and the resulting values are run through the regression function to attain an algorithm prediction. If we can successfully perform this algorithm prediction task, we can form the basis of a generic recommender system, which can employ cutting edge filtering techniques to a given system without having to manually tailor the recommendation engine for that system. The systems design is completely modular, which has the advantage of allowing new techniques to be added as they develop.

A linear regression model [11] is built up using our evaluations in [7], this is based on a predictive function of several variables, as described in [9].

$$E\{Y\} = \beta_0 + \beta_1 X_1 + \beta_2 X_2 \qquad (1)$$

Values for the $\beta_i's$ are gotten by going over all the classification metric values for each dataset, and the best performing algorithm for that set, and then solving a resulting system of simultaneous equations. The SmartRadio dataset was classified according to the same metrics as the others and was found to be over 99% sparse and have user-item ratio of 1:9. This information was put through the regression function, which predicted the user-based algorithm for best performance.

3   Experimental Data and Evaluation

We aim to predict the best-performing algorithm using only the regression function learned from the classification metrics of the other datasets, and the values the new dataset has for these metrics. Having calculated our regression function

Table 1. Classification of Experimental Data

Dataset	Users-Items	Sparsity	Type
PTV	1:6	94.25%	TV Progs
MovieLens	9:13	93.7%	Movie Ratings
Jester	9:1	54%	Jokes Ratings
EachMovie	9:17	93%	Movie Ratings
SmartRadio	1 : 9(approx)	99.98 %	Music Ratings

from tests shown in [7], we run all of the algorithms again on the new dataset. Our predictive accuracy tests are simplified by keeping the neighbourhood size k and the test-train ratio constant at 30 and 80 respectively. These are optimal values we found in [7].

For the initial training phase of the system, four experimental datasets are used: Jester [3], EachMovie, PTV [2], and MovieLens [10]. We selected subsets of 900 profiles from each of the above datasets comprised of the largest profiles. (with the exception of PTV which only contains 622 profiles).

3.1   Experimental Procedure and Results

In this paper, we use predictive accuracy as the performance metric for the rec-ommendation algorithms. For each dataset, if a users rating is beyond a certain threshold, the item is considered liked by that user. This level of granularity was chosen because people will use the rating scales differently. We tailored this threshold value for each individual scale, based on distribution of ratings. We predict the "liked" items for the unseen test data and record accuracy on each dataset. User profiles are split into training and test data. The training data is fed to each filtering component individually and each generates its own predic-

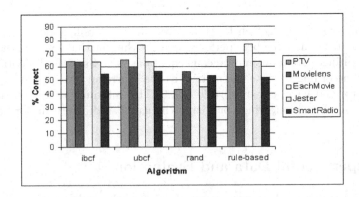

Fig. 1. Recommendation Accuracy for each algorithm. (Keeping neighbourhood size k constant at 30 and test-train ratio at 80%)

tions for the unseen test data. To build our regression model, we use our results from [7].

To validate our earlier proposal, we need to show that the algorithm predicted by the regression function performs better than its competitors on our new dataset. The graph below clearly shows that the user-based CF algorithm (predicted as the best-performer by our regression function) does in fact have a better predictive accuracy than all of its competitors.

4 Conclusion and Future Work

The approach adopted by our system is based on a predictor for filtering techniques. More than simply developing specific filtering implementations, we produce an information filtering architecture, capable of incorporating new technologies as they arrive. One application of this adaptive recommender could be commercially deployed in cases where system developers do not have the time or expertise available to assess which information filtering technique best suits the individual requirements of their application. The testing procedure in this paper will be reviewed in a further paper to incorporate 10-fold cross validation and decision support metrics such as Receiver Operator Characteristic (ROC) and better statistical accuracy in the form of mean absolute predictive error. Future work will also include extension of the scope of test data to other domains. These improvements should provide a more reliable test-bench and therefore a better regression function upon which to base our algorithm predictions.

References

1. Daniel Billsus and Michael J. Pazzani. Learning collaborative information filters. In *Proc. 15th International Conf. on Machine Learning*, pages 46–54. Morgan Kaufmann, San Francisco, CA, 1998.
2. Paul Cotter and Barry Smyth. PTV: Intelligent personalised TV guides. In *Proceedings of the 7th Conference on Artificial Intelligence (AAAI-00) and of the 12th Conference on Innovative Applications of Artificial Intelligence (IAAI-00)*, pages 957–964, Menlo Park, CA, July 30–3 2000. AAAI Press.
3. Ken Goldberg, Theresa Roeder, Dhruv Gupta, and Chris Perkins. Eigentaste: A constant time collaborative filtering algorithm. *Information Retrieval*, 4(2):133–151, 2001.
4. C. Hayes, P. Cunningham, P. Clerkin, and M. Grimaldi. Programme-driven music radio, 2002.
5. George Karypis. Evaluation of item-based top-n recommendation algorithms. In *CIKM*, pages 247–254, 2001.
6. P. Melville, R. Mooney, and R. Nagarajan. Content-boosted collaborative filtering, 2001.
7. John O'Donovan and John Dunnion. A comparison of collaborative recommendation algorithms over diverse data. In *Proceedings of the National Conference on Artificial Intelligence and Cognitive Science (AICS), Ireland*, pages 101–104, September 17 – September 19 2003.

8. Michael P. O'Mahony, Neil Hurley, and Guenole C. M. Silvestre. An attack on collaborative filtering. In *Proceedings of the 13th International Conference on Database and Expert Systems Applications*, pages 494–503. Springer-Verlag, 2002.

9. Adrian E. Raftery, David Madigan, and Jennifer A. Hoeting. Bayesian model averaging for linear regression models. *Journal of the American Statistical Association*, 92(437):179–191, 1997.

10. Paul Resnick, Neophytos Iacovou, Mitesh Suchak, Peter Bergstrom, and John Riedl. Grouplens: An open architecture for collaborative filtering of netnews. In *Proceedings of ACM CSCW'94 Conference on Computer-Supported Cooperative Work*, Sharing Information and Creating Meaning, pages 175–186, 1994.

11. Badrul M. Sarwar, George Karypis, Joseph A. Konstan, and John Reidl. Item-based collaborative filtering recommendation algorithms. In *World Wide Web*, pages 285–295, 2001.

12. B. Smyth, D. Wilson, and D. O'Sullivan. Improving the quality of the personalised electronic programme guide. In *In Proceedings of the TV'02 the 2nd Workshop on Personalisation in Future TV, May 2002.*, pages 42–55, 2002.

Lexical Chains versus Keywords for Topic Tracking

Joe Carthy

Department of Computer Science,
University College Dublin, Ireland.
Joe.Carthy@ucd.ie

Abstract. This paper describes research into the use of lexical chains to build effective Topic Tracking systems and compares the performance with a simple keyword-based approach. Lexical chaining is a method of grouping lexically related terms into so called *lexical chains*, using simple natural language processing techniques. Topic tracking involves tracking a given news event in a stream of news stories i.e. finding all subsequent stories in the news stream that discuss the given event. This paper describes the results of a novel topic tracking system, LexTrack, based on lexical chaining and compares it to a keyword-based system designed using traditional IR techniques.

1 Introduction

Topic detection and tracking research has grown out of a DARPA-sponsored initiative to investigate the computational task of finding new events and tracking existing events in a stream of textual news stories from multiple sources [1]. These sources include news broadcast programs such as CNN news and newswire sources such as Reuters. The information in these sources is divided into a sequence of stories that provide information on one or more events. The tracking task is defined as that of associating incoming stories with events known to the system. An event is defined as "known" by its association with stories that discuss the event. So, each target event is defined by a list of stories that define it. If we take an event such *as "the Kobe earthquake"*, then the first story (or first N stories) in the corpus describing the Kobe earthquake could be used as the definition of that event.

A TDT test corpus was constructed to facilitate the TDT initiative. This corpus includes 15,863 news stories from July 1, 1994 to June 30, 1995. The corpus included relevance judgments for a set of 25 events covering a broad spectrum of interests such as disaster stories (e.g. Kobe earthquake in Japan) and crime stories (e.g. OJ Simpson trial). Every story in the corpus was judged with respect to every event by two sets of assessors and any conflicts were reconciled by a third assessor.

2 Lexical Chaining

The notion of lexical chaining derives from work in the area of textual cohesion by Halliday and Hasan [2]. The linguistics term *text* is used to refer to any passage

A. Gelbukh (Ed.): CICLing 2004, LNCS 2945, pp. 507–510, 2004.
© Springer-Verlag Berlin Heidelberg 2004

spoken or written that forms a unified whole. This unity or cohesion may be due, for example, to an anaphoric reference, which provides cohesion between sentences. In its simplest form it is the presupposition of something that has gone before, whether in the preceding sentence or not. Where the cohesive elements occur over a number of sentences a cohesive *chain* is formed. For example, the following lexical chain, *[mud pie, dessert, mud pie, chocolate, it]* could be constructed given the sentences: *John had mud pie for dessert. Mud pie is made of chocolate. John really enjoyed it.* The word *it* in the third sentence refers back to *dessert* in the first sentence. In this example repetition (*mud pie* in the first and second sentences) also contributes to the cohesion of the text.

A *lexical chain* is a sequence of related words in the text, spanning short (adjacent words or sentences) or long distances (entire text). A chain is independent of the grammatical structure of the text and in effect it is a list of words that captures a portion of the cohesive structure of the text. A lexical chain can provide a context for the resolution of an ambiguous term and enable identification of the concept the term represents. Morris and Hirst [3] were the first researchers to suggest the use of lexical chains to determine the structure of texts. A number of researchers such as Stairmand [4], Green [5] and Kazman[6] have developed IR applications using lexical chains as an aid to representing document content. Stairmand and Black [7] point out that the lexical chains may help identify the focus of a document

A key factor in the design of any IR system is the notion of aboutness and how we represent what a document is *about*. The vast majority of IR systems represent document content via lists of keywords. Any given document and in particular a news story, will typically have a central theme or focus. Lexical chain generation is one method that can be used to identify the central theme of a document. By utilising the lexical chains we postulated that it would be possible to build more effective systems than the simple keyword-based ones that dominate in current IR systems. In our research we designed and built a topic tracking system called LexTrack based on lexical chains. The goal was to investigate if this computational linguistic approach would outperform a simple keyword-based approach.

2.1 LexTrack Lexical Chaining Algorithm

A lexical resource is required to identify the relations between words in order to construct lexical chains. In this research we used WordNet in the construction of lexical chains [8]. WordNet uses synsets to represent concepts. The lexical chaining module of LexTrack operates as follows.

1. Take $term_i$ in a story and using WordNet generate the *Neighbour* set called *Neighbour$_i$* of its related synset identifiers using the hyponym/hypernym (is-a) and meronym/holonym (part-of) relationships.
2. For each other term in the story, if it is a repetition of $term_i$ or if it is a member of the set Neighbour$_i$ then add its synset identifier to the lexical chain for $term_i$.
3. A word sense disambiguation process is also carried out at this time (described in [9]). If a word sense is disambiguated, then discard all non-relevant senses from the set Neighbour$_i$.
4. Repeat steps 1, 2 and 3 for all terms in the story.

LexTrack computed the similarity between all chains in a target event and each incoming document. If this similarity exceed a given theshold (computed empirically), then the incoming document was flagged to track the given event. The Overlap Coefficient was used to compute lexical chain similarity [10]. It may be defined as follows, for two lexical chains c_1 and c_2:

$$\text{Overlap Coefficient} = \frac{|c_1 \cap c_2|}{\min(|c_1|, |c_2|)}$$

3 Experimental Results of Tracking Based on Lexical Chains

In Figure 1 shows the Precision-Recall performance of LexTrack relative to a baseline keyword-based system, KeyCos, that we implemented. KeyCos was based on traditional IR techniques and in this case on using Cosine Similarity to measure the similarity between a tracking story and an incoming story. We can see that KeyCos clearly outperforms the LexTrack system. This is a disappointing result. We believe that the Topic Tracking task may not be a suitable one for a lexical chain-based system. This is because lexical chains have been mainly used in the analysis of a **single** document for discourse analysis and summarization purposes. The lexical chains are useful at identifying topics and themes in a single document. In the Tracking Task we are concerned with comparing lexical chains between many documents. We have applied lexical chaining-based approach to the problem of text segmentation with very promising results – this is a task where lexical chains are used to identify topics in a single document [11].

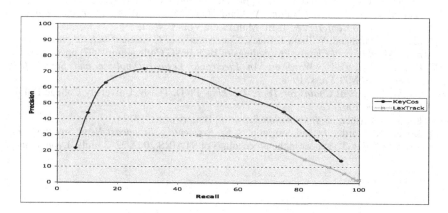

Fig. 1. Precision-Recallgraph of LexTrack versus KeyCos

4 Conclusions and Future Work

In this paper we have described a novel approach to topic tracking based on lexical chaining. Lexical chaining has been used in a number of IR applications previously but with very poor results. We have shown that lexical chaining also yields poor results in topic tracking by comparing the performance of LexTrack, a topic tracking system using lexical chains with a system based on traditional IR techniques. It may be possible that the performance of LexTrack can be improved in the future by taking special account of proper nouns looking at enhanced word sense disambiguation techniques. The chain matching process can also be improved to take account of chain metrics such as the span of the lexical chains and the number of elements in each chain. However, we believe that lexical chaining is more suited to tasks involving the detailed analysis of single documents as opposed to IR-like tasks which involve inter-document analysis.

References

[1] James Allan et al., *Topic Detection and Tracking Pilot Study Final Report*, In the proceedings of the DARPA Broadcasting News Transcript and Understanding Workshop, February 1998.
[2] M Halliday, R Hasan, *Cohesion in English*, Longman, 1976.
[3] Jane Morris, Graeme Hirst, *Lexical Cohesion by Thesaural Relations as an Indicator of the Structure of Text*, Computational Linguistics 17(1), March 1991.
[4] Mark Stairmand, *A Computational Analysis of Lexical Cohesion with applications in information Retrieval*, Ph.D. Thesis, UMIST, 1996.
[5] Stephen J Green, *Automatically Generating Hypertext By Comparing Semantic Similarity*, University of Toronto, Technical Report number 366, October 1997.
[6] Rick Kazman, Reem Al-Halimi, William Hunt, Marilyn Manti, *Four Paradigms for Indexing Video Conferences*, IEEE Multimedia Vol. 3, No. 1.
[7] Mark A. Stairmand, William J. Black, *Conceptual and Contextual Indexing using Word-Net-derived Lexical Chains*, Proceedings of BCS IRSG Colloquium 1997, pp. 47–65.
[8] Fellbaum, C., (Ed.), *WordNet: An Electronic Lexical Database and Some of its Applications*, MIT Press, 1998.
[9] Carthy, J., *Lexical Chains for Topic Tracking*, Ph.D. Thesis, University College Dublin, Ireland, June 2002.
[10] Keith van Rijsbergen, *Information Retrieval*, Butterworths, 1979.
[11] Stokes, N., Carthy J., and Smeaton, A.F., *Segmenting Broadcast News Streams using Lexical Chains*, To appear in the proceedings of STAIRS 2002, 22–23 July, Lyon, France.

Filtering Very Similar Text Documents: A Case Study

Jiří Hroza[1], Jan Žižka[1], and Aleš Bourek[2]

[1] Faculty of Informatics, Department of Information Technologies
Masaryk University, Botanická 68a, 602 00 Brno, Czech Republic
{xhroza1,zizka}@informatics.muni.cz
[2] Faculty of Medicine, Department of Biophysics
Masaryk University, Joštova 10, 662 43 Brno, Czech Republic
bourek@med.muni.cz

Abstract. This paper describes problems with classification and filtration of similar relevant and irrelevant real medical documents from one very specific domain, obtained from the Internet resources. Besides the similarity, the documents are often unbalanced—a lack of irrelevant documents for the training. A definition of similarity is suggested. For the classification, six algorithms are tested from the document similarity point of view. The best results are provided by the back propagation-based neural network and by the radial basis function-based support vector machine.

1 Introduction

After downloading many textual documents from the Internet resources, users often need subsequent filtration of the resulting data. Typically, only a small part of these documents is relevant for a user. If the documents are sufficiently different, it is possible to use an effective filtering method like, for example, the naïve Bayes classifier provided that there are balanced and good training sets of instances, see [6]. However, if a user looks for documents from a very specific and narrow area and moreover he or she defines efficient search conditions, the outcome of a web-browser searching can include very similar relevant and irrelevant documents. The similarity is usually based on a high incidence of identical words so a classifier can make many errors when filtering irrelevant documents even if it is trained using carefully selected examples. An additional problem is often in very unbalanced numbers of training positive and negative examples because users usually need processing of data that they simply obtained and it is not possible to create more positive or negative examples to fulfil conditions required by algorithms for the reliable training, see [9]. Thus the existing methods based on extensive balanced training, such as [4], or on general-purpose onthologies, such as [5], are not efficient for similar special-purpose texts.

The described situation occurs very often in various medical domains and this paper describes a study with documents in the area of gynecology, infertility, and assisted reproduction. Any suitable solution of the problem is naturally

A. Gelbukh (Ed.): CICLing 2004, LNCS 2945, pp. 511–520, 2004.
© Springer-Verlag Berlin Heidelberg 2004

very important because physicians usually obtain too many documents from the WWW (e.g., from the MEDLINE resource) and they do not have time enough to go through all the data to select relevant documents manually.

2   Investigated Data and Their Characteristics

This study dealt with three types of real textual documents from the Internet. The first and the second group [3] consisted of medical articles and abstracts, while the third group included quite different instances of 20 various WWW-newsgroups, see [1]—those newsgroups were used only for the comparison and verification of results. The Internet documents obtained by physicians were filtered by six selected algorithms and the results were compared with the ones provided by experiments with sets of documents from the newsgroups.

2.1   Basic Description of the Textual Documents

Table 1 shows the basic characteristics of the three document sets.

The first group (1 ⊕ and 1 ⊖ in Table 1) presented a great problem: new important medical documents, however, with a low number of instances that were poorly balanced. Physicians also could not provide more irrelevant examples of documents to balance ⊕ and ⊖ training instances because the aim was to filter similar documents from the same medical category—not to separate the category from arbitrary text units. Therefore, it was not possible to use arbitrary documents as negative examples to fill in the missing instances.

In the second data set, the medical texts were better balanced, having sufficient numbers of relevant (2 ⊕) and irrelevant (2 ⊖) documents. Particular classification results with these data sets were published, e.g., in [12,13]. Nevertheless certain document-similarity problems with this data set were detected when these documents were processed for the first time so the data was again

Table 1. Basic characteristics of three textual document sets used in experiments. ⊕ means positive (relevant) training examples, ⊖ means negative (irrelevant) training examples

Document group	Number of documents	Average number of words
1 ⊕	191	271.4
1 ⊖	40	294.6
2 ⊕	295	125.3
2 ⊖	295	107.0
3a ⊕	990	280.0
3b ⊖	990	257.2
3c ⊕	990	327.5
3d ⊖	990	383.4

included in the tests described here. In the new experiments the number of relevant (positive) examples was decreased to 295 documents to get two perfectly balanced sets of relevant and irrelevant examples.

Finally, the third data was large enough and perfectly balanced. In this last group, data experiments employed just four selected newsgroups from 20 ones because the aim was to show and compare possible results with those relatively very good training sets. Moreover, here it was easy to select examples of reliable and balanced documents from two quite topically dissimilar computer- and sport-domains (*comp.graphics* as 3a $\oplus$ and *rec.sport.hockey* as 3b $\ominus$) and two topically similar religion-domains (*talk.religion.misc* as 3c $\oplus$ and *soc.religion.christian* as 3d $\ominus$) of newsgroups—of course, here it was selected just randomly whether a domain was in the class $\oplus$ or $\ominus$, without any relation to the relevance or irrelevance. The actual aim was to obtain results from separating a certain topic from another one, both for similar and dissimilar topics. The similarity and dissimilarity was primarily determined from the human point of view.

2.2 Preprocessing of Documents

Before starting the experiments with textual data, it is usually necessary to adjust words in the documents so that employed algorithms provide as reliable results as possible. Experiments described in further sections used only a simple adjustment: *stripping word-suffixes* to obtain the same word if it had more forms in a document. For example, *classified, classify, classifies*, etc., should provide just one form, or a plural and singular of a noun should also have the same form, and so like. For this purpose, the words in the documents were modified using a commonly applied algorithm described in [7]. Without using these modifications, results were mostly significantly worse even if the documents were really very similar from a common human point of view—computers only could see too many different words knowing nothing about relations among words and sentences.

3 Determination of the Similarity Measure

It is not quite obvious how to automatically determine the degree of similarity (or dissimilarity) among textual documents. Having no deep linguistic representation of specific documents to help a computer calculate a certain similarity degree, one possible way is employing a function based on selected attributes of documents. These attributes are mainly words.

3.1 Hamming Distance

As the first and simple possibility, just the use of the occurrence of words in documents suggests itself. A commonly used tool in many scientific branches, the *Hamming distance*, is here principally based on the comparison of the number of the same words in documents: the higher is the number the more similar are the documents. However, experiments with the *Hamming distance* using the

Table 2. The Hamming distances for textual documents used in experiments

Document group	Hamming distance
1 $\oplus$ and 1 $\ominus$	220.6
2 $\oplus$ and 2 $\ominus$	106.5
3a $\oplus$ and 3b $\ominus$	211.8
3c $\oplus$ and 3d $\ominus$	252.4

specific data sets (described in the previous section) did not provide satisfactory results because opinions of human medical experts were quite different. The non-medical newsgroups sets also obtained degrees that were improper from the common human point of view. In all the cases, the *Hamming distance* was generally higher for larger documents and lower for shorter documents, almost without any reflecting of the real (dis)similarity. The reason was obviously the form and type of the available data because many documents were relatively short—frequently just abstracts of articles or typical contributions to newsgroups discussions. The results provided by the *Hamming distance* are in Table 2.

3.2   The Alternative Common-Word-Based Similarity

To measure the document (dis)similarities, a heuristic similarity function based on relative numbers of the same (common) words was suggested. Let us suppose there are two sets of documents, a set $A = \{a_1, ..., a_n\}$ having an average number of n_A words in a document and similarly a set $B = \{b_1, ..., b_m\}$ having an average number of n_B words in a document. The average absolute number of common words between A and B is determined using each pair of documents, (a_i, b_i), and the result is an average number. (If $A = B$, then the average absolute number is determined for each distinct pair of documents, (a_i, a_j), $i \neq j$.) For the two sets, it is possible to determine their mutual similarity degree knowing their average absolute number of the same words of A in B (or B in A), which is $a_{AB} = a_{BA}$.

Let documents in the same set have the average absolute number of the same words a_{AA} and b_{BB}. The relative rate of the same words of the set A in B is then $r_{AB} = a_{AB}/n_A$ and for B in A it is $r_{BA} = a_{BA}/n_B$. Similarly, $r_{AA} = a_{AA}/n_A$ and $r_{BB} = a_{BB}/n_B$. Now it is possible to compute the similarity of A to B related to the similarity of A to A, which is r_{AB}/r_{AA}, and vice versa, B to A related to the similarity of B to B, which is r_{BA}/r_{BB}.

The result of the multiplication of r_{AB}/r_{AA} and r_{BA}/r_{BB} provides a coefficient that determines the degree of (dis)similarity: the higher is the coefficient the more similar are the documents because they have more common words, and vice versa. Therefore, it is enough to use only the average absolute numbers of the common words between A and B:

$$Similarity(A, B) = \frac{r_{AB}}{r_{AA}} \cdot \frac{r_{BA}}{r_{BB}} = \frac{a_{AB}}{a_{AA}} \cdot \frac{a_{BA}}{a_{BB}} = \frac{a_{AB}^2}{a_{AA} \cdot a_{BB}}. \tag{1}$$

The main idea of the suggested function $Similarity(A, B)$ is in the following: If the relative average number of common words of the set A in the set B, r_{AB}, is divided by the relative average number of common words of the documents just in the set A, r_{AA}, the result represents the distance of B to A. Similarly, it is also possible to obtain the distance of A to B. A certain disadvantage of this approach is in the case when there are two unbalanced coefficients due to the different average length of documents in the processed sets. By multiplying these two numbers, a measure of the similarity between two sets of documents is obtained. This measure is symmetric considering A and B, thus only one number is sufficient. For two absolutely identical document sets, the similarity equals to 1 and if two document sets have no common word, the similarity equals to 0 provided that the documents are correctly put into their sets A and B.

The function $Similarity(A, B)$ was applied to the tested textual document sets with quite acceptable results that agreed with subjective human points of view despite the fact that humans cannot express their opinions using just numbers—they can express their opinions, for example, on a scale 0-100% which somehow corresponded to the similarity degrees obtained from the suggested similarity function. However, those human opinions were subjective and they were used only to know if the similarity of the processed documents could be reliably measured by computers. The results provided by $Similarity(A, B)$ are shown in the following table: Table 3 depicts similarities determined by individual documents in each document set A and B.

Table 3 also shows far better similarity results for the processed documents than the originally applied *Hamming distance*. Clearly, the third document sets taken from the newsgroups 3a $\oplus$ *comp.graphics* and 3b $\ominus$ *rec.sport.hockey* have the lowest similarity degree which could be naturally expected. On the other hand, both *religion* topics from the newsgroup show higher similarity. The similar situation is also valid for the medical documents where the results were quite acceptable by physicians who provided the document groups 1 and 2 containing relevant and irrelevant textual training documents.

Table 3. The results of the alternative similarity function

Document group	Common words in the same group	Common words between two subgroups	Similarity between two subgroups
1 $\oplus$	25.7	26.5	0.95
1 $\ominus$	29.0		
2 $\oplus$	22.3	20.8	0.98
2 $\ominus$	19.8		
3a $\oplus$	17.0	16.7	0.74
3b $\ominus$	22.2		
3c $\oplus$	31.1	33.1	0.93
3d $\ominus$	37.8		

However, the most important piece of knowledge resulting from the automatically determined similarities is the fact that the greatest filtering problems were really caused by high degrees of similarity between $\oplus$ and $\ominus$ document classes. The following sections describe experiments with various filtering algorithms where the results were influenced by the similarity degree.

4 Filtering Experiments and Results

For testing the textual documents mentioned above, the six following algorithms were applied:

- SVM_{RBF} : Support Vector Machine with Radial Basis Kernel [10], software BSVM [2] with parameters $C = 1000$ and $gamma = 0.005$;
- SVM_{LIN} : Support Vector Machine with Linear Kernel [10], software BSVM with $C = 10000$ and $e = 0.1$;
- $c4.5$: Decision Trees c4.5 [8] with default settings;
- $c5.0_{boosting}$: Decision Trees c5.0 with 10-times boosting [8], default settings;
- $NN_{BackProp}$: Artificial Neural Networks with Back Propagation and automatic adaptation of the learning speed, five sigmoidal units in the hidden layer, 300 iterations, and
- $Bayes$: Naïve Bayes Classifier [6].

All the documents except the naïve Bayes classifier were encoded using binary vectors where positions representing words were set to 1 if a word was present, otherwise 0. The naïve Bayes classifier had a word frequency in every position.

The algorithms were used generally with the 10-times cross-validation to obtain statistically more reliable results. However, for the data set 1 (highly unbalanced medical documents), it was not possible to use the cross-validation because this data contained too low number of negative examples. Therefore, here was used the 10-times random selection: a certain percentage of negative examples was selected so that the number of documents was the same in the positive and negative subsets. For example, in the Table 4, 18.8% of positive and 90% of negative examples were used, which were approximately 36 examples for the training process and the rest for the testing process. Naturally, this procedure had certain disadvantages from the statistical point of view if it is necessary to compare the results with other data sets, however, for the real data it was not possible to obtain acceptable larger sets. However, the results should have been somehow compared to know whether and how the difficult data set 1 could be also processed.

The graph in Fig. 1 shows the dependence of the filtering accuracy on the document-similarity degree for all the six algorithms that classified $\oplus$ and $\ominus$ documents. The next graph in Fig. 2 depicts the dependence of the filtering accuracy on the number of training documents for the difficult data set 1 using the six classification algorithms (10-times random selection of the training and testing instances was used to obtain these data)—the effect of the low number of negative training instances is quite evident, especially for the decision trees.

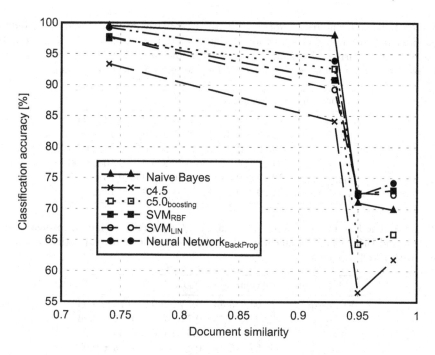

Fig. 1. The dependence of the filtering accuracy on the document-similarity degree

Tables 4, 5, 6, and 7 depict the results of experiments with the documents. The columns *Accuracy* show the accuracy of the classification related to both the $\oplus$ and $\ominus$ sets. In the columns $F_1 \oplus$ and $F_1 \ominus$, there are so called F_1-*measures*, which combine precisions and recalls according to the definition in [11]:

$$F_1(R, P) = \frac{2RP}{R + P}, \tag{2}$$

where R stands for the *recall* and P stands for the *precision*, $\oplus$ stands for the relevant and $\ominus$ for the irrelevant text documents.

5   Conclusions

The experiments, which were based on real medical documents, showed clearly that the classification and filtration depended strongly on the fact whether and how the classified documents are similar or dissimilar. The similarity measure, which was defined in this paper and was based on the rate of numbers of common words between relevant and irrelevant textual documents, corresponded to expectations of human medical experts. Generally applied machine-learning classification algorithms provided worse results for more similar documents, especially the naïve Bayes classifier—which is otherwise a very useful tool—had a relatively rapid descent of its accuracy. The decision trees c4.5 and c5.0, based on

Table 4. The filtering results for the data set 1 (very similar unbalanced medical documents) and the applied classification algorithms—10-times random selection. Because the relevant and irrelevant examples could not be balanced, 18.8% of relevant and 90% of irrelevant examples were used for training, the rest was used for testing

Algorithm	Accuracy	$F_1 \oplus$	$F_1 \ominus$
SVM_{RBF}	72.50 ± 8.07 %	0.85 ± 0.02	0.14 ± 0.02
SVM_{LIN}	72.63 ± 8.07 %	0.83 ± 0.04	0.14 ± 0.02
c4.5	56.52 ± 12.19 %	0.77 ± 0.07	0.08 ± 0.03
$c5.0_{boosting}$	64.30 ± 8.45 %	0.80 ± 0.04	0.10 ± 0.03
$NN_{BackProp}$	72.19 ± 9.03 %	0.80 ± 0.05	0.13 ± 0.03
Naïve Bayes	71.00 ± 9.11 %	0.81 ± 0.02	0.13 ± 0.03

Table 5. The filtering results for the data set 2 (very similar balanced medical documents) and the applied classification algorithms—10-times cross-validation, $\oplus$ and $\ominus$ sets with 295 documents

Algorithm	Accuracy	$F_1 \oplus$	$F_1 \ominus$
SVM_{RBF}	73.03 ± 5.56	0.73 ± 0.04	0.72 ± 0.06
SVM_{LIN}	72.31 ± 5.43	0.72 ± 0.04	0.72 ± 0.06
c4.5	61.84 ± 4.46	0.65 ± 0.03	0.56 ± 0.08
$c5.0_{boosting}$	65.91 ± 5.44	0.67 ± 0.04	0.63 ± 0.07
$NN_{BackProp}$	74.23 ± 5.12	0.74 ± 0.04	0.74 ± 0.06
Naïve Bayes	69.90 ± 4.58	0.70 ± 0.05	0.69 ± 0.04

Table 6. The filtering results for the data set 3ab (*comp.graphics* vs. *rec.sport.hockey* newsgroups) and the applied classification algorithms—10-times cross-validation

Algorithm	Accuracy	$F_1 \oplus$	$F_1 \ominus$
SVM_{RBF}	97.75 ± 1.93 %	0.97 ± 0.01	0.97 ± 0.02
SVM_{LIN}	97.71 ± 1.92 %	0.97 ± 0.01	0.97 ± 0.02
c4.5	93.36 ± 1.91 %	0.93 ± 0.02	0.92 ± 0.02
$c5.0_{boosting}$	97.53 ± 0.70 %	0.97 ± 0.00	0.97 ± 0.00
$NN_{BackProp}$	99.21 ± 0.79 %	0.99 ± 0.00	0.99 ± 0.00
Naïive Bayes	99.49 ± 0.62 %	0.99 ± 0.00	0.99 ± 0.00

Table 7. The filtering results for the data set 3cd (*religion* newsgroups) and the applied classification algorithms—10-times cross-validation

Algorithm	Accuracy	$F_1 \oplus$	$F_1 \ominus$
SVM_{RBF}	90.93 ± 1.30 %	0.90 ± 0.01	0.90 ± 0.02
SVM_{LIN}	89.94 ± 1.61 %	0.89 ± 0.01	0.89 ± 0.02
c4.5	86.76 ± 2.79 %	0.85 ± 0.03	0.87 ± 0.03
$c5.0_{boosting}$	92.13 ± 2.07 %	0.91 ± 0.02	0.92 ± 0.02
$NN_{BackProp}$	94.30 ± 1.52 %	0.94 ± 0.01	0.94 ± 0.01
Naïve Bayes	97.98 ± 1.11 %	0.97 ± 0.01	0.97 ± 0.01

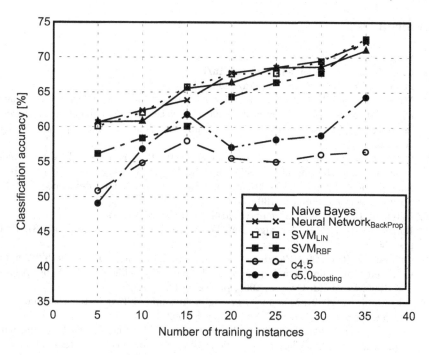

Fig. 2. The dependence of the filtering accuracy on the number of training documents for the data set 1

the entropy minimization, also failed, even if the c5.0 with the 10-times boosting method worked dependably for dissimilar documents in relevant and irrelevant document groups.

On the other hand, the back propagation-based artificial neural network provided the best results together with the SVM (*support vector machine*) algorithms, where the SVM based on radial basis functions overcome the linear SVM. All the three latter methods were more resistant to the similarity than the decision trees. However, the SVM algorithms were 30-50 times faster than the artificial neural network during the training process, which is not a negligible feature. The real documents from very specific domains are often very similar, however, human physicians can differentiate such medical documents— they just do not have time enough because of too high numbers of documents so an automatic tool would be welcome.

Acknowledgments. This research was partly supported by the Grant Human-computer interaction, dialog systems and assistive technologies CEZ:J07/98: 143300003.

References

1. http://www.ai.mit.edu/~jrennie/20Newsgroups/
2. http://www.csie.ntu.edu.tw/~cjlin/bsvm/
3. http://www.fi.muni.cz/~zizka/medocs/
4. M. Alexandrov, A. Gelbukh, G. Lozovoi (2001): Chi-square Classifier for Document Categorization. In: Computational Linguistics and Intelligent Text Processing (CICLing-2001). Lecture Notes in Computer Science, N 2004. Springer-Verlag, 2001, pp. 455–457.
5. Gelbukh, A., G. Sidorov, A. Guzman-Arenas (1999): Use of a weighted topic hierarchy for text retrieval and classification. In: Václav Matousek *et al.* (Eds.). Text, Speech and Dialogue (TSD-99). Lecture Notes in Artificial Intelligence, N 1692. Springer-Verlag, 1999, pp. 130–135.
6. Mitchell, T. M. (1997): Machine Learning. McGraw Hill, 1997.
7. Porter, M. F. (1980): An Algorithm For Suffix Stripping. Program 14 (3), 1980, pp. 130–137.
8. Quinlan, J. R. (1996): Bagging, Boosting, and C4.5. In: Proc. of the 8th Annual Conference on Innovative Applications of Artificial Intelligence, AAAI'96, August 4–8, 1996, Portland, Oregon, 1996, pp. 725–730.
9. Sebastiani, F. (2002): Machine Learning in Automated Text Categorization. ACM Computing Surveys, Vol. 34, No. 1, March 2002, pp. 1–47.
10. Tong, S. and Koller, D. (2001): Support Vector Machine Active Learning with Applications to Text Classification. Journal of Machine Learning Research, Vol. 2, November 2001, pp. 45–66.
11. Van Rijsbergen, C. J. (1979): Information Retrieval, 2nd Edition. Department of Computer Science, University of Glasgow, 1979.
12. Žižka, J., Bourek, A., and Frey, L. (2000): TEA: A Text Analysis Tool for the Intelligent Text Document Filtering. In: Proc. of the Third International Conference TSD-2000 Text, Speech, and Dialogue, Brno, Czech Republic, September 2000, Springer-Verlag Berlin Heidelberg New York, LNAI 1902, pp. 151–156.
13. Žižka, J. and Bourek, A. (2002): Automated Selection of Interesting Medical Text Documents by the TEA Text Analyzer. In: A. Gelbukh (Ed.): Proc. of the Third International Conference CICLing-2002, Mexico City, Mexico, February 2002, Springer-Verlag Berlin Heidelberg New York, LNCS 2276, pp. 402–404.

Using Information Extraction to Build
a Directory of Conference Announcements

Karl-Michael Schneider

University of Passau, Department of General Linguistics
Innstr. 40, 94032 Passau, Germany
schneide@phil.uni-passau.de
http://www.phil.uni-passau.de/linguistik/schneider/

Abstract. We describe an application of information extraction for
building a directory of announcements of scientific conferences. We employ a cascaded finite-state transducer to identify possible conference
names, titles, dates, locations and URLs in a conference announcement.
In order to cope with agrammatical text that is typical for conference
announcements, our system uses orthographic features of the text and a
domain-specific tag set, rather than general purpose part-of-speech tags.
Extraction accuracy is improved by recognizing other entities in the text
that are not extracted but could be confused with slot values. A scoring
scheme based on some simple heuristics is used to select among multiple
extraction candidates. We also present an evaluation of our system.

1 Introduction

A conference directory lists conferences, workshops and other meetings, often in
one scientific field, such as Computer Science, Computational Linguistics or Artificial Intelligence.[1] A conference directory is a valuable resource for researchers
who want to present their research to an interested audience, or are themselves
interested in the research of others in their field, and for this purpose are looking
for an appropriate conference.

An entry in a conference directory consists of at least the conference name
(e.g. *CICLing 2004*), title (*International Conference on Intelligent Text Processing and Computational Linguistics*), date, location and a link to the conference
web page that contains the full announcement and call for papers. New conference announcements are posted in newsgroups and distributed by electronic mail
through mailing lists. Upcoming conferences should be included in the directory
with little or no delay in order to keep the directory up-to-date.

Maintaining a conference directory requires to extract the relevant information from each incoming conference announcement. Doing this automatically

---

[1] See for example:
   http://www.aaai.org/Magazine/Departments/calendar.html
   http://www.conferencealerts.com/
   http://www.cs.jhu.edu/~yarowsky/sigdat.html

A. Gelbukh (Ed.): CICLing 2004, LNCS 2945, pp. 521–532, 2004.
© Springer-Verlag Berlin Heidelberg 2004

using Information Extraction (IE) techniques instead of reading each conference announcement and extracting the relevant information manually makes maintaining a conference directory much easier.

This paper describes a system that uses IE to extract relevant pieces of information from conference announcements for inclusion in a conference directory that is part of a comprehensive hyperlink collection for the field of linguistics, computational linguistics and related areas.[2] The conference subdirectory currently contains more than 1,000 links. Each hyperlink is assigned to a node in a topic hierarchy using a statistical text classifier (not described in this paper).

We employ a cascaded finite-state transducer [1] that identifies possible conference names, titles, dates, locations and URLs in a conference announcement, plus some simple heuristics to select among multiple candidates of names, titles, etc. Finite-state techniques for IE have been applied mostly to free text, i.e. text composed of grammatically well-formed sentences [1,2]. In contrast, a conference announcement usually consists of a mixture of free text and specially formatted text that does not consist of complete sentences, but often contains important information about the conference. In the absence of full syntax, linguistic analysis methods cannot be used (e.g. part-of-speech tagging normally relies on full sentences).

We deal with this situation by relying on orthographic features (capitalization) and a tagging dictionary that encodes domain-specific knowledge about the use of words in conference announcements, rather than on general syntactic properties, plus a gazetteer list for recognizing locations.

The paper is structured as follows. In Sect. 2 we describe our cascaded finite-state transducer and the selection heuristics that we use to extract the relevant information from conference announcements. Sect. 3 presents an evaluation of our system. Sect. 4 discusses related work. Finally, in Sect. 5 we draw some conclusions and discuss future work.

2   Extracting Information from Conference Announcements

2.1   Overview

Information extraction is the task of extracting certain pieces of information from a text, e.g. for inclusion of the extracted information in a database. Typically, there will be a given set of *slots*, and the goal is to fill these slots with information from the input text. In our domain of conference announcements the slots are *name, title, date, location* and *url*.

Fig. 1 shows a portion of a conference announcement. Table. 1 shows the values for the slots from this announcement. Note that all the conference information is separated from the free text portion of the message (although sometimes it is repeated in the free text), and there is no structural or linguistic context (except line breaking). Instead, we can use lexical and orthographic properties

---

[2] http://www.phil.uni-passau.de/linguistik/linguistik_urls/

```
                        CALL FOR PAPERS

CoNLL-2003: Seventh Conference on Natural Language Learning

       Organized at HLT-NAACL-02, Edmonton, Canada

                     May 31 - June 1 2003

                http://cnts.uia.ac.be/conll2003/


CoNLL is an international forum for discussion and presentation of
research on natural language learning. We invite submission of papers
about natural language learning topics, including, but not limited to:
```

Fig. 1. Example portion of a conference announcement.

Table 1. Slots and their values from the conference announcement in Fig. 1.

name	CoNLL-2003
title	Seventh Conference on Natural Language Learning
date	May 31 - June 1 2003
location	Edmonton, Canada
url	http://cnts.uia.ac.be/conll2003/

of the text in order to identify the relevant pieces. For example, note that the conference title contains the word Conference, preceded by the number word Seventh and followed by a prepositional phrase headed by the preposition on, and all words in the title except on are capitalized. In contrast, only words at the beginning of sentences and proper names are capitalized in the free text part.

Our cascaded finite-state transducer (described below) uses the following sources of information in order to identify relevant pieces of text:

- orthographic features (i.e. whether a token begins with an uppercase letter, is all uppercase, etc.),
- a small dictionary containing words that commonly appear in slot values, as well as words that cannot appear in slot values,
- a gazetteer for recognizing locations,
- a very limited amount of syntactic context.

Sometimes a conference announcement contains more than one conference name or title, e.g. when a call for an annual conference refers to last year's conference, or in a workshop announcement when the workshop is part of a conference. Almost all conference announcements contain several dates and locations (deadline for paper submission, notification of author, addresses of program committee members). In these cases we use some heuristics to assign a score to each candidate value and extract the highest scoring candidate for each slot. After normalizing (removal of tags, removal of white space before punctuation, case and date normalization, removal of syntactic context extracted along with a slot value), the slot values can then be inserted into a database.

2.2   Recognition of Candidate Slot Values

We use a cascade of finite state transducers for tokenization, tagging and bracketing to identify potentially relevant pieces of text in a conference announcement. The tokenization stage transforms an input text into a stream of tokens separated by blanks. The tagging stage appends a tag to each token that specifies the role of the token in the text. Finally, the bracketing stage matches token and tag sequences against specially handcrafted regular patterns and inserts labeled brackets around matching sequences.

Tokenization. In general, tokenization is a non-trivial problem [3]. For example, a sequence of alphabetic characters followed by a period can be a single token (abbreviation) or a sequence of two tokens (end of sentence).

We recognize the following sets of tokens: words, numbers, time expressions, URLs, e-mail addresses, punctuation and paragraph boundaries (a sequence of white-space characters containing at least two newline characters), plus the two special tokens Int. and Conf.

Tagging. The most striking difference to existing IE systems is the set of tags that we use. These tags are different from general purpose part-of-speech (POS) tag sets that mark words according to their syntactic function (e.g. verbs, nouns, adjectives, etc.). In contrast, the tags employed by our system are used to classify words according to the role they play in recognizing conference information in conference announcements, for instance whether a word is the head word of a conference title or an organization, a conference attribute, or a word that is likely to appear in a conference announcement but cannot be part of a conference title. Thus our tags encode specific knowledge about the target domain.

Tags are assigned to tokens using a small dictionary, a gazetteer and orthographic features. No context is used during tagging. The dictionary is used to tag words that typically appear in conference titles and related expressions like names of associations, institutions, etc. (see Table 2). HD (header) is assigned to words that are used to explicitly mark certain types of information. The purpose of the NM and UN tags is explained below. The dictionary also contains lists of prepositions and conjunctions (not shown in Table 2).

In addition to the words in the dictionary, the tag NM (name) is assigned to all tokens that consist of alphabetic characters and start with an uppercase letter and do not appear in the dictionary or on a list of location names compiled from a gazetteer.[3] Tokens that (after normalizing the case of all uppercase tokens) appear on the gazetteer list are assigned the tag LO (location). Note that tokens tagged with NM are not necessarily names of persons, companies,

---

[3] Obtained from http://www.world-gazetteer.com/st/overview.htm

Table 2. The tagging dictionary (prepositions, conjunctions and upper and lower case variants not shown).

Tag	Words
UV	University
CE	Center, Centre, Institute, School, Department, College
OR	Society, Association, Council, Consortium
EV	Conference, Conf., Workshop, Symposium, Meeting, Congress, Roundtable, ...
AN	Annual, International, Int., Interdisciplinary, Special, Joint, European, ...
MO	January, February, March, ...
SM	Jan, Feb, Mar, ...
DA	Monday, Tuesday, Wednesday, ...
SD	Mon, Tue, Wed, ...
HD	Title, Date, Location, Contact, Email, URL, Website
DL	Deadline, Reminder, Submission
DT	the, this, its, their
TH	st, nd, rd, th
NT	First, Second, Third, ...
NM	computational, cognitive, linguistics
UN	Dr, Call, Papers, Paper, CFP, See, Copyright, Collocated, ASCII, Format, PhD

etc. Rather they represent words that are likely to occur in conference titles, because conference titles have a strong tendency to be capitalized. Nevertheless we shall call them "names" in the sequel.

In addition we have tags for numbers, roman numbers, time expressions, e-mail addresses, URLs, punctuation and paragraphs. The tag UN (no name) is assigned to all other tokens, in particular lowercase words except those that appear in the dictionary, and to a small list of capitalized words in the dictionary that usually never occur in a conference title, like *Papers*, *LaTeX*, etc. The total number of tags is 36.

Bracketing. This stage performs a greedy search for sequences of tokens whose tags match certain regular patterns. Whenever a match is found, a labeled pair of brackets is inserted into the stream of tagged tokens. Table 3 lists the recognized entities. Fig. 2 shows the patterns for CONF entities (conference titles).[4] nth, name, conjunction, etc. represent tokens with appropriate tags. event represents tokens tagged with EV, called *event keywords*. A conference title must contain an event keyword. conference1 matches titles such as *Workshop on Natural Language Processing* and *Canadian Linguistics Association Symposium on Language Acquisition*, while conference2 matches titles like *Conference of the Association for Computational Linguistics*.

An optional prefix (e.g. *First*, *2nd*), or a year, followed by a sequence of words like *Annual*, *Int.* etc. is recognized as a prefix of the conference title. confsuffix matches suffixes such as *'2003* or *IX*. Thus we can have conference titles such as *2003 Annual Conference of the Association for Cognitive Linguistics* or *2nd*

---

[4] The patterns in Fig. 2 were simplified for the purpose of presentation.

Table 3. Recognized entities.

Entity	Example
NAME	CoNLL-2003
NAMEAFFIX	CoNLL-2003:
NAMESIMPLE	CoNLL
ATCONF	at HLT-NAACL-02
CONF	Seventh Conference on Natural Language Learning
ORG	Association for Computational Linguistics
HEADERDATE	Conference: May 31-June 1 2003
DATE	May 31 - June 1 2003
SHORTDATE	Friday, April 5
YEAR	2003
HEADERLOC	Location: Edmonton, Canada
INLOC	in Madrid
ATLOC	at the University of Antwerp
LOC	Edmonton, Canada
INST	University of Antwerp
HEADERURL	Website: http://cnts.uia.ac.be/conll2003/
URL	http://cnts.uia.ac.be/conll2003/
DEADLINE	Submission: March 16, 2003

```
names        ::= nth? name ('-'? name)*
nameconj     ::= ','|'/'|(',' conjunction|preposition) article?
namephrase   ::= names (nameconj names)*
quotedphrase ::= ('"'|''' ''')?) (word|'-')+ ('"'|''' ''')?)
eventattr    ::= attribute (conjunction? attribute)*
confprefix   ::= (nth|year)? eventattr*
confsuffix   ::= '''? (year|shortyear)|romannumber
conftheme    ::= (on|in|':') namephrase|(on|in|':')? quotedphrase
conference1  ::= (organization|namephrase)? event conftheme
conference2  ::= event of article organization
conference   ::= confprefix? (conference1|conference2) confsuffix?
```

Fig. 2. Patterns for recognizing conference titles.

Int. Workshop on Dialogue Modeling. The patterns for recognizing associations, organizations, institutions, etc. are similar.

Note how the recognition of conference titles relies on orthographic features. Words in conference titles (except function words) tend to be capitalized, whereas most words (excluding person and location names) are usually not capitalized in free text, except at the beginning of a sentence. Since only uppercase words are recognized in conference titles (in addition to prepositions, conjunctions and some classes of words in the dictionary), conference titles are quite reliably recognized also in running text. In order to capture some rare cases where a conference title is not capitalized, we have included some lowercase words that can appear in conference titles as names in the dictionary.

```
CALL/UN FOR/FO PAPERS/UN PA/PA [NAMEAFFIX CoNLL/NM -/PU 2003/NB :/PU ]
[CONF Seventh/NM Conference/EV on/ON Natural/NM Language/NM Learning/NM ]
PA/PA Organized/NM [ATCONF at/AT HLT/NM -/PU NAACL/NM -/PU 02/NB ] ,/PU
[LOC Edmonton/LO ,/PU Canada/LO ] PA/PA [DATE May/MO 31/NB -/PU June/MO
1/NB 2003/NB ] PA/PA [URL http://cnts.uia.ac.be/conll2003//UR ] PA/PA
[NAMESIMPLE CoNLL/NM ] is/UN an/UN international/AN forum/EV for/FO
discussion/UN and/CJ presentation/UN of/OF research/UN on/ON natural/UN
language/UN learning/UN ./PU We/NM invite/UN submission/DL of/OF
papers/UN about/AB natural/UN language/UN learning/UN topics/UN ,/PU
including/UN ,/PU but/UN not/UN limited/UN to/TO :/PU
```

Fig. 3. Portion of the tagged and bracketed conference announcement from Fig. 1.

Note also the role of the words tagged with UN in the dictionary. This list prevents the sequence *Papers Conference in Linguistics* to be recognized as a conference title when the string *Call for Papers* immediately precedes the string *Conference in Linguistics*. It also prevents *CFP* to be recognized as a conference name.

Fig. 3 shows the tagged portion of text from Fig. 1 with brackets inserted.

2.3   Selection from Multiple Candidates

The output of the finite state cascade described in the previous section is a list of potential slot values, along with their position in the input text and their type as given in Table 3. Table 4 shows some of the entities found in the conference announcement in Fig. 1. Altogether 61 entities have been identified in this example.

Each one of the identified entities (except DEADLINE) is a candidate value for one of the five slots (name, title, date, location, url). The assignment of entity types to slots is as follows:

- name: NAME, NAMEAFFIX, NAMESIMPLE, ATCONF
- title: CONF, ORG
- date: HEADERDATE, DATE, SHORTDATE, YEAR
- location: HEADERLOC, INLOC, ATLOC, LOC, INST
- url: HEADERURL, URL

We use a scoring scheme to select the best value for each slot. The score for a candidate value is determined based on the following properties:

- its position in the text,
- its length (number of tokens),
- its type,
- its distance to the nearest candidate value of a certain type in the text.

The score for a candidate value e is computed by the formula

$$S_e = P_\tau \cdot Pos_e + L_\tau \cdot Length_e + T_t + \sum_{\tau'} D_{\tau,\tau'} \cdot Dist_{e,\tau'} \qquad (1)$$

Table 4. Some extracted entities from the conference announcement in Fig. 1.

Pos.	Entity	Extracted tokens
5	NAMEAFFIX	CoNLL - 2003 :
9	CONF	Seventh Conference on Natural Language Learning
17	ATCONF	at HLT - NAACL - 02
24	LOC	Edmonton , Canada
28	DATE	May 31 - June 1 2003
35	URL	http://cnts.uia.ac.be/conll2003/
37	NAMESIMPLE	CoNLL
172	NAMESIMPLE	SNoW
227	ORG	Association for Computational Linguistics
245	INLOC	in Madrid
248	YEAR	1997
251	LOC	Sydney
278	URL	http://www.aclweb.org/signll
597	DATE	March 16 , 2003
688	INST	University of Antwerp , Universiteitsplein
698	LOC	Antwerpen , Belgium
844	DEADLINE	Submission : March 16 , 2003
872	DATE	April 10 , 2003
876	HEADERDATE	Conference : May 31 - June 1 2003
921	NAMEAFFIX	(UK)

where t is the type of e (Table 3), τ is the corresponding slot type, Pos_e and $Length_e$ are the position and length of e, respectively, $Dist_{e,\tau'}$ is the distance of e to the nearest entity with corresponding slot type τ', and P_τ, L_τ, T_t, $D_{\tau,\tau'}$ are parameters that depend on t, τ, τ'.

A negative value of P_τ favors earlier occurrences of entities over later ones. Similarly, a positive value of L_τ favors longer entities over shorter ones. T_t can be used to select among entities with different types that belong to the same slot. For example, an INLOC entity may be more likely to contain the city and state of a conference than an ATLOC entity, and header entities (HEADERDATE, HEADERLOC, HEADERURL) are often more reliable than non-header entities. Finally, $D_{\tau,\tau'}$ can be used to favor entities that are near to other entities. For example, a location that is preceded or followed by a date is often more likely to be the location of a conference than a location that occurs without a date in a paragraph. A NAME entity next to a conference title is more likely to be the true name of the conference than one that is farther off a conference name, which might refer to a different conference.

Note that $Dist_{e,\tau'}$ can be computed in time linear in the number of identified entities by maintaining lists of identified entities, one for each slot, where entities are ordered by position. For each slot, we select the candidate value of appropriate type with the highest score.

3   Evaluation

For the evaluation, a test collection consisting of conference announcements received by the author between November 4, 2002 and September 16, 2003 was compiled. After removal of duplicates and near duplicates there were 88 announcements in the collection. Each announcement was tokenized and the correct slot values were manually tagged. When a conference announcement contained different entities that were considered valid fillers for one slot, all of them were tagged.

We used the following parameter values:

$$P_{name} = -1,\ P_{title} = -1,\ P_{date} = -0.1,\ P_{location} = -0.1,\ P_{url} = -0.01,$$
$$L_{title} = 1.5,\ T_{HEADERNAME} = 1,\ T_{NAMESIMPLE} = -1,$$
$$T_{HEADERDATE} = 2,\ T_{SHORTDATE} = -10,\ T_{YEAR} = -3,$$
$$T_{ATLOC} = -10,\ T_{INLOC} = -10,\ T_{INST} = -10,\ T_{HEADERURL} = 2,$$
$$D_{name,title} = -1,\ D_{loc,date} = -1.$$

All other parameters were set to zero. These parameter settings generally favor header entities over non-header entities, and earlier occurrences over later ones. We also prefer locations that are near to a date. These values were found experimentally using the first half of the test set. The extracted slot values were then compared to the true (annotated) values. For each slot type τ we collected the following statistics [2]:

- C_τ = number of times one of the correct values was extracted when there was at least one correct value for slot τ.
- E_τ = number of times a value for slot τ was extracted.
- V_τ = number of announcements containing at least one value for slot τ.

The evaluation metrics precision and recall are defined as follows:

$$prec_\tau = \frac{C_\tau}{E_\tau} \qquad recall_\tau = \frac{C_\tau}{V_\tau} \tag{2}$$

If $E_\tau = 0$ we set $prec_\tau = 1$ (note that $E_\tau = 0$ implies $C_\tau = 0$). Thus perfect precision can be reached by extracting nothing, however at the cost of zero recall. Precision assesses how many of the extracted values are correct. Extracting a value when there is no true value counts as an error. Recall assesses how many of the true values are extracted. Here, extracting nothing when there is a true value counts as an error. The common measure $F1$ combines precision and recall into a single figure. It is defined by $F1_\tau = 2 \cdot prec_\tau \cdot recall_\tau / (prec_\tau + recall_\tau)$. Table 5 shows the results for all five slots on the test set using the parameter values shown above.

Precision and recall reflect the extraction properties of the system. For a user a more interesting question is how many extraction errors the system is expected to make. From the user's perspective the system acts correctly if for a slot τ, either (i) there is at least one correct value for τ and the system extracts one of them, or (ii) the slot has no value and the system extracts nothing for this slot.

Table 5. Results on the test set.

Slot	C	E	V	Prec	Recall	F1	Acc
name	42	82	50	0.5122	0.8400	0.6364	0.5455
title	62	81	88	0.7654	0.7045	0.7337	0.7045
date	84	87	88	0.9655	0.9545	0.9600	0.9545
loc	65	87	87	0.7471	0.7471	0.7471	0.7500
url	75	82	80	0.9146	0.9375	0.9259	0.9091

Everything else counts as an extraction error. Accuracy for slot τ with respect to a test set is defined as the number of announcements in the test set with no extraction error for τ, divided by the total number of announcements in the test set. Table 5 also contains accuracy results for our test set and parameter values.

The most common extraction errors are the following:

- When there is a reference to a related or conjoined conference (e.g. *in conjunction with EACL 2003*) but the announced conference itself has no name, the name of the related or conjoined conference is extracted.
- When a workshop title contains the name of the main conference (e.g. *ACL-2003 Workshop on Multiword Expressions*), the conference name is extracted separately from the workshop title, i.e. name = *ACL-2003*, conf = *Workshop on Multiword Expressions*.
- Conference titles that do not contain an event keyword (e.g. *The Lexicon and Figurative Language*) are not extracted.
- Sometimes names of persons are extracted as conference names, especially when there is no conference name.

The first type of error could be fixed by adding patterns that extract phrases like *in conjunction with EACL 2003* as a CONJOINED entity so that the conference name would be inaccessible to the NAME pattern. The second type of error is hard to fix because it seems to require a thorough semantic analysis to decide whether a conference name preceding a title is part of the title or the name of a superordinate conference. The same is true for the third type of error. The fourth type of error could be fixed by identifying person names, using a dictionary of names, and thus make person names inaccessible to the NAME patterns.

4   Related Work

Kruger et. al. [4] have described DEADLINER, a domain-specific web search engine for scientific conferences. DEADLINER extracts conference titles, dates, locations, submission deadlines, program committee members, topics and other entities, which are then used for indexing conference web pages. Robustness is achieved by combining simple detectors based on regular templates in a probabilistic fashion. In order to avoid false extractions, DEADLINER first detects portions of the text that contain relevant information and then limits the application of extraction rules to these portions. This strategy is replaced by the scoring of candidate slot values in our system.

McCallum et al. [5] employed information extraction to extract bibliographic information such as authors, title, journal and publication date form research papers, in order to to build a computer science research paper directory automatically by using machine learning techniques.

Another popular domain for work on information extraction is seminar announcements, where the task is to extract the speaker, location, start and end time from announcements of seminar talks [6]. In talk announcements, these entities are often preceded by header words (*Date:*, *Time:*, *Place:*) which makes their recognition easier. However, the title of a talk is usually not extracted; we suspect that extracting the talk title from an announcement is more difficult and requires other techniques than those presented in this paper because talk titles usually do not contain an event keyword (*Conference, Workshop*, etc.) that would help to identify them. In addition, talk announcements (mostly for invited talks) often contain additional information about the speaker (e.g. affiliation) that is capitalized and thus difficult to distinguish from the talk title when only orthographic features are used.

Finite-state techniques have been employed for a variety of natural language processing tasks, mostly in the context of free text (consisting of grammatically well-formed sentences), such as shallow parsing [7], noun phrase recognition [8], named entity recognition [9] and information extraction [1]. Also, many IE systems make use of specialized dictionaries containing keywords that play a special role in the target domain [2].

Recently, machine learning techniques have been employed to learn extraction rules or patterns from training data and thus to avoid the need to write patterns by hand. These systems either induce extraction rules [10] or statistical models, e.g. Hidden Markov Models (HMM) or variants of HMMs and estimate the HMM parameters from training texts given a fixed model structure [11], or even learn the structure of the model [12]. Chieu and Ng present a statistical approach to IE that uses stateless maximum entropy models [13].

5   Conclusions

We have presented a system that extracts conference information from conference announcements. The system uses a cascaded finite-state transducer to identify candidate values, and some simple heuristics to select among multiple candidate values. Because of its finite-state architecture, the system is very fast.

Current limitations of the system are: (i) its limitation to announcements written in English (though the large majority of conference announcements is in English); (ii) some systematic extraction errors, like the extraction of something that looks like a conference name when there is no conference name. An obvious extension that could fix the latter problem would be to add a threshold parameter in order to rule out candidate values when their score is too low.

Future work includes: (i) experiments with other (possibly non-linear) scoring functions; (ii) automatic estimation of good parameters for the selection heuristics from annotated conference announcements; (iii) a comparison of the cascaded finite-state approach to a machine learning approach such as WHISK [10] or the stateless maximum entropy approach of Chieu and Ng [13].

References

1. Hobbs, J.R., Appelt, D., Bear, J., Israel, D., Kameyama, M., Stickel, M., Tyson, M.: FASTUS: A cascaded finite-state transducer for extracting information from natural-language text. In Roche, E., Schabes, Y., eds.: Finite-State Language Processing. MIT Press, Cambridge, MA (1997)
2. Grishman, R.: Information extraction: Techniques and challenges. In Pazienza, M.T., ed.: Information Extraction: A Multidisciplinary Approach to an Emerging Information Technology. LNAI 1299. Springer-Verlag, Heidelberg (1997) 10–27
3. Grefenstette, G., Tapanainen, P.: What is a word, what is a sentence? Problems of tokenization. In: 3rd International Conference on Computational Lexicography (COMPLEX'94), Budapest (1994) 79–87
4. Kruger, A., Giles, C.L., Coetzee, F.M., Glover, E., Flake, G.W., Lawrence, S., Omlin, C.: DEADLINER: Building a new niche search engine. In: Proc. Ninth International Conference on Information and Knowledge Management (CIKM'2000), Washington, DC (2000)
5. McCallum, A., Nigam, K., Rennie, J., Seymore, K.: A machine learning approach to building domain-specific search engines. In: 16th International Joint Conference on Artificial Intelligence (IJCAI-99). (1999)
6. Freitag, D.: Machine learning for information extraction in informal domains. Machine Learning **39** (2000) 169–202
7. Abney, S.: Partial parsing via finite-state cascades. In: ESSLLI'96 Workshop on Robust Parsing, Prague (1996) 8–15
8. Schiller, A.: Multilingual finite-state noun phrase extraction. In: Proc. ECAI-96 Workshop on Extended Finite State Models of Language. (1996)
9. Friburger, N., Maurel, D.: Finite-state transducer cascade to extract proper names in texts. In Watson, B.W., Wood, D., eds.: Implementation and Application of Automata, 6th International Conference, CIAA 2001. LNCS 2494, Berlin, Springer-Verlag (2002) 115–124
10. Soderland, S.: Learning information extraction rules for semi-structured and free text. Machine Learning **34** (1999) 233–272
11. McCallum, A., Freitag, D., Pereira, F.: Maximum entropy markov models for information extraction and segmentation. In: Proc. 17th International Conference on Machine Learning (ICML-2000), San Francisco, CA, Morgan Kaufmann (2000) 591–598
12. Seymore, K., McCallum, A., Rosenfeld, R.: Learning hidden markov model structure for information extraction. In: AAAI'99 Workshop on Machine Learning for Information Extraction. (1999)
13. Chieu, H.L., Ng, H.T.: A maximum entropy approach to information extraction from semi-structured and free text. In: Proc. 18th National Conference on Artificial Intelligence (AAAI-2002), Edmonton (2002) 786–791

Unsupervised Event Extraction from Biomedical Text Based on Event and Pattern Information

Hong-woo Chun, Young-sook Hwang, and Hae-Chang Rim

Natural Language Processing Lab., Dept. of CSE,
Korea University, Anam-dong 5-ga, Seongbuk-gu, 136-701, Seoul, Korea
{hwchun,yshwang,rim}@nlp.korea.ac.kr

Abstract. In this paper, we proposed a new event extraction method from biomedical texts. It can extend patterns by unsupervised way based on event and pattern information. Evaluation of our system on GENIA corpus achieves 90.1% precision and 70.0% recall.

1 Introduction

The current electronic revolution taking place via the internet and other networked resources giving easy online access to large collections of texts and data to researchers offers lots of new challenges in the field of automatic information extraction. In genomics, electronic databases are increasing rapidly, but a vast amount of knowledge still resides in large collections of scientific papers such as Medline [1]. In order to extract meaningful information from these data, the study of interactions between genes and proteins is very important.

Most of current approaches usually use predefined patterns of event verbs. However it is impossible for humans to define all the patterns of the event verbs. To make matters worse, there are also insufficient annotated corpora for learning. Thus, our proposed method is to use not only the patterns of event verbs but also statistical measures. These measures determine the frequency of verbs, nouns and their co-occurrence information, and the dependency relation. As a result, we show the ranking of events and patterns, thereby allowing us to extract reliable events.

In this paper, *Entity* is a biomedical class name such as protein, gene, cell, tissue, etc. *Event* is defined as the binary relation between subject entity and object entity for special event verbs.

2 System Architecture

The ultimate goal of our research is to build a network of gene or protein interaction using events extracted from biomedical texts. An illustration of the relevant portion of the architecture is shown in Figure 1.

In order to extract reliable events, we need a preprocessing procedure [Figure 1]. The first module is POS tagging and chunking. These processes transform raw corpus into POS tagged and chunked corpus [2]. The second module is

A. Gelbukh (Ed.): CICLing 2004, LNCS 2945, pp. 533–536, 2004.
© Springer-Verlag Berlin Heidelberg 2004

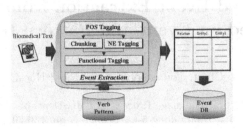

Fig. 1. System Architecture

NE tagging which tags named entities - such as proteins, genes, cells, virus, tissu, etc. - to POS tagged and chunked corpus [3]. The third module is dependency relations tagging that analyzes dependency relations both between subject and verb, and between object and verb [4].

3   Event Extraction Method

Our unsupervised event extraction method uses not only pattern information but also the co-occurrence and the dependency relation information. At that time, our approach automatically generates all patterns of the candidate events. We calculate the events and patterns confidence by using above three information. These confidence have reciprocal effects on each other, so each confidence updates, iteratively, other confidence until the ranks of candidate events remains unchanges. We extract reliable events based on the ranking of the candidate events. Consequently, our approach minimizes the handwork and achieves high recall (70.0%) as well as high precision (90.1%).

3.1   Sentence Normalization for Event Extraction

After the preprocessing procedure, we did not need the information of all words in a raw sentence. That is to say, there are essential arguments for event extraction. Figure 2 shows an example of sentence normalization. While normalizing the sentence, we consider peculiar features which are given in Table 1.

... lipoxygenase metabolites activate ROI formation which then induce
     Protein   EV   Other   WDT   EV
IL-2 expression via NF-kappa B activation.
Protein   PP   Other

Fig. 2. An example of sentence normalization

Table 1. Normalization Rules

Normalization Items	Examples
Entities	Protein, Gene, Tissue, Cell
Event verbs	Activate, Bind, Induce
Not event verbs	Be, Understand, Present
Preposition	of, by, with, in
Relative	Which, That
Conjunctions	and, but, or
Symbols	'(',')',',',':',';'

3.2   Generation of Candidate Events and Patterns

Candidate events are extracted from sentences which contain at least one event verb and two entities. For extracting candidate events, we began by finding all event verbs in a sentence, and then we coupled all possible entity pairs for each event verb in a sentence. These are called *Candidate Events*. After that, we built patterns using arguments for each candidate event. We also relied on common English grammar for choosing candidate events.

3.3   Ranking Events and Patterns

We had to choose reliable events from the candidates. Thus, we ranked candidate events by the event score which is calculated by 3 measures. The first measure is co-occurrence information both between entities, and between an entity and a verb in an event. The second measure is dependency relations between them. The last measure is the score of the averaging patterns which are generated by a candidate event. Event score is modeled as:

$$Score(E) = [\alpha Cooccurrence + \beta Dependency\ Relation] \times \frac{\sum_i Score(P_i^E)}{|P^E|} \quad (1)$$

where α, β and γ are score which are calculated by empirical experiments and P^E means all patterns which are generated by an event E.

The pattern score($Score(P)$) is calculated as:

$$Score(P) = \frac{|\{E_j^P | \forall j, Score(E_j^P) > \delta\}|}{|E^P|} \quad (2)$$

where δ is a current averaging event score and E^P means all candidate events which are represented by a pattern P.

We can see that two equations [Equation 1] and [Equation 2] have an effect on each other. Thus we can rerank the candidate events by recalculating events score and patterns score iteratively. This iteration continues until the ranking of candidate events no longer changes.

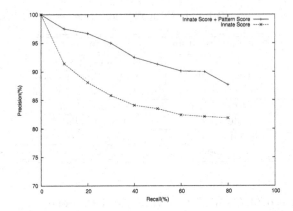

Fig. 3. Precision-Recall Graph for 241 Events

4   Experimental Results

We experimented in the GENIA corpora [5] which consist of 18,544 sentences. We selected 372 sentences which contained 241 events. Figure 3 shows the result of two experiments. One used pattern information, the other didn't. According to the graph, the precision of the experiment considering *pattern score* is higher than the other over all recall range.

5   Conclusions and Future Works

In this paper, we extracted reliable events from biomedical texts by an unsupervised method which extended patterns automatically. In the future, more experiments are required to do further analysis.

References

1. D. Proux: A pragmatic information extraction strategy for gathering data on genetic interactions. ISMB. **8** (2000) 279–285.
2. Y.S. Hwang: Weighted Probabilistic Sum Model based on Decision Tree Decomposition for Text Chunking. International Journal of Computer Processing of Oriental Languages. (2003) vol 16, no 1.
3. K.J. Lee, Y.S. Hwang, H.C. Rim: Two-Phase Biomedical NE Recognition based on SVMs. Proc.of the ACL 2003 Workshop on Natural Language Processing in Biomedicine. (2003) 33–40
4. K.M. Park: Grammatical Relation Analysis Using Support Vector Machine in Biotext. Proc. of the 15th Conference of Hangul and Korean Information Processing. (2003) 287–292
5. GENIA Corpus 3.0p: Available at http://www-tsujii.is.s.u-tokyo.ac.jp/genia/topics/Corpus/3.0/GENIA3.0p.intro.html

Thai Syllable-Based Information Extraction Using Hidden Markov Models

Lalita Narupiyakul[1], Calvin Thomas[1], Nick Cercone[1], and
Booncharoen Sirinaovakul[2]

[1] Faculty of Computer Science, Dalhousie University 6050 University Avenue,
Halifax, NS, CANADA B3H 1W5
{lalita, thomas,nick}@cs.dal.ca
[2] King Mongkut's University of Technology Thonburi 91 Pracha Uthit, Thungkru,
Bangkok, THAILAND 10140
boon@cpe.kmutt.ac.th

Abstract. Information Extraction (IE) is a method which analyzes the
information and retrieves significant segments or fields for insertion into
tables or databases by automatic extraction. In this paper, we employ a
statistical model for an IE system. Thai syllable-based information extraction using Hidden Markov Models (HMM) is our proposed method
for automated information extraction. In our system, we develop a non-
dictionary based method which requires a rule-based system for syllable
segmentation. We employ a Viterbi algorithm, which is a statistical system for learning/testing our corpus, and extract the required fields from
the information in corpus.

1 Introduction

In electronic communication systems, there are many ways to communicate or
send information to others using hi-tech digital devices. Sending printed information via telephone lines is a basic method of communication. Electronic mail
and webboard are the most popular communication tools. They are used to
send various kinds of information to people such as news, advertisements and
announcements. These information are broadcasted to subscribers. A tremen-
dous amount of information is sent via electronic documents directly to people.
Tools to manipulate this information are desirable. Therefore, information extraction (IE) is one of various methods proposed to analyze information and
retrieve significant segments or fields for insertion into tables or databases by
automatic extraction.

Developing IE in Thai is at a preliminary stage and there are a small number
of researchers working on Thai IE [1],[2]. For example, Sukhahuta [1] develops
information extraction strategies for Thai documents. His work is based on natural language techniques (grammar parsing, syntactic and concept analysis) to
extract information from a prepared template corpus. Information extraction
in Thai is difficult because Thai is distinguished from other languages including reading and writing structures. A characteristic of Thai written structures

A. Gelbukh (Ed.): CICLing 2004, LNCS 2945, pp. 537–546, 2004.
© Springer-Verlag Berlin Heidelberg 2004

is that no boundary separates words. Therefore Thai word segmentation is an important problem to work on natural language processing in Thai [3]. Furthermore, a Thai character cannot represent a word or a meaning like Chinese or Japanese. In Thai, a smallest unit which can represent a word or a meaning is a syllable. Based on various research [3],[4], syllable segmentation in Thai can be successful at high accuracy compared with Thai word segmentation. This is a reason why we develop Thai information extraction at the syllable level. Another reason is that we would like to develop our system without a dictionary, or use a non-dictionary based system.

In this paper, we apply syllable segmentation in the Thai language for our IE system using a housing advertisement corpus collected from a webboard. The necessary information that we intend to extract from this housing advertisement, is composed of 4 fields: number of bedrooms and bathrooms, type of house and location fields are also exhibited the objective of each advertisement. Our system is composed of two main processes; Thai syllable segmentation and a statistical IE system using a Hidden Markov Model (HMM). Because of no boundaries in Thai written strings, our system requires a method to separate the connected input string into small units. We employ Thai syllable segmentation using a Markov Chain[5]. The system separates the written string into syllable units. Then the system will send these syllables to the statistical IE system using HMM for training/testing the information and then extract the required fields from the corpus.

For the extraction technique, our work utilizes a HMM inspired from Freitag[6]. HMM is known as one of the most effective techniques for discrete and continuous information for various problems such as speech [7], and information retrieval[8]. The advantage of HMM for IE is no syntactic and semantic analysis is necessary. HMM can learn directly from original documents. The basic idea of HMM, related to Bayes's theorem, is a stochastic technique, which leads to good reliability. For the IE problem, researchers also prove that HMMs have been a successful approach making use of the wealth of efficient algorithms available, including Baum-Welch and Viterbi algorithm[9]. In the last section, we evaluate the performance of IE using HMM by precision, recall and F-measure.

2 Problems of Thai Syllable-Based IE Using HMMs

Generally, we obtain much information from electronic documents such as a webboard. Humans have difficulty to manage many advertisements, such as cancelling or updating the information. To support humans, IE can retrieve the important information from news or advertisements and transfer this information to special devices, such as organizer. In a syllable segmentation system, there is a problem which occurs because of the ambiguity of some words. Our segmentation process is based on a rule-based approach. Some distinct words are not amenable to rule processing.

Another significant problem when applying HMMs to information extraction is the selection of a state-transition model. This model describes the number of target, prefix and suffix states. Target states emit observables that the IE system should extract, prefix transition into targets and suffix trail targets. Primarily of interest is the number of prefix and suffix states since optimal values depend on the data. For example, considered the extraction of a type of houses. A simple model consists of one prefix state and one suffix state. Clearly, finding optimal models that correspond to the structure of natural language context is quite difficult.

3   Thai Syllable-Based IE Using HMM System

Our system follows two processes; Thai syllable segmentation and statistical information extraction. The syllable segmentation, which is a rule-based approach, is used to separate a Thai written string into syllable units while statistical information extraction employs the Viterbi algorithm to extraction the required fields or segmentations for our corpus.

3.1   Syllable Segmentation

Syllable segmentation includes two processes; syllable analysis and alternative selection. The syllable segmentation proceeds by initially preprocessing text to query the special words in the exception dictionary, which contains some special words. These words are the distinctive words; they are not amenable to rule processing, such as some loan words.

Syllable analysis is represented with a rule-based approach to find the the basic components of syllables. The analyzed system is separated into two elements: syllable rules[5] and the rule inference engine. Syllable rules gather the analysis rules of syllable components, composed of consonant rules, and syllable structure rules [5]. The function of these rules is to recognize the components of each syllable from the written strings. Thai syllable structures or components are composed of initial consonant (Ci), second initial consonant (Cc), vowel (Vw), tone (Tn) and final consonant (Cf) but tone, second initial consonant and final consonant are optional characters for Thai syllables. Thai syllable structures are shown in following pattern.

$$Syllable \Rightarrow Ci + [Cc] + Vw + [Tn] + [Cf]$$

The design of rules are defined as transition rules by every syllable structures or components in the right-hand side and mapping with the other structures on the other side. The rule inference, the second element, is the engine which controls searching rule. Rule inference starts by checking their factors in each character. The process runs using a left look-ahead parsing strategy. It scans an input string from left to right, looks up the suitable rule from syllable rule-base, and transforms the left-hand side of the input structure expression into another expression on the right-hand side as syllable components, and it will recurse until the end of input string.

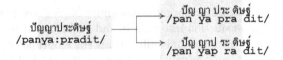

Fig. 1. The alternative selection for Thai syllable segmentation

To determine proper syllable segmentation, alternative selection process [5] selects the best output from the output alternatives given by the previous processes. In this process, we propose checking syllables used to determine syllable separation and decrease the ambiguity of syllable components. For example, a consonant may be the final consonant of the current syllable or the initial consonant of the next syllable, which is in accord with Thai text characteristics. Furthermore, our system does not include the entire dictionary when checking syllable separation and possible syllable components of Thai syllables, so we design syllable checking based on statistical properties, that is, as Markov chains [10] to determine suitable syllable components in Thai written strings. Consequently, the probabilistic model is applied in this process as weighted automata. We use a probabilistic finite state machine to model each word's pronunciation variations. The whole system is reported in [5]. The example in Fig. 1 can be pronounced in two ways. The probability, that each arc indicates how likely that path is to be taken. Following the syllable segmentation, the result will be sent to the statistical extraction system to retrieve the required fields.

3.2   The Statistical Extraction System

Our IE system employs the Viterbi algorithm[9] to extract the necessary fields. That is: type of houses, location, number of bedrooms and bathrooms. This system is composed of three main steps, namely data preparation, HMM using Viterbi algorithm, and testing with the Viterbi algorithm.

Data Preparation. This process will prepare the data or input from the housing advertisement corpus before it is sent to the HMM process. We load all advertisements and keep them in memory. For each advertisement, the process eliminates unnecessary tokens. It adjusts the abbreviations and address formats in the same pattern. Next, the process tags each syllable with number to represent prefix, target, suffix and unnecessary words. Finally, it will put tagging numbers in the temporary file to prepare the information for learning and testing. An example illustration is shown below;

 - 0 for word or token which is insignificant to extraction
 - 10, 11, 12, ..., 19 are prefix before words or a phrase and order by running number.
 - 20 is target or field as number of bedrooms.
 - 30 is target or field as number of bathrooms.

Target : Location
... ขาย 0 บ้าน 0 พร้อม 0 ที่ 10 ดิน 11 ถนน 12 แจ้ง 40 วัท 40 ทนะ 40 อยู่ 60 ใกล้ 61 ทาง 62 ด่วน 0 ...

Fig. 2. The example of temporary file for data preparation

- 40 is target or field as location
- 50 is target or field as type of houses
- 60, 61, 62, ..., 69 are suffix after words or a phrase and order by running number.

HMM Using Viterbi Algorithm. Efficient training of the Hidden Markov Model is available through use of the Expectation Maximization (EM) algorithm. HMMs learn by estimating the parameter model that best supports the training data, consisting of observables tagged with their state. The basic idea of HMM is based on state-transition with probability, and ideally a large training corpus is desired. In this system, we have two steps for HMM; learning and testing.

Statistical learning occurs via studying the training data, counting triples consisting of an observable W_i, its state V_i and the previous state V_{i-1} where i is the state number. The process learns initial state probabilities, state-emission probabilities (the probability of a particular word given a state) and state-transition probabilities (the probability of another state given a current state).

- Initial State Probability: $P(V_1)$
- State-Emission Probability: $P(W_i|V_i)$;
  (the probability of word W_i in state V_i)

$$P(W_i|V_i) = \frac{C(W_i, V_i)}{C(V_i + \varepsilon)} \tag{1}$$

$C(W_i, V_i)$ is observed count of word W_i within state V_i while $C(V_i)$ is total number of words in state V_i and ε represents "smoothing constant".
- State-Transition Probability: $P(V_i|V_{i-1})$;
  (the probability of state V_i from state V_{i-1})

$$P(V_i|V_{i-1}) = \frac{C(V_{i-1}, V_i)}{C(V_i)} \tag{2}$$

$C(V_{i-1}, V_i)$ is number of state transition V_{i-1} followed by V_i while $C(V_i)$ is total number of state-transition from state V_i

Finally, the probabilistic data of each entry is created using the observable, state and state-transition information it learns. For reasons of efficiency and accuracy, the log of entries is stored for use later in the Viterbi algorithm.

V₁	log(P(V₁))	Vᵢ₋₁	Vₙ	log(P(Vᵢ|Vᵢ₋₁))	Vᵢ	Wₙ	log(P(Wᵢ|Vᵢ))
0	-0.254892	0	0	-0.016074	0	กค	-7.829166
		0	10	-4.138589		กา	-8.927779
		10	11	0.000000		กาย	-8.927779
		11	12	0.000000		กาว	-8.927779
		⋮	⋮	⋮	⋮	⋮	⋮

Fig. 3. The example of learning probabilistic table

Testing with the Viterbi Algorithm. From the learning process, we will get the probabilistic data and we will get data that has already tagged each word from preprocessing and keep them on the temporary file. The testing process uses the Viterbi algorithm to find the most likely state sequence given particular text. This algorithm is one of the efficient algorithms for computing the most likely state sequence. This algorithm is defined as

$$\delta(t) = \max_{x_1 \ldots x_{t-1}} P(x_1 \ldots x_{t-1}, o_1 \ldots o_{t-1}, x_t = j|\mu) \tag{3}$$

$\delta(t)$ is the probability of the most likely state sequence at time t and o is the observation sequence while x is the state sequence. The Viterbi algorithm[11] is composed of three steps; initialization, induction, and termination, using dynamic programming to find the most probable path as follows:

The Viterbi Algorithm [11]

1. Initialization

$$\delta_j(t) = \pi_j, \qquad 1 \leq j \leq N \tag{4}$$

2. Induction

$$\delta_j(t+1) = \max_{1 \leq i \leq N} \delta_i(t) a_{ij} b_{ijo_t}, \qquad 1 \leq j \leq N \tag{5}$$

Store Backtrace

$$\psi_j(t+1) = \arg\max_{1 \leq i \leq N} \delta_i(t) a_{ij} b_{ijo_t}, \qquad 1 \leq j \leq N \tag{6}$$

3. Termination

$$\hat{X}_{T+1} = \arg\max_{1 \leq i \leq N} \delta_i(T+1) \tag{7}$$

$$\hat{X}_t = \psi_{\hat{X}_{t+1}}(t+1) \tag{8}$$

$$P(\hat{X}) = \max_{1 \leq i \leq N} \delta_i(T+1) \tag{9}$$

N is the number of states, a_{ij} is state transition probability and b_{ijo_t} is the symbol emission probability

Therefore, the result is the path corresponding to the state sequence that has the maximum probability. As stated earlier, efficiency and accuracy dictate the exploitation of the relationship between $P(A) \cdot P(B)$ and $\log(P(A)) + \log(P(B))$, where P(A) and P(B) are the probability of A and B, respectively. When attempting to maximize the state-sequence probabilities, not only are multiplications expensive, but accuracy is lost with every operation. Substituting additions for multiplications in the Viterbi algorithm and log of probabilities for actual probabilities, we realize cost savings and increased accuracy.

4   Evaluation and Experimental Results

Precision and recall are common evaluation measures. Precision is a measure of the proportion of selected items that the system got right. Recall is defined as the proportion of the target items that the system selected. F-measure is used to combine precision and recall in to a single measure of overall performance.

$$Precision = \frac{tp}{tp + fp} \tag{10}$$

$$Recall = \frac{tp}{tp + fn} \tag{11}$$

tp (true positives) are the cases that system selected right, fp (false positives) are the cases that system selected wrong and fn (false negative) are the cases that system failed to be selected.

$$F = \frac{1}{\alpha \frac{1}{p} + (1 - \alpha)\frac{1}{R}} \tag{12}$$

P is precision, R is recall and is a factor which determines the weighting of precision and recall. Basically, a value of $\alpha = 0.5$ is often chosen for equal weighting of P and R.

In preliminary work, our training and testing corpus consisted of housing advertisements. Our training and testing corpus consisted of 200 housing advertisements. The training and testing are performed for each field. We wish to extract required fields, since a different optimal model is expected for each field. The number of prefix, target and suffix states for each field is dependent on the environment of the extracted field. Therefore, we experiment by setting various numbers of prefix, target and suffix states and report precision, recall and F-measure in Fig. 4 for "Type of houses" field and Fig. 5 for "number of bathrooms" field. The results are averaged over 4-fold cross-validation of the training data.

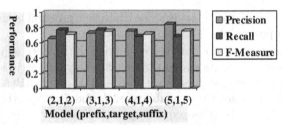

Performance	Model (prefix,target,suffix)			
	(2,1,2)	(3,1,3)	(4,1,4)	(5,1,5)
Precision	0.66	0.73	0.75	0.84
Recall	0.77	0.77	0.68	0.68
F-Measure	0.71	0.74	0.71	0.75

Fig. 4. The experimental results of IE using HMM with different number of prefixes, target and suffixes on "type of house" field

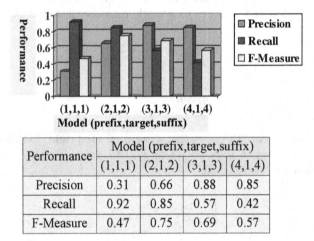

Performance	Model (prefix,target,suffix)			
	(1,1,1)	(2,1,2)	(3,1,3)	(4,1,4)
Precision	0.31	0.66	0.88	0.85
Recall	0.92	0.85	0.57	0.42
F-Measure	0.47	0.75	0.69	0.57

Fig. 5. The experimental results of IE using HMM with different number of prefixes, target and suffixes on "number of bathrooms" filed

5   Discussion and Concluding Remarks

From Fig. 4 and 5, the highest precision shows 84% with 5 prefixes and 5 suffixes for "type of houses" field while the highest precision shows 88% with 3 prefixes and 3 suffixes for "number of bathrooms" field. Based on the experiment, we observe that assigning the number of prefixes and suffixes affects the performance of the HMM. For example, if we increase the number of prefixes and suffixes for some fields, such as number of bathrooms, the accuracy of the experimental results will decrease. The process generates too many transition states to analyze environments of extracted fields.

Moreover, the state-transition models will contaminate with noise or unnecessary information and the extraction system will bias because of noise. If we assign a small number of prefixes and suffixes for some fields, such as types of house. The process will have too few transition states to analyze the environment of the field. Therefore, the state-transition models may not cover all necessary information to predict the extracted field. However, we evaluate our model with the small dataset which is the preliminary testing. HMM shows good performance and the experimental results are satisfactory. HMM are very flexible to adapt to the information extraction problem.

In this paper, we develop Thai syllable-based information extraction using HMM for housing advertisement from a webboard. Our system has two main parts; syllable segmentation and statistical IE system which composed of data preparation, HMM using Viterbi algorithm and evaluation process. The system segments the Thai written string to syllable units. Then the IE system learns a set of tagged housing advertisement and tests with another set of these advertisements. The experimental results report precision, recall, and F-measure. We can conclude satisfactory results and its performance of Thai syllable-based IE system is also fine for our work. In future work, we plan to perform an evaluation for large datasets. We expect that syllable-based information extraction using HMM could be one of the efficient methods to solve the information extraction problem in Thai.

Acknowledgements. This work is supported by NSERC, Canada and Royal Golden Jubilee Ph.D. program, Thailand Research Fund, Thailand.

References

1. Sukhahuta R., Smith D.: Information Extraction Strategies for Thai Documents: International Journal of Computer Processing of Oriental Languages, Vol. 14 No. 2 (2001) 153–172.
2. Sornlertlamvanich V., Potipiti T., Charoenporn T.: Automatic Corpus-based Thai Word Extraction with the C4.5 Learning Algorithm: Proceedings of the 18th International Conference on Computational Linguistics (COLING2000), Saarbrucken, Germany, July-August (2000) 802–807.
3. Tarsaku P., Sornlertlamvanich V., Thongpresert R.: Thai Grapheme-to-Phoneme Using Probabilistic GLR Parser: Proceeding of Eurospeech 2001, Aalborg, Denmark, September (2001)
4. Chotimongkol A., Black A.: Statistcally Trained orthographic to sound models for Thai: Proceeding of ICSLP 2000, Beijing, China (2000)
5. Narupiyakul L., Khumya A., Sirinaovakul B.: Syllable Segmentation by Using Markov Chains: 2001 International Symposium on Communications and Information Technology (ISCIT' 2001), November 14–16, Chiang Mai, Thailand (2001)
6. Freitag D., McCallum A.: Information extraction with HMM structures learned by stochastic optimization: Proceedings of AAAI-2000, (2000)

7. Renals S., Morgan N., Bourlard H., Cohen M., Franco H.: Connectionist Probability Estimators in HMM Speech Recognition: IEEE Transactions Speech and Audio Processing (1993)

8. Miller D.R., Leek T., Schwartz R.M.: A hidden Markov model information retrieval system, Proceedings of SIGIR-99: 22nd ACM International Conference on Research and Development in Information Retrieval, Berkeley, US, (1999) 214–221

9. Forney, G.D.: The Viterbi algorithm: Proceeding of IEEE 61(3) (1973) 268–278

10. Huang X., Acero A., Han H.W.: Spoken Language Processing: A Guide to Theory, Algorithm, and System Development: Prentice-Hall, New Jersy, USA, (2001) 378–380.

11. Manning C., Schütze H.: Foundations of Statistical Natural Language Processing: MIT Press. Cambridge, MA: May (1999) 332–333

The Impact of Enriched Linguistic Annotation
on the Performance of Extracting Relation Triples

Sanghee Kim, Paul Lewis, and Kirk Martinez

Intelligence, Agents, MultiMedia Group, Department of Electronics and Computer Science,
University of Southampton, U.K.
{sk,phl,km}@ecs.soton.ac.uk

Abstract. A relation extraction system recognises pre-defined relation types between two identified entities from natural language documents. It is important for a task of automatically locating missing instances in knowledge base where the instance is represented as a triple ('entity – relation – entity'). A relation entry specifies a set of rules associated with the syntactic and semantic conditions under which appropriate relations would be extracted. Manually creating such rules requires knowledge from information experts and moreover, it is a time-consuming and error-prone task when the input sentences have little consistency in terms of structures and vocabularies. In this paper, we present an approach for applying a symbolic learning algorithm to sentences in order to automatically induce the extraction rules which then successfully classify a new sentence. The proposed approach takes into account semantic attributes (e.g., semantically close words and named-entities) in generalising common patterns among the sentences which enable the system to cope better with syntactically different but semantically similar sentences. Not only does this increase the number of relations extracted, but it also improves the accuracy in extracting relations by adding features which might not be discovered only with syntactic analysis. Experimental results show that this approach is effective on the sentences of the Web documents obtaining 17% higher precision and 34% higher recall values.

Keywords: relation extraction, information extraction, inductive logic programming

1 Introduction

When organisations (e.g. 'museum' or 'gallery') hold an immense quantity of information in the formats of electronic documents or databases, missing values for some data can occur. Examples are the names of people who participated in the creation of an art work or historical events which influenced the artists. To extract such missing values, we might need to rely on additional information sources, like the Web. The Web exists as the largest information repository and new data are continuously added. The observation that most of the Web documents are free-texts in various structures and vocabularies emphasizes the importance of techniques that can extract a piece of information of interest.

A. Gelbukh (Ed.): CICLing 2004, LNCS 2945, pp. 547–558, 2004.
© Springer-Verlag Berlin Heidelberg 2004

Information extraction (IE) systems aims to provide easy access to natural language documents by organising data into pre-defined named-entity types and relations. Entities can be the name of 'person' or 'organisation' and 'location_of' is an example relation that defines geographical information between two entities. IE systems can rely on extraction rules created from example documents by inducing regular patterns among the examples based on machine learning and/or natural language techniques [4,17]. The accuracy of entity recognition depends on the nature of entity type, for example, 'painting' is more difficult to learn than 'person' since a 'painting' has less distinctive attributes differentiating it from other types. When it is hard to discover consistent patterns among the documents (e.g. Web pages), using gazetteers for a pattern-based matching can be an alternative [6]. With respect to end-users efforts, it does not require any extra annotations unless new types of entities are to be learned. One of the shortcomings this approach is that most entities are pre-defined with specific types such that new entities may not be easily identified.

The task of relation extraction is to extract pre-defined relation types between two identified entities. Many IE systems mainly focus on recognising named-entities (e.g. GATE [6]) and recent experimental results showed that the performance could reach over 80% F-measure [10]. Whereas some systems try to extract relations, the number of relation types is rather small or no relations are extracted [2]. For example, whereas GATE can recognize "*Museum France*" as a type of "*organization*", but it does not extract the fact that the "*Museum France*" holds a masterpiece of "*Courbet*". Rather than treating the tasks of entity recognition and relation extraction separately, we regard the relation learning as depending on the entity identifications which provide the conditions under which relations can be extracted. Approaches like [4,18] learn rules for relation extraction over examples annotated by end-users. When the number of relations exceeds dozens, it is infeasible to ask end-users to provide such examples since the users need to annotate a large number of documents.

The relation extraction system tends to achieve a reasonable performance when tested with semi-structured texts or when relations to be learned have distinctive features [18]. For example, 'date_of_birth' that holds the date of when a 'Person' was born, is easier than that of 'was_used_for' which specifies explanations why the art object is important, or its influence on other objects. One of reasons is that there are more ways of describing the latter relation such that it is hard to discover common patterns among examples collected. It is also feasible that more efforts are required to gather examples for such relations. Applying machine learning techniques to derive the distinctive features automatically hence supports a reduction in human efforts to provide such services, or examples. Inducing rules by mining common attributes of the given examples can be supported by using inductive logic programming (ILP), which is a supervised learning system [12]. ILP enables the learner to make use of background knowledge provided and allows the input data to be represented as a Prolog style. Using the ILP to learn the relation extraction rules hence is suitable for our task.

Semantic variations among the Web documents are considerable since authors use their own styles and vocabularies defining similar statements. Two sentences might be semantically interchangeable even though they share few similar syntactic structures. It is preferred to extract multiple instances for certain types of relations meaning that such semantic variations needed to be considered in generating extraction rules. For example, extending the rules with semantically close terms can be of use.

In this paper, we describe Ontotriple, a semantic-oriented machine learning algorithm that creates rules for relation extractions. The types of relations considered here are the ones defined across different syntactic functions (e.g. 'noun', 'verb') such that semantic analysis is required in extracting such relations. Since the relations extracted are not limited in the descriptions of attributes, the number of relations extracted will be increased. As a supervised learning, Ontotriple needs a set of examples to be marked-up according to the algorithm used. In an effort to reduce workloads on locating and manually annotating the dataset, we use the Web for downloading the examples, and apply a natural language processing technique to automatically annotate them with the algorithm specifications. To cope with semantic variations among the documents, WordNet [11] is used for comparing similarity between two sentences. We evaluate Ontotriple with a small text dataset, and the experiment shows considerably improved performance compared to a simple bag-of-word approach which converts a document into a list of words. This paper is organized as follows: in Section 2, reviews of the related work are given; Section 3 describes Ontotriple beginning with an introduction to ILP on which Ontotriple is based, and discusses how to encode texts appropriate for mining. An experimental result is reported in Section 4 followed by conclusions and directions for future work in Section 5.

2 Related Work

Roth presented a probabilistic method for recognising both entities and relations together [15]. The method measures the inter-dependency between entities and relations and uses them to restrain the conditions under which entities are extractable given relations and vice versa. Local classifiers for separately identifying entities and relations are first calculated. Global inferences are derived from the local classifiers by taking the outputs in conditional probabilities as inputs for determining the most appropriate types. An evaluation with test documents showed over 80% accuracy on entities and a minimum 60% on relations. However, the computational resources for generating such probabilities are generally intractable.

The use of ILP to learn the extraction rules in texts has been attempted in [1, 9, 13]. [9] developed a system that classified e-mail messages into either interesting or non-interesting ones after learning user preferences from e-mail messages read. Message contents were converted into attribute-value pairs describing under which conditions the users are interested in reading a new message. ILP was appropriate for this task since it discovered inter-relatedness among the attributes which were often difficult to induce with statistical methods (e.g. a naïve Bayesian probability). [1] applied ILP to learn relation extraction rules where associated entities are symbols (e.g., 'high', 'low'). It is more concerned with discovering hidden descriptions of entity attributes than creating binary relations between two entities which we are interested in. For example, in the sentence "*Higher levels of CO2 can clearly make plants grow better*", the fact that CO_2 has 'high' level can be understood by deducing certain hidden descriptions whereas Ontotriple has interests in identifying causal relations between CO_2 and plants in the sentence. [13] used Progol to learn user preferences concerning WWW pages. Users rated the pages as either interesting or uninteresting when they browsed them, and then Progol generated rules for describing under which conditions users make decisions concerning these classifications. Experimental results showed that Progol achieved a higher or comparable performance to human defined rules.

REES, developed by [3] is a lexicon-driven relation extraction system aiming at identifying a large number of event-related relations. Similarly to the approach here, it depends on a verb for locating an event-denoting clue and uses a pre-defined template which specifies the syntactic and semantic restrictions on the verb's arguments. Ontotriple aims at generating the template automatically from the collected examples instead of relying on knowledge experts or end-users. Craven et al. implemented the WEBKB project, which aimed to build a knowledge base of Web pages by identifying hidden relationships, which may exist in the pages represented by words and hyperlink definitions [5]. An example of the relations is 'instructors_of(A,B)' which discovers a relationship between course page (A) and instructor's homepage (B) in terms of hyperlink definition. Its main task was to classify Web pages into pre-defined six categories according to the rules created by a rule learning algorithm. To resolve the conflicting predictions that resulted from multi-category problems, a confidence value for each generated rule was computed and compared to other predictions in order to decide which class was assigned.

Ontotriple uses an existing named-entity recogniser (GATE) and a lexical database (WordNet [11]) for annotating an entity with pre-defined types. Similarly to the relation extraction, applying machine learning algorithms to induce entity recognition rules has been proposed. [7] uses SRV, a token-basis general-specific rule learning algorithm for online texts. It makes use of grammatical inferences for generating pattern-based extraction rules appropriate for HTML structures. The evaluation shows lower performance of the multiple-value (e.g. project members) instantiations compared to that of single-value (e.g. project title) entities implying that the former is harder to extract. [4] uses a supervised wrapper induction system that generalizes extraction rules based on a bottom-up approach [4]. The generalization starts with word string features suitable for highly structured texts and gradually adds linguistic attributes to induce more appropriate patterns. The generated rules are corrected from mislabeled tags by inducing correct tag positions from a corpus provided. This correction step is one of contributions that enables the algorithm to show a higher performance compared to other existing entity rule induction systems (e.g. SRV).

3   Ontotriple

3.1   Relation Extraction

Ontotriple extracts pre-defined binary relations between two identified entities in a natural language document. The relation is represented as a triple, i.e. $predicate(e_1, e_2)$, where e_1, e_2 are entities. Associated entities restrict the types of arguments to be linked with the predicate. The relation extraction is dependent on the availability of named entities in that mislabelled entities can decrease the number of relations correctly identified. A relation can be implicitly implied in a phrase, for example, [2] extracts an 'employee_of' relation from the phrase of '*an analyst at ING Barrings*', where the analyst is a person type and 'ING Barrings' is an organisation. In this paper, we are interested in relations defined in a sentence-level. An example is

'*John works for ING Barrings*', where the verb 'work' links two entities ('John' and 'ING Barrings') with 'work_for' relation. As such, it is necessary to analyse the sentence both from syntactic and semantic perspectives.

There can be various ways of mapping between the structures of sentence to its predicate-argument relations. For example, in a sentence of '*His final death happened in 1820*', noun phrases (i.e. His final death) in a subject maps to the relation of 'date_of_death'. In this paper, we are interested in the relation that can be extracted from a verb. A verb as the central organizer of a sentence posits a core element in recognizing relations between entities. It asserts something about the subject of a sentence for asserting additional information or expresses actions, events, or states of being. For example, in the sentence '*John died on 6th Jan 1900*', the verb 'died' describes an existential status of a person 'John'. As an object, '6th Jan 1900' modifies the verb giving an additional fact of the death event. As such, the verb 'died' acts as a linking word between two identified entities ('John'-person, '6th Jan 1900'-date) and conveys a writer's intention of making the statement. Ontotriple relates the verb to pre-defined relations by considering conditions defined in the relation entry. According to WordNet definitions, each relation is described with a corresponding verb and a sense entry. A word can have multiple meanings (i.e. senses) and it is important to know in which sense the word is used in a given sentence when the semantically close words are collected. Including similar verbs has a purpose of reducing semantic variations between the defined verb and a verb in a given sentence, so that it can increase the number of relations extracted. We rely on Resnik's approach that defines the similarity between two concepts based on the information content of their least common subsumer in a semantic network [14].

3.2 Progol: Inductive Logic Programming

Inducing rules from given examples can be supported by the inductive logic programming technique. ILP can be defined as the intersection of machine learning and logic programming. Contrasted with other learning methods (e.g. Decision Trees), by using computational logic as the representational mechanisms, ILP can learn complex, structured, or recursive descriptions and generate the outputs in first-order logic. A system is said to learn from E (formed as positive or negative) and background knowledge B by constructing a set of hypotheses that can explain new examples. The positive examples are the facts that are true for task T while the negative examples are the facts that should be excluded from the set of hypotheses.

Progol is one of the ILP systems and selects one positive example, constructs the most specific clause and this becomes a search space for the hypotheses [12]. A compression measure is used to compare hypotheses, and is computed by counting the number of positive examples explained, the number of negative examples incorrectly explained, and the number of further atoms to complete the clause. If the hypothesis is confirmed, then Progol looks at the remaining positive examples, and deletes redundant ones. Progol continues until there are no more positive examples left. Input features in the background knowledge are associated with one of three 'mode-type' declarations. '+A' implies that the literal A is an input type in the hypothesis created, '-A' specifying that A is an output variable, and '#A' defines that the literal A is a constant type. This mode type is of use to connect two clauses by allowing one clause to take the output of the other clause as an input.

Table 1. Clauses used for relation learning by Progol

Annotation	Progol clause
Common attributes	has_word(+sentence,-word). has_words(+sentence,-words). consist_of(+words,-word).
Semantic feature	has_verb(+sentence,#verb) has_verbtense(+sentence,#verb,#tense) has_verbmood(+sentence,#verb,#mood) has_subject_word(+sentense,#word) has_subject_words(+subject,#words) has_object_words(+sentence,#words) has_object_word(+sentence,#word)
Named entity	has_entitytype(+sentence,+words,#type) has_gender(+sentence,+words,#gender)
Postag	has_postag(+sentence,+word,#postag). has_postagtype(+sentence,#postype) has_subject_pos(+subject,#postag) has_object_pos(+sentence,#postag)
Word sequence	has_prev(+sentence,+word,#word) has_prevs(+sentence,+words,#words) has_next(+sentence,+word,#word) has_nexts(+sentence,+words,#words)
Word sequence & Postag	has_prev_postag(+sentence,+postag,#postag) has_next_postag(+sentence,+postag,#postag)
Semantic feature & named entity	has_object_type(+sentence,#type) has_subject_type(+sentence,#type)
Semantic feature & Postag	has_subject_pos(+sentence,#postag) has_subject_postype(+sentence,#postype) has_object_pos(+sentence,#postag),has_object_postype(+sentence,#postype)

Since a generalisation is only based on the selected clauses, decisions on how to represent these or what to select normally influence the results. For instance, we have experimented with other representations, and in one of the cases a single clause was tested. It took a long time to construct hypotheses with these complex clauses, and moreover, it required a large number of examples. As such, each relation is represented as simply as possible in a Prolog style. The target clause to be learned is prediction (A,B), where B is the predicted relation entry with which the sentence A is to be associated, e.g. prediction(sentence1, 'place_of_birth'). Each sentence is represented with clauses as described in Table 1.

The common attributes in table 1 are the lists of a single word or words that correspond to the identified entity types. For example, 'Diego Rodriguez' is converted into 'has_words(sen1,'Diego Rodriguez')', 'has_word('Diego')' and 'has_word ('Rodriguez')'. It is of use when a concept is referred with different names, as in the case when a person's full name is used first and the first name is cited afterwards. Semantic feature contains clauses about 'verb', 'subject', and 'object' including temporal data of the verb (e.g. 'past', 'present') as well as the way the sentence is to be voiced (e.g. 'active/passive'). Named entities encode the identified entities with available gender information (e.g. 'male/female'). As a result of syntactic analysis, a word is associated with Pos-tagging and in order to reduce the influence of mistagging on relation extraction, 'has_postagtype(+sentence,#postype)' is used for grouping sub-categories of nouns into one type, e.g. 'p-noun' for NNPX, NNPS, NNP. The word sequence defines the ordering of a single word and words. Some annotations are combined in order to test if the combination improves the prediction result. For example, the row denoted as 'Word sequence & postag' in table 1 combines the annotations of 'word sequence' and of 'postag' as well as two clauses specially added to this relation, i.e. 'has_prev_postag(+sentence,+postag,#postag), has_next_postag(+sentence,+postag,#postag).

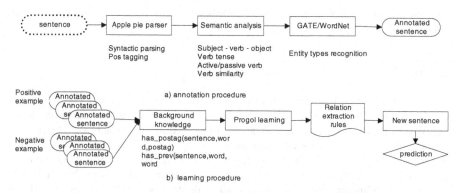

Fig. 1. The procedure for learning relation extractions with Ontotriple

Figure 1 shows the overall procedure of 'Ontotriple', divided into annotation and learning steps. 'Ontotriple' uses the Apple Pie Parser [16] for a syntactic analysis and parts of the semantic analysis tools used in the Artequakt project [8]. Diagram (a) shows the procedure of annotating a sentence through syntactic, semantic and named-entity analysis. With regard to named-entity recognition, Ontotriple uses GATE and WordNet. GATE provides four different types of entities (i.e. 'person', 'orgranisation', 'date', 'location') and a new type can be recognized if the gazetteers are updated with this information or corresponding extraction rules are created. A diagram (b) in Fig. 1 shows that the background knowledge is constructed from the features of the annotated sentences, and extraction rules are generated by the Progol. The rules then are applied to a new sentence to make a prediction of which relations are most appropriate to be associated with.

4 Experiment

This experiment tests the effectiveness of the proposed approach in identifying relations in natural language documents. It evaluates how automatically generated rules by Ontotriple successfully assign appropriate relations to new sentences. Two used measurements are precision and recall. Precision is the proportion of the correctly predicted relations by Ontotriple to the total number of relations predicted. Recall is the proportion of the number of the correctly predicted relations to the total number of correct relations. A contribution is summarised in the following. Ontotriple is capable of extracting relations from a sentence-level unit without restricting the relations to be defined in phrases. Since it can identify relations between syntactic tags which might not be feasible with phrase analysis, more various types of relations can be identified. For example, a relation like 'depict_person' is easily extractable in the sentence *'The exterior of the altar depicts Jodocus Vijdt, the donor'* by recognizing the main verb and its meanings. Ontotriple increases the number of the correctly extracted relations by exploring the idea of semantic closeness between a pre-defined verb and a verb in a given sentence. In addition, Ontotriple reduces the effort of experts in manually annotating extraction rules which can be a time-consuming and difficult task. The performance of Ontotriple is compared to that of a baseline which is encoded with a list of words occurring without taking into account either their syntactic roles or semantic meanings.

4.1 Dataset

Supervised learning requires a set of examples to be prepared according to its specifications. The lack of easily accessible datasets restrains the algorithm to be easily applied to new domains. In an effort to reduce workloads due to manual annotations, we used the Web to automatically provide both training and testing documents. That is, one Web site is mined for training, and then we apply the rules generated to a similar site to the one for training. The Web Museum site (http://www.ibiblio.org/wm/about/) has a short biography of some of artists and this site is being maintained well, therefore a dataset was created based on this site. A total of 166 pages were retrieved and downloaded. Each page was analysed following the annotation steps described in section 3.2. It took over two hours to annotate the sentences. Table 2 shows the relation definitions evaluated in this experiment. 'place_of_birth' is about where a person is born, 'work_in' relates to places where a person did/does work, 'work_as' similarly refers to employee information of a person, and 'represent_person' specifies a subject person that a specific painting is about. Currently, the named-entity recognizer used is not able to extract 'painting' type so that we examined the sentences collected in order to annotate the painting type manually.

As described in section 3.1, to cope with semantic variations, semantic similarity between a target verb in Table 2 and a verb in a given sentence is measured and if it exceeds a similarity value (set as 6.0 for this experiment), the sentence is collected. For example, a sentence '*Expressing human misery, the paintings portray blind figures, beggars, alcoholics*' is matched with a predicate, 'represent_person' since the similarity between 'represent (sense '9') and 'portray' is computed as over 7.0.

Progol induces rules over positive and negative examples, and has an option of running only on positive examples (see details in section 3.2). Whereas this option is of use when it is difficult to supply the negative examples, we found that it took a long time to construct the rules with positive examples only and moreover it required a large number of examples. Hence, in this experiment, Progol learns with both positive and negative examples.

A sentence was entered into a training example if the sentence has a main verb corresponding to the verb classes in Table 2. For two aims, we manually examined the sentences collected. First, we removed sentences which are duplicate, or inappropriate for training. It includes sentences either parsed inaccurately by Apple pie parser or associated with incorrect named-entities. The misclassifications of subject-verb-object identification also cause the sentences to be removed. Secondly, we selected sentences as negative examples when verbs were matched with one of the verbs in Table 2 but have different WordNet senses. For example, a sentence, '*Leonardo was the illegitimate son of a local lawyer (employee) in the small town of Vinci (place) in the Tuscan region*', is a negative example both for 'Work_in' and 'Work_as' relations. The reason is that whereas 'be' is one of synonyms of 'work' (sense 4), here it is a linking verb that complements the subject ('Leonardo') as described in the object, irrelevant to the 'work' information.

Table 2. A relation entry specifying the details of triples used for the experiment

Verb	WordNet sense	Predicate	Entity	Entity
Bear	2	Place_of_birth	Person	Place
Work	4	Work_in	Person	Place
		Work_as	Person	Employment
Represent	9	Represent_person	Painting	Person

Each annotation described in Table 1 was tried separately with Progol. The following shows examples of generated rules specifying under which conditions a new sentence would be assigned as 'work_as' relation. The first example defines that if a sentence has a word pos-tagged as 'NN' (singular noun) in the object and the sentence has 'a' (an article) as a previous word, then the 'work_as' relation is extractable. In the second example, if a subject has a word tagged as 'noun' and if a word tagged as 'DT' occurred in an object, then the sentence is predicted as related to 'work_as'. The third example specifies that if a sentence has an entity tagged as 'job' and if a 'DT' tagged word occurred in an object, then the sentence is related to 'work_as' relation.

```
prediction(A,workas) :- has_word(A,B), has_prev(A,B,a), has_object_pos(A,'NN').
prediction(A, workas) :- has_subject_postype(A,'noun'), has_object_pos(A,'DT').
prediction(A, workas) :- has_words(A,B), has_entitytype(A,B,'Job'), has_object_pos(A,'DT').
```

4.2 Results

To evaluate the rules generated above, testing documents were downloaded from a Web site called 'A virtual art museum' (http://cgfa.sunsite.dk/) where a list of artist information is retrieval. A total of 88 pages were selected. Negative examples were sorted in the same way as the training examples. A total of 102 ('place_of_birth' (37), 'work_in' (19), 'work_as' (23), 'represent_person' (23)) sentences were used for this evaluation. Table 3 summarizes precision and recall values both of Ontotriple and the baseline. The baseline used only 'has_word(+sentence,#word)' clause, which defines a list of word occurred in the sentence for rule generations. The precision and recall for Ontotriple was the highest value among the predictions made by the five different relation clauses.

Table 3. Precision and recall values comparing the performance of Ontotriple to that of baseline

Relation	Ontotriple		Baseline	
	Precision	recall	Precision	Recall
Place_of_birth	1	0.97	1	0.91
Work_in	0.67	0.75	0.11	0.25
Work_as	1	0.89	1	0.38
Represent_place	0.89	0.82	0.75	0.55
Average	0.89	0.86	0.72	0.52

Table 4. Precision and recall values for the attributes used by Ontotriple

	Annotation	Place_of_birth	Work_in	Work_as	Represent_place
precision	SF	1	0.33	1	0.47
	NE	1	0.57	1	0.78
	WS & postag	1	0.27	1	0.75
	SF & NE	1	0.67	1	0.53
	SF & postag	1	0.25	0.88	0.89
recall	SF	0.88	0.5	0.28	0.73
	NE	0.97	1	0.89	0.64
	WS & postag	1	0.75	0.78	0.55
	SF & NE	0.85	1	0.89	0.82
	SF & postag	1	0.5	0.78	0.73

It is noticeable that the recall value of the baseline was considerably lower than that of Ontotriple except for the 'place_of_birth' relation in which only little difference was observed. On average, Ontotriple obtained 17% higher precision and 34% higher recall. The difference of the precision between Ontotriple and the baseline is most evident for the 'work_in' relation. This relation extracts the description that a person works/worked in a specific location. It is feasible to have erroneous rules with the baseline since analyzing the sentence only in the perspective of word occurrence is not sufficient to cope with sentences in various formats. Taking into account the following two examples, '*From 1652 Alonso worked mainly in Granada, where he designed the façade of the cathedral (1667)*' (positive sentence), '*During the 1930s he worked in the manner of the Regionalists*' (negative sentence), we can infer that the entity types of the direct object syntax are of use in differentiating the positive example from the negative one. Table 4 shows the detailed performance results of different types of attributes used by Ontotriple. It uses symbols, i.e. SF (semantic feature), NE (named entity), WS (word sequence).

It is difficult to conclude which annotation performs best across the relations evaluated. For the 'work_in' predicate, using both semantic feature and named entity produces the highest precision and recall values. However, this combination shows lower performance when it is applied to the 'represent_place' relation. This observation is though not surprising since each relation is best characterized with different attributes. For example, the word which pos-tagged with 'IN' (e.g. 'as') is of great use in identifying 'work_as' relation, whereas it is of little use for 'work_in' relation (e.g. 'in') since not only the 'in' word refers to a location, but it also relates to 'style' or 'manner' information. This confirms that it is advantageous to learn rules separately for each relation in order to discover the best strategy.

5 Conclusions and Future Work

We presented an overview of 'Ontotriple' that automatically generates the rules of relation extraction from examples and applies them to classify a new sentence. Ontotriple falls into a supervised learning system and requires a set of examples to be annotated according to the attribute-value pairs defined. A manual annotation is limited in that an expert intervention is needed so that the portability of the approach can be decreased. Ontotriple uses the Web as a repository of trainable examples and applies natural language techniques to automatically construct the examples. Since there could be errors either in syntactic or semantic understanding including named-entity recognition, human intervention is needed in order to correct the mistaggings. Syntactic functions as well as morphological features and named-entities are used for generalising common patterns. The evaluation shows a higher accuracy of Ontotriple compared to the baseline which models a sentence without considering any semantic or syntactic features confirming the benefits of adding more linguistic knowledge.

We examined a few issues for further improvement of the proposed approach that could be made in the future. Currently, misclassified pos-taggings or entities are manually corrected in order to use them for training. Similarly to the approach by [4], it might be of use to explore the idea of the 'correct' procedure that re-applies Progol to the generated rules in order to correct mislabeled tags. In Ontotriple, a relation is assigned as a result of classifying a verb in a given sentence into pre-defined verb classes. It is based on the assumption that a verb acts as a core element for conveying the intended statement of a sentence by linking entities. It implies that a relation can be extracted by identifying two entities that are linked by the verb. This is the reason why we collected semantically close sentences by tracing the synonyms of the verb used. However, we observed that there are semantically similar sentences which can not be located by comparing the similarity between the two verbs mentioned. For these sentences, the use of other features, like words in the object tag for measuring similarity might be of use.

Acknowledgements. The authors wish to thank the EU for support through the SCULPTEUR project under grant number IST-2001-35372. They are also grateful to their collaborators on the project for many useful discussions, use of data and valuable help and advice. We also thank S. Banerjee and T. Pedensen for software implementing Resnik's similarity measurement approach.

References

[1] Aitken, J. S.: Learning information extraction rules: An inductive logic programming approach, Proc. of European Conf. on Artificial Intelligence ECAI, France, (2002), 335–359

[2] Aone, C., Halverson, L., Hampton, T., Ramos-Santacruz, M.: SRA: Description of the IE system used for MUC-7, MUC-7, (1998)

[3] Aone, C. , Ramos-Santacruz, M.: REES: A Large-Scale Relation and Event Extraction System, Proc. of the 6th Applied Natural Language Processing Conference, U.S.A, (2000), 76–83

[4] Ciravegna, F.: Adaptive Information Extraction from Text by Rule Induction and Generalisation, Proc. 17th Int. Joint Conf. on Artificial Intelligence, Seattle,(2001)

[5] Craven, M., DiPasquo, D., Freitag, D., McCallum, A., Mitchell, T., Nigam, K., Slattery, S.: Learning to Extract Symbolic Knowledge from the World Wide Web, In Technical report, Carnegie Mellon University, U.S.A, CMU-CS-98-122,1998

[6] Cunningham, H., Maynard, D., Bontcheva, K., and Tablan, V.: GATE: a framework and graphical development environment for robust NLP tools and applications. Proc. of the 40th Anniversary Meeting of the Association for Computational Linguistics, Philadelphia, USA, (2002), 168–175

[7]   Freitag, D.: Information Extraction from HTML: Application of a General Machine Learning Approach, Proc. AAAI 98, (1998), 517–523

[8]   Kim, S., Alani, H., Hall, W., Lewis, P.H., Millard, D.E., Shadbolt, N.R., Weal, M.W.: Artequakt: Generating Tailored Biographies with Automatically Annotated Fragments from the Web, Proc. of the Workshop on the Semantic Authoring, Annotation & Knowledge Markup in the 15th European Con. on Artificial Intelligence, France, (2002), 1–6

[9]   Kim, S., Hall, W., Keane, A.: Natural Language Processing for Expertise Modelling in E-mail Communication, Proc. of the 3rd Int. Con. On Intelligent Data Engineering and Automated Reasoning, England, (2002), 161–166

[10] Marsh, E., Perzanowski, D.: MUC-7 Evaluation of IE Technology: Overview of Results, available at http://www.itl.nist.gov/iaui/894.02/related_projects/muc/index.html, (1998)

[11] Miller, G.A., Beckwith, R. , Fellbaum, C., Gross, D. ., Miller, K.: Introduction to wordnet: An on-line lexical database. Technical report, University of Princeton, U.S.A.,(1993)

[12] Muggleton, S.: Inverse entailment and Progol, New Generation Computing, 13, (1995), 245–286

[13] Parson, R. and Muggleton, S.: An experiment with browsers that learn, In K. Furukawa, D. Michie and S. Muggleton (Eds.), Machine Intelligence, 15, Oxford University Press, (1998)

[14] Resnik, P.: Using Information Content to Evaluate Semantic Similarity in Taxonomy, Proc. of the 14th Int. Joint Con. On Artificial Intelligence, (1995), 448–453

[15] Roth, D. , Yih, W. T.: Probabilistic reasoning for entity & relation recognition, In COLING'02, (2002).

[16] Sekine, S., Grishman, R.: A corpus-based probabilistic grammar with only two non-terminals, Proc. of the 1st International Workshop on Multimedia annotation, Japan, (2001)

[17] Staab, S., Maedche, A., Handschuh, S.: An annotation framework for the semantic web, Proc. of the 1st International Workshop on MultiMedia Annotation, Japan, (2001)

[18] Vargas-Vera, M., Motta, E., Domingue, J.: Knowledge extraction by using an ontology-based annotation tool, Proc. of the Workshop on Knowledge Markup and Semantic Annotation, KCAP' 01,Canada, (2001)

An *k*NN Model-Based Approach
and Its Application in Text Categorization

Gongde Guo[1], Hui Wang[1], David Bell[2], Yaxin Bi[2], and Kieran Greer[1]

[1] School of Computing and Mathematics, University of Ulster
Newtownabbey, BT37 0QB, Northern Ireland, UK
{G.Guo,H.Wang,Krc.Greer}@ulst.ac.uk
[2] School of Computer Science, Queen's University Belfast
Belfast, BT7 1NN, UK
{DA.Bell,Y.Bi}@qub.ac.uk

Abstract. An investigation has been conducted on two well known similarity-based learning approaches to text categorization. This includes the *k*-nearest neighbor (*k*-NN) classifier and the Rocchio classifier. After identifying the weakness and strength of each technique, we propose a new classifier called the *k*NN model-based classifier by unifying the strengths of *k*-NN and Rocchio classifier and adapting to characteristics of text categorization problems.

A text categorization prototypes system has been implemented and then evaluated on two common document corpora, namely, the 20-newsgroup collection and the ModApte version of the Reuters-21578 collection of news stories. The experimental results show that the *k*NN model-based approach outperforms the *k*-NN, Rocchio classifier.

1 Introduction

Text categorization (TC) is the task of assigning a number of appropriate categories to a text document. This categorization process has many applications such as document routing, document management, or document dissemination [1]. Traditionally each incoming document is analyzed and categorized manually by domain experts based on the content of the document. A large amount of human resources have to be spent on carrying out such a task. To facilitate the process of text categorization, automatic categorization schemes are required. The goal of text categorization is to learn such categorization schemes that can be used to classify text documents automatically.

There are many categorization schemes addressed for this automatic text categorization task in text categorization literature. This includes Naïve Bayes (NB) probabilistic classifiers [2], Decision Tree classifiers [3], Decision Rules [4], regression methods [5], Neural Network [6], *k*-NN classifiers [5, 7], Support Vector Machine (SVMs) [8, 9], and Rocchio classifiers [10, 11] etc. In many applications, such as web mining for a large repository, the efficiency of those schemes is often the key element to be considered. Sebastiani has pointed this out in his survey on text categorization [12].

k-NN and Rocchio are two classifiers frequently used for TC, and they are both similarity based. The *k*-NN algorithm directly uses the training examples as a basis

A. Gelbukh (Ed.): CICLing 2004, LNCS 2945, pp. 559–570, 2004.
© Springer-Verlag Berlin Heidelberg 2004

for computing similarity. For a data record t to be classified, its k nearest neighbors are retrieved, and this forms a neighborhood of t. Majority voting among the data records in the neighborhood is used to decide the classification for t. However, to apply k-NN we need to choose an appropriate value for k, and the success of classification is very much dependent on this value. Moreover, k-NN has a high cost of classifying new instances. This is single-handedly due to the fact that nearly all computation takes place at classification time rather than when the training examples are first encountered. However, k-NN has been applied to text categorization since the early days of its research [12] and is known to be one of the most effective methods on Reuters corpus of newswire stories – a benchmark corpus in text categorization.

The Rocchio method [10, 11] however can deal with those problems to some extent. It uses the generalized instances to replace the whole collection of training instances by summarizing the contribution of the instances belonging to each category. Besides its efficiency this method is easy to implement, since learning a classifier basically comes down to averaging weights and classifying a new instance only needs computing the inner product between the new instance and the generalized instances. It can be regarded as a similarity-based algorithm. Moreover, the Rocchio method can deal with noise to some extent via summarizing the contribution of the instances belonging to each category. For example, if a feature mainly appears in many training instances of a category, its corresponding weight in the generalized instance will have a larger magnitude for this category. Also if a feature mainly appears in training instances of other categories, its weight in the generalized instance will tend to zero [1]. Therefore, the Rocchio classifier can distill out certain relevant features to some extent. On the other hand, one drawback of the Rocchio classifier is it restricts the hypothesis space to the set of linear separable hyper-plane regions, which has less expressiveness power than that of k-NN algorithms [1].

The generalized instance set (GIS) algorithm proposed by Lam et al [1] is an attempt to overcome the weakness of the k-NN algorithms and linear classifiers. The main idea for the GIS algorithm is to construct more than one generalized instance (GI) for a category in contrast to only one generalized instance for a category in linear classifiers like the Rocchio method. Though better performance was obtained in experiments, some drawbacks still exist. One drawback is that the performance of GIS depends on the order in which positive instances are chosen, and on the value of k. The other drawback is that the removal of the top-k instances from the training collection after obtaining a generalized instance will directly affect the calculation of further generalized instances.

Having identified the weakness and strength of each technique, we propose a new method called the kNN model-based algorithm (represented as kNNModel for short) by combining the strengths of the k-NN and Rocchio classifiers (details to be presented later). The proposed method has been implemented and integrated into our text categorization prototype system along with the standard k-NN algorithm, and the Rocchio algorithm. Extensive experiments have been conducted on two common document corpora so that we can compare the categorization performance of different approaches. The results show that the proposed new method outperforms the k-NN algorithm and the Rocchio classifier in all experiments.

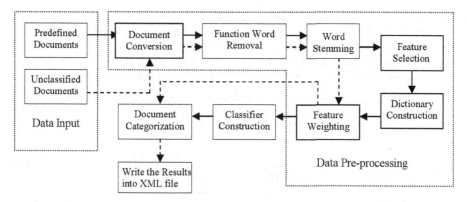

Fig. 1. The architecture of text categorization

2   The Architecture of Text Categorization

In this section, we give an overview of the architecture of text categorization and describe the functionality of each component in text categorization. The text categorization usually comprises three key components: data pre-processing, classifier construction, and document categorization. Data pre-processing implements the function of transferring initial documents into a compact representation and will be uniformly applied to training, validation, and classification phases. Classifier construction implements the function of inductive learning from a training dataset, and document categorization implements the function of document classification. All these components together make the text categorization practicable.

In Fig. 1, the arrow with dashed line represents the data flow in the categorization process as the arrow with the solid line represents the data flow in the classifier construction process.

2.1   Data Pre-processing

Data pre-processing comprises six components including document conversion, function word removal, word stemming, feature selection, dictionary construction, and feature weighting. The functionality of each component is described as follows:

(1) Document conversion – converts different types of documents such as XML, PDF, HTML, DOC format to plain text format.
(2) Function word removal – removes topic-neutral words such as articles (a, an, the), prepositions (in, of, at), conjunctions (and, or, nor), etc. from the documents.
(3) Word stemming – standardizes word's suffixes (e.g., labeling-label, introduction-introduct).
(4) Feature selection – reduces the dimensionality of the data space by removing irrelevant or less relevant features. In our prototype, we choose information gain as a feature selection criterion.

(5) Dictionary construction – constructs a uniform dictionary which is used as a reference for converting the text document to a vector of features. Each feature in the vector corresponds to a word in the dictionary.

(6) Feature weighting – assigns different weights to words in the dictionary. We use standard normalized *tfidf* as the weighting function in our TC prototype system.

The information gain and the *tfidf* function are defined respectively as follows:

$$IG(t_k, c_i) = \sum_{c \in \{c_i, \bar{c}_i\}} \sum_{t \in \{t_k, \bar{t}_k\}} P(t,c) . \log \frac{P(t,c)}{P(t).P(c)} \tag{1}$$

$$tfidf(t_k, d_i) = \#(t_k, d_i) . \log \frac{|T_r|}{\#T_r(t_k)} , \quad w_{ki} = \frac{tfidf(t_k, d_i)}{\sqrt{\sum_{i=1}^{|T_r|} (tfidf(t_k, d_i))^2}} \tag{2}$$

where $\#(t_k, d_i)$ is the number of times t_k occurs in d_i, and $\#T_r(t_k)$ denotes the document frequency of term t_k, that is the number of documents in T_r in which t_k occurs. $|T_r|$ is the number of documents in the training dataset, and w_{ki} is the normalized term weight.

Each document will be converted to a compact representation and will be applied to training, validation, and classification phases.

2.2 Classifier Construction

Classifier construction is the key component of automatic text categorization. The role of this component is to build a classifier by learning from predefined documents, which will be used to classify unknown documents. In our TC prototype system, we have implemented three categorization algorithms: k-NN, Rocchio, and the kNNModel. We give a brief description for each algorithm except for the kNNModel, which will be described in detail in section 3.

2.2.1 k-NN Algorithm

k nearest neighbor (k-NN) is a similarity-based learning algorithm and is known to be very effective for a variety of problem domains including text categorization [5, 7]. Given a test document d_r, the k-NN algorithm finds its k nearest neighbors among the training documents, which forms a neighborhood of d_r. Majority voting among the documents in the neighborhood is used to decide the category for d_r.

2.2.2 Rocchio Algorithm

The Rocchio's method is a linear classifier. Given a training dataset T_r, it directly computes a classifier $\vec{c}_i = < w_{1i}, w_{2i}, ..., w_{ri} >$ for category c_i by means of the formula:

$$w_{ki} = \beta \cdot \sum_{\{d_j \in POS_i\}} \frac{w_{kj}}{|POS_i|} - \gamma \cdot \sum_{\{d_j \in NEG_i\}} \frac{w_{kj}}{|NEG_i|} \tag{3}$$

where w_{kj} is the weight of t_k in document d_j, $POS_i = \{d_j \in T_r \mid \hat{\Phi}(d_j, c_i) = T\}$, and $NEG_i = \{d_j \in T_r \mid \hat{\Phi}(d_j, c_i) = F\}$. $\hat{\Phi}(d_j, c_i) = T$ (or F) means document d_j belonging to (or not belonging to) category c_i. In formula 6, β and γ are two control parameters used for setting the relative importance of positive and negative examples. The profile of c_i is the centroid of its positive training examples. A classifier built by means of the Rocchio method rewards the closeness of a test document to the centroid of the positive training examples, and its distance from the centroid of the negative training examples [12].

2.3 Document Categorization

The document categorization component directly uses the model created in the classifier construction phase to classify new instances. All documents to be classified must be pre-processed as in the classifier construction phase.

3 *k*NN Model-Based Algorithm

3.1 The Basic Idea of *k*NNModel

*k*NN is a case-based learning method, which keeps all the training data for classification. Being a lazy learning method prohibits it in many applications such as dynamic web mining for a large repository. One way to improve its efficiency is to find some representatives of the whole training data for classification, viz. building an inductive learning model from the training dataset and using this model (set of representatives) for classification. *k*NN is a simple but effective method for classification and has been shown to be one of the most effective methods on the Reuters corpus of newswire stories in text categorization. This motivates us to build a model for *k*NN to improve its efficiency whilst preserving its classification accuracy. Rochhio, on the other hand, is quite efficient as learning a classifier comes down to building a generalized instance for each category, which are then used as a basis for classification. A well-known disadvantage for Rocchio is its linear characteristic of dividing the space of data points linearly. As an example, consider Fig. 2, the small crosses and circles are two classes of instances with different categories. The big circle denotes the inference area of the classifier for the cross category. As the data points for the cross category occur in disjoint clusters, it causes the classifier built by the Rocchio method to miss most of them, as the centroid of these data points may fall outside all of these clusters. One way to overcome this drawback is to build several local centroids for one category. The number of centroids for a category depends on the dataset given for training. Fig. 3 shows the modeling result of *k*NNModel for category '+'.

Note that, for ease of illustration, document similarities are viewed here (also in the following graphical illustration) in terms of Euclidean distance rather than, as is more common, in terms of dot product or cosine.

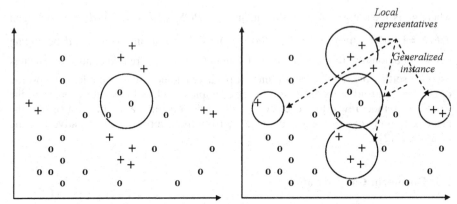

Fig. 2. The generalized instance of category "+"(Rocchio classifier)

Fig. 3. The representatives of category "+" (*k*NNModel algorithm)

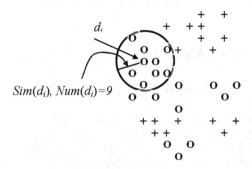

Fig. 4. The first obtained representative

If we use Euclidean distance as our similarity measure for illustration, it is clear that many data points with the same class label are close to each other in many local areas. In each local region, the central data point d_i, called *centroid*, looking at Fig. 4 for example, with some extra information such as $Num(d_i)$ - the number of data points inside the local region and $Sim(d_i)$ - the similarity of the most distant data point inside the local region to d_i, might be a good representative of this local region. If we take these representatives plus the generalized instances of each category as a model to represent the whole training dataset, one merit is that it better reflects the data distribution of each category via both local and global generalization, thus probably improving its classification accuracy; the other merit is that it significantly reduces the number of data points used for classification, thereby improving efficiency. Creating more than one representative for a category readily solves the disjoint clusters problem. For a new data point to be classified, we take into account its distance to each generalized instance and whether if falls into each representative's inference area, and then decide the category it belongs to. See section 3.2 for more detail.

In the model construction process, each data point has its largest neighborhood which covers the maximal number of data points with the same class label. This largest neighborhood is called *local neighborhood*. Based on these local neighborhoods, the largest local neighborhood, called *global neighborhood*, can be obtained and seen as a representative of all the data points covered by it. For data points not covered by any representatives, we repeat the above operation until all the data points have been covered by some representatives. The model comprises both the created representatives and the generalized instances of each category. Obviously, we don't need to choose a specific *k* for our method in the model construction process, the number of data points covered by a representative can be seen as an optimal *k*, but it is different for different representatives. The *k* is generated automatically in the model construction process. Further, using a list of chosen representatives plus the generalized instances of each category as a model not only reduces the amount of data used for classification, but also significantly improves its efficiency. Moreover, as the model reflects the true distribution of each category from both local and global aspects, it probably results in improvement of classification accuracy. Finally, multi-representatives for a category resolve the disjoint clusters problem.

3.2 Modeling and Classification Algorithm

Let D be a collection of n pre-labeled documents $\{d_1, d_2, ..., d_n\}$ with m categories. Document $d_i \in D$ is represented by a feature vector of the form $<w_{i1}, w_{i2}, ..., w_{il}>$, where w_{ij} is the numeric weight for the j-th feature and l is the total number of features. Typically, each feature corresponds to a word or phrase appearing in the training corpus after the removal of function words, word stemming, and feature selection. In the *k*NN model-based algorithm without any extra explanation, we will use the information gain (IG) as the default feature selection criterion, the term frequency combined with inverse document frequency (TFIDF) as the default weighting measure, and the cosine similarity Δ as the default similarity metric.

$$\Delta (d_i, d_j) = \frac{\sum_{k=1}^{l} w_{ik} \cdot w_{jk}}{\sqrt{\sum_{k=1}^{l} w_{ik}^2} \sqrt{\sum_{k=1}^{l} w_{jk}^2}} \tag{4}$$

In the following algorithms, we will use the term *data tuple* to represent a document with or without compact representation after data preprocessing as a convention. Additionally, a data tuple d_i is said to be covered by a representative $<Cls(d_j), Sim(d_j), Num(d_j), Rep(d_j)>$ if $\Delta (d_i, d_j) >= Sim(d_j)$.

The detailed model construction algorithm is described as follows:

(1) Create a similarity matrix from the given training dataset.
(2) Label all data tuples as 'ungrouped'.
(3) For each 'ungrouped' data tuple, find its local neighborhood.
(4) Among all the local neighborhoods obtained in step 3, find its global neighborhood N_i. Create a representative $<Cls(d_i), Sim(d_i), Num(d_i), Rep(d_i)>$ into M to represent all the data tuples covered by N_i, and then label as 'grouped' all the data tuples covered by N_i.
(5) Repeat step 3 and step 4 until all the data tuples in the training dataset have been set to 'grouped'.

(6) Calculate the generalized instance $\overrightarrow{c_i}$ for each category c_i and add $<c_i, 0, n,$
$Rep(\overrightarrow{c_i})$ to M.

(7) Model M consists of all the representatives collected from the above learning process.

In the above algorithm, M represents the created model. The elements of representative $<Cls(d_i), Sim(d_i), Num(d_i), Rep(d_i)>$ represent respectively the class label of d_i; the lowest similarity to d_i among the data tuples covered by N_i; the number of data tuples covered by N_i; and a representation of d_i itself. In step (4), if more than one local neighborhood has the same maximal number of neighbors, we choose the one with the maximal value of $Sim(d_i)$, viz. the one with the highest density, as representative. In step (6), n is the number of data tuples for training. As the minimal value of cosine similarity is 0, we assign $Sim(\overrightarrow{c_i})=0$. This setting allows the global distribution of data tuples belonging to each category to have the certain inference on classifying new instances.

The classification algorithm is described as follows:

(1) For a new data tuple d_t to be classified, calculate its similarity to all representatives in the model M as follows:
For each representative in the model, if d_t is covered by a representative $<Cls(d_j), Sim(d_j), Num(d_j), Rep(d_j)>$, that is, $\Delta(d_t, d_j)$ is larger than or equal to $Sim(d_j)$, then add the contribution $\Delta(d_t, d_j)$ of d_t to $Cont(Cls(d_j))$, viz. $Cont(Cls(d_j)) = Cont(Cls(d_j)) + \Delta(d_t, d_j)$.

(2) Classify d_t by $Cls(d_x)$ if $Cont(Cls(d_x)) = \max\{Cont(Cls(d_i)) \mid i=1,2,...,m\}$.

In text categorization, it is quite common that instances in the training collection contain some level of noise due to the various reasons such as missing appropriate features, typographical errors in texts, or wrong category assigned by a human [1]. In an attempt to improve the classification accuracy for kNNModel, we integrated the pruning work into the process of model construction by modifying step (3) in the model construction algorithm to allow each local neighborhood to cover ε data tuples (called error tolerant degree) with different categories to the majority category in this neighborhood. Experimental results are reported in the next section.

4   Experiment and Evaluation

We have conducted experiments on two commonly used corpora in text categorization research: 20-newsgroups, and Modapte version of the Reuters-21578 collection of news stories. All documents for training and testing involve a pre-processing step, which includes tasks of function word removal, word stemming, feature selection, and feature weighting. We use information gain as the feature selection criterion and the normalized *tfidf* as the weighting function in our text categorization prototype system.

Experimental results reported in this section are based on the so-called "F_1-measure", viz. the harmonic mean of precision and recall.

$$F_1(recall,\ precision) = \frac{2 \times recall \times precision}{recall + precision} \qquad (5)$$

In the above formula, precision and recall are two standard measures widely used in text categorization literature to evaluate the algorithm's effectiveness [12] on a given category, where

$$precision = \frac{true \quad positive}{(true \quad positive) + (false \quad positive)} \times 100 \qquad (6)$$

$$recall = \frac{true \quad positive}{(true \quad positive) + (false \quad negative)} \times 100 \qquad (7)$$

We also use the *macroaveraged* F_1 to evaluate the overall performance of the algorithms on given datasets. The macroaveraged F_1 computes the F_1 values for each category and then takes the average over the per-category F_1 scores. Given a training dataset with m categories, assuming the F_1 value for the i-th category is $F_1(i)$, the *macroaveraged* F_1 is defined as:

$$macroaveraged\ F_1 = \frac{\sum_{i=1}^{m} F_1(i)}{m} \qquad (8)$$

4.1 Datasets for Experiment

4.1.1 Reuters-21578 Corpus
The Reuters dataset has been used in many text categorization experiments. The data was originally collected by the Carnegie group from the Reuters newswire in 1987. There are now at least five versions of the Reuters dataset widely used in the TC community. We choose the ModApte version of the Reuters-21578 collection of news stories from www.daviddlewis.com/resources/testcollections/reuters21578. In our experiments, we used the seven most frequent categories from this corpus as our dataset for training and testing. Each category in this subset contains 200 documents. The seven most frequent categories are: {Acq, Corn, Crude, Earn, Interest, Ship, Trade}.

4.1.2 20-Newsgroup Corpus
The 20-newsgroups contains approximately 20,000 newsgroup documents being partitioned (nearly) evenly across 20 different newsgroups. We used the 20-news-18828 version downloaded from www.ai.mit.edu/~jrennie/20Newsgroups/. In this dataset duplicates have been removed and we only keep "From" and "Subject" headers in each document. In experiments, we choose a subset from this corpus for training and testing. The subset includes 20 categories, and each category contains 200 documents.

4.2 Evaluation

In our experiments, we use the ten-fold cross validation method to evaluate the *macroaveraged* F_1 of different algorithms on above two datasets. The basic settings of parameters for each algorithm as well as the F_1 value and the *macroaveraged* F_1 value are shown in Table 1 to Table 3 respectively. Different values of parameters have been tried on each algorithm to ensure that the experimental results faithfully reflect the best performance of the algorithms. The value of k for k-NN algorithm includes 5, 15, 25, 35, 45, 55, 65; the pair value of (β, γ) used for the Rocchio algorithm includes $(1, 0.1), (1, 0.2),..., (1, 1)$; the value of ε for the kNNModel method includes 3, 4, 5, 6, 7. The experimental results are listed in Table 2 to Table 3.

In Table 1, heading IG is short for Information Gain. The values in this column are the thresholds for feature selection on different datasets. Others headings in Table 1 have been introduced in section 2.2.

From the experimental results, it is clear that the *macroaveraged* F_1 of our proposed kNNModel method outperforms the k-NN algorithm and Rocchio classifier on both datasets in ten-fold cross validation. The kNNModel method is more efficient than k-NN as it keeps only a few representatives for classification, and is comparable to the Rocchio algorithm.

Table 1. The basic settings of parameters for each algorithm

Dataset	IG	k-NN	Rocchio	KNNModel
Reuters-21578	0.003	$k=35$	$\beta=1, \gamma=0.2$	$\varepsilon=5$
20-newsgroup	0.006	$k=45$	$\beta=1, \gamma=0.2$	$\varepsilon=5$

Table 2. The comparison of performance (F_1) on Reuters-21578 subset

Category	k-NN	Rocchio	kNNModel
Acq	78.81	84.03	86.08
Corn	87.08	87.74	91.85
Crude	84.12	84.51	84.72
Earn	88.02	90.39	89.45
Interest	79.67	80.84	83.26
Ship	84.02	86.22	86.73
Trade	80.69	81.64	80.00
macroaveraged F_1	83.20	85.05	86.01

Table 3. The comparison of performance (F_1) on 20-newsgroup subset

Category	*k*-NN	Rocchio	*k*NNModel
alt.atheism	88.67	83.85	91.38
comp.graphics	65.47	70.00	68.06
comp.os.ms-windows.misc	65.27	66.67	67.40
comp.sys.ibm.pc.hardware	55.78	55.89	58.70
comp.sys.mac.hardware	56.92	57.91	61.04
comp.windows.x	80.00	80.21	80.10
misc.forsale	67.92	72.68	73.13
rec.autos	76.17	75.81	77.75
rec.motorcycles	88.50	88.42	89.41
rec.sport.baseball	85.86	88.61	90.00
rec.sport.hockey	90.12	93.27	92.73
sci.crypt	89.16	89.43	88.61
sci.electronics	70.17	69.09	73.60
sci.med	88.40	88.22	90.54
sci.space	83.45	86.76	86.83
soc.religion.Christian	83.17	81.00	83.33
talk.politics.guns	89.05	85.51	88.94
talk.politics.mideast	91.39	93.09	91.54
Talk.politics.misc	85.11	75.37	83.29
Talk.religion.misc	80.83	74.18	79.47
macroaveraged F$_1$	79.07	78.80	80.79

5 Conclusions

In this paper, we have investigated several recent approaches for text categorization under the framework of similarity-based learning. They include the *k*-NN algorithm and the Rocchio classifier. We analyzed both algorithms and identified some shortcomings of them. Based on the analysis, we developed a new approach called the *k*NN model-based algorithm which combines the strengths of *k*-NN and the Rocchio classifier. We implemented our *k*NN model-based algorithm, along with a standard *k*-NN algorithm, and Rocchio algorithm in our TC prototype system. Extensive experiments were conducted on two common document corpora, namely the 20-newsgroup collection and the Reuters-21578 collection. All experimental results show that our proposed *k*NN model-based approach outperforms other approaches. Further research is required into how to improve the classification accuracy of marginal data which falls outside the regions of representatives.

Acknowledgements. This work was partly supported by the European Commission project ICONS, project no. IST-2001-32429.

References

1. Lam, W. and Ho, C.Y. (1998). Using a Generalized Instance Set for Automatic Text Categorization. SIGIR'98, pages 81–89.
2. Lewis, D. D. (1998). Naïve (Bayes) at forty: The independent assumption in information retrieval. In Proceedings of ECML-98, 10th European Conference on Machine Learning, pages 4 –15.
3. Cohen, W. W. and Singer, Y. (1999). Context–Sensitive Learning Methods for Text Categorization. ACM Trans. Inform. Syst. 17, 2, pages 141–173.
4. Li, H. and Yamanishi, K. (1999). Text Classification Using ESC-based Stochastic Decision Lists. In Proceedings of CIKM-99, 8th ACM International Conference on Information and Knowledge Management, pages 122–130.
5. Yang, Y. and Liu, X. (1999). A Re-examination of Text Categorization Methods. In Proceedings of SIGIR-99, 22nd ACM International Conference on Research and Development in Information Retrieval, pages 42–49.
6. Ruiz, M. E. and Srinivasan, P. (1999). Hierarchical Neural Networks for Text Categorization. In Proceedings of SIGIR-99, 22nd ACM International Information Retrieval, pages 281–282.
7. Mitchell, T.M. (1996). Machine Learning. McGraw Hill, New York, NY.
8. Joachims, T. (1998). Text Categorization with Support Vector Machines: Learning with Many Relevant Features, In Proceedings of 10th European Conference on Machine Learning, Chemnitz, Germany, pages 137–142.
9. Joachims, T. (2001). A Statistical Learning Model of Text Classification for Support Vector Machines. In Proceedings of SIGIR-01, 24th ACM International Conference on Research and Development in Information Retrieval, pages 128–136.
10. Rocchio, Jr. J. J. (1971). Relevance Feedback in Information Retrieval. The SMART Retrieval System: Experiments in Automatic Document Processing, editor: Gerard Salton, Prentice-Hall, Inc., Englewood Cliffs, News Jersey, 1971.
11. Joachims, T. (1997). A Probabilistic Analysis of the Rocchio Algorithm with TFIDF for Test Categorization. In Proceedings of ICML-97, 14th International Conference on Machine Learning, pages 143–151.
12. Sebastiani, F. (2002). Machine Learning in Automated Text Categorization. ACM Computing Surveys, Vol.34, No.1, March 2002, pages 1–47.
13. Cortes, C. and V. Vapnik (1995). Support-Vector Network. Machine Learning 20, pages 273–297.

Automatic Learning Features Using Bootstrapping for Text Categorization

Wenliang Chen, Jingbo Zhu, Honglin Wu, and Tianshun Yao

Natural Language Processing Lab
Northeastern University, Shenyang, China
{chenwl,zhujingbo,wuhl,tsyao}@mail.neu.edu.cn

Abstract. When text categorization is applied to complex tasks, it is tedious and expensive to hand-label the large amounts of training data necessary for good performance. In this paper, we put forward an approach to text categorization that requires no labeled documents. The proposed approach automatically learns features using bootstrapping. The input consists of a small set of keywords per class and a large amount of easily obtained unlabeled documents. Using these automatically learned features, we develop a naïve Bayes classifier. The classifier provides 82.8% F1 while classifying a set of web documents into 10 categories, which performs better than naïve Bayes by supervised learning in small number of features cases.

1 Introduction

The goal of text categorization is to classify documents into a certain number of predefined categories. When provided with enough labeled training examples, a variety of techniques for supervised learning algorithms have demonstrated reasonable performance for text categorization [Yang, ml1997; Yang and Liu, 1999], such as Rocchio[Ittner et al, 1995; Lewis et al, 1996], SVM[Joachims, 1998], decision tree[Lewis, 1994], Maximum Entropy[Nigam et al., 1999], and naïve Bayes [McCallum and Nigam, 1998]. However, when applied to complex domains with many classes, these algorithms often require extremely large training sets to reach useful classification accuracy. Creating these sets of labeled data is tedious and expensive, because labeled documents should be labeled by hand. So in this paper, we consider learning algorithms that do not require such labeled documents [Nigam et al., 2000].

Obtaining labeled data is difficult; on the contrary, unlabeled data is readily available and plentiful. Unlabeled data can often be obtained by fully automatic methods. It can be easy to download unlabeled examples of news articles from Internet.

In this paper, we propose a new automatic text categorization method based on unsupervised learning. Without labeled documents, we automatically learn features for each category using a small set of keywords per class and a large amount of unlabeled documents. And then, using these features, we develop a naïve Bayes text classifier. Keywords are generated more quickly and easily than labeling even a small number of documents. Using these keywords, our algorithm generates features for

A. Gelbukh (Ed.): CICLing 2004, LNCS 2945, pp. 571–579, 2004.
© Springer-Verlag Berlin Heidelberg 2004

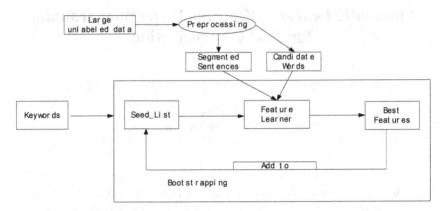

Fig. 1. FLB process

each category by bootstrapping [Abney, 2002; Blum and Mitchell, 1998; Li and Li, 2002; Riloff, 1999; Yarowsky, 1995], which we refer to as *"Feature Learning Bootstrapping"* (**FLB**).

In this paper, we use Chinese documents as test data set. Experimental evaluation of this bootstrapping approach is performed on a data set of 13,450 documents. In total 10 categories, 10 keywords for each category and 1,630,000 unlabeled sentences are provided as input. Our bootstrapping algorithm uses these as input and outputs the features for each category to a naïve Bayes [Mitchell, 1997] text classifier. Using these features, naïve Bayes achieves 83% F1. When the feature set is small, naïve Bayes with FLB outperforms naïve Bayes by supervised learning.

This paper is organized as follows. In Section 2 we describe in detail the idea behind FLB Algorithm. In Section 3 we introduce how to learn a naïve Bayes classifier. In Section 4 we present the results of experiments on data set. Finally we draw a conclusion.

2   Feature Learning Bootstrapping

FLB makes use of, in learning, a small number of keywords and a large amount of unlabeled corpus. Using bootstrapping, it learns features in the corpus. And such a process repeatedly learns from keywords by *"Feature Learner"*. Note that *"Feature Learner"* is used to learn new features based on the set of seed words, and it can be constructed in many ways. In this paper, it considers the co-occurrence of the word and seed words in the same sentence. Figure 1 shows the FLB process. The process described in this paper consists of the following steps:

- Preprocessing: Segmentation, Extracting candidate words
- Initialization: A small number of keywords for each category are added to the set of Seed_List(list of seed words)
- Iterate Bootstrapping:
    - Feature Learner: Learn new features using Seed_List
    - Select new Seeds: Select some features from learned features as new seeds

Table 1. Examples of keywords

Category	Keywords
金融(*finance*)	股票(*stock*),金融(*finance*), 税收(*tax*), 贷款(*loan*)
军事(*military*)	军事(*military*), 武器(*weaponry*) ,军队(*army*) ,战争(**war**)
体育(*sports*)	体育(sports) ,选手(player) ,足球(football) ,联赛(league)
法律(*law*)	法律(*law*) ,法院(*court*) ,律师(*lawyer*)

2.1 Preprocessing

First, the html tags and special characters in the collected documents are removed. And then, the contents of the documents are segmented into sentences, and the sentences are segmented into words. We extract candidate words from the documents: First we use a stoplist to eliminate no-informative words, and then we remove the words whose frequencies are less than F_{min}.

2.2 Initialization

In FLB, seed information is provided in the form of keywords. Table 1 shows examples of keywords used in our experiments. Each category will be provided with 10 keywords. In initialization, we will add all keywords for each category to seed words list.

2.3 Iterative Bootstrapping

We can regard bootstrapping as iterative clustering. Given the initial class-based seed words provided as input, we learn more features, and output a new set of features for each category.

Our bootstrapping algorithm begins with seed word list that belongs to a category. From the set of candidate words, we can learn the reliable features using these seed words. These learned features are of the same category as the seed words. And we call this learner "*Feature Leaner*". The best of the features are then added to the set of seed words that are used to generate new features, and the process repeats.

Feature learner can be constructed in many ways. In this paper, it is based on sentences, and it considers the co-occurrence of the word and seed words in the same sentence. We score each word with the RlogF metric previously used by [Riloff, 1999]. The score is computed as:

$$M(w_i) = Log_2 F(w_i, X) \times R_i,$$

where $F(w_i, X)$ is the frequency of co-occurrence of w_i and X(set of seed words) in the same sentence, $F(w_i)$ is the frequency of w_i in the corpus, and $R_i=F(w_i,X)/F(w_i)$. The RlogF metric tries to strike a balance between reliability and frequency: R is high when the word is highly correlated with set of seed words (the category), and F is

Table 2. First 10 Learned Features of "finance"

Feature	$F(w_i,X)$	$F(w_i)$	M	Feature	$F(w_i,X)$	$F(w_i)$	M
国有(*state owned*)	10844	12322	11.796	批发(*wholesale*)	1471	1896	8.163
大中型(*large and middle scale*)	2325	2618	9.931	筹集(*raise*)	924	1118	8.142
外商(*foreign businessmen*)	3534	4498	9.260	贷款(*loan*)	3665	5539	7.833
三资(*enterprises in the three forms*)	777	817	9.131	兼并(*annex*)	1130	1505	7.615
股份制(*joint-stock*)	2657	3509	8.613	筹措(*financing*)	568	694	7.488

high when the word and X highly co-occur in the same sentence. In this paper, if w_i wants to be a feature, both of the following two conditions must be satisfied: 1) R_i of w_i should be greater than R_{min}; 2) M of w_i should be greater than M_{min}. Table 2 shows the first 10 features learned in our following experiments in "finance" category, in which features are sorted by M.

After *Feature Learner* learns new features, we select top 10 features by the value of M as new seeds. Then we add them to the seed word list.

2.4   FLB Algorithm

Figure 2 outlines the *Feature Learning Bootstrapping* (**FLB**) algorithm, which iteratively learns features from the seed words and a large amount of unlabeled documents. At iteration, the algorithm saves the seed words for the category to a seed word list. Then the new features are identified by *Feature Learner* (Step a – Step e in Figure 2), based on both the original seed words and the new seed words that were just added to the seeds list. And then the process repeats. The output of the process is the set of learned features.

In Figure 2, C denotes a large size of unlabeled data, W a set of candidate words, and K a set of hand selected keywords as shown in Table 1. F denotes a set of learned features as results. S denotes a set of seed words. In initialization, all k in K are put into S.

```
Input: C, W, K
Output: F
Put all k in K into S
Rmin = R_Init_Value;
Features Learner Bootstrapping
    a)   Select w whose R(w) > Rmin from W, and add w to W1
    b)   If W1 ⊂ Φ , Rmin -=R_Step, go to a
    c)   Score all words in W1
    d)   F_New = the words whose M is greater than Mmin
    e)   Put all f in F_New into F
    f)   F_Best = the top 10 scoring words from F not already in S
    g)   Put all f in F_Best into S
    h)   Go to a)
```

Fig. 2. FLB Algorithm

3 Text Classifier

We use naïve Bayes for classifying documents. We only describe naïve Bayes briefly since full details have been presented in the paper [McCallum and Nigam, 1998]. The basic idea in naïve Bayes approach is to use the joint probabilities of words and categories to estimate the probabilities of categories when a document is given. Given a document d for classification, we calculate the probabilities of each category c as follows:

$$P(c \mid d) = \frac{P(c)P(d \mid c)}{P(d)} = P(c) \prod_{i}^{|T|} P(t_i \mid c)^{N(t_i \mid d)}$$

where $N(t_i \mid d)$ is the frequency of word t_i in document d, T is the vocabulary and $|T|$ is the size of T, t_i is the ith word in the vocabulary, and $P(t_i \mid c)$ thus represents the probability that a randomly drawn word from a randomly drawn document in category c will be the word t_i. The probability is estimated by the following formulae:

$$P(t_i \mid c) = \frac{M(t_i, X_c) + 0.1}{\sum_{j=1}^{|T|} M(t_j, X_c) + 0.1 |T|}$$

where X_c denotes the set of seed words for category c. $M(t_i, X_c)$ denotes value of RlogF between t_i and X_c.

4 Evaluation

In this section, we provide empirical evidence to prove that the text classifier with features learned from unlabeled data based on bootstrapping is a high-accuracy text classifier.

4.1 Performance Measures

In this paper, a document is assigned to only one category. We use the conventional recall, precision and F1 to measure the performance of the system. For evaluating performance average across categories, we use the micro-averaging method. F1 measure is defined by the following formula [Ko and Sco, 2002]:

$$F_1 = \frac{2rp}{r + p},$$

where r represents recall and p represents precision. It balances recall and precision in a way that gives them equal weight.

4.2   Experimental Setting

We use the People's Daily corpus (Including articles of 30 months) as unlabeled data. We name the corpus as PDC. The data set contains 1,630,000 sentences. We use the toolkit *CipSegSDK*[Yao, et al, 2002] for segmentation.

The NEU_TC data set contains web pages collected from web sites. The pages are divided into 10 categories: IT, finance, military, education, sports, recreation, house, law, profession and travel. It consists of 14,405 documents. We do not use tag information of pages. For experiments, we use 3000 documents (300 documents for each category) for training NB by supervised learning. The rest of data set is used to test, and it consists of 11,405 documents.

The algorithm FLB described in Section 2 is applied using the following setting: $F_{min}=10$, R_Init_Value=0.5, R_Step=0.05, $M_{min}=\log_2(10)*0.5$, at each iteration we select less than 10 new seed words.

Here we name *naïve Bayes by supervised learning* as **NB_SL** and *naïve Bayes with FLB* as **NB_FLB**.

4.3   Experimental Results

4.3.1   Experiment: FLB

In our experiments, we study the effect of feature set size and corpus size on performance with varying the number of learned features for each category and the size of PDC. In Figure 3 we consider the effect of varying the amount of features with 5 different amounts of sentences for FLB. In Figure 3, *All* refers to using 1,630,000 sentences; *1400* refers to using 1,400,000; *200* refers to using 200,000. For five different quantities of sentences for training, we keep the number of features constant, and vary the number of sentences in the horizontal axis. Naturally, the more sentences for training are used, the better the performance is. With 200 thousand sentences, the best result of NB_FLB provides 78.9% F1. And NB_FLB reaches 82.8% F1 with 1.63 million sentences, when the number of features is 200.

Note that adding more features actually hurts the performance. With 1.63 million sentences, NB_FLB provides 81.3% F1 when the number of features is 500. The result of NB_FLB with 200 features provides 1.5% above with 500 features.

4.3.2   NB by FLB Vs NB by Supervised Learning

We compare NB_FLB with NB_SL. The number of features used in our experiment is selected by ranking features according to their information gain (IG) with respect to the category. Information gain is a commonly used technique for feature selection in naïve Bayes text categorization.

Table 3 shows categorization results for the two algorithms on test dataset, in which the first row indicates the number of labeled documents for NB_SL (For instance, *IG_100* refers to the number of labeled documents for training is 100). We use all the sentences for training NB_FLB, and vary the number of labeled documents for training NB_SL. Note that in small number of features cases, NB_FLB always performs better than NB_SL with IG. Even using 3000 documents for training, NB_SL with IG provides a F1 of 2.5% lower than NB_FLB when the number of features is 200. However, with more features performance of NB_FLB starts to decline while performance of NB_SL with IG increases continually.

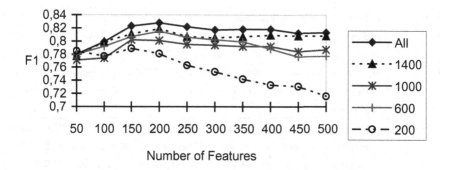

Fig. 3. Performance while varying the number of features

Table 3. NB_FLB VS NB_SL

	100	200	300	400	500	600	800	1000	1500
NB_FLB	*0.799*	*0.828*	*0.817*	*0.818*	0.813	0.801	0.802	0.791	0.778
IG_100	0.727	0.750	0.758	0.760	0.761	0.784	0.798	0.826	0.832
IG_200	0.764	0.779	0.788	0.791	0.797	0.817	0.835	0.854	0.881
IG_300	0.771	0.789	0.792	0.791	0.793	0.800	0.817	0.842	0.869
IG_500	0.780	0.789	0.790	0.794	0.797	0.797	0.802	0.811	0.840
IG_3000	0.788	0.803	0.809	0.812	*0.815*	*0.815*	*0.819*	*0.824*	*0.882*

4.4 Discussion

First we investigate the reason why adding more features actually hurts performance in NB_FLB according to the following observations. We collect the words for each category. It is obvious that the set of later learned features has more "irrelevant words" than the set of previously learned features. Here "relevant words" for each category refer to the words that are strongly indicative to the category on the basis of human judgments.

Table 4 shows the top twenty features of "finance" VS the features from No.481 to No.500, in which irrelevant words are underlined. For iterative learning based on unreliable learned features, irrelevant words will be learned as features for the category. These words hurt performance.

Second we investigate the reason why NB_FLB outperforms NB_SL with IG in small number of features cases. We also collect the words for each category in both NB_FLB and NB_SL. And we find NB_FLB obviously has more "relevant words" than NB_SL with IG.

Tables 5 shows the top twenty words of "finance" with respect to NB_FLB (not including keywords) and NB_SL, in which irrelevant words are underlined.

Table 4. Examples: features of "finance"

No.1-No.20	国有(state owned) 大中型(large and middle scale) 外商(foreign businessmen) 三资(enterprises in the three forms) 股份制(joint-stock) 筹集(raise) 兼并(annex) 批发(wholesale) 贷款(loan) 筹措(financing) 破产(bankrupt) 固定资产(capital assets) 控股(holding company) 自筹(self-financing) 预算外(extra budget) 亏损(loss) 私营(private sector) 民营(nongovernmental business) 拆借(inter-bank borrowing) 经营(manage)
No.481-No.500	做到(manage to do) 野生(wildness) 合法(legality) 路线(route) 办理(transact) 行政管理(administration management) 消费(consume) 立法(legislation) 健康(health) 检查(check) 现有(existing) 分析(analyze) 安排(arrange) 具备(possess) 培育(foster) 前提(premise) 探索(explore) 股份合作制(the joint stock cooperative system) 吸收(absorb) 进展(advance)

Table 5. Top 20 words of "finance"

NB_FLB	国有(state owned) 大中型(large and middle scale) 外商(foreign businessmen) 三资(enterprises in the three forms)股份制(joint-stock) 筹集(raise) 兼并(annex) 批发(wholesale) 贷款(loan) 筹措(financing) 破产(bankrupt) 固定资产(capital assets) 控股(holding company) 自筹(self-financing) 预算外(extra budget) 亏损(loss) 私营(private sector) 民营(nongovernmental business) 拆借(inter-bank borrowing) 经营(manage)
NB_SL	汇市(exchange market) 承销(sell goods on a commission basis) 下挫(down) 监管部门(regulation department) 承销商(consignee) 报收(close at [stock market]) 汇价(exchange rate) 周小川(Zhou Xiaochuan,president of the people's bank of china) 汇丰(HSBC) 油价(oil price) 票面(face) 债市(bond market) 原油(crude oil) 空头(short position) 增发 (additional) 国际货币(international currency) 基金组织(fund) 年率(annual rate) 股民(stockholder) 吴定富(Wu Dingfu,chairman of China Insurance Regulatory Commision)

5   Conclusion

We have addressed here the problem of automatic text categorization. Specifically we use bootstrapping to learn features from a small set of keywords and a large amount of unlabeled data. Using these learned features, we develop a naïve Bayes classifier without any labeled documents that performs better than supervised learning in small number of features cases.

Acknowledgments. This research was partially funded by the National Natural Science Foundation of China and Microsoft under Grant No. 60203019.

References

[Abney, 2002] Steven Abney, Bootstrapping, Proceedings of the 40th Annual Meeting of the Association for Computational Linguistics (ACL-02) 2002

[Blum and Mitchell, 1998] A. Blum and T. Mitchell, Combining labeled and unlabeled data with co-training. In COLT: Proceedings of the Workshop on Computational Learning Theory. 1998

[Ittner et al, 1995] David J. Ittner, David D. Lewis, and David D. Ahn, Text categorization of low quality images. In Symposium on Document Analysis and Information Retrieval, pages 301–315, Las Vegas, NV, ISRI; Univ. of Nevada, Las Vegas. 1995.

[Joachims, 1998] T. Joachims, Text categorization with Support Vector Machines: Learning with many relevant features. In Machine Learning: ECML-98, Tenth European Conference on Machine Learning, pp. 137–142. 1998

[Ko and Sco, 2002] Youngjoong Ko and Jungyun Sco, Automatic Text Categorization by Unsupervised Learning, COLING02,2002

[Lewis, 1994] D. Lewis, A Comparison of Two Learning Algorithms for Text Categorization, Symposium on Document Analysis and IR, 1994

[Lewis et al, 1996] D. Lewis, R. Schapire, J. Callan, and R. Papka, Training Algorithms for Linear Text Classifiers, Proceedings of ACM SIGIR, pp.298–306, 1996.

[Li and Li, 2002] Cong Li and Hang Li, Word Translation Disambiguation Using Bilingual Bootstrapping. Proceedings of the 40th Annual Meeting of Association for Computational Linguistics (ACL'02), pp.343–351, 2002.

[Mitchell, 1997] T. M. Mitchell. Machine Learning. The McGraw-Hill Companies, Inc.1997

[McCallum and Nigam, 1998] A.McCallum and K.Nigam, A Comparison of Event Models for naïve Bayes Text Classification, In AAAI-98 Workshop on Learning for Text Categorization,1998

[Nigam et al., 1999] K. Nigam, John Lafferty, and Andrew McCallum, Using maximum entropy for text classification. In IJCAI-99 Workshop on Machine Learning for Information Filtering, pages 61–67, 1999

[Nigam et al., 2000] K. Nigam, A.K. McCallum, S. Thrun, and T. Mitchell Text Classification from Labeled and Unlabeled Documents using EM, Machine Learning, 39 2–3 (2000) 103–134.

[Riloff, 1999] Ellen Riloff, Rosie Jones, Learning Dictionaries for Information Extraction by Multi-Level Bootstrapping, Proceedings of the Sixteenth National Conference on Artificial Intelligence(AAAI-99),1999

[Yang and Liu, 1999] Yiming Yang , Xin Liu, A re-examination of text categorization methods. sigir99,1999

[Yang, ml1997] Yiming Yang, A Comparative Study on Feature Selection in Text Categorization, ml97,1997

[Yao, et al, 2002] T.S. Yao, et al, Natural Language Processing – A research of making computers understand human languages, Tsinghua University Press,2002,(In Chinese).

[Yarowsky, 1995] David Yarowsky, Unsupervised word sense disambiguation rivaling supervised methods. In Proceedings of the 33rd Annual Meeting of the Association for Computational Linguistics (ACL), 1995

Recomputation of Class Relevance Scores for Improving Text Classification

Sang-Bum Kim and Hae-Chang Rim

Dept. of Computer Science and Engineering, Korea University,
Anam-dong 5 ka, SungPuk-gu, SEOUL, 136-701, KOREA
{sbkim,rim}@nlp.korea.ac.kr

Abstract. In the text classification task, bag-of-word representation causes a critical problem when the prediction powers for a few words are estimated terribly inaccurately because of the lack of the training documents. In this paper, we propose recomputation of class relenvace scores based on the similarities among the classes for improving text classification. Through the experiments using two different baseline classifiers and two different test data, we prove that our proposed method consistently outperforms the traditional text classification strategy.

1   Introduction

Text categorization (or classification, filtering, routing, etc.) is the problem of assigning predefined categories to free text documents. This problem is of great practical importance given the massive volume of online texts available through the World Wide Web, internet news feeds, electronic mail, corporate databases, medical patient records, digital libraries, etc. Learning methods are frequently employed to automatically construct classifiers from labeled documents. A growing number of statistical learning methods have been applied to this problem in recent years, including nearest neighbor classifiers[4], perceptron classifiers[3], Bayesian probabilistic classifiers[2], and support vector machines[1], etc. Most text classification approaches are based on bag-of-word representation of documents. Each word has its own class prediction power learned by specified learning algorithm, and they are combined to predict the class of each document. A bag-of-word representation scheme is widely used in many other IR applications because of its simplicity and efficiency. However, this representation causes a critical problem when the prediction powers for a few words are estimated terribly inaccurately because of the lack of the training documents. For example, suppose that the word *"model"* has appeared all the three training documents for class airplane, but has not appeared in any other documents. In this case, the word *"model"* has extreme weight, i.e., prediction power, to favor the class airplane. Thus, if a new test document including the word *"model"* will be classified into the class airplane although the test document is about *"Recent various computer models"*. It is obvious that the proper class can be assigned to the test document if the document has many informative terms such as *"computer"*, *"CPU"* which favor the class computer. For this problem, some studies

A. Gelbukh (Ed.): CICLing 2004, LNCS 2945, pp. 580–583, 2004.
© Springer-Verlag Berlin Heidelberg 2004

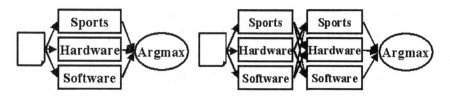

Fig. 1. Traditional classification process(left) and proposed classification process(right)

have tried n-gram feature based representation to reduce the ambiguities of the unigrams, but they have often failed to improve the performances compared to its overhead to use of multiword features. In this paper, we propose a solution of a different style: recomputation of class relevance scores based on the similarities among the classes.[1] First, the original classifier trained using any machine-learning algorithm calculates the relevance scores of the document for each class. Then the relevance score for the class is recomputed using similarities between other classes and relevance scores for the classes.

2   Motivation and Approach

One of the distinguished characteristics of text classification is that many classes have their conceptually similar classes. For example, the class "Computer" is conceptually most similar to the class "Software", then the class "Electronic product", and so on. Thus, we can assume that if the relevance score between a document and a class c is high, the score between the document and the similar class to the class c should be also high. For this reason, we propose the recomputation of class relevance scores based on the class similarities.

2.1   Recomputation of Class Relevance Scores

In our method, a class of a given text is determined through the following two steps. First, the relevance scores of the document for all the classes are calculated by the original classifier trained using any traditional machine learning algorithm. Then the relevance score for the class is recomputed using similarities between other classes and relevance scores for the classes as follows:

$$ReScore(d_k, c_j) = Score(d_k, c_j) + \sum_{\forall i, i \neq j} Score(d_k, c_i) \cdot \frac{Sim(c_j, c_i)}{N_j} \quad (1)$$

where, $Score(d_k, c_j)$ is initial relenvace score between document k and class j by the original classifier, $Sim(c_j, c_i)$ is a similarity between class k and class i. N_j is a normalization factor for class c_j, which is $\sum_{\forall i, i \neq j} Sim(c_j, c_i)$.

---

[1] Demo Website : http://term.korea.ac.kr/~sbkim/ (Korean Only)

For the class similarities, we use cosine similarities between two centroid vectors $\boldsymbol{w_i}$, $\boldsymbol{w_j}$ for each class c_i and c_j defined by:

$$\boldsymbol{w_i} = (w_{1i}, w_{2i}, \cdots, w_{|V|i}), w_{ti} = \frac{1}{|D_i|} \sum_{d_k \in c_i} tf_{tk} \cdot idf_t \tag{2}$$

where, $|V|$ is a size of vocabulary, $|D_i|$ is a number of training documents for class c_i, tf_{tk} is a term frequency of term t in a document d_k, and idf_t is inverse document frequency of term t. Figure 1 shows the difference between traditional text classification process and our proposed classification process.

2.2   Baseline Text Classifiers

We have used two different classifiers for evaluating our method: Naive Bayes text classifier[2] and Perceptron classifier[3]. Naive Bayes text classifier is based on the generative model of a document. We choose the multinomial naive Bayes classifier in [2], and the relevance score is computed as follows:

$$Score(d_k, c_j) = \sum_{t=1}^{|V|} tf_{tk} \cdot \log p(w_t|c_j) \text{ , where } p(w_t|c_j) = \frac{\sum_{d_k \in c_j} tf_{tk}}{\sum_i \sum_{d_k \in c_j} tf_{ik}} \tag{3}$$

For the perceptron classifiers, we use general perceptron learning algorithm with the training documnet vectors with $tf \cdot idf$ values. With the final perceptron weight $\boldsymbol{PW_j}$ for each class, the relevance score between new document vector $\boldsymbol{d_k}$ and class c_j is computed by inner product as follows:

$$Score(d_k, c_j) = \boldsymbol{d_k} \cdot \boldsymbol{PW_j} \tag{4}$$

3   Experimental Results

We have used two different test collections: Reuters 21578 collection and Korean Web Documents collection. Reuters 21578 collection consists of 9,603 training documents and 3,299 test documents. There are 90 categories, and each document has one or more of the categories. Korean Web Document collection has 4,234 training documents and 1,061 test documents, and these documents are exclusively classified into 90 classes. Accuracy measure is used to evaluate the performances. Since a few categories can be assigned to a document in the reuters 21578 collection, we count as the right classification if the output class of the classifiers is one of the answer classes of the test document.

Table 1 shows the performances of naive Bayes and perceptron baseline classifiers and their recomputation results on the two different test data. Our proposed recomputation method consistently improved the baseline classifiers in any cases though the degree of the improvement is somewhat discouraging.

We have found that our method reduced the cases where the document is classified into wholly unrelated class, but there are a number of misclassifications among the similar classes. Our method generally raises the relevance score

Table 1. Summary of the performances : Baseline vs. Baseline+Re

	Reuters 21578	Korean Web Documents
Naive Bayes	88.34	63.08
Naive Bayes+Re	**88.92(+0.66%)**	**64.00(+1.46%)**
Perceptron	90.16	67.02
Perceptron+Re	**90.40(+0.27%)**	**68.28(+1.90%)**

between a document and the class that is similar to the highly ranked classes for the given document. For this reason, if two similar classes are ranked at top and the second, their ranks are often reversed according to similarities between these two classes and the classes at the lower ranks. This happens especially when the right answer ranks the top, and many of its similar classes rank at the second, third, and so on.

4 Conclusions and Future Works

In this paper, we propose the method of recomputation of class relevance scores to alleviate the problems caused by a few terms which prediction powers are estimated terribly. Through the experiments using two different baseline classifiers and two different test data, we prove that our proposed method consistently outperforms the traditional text classification strategy. It is because that our method reduces many of the entirely wrong misclassification in the test data. Our proposed method, however, also has a problem that discriminative powers among the similar classes become weakened. For the future work, we try to develop a modified version of proposed method that keeps the discriminative power among the similar classes using hierarchical manner.

References

1. T. Joachims. Text categorization with support vector machines: learning with many relevant features. In *Proceedings of ECML-98, 10th European Conference on Machine Learning*, pages 137–142, 1998.
2. A. K. McCallum and K. Nigam. A comparison of event models for naive bayes text classification. In *Proceedings of AAAI-98 Workshop on Learning for Text Categorization*, pages 137–142, 1998.
3. H. T. Ng, W. B. Goh, and K. L. Low. Feature selection, perceptron learning, and a usability case study for text categorization. In *Proceedings of SIGIR-97*, pages 67–73, 1997.
4. Y. Yang and C. G. Chute. An example-based mapping method for text categorization and retrieval. *ACM Transactions on Information Systems*, 12(3):252–277, 1994.

Raising High-Degree Overlapped Character Bigrams into Trigrams for Dimensionality Reduction in Chinese Text Categorization

Dejun Xue and Maosong Sun

National Key Laboratory of Intelligent Technology and Systems
Department of Computer Science and Technology, Tsinghua University
Beijing, China 100084
xdj00@mails.tsinghua.edu.cn; lkc-dcs@mail.tsinghua.edu.cn

Abstract. High dimensionality of feature space is a crucial obstacle for Automated Text Categorization. According to the characteristics of Chinese character N-grams, this paper reveals that there exists a kind of redundancy arising from feature overlapping. Focusing on Chinese character bigrams, the paper puts forward a concept of δ-overlapping between two bigrams, and proposes a new method of dimensionality reduction, called δ-Overlapped Raising ($\delta - OR$), by raising the δ-overlapped bigrams into their corresponding trigrams. Moreover, the paper designs a two-stage dimensionality reduction strategy for Chinese bigrams by integrating a filtering method based on *Chi-CIG* score function and the $\delta - OR$ method. Experimental results on a large-scale Chinese document collection indicate that, on the basis of the first stage of reduction processing, $\delta - OR$ at the second stage can significantly reduce the dimension of feature space without sacrificing categorization effectiveness. We believe that the above methodology would be language-independent.

1   Introduction

Nowadays, a large volume of information in digital form is available. Automated Text Categorization (*TC*), which automatically classifies natural language documents into a predefined set of thematic categories, is becoming a key approach in content-based document management tasks [1]. A range of statistic and machine learning methods have been employed in *TC*, such as Probabilistic Model [2, 3], Neural Network [4], K-Nearest Neighbors [5], Decision Tree [6], Centroid-Based Classifier [7], Rocchio Classifier [8], Support Vector Machine [9], as well as Classifier Committee [10], etc. In this kind of inductive classifier learning, text documents are usually indexed to weighted feature vectors with an indexing language, such as words or phrases [11]. Although phrases have intuitively better semantic qualities than words, previous works show that more sophisticated representations have not led to significant improvement over word indexing due to their inferior statistical qualities on some occasions [1, 12].

A. Gelbukh (Ed.): CICLing 2004, LNCS 2945, pp. 584–595, 2004.
© Springer-Verlag Berlin Heidelberg 2004

High dimensionality of feature space is a crucial obstacle for *TC*. In English word indexing, for instance, the size of feature set is often above tens of thousands, and in English phrasal indexing, features are far more than these. It is highly desirable to automatically reduce the dimensionality of original large-size feature space without sacrificing categorization effectiveness [13]. Published works claimed that the processing of dimensionality reduction in *TC* can not only decline overfitting of learning, but also lead to effectiveness improvement to a certain extent [12, 13].

One way of tackling the issue is Feature Selection which tends to select a subset of features from original feature set to maximize the categorization effectiveness. The filtering approach, which selects the highest-scored features according to a numerical function, is widely used in feature selection procedure [14]. By controlling the score threshold, the filtering approach can usually achieve a sharp dimensionality reduction. The commonly used score functions include Term Frequency (*TF*, *tf*), Document Frequency (*DF*, *df*), Chi-square (*Chi*), Correlation Coefficient, Simplified Chi, Mutual Information (*MI*) and Information Gain (*IG*), etc [1]. Yang et al.[13] compared five score functions on Reuters21578 collection, and concluded that *DF*, *IG*, and *Chi* are more effective than the others.

Feature Extraction (also known as Reparameterization) is another way to address the problem. By mapping original high dimension feature space into a lower dimension space, feature extraction eliminates redundancy in feature space and creates a new set of independent feature dimensions. Feature Clustering, Principal Component Analysis (*PCA*), and Latent Semantic Indexing (*LSI*) are this kind of approaches [12, 15, 16, 17]. *PCA* and *LSI* coming from linear algebra are not applicable for high dimension space for their high computation complexity. Feature clustering reduces dimensionality by grouping features which share a high degree of semantic relatedness into clusters. Through investigating the impact of feature clustering on *TC*, Lewis concluded that the clustering of both words and phrases is inferior to non-clustering indexing language because the relationships captured in the clusters are mostly accidental [12]. Li et al. experimented with feature clustering on a small data set (814 docs) and reported that clustering contributes marginally to categorization [15]. In these works, clustering processing was implemented according to co-occurrence *df* of features (called as metafeature in [12]). We think that this is one reason for the discouraging results as most co-occurring features in documents are independent entities. Another reason is that the scope of clustering upon the whole feature space is too wide, so a great deal of noise is incorporated into clusters.

Unlike English, Chinese text has no explicit segmentation tokens. Hence, Chinese character N-gram serves as a reasonable candidate for document indexing in *TC*. Nie et al. studied Chinese words and Chinese N-grams with respect to their performances in Chinese Information Retrieval (*IR*), and claimed that N-grams (in particular bigrams) perform as well as, or even better than words. Moreover, the performance of word indexing is affected by the size of dictionary and segmentation accuracy [18]. Following the suggestions, some works on Chinese *TC* on bigrams achieved satisfied performances [19].

We found that there exists a kind of redundancy arising from feature overlapping after analyzing the characteristics of Chinese character N-grams. Focusing on bigrams, this paper puts forward a concept of δ-Overlapped Bigrams, and proposes a new method of dimensionality reduction, called δ-Overlapped Raising ($\delta - OR$), by raising the δ-overlapped bigrams into corresponding trigrams which are concatenations of the overlapped bigrams. Moreover, the paper designs a two-stage strategy for dimensionality reduction over Chinese bigrams by integrating the filtering method based on *Chi-CIG* score function and the $\delta - OR$ method. Experimental results on a large-scale Chinese document collection indicate that, on the basis of the first stage of dimensionality reduction, δ -*OR* can effectively reduce the dimension of feature space without sacrificing categorization effectiveness.

The remainder of this paper is organized as follows. In Section 2, we analyze the characteristics of Chinese character N-grams. In Section 3, we give the definitions about Chinese character δ -overlapped bigrams, and propose the $\delta - OR$ method. In Section 4, we give a two-stage dimensionality reduction strategy for Chinese bigrams. Section 5 is about experiment conditions, including data set, classifier, and evaluation. In Section 6, we analyze the experimental results. Conclusions are given in the last section.

2   Chinese Character N-grams

As the length of Chinese character is fixed at 2 bytes in computer, and a sentence is written as a continuous string of characters, it is very easy to index Chinese document with N-grams in which a feature has a fixed length. For example, a Chinese sentence:

中华人民共和国 (The People's Republic of China).

The bigram indexing is:

t_1	t_2	t_3	t_4	t_5	t_6	t_7
中	华	人	民	共	和	国
T_1	T_2	T_3	T_4	T_5	T_6	

And the trigram indexing is:

t_1	t_2	t_3	t_4	t_5	t_6	t_7
中	华	人	民	共	和	国
T_1	T_2	T_3	T_4	T_5		

In Chinese character N-grams, especially bigrams, many are real words. For example, in the Chinese Thesaurus (Tong Yi Ci Ci Lin) which has 52,260 Chinese words, 33,624 words (64.34%) are composed of two characters, i.e. bigrams, 14,763 words (28.20%) have three or more characters and the rest 3874 words (7.46%) are unigrams [20]. Moreover, many N-grams which are not included in Chinese thesaurus act as real words in reality to convey definite meanings. They are primarily Chinese phrases (such as compound words, idioms, and so on). Both the two types of character strings are often selected from original N-gram set during feature selection procedure for their high frequency and semantic independency. We think that this is one of the reasons that bigram indexing is superior to word indexing in Chinese IR and *TC*.

According to Lewis' claims, optimal effectiveness of *TC* will occur at a feature set size substantially below the size of full indexing language [12]. And Xue et al. [19] suggested that the most important features for category prediction are those that both represent semantically the content of documents, and distribute unevenly between relevant documents and irrelevant documents. Dimensionality reduction processing should pay more attention on categorization capability of features. N-gram feature set (not including unigrams) provides us with a much more freedom space to select important features as its large size.

Although N-gram feature space has a far better dimensionality independency than word space, it incorporates a great deal of noisy as well. Hence, dimensionality reduction is a necessary step for *TC* based on N-gram indexing.

3   Raising High-Degree Overlapped Character Bigrams into Trigrams

Although Chinese character N-gram indexing (N>=2) has some positive characteristics over Chinese word indexing, it creates a great deal of redundancy resulting from character overlapping. As the paper focuses on Chinese character bigrams, here, we just discuss about this kind of redundancy over bigrams. First, let us give several definitions and a corollary.

Two Bigrams are Equal ($=$): Given two bigrams T_1 ($t_{11}t_{12}$) and T_2 ($t_{21}t_{22}$). If ($t_{11}=t_{21}$ AND $t_{12}=t_{22}$), then T_1 is equal to T_2, which is abbreviated to $T_1=T_2$. Here, t_i is a Chinese character, and it is the same in the following definitions.

Two Bigrams are not Equal ($\neq$): Given two bigrams T_1 ($t_{11}t_{12}$) and T_2 ($t_{21}t_{22}$). If ($t_{11} \neq t_{21}$ OR $t_{12} \neq t_{22}$), then T_1 is not equal to T_2, which is abbreviated to $T_1 \neq T_2$.

A Trigram Contains a Bigram ($\supset$): Given bigram T_1 ($t_{11}t_{12}$) and trigram T_2 ($t_{21}t_{22}$ t_{23}). If ($t_{11}=t_{21}$ AND $t_{12}=t_{22}$) OR ($t_{11}=t_{22}$ and $t_{12}=t_{23}$), then trigram T_2 contains T_1, which is abbreviated to $T_2 \supset T_1$.

Overlapped Bigrams (OB): Given two bigrams T_1 ($t_{11}t_{12}$) and T_2 ($t_{21}t_{22}$), and $T_1 \neq T_2$. If $t_{12}=t_{21}$, then T_1 and T_2 overlap each other, which is abbreviated to (T_1 OB T_2).

δ **- Overlapped Bigrams** ($\delta-OB$): Given a document collection D, bigrams T_1 ($t_{11}t_{12}$) and T_2 ($t_{21}t_{22}$), and trigram T_3 ($t_{31}t_{32}t_{33}$). T_1, T_2 and T_3 occur in D, and $T_1 \neq T_2$. If T_1, T_2 and T_3 are subject to the following constraints simultaneously:

(1). T_1 OB T_2 AND $T_3 \supset T_1$ AND $T_3 \supset T_2$;

(2). $\dfrac{\left| tf(T_1) - tf(T_2) \right|}{\max \left(tf(T_1), tf(T_2) \right)} \leq 1 - \delta$;

(3). $\dfrac{\left| df(T_1) - df(T_2) \right|}{\max \left(df(T_1), df(T_2) \right)} \leq 1 - \delta$;

(4). $\dfrac{\min \left(\left| tf(T_1) - tf(T_3) \right|, \left| tf(T_2) - tf(T_3) \right| \right)}{\max \left(tf(T_1), tf(T_2) \right)} \leq 1 - \delta$.

then T_1 and T_2 are δ-overlapped with a degree of δ over D, which is abbreviated to (T_1 $\delta - OB$ T_2). Here, $tf(T_1)$ is the occurrence frequency of bigram T_1 over D, $df(T_1)$ the number of documents in which T_1 occur, and δ the maximum real value falling in [0, 1.0] indicating the overlapping degree between T_1 and T_2.

Corollary 1: Given Chinese document collection D and bigram T_1 ($t_{11}t_{12}$) and trigram T_2 ($t_{21}t_{22}$ t_{23}). If $T_2 \supset T_1$, then $tf(T_1) \geq tf(T_2)$, and $df(T_1) \geq df(T_2)$.

Relationship (T_1 OB T_2) only requires the characters in T_1 and T_2 to occur continuously in a sentence. It is a very relax relationship between bigrams, and there are numerous bigrams meeting it in a Chinese document collection. Based on OB, relationship (T_1 $\delta - OB$ T_2) introduces trigram constraints and *tf/df* constraints to emphasize that T_1 and T_2 should overlap each other with a degree of δ. When δ =0, it indicates that T_1 and T_2 do not overlap at all, and T_1 and T_2 are different entities in feature space; when $\delta = 1$, it indicates that T_1 and T_2 are completely overlapped, and they contribute similarly for categorization. On the other words, in this case, both T_1 and T_2 can be raised into a single trigram T_3 which is concatenated by T_1 and T_2. With the raising operation, the original feature set is reduced. By adjusting the parameter δ, we can relax the constraints of bigram overlapping, and gain more aggressive dimensionality reduction.

$\delta - OB$ often happens during indexing Chinese proper names, technology nomenclatures, Chinese idioms, and specific phrases. These character strings are relatively independent entities in Chinese language, and their two-character components are almost exclusively used in the strings. In the case, the pairs of bigrams can be raised into the corresponding trigrams which contain the bigrams, which we call as δ-Overlapped Raising ($\delta - OR$). For example, the Chinese three-character string: 毛泽东 (Name of Chairman Mao's, the founder of the People's Republic of China), its two bigrams 毛泽 and 泽东 are exclusively used as components of Chairman Mao's name in our document collection. So, we think that the two bigrams are high-degree overlapped, and can be raised into the trigram 毛泽东.

4   Two-Stage Dimensionality Reduction Strategy

Because the size of index features in our data set is very large, about 1.75 million bigrams, we devise a two-stage strategy for global dimensionality reduction. In the first stage, we use two filtering schemes to reduce dimensionality. First, we remove the rare features whose *tf* is below 10. The size of feature set declines to about 0.41 million (it acts as the original feature set for next processing), with a reduction degree of 76.4% at this step. Then, we use *Chi-CIG* weighting function which combines *Chi* and *CIG* functions to select the highest scored features. *Chi*, *CIG*, and *Chi-CIG* functions are demonstrated as Formula 2, 3 and 4 respectively [13, 20]. At this step, we set up 7 feature subsets whose size falls in the range of [10,000, 70,000] with the interval of 10,000 from the original feature set.

$$Chi(T_k, c_j) = \frac{N[P_d(T_k, c_j) \times P_d(\overline{T_k}, \overline{c_j}) - P_d(T_k, \overline{c_j}) \times P_d(\overline{T_k}, c_j)]^2}{P_d(T_k) \times P_d(c_j) \times P_d(\overline{T_k}) \times P_d(\overline{c_j})}. \qquad (1)$$

where N is the size of training documents, $P_d(T_k, c_j)$ is the number of documents belonging to category c_j and containing feature T_k over N, $P_d(T_k)$ is the number of documents containing T_k over N, and $P_d(c_j)$ is the number of documents involved in category c_j over N. For the whole category set, *Chi* value of feature T_k can be defined in Formula 2 [13, 20], where M is the size of category set.

$$Chi(T_k) = \max_{j=1}^{M} \{Chi(T_k, c_j)\}. \qquad (2)$$

$$CIG(T_k) = -\sum_{j=1}^{M} P_d(c_j) \log P_d(c_j) \tag{3}$$

$$+ P_d(T_k) \sum_{j=1}^{M} \left[P_d(c_j \mid T_k) \log P_d(c_j \mid T_k) \right] \times R(c_j, T_k)$$

$$+ P_d(\overline{T_k}) \sum_{j=1}^{M} \left[P_d(c_j \mid \overline{T_k}) \log P_d(c_j \mid \overline{T_k}) \right] \times R(c_j, T_k).$$

where $R(c_j, T_k) \in \{0,1\}$ indicates whether feature T_k appears in the documents of category c_j or not, and $P(c_j \mid T_k)$ is the number of documents which contain T_k in c_j over the number of documents containing T_k in training set.

$$Chi\text{-}CIG(T_k) = Chi(T_k) \times CIG(T_k). \tag{4}$$

At the second stage, we use the $\delta - OR$ method to further reduce dimensionality on the basis of the feature subsets created at the first stage. The procedure is formalized as the following steps:

(1). Do dimensionality reduction processing over all of the document vectors in collection (including training document vectors and test document vectors), according to the feature subset created at the first stage;

(2). Given a δ, find out the $\delta - OB$ bigrams and corresponding trigrams from the original bigram set and trigram set;

(3). According to the $\delta - OB$ bigram list and corresponding trigram list, implement $\delta - OR$ operation over all of the document vectors: Given a document vector d, $\delta - OB$ bigrams T_1 and T_2, as well as corresponding trigram T_3, if T_3 does not occur in d, then remove T_1 and T_2 from d (if they exist); if T_3 occurs in d, and either T_1 or T_2 or both occur in d as well, then raise T_1 or T_2 or both into T_3, and replace their *tf*s with T_3's $h*tf$ in d. Here, h is an integer determined in experiments. In the paper, it is fixed at 10 at which the categorization effectiveness is optimal in our experiments. Enlarging T_3's *tf* by h times aims to emphasize its contribution for category prediction. We think that T_3 is narrower than both T_1 and T_2. So, raising T_1 and T_2 into T_3 is benefit to categorization precision. And according to the statements in Section 3, T_3 is usually an independent and specific language entity, such as Chinese person name, Chinese idiom, which could give strong evidence for categorization.

(4). Sum up the *tf*s of same features within document vectors, and remove the duplicated features from vectors. Then, go to the classifier induction process (Section 5.2).

5   Experiment Design

5.1   Data Set

We adopt the categorization system of Encyclopedia of China as the predefined category set which comprises 55 categories. According to the categorization system, we build up a Chinese document collection consisting of 71,674 texts with about 74 million Chinese characters. Each text is manually assigned a single category label. The number of documents in the categories is quite different, ranging from 399 (Solid Earth Physics Category) to 3,374 (Biology Category). The average number of documents in a category is 1,303. The average length of documents is 921 Chinese characters. We randomly divide the document collection into two parts: 64,533 texts for training and 7,141 texts for test in proportion of 9:1.

5.2 Classifier

In the *TC* system, we adopt centroid-based classifier which is a kind of profile-based classifier, because of its simplification and fast speed [7, 20]. After bigram indexing and feature dimensionality reduction, we build *tf* vectors for documents, then sum up *tf* vectors within each category to get the *tf* vector for the category, and further weight the features based on the summed *tf* vectors of categories with the well-known *tf*idf* weighting criterion (shown as Formula 5) to create weighted feature vectors for categories. The resulting feature vectors are considered as the centroids of the categories.

$$w(T_k, c_j) = TF(T_k, c_j) \times IDF(t_k) = \log(tf_{kj} + 1.0) \times \log(N / df_k). \tag{5}$$

where tf_{kj} is the frequency of feature T_k occurring in the training documents which belong to category c_j, df_k the document frequency of T_k in training set, and N the size of training set.

Then, a document-pivoted classifier f can be set up:

$$f = \arg \max_{j=1}^{M} (V_j \bullet d). \tag{6}$$

where V_j is the centroid vector of category c_j, and d the weighted feature vector of a free document.

5.3 Evaluation

For a category, classification effectiveness is evaluated in features of precision (*Pr*) and recall (*Re*). For the categorization system, we adopt F_1-measure with micro-averaging of individual *Pr* and *Re*, shown as Formula 7. As for the level of dimensionality reduction, we use aggressivity (abbreviated to *Agg*) as evaluation measure [1], shown as Formula 8.

$$F_1 = \frac{2 Pr \times Re}{Pr + Re}. \tag{7}$$

$$Agg = 1 - \frac{\text{the number of features after dimensionality reduction}}{\text{the number of features before dimensionality reduction}}. \tag{8}$$

6   Experiment Results and Analysis

The impacts on categorization effectiveness resulting from the first stage of dimensionality reduction are plotted in Fig1. The curve shows that as selecting more features, we get better effectiveness performance. As the selected features are above 30,000, however, the improvement tendency declines. It indicates that with the increase of the size of selected features, the system will get to the optimal point of effectiveness. At the first stage of dimensionality reduction, we gain sharp $Aggs$ from 83.0% to 97.6% (the size of original feature set is 412,908). It shows that, in Chinese TC based on N-gram indexing language, it is a desirable step to reduce dimensionality with an effective feature selection score function for original large-size feature space.

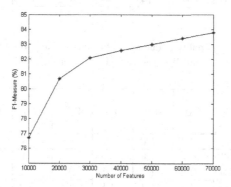

Fig. 1. Categorization Effectiveness with *Chi-CIG* Score Function at the First Stage of Dimensionality Reduction

Table 1 shows the number of reduced features achieved by using $\delta - OR$ dimensionality reduction method. As parameter δ is set at 1.0, i.e. two bigrams are required to overlap completely when they are raised into the corresponding trigram, the number of reduced features is small, in the range of [30-300]. As δ decreases, the constraints on $\delta - OB$ are relaxed, i.e. two bigrams are just subject to overlap at most times, the number of raised features increases. When δ decreases to 0.3, the number of reduced features gets to 4,358 on the 70,000-size feature set. Moreover, the larger of the size of original feature set, the more features are reduced at the second reduction stage with a same δ.

The $Aggs$ of dimensionality reduction coming from the second dimensionality reduction stage are shown in Table 2. As we can see, $Aggs$ of dimensionality reduction gained at this stage are primarily affected by δ, and slightly by the size of feature set. This indicates that bigram overlapping exists in various sizes of feature sets, and $\delta - OR$ dimensionality reduction processing can be implemented on various feature sets built at the first stage. However, the $Aggs$ gained at the second stage (less than 10%) are far less than those gained at the first stage (about 90%).

Table 1. Number of Reduced Features Achieved By Using $\delta - OR$ Method. A is the Parameter δ, C the 7 Feature Sets Created at the First Stage of Dimensionality Reduction, and B the Number of Reduced Features at the Second Stage

B \ A \ C	1.0	0.9	0.8	0.7	0.6	0.5	0.4	0.3
70000	270	692	1135	1569	2040	2623	3359	4358
60000	245	627	1020	1399	1798	2308	2947	3808
50000	211	546	881	1207	1543	1968	2513	3222
40000	170	458	722	993	1261	1618	2066	2645
30000	126	369	572	765	966	1211	1558	2004
20000	88	252	405	534	660	819	1057	1352
10000	30	114	199	266	334	416	540	684

Table 2. Aggs of Dimensionality Reduction Achieved by Using $\delta - OR$ Method. A and C are as the Same as in Table 1, and B the Aggs of Dimensionality Reduction at the Second Stage (%)

B \ A \ C	1.0	0.9	0.8	0.7	0.6	0.5	0.4	0.3
70000	0.4	1.0	1.6	2.2	2.9	3.7	4.8	6.2
60000	0.4	1.0	1.7	2.3	3.0	3.8	4.9	6.3
50000	0.4	1.1	1.8	2.4	3.1	3.9	5.0	6.4
40000	0.4	1.1	1.8	2.5	3.2	4.0	5.2	6.6
30000	0.4	1.2	1.9	2.6	3.2	4.0	5.2	6.7
20000	0.4	1.3	2.0	2.7	3.3	4.1	5.3	6.8
10000	0.3	1.1	2.0	2.7	3.3	4.2	5.4	6.8

Table 3 demonstrates the categorization performances using the two-stage dimensionality reduction strategy, and Table 4 is about the contribution for categorization effectiveness coming from the $\delta - OR$ method alone. When the size of feature sets created at the first stage is above 40,000, the categorization performances are improved by using $\delta - OR$ method to reduce dimensionality at various δ. The improvement tendencies are in the shape of arcs. The optimal points of effectiveness improvement occur as δ falls in the range of [0.7, 0.8] with about 0.5% effectiveness improvement and about 2% Agg of dimensionality reduction. As δ is above 0.8, it reduces dimensions of feature space without sacrificing effectiveness on 7 feature sets, even with a slight improvement. Hence, it is convinced that the $\delta - OR$ method is an effective way of feature extraction, in comparison with the previous approaches, such as feature clustering, which focus on all the features according to their co-occurrence df. The $\delta - OR$ method fines data grain from df to tf, and limits the processing of feature raising over the δ-overlapped bigrams. Furthermore, it shows us a new direction of dimensionality reduction through making full use of the characteristics of indexing language itself.

Table 3. F1-measure of Categorization Effectiveness resulting from the Two-Stage Dimensionality Reduction Strategy. A is the parameter δ, C the 7 Feature Sets and their F1-measure Effectiveness by Using *Chi-CIG* Score Function Alone (%), and B the F1-measure Resulting from the Two-Stage Reduction Strategy (%)

B \ A C	1.0	0.9	0.8	0.7	0.6	0.5	0.4	0.3
70000	83.8	83.9	84.2	84.3	84.3	84.1	84.0	84.0	83.9
60000	83.4	83.5	83.7	83.8	83.8	83.7	83.7	83.5	83.3
50000	83.0	83.1	83.3	83.4	83.4	83.3	83.3	83.2	82.9
40000	82.6	82.6	82.8	82.7	82.8	82.8	82.8	82.7	82.5
30000	82.1	82.1	82.2	82.2	82.2	82.1	82.0	81.7	81.5
20000	80.7	80.7	80.8	80.8	80.6	80.4	80.4	80.5	80.2
10000	76.7	76.7	76.8	76.8	76.6	76.6	76.4	76.4	76.2

Table 4. Improvement Degree of Categorization Effectiveness Contributed by $\delta - OR$ Method. A and C are as the Same as in Table 1, and B the Improvement Degree of Categorization Effectiveness Coming from the Second Dimensionality Reduction Stage (%)

B \ A C	1.0	0.9	0.8	0.7	0.6	0.5	0.4	0.3
70000	0.1	0.4	0.5	0.5	0.3	0.2	0.2	0.1
60000	0.1	0.3	0.4	0.4	0.3	0.3	0.1	-0.1
50000	0.1	0.3	0.4	0.4	0.3	0.3	0.2	-0.1
40000	0	0.2	0.1	0.2	0.2	0.2	0.1	-0.1
30000	0	0.1	0.1	0.1	0	-0.1	-0.4	-0.6
20000	0	0.1	0.1	-0.1	-0.3	-0.3	-0.2	-0.5
10000	0	0.1	0.1	-0.1	-0.1	-0.3	-0.3	-0.5

7   Conclusions

The paper first analyses the characteristics of Chinese character N-grams, and points out that there exists a kind of redundancy arising from feature overlapping. Focusing on Chinese bigrams, the paper gives several definitions about Chinese bigram overlapping, and puts forward the concept of δ-Overlapped Bigrams by introducing trigram constraints and *tf/df* constraints. Upon the idea of $\delta - OB$, the paper then proposes the method of δ-Overlapped Raising for dimensionality reduction by raising the δ-overlapped bigrams into the corresponding trigrams. Furthermore, the paper suggests a two-stage dimensionality reduction strategy for Chinese bigrams by integrating the filtering method based on *Chi-CIG* score function and the $\delta - OR$ method. Experimental results on a large-scale Chinese document collection indicate that, on the basis of the first stage of dimensionality reduction processing, the $\delta - OR$ method is capable of effectively reducing the dimension of feature space without sacrificing categorization effectiveness.

Due to that δ-overlapping is in fact a general characteristic of bigrams for any natural languages, $\delta - OR$ would be likely to be regarded as a language-independent method for dimensionality reduction. In the future, we will experiment with the method on Reuters-21578 collection for English language, where $\delta - OR$ will take word rather than character as its basic unit.

References

1. Fabrizio Sebastiani: Machine Learning in Automated Text Categorization. ACM Computing Surveys, Vol. 34(1). ACM Press New York (2002) 1–47
2. David D. Lewis: Naïve Bayes at Forty: The Independence Assumption in Information Retrieval. In Proceedings of 10th European Conference on Machine Learning (1998) 4–15
3. Andrew McCallum, Kamal Nigam: A Comparison of Event Models for Naïve Bayes Text Classification. In AAAI-98 Workshop on Learning for Text Categorization (1998) 41–48
4. Erik Wiener, Jan O. Pedersen, Andreas S. Weigend: A Neural Network Approach to Topic Spotting. In Proceedings of 4th Annual Symposium on Document Analysis and Information Retrieval (1995) 317–332
5. Yiming Yang: Expert Network: Effective and Efficient Learning from Human Decisions in Text Categorization and Retrieval. In Proceedings of 17th Annual International ACM SIGIR Conference on Research and Development in Information Retrieval (1994) 11–21
6. Chidanand Apte, Fred Damerau, Sholom M. Weiss: Automated Learning of Decision Rules for Text Categorization. ACM Transactions on Information Retrieval, Vol. 12(3). ACM Press New York (1994) 233–251
7. Veravuth Lertnattee, Thanaruk Theeramunkong: Improving Centroid-Based Text Classification Using Term-Distribution-Based Weighting and Feature Selection. In Proceedings of International Conference on Intelligent Technologies (2001) 349–356
8. Thorsten Joachims: A Probabilistic Analysis of the Rocchio Algorithm with TFIDF for Text Categorization. In Proceedings of 14th of International Conference on Machine Learning (1997) 143–151
9. Thorsten Joachims: Text Categorization with Support Vector Machines: Learnging with Many Relevant Features. In Proceedings of 10th European Conference on Machine Learning (1998) 137–142
10. Robert E. Schapire, Yoram Singer: BoosTexter: A Boosting-Based System for Text Categorization. Machine Learning, Vol. 39(2/3), (2000) 135–168
11. Gerard Salton, Michael J. McGill: Introduction to Modern Information Retrieval. McGraw-Hill Book Company, New York (1983)
12. David D. Lewis: An Evaluation of Phrasal and Clustered Representations on a Text Categorization. In Proceedings of 15th Annual International ACM SIGIR Conference on Research and Development in Information Retrieval (1992) 37–50
13. Yiming Yang, Jan O. Pedersen: A Comparative Study on Feature Selection in Text Categorization. In Proceedings of 14th International Conference on Machine Learning (1997) 412–420
14. Luis Carlos Molina, Lluis Belanche, Angela Nebot: Feature Selection Algorithms: A Survey and Experimental Evaluation. In Proceedings of 2nd IEEE International Conference on Data Mining. Maebashi City, Japan (2002) 306–313
15. Y. H. Li, Anil K. Jain: Classification of Text Document. The Computer Journal. Vol. 41, No.8, (1998)537–546
16. Scott Deerwester, Suan T. Dumais, George W. Furnas, Thomas K. Landauer, Richard Harshman: Indexing by Latent Semantic Indexing. Journal of the American Society for Information Science, Vol. 41, No.6, (1990)391–407

17. Hinrich Schutze, David A. Hull, Jan O. Pedersen: A comparison of Classifiers and Document Representations for the Routing Problem. In Proceedings of 18th Annual International ACM SIGIR Conference on Research and Development in Information Retrieval (1995) 229–237
18. Jianyun Nie, Fuji Ren: Chinese Information Retrieval: Using Characters or Words? Information Processing and Management Vol. 35, (1999) 443–462
19. Dejun Xue, Maosong Sun: A Study on Feature Weighting in Chinese Text Categorization. In Proceedings of the 4th International Conference on Computational Linguistics and Intelligent Text Processing. Mexico City (2003) 594–604
20. Shenfeng Luo: Statistic-Based Two-Character Chinese Word Extraction. Master Thesis of Tsinghua University, China (2003)

Information Retrieval and Text Categorization with Semantic Indexing[*]

Paolo Rosso, Antonio Molina, Ferran Pla,
Daniel Jiménez, and Vicent Vidal

Dpto. de Sist. Informáticos y Computación, U. Politécnica de Valencia, Spain
{prosso,amolina,fpla,djimenez,vvidal}@dsic.upv.es

Abstract. In this paper, we present the effect of the semantic indexing using *WordNet* senses on the Information Retrieval (IR) and Text Categorization (TC) tasks. The documents have been sense-tagged using a Word Sense Disambiguation (WSD) system based on Specialized Hidden Markov Models (SHMMs). The preliminary results showed that a small improvement of the performance was obtained only in the TC task.

1   WSD with Specialized HMMs

We consider WSD to be a tagging problem. The tagging process can be formulated as a maximization problem using the Hidden Markov Models (HMMs) formalism. Let S be the set of sense tags considered, and W, the vocabulary of the application. Given an input sentence, $W = w_1, \ldots, w_T$, where $w_i \in W$, the tagging process consists of finding the sequence of senses ($S = s_1, \ldots, s_T$, where $s_i \in S$) of maximum probability on the model, that is:

$$\widehat{S} = \arg\max_S P(S|W)$$

$$= \arg\max_S \left(\frac{P(S) \cdot P(W|S)}{P(W)} \right); \, S \in S^T \tag{1}$$

Due to the fact that the probability $P(W)$ is a constant that can be ignored in the maximization process, the problem is reduced to maximizing the numerator of equation 1. To solve this equation, the Markov assumptions should be made in order to simplify the problem. For a first-order HMM, the problem is reduced to solving the following equation:

$$\arg\max_S \left(\prod_{i:1\ldots T} P(s_i|s_{i-1}) \cdot P(w_i|s_i) \right) \tag{2}$$

The parameters of equation 2 can be represented as a first-order HMM where each state corresponds to a sense s_i, $P(s_i|s_{i-1})$ representing the transition probabilities between states and $P(w_i|s_i)$ representing the probability of emission

[*] This work was supported by the Spanish Research Projects CICYT TIC2000-0664-C02 and TIC2003-07158-C04-03. We are grateful to E. Ferretti for sense-tagging the data.

A. Gelbukh (Ed.): CICLing 2004, LNCS 2945, pp. 596–600, 2004.
© Springer-Verlag Berlin Heidelberg 2004

of words, w_i, in every state, s_i. The parameters of this model are estimated by maximum likelihood from semantic annotated corpora using an appropriate smoothing method (e.g. linear interpolation).

The HMM approach above presented cannot include different kinds of available linguistic information which can be useful in solving WSD. In particular, the *SemCor* corpus was used to learn the models, because it is the only available english corpus in which all content words have been semantically tagged. It provided the following input features: words ($\mathcal{W}$), lemmas ($\mathcal{L}$) and the corresponding POS tags ($\mathcal{P}$). Therefore, in the formulation presented above, the input vocabulary ($\mathcal{W}$) can be redefined as $\mathcal{I} = \mathcal{W} \times \mathcal{L} \times \mathcal{P}$. Then, an input sentence will be a sequence of tuples of words, lemmas and POS.

In order to incorporate this kind of information to the model we used Specialized HMMs [5]. Basically, a SHMM consists of changing the topology of the HMM in order to get a more accurate model which includes more information. This is done by means of an initial step previous to the learning process. It consists of the redefinition of the input vocabulary and the output tags. Therefore, no changes are needed in the usual HMM learning task. This redefinition is done by means of two processes: the *selection* process, which is applied to the input vocabulary, and the *specialization* process, which redefines the output tags.

The aim of the *selection* process is to choose which input features are relevant to the task. This process applies a determined *selection criterion* to $\mathcal{I}$ that produces a new input vocabulary ($\hat{\mathcal{I}}$). This new vocabulary consists of the concatenation of the relevant features selected. The *selection criteria* used in this work is as follows: if a word has a sense in *WordNet* we concatenate the lemma and the POS (Part-Of-Speech) associated to the word as input vocabulary. For non-content words (i.e., words without meaning), we only consider their lemma as input.

The *specialization process* allows for the codification of certain information into the context (i.e., into the states of the model). It consists of redefining the output tag set by adding information from the input. This redefinition produces some changes in the model topology, in order to allow the model to better capture some contextual restrictions and to get a more accurate model. The application of a *specialization criterion* to $\mathcal{S}$ produces a new output tag set ($\hat{\mathcal{S}}$), whose elements are the result of the concatenation of some relevant input information to the original output tags.

In the WSD system used here, we defined the output semantic tag set by considering certain statistical information which was extracted from the annotated corpora. In the *SemCor* corpus, each annotated word is tagged with a *sense_key* which has the form *lemma%lex_sense*. In general, we considered the *lex_sense* field of the *sense_key* associated to each lemma as the semantic tag in order to reduce the size of the output tag set. This does not lead to any loss of information because we can obtain the *sense_key* by concatenating the lemma to the output tag. For certain frequent lemmas, we can specialize their output tags to produce a more fine-grained semantic tag (which is equivalent to the *sense_key*). These choices were made experimentally by taking into account a set of frequent lemmas, which were extracted from the Semcor corpus.

The evaluation of the WSD system was previously carried out on the *Semcor* corpus (73.3% of precision) and on the English all-word task of the *Senseval-2* competition (60.2% of precision) [5]. These results are in line with the results provided for the best WSD systems in the literature on the same tasks.

2   Semantic IR and TC: Experimental Results

The classical vector space model for IR was shown by Gonzalo [2] to give better results if WordNet synsets are chosen as the indexing space instead of terms (up to 29% improvement in the experimental results was obtained for a manually disambiguated test collection derived from the SemCor corpus). Therefore, in our research work, we decided to represent each document through a vector of relevant synsets instead of a vector of relevant terms. The disambiguation of the meaning of each term was obtained using the WSD system based on SHMMs presented above.

When searching for a document, it could be often useful to previously group, or cluster, the documents of the collection. Therefore, the IR task was initially carried out employing the Bisecting-Spherical K-Means clustering technique. Its algorithm tries to join the advantages of the bisecting K-Means algorithm with the advantages of a modified version of the Spherical K-Means [4]. The corpus used for the experiments contains articles from the *1963 Times Magazine*[1]. Query statistics were also obtained for the query collection, formed by a total of 83 queries with an average of 15 words and one line per query. The optimal number of clusters for the Times Magazine corpus was set equal to 8. From a general viewpoint, less clusters imply a lower precision and a higher recall, whereas more clusters imply the opposite.

The same experiments were also carried out using the Singular Value Decomposition (SVD) technique of the Latent Semantic Indexing (LSI) model. The initial size of the vocabulary (i.e., the number of relevant terms of the document collection), was approximately equal to 6,500 terms. The SVD technique did not change this size and projected the vocabulary on a smaller dimensional subspace. The vector of each query was built the same way and during the evaluation, it was projected on a space whose dimension was equal to the number of singular values used for modelling the information system.

For both clustering and LSI models a worse precision was obtained when semantics was taken into account: 42.41% (sense indexing) vs. 63.58% (term indexing) for the Bisecting-Spherical K-Means technique, and 51.72% (sense indexing) vs. 67.95% (term indexing) for the SVD technique [3]. This could be due to the length of the queries because such long queries implicitly have a disambiguation effect. At the moment of writing this paper, some experiments have been carrying out using the *TREC document collection*[2] in which queries are shorter on average.

---

[1] Available at ftp.cs.cornell.edu/pub/smart/time/

[2] Text Retrieval Conference document collection; at www.trec.nist.gov

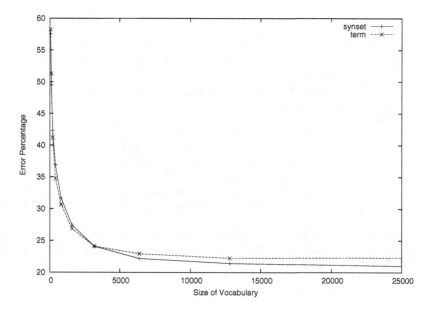

Fig. 1. Text Categorization: term vs. sense indexing

The K Nearest Neighbours (K-NN) is the technique we used in the TC task. The TC was performed using the K-NN method provided by the Rainbow system[3], with the value for the parameter K which was established as 30. Different experiments were carried out on the *20 Newsgroups* corpus[4] for the semantic TC task. This corpus contains about 20,000 news messages from 20 UseNet discussion groups (i.e., categories) that were sent in 1993. The task consisted of predicting which group each test document was sent to. The training set was composed of 16,000 documents (the first 800 ones of each category), whereas the other 3,997 documents were used as test set.

The introduction of semantics allowed for a small improvement of the precision: 79% (sense indexing) vs. 77.68% (term indexing). Figure 1 shows the comparison of the error percentage obtained with and without the introduction of the semantics with respect to the size of the vocabulary. The *Information Gain* technique was employed to reduce the vocabulary size [1].

As further work, we plan to study the TC and the IR tasks on just one corpus of the TREC collection, in order to better understand and compare the influence of semantics on both the TC and the IR tasks. Moreover, the two vector representations of each document should be combined, in order to take into account with different weights, terms and WordNet synsets at the same time.

---

[3] The Bow: A toolkit for Statistical Language Modelling, Text Retrieval, Classification and Clustering is available at www.cs.cmu.edu/~mccallum/bow/

[4] Available at www.ai.mit.edu/~jrennie

References

1. E. Ferretti, J. Lafuente, P. Rosso. Semantics Text Categorization using the K Nearest Neighbours Method. In: Proc. of the 1st Indian International Conference on Artificial Intelligence, 2003.
2. J. Gonzalo, F. Verdejo, I. Chugur, J. Chigarrán. Indexing with WordNet Synsets can improve Text Retrieval. In: Proc. of the Workshop on Usage of WordNet for NLP, 1998.
3. D. Jiménez, E. Ferretti, V. Vidal, P. Rosso, C.F. Enguix. The Influence of Semantics in IR using LSI and K-Means Clustering Techniques. In: Proc. of the Workshop on Conceptual Information Retrieval and Clustering of Documents, ACM Int. Conf. on Information and Communication Technologies, 2003.
4. D. Jiménez, V. Vidal, C.F. Enguix. A Comparison of Experiments with the Bisecting-Spherical K-Means Clustering and SVD Algorithms. In: Proc. of JOTRI, 2002.
5. A. Molina, F. Pla, E. Segarra. A Hidden Markov Model Approach to Word Sense Disambiguation. In: Proc. of VIII Conf. Iberoamericana de Inteligencia Artificial (IBERAMIA2), Sevilla, Spain, 2002.

Sampling and Feature Selection in a Genetic Algorithm for Document Clustering

Arantza Casillas[1], Mayte T. González de Lena[2], and Raquel Martínez[2]

[1] Dpt. Electricidad y Electrónica
Universidad del País Vasco
arantza@we.lc.ehu.es

[2] Dpt. Informática, Estadística y Telemática
Universidad Rey Juan Carlos
{m.t.gonzalez,r.martinez}@escet.urjc.es

Abstract. In this paper we describe a Genetic Algorithm for document clustering that includes a sampling technique to reduce computation time. This algorithm calculates an approximation of the optimum k value, and solves the best grouping of the documents into these k clusters. We evaluate this algorithm with sets of documents that are the output of a query in a search engine. Two types of experiment are carried out to determine: (1) how the genetic algorithm works with a sample of documents, (2) which document features lead to the best clustering according to an external evaluation. On the one hand, our GA with sampling performs the clustering in a time that makes interaction with a search engine viable. On the other hand, our GA approach with the representation of the documents by means of entities leads to better results than representation by lemmas only.

1 Introduction

Clustering involves dividing a set of n objects into a specified number of clusters k, so that objects are similar to other objects in the same cluster, and different from objects in other clusters. Clustering algorithms can work with objects of different kinds, but we have focused on documents.

Several clustering approaches assume that the appropriate value of k is known. However, there may be numerous situations in which it is not possible to know the appropriate number of clusters, or even an approximation. For instance, if we want to divide into clusters a set of documents that are the result of a query to a search engine, the value of k can change for each set of documents that results from interaction with the engine. Amongst the first to recommend that automatic clustering might prove useful in document retrieval were [Good 58], [Fairthorne 61], and [Needham 61].

In our first approach [Casillas et al. 03], we dealt with the problem of clustering a set of documents without prior evidence on the appropriate number of clusters. Our main aim was to provide an approximation of an appropriate value of k, with an acceptable computation cost, for a small number of documents.

A. Gelbukh (Ed.): CICLing 2004, LNCS 2945, pp. 601–612, 2004.
© Springer-Verlag Berlin Heidelberg 2004

In this approach we have introduce a sampling technique in order to deal with more documents without increasing the computation time.

There are various approaches for obtaining the optimum number, k, of clusters given a set of objects. We have focused on global stopping rules. These rules evaluate a measure, $C(k)$, of the goodness of the partition into k clusters, and calculate the value of k for which $C(k)$ is optimal. This $C(k)$ measure is usually based the within-cluster and between-cluster similarity or distance. A drawback of many of these rules is that $C(1)$ is not defined [Gordon 99], so the set of data is always assumed to be partitioned. Another general drawback of stopping rules is the high computation cost of calculating the best value of k, even with a moderate number of documents, n. In this work we present a solution to both drawbacks combining our Genetic Algorithm (GA) with sampling.

Many different stopping rules have been proposed. In [Milligan & Cooper 85] a comparative study of 30 stopping rules is presented. That study was the result of a simulation experiment carried out with artificial data sets containing nonoverlapping clusters. Although the results of that experiment depend on the cluster generating strategy, the study is useful in identifying which stopping rules perform better. One of the rules which performed best in that experiment was Calinski and Harabasz's rule. This is the stopping rule which we have selected as base of our GA.

The Calinski and Harabasz [Calinski & Harabasz 74] stopping rule calculates an informal indicator of the best number of clusters. With this rule we have designed and implemented a GA that finds an approximation of the optimal value of k, with significantly lower computation time than the former in most cases.

There are earlier works that apply GA and evolutionary programming to clustering. Some of them deal with clustering a set of objects by assuming that the appropriate value of k is known ([Estivill-Castro & Murray 98], [Chu et al. 02], [Murthy & Chowdhury 96], [Mertz & Zell 02], [Lucasius et al. 93]). However, in [Sarkar et al. 97] and [Imai et al. 00] evolutionary programming-based clustering algorithms are proposed in order to group a set of data into an optimum unknown number of clusters. The former is based on the well known K-means algorithm. Two objective functions are used that are minimized simultaneously: one gives the optimum number of clusters, and the other leads to proper identification of each cluster's centroids. The latter assumes that every cluster has the normal distribution; the standard deviation gives the probability of the membership degree of each object of a cluster. In both approaches the computation time is very high. In [Makagonov et al. 02] other heuristics are discussed to split the dendrite in an optimal way without fixing the number of clusters.

In our approach, only one objective function is maximized, so we calculate both aspects of the solution at the same time: an approximation of the optimum k value, and the best grouping of the objects into these k clusters. In addition, the sampling provides the condition of non partition of the input set of objects, which was one of the drawbacks of the global stopping rules.

The remainder of the paper is organized as follow: Section 2 describes the Genetic Algorithm. The sampling technique is explained in Section 3. Section 4 presents the clustering algorithm. Section 5 shows how the documents are represented. Section 6 describes the experiments and the evaluation methods. Finally, Section 7 includes the main conclusions and suggestions for future work.

2   The Genetic Algorithm

Genetic Algorithms were developed by John Holland at the University of Michigan. They are search algorithms based on the mechanics of natural selection and natural genetics [Holland 75]. The algorithm begins with an initial solutions population of the problem. This population is generated randomly. Each one of these solutions must be evaluated by means of a fitness function; the result of this evaluation is a measure of individual adaptation. The individuals with the best adaptation measure have more chance of reproducing and generating new individuals. Each individual (chromosome) is represented by a set of parameters (genes). An up to date description of GA can be found in [Goldberg 02] and [Michalewicz 96].

In this section, we describe first the stopping rule which is the base of our GA; then, the reproducing and generating mechanisms and other parameters of the GA.

2.1   The Calinski and Harabasz Stopping Rule

In [Calinski & Harabasz 74] a method for identifying clusters of points in a multidimensional Euclidean space is presented. An informal indicator of the best number of clusters k is also calculated. The method assumes there are n individuals with values of the same v variables for each individual. These individuals can be represented by n points in a v-dimensional Euclidean space. An $n \times n$ distance matrix is then calculated. Next, the method needs to calculate the Minimum Spanning Tree (MST), so that the enormous number of possible partitions of a set of points is reduced to those which are obtainable by splitting the MST.

This tree is then partitioned by removing some of its edges. If we want to divide the n points into k clusters, $k-1$ edges have to be removed. For each possible partition, the within-cluster sum of squared distances about the centroids ($WGSS$) is computed. In order to calculate the optimal value of k, first $k = 2$ is taken, then $k = 3$, and so on. For each value of k, the best partition is calculated with the minimum $WGSS$ and the Variance Ratio Criterion (VRC):

$$VRC = \frac{\frac{BGSS}{k-1}}{\frac{WGSS}{n-k}}, \tag{1}$$

where $BGSS$ is the total between-cluster sum of squared distances.

The authors suggest using VRC as an informal indicator for the best value of k. They also suggest the computation of VRC for $k = 2, 3, \ldots$ choosing the value on k for which the VRC has an absolute or local maximum. The computation can be stopped when the first local maximum is reached.

Although working with the minimum spanning tree instead of the whole graph reduces the number of partitions to be examined, this number,

$$\binom{n-1}{k-1} = \frac{(n-1)!}{(k-1)! \times (n-k)!},$$

(2)

is high enough for this method to be used with even moderate values of n.

2.2   Our Genetic Algorithm Characteristics

Our Genetic Algorithm is based on the Calinski and Harabasz Stopping Rule, and thus it uses the Variance Ratio Criterion (VRC) as its fitness function.

Population Representation. We use a chromosome (individual) description that allows us to represent two different points: the value of k, and which edges of the MST have to be eliminated. A vector with $n-1$ binary elements can deal with both points. The $n-1$ elements represent the $n-1$ edges of the MST. A vector element with value "0" means that this edge remains, whereas a vector element with value "1" means that this edge is eliminated. The number of elements with value "1" represents the value of $k-1$.

For instance, with 5 documents the MST will have 5 nodes and 4 edges. One chromosome could be the vector $(0,0,1,1)$, where $k = 3$ and the edges removed are the third and fourth ones. We have selected this representation because it is straightforward and permits us to create valid chromosomes.

Initial Population. The initial population has to take into account the solution space of the problem. The size of the solution space (search space) in the Calinski and Harabasz rule is shown in formula (2), where $k = 2, \ldots, n-1$, and n is the number of documents. This solution space is not equiprobable, and there are more individuals when $k = \frac{n-1}{2} + 1$. We have adapted our GA to search for an optimal solution in this specific search space. The probability of generating a chromosome with a value of k near that maximum is greater than with a value of k distant from that maximum. In order to estimate that combinatorial number we use the Laplace distribution.

Fitness Function. The fitness function of the GA is the VRC of Calinski and Harabasz's stopping rule (see formula (1)). An individual with a higher value of VRC is considered as better adapted by the algorithm.

Selection Operator. The selection operator mimics the selection concept of natural genetic systems: the best chromosome survives. The probability of any chromosome being selected is directly proportional to the VRC value (formula (1)). The chromosomes with the highest VRC values have more chance of reproducing and generating new chromosomes.

Crossover Operator. Once two parents are selected, two offspring are generated. These offspring will receive information from both parents. The classical genetic methods use only one crossing point chosen at random, however we use a number of crossing points chosen at random (every number has the same probability).

Mutation Operator. Before evaluating each next generation mutation is applied, so that each chromosome is subjected to a low probability of change or mutation. The mutation operator guarantees that all the search space can be explored. We assume that at the beginning a high probability of mutation can help to obtain a more varied population. But as the GA advances, the mutation probability must decrease so that the algorithm can converge towards the solution. We have therefore introduced a variable mutation operator which decreases from one generation to the next.

Stopping Criterion. There is no stopping criterion in the relevant literature which ensures the convergence of a GA to an optimal solution. We have used the most usual criteria. Our GA stops when:

- After a number x of iterations, the best chromosome does not change. We have set $x = 3$.
- The maximum number of generations is reached. We choose n, the number of documents (GA without sampling) or the sample size (GA with sampling), as this number.
- Computation time is spent.

3   Sampling

Calculating value of k optimum using all the documents may be unnecessary if we are capable of selecting a representative sample of them. Sampling techniques are used to draw conclusions on a population by obtaining information on a representative subset rather than on every individual. Two aspects are crucial so that the conclusions can be applied to the whole population: the way the sample is selected, and the sample size.

We can calculate the sample size by setting the sampling error $e(x)$:

$$e(x) = \sqrt{\sigma(x)} = \sqrt{\frac{1}{N} \sum_{i=1}^{N} (x_i - \bar{x})^2},\qquad(3)$$

where N is the number of individuals in the population, x_i is the value of variable x for individual i, and $\bar{x} = \frac{1}{N} \sum_{i=1}^{N} x_i$ is the mean.

When document clustering is the problem, the total population is a feature matrix where each row represents the features vector of a document. Each document feature is relevant, so we calculate the sampling error for each of them; then we select the highest and the lowest sampling errors. These two figures allows us to set a range of sampling errors where we can select the value according to the particular problem. In this way, we can ensure that the sample is representative for each of the document features with a known percentage of error.

Once the sampling error is set, the sample size can be calculated with the following formula:

$$n = \frac{N \times S^2}{N \times e^2 + S^2},$$ (4)

where n is the sample size, N is the number of individuals in the population, e is the percentage of sampling error, and $S = \sqrt{\frac{1}{N-1} \sum_{i=1}^{N} (x_i - \bar{x})^2}$.

Once the sample size is calculated with a known error, the sample is chosen at random and without replacement (repeated documents are not allowed).

Since the sampling indicates the number of representative documents of the population, if the sample size is 1, that is, one document can represent all of them, we consider that the set of documents does not have to be partitioned. This is the non partition condition which is missing from the Calinski and Harabasz stopping rule.

Our GA can calculate the value of k over the sample. Afterwards, with that value of k, clustering all documents into k clusters can be resolved using a classic partition method. This approach allows us to reduce the computation cost.

4   Clustering Algorithm

Our clustering algorithm combines different performances which can be selected depending on the number of documents to be clustered:

- If the number of documents is small the Calinski and Harabasz stopping rule can be applied.
- If the number of documents is not too large the GA algorithm can be used.
- For a large number of documents first the sample size is calculated, then the GA is used with the sample of the documents in order to calculate the optimum number of clusters k. Then a classical partition clustering algorithm can be used with all documents. We are currently using a partition algorithm from the well known CLUTO library [Karypis].

5   Document Representation

We are working with a corpus of Spanish news. The documents have been preprocessed so that we can work with lemmas instead of inflected forms. The entities of the documents have been identified (we use "entity" in the meaning give in [MUC-6 95]). In addition, the words on a stoplist used in Information Retrieval (with articles, determinants, etc.) have been eliminated from the documents.

In order to determine which document features lead to the best clustering solution using our algorithm, we created three representation versions for each document by using different features:

- The lemmas of the first paragraph (L).
- The entities of the whole document (E).
- The lemmas of the first paragraph, and the entities of the whole document (L+E).

Using these three types of feature, documents are represented using the vector space model. In this model, each document is considered to be a vector, where each component is the weight of a feature in the document. We have used the version of this model that weights each feature based on its Term Frequency (TF), so that each term is assumed to have importance proportional to the number of times it occurs in a document.

6 Experiments

For the experiments we have tried the following performances of the algorithms:

- The Calinski and Harabasz stopping rule searching the first local maximum.
- The genetic algorithm applied to all the documents.
- The genetic algorithm with sampling.

We used a collection of 14,000 news items from a Spanish newspaper. The documents that are the input of the algorithms are those resulting from a query with a search engine concerning that collection of news items. In this framework, no evidence of an appropriate number for k is known, and a quick clustering solution has to be reached.

We have carried out two types of experiment in order to test different capabilities of our approach:

- To evaluate the time that the GA with sampling needs to cluster the documents resulting from a query with a search engine.
- To evaluate the goodness of the k value calculated.
- To evaluate which document features lead to the best clustering solution.
- To evaluate the quality of the clustering solution by means of external, and internal evaluation measures.

The goodness of the k value will be represented by means of the VRC value in the Calinski and Harabasz rule; the bigger VRC, the better k, so that the value of VRC is the measure of the quality of the clustering solution according to the method. The time taken in obtaining that k value and the corresponding partition of the documents into these k clusters will give an idea of the viability of our approach in working with a search engine.

The internal evaluation (without reference to external knowledge) is carried out by means of the cohesiveness of clusters, whereas the external evaluation of clustering quality is determined by means of the F-measure [van Rijsbergen 74].

Cluster cohesiveness is computed through the weighted similarity of the internal cluster similarity:

$$\frac{1}{|D|^2} \sum_{d \in D, d' \in D} cosine(d', d), \tag{5}$$

where D represents the set of documents, d' and d represent document items, and $cosine(d', d)$ is the cosine measure between the documents d' and d. The average cohesiveness of the clustering solution is the mean of the cohesiveness of all the clusters.

The F-measure combines the precision and recall measures:

$$F(i, j) = \frac{2 \times Recall(i, j) \times Precision(i, j)}{(Precision(i, j) + Recall(i, j)}, \tag{6}$$

where $Recall(i, j) = \frac{n_{ij}}{n_i}$, $Precision(i, j) = \frac{n_{ij}}{n_j}$, n_{ij} is the number of members of cluster human solution i in cluster j, n_j is the number of members of cluster j and n_i is the number of members of cluster human solution i. For all the clusters:

$$F = \sum_i \frac{n_i}{n} max\{F(i, j)\} \tag{7}$$

We have not been able to use the same sets of documents to evaluate the different capabilities. To carry out the external evaluation a manually clustered collection is needed. Two human judges have evaluated the results of the clustering of some queries involving few documents. These experiments were carried out on a Pentium IV at 2.6 GHZ with 1 GB of RAM.

Both genetic algorithms work with an initial population of $n \times 10$ chromosomes, and the maximum number of generations is n. In the GA with sampling, n is the sample size, whereas in the GA n is the number of documents. The sampling error has been fixed at 5%, and the probability of mutation starts at $\frac{1.25}{t}$, where t is number of generation.

In Table 1 the results of the experiments of Calinski and Harabasz, and Genetic Algorithm with sampling implementations can be seen in terms of VRC value, k value, and time. The "N. Fe." column shows the number of features of each set of documents. The results for time in Table 1 of the GA with sampling refer to the average time after running the algorithm 10 times. We can observe that the Calinski and Harabasz stopping rule performs well in connection to time when the set has few documents, and the k value is close to 2. However, for other values of k, or when the set has more than a few documents the time is unacceptable for interacting with a search engine. This is because this stopping rule starts the exploration with $k = 2$, then 3, and so on, finishing when a local VRC maximum is found.

Table 1 shows that GA with sampling proposes a clustering solution in less time; however, the value of k does not always coincide with that of the Calinski and Harabasz stopping rule. The values of VRC are lower with the GA with sampling because the partition algorithm which we use after obtaining the value of k with the sample, does not try to optimize the VRC function. As can be seen in Table 1, our GA with sampling would allow interaction with a search engine offering the clustering of 350 documents in 4 seconds.

Table 2 represents the results of the internal (cohesiveness) and external evaluation (F-measure) of: (1) the Calinski and Harabasz stopping rule, (2) the GA with sampling, and (3) the GA over the whole set of documents. Five sets

Table 1. Results of Calinski and Harabasz, and Genetic Algorithm with sampling implementations in connection with time, k, and VRC values

N. Documents	N. Fe.	k	Time	VRC	Sample Size	k	Aver. Time	VRC
		Cal. and Har.			**GA + sampling**			
350	2672	2	59.9 s	8.211	19	2(30%)	3.2 s	0.931
						3(50%)	3.8 s	1.095
						4(20%)	4 s	1.480
122	1377	3	45.7 s	2.983	16	2(50%)	0.7 s	1.047
						3(20%)	0.8 s	1.508
						4(30%)	0.8 s	1.497
119	1053	3	41.1 s	4.530	16	2(40%)	0.4 s	1.645
						3(20%)	0.5 s	2.030
						5(40%)	0.5 s	1.492
117	1058	4	19m,43.2s	3.254	16	3(20%)	0.5 s	1.133
						4(20%)	0.6 s	1.237
						5(40%)	0.6 s	1.221
						6(20%)	0.6 s	1.220
116	1320	2	1.4 s	4.185	16	3(50%)	0.7 s	1.377
						4(50%)	0.7 s	1.181
104	1267	3	22.8 s	7.989	16	2(20%)	0.5 s	1.225
						3(20%)	0.5 s	1.06
						4(40%)	0.6 s	1.22
						5(20%)	0.6 s	1.303
71	791	2	0.3 s	2.630	14	3(40%)	0.4 s	2.873
						4(30%)	0.4 s	2.195
						5(30%)	0.4 s	3.413

of documents have been manually clustered in order to calculate the F-measure. X-L, X-E, and X-L+E denote respectively the representation by the lemmas of the first paragraph, by the entities of the whole document, and the lemmas of the first paragraph and the entities of the whole document of each one of the five sets of documents. The "H-J" column represents the value of k proposed by the two human judges, and the "N. Fe." column shows the number of features of each representation.

The F-measure values of both genetic solutions are better than the values of the Calinski and Harabasz stopping rule F-measure most of the times. This is not the case for cohesiveness, which in half the experiments is better in the Calinski and Harabasz stopping rule than in the GA with sampling. From the external evaluation point of view, both genetic solutions lead to better clustering results. In comparing the two genetic solutions, the F-measure of the GA with sampling is slightly better than that of the GA. However, the cohesiveness is better with the GA algorithm because it tends to increase with a higher number of clusters (the best cohesiveness is obtained when each cluster contains exactly one document). As we can observe, the internal and external evaluations do not always coincide.

Table 2. Results of Clustering Algorithm in connection with external evaluation

Doc. Set	N. doc	Cal. and Har. stop. rule			GA + sampling				GA			H-J	N. Fe.
		k	F-m.	cohe.	size sam.	k	F-me.	cohe.	k	F-me.	cohe.	k	
1-L	12	3	0.482	0.733	6	3(40%)	0.607	0.537	6(50%)	0.696	0.879	7	153
						4(30%)	0.766	0.575	8(20%)	0.713	0.917		
						2(30%)	0.483	0.355	7(20%)	0.788	0.904		
									5(10%)	0.621	0.850		
1-E		3	0.451	0.728	8	4(60%)	0.769	0.619	7(80%)	0.711	0.863	7	205
						6(20%)	0.944	0.796	9(20%)	0.722	0.927		
						3(20%)	0.618	0.546					
1-L+E		2	0.412	0.450	8	5(60%)	0.839	0.768	8(70%)	0.663	0.909	7	358
						4(30%)	0.764	0.601	3(20%)	0.337	0.724		
						6(10%)	0.914	0.849	6(10%)	0.483	0.868		
2-L	20	2	0.214	0.570	9	3(100%)	0.377	0.292	13(100%)	0.704	0.941	14	286
2-E		4	0.321	0.774	11	7(70%)	0.726	0.552	15(100%)	0.716	0.947	14	370
						6(20%)	0.666	0.457					
						8(10%)	0.780	0.581					
2-L+E		3	0.267	0.706	11	4(60%)	0.459	0.365	12(100%)	0.613	0.894	14	656
						5(20%)	0.526	0.531					
						3(20%)	0.377	0.292					
3-L	14	4	0.408	0.792	6	4(40%)	0.507	0.398	10(50%)	0.669	0.903	9	253
						2(30%)	0.366	0.234	9(20%)	0.733	0.840		
						3(20%)	0.460	0.341	8(20%)	0.671	0.814		
						5(10%)	0.545	0.479	7(10%)	0.606	0.785		
3-E		9	0.568	0.918	9	5(50%)	0.783	0.510	9(100%)	0.568	0.918	9	330
						4(30%)	0.707	0.435					
						6(10%)	0.790	0.563					
						3(10%)	0.595	0.346					
3-L+E		2	0.313	0.587	9	5(60%)	0.625	0.512	9(100%)	0.517	0.916	9	583
						7(20%)	0.685	0.684					
						6(10%)	0.640	0.556					
						3(10%)	0.542	0.349					
4-L	17	4	0.408	0.792	10	5(70%)	0.428	0.496	11(100%)	0.550	0.928	8	264
						4(20%)	0.414	0.465					
						6(10%)	0.488	0.532					
4-E		9	0.568	0.336	10	5(60%)	0.570	0.499	11(100%)	0.555	0.925	8	313
						6(30%)	0.544	0.524					
						4(10%)	0.531	0.367					
4-L+E		2	0.313	0.587	10	6(50%)	0.570	0.499	12(100%)	0.637	0.908	8	577
						7(30%)	0.586	0.538					
						5(20%)	0.532	0.451					
5-L	15	2	0.464	0.577	7	3(30%)	0.925	0.348	2(50%)	0.465	0.578	4	204
						4(40%)	0.798	0.397	5(30%)	0.390	0.723		
						5(30%)	0.812	0.461	6(20%)	0.394	0.672		
5-E		2	0.465	0.629	9	6(50%)	0.691	0.729	11(100%)	0.417	0.913	4	278
						7(50%)	0.691	0.791					
5-L+E	15	2	0.464	0.577	9	3(30%)	0.672	0.4	11(100%)	0.528	0.906	4	482
						4(50%)	0.602	0.471					
						5(20%)	0.726	0.545					

As regards document representation, from the external evaluation point of view the representation with entities is involved in most of the better solutions. Between only entities (X-E), and lemmas plus entities (X-L+E), the X-E representation is slightly better in these experiments.

7   Conclusions

We propose a clustering algorithm that calculates an approximation of the optimum k value, and finds the best grouping of the objects into these k clusters. The algorithm combines the use of a global stopping rule, a genetic algorithm based on that rule, and sampling techniques. The use of sampling allows us to reduce the computation time, and at the same time provides the condition for not partitioning the input set of documents.

On the one hand, the first experiment shows that the Calinski and Harabasz stopping rule performs well in relation to time when the document set has few documents and the k value is close to 2. However, for other values of k, and when the set has more than a few documents the time is unacceptable if we want to solve the clustering to interact with a search engine. Our GA with sampling clusters the same documents in a few seconds, so it could be used for interacting with a search engine when the number of clusters for partitioning the set of documents is completely unknown.

On the other hand, the experiments show that both genetic solutions lead to better clustering results from an external evaluation point of view (F-measure values). From the same point of view, the representation of the documents by means of entities leads to better results that representation only by lemmas. So the entity identification is a preliminary process that can improve the clustering results of news documents.

Our GA approach offers a plausible solution for document clustering, when there is no evidence of the number of clusters, from both time and quality view points. More experiments using evaluated document collections should be done in order to confirm these results.

Acknowledgments. This research is supported by the Madrid Research Agency, project 07T/0030/2003 1 and by the Rey Juan Carlos University project PPR-2003-38.

References

[Calinski & Harabasz 74] Calinski, T., Harabasz, J.: "A Dendrite Method for Cluster Analysis". *Communications in Statistics*, 3(1), (1974), 1–27.

[Casillas et al. 03] Casillas A., González de Lena M.T., Martínez, R.: "Document Clustering into an unknown number of clusters using a Genetic Algorithm". *Lecture Notes in Artificial Intelligence 2807, Subseries of Lecture Notes in Computer Science*, Springer-Verlag Heidelberg (2003), 43–49.

612   A. Casillas, M.T. González de Lena, and R. Martínez

[Chu et al. 02] Chu S.C., Roddick J.F., Pan J.S.: "An Incremental Multi-Centroid, Multi-Run Sampling Scheme for k-medoids-based Algorithms-Extended Report". *Proceedings of the Third International Conference on Data Mining Methods and Databases, Data Mining III*, (2002), 553–562.

[Estivill-Castro & Murray 98] Estivill-Castro V., Murray A.T.: "Spatial Clustering for Data Mining with Genetic Algorithms". *Proceedings of the International ICSC Symposium on Engineering of Intelligent Systems, EIS-98*, (1998).

[Fairthorne 61] FAIRTHORNE, R.A.: "The mathematics of classification". *Towards Information Retrieval*, Butterworths, London, (1961), 1–10.

[Goldberg 02] Goldberg, D.E.: *Genetic Algorithms in Search, Optimization, and Machine Learning*, Addison Wesley Longman, Inc., (2002).

[Good 58] GOOD, I.J.: "Speculations Concerning Information Retrieval", Research Report PC-78, IBM Research Center, Yorktown Heights, New York, (1958).

[Gordon 99] Gordon, A. D.: *Classification*, Chapman & Hall/CRC, (1999).

[Holland 75] Holland, J. H.: *Adaptation in natural and artificial system*, Ann Arbor: The University of Michigan Press, (1975).

[Imai et al. 00] Imai K., Kaimura N., Hata Y.: "A New Clustering with Estimation of Cluster Number Based on Genetic Algorithms". *Pattern Recognition in Soft Computing Paradigm*, World Scientific Publishing Co., Inc. (2000), 142–162.

[Karypis] Karypis G.: "CLUTO: A Clustering Toolkit". Technical Report: 02-017. University of Minnesota, Department of Computer Science, Minneapolis, MN 55455.

[Lucasius et al. 93] Lucasius C.B., Dane A.D., Kateman G.: "On k-medoid clustering of large data sets with the aid of Genetic Algorithm: background, feasibility and comparison". *Analytica Chimica Acta*, Elsevier Science Publishers B.V. 283(3), (1993), 647–669.

[Makagonov et al. 02] Makagonov, P., Alexandrov, M., Gelbukh, A.: "Selection of typical documents in a document flow". *Advances in Communications and Software Technologies*, WSEAS Press (2002), 197–202.

[Mertz & Zell 02] Merz P., Zell A.: "Clustering Gene Expression Profiles with Memetic Algorithms". *Lecture Notes in Computer Science 2439*, Springer-Verlag Berlin (2002), 811–820.

[Michalewicz 96] Michalewicz, Z.: *Genetic algorithms + data structures = evolution programs*, Springer Comp. (1996).

[Milligan & Cooper 85] Milligan, G. W., Cooper, M.C.: "An Examination of Procedures for Determining the Number of Clusters in a Data Set". *Psychometrik*, 58(2), (1985), 159–179.

[MUC-6 95] MUC-6. *Proceedings of the Sixth Message Understanding Conference (MUC-6)*. Morgan Kaufman.

[Murthy & Chowdhury 96] Murthy C.A., Chowdhury N.: "In search of Optimal Clusters Using Genetic Algorithms". *Pattern Recognition Letters*, 17(8), (1996), 825–832.

[Needham 61] Needham, R.M.: *Research on information retrieval, classification and grouping* 1957-1961, Ph.D. Thesis, University of Cambridge; Cambridge Language Research Unit, Report M.L. 149, (1961).

[van Rijsbergen 74] van Rijsbergen, C.J.: "Foundations of evaluation". *Journal of Documentation*, 30 (1974), 365–373.

[Sarkar et al. 97] Sarkar, M., Yegnanarayana, B., Khemani, D.: "A clustering algorithm using an evolutionary programming-based approach". *Pattern Recognition Letters*, 18, (1997), 975–986.

A New Efficient Clustering Algorithm
for Organizing Dynamic Data Collection*

Kwangcheol Shin and Sangyong Han**

School of Computer Science and Engineering, Chung-Ang Univ.
221 HukSuk-Dong DongJak-Ku, Seoul, Korea
kcshin@archi.cse.cau.ac.kr, hansy@cau.ac.kr

Abstract. We deal with dynamic information organization for more efficient
Internet browsing. As the appropriate algorithm for this purpose, we propose
modified ART (artificial resonance theory) algorithm, which functions similarly
with the dynamic Star-clustering algorithm but performs a more efficient time
complexity of $O(nk)$, $(k \ll n)$ instead of $O(n^2 log^2 n)$ found in the dynamic Star-
clustering algorithm. In order to see how fast the proposed algorithm is in
producing clusters for organizing information, the algorithm is tested on
CLASSIC3 in comparison with the dynamic Star-clustering algorithm.

1 Introduction

From the very beginning of the information-oriented society era, gathering
information has been very important issue. However, in current Internet environment
there are too many documents; this makes users to waste time. Information
organization techniques capable of automatically grouping related documents make it
easy for users to recognize the contents of documents and to find what they want [1].

The most recent study on information organization deals with Star-clustering [2].
The Star-clustering algorithm presents the information system by applying the
undirected, weighted similarity graph $G=(V,E,\omega)$ and forms a dense subgraph
$G'=(V,E)$ based on G in order to organize the information. The Star-clustering
algorithm also can be executed dynamically, which means each document clustered
one by one. Compared to the formerly used average link or single link algorithm, the
Star-clustering algorithm scored higher in the recall-precision measurement.
However, in order to execute dynamic Star-clustering algorithm, the required time
complexity is $O(n^2 log^2 n)$. And $O(n^2 log^2 n)$ is too mush time wasting when one has a
massive amount of document groups to process in real time.

In this study, we suggest a new algorithm, which retains the benefits of the Star-
clustering algorithm but has complexity only $O(kn)$, where k is the number of
produced clusters. Our algorithm combines ART (artificial resonance theory) [3], a
real time clustering algorithm, and concept vector [4]. By controlling the vigilance
parameter in ART, we can form clusters that have certain number of documents and
certain coherence.

---

* Work supported by the ITRI of the Chung-Ang University.
** Corresponding author.

A. Gelbukh (Ed.): CICLing 2004, LNCS 2945, pp. 613–616, 2004.
© Springer-Verlag Berlin Heidelberg 2004

2 Suggested Method

Our algorithm uses the vector space model based on the cosine similarity, which applies the concept vector [4], and assigns a different vigilance parameter to each cluster in order to use the dynamic vigilance parameter changes for each cluster. So in order to have newly produced clusters to have coherent vigilance parameter values, the global vigilance parameter ρ_g is applied, and vigilance parameter ρ_j is applied to cluster π_j to control the vigilance parameter of each cluster.

Initialization: The number of clusters is initialized as 1, and the input patterns (document vectors) are normalized to be formed in units of the L_2 norm. Then a cluster is made with the first input pattern and the global vigilance parameter $\rho_g^{(0)}$ and the vigilance parameter of the first cluster $\rho_1^{(0)}$ is set at a value over 0.3.

$$w_1^{(0)} = x_1, \ \rho_g^{(0)} \in [0.3,1], \ \rho_1^{(0)} = \rho_g^{(0)} \tag{1}$$

Since the amount of matches between the input pattern x_i and cluster π_j is perceived by the cosine similarity, the number of clusters to be produced can be increased by setting the initial vigilance parameter at a higher level.

Activation Function (AF): The activation function used for measuring the compatibility between the input pattern and the weighting vector is calculated as the cosine similarity between the two vectors as shown below.

$$AF(w_j^{(t)}, x_i) = \cos(\theta(w_j^{(t)}, x_i)) = x_i \cdot \frac{w_i^{(t)}}{\left\| w_j^{(t)} \right\|} = x_i^T \cdot c_j^{(t)} \tag{2}$$

Here, the weighting vector is the sum of cluster π_j's input patterns:

$$w_j^{(t)} = \sum_{x_i \in \pi_j} x_i$$

Unlike *fuzzy* ART [3], the suggested algorithm does not have the *Matching Function* calculated. The *Activation Function* substitutes it. In other words, the activation function (2) also serves as the matching function. So no additional calculation is necessary for the matching function.

Selecting the Resonance Cluster and Modulating the Vigilance Parameter: Because the activation function takes over the place of the matching function, the resonance cluster is obtained by applying the following formula.

$$AF(w_{j*}^{(t)}, x_i) \geq \rho_j^{(t)}, \ j* = \arg_{j=1,\cdots,k}^{\max} \{AF(w_j^{(t)}, x_i)\} \tag{3}$$

It is checked whether the weighting vector of the cluster that is the most similar to the input pattern meets the condition of the cluster's vigilance parameter.

When the cluster is not applicable to formula (3), then the next closest cluster is selected and tested on the formula. If no cluster meets the vigilance parameter conditions, then a new cluster is formed and the input pattern in concern is allocated. Here, the newly produced cluster π_j's vigilance parameter $\rho_j^{(t)}$ must be set as $\rho_g^{(t)}$. This is to have the new cluster's vigilance parameter to accord to the global vigilance parameter. If the newly produced cluster's vigilance parameter is too high, the input pattern cannot be allocated and the cluster becomes isolated.

During the production of new clusters, the vigilance parameter of all clusters and the global vigilance parameter are lowered the same amount according to the following formula. This is to reduce the probability of continuous cluster production and have the input patterns accord to the current cluster.

$$\rho_j^{(t+1)} = \rho_j^{(t)} - \zeta, \; \zeta \in [0,0.02] \; (j = 1, \cdots, k),$$

$$\rho_g^{(t+1)} = \rho_g^{(t)} - \zeta, \; where \; \zeta \; is \; a \; control \; parameter \tag{4}$$

Renovating the weighting and controlling the vigilance parameter: If for the selected cluster π_{j*} satisfies (3), the input pattern is allocated to π_{j*} and the weighting vector and concept vector of π_{j*} is modulated by the following formula.

$$w_{j*}^{(t+1)} = w_{j*}^{(t)} + x_i, \quad c_{j*}^{(t+1)} = \frac{w_{j*}^{(t+1)}}{\left\| w_{j*}^{(t+1)} \right\|} \tag{5}$$

Applying the formula below changes the vigilance parameter for the cluster in concern.

$$\rho_{j*}^{(t+1)} = \rho_{j*}^{(t)} + \delta, \; \delta \in [0,0.002] \tag{6}$$

where δ is a control parameter.

Cluster π_{j*}'s vigilance parameter ρ_{j*} is modulated in order to prevent the input pattern being allocated entirely to a single cluster. If the number of input patterns in a certain cluster continues to increase, the non-zeroes among the cluster's weighting vector elements also increase. In this case, the cosine similarity measured by using the vector's inner product is relatively higher than that of other clusters. This results in having the input patterns all gather in a single cluster and ultimately lowers the clustering coherences. Therefore, heightening the vigilance parameter of the clusters where the input patterns are to be allocated must prevent such cases.

3   Experimental Results

To verify its speed, the suggested algorithm has been tested on data set CLASSIC3 (ftp.cs.cornell.edu/pub/smart) composed of 3893 documents extracted from the well-known data sets MEDLINE, CISI, and CRANFIELD. First, the MC program (www.cs.utexas.edu/users/jfan/dm/) vectorizes the 3893 data. In this process, stopwords and words of the frequency below 0.5% and above 15% are deleted. From the remaining 4262 terms, the *tfn* scheme makes 3893 document vectors.

For the experiments, besides dynamic Star-clustering algorithm, we also implemented ART, which clusters data dynamically, and *k*-means, fast static clustering algorithm.

At first, we make experiments with suggested algorithm, namely Modified ART, and as a result, we extracted five clusters, which has at least 20 data, in order of coherence. In five clusters, 195 data has been extracted and average coherence of clusters is 0.597. And run time is 14.04 seconds. Parameters of ART and dynamic Star are modulated to have similar number of data with modified ART, and in case of *k*-means, *k* is set to 57 to get same number of produced clusters as modified ART for

Table 1. The Result over CLASSIC3. RT stands for the run time, TNC for the total number of produced clusters and ND for the number of data.

	Modified ART $(\rho_1^{(0)}=0.35, \delta=0.0015, \zeta=0.017)$			ART $(\rho=0.1, \alpha=10^{-5}, \beta=1)$			k-means $(k=57)$			Dynamic Star $(\rho=0.3)$		
	ND	Coherence		ND	Coherence		ND	Coherence		ND	Coherence	
		Total	Avr		Total	Avr		Total	Avr		Total	Avr
Cluster1	21	15.10	0.719	27	13.52	0.501	22	11.93	0.542	25	33.00	0.606
Cluster2	71	41.10	0.579	45	22.10	0.491	92	48.77	0.530	22	41.62	0.585
Cluster3	26	14.84	0.571	24	11.61	0.484	59	30.78	0.522	28	44.57	0.585
Cluster4	20	11.27	0.564	21	9.51	0.453	80	41.69	0.521	22	35.98	0.579
Cluster5	57	31.55	0.553	34	15.31	0.450	33	16.78	0.508	54	39.06	0.578
Sum	195	270.1		151	72.0		286	149.9		151	194.2	
Average			0.597			0.476			0.525			0.587
RT(sec.)	14.04			13.94			50.59			83.34		
TNC	57			72			57			1293		

the fair comparisons. Table 1 shows that suggested modified ART can produce more coherent clusters with 4 or 6 times faster than k-means and dynamic Star, and in case of ART, within almost same time, modified ART can produce clusters with 25% better coherence.

References

1. Montes-y-Gomez, M., Lopez-Lopez A., and Gelbukh A.: Information Retrieval with Conceptual Graph Matching. Database and Expert Systems Applications (DEXA-2000), Lecture Notes in Computer Science, N 1873, Springer-Verlag, pp. 312–321, (2000)
2. Aslam J., Pelekhov K. and Rus D.: A Practical Clustering Algorithm for Static and Dyamic Information Organization. In Proceedings of the 1999 Symposium on Discrete Algorithms, Baltimore, MD, (1999)
3. Carpenter G. A., Grossberg S. and Rosen D. B.: Fuzzy ART : An Adaptive Resonance Algorithm for Rapid, Stable Classification of Analog Patterns, Proceedings of 1991 International Conference Neural Networks, Vol.II, (1991)
4. Dhillon I. S. and Modha, D. S.: Concept Decomposition for Large Sparse Text Data using Clustering. Technical Report RJ 10147(9502), IBM Almaden Research Center, (1999)

Domain-Informed Topic Detection

Cormac Flynn and John Dunnion

Department of Computer Science,
University College Dublin,
Ireland.
{cormac.flynn,john.dunnion}@ucd.ie

Abstract. We discuss *Topic Detection*, a sub-task of the *Topic Detection and Tracking (TDT)* Project, and present a system that uses the linguistic and temporal features of news reportage to enhance the discovery of events in a collection of news articles. We describe an online application of these techniques that constructs topical clusters from live news feeds. We conclude that these approaches promise more coherent and useful clusters and suggest some areas of future work.

1 Introduction

The *Topic Detection and Tracking (TDT)* Project [1] is a DARPA-sponsored initiative [1] that aims to develop systems that monitor news-wire, broadcast news and other topical information sources, detect breaking stories and new events, and track these as they change over time.

The most recent phase of the project defined five tasks that are necessary for an effective TDT system: Story Segmentation, Topic Tracking, Topic Detection, New Event Detection and Link Detection. We concentrate on *Topic Detection*, i.e. the grouping together of related documents into topically cohesive clusters that correspond to distinct news events. This can be performed on a retrospective collection of documents or on a live stream. Such a system could be used to group an accumulation of time-ordered news articles into topical clusters, or to monitor the many online sources of news reportage.

This paper consists of six sections. We describe our basic Topic Detection system in Section 2. Section 3 discusses those features that distinguish problems in the TDT domain from general information filtering. Section 4 describes extensions to the basic system that exploit these features. Section 5 presents a Topic Detection system that operates on live news feeds. Finally, we give our conclusions and suggest future work in Section 6.

2 Baseline Topic Detection System

Our baseline Topic Detection system accepts documents from a variety of sources; from the TDT corpora, the TREC collection, or from online RSS feeds.

---

[1] http://www.nist.gov/speech/tests/tdt/

A. Gelbukh (Ed.): CICLing 2004, LNCS 2945, pp. 617–626, 2004.
© Springer-Verlag Berlin Heidelberg 2004

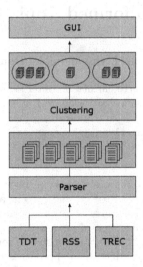

Fig. 1. Topic Detection System Diagram

For the purposes of this study, we concentrate primarily on the TDT1 corpus. We use the standard vector space model, where documents are represented as vectors of weighted term frequencies and distance judged according to some similarity measure. The set of documents is then grouped into topical clusters using the distance metric and an appropriate clustering algorithm. In the following sub-sections we outline each processing stage of the baseline system.

2.1 Feature Selection

We aim to represent each news article using the smallest and most salient set of terms possible. Words are chosen for each document according to the following criteria.

- The term is not a member of a stop-list.
- The term has a *global frequency* that is greater than one. The global frequency of a term is the number of times it appears in the entire corpus. Since infrequently occurring words are often representative of short documents or brief events, we discard only those features with a single corpus-wide occurrence.
- Words are chosen irrespective of their *local frequency*. The local frequency of a term is the number of times it appears in a particular document. Intuitively, those words with the greatest local frequency would seem to be the most important. For the TDT domain this is not always the case, due to the phenomenon of *topic shift* [2]. Topic shift is when the focus of an event suddenly changes, perhaps signalling a new or unexpected development. In these instances, a previously infrequent term can suddenly increase in both frequency and importance.

- Features are selected independent of their *document frequency*, i.e. the number of documents in which the term appears. Terms with a very low document frequency are often presumed to be unimportant. However, excluding such features makes it more difficult to classify articles for small or briefly occurring events, e.g. the "Cuban Riot in Panama" event in the TDT1 corpus spans six days and contains only four on-topic articles.

2.2   Similarity Measure

We examined three similarity metrics, *cosine*, *chord* and *dice*, and also the *Euclidean distance* measure. Cosine similarity is currently favoured, as it is considered most suitable for a vector space model. The cosine similarity formula is:

$$\frac{\sum_{i=1}^{n} V_i \cdot W_i}{\sqrt{\sum_{i=1}^{n} (V_i)^2} \sqrt{\sum_{i=1}^{n} (W_i)^2}}$$

where V and W are vectors of weighted term frequencies.

2.3   Term Weighting

Statistical information based on term frequency is commonly used to improve the performance of IR systems. Typically, the overall weight of a term is the product of three factors.

Local Weighting produces a weight based on the frequency of a term within individual documents. We examined three local weighting schemes, *term frequency*, *normalised log* and *augmented normalised term frequency*. Although experiments have yet to be completed, normalised log appears to work best for the TDT1 corpus. The normalised log formula is:

$$\frac{1 + \log f_{ij}}{1 + \log a_j} \text{ if } f_{ij} > 0$$
$$0 \qquad \text{if } f_{ij} = 0$$

where f_{ij} is the frequency of term i in document j and a_j is the average frequency of all the terms in the document.

Global Weighting produces a measure of the discriminating power of a term based on its corpus-wide document frequency. We use a retrospective collection of news articles to calculate the weighting scores, and evaluated four global weighting schemes, *inverse document frequency (IDF)*, *global frequency IDF*, *probabilistic inverse* and *entropy*. Again, provisional results indicate that IDF performs best. IDF is calculated in the following manner:

$$\log\left(\frac{N}{n_i}\right)$$

where N is the total number of documents in the collection and n_i is the number of documents in which term i appears.

Finally, the *normalisation factor* ensures that long documents are not assigned a disproportionate importance due solely to their length. We chose to normalise each document vector to unit length. This also allows the cosine similarity to be simplified to dot product.

2.4   Document Clustering

Document clustering techniques fall into one of two categories. *Partitional Clustering* starts with all items in a single cluster and attempts to split this until K disjoint clusters have been created. *Agglomerative Clustering* begins with each document in its own cluster and aims to merge those pairs that are most similar until K remain. We have concentrated on agglomerative techniques since these have proven effective in previous research [3,4]. Furthermore, we chose an agglomerative hierarchical clustering algorithm [5]. Hierarchical methods produce a hierarchy of clusters, with broadly related documents placed in large clusters towards the top of the hierarchy and more topic-specific clusters towards the bottom. This allows the document collection to be examined at varying degrees of topic granularity.

We examined three agglomerative hierarchical clustering algorithms, *single-link*, *complete-link* and *group-average*. These methods differ in how they decide the similarity between two clusters. For single-link clustering, we consider this similarity to be the *greatest* similarity between any member of one cluster and any member of the other cluster. Conversely, complete-link clustering takes the *smallest* similarity between members of the cluster pair. Group-average falls between these two extremes; the similarity score for two clusters is judged to be the *average* similarity between the cluster members. Previous research has shown that Group Average Hierarchical Clustering (GAC) is the most effective for the TDT domain [6].

Agglomerative methods are among the most computationally expensive approaches to document clustering. Group-average methods in particular have an $O(n)$ space and $O(n^2)$ time complexity. For large highly-dimensional document collections, such as the TDT corpora, performance issues most commonly arise in the construction and updating of the *similarity matrix*. A similarity matrix is a diagonal matrix that holds the similarity scores between every cluster in the set. To address this problem, we implemented a number of optimisations to reduce both the time and space requirements of the matrix and its operations.

The simplest way to reduce the size of the similarity matrix is to compress the data. We chose to use the **Compressed Column Storage (CCS)** [7] method. For very large corpora, there are typically a considerable number of dissimilar clusters. If we were to store only those similarities that pass a certain threshold, our similarity matrix would be composed of very many zero entries. CCS exploits this sparsity. Columns are represented as a pair of arrays, one for the non-zero entries and the other for their indexes in the original column, eliminating the space requirements of the zero values.

Fractionation [8] is a "divide and conquer" strategy that aims to further minimise the size of the matrix. At each iteration, we divide the group of clusters into a set of non-overlapping buckets. Only documents that lie in the same bucket are compared to one another. So, rather than a single massive matrix for the entire collection, we construct a set of smaller similarity matrices for each bucket. These matrices are much quicker to scan and update, offering a significant improvement in performance.

For each iteration of a document clustering algorithm, we merge those clusters that are most similar. This requires a rebuild of the similarity matrix - removing the scores for the old clusters and updating the matrix with similarities for the new merged cluster. Performing this operation naïvely requires a large number of expensive comparisons to be performed. We first limit the number of matrix re-builds by using the **Partial Maximum Array** techniques described in [9]. The **Lance-Williams Update Formulae** [10] were then used to significantly improve matrix update performance. For a particular set of clustering algorithms, we can derive a formula that describes the similarity between a pair of clusters as a function of the similarities between their individual members. This means that we need only perform a full build of the similarity matrix once, at its initialisation. Subsequent iterations require only the appropriate Lance-Williams formula and the similarity scores in the original matrix.

Finally, we present the resulting set of event clusters to the user in a GUI. For each cluster, we compute the *centroid*, i.e. the average of the term vectors for all members of the cluster. The representative document for a particular cluster is the document that lies closest to the centroid. Figure 2 shows the set of event clusters displayed as a tree; each cluster is represented as a node and labelled with the title of its representative document. Non-singleton clusters can be expanded to reveal all on-topic news reports for that event, with the full text of the document displayed in a frame.

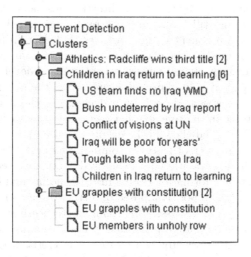

Fig. 2. Event Cluster Tree

3   Analysis of the TDT Corpus

In general, we define a topic over a corpus to be that set of documents that share a consistent theme or concept. Two documents can lie in the same topic yet still discuss different specific issues, e.g. reports on separate earthquakes are both members of the topic "natural disasters". It is possible to imagine any number of equally valid topic boundaries for a particular dataset. A typical clustering algorithm attempts to discover these broad groupings in an unsupervised and domain-independent way; an unordered corpus is ordered into a set of cohesive clusters corresponding to topics.

Topic Detection in the TDT domain diverges from standard clustering in a number of significant ways. Unlike a random collection of articles, the TDT corpus already has an underlying structure. It is time-ordered; news reports are date-stamped and the set arranged starting with the earliest. Moreover, there are distinct and specific entities already present in the dataset. If a human were to browse a collection of news articles, he would recognise a number of narrative threads running through the set. These discourses correspond to the events that occurred during the period covered by the corpus. A Topic Detection system aims to construct clusters that correspond to these narratives. Unlike a set of topics, there are a finite number of valid events that could take place for a collection of TDT documents. Furthermore, we are clustering documents from a single specific genre, that of news reportage.

A *News Event* is defined as something that happens at a particular place at a particular time. It is the latter attribute, the temporal nature of news, that is most characteristic of an event. Events have a beginning and an end, a date we associate with the occurrence and a time by which the incident has played out in full or the media's focus has shifted elsewhere. Between these two points, there is a broad pattern of development common across news events. The initial stages of an event are characterised by a flurry of directly on-topic news reports. At this point, the occurrence is still recent and the reader presumed to be unfamiliar with all the details. Consequently, those articles that contain the most directly on-topic information tend to occur early in the course of an event. This burst of articles starts to drop off as the event continues to develop; as the issues are resolved, the incident splits into sub-events or as the occurrence lessens in importance. This is represented both by a decrease in the number of relevant articles and an increase in the time gap between successive stories, and is visible in the histograms for the labelled TDT1 events (Figure 3).

There are also a number of features common amongst the individual news reports. News articles are traditionally structured in an "inverted triangle" style, i.e. the most important information occurs in the headline and lead paragraphs, with the remainder of the report composed of further discussion and background details [11,12]. In [13], Bell discusses this common structure and emphasises the significance of the opening paragraph, which typically summarises all the important details of an event. News stories are often characterised by six properties - *who, when, where, what, how,* and *why.* The lead paragraph commonly contains the most important of these - *who, where* and *what.* The *when* attribute is de-

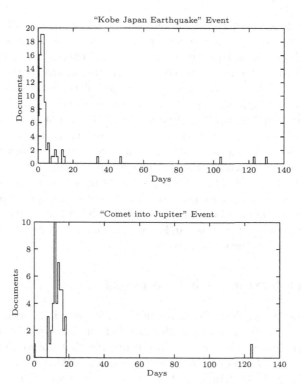

Fig. 3. TDT1 Event Histograms

rived from the document date stamp, or appears later in the text, illustrating that both words and dates are important details for describing an event.

4   Extensions

We aim to exploit those features peculiar to the TDT domain to enhance the basic Topic Detection system. This requires changes at each of the processing stages.

Feature Selection. We extract both words and dates from the text, mapping each date to a universal format. Simple date references such as *Today*, *Yesterday*, etc. are also captured in the same format. In addition, we allow indexing to be restricted to a percentage of the document. This allows us to extract only those features that occur towards the top of the news report, typically those that are most salient to the event being discussed.

Term Weighting. Topic shift means that the set of representative terms can change significantly from the early to the later stages of an event. Moreover, those documents that occur toward the beginning of an event tend to discuss the incident more precisely. If we suppose that the centroid ideally represents an event's core features, deriving the centroid for an occurrence whose focus has shifted may not produce a fully representative term vector. If we were to weight more highly those terms that appear in early documents, we might force the event centroid to better represent the main characteristics of the incident. In addition, we favour those terms that appear toward the top of a document, to exploit the "inverted triangle" structure of news reports.

Document Clustering. It is often noted in TDT literature that documents occurring close together in time are more likely to discuss the same event [14]. We noted earlier that the later stages of an incident are characterised by a drop in the number of reports and an increase in the time gap between them. Therefore, related news stories are only proximate in the early stages of an event. We propose establishing an adaptive time window for the document clustering. Articles would be compared to one another only when they are sufficiently close together in time. Moreover, this window would increase in size as a function of the period covered by the event cluster.

5   Topic Detection with Live Feeds

To illustrate how a complete system might work, we have implemented an example Topic Detection system that downloads data from live feeds over the Internet. The current implementation accepts an OPML file that points to a number of RSS feeds. *Outline Processor Mark-up Language (OPML)* is an XML format designed to allow the exchange of structured information. *RDF Site Summary (RSS)* is a web-content syndication format that delivers online information to the user as a data stream. Many Internet news services and websites deliver their content in this manner. The system parses the OPML file, extracting the URLs for each RSS feed and downloading the most recent entries. This set of articles is then passed to the clustering component, where it is grouped into event clusters and displayed to the user.

Deciding the value of an event cluster is a subjective judgement. However, although still quite basic, we found that the online system produced interesting and potentially useful clusters, such as those shown in Figure 2.

6   Conclusions and Future Work

Although we have yet to complete a full set of experiments, we have observed promising results for the current implementation of the Topic Detection system. Using GAC clustering with cosine similarity and simple term weighting, we have produced event clusters for the TDT1 corpus and provided a means for them to be browsed by the user. Furthermore, our online Topic Detection system creates interesting clusters despite receiving data of limited length and varying quality. This component will be further developed as a Java Servlet, and made available over the Internet. We expect that, following parameter setting and full implementation of the extensions described in Section 4, both the offline and online Topic Detection systems will produce clusters that are further refined and more cohesive. Independent of this, there are a number of areas that are open to future work.

The TDT1 corpus is composed of reports taken from across the news media, and subsequent updates have significantly increased both the number of articles and the breadth of sources. Consequently, a large percentage of the document collection is composed of transcripts of broadcast news and translations from non-English language sources, some automatically generated and others produced by hand. It is unclear whether the observations outlined in Section 3 hold for the more conversational nature of broadcast news. Moreover, transcripts and translated articles have considerably more errors than data derived from print or English language media. This suggests that clustering transcripts separately may be a useful approach, perhaps using methods similar to those described in [15] that are less sensitive to noisy data. Furthermore, articles from the TDT corpora differ from other natural-language documents in the importance of proper nouns. The *who* and *where* characteristics of a news story are both proper nouns, and events can often be represented by named entities alone. A further extension to the term weighting component might be a means of favouring proper nouns over other terms in the report.

Agglomerative clustering techniques are greedy algorithms. The operation of merging two clusters cannot be reversed, allowing a mistake early in the process to affect all subsequent iterations. *Cluster Refinement* [16] attempts to avoid this problem by periodically refining the set of clusters to remove those documents that have been assigned to a cluster in error. Since the core of a Topic Detection system is its clustering component, cluster refinement might offer a further performance improvement.

There are also a number of possible enhancements to the online Topic Detection system. Papka and Allan [17] have found that *single-pass* clustering is more appropriate for topic detection on a live feed. In addition, there are improvements that could be made to better exploit the meta-data present in RSS.

Finally, the system is currently implemented only for the TDT1 and TDT2 corpora. Moving to the new TDT4 corpus and participating in the official evaluation is an important goal.

References

1. Allan, J., Carbonell, J., Doddington, G., Yamron, J., Yang, Y.: Topic Detection and Tracking Pilot Study Final Report. In: Proc. DARPA Broadcast News Transcription and Understanding Workshop. (1998)
2. Arampatzis, A., van der Weide, T., Koster, C., van Bommel, P.: Term Selection for Filtering based on Distribution of Terms over Time. In: Proc. RIAO'2000 Content-Based Multimedia Information Access, Paris, France (2000) 1221–1237
3. Hatzivassiloglou, V., Gravano, L., Maganti, A.: An Investigation of Linguistic Features and Clustering Algorithms for Topical Document Clustering. In: Proc. 23rd Annual International ACM SIGIR Conference. (2000) 224–231
4. Yang, Y., Carbonell, J., Brown, R., Pierce, T., Archibald, B.T., Liu, X.: Learning Approaches for Detecting and Tracking News Events. IEEE Intelligent Systems **14** (1999) 32–43

5. Griths, A., Robinson, L., Willett, P.: Hierarchic Agglomerative Clustering Methods for Automatic Document Classication. Journal of Documentation **40** (1984) 175–205

6. Carbonell, J., Yang, Y., Lafferty, J., Brown, R., Pierce, T., Liu, X.: CMU Report on TDT-2: Segmentation, Detection and Tracking. In: Proc. of the DARPA Broadcast News Conference. (1999)

7. Gundersen, G., Steihaug, T.: Data Structures in Java for Matrix Computations. In: Proc. Norsk Informatikkkonferanse NIK'2002. (2002) 97–108

8. Cutting, D.R., Karger, D.R., Pedersen, J.O., Tukey, J.W.: Scatter/Gather: a Cluster-based Approach to Browsing Large Document Collections. In: Proc. 15th Annual International ACM SIGIR Conference. (1992) 318–329

9. Jung, S., Kim, T.S.: An Agglomerative Hierarchical Clustering Using Partial Maximum Array and Incremental Similarity Computation Method. In Cercone, N., Lin, T.Y., Wu, X., eds.: Proc. 2001 IEEE International Conference on Data Mining, San Jose, California, USA, IEEE Computer Society (2001) 265–272

10. Lance, G., Williams, W.: A General Theory of Classificatory Sorting Strategies I Hierarchical Systems. Computer Journal **9** (1967) 373–380

11. Delin, J.: The Language of Everyday Life. Sage, London (2000)

12. van Dijk, T.: News as Discourse. Lawrence Erlbaum, Hillsdale, NJ (1988)

13. Bell, A.: The Language of News Media. Blackwell Publishing, Oxford (1991)

14. Yang, Y., Pierce, T., Carbonell, J.: A study on retrospective and on-line event detection. In: Proc. of SIGIR-98, 21st ACM International Conference on Research and Development in Information Retrieval, Melbourne, AU (1998) 28–36

15. Ibrahimov, O., Sethi, I., Dimitrova, N.: Clustering of Imperfect Transcripts Using a Novel Similarity Measure. In: Proc. of the SIGIR'01 Workshop on Information Retrieval Techniques for Speech Applications. (2002)

16. Liu, X., Gong, Y., Xu, W., Zhu, S.: Document Clustering with Cluster Refinement and Model Selection Capabilities. In: Proc. of the 25th Annual International ACM SIGIR Conference on Research and Development in Information Retrieval, ACM Press (2002) 191–198

17. Papka, R., Allan, J.: On-line New Event Detection using Single-pass Clustering. Technical Report UMASS Computer Science Technical Report, Department of Computer Science, University of Massachusetts (1998)

Assessing the Impact of Lexical Chain Scoring Methods and Sentence Extraction Schemes on Summarization

William Doran, Nicola Stokes, Joe Carthy, and John Dunnion

Department of Computer Science,
University College Dublin, Ireland.
{William.Doran,Nicola.Stokes,Joe.Carthy,John.Dunnion}@ucd.ie

Abstract. We present a comparative study of lexical chain-based summarisation techniques. The aim of this paper is to highlight the effect of lexical chain scoring metrics and sentence extraction techniques on summary generation. We present our own lexical chain-based summarisation system and compare it to other chain-based summarisation systems. We also compare the chain scoring and extraction techniques of our system to those of several other baseline systems, including a random summarizer and one based on tf.idf statistics. We use a task-oriented summarisation evaluation scheme that determines summary quality based on TDT story link detection performance.

1 Introduction

Summarisation is a reductive transformation of a source text into a summary text by extraction or generation [13]. It is generally agreed that automating the summarisation procedure should be based on text understanding that mimics the cognitive processes of humans. However, this is a sub-problem of Natural Language Processing (NLP) and is a very difficult problem to solve at present. It may take some time to reach a level where machines can fully understand documents, in the interim we must utilise other properties of text, such as lexical cohesion analysis, that do not rely on full comprehension of the text.

Lexical cohesion is the textual property responsible for making the sentences of a text seem to "hang together", indicated by the use of semantically related vocabulary [10]. Cohesion is thus a surface indicator of the discourse structure of a document. One method of representing this type of discourse structure is through the use of a linguistic technique called lexical chaining. Lexical chains are defined as clusters of semantically related words. For example, {*house, loft, home, cabin*} is a chain, where *house* and *home* are synonyms, *attic* is part of a *house* and *cabin* is a specialisation of *house*. The lexical chaining algorithms discussed in this paper identify such lexical cohesive relationships between words using the WordNet taxonomy [9].

Since lexical chains were first proposed by Morris and Hirst [10], they have been used to address a variety of Information Retrieval (IR) and NLP applications, such as term weighting for IR tasks [15], malapropism detection [14], hypertext generation [6] and topic detection in broadcast news streams [16], to name but a few. More importantly however, in the context of this paper, lexical chains have been successfully used as an intermediate source text representation for document

A. Gelbukh (Ed.): CICLing 2004, LNCS 2945, pp. 627–635, 2004.
© Springer-Verlag Berlin Heidelberg 2004

summarisation. This application of lexical chaining was first implemented by Barzilay and Elhadad [3]. They used lexical chains to weight the contribution of a sentence to the main topic of a document, where sentences with high numbers of chain words are extracted and presented as a summary of that document.

In this paper, we put forward novel methods of building extractive summaries of single documents using lexical chains. However, unlike other attempts to improve upon Barzilay and Elhadad's work [1, 4, 12], we evaluate our weighting and extraction schemes directly with theirs using an extrinsic or task-based evaluation technique. An intrinsic evaluation is the preferred method of evaluating summary quality used by most summarisation researchers. This type of evaluation requires a set of human judges to either create a set of gold standard summaries or score summary quality compared to the original text. However, this evaluation method is time consuming, expensive and quite often subjective and hence is inappropriate for estimating the effect of different schemes on summary performance. Therefore in this paper we propose a more efficient evaluation alternative based on the TDT story-link detection task [2], where summary quality is evaluated with respect to how well a story link detection system can determine if a pair of document summaries are similar (on-topic) or dissimilar (off-topic). We are also interested in finding out whether this type of evaluation is sensitive enough to pick up differences in the summary extraction techniques discussed in this paper. In the remainder of the paper, we explain in more detail how lexical chaining based summarisation works. We evaluate our scoring metrics and compare the best performing metric to Barzilay and Elhadad's metric. We also present our experimental methodology and results. The final section discusses our conclusions and some future work.

2   Lexical Chaining and Text Summarisation

The basic chaining algorithm follows the following steps. First, the algorithm select a set of candidate words, in our case, nouns. Then it searches through the list of chains and if a word satisfies the relatedness criteria with a chain word then the word is added to the chain, otherwise a new chain is created.

The relatedness criteria are the relationships outlined by St Onge [14]. St Onge used WordNet [9] as the knowledge source for lexical chaining. He devised three different relationships between candidate words: extra-strong, strong and medium-strong. Extra-strong relations are lexical repetitions of a word and strong relations are synonyms or near-synonyms. Strong relations can also indicate a shared hypernym/hyponym or meronym/holonym, such that one word is a parent-node or child-node of the other in the WordNet topology. Medium-strength relations follow sets of rules laid out by St Onge. These rules govern the shape of the paths that are allowable in the WordNet structure. St Onge's algorithm uses a greedy disambiguation procedure where a word's sense is determined only by the senses of words that occur before it in the text. In contrast, a non-greedy approach waits until all words in the document are processed and then calculates the appropriate senses of all the words.

In general, most lexical chain based summarizers follow the same approach by firstly generating lexical chains, then the 'strongest' of these chains are used to weight and extract key sentences in the text. Barzilay and Elhadad [3] form chains using a non-greedy disambiguation procedure. To score chains they calculate the product of two chain characteristics: the length of the chain, which is the total number of words in the chain plus repetitions and, the homogeneity of the chain, which is equal to 1 minus the number of distinct words divided by the length of the chain. Chain scores that exceed an average chain score plus twice the standard deviation are considered 'strong' chains. Barzilay et al. then select the first sentence that contains a 'representative' word from a 'strong' chain, where a 'representative' word has a frequency greater than or equal to the average frequency of words in that chain.

Most other researchers use this approach to building extractive summaries using lexical chains [1, 12], with the exception of Brunn et al. [4] who calculate chain scores as the pair-wise sum of the chain word relationship strengths in the chain. In the latter, sentences are ranked based on the number of 'strong' chain words they contain.

3   The LexSum System

Our chaining algorithm LexSum is based on [14, 16] and uses a greedy lexical chaining approach. The first step in our chain formation process is to assign parts-of-speech to an incoming document. The algorithm then identifies all noun, proper nouns and compound noun phrases by searching for patterns of tags corresponding to these types of phrases e.g. presidential/JJ campaign/NN, or U.S/NN President/NN Bush/NP where /NN is a noun tag and /NP is a proper noun tag.

The nouns and compound nouns are chained by searching for lexical cohesive relationships between words in the text by following constrained paths in WordNet similar to those described in [14] using lexicographical relationships such as synonymy (*car, automobile*), specialisation/generalisation (*horse, stallion*), part-whole/whole-part (*politicians, government*). However, unlike previous chaining approaches our algorithm produces two disjoint sets of chains: noun chains and proper noun chains. Finding relationships between proper nouns is an essential element of modelling the topical content of any news story. Unfortunately, WordNet's coverage of proper nouns is limited to historical figures (e.g. Marco Polo, John Glenn) and so our algorithm uses a fuzzy string matching function to find repetition relationships between proper nouns phrases like George_*Bush* ⟺ President_*Bush*.

In this paper we present five different chain scoring metrics, three of which are based on semantic relationships between the words of the chain, another is based on corpus statistics, and the final metric assigns the same score to each chain. Unlike Barzilay et al.'s approach, the first three metrics calculate chain scores based on the number of repetitions and the type of WordNet relations between chain members. The differences between the three lie in the way relations in the chain are handled. More specifically, as shown in equation (1), the chain score is the sum of each score assigned to each word pair in the chain. Each word pair's score is calculated as the sum of the frequencies of the two words, multiplied by the relationship score between them,

$$chain\_score1(chain) = \sum (reps_i + reps_j) * rel(i,j). \tag{1}$$

where $reps_i$ is the frequency of word i in the text, and $rel(i,j)$ is a score assigned based on the strength of the relationship between word i and j, where a synonym relationship gets assigned a value of 0.9, specialisation/generalisation and part-whole/whole-part 0.7. Proper nouns chain scores are calculated depending on the type of match, 1.0 for an exact match, 0.8 for a partial match and 0.7 for a fuzzy match.

The second metric, equation (2), assigns a score to each word in the chain depending on its relation to the most frequent member of the chain. Therefore, the most frequent word will get the highest score, the next frequent will get a lesser score depending on its frequency and how it is related to the most frequent word in the chain. If a word is not related to the most frequent word in the chain, we then take into account the word in the chain that it is related to.

$$chain\_score2(chain) = \sum (reps_i * rel(i,j)).\tag{2}$$

where $reps_i$ is the frequency of word i in the text, and $rel(i,j)$ is a score assigned based on the strength of the relationship between word i and j, where word i is the most frequent word in the chain. The scores of the relationships are the same as in equation (1).

The third scoring metric, equation (3), assigns a score to each chain depending on the number of words and number of relations in the chain. The first word added is deemed the most important and any subsequent additions simply add to the total score of the chain. The scores of subsequent additions are not adversely affected as in equation (1) and equation(2).

$$chain\_score3(chain) = \sum (reps_i) + \sum rel(i,j).\tag{3}$$

where $reps_i$ is the frequency of word i in the text, and $rel(i,j)$ is a score assigned based on the strength of the relationship between word i and j as in equation(1).

The fourth scoring metric proposed in this paper is based on corpus statistics from an auxiliary corpus. The reason we use a different corpus is because our evaluation corpus only comprises 625 documents [5] and these documents are grouped into similar clusters. These documents have similar word distributions thus overly biasing the statistics. We use a larger corpus of roughly 16,000 documents taken from the TDT pilot corpus [17].

$$chain\_score4(chain) = \sum (reps_i + idf(word_i))\tag{4}$$

where $reps_i$ is the frequency of word i in the text, and $idf(word_j)$ is a score assigned based on the inverse document frequency of the word taken from the auxiliary corpus [17]. If a chain word is a phrase, the score of the phrase is the score of the individual words comprising it. In the previous four weighting schemes we calculate a relative score for each chain, by dividing each chain's score by the largest chain score.

The final scoring scheme, equation (5), assigns the same default score of 1 to all the chains.

$$chain\_score5(chain) = 1\tag{5}$$

The next step in the algorithm ranks sentences based on the sum of the scores of the words in each sentence. The summary will be based on the top ranking sentences. We have implemented three different ranking schemes: the first is based on the 'burstiness' of chain words, the second is based simply on the chain scores and the third is a variant of the first scheme that incorporates a bonus score for words that occur in the first paragraph.

In the first sentence-ranking scheme, equation (6), a word's score is a scaled version of its chain's score. The scaling factor is the minimum distance between a word and its predecessor or its successor in the chain. This idea is based on the fact that general topics tend to span large sections of a discourse whereas subtopics tend to populate smaller areas. [7]. Therefore, the score of a word will be increased if semantically similar words are close by it in the text i.e. the topic is in the focus of the reader,

$$word\_score(\ word_i) = \ \alpha * chain\_score(\ chain(\ word_i)) \qquad (6)$$

$$\alpha = 1 - (\min[dist(w_{i-1}, w_i), dist(w_i, w_{i+1})]/\ dist(w_1, w_n)) \qquad (7)$$

where $dist(w_i, w_j)$ is the number of words that separate two words in the text and $chain(word_i)$ is the chain $word_i$ belongs to. As explained earlier the sentence score is the sum of these word scores normalized with respect to the length of the sentence and the number of chain words it contains.

The second ranking scheme, equation (8), simply gives each word in a sentence the score of the chain to which it belongs,

$$word\_score(\ word_i) = \ chain\_score(\ chain(\ word_i)) \qquad (8)$$

where $chain(word_i)$ is the chain $word_i$ belongs to.

The final ranking scheme is identical to the first scheme, except that if a word occurs in the first paragraph then its score is doubled, thus biasing chain words that occur in the first paragraph. This takes into account the structure of news documents where the first paragraph tends to contain a summary of the article and subsequent articles elaborate and expand the story. So for all the ranking schemes we total the scores for each word in the sentence. This sentence score is then normalised by the number of chain words per unit length.

In the next section we will compare all possible combinations of the scoring and sentence ranking metrics. We will evaluate all these summarization systems and compare the best performing system against several baseline systems.

4 Experimental Methodology

As explained above, we use a task-oriented evaluation methodology to determine the performance of our lexical chain based summarizers, this type of evaluation can be automated and hence more efficient than an intrinsic evaluation that involves the time and effort of a set of human judges. It also provides us with a means of evaluating summary performance on a larger than normal data set of news stories used in the DUC evaluation, i.e. 326 TDT documents and 298 TREC documents [5]. While intrinsic evaluation gauges summary quality directly by rating summary informativeness and coherency, extrinsic evaluation gauges the impact the summary generation procedure has on some task, thus indirectly determining summary quality. Several such tasks have been outlined as useful by TIPSTER [8], such as ad-hoc retrieval, categorization and question answering tasks.

In this paper we use the TDT Story Link Detection Task [2]. TDT is a research initiative that investigates the event-based organisation of news stories in a broadcast news stream. Story Link Detection (SLD) is the pair-wise comparison of stories to establish whether they discuss the same event. Thus for each distinct set of summaries generated (by each system), we evaluate summary quality by observing whether the SLD system can distinguish between on-topic and off-topic document summary pairs. Hence, the hypothesis underlying this type of summary evaluation is that an SLD system will perform well on summaries that have retained the core message of each news story, while it will perform poorly on summaries that in general failed to recognise the central theme of the documents in the data set. Our SLD system is based on an IR vector space model where document similarity is determined using the cosine similarity function [18]. As in the TDT initiative, we evaluate story link detection performance using two error metrics: percentage misses (document pairs that are incorrectly tagged as off-topic) and false alarms (document pairs that are incorrectly tagged as on-topic). A Detection Error Trade-off (DET) graph is then plotted for misses and false alarms rates at various similarity thresholds (ranging from 0 to 1) where a DET curve is produced for each set of generated summaries. Optimal SLD performance can then be determined by observing which of these curves lies closest to the origin, i.e. has the lowest miss and false alarm rates.

5   Results

Firstly, we evaluated all possible combinations of the five scoring metrics and three ranking metrics. These combinations are listed in Table1 below.

We generated summaries for all fifteen of the systems at summary compression rates of 10, 20, 30, 40, 50 and 60 percent. Each of these summary sets was given as input to the SLD system and DET graphs were produced. Below we have Figure 1 which shows the best performing systems of the second ranking scheme, where sentence words are given the score of the chain to which they belong. We have left out the results of the two lesser performing metrics for the sake of clarity in the graph. Also, the results shown in this graph are indicative of the general trend for all compression rates.

The results of this experiment lead us to believe that the differences between scoring metrics is very small. However, the best performing sentence ranking scheme across the five scoring metrics is the second ranking scheme, equation (8), and the best performing scoring metric is the second scoring metric, equation (2). These facts are reinforced by the fact that system G marginally outperforms other summarization system. (System G is the combination of the best sentence ranking and scoring metrics).

Table 1. This table contains the system letters assigned to all the possible combinations of the five scoring metrics and the three ranking schemes.

	Chain_score1	Chain_score2	Chain_score3	Chain_score4	Chain_score5
Ranking_1	A	B	C	D	E
Ranking_2	F	G	H	I	J
Ranking_3	K	L	M	N	O

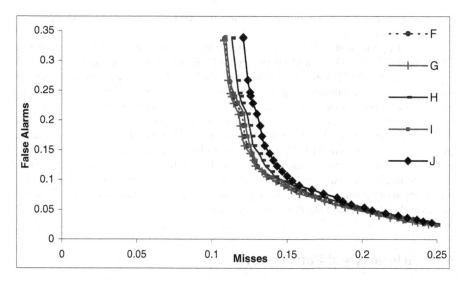

Fig. 1. This DET graph shows the Story Link Detection comparison of the different combinations of scoring and ranking metrics for a compression rate of 50%

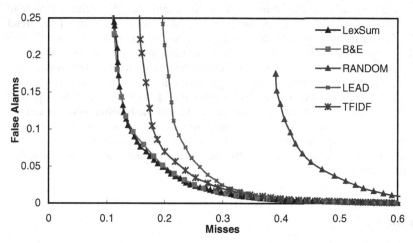

Fig. 2. This DET graph shows the Story Link Detection results of summaries (at a compression rate of 50%)

We also evaluate our best combination, LexSum, against three baseline systems LEAD, TF-IDF, and RANDOM, using the same evaluation strategy as above. The LEAD system creates summaries from the lead paragraph of each document, since news stories tend to contain a summary of the article in the first paragraph. The TF-IDF system extracts sentences which have high *tf-idf* weights values, where *tf-idf* is a term weighting scheme that is commonly used in IR research [18]. The final baseline extracts sentences at random from the source document and uses these as a summary. We also created a system, B&E that replicates Barzilay and Elhadad's scoring metric.

We modified the B&E extraction technique to enable us to generate summaries of different lengths.

We again generated summaries for all the summarizers at summary compression rates of 10, 20, 30, 40, 50 and 60 percent (of the top ranked sentences in the text). Figure 2 is a DET graph illustrating the results for each summarisation system running at 50% compression. Again, this graph is indicative of the general trend for all the compression rates. Both lexical chain systems outperform the baseline systems for all percentages except at 10% where the LEAD performs better. As expected the RANDOM summariser has the worst performance. The fact that lexical chain based summarisers outperform TFIDF, suggests that observing patterns of lexical cohesion is a more accurate means of identifying core themes in documents than using corpus statistics like *tf.idf*. Another observation from these experiments is that B&E's weighting scheme marginally outperforms ours at high false alarm and low miss rates; however this result is not statistically significant.

6   Conclusions and Future Work

In this paper, we have analysed some of the factors that affect lexical chain based summarisation using an extrinsic evaluation methodology. We found that the effect of the weighting scheme has little effect on the summaries. It is likely that both lexical chain based systems are selecting the same sentences, the extent of this trend warrants further investigation. Both chaining systems perform better than the TF.IDF and LEAD systems, justifying the extra computation involved in lexical chaining. We have also shown that combining different scoring and ranking schemes can have an effect on performance, this is only a slight effect at the moment but it may prove useful at finer levels of system granularity. Also, the SLD evaluation method proved to be sensitive enough to show the differences between the baseline systems and the lexical chain based systems. It is our intention to carry out an intrinsic evaluation of the summarisation systems described in this paper and compare these human-deduced summary quality ratings with the results of the automated evaluation presented above.

References

[1]   Alemany, L. and Fuentes M., 2003, *Integrating Cohesion and Coherence for Text Summarization.* In the Proceedings of the EACL Student Workshop, 2003.

[2]   Allan J., 2002, Introduction to Topic Detection and Tracking, In *Topic Detection and Tracking: Event-based Information Organization*, Kluwer Academic Publishers, pp. 1–16.

[3]   Barzilay R. and Elhadad M., 1997, Using Lexical Chains for Summarisation. In *ACL/EACL-97 summarisation workshop.* pp 10–18, Madrid.

[4]   Brunn M., Chali Y., and Pinchak C. 2001,Text summarisation using lexical chains, In *Workshop on Text Summarisation in conjunction with the ACM SIGIR Conference 2001*, New Orleans, Louisiana, 2001.

[5]   DUC 2003 http://www-nlpir.nist.gov/projects/duc/

[6]   Green, S. 1997, *Automatically generating hypertext by computing semantic similarity*, PhD thesis, University of Toronto.

[7] Hearst, M. 1994, Multi-paragraph segmentation of expository text, In *Proceedings of the 32th Annual Meeting of the Association for Computational Linguistics,* 9–16. Las Cruces, New Mexico: Association for Computational Linguistics.

[8] Mani I., House, D., Klein, G., Hirschman, L., Obrst, L., Firmin, T., Chrzanowski, M. and Sundheim, B. 1998, The TIPSTER SUMMAC text summarisation evaluation: Final report. MITRE Technical Report MTR 98w0000138, MITRE.

[9] Miller G.A., Beckwith R., Fellbaum C., Gross, D., and Miller, K. 1990, *Five papers on WordNet.* Technical Report, Cognitive Science Laboratory, 1990.

[10] Morris, J. and Hirst, G. 1991. Lexical cohesion computed by thesaural relations as an indicator of the structure of text, *Computational Linguistics* 17(1): 21–43.

[11] Salton, G., Singhal, A., Mitra, M., and Buckley, C. 1997, Automatic text structuring and summarisation. *Information Processing and Management* 33(2):193–208.

[12] Silber, G. and McCoy, K.. 2000, Efficient Text Summarisation Using Lexical Chains, In *Proceedings of the ACM Conference on Intelligent User Interfaces (IUI'2000).*

[13] Spark-Jones, K. 2001, Factorial Summary Evaluation, In *Workshop on Text Summarisation in conjunction with the ACM SIGIR Conference 2001.* New Orleans, Louisiana.

[14] St. Onge, D. 1995, *Detection and Correcting Malapropisms with Lexical Chains,* M.Sc Thesis, University of Toronto, Canada.

[15] Stairmand, M. 1996, *A Computational Analysis of Lexical Cohesion with Applications in Information Retrieva,.* Ph.D. Dissertation, Center for Computational Linguistics, UMIST, Manchester.

[16] Stokes, N., J. Carthy, A.F Smeaton, SeLeCT: A Lexical Chain-based News Story Segmentation System. To appear in the AI Communications Journal.

[17] TDT Pilot Corpus, http://www.nist.gov/speech/tests/tdt/

[18] van Rijsbergen, C.J., Information Retrieval, Butterworths, 1979

A Term Weighting Method Based on Lexical Chain for Automatic Summarization

Young-In Song, Kyoung-Soo Han, and Hae-Chang Rim

Natural Language Processing Lab., Dept. of CSE,
Korea University, Anam-dong 5-ga, Seongbuk-gu, 136-701, Seoul, Korea
{sprabbit,kshan,rim}@nlp.korea.ac.kr

Abstract. We suggest a new term weighting method based on lexical cohesion in a text. To compute cohesion, we use lexical chain with a new lexical chain disambiguation method considering association between words and characteristics of WordNet. In our experiment, the methods show a better result than traditional term weighting methods such as tf and tf.idf.

1 Introduction

Summarization can be defined as the work of extracting essential part of a document as a readable form and deleting some redundant information. From this point of view, finding thematic terms of a document is one of the important tasks in the automatic summarization, and various term weighting methods such as tf.idf have been used for it.

In this paper, we try to develop a new term weighting scheme considering the lexical cohesion, that is to say, semantic relations (e.g. synonym, antonym, etc.) between words. Our motivation is quite simple but reasonable; Thematic words have more semantic relation than others in a text.

One of the efficient methods to compute the lexical cohesion is to use the lexical chain. The lexical chain can be defined as groups or sequences of semantically related words, and the work of [1] and [2] suggest successful ways to use the lexical chain for the automatic summarization. To use the lexical chain for summarization task, there are two problems to be solved;

1. Ambiguity of the lexical chain: A semantic relation between words is dependent on the meaning of each word. If the ambiguity of word sense cannot be resolved, lexical chain also has an ambiguity.

2. Relevance of the lexical chain: All of lexical chains are not relevant to the topic of the document. A method to distinguish useful chains from useless ones is needed.

In previous works, heuristic methods were used for above two problems, based on the number and kind of semantic relations in a chain[2, 3]. However, they are so simple that they cannot help containing some errors. They do not consider anything about words which make a semantic relation. Thus we suggest a new disambiguation method considering word association and term weighting methods based on it.

A. Gelbukh (Ed.): CICLing 2004, LNCS 2945, pp. 636–639, 2004.
© Springer-Verlag Berlin Heidelberg 2004

2 Disambiguation of Lexical Chain

We compute chains as same manner with Barzilay's system except one, a relation weight scheme for chain disambiguation[2]. We will describe it in this section.

To resolve ambiguities of chains, we design a scoring function f_s which indicates a possibility that a word relation is a correct one. It consists of three parts as follows:

Word association score (*Assoc*): A high frequency of co-occurrence between two words should be the evidence that there is a semantic relation. On this intuition, we design a *word association score (Assoc)*:

$$Assoc(w_1, w_2) = \frac{\log(p(w_1, w_2) + 1)}{N_s(w_1) \times N_s(w_2)}, \tag{1}$$

where w1, w2 are the candidate words with some relation in WordNet, and p(w1, w2) is a co-occurrence probability of a word pair. Ns(w) is a kind of normalization factor. It means the number of senses which a word w has.

Depth in Wordnet hierarchy (*DepthScore*): Thematic words in a document have a tendency to belong to a lower synset in WordNet hierarchy, because it has a specific meaning rather than a broader meaning in many cases. To reflect this tendency, we define *DepthScore* as follows:

$$DepthScore(w_1, w_2) = Depth(w_1)^2 \times Depth(w_2)^2 \tag{2}$$

Depth (w) is the depth of word *w* in WordNet.

Semantic relation weight (*RelationWeight*): We also weight a relation according to its type. Experimentally, we fixed the weight of reiteration to 1, synonym to 0.2, antonym to 0.3, mero/holonym to 0.4, hyper/hyponym to 0.2, and sibling to 0.05.

Finally, scoring function f_s is defined using above three. Given two words w_1, w_2, scoring function f_s via relation r is defined as the following formula.

$$fs(w_1, w_2, r) = Assoc(w_1, w_2) \times DepthScore(w_1, w_2) \times RelationWeight(r) \tag{3}$$

The score of lexical chain C_i is calculated as the sum of the score for each relation r_j in C_i.

$$Score(C_i) = \sum_{r_j \, in \, C_i} f_s(w_{j1}, w_{j2}, r_j) \tag{4}$$

If ambiguities of a chain would occurs at a chain generation step, the chain score is calculated for each one, and the chain with the highest score is regarded as a correct one.

3   Term Weighting Method and Sentence Extraction

In this section, we propose a term weighting method based on the lexical chain and a sentence extraction method using it. Our method is started from the following assumptions:

Assumption 1: All words in the same chain represent one concept.
Assumption 2: The number of word relations in a chain implies a degree of cohesion. As a chain has more connectivity, it is more important.
Assumption 3: As a word is more connected in a chain, it is more important in the chain.

From this point of view, we design new term weighting formula, namely *ConceptFreq* as follows:

$$ChainFreq(w_{ij}, c_j) = WordConnectivity(w_{ij}) \times ChainConnectivity(c_j) \tag{5}$$

$$WordConnectivity(w_{ij}) = Frequency(w_{ij}) \times \frac{r(w_{ij}, c_j) + \alpha}{\displaystyle\sum_{j=1}^{J}\sum_{k=1}^{N} r(w_{kj}, c_j)}$$

$$ChainConnectivity(c_j) = \frac{\displaystyle\sum_{k=1}^{N} r(w_{kj}, c_j)}{|c_j|},$$

where r(wij, cj) is the number of relations that include wij in chain cj, | cj | is the number of unique words in chain cj, and α is a constant of small value.

WordConnectivity (w_{ij}) is a function for measuring the degree of the connectivity of a word w_{ij} in a chain c_j, and *ChainConnectivity* (c_j) is that for the degree of the connectivity of a chain c_j. *ConceptFreq* is the product of them.

Because our aim is not to achieve higher performance of the sentence extraction, but to find an elaborate term weighting method, we make a simple sentence scoring function. The score of a sentence *Sentence*$_k$ which consists of words $w_1,...,w_n$ is calculated as the sum of term weights.

$$SentenceScore(Sentence_k) = \sum_{i=1}^{N}\sum_{j=1}^{C} ConceptFreq(w_{ij}, C_j), \tag{6}$$

where cj is a chain in the text, wij is a word belong to the chain cj, n is the number of words, and C is the number of chains.

Table 1. The result of sentence extraction: tf is the system using tf weighting scheme, tf.idf is the system using tf.idf, and LC is the proposed system using lexical chains

	P1	P3	P5	P10	P20	R-prec
Tf	0.57	0.47	0.41	0.32	0.23	0.392
tf.idf	0.64	0.45	0.41	0.31	0.23	0.364
LC	**0.64**	**0.52**	**0.45**	**0.36**	**0.26**	**0.431**

4   Experimental Results

The experiments were carried out with 20 documents randomly selected from DUC 2001 training document collection, and the abstracts were manually aligned to the sentences which contain similar information to it. The average number of sentences in the documents is 52, and the average number of sentences aligned to an abstract is 5.4.

We implemented two systems to be compared with ours; the system using tf as a term weight and the system using tf.idf as a term weight. All systems in our experiments have a common sentence extraction module described in section 3.2. System output is the ranked sentences of an input document.

Table 1 shows our experimental results. Our system shows better performance than others by the whole evaluation measures. Our term weighting method seems reasonable in the general case, but in some cases, especially tense expression such as year and month which have a lot of relation naturally, it is erroneous and causes a wrong weighting. Proper nouns and semantic relations which do not exist in WordNet dictionary are also problematic in our term weighting method.

5   Conclusions

We proposed a weighting method for the lexical chain disambiguation and a new term weighting method based on lexical chain. Our proposed method outperformed the traditional methods such as tf and tf.idf in our experiments, but we found some problems also.

In our term weighting method, proper nouns and semantic relations which do not exist in WordNet dictionary are problematic. In the case of proper nouns, some ways to recognize the class of proper nouns, named entity, can be one of solutions. The problem of semantic relations looks very difficult to be solved. It requires more knowledge about semantic relations. These remained as future work.

References

1. J.Morris and G.Hirst: Lexical cohesion computed by thesaural relations as indicator of the structure of text. Computational linguistics, (1991) 17(1) 21–45
2. Barzilay, Regina and Michael Elhadad: Lexical Chains for Text Summarization. Master's thesis, Ben-Gurion University (1997)
3. Siber, H.G and McCoy, K.F: Efficient Text Summarization using Lexical Chains. In Proceedings of the ACM Conference on Intelligent User Interfaces (2000)

Centroid-Based Language Identification Using Letter Feature Set

Hidayet Takcı and İbrahim Soğukpınar

Gebze Institute of Technology 41400 Gebze/Kocaeli-Turkey
{htakci,ispinar}@bilmuh.gyte.edu.tr

Abstract. In recent years, an unexpected amount of growth of the text documents volume has been observed on the internet, intranet, in digital libraries and newsgroups. To obtain useful information and meaningful patterns from these documents, a great many researchers known under the term "text mining" have been carried out. Among them text categorization is to be mentioned that covers the problem of classifying documents relative to their similarities. One of techniques applied in this area is called centroid-based document classification method. All researchers on text categorization use the notion of frequency somehow or other. In this study, letter frequencies (LF) have been used for text categorization. By making use of letter frequencies information, the centroid-based document classification has been carried out. An experiment has been done on language detection for text documents. Its results allow propose that the letter-based text categorization should be done prior to term based text categorization.

1 Introduction

With the current spread of worldwide access, the volume of available texts increased written in different languages. Automated treatment of these texts that anyway requires natural language processing, necessitate a preliminary identification of the language used [2]. Language identification problem can be seen as a specific instance of the more general problem of an item classification through its attributes [3].

Language identification is one of the text categorization applications [8]. In language identification study languages will be pre-defined categories. So, we can identify a language by using a text categorization algorithm. As far as centroid-based document classification is one of techniques of text classification algorithm can be applied with the purpose of language identification. It has a linear time complexity, and it is easy for use [7].

Generally, in language identification studies, short words or common words [9], n-grams [4, 11], unique letter combinations [10] etc. are used as feature set. Usage of too many features is a disadvantage for fast language identification processes. Instead, we could alternatively use letter feature sets. In a study, it has been mentioned that, letters could be used for characterization of documents [5]. In addition to, sometimes, word based identification techniques are not easily applied to Japanese and Chinese. Therefore character-based methods are also used for language identification in

A. Gelbukh (Ed.): CICLing 2004, LNCS 2945, pp. 640–648, 2004.
© Springer-Verlag Berlin Heidelberg 2004

Japanese and Chinese languages [1, 12]. Consequently, letters can be used as an alternative solution and letters can be used to reduce the size of feature sets.

In this study, letter feature sets are proposed to use with the aim of increasing speed of centroid-based languages identification. The document languages were tried for recognition and successful results were obtained by using the proposed method.

Our approach is based on calculating and comparing profiles (centroids) of letter frequencies. First, profiles on training data sets that represent various categories are computed. Training data may be language samples or other content samples. Then is calculated a profile for a particular text document that is to be classified. Finally, to detect the language of new text documents, the method computes a similarity measure between the document's profile and each of the category profiles. Our method selects the category whose profile is the nearest to the document's profile.

The rest of the paper is organized as follows: in the second section of this paper, motivation of letter-based classification is described. In the third chapter, theoretical approach and procedural principles of proposed method are described. In the fourth section, experimental results and analysis are given. The last section contains conclusions

2 Using Letter Feature Set in Language Identification

In language identification studies, one of main problems is the dimension of the feature set. Generally, feature sets are constructed from n-grams or short terms and these are very large in size. Therefore, reducing their dimension is necessary in language identification studies.

Using letters in the language identification process will indeed solve the dimension problem. For example, the numbers of n-grams and common words are estimated as 2550-3560 and 980-2750, correspondingly [2], while in an alphabet there are 25 – 30 letters on the average using letters has more advantages.

When taking speed using of letters has more advantage over the others. However, what about the adequate identification of documents when letters are used? To investigate this issue, letters from four languages have been analyzed and distributions of letter frequencies have been determined relative to different languages. Average letter frequencies belonging to documents from different languages are shown in Figure 1.

Figure 1 shows the differences of letter frequencies from one language to other. The closeness of frequencies of some letters is sourced from the neighbor of languages. This situation is from the historical basis of languages. Figure 1 obviously depicts that letters provide distinguishing information for documents. Letter distributions in documents depend not only on language but also on subject and writer as well.

Documents are represented by short terms or n-grams in usual language identification, but in letter based language identification documents are represented by letter frequencies. Using letters as feature set reduces the dimension significantly and this situation maintain the greatest motivation for letter based language identification.

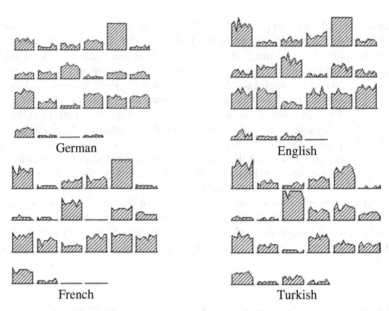

German   English

French   Turkish

Fig. 1. Letter frequencies of each language

3   Letter Based Language Identification System

Two most important features of letter based language identification system are letter feature set and centroid based classification. Architecture of the proposed system is shown in Figure 2 and represented by two main steps. At the first step, system is trained with training data and centroid values (category profiles) are learned from training data. At the second step test documents are assigned to categories according to centroid values. Similarities are used to classify documents in categories. During these processes, documents are represented by letter frequencies (document profile). The most important difference of this system from the other language identification systems is usage of letter feature set.

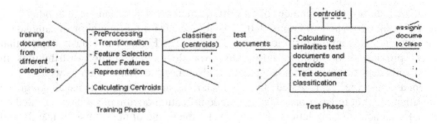

Fig. 2. Proposed language identification system

3.1 Training Phase

Training phase is the most important step in all classification applications and in this step; classifiers are trained with labeled data. First step of training phase is pre-processing. In this phase, documents from different categories are pre-processed.

3.1.1 Pre-processing
In letter-based method, cleaning, stemming and parsing are not necessary. Only, transformation is done on text documents. Text documents are transformed to letter frequencies.

3.1.2 Feature Selection
Feature Selection is the next step after pre-processing of documents. The aim of this process is to find the best features that will represent the documents. In letter-based language identification, letters are chosen as features.

Letter Features
Letter feature sets are constructed of letters (a ... z) chosen from Latin alphabet. Four languages that have been chosen for the experiment use these letters. The usage of letters as feature set reduces the volume of the feature set dramatically. By this, an important increase in speed is observed classifying the documents.

3.1.3 Representation
A suitable model is necessary for the chosen features representation. Documents are represented using the vector space model in Centroid-based document classification [6]. In this model, each document d can be thought of as a vector in a letter space. In the simplest form each document can be represented via a letter frequency vector,

$$\vec{d}_{lf} = (lf_1, lf_2, ..., lfn)$$ where lfi is the frequency of ith letter in the document.

As a weighting model for the LF vector, the frequency-weighting vector is chosen. Therefore, for each document LF vector will also be its weighting vector. At the last step, normalization is achieved by transforming each document vector into a unit vector.

In this model, documents can be imagined as points in a letter space and therefore the similarities between documents can be calculated by geometrical methods.

3.1.4 Calculating Centroids (Category Profiles)
Last step of training phase is calculating centroid values for each class. If there are k classes in training set, then, k centroid vectors are calculated.

$\{\vec{C}_1, \vec{C}_2, ..., \vec{C}_k\}$, Each $\vec{C}_i$, is centroid value of the *ith* class. Centroid value mentioned the mean of elements in the class. Mean value for a class is assumed to characterize the whole class.

If $\vec{C}$ is to be defined as a centroid value for a document set (category or class) formed by S documents, the value of this vector is obtained as follows:

$$\vec{C} = \frac{1}{|S|} \sum_{d \in S} \vec{d}$$
(1)

3.2 Test Phase

As in the training phase, pre-processing, feature selection and representation processes are done in this phase. At the last step, similarities between test documents, weighting vectors of which are calculated and centroid values are measured and classification is carried out.

3.2.1 Calculating Similarities (between Document Profile and Category Profiles)

To find calculated class that test documents will be assigned to, similarities are to be. In vector space model, to calculate similarity between two documents (di and dj) cosine function (Equation 2) is generally used.

$$sim(\vec{d}_i, \vec{d}_j) = \frac{\vec{d}_i . \vec{d}_j}{\left\| \vec{d}_i \right\|_2 * \left\| \vec{d}_j \right\|_2}$$
(2)

To calculate similarity between a new (x) document and centroid vectors, Equation 3 can be used.

$$sim(\vec{x}, \vec{C}) = \frac{\vec{x} . \vec{C}}{\left\| \vec{x} \right\|_2 * \left\| \vec{C} \right\|_2}$$
(3)

3.2.2 Document Classification (Language Identification)

To find the class of a new x document, similarities are calculated between letter frequencies of x document and letter frequencies of k categories (centroid values) (Equation 4).

$$sim(\vec{x}, \vec{C}_{j, j \in k}) = \frac{\vec{x} . \vec{C}_j}{\left\| \vec{x} \right\|_2 * \left\| \vec{C}_j \right\|_2}$$
(4)

Consequently, based upon these similarities, x document is assigned to a class, which gives the most similar centroid value. This situation can be defined as follows:

$$\arg \max_{j=1,.....,k} (sim(\vec{x}, \vec{C}_j))$$
(5)

At the end of training and test phases documents are to be classified (identified). A further process is entering the output of test sub-system into training sub system. This will provide more precise centroid values.

Operation complexities of training phase for centroid-based classifiers (centroid-based identifier) are related to the documents number and letters number in the training set. Thus, the algorithm has a linear complexity. Almost all k centroid values can be calculated at unique step in training set, each centroid is calculated depending on the means of documents of related class.

Time complexity of classifying a new x document is O (km), where m is the number of letters represented in x document. In letter-based method, m is very small, therefore operation complexity of algorithm is really low and algorithm is as fast classifier as NB (Naive Bayesian) [7].

3.3 Advantage of Using Letter Frequency

When carefully looked at, operation complexity of centroid based document classification is depending on k and m values. k is the number of centroids whereas m is the dimension of the feature set. For example, dimension of the feature set in the space of n-grams takes its value between 2550 and 3560 [2]. However, according to the proposed method dimension of feature set is only between 20 and 30. Therefore, using letter feature set lowers m value and algorithm speeds up.

4   Experimental Results and Analysis

In order to obtain successful results from automatic text classification process, training set must contain as much text documents as possible. Today it is obvious that the biggest data and documents storage is Internet. Therefore, it is the most practical solution to get training documents from Internet. To accomplish language classification about 1000 documents from different languages were taken from Internet and training set was constructed of these documents. In the test, German, French, English and Turkish were used as document languages.

Next step after collecting training documents is to decide how will representation take place and with which features. In this proposed system, texts are represented with letters and vector space model is preferable model for representation. By this representation, documents are points in letter space and similarities between documents and centroid values can be calculated by geometrical methods. Cosine similarity finding method is used for finding similarities between documents.

Table 1. Sample LF data (Training)

A	B	C	D	E	F	G	H	I	K	L	M	N	O	P	R	S	T	U	V	Y	Z	Class
6	1	4	3	10	3	1	2	7	1	4	2	6	6	3	4	6	4	1	1	2	0	Eng
7	1	3	4	9	1	1	3	6	1	3	2	7	5	1	5	5	8	2	1	1	0	Eng
7	1	3	3	10	2	1	4	4	0	2	2	6	6	1	6	5	8	2	1	1	0	Eng
-	-	-	-	-	-	-	-	-	-	-	-	-	-	-	-	-	-	-	-	-	-	-
11	1	1	5	8	0	1	2	10	4	5	2	7	3	0	6	5	3	5	1	2	1	Trk

After representing documents in the form of LF as in Table 1, centroid values are found for each class. Centroid values are vectors formed by mean values belonging to each class. Centroid values for classes are shown in Table 2.

Table 2. Centroid values (profile) for each class

Ctr	A	B	C	D	E	F	G	H	I	K	L	M	N	O	P	R	S	T	U	V	Y	Z
Eng	7	1	2	3	9	2	2	4	6	1	3	2	6	6	2	5	5	7	2	1	1	0
Fre	7	1	3	3	10	1	1	1	6	0	4	2	6	4	2	5	6	5	4	1	0	0
Ger	5	2	2	4	13	2	2	3	6	1	3	2	8	3	1	7	5	5	4	1	0	1
Trk	10	2	2	4	8	0	1	1	11	4	6	2	7	3	1	6	4	3	4	1	2	1

Table 3. Similarities and identification

Test #	Centroid ENG Sim(X,CE)	Centroid FRE Sim(X,CF)	Centroid GER Sim(X,CG)	Centroid TRK Sim(X,CT)	Class
1	0,932314	0,952898	0,888573	0,953312	TRK
2	0,949568	0,987048	0,938987	0,897538	FRE
3	0,968011	0,997052	0,958592	0,918897	FRE
4	0,981157	0,954467	0,931332	0,889439	ENG
5	0,944211	0,987453	0,955896	0,86248	FRE
6	0,956026	0,961698	0,991222	0,873209	GER
7	0,945303	0,943066	0,983479	0,837987	GER
8	0,969726	0,92507	0,920181	0,859946	ENG
9	0,989622	0,965286	0,951085	0,875783	ENG
10	0,930377	0,942804	0,992805	0,859377	GER
11	0,939923	0,955379	0,99473	0,876561	GER
12	0,950932	0,950191	0,989647	0,869499	GER
13	0,977641	0,941941	0,92853	0,822313	ENG
14	0,988565	0,951834	0,928819	0,865981	ENG
15	0,952515	0,969922	0,93636	0,869801	FRE
16	0,940653	0,939225	0,914569	0,952135	TRK
17	0,989995	0,958084	0,945594	0,880828	ENG
18	0,981713	0,955529	0,918548	0,89283	ENG
19	0,98662	0,962032	0,941372	0,889497	ENG
20	0,879177	0,904178	0,874561	0,992723	TRK
21	0,878454	0,90557	0,878923	0,985379	TRK
22	0,86145	0,886392	0,854575	0,990326	TRK
23	0,952286	0,985618	0,96148	0,877442	FRE
24	0,919414	0,939859	0,981203	0,873904	GER
25	0,947466	0,948114	0,989841	0,875668	GER
26	0,880619	0,916897	0,906696	0,980385	TRK
27	0,870538	0,904094	0,854991	0,980893	TRK
28	0,8636	0,89436	0,862376	0,984322	TRK
29	0,886043	0,918653	0,903683	0,972853	TRK
30	0,987823	0,954797	0,93075	0,897022	ENG
---	---	---	---	---	---
N	0,9048986	0,922463	0,8921037	0,9836408	TRK

Table 4. Detection rates according to categories

Category Names	Training Set Size	Test Set Size	Detection Rate
English	312	126	0,9880
French	270	108	0,9722
German	276	116	0,9740
Turkish	270	113	0,9866

Centroid based classification is based on similarities between centroid values and test documents. These similarities are calculated according to the method of similarity finding. Test documents differ from training ones in that the first ones are not labeled.

Cosine similarity function is used for finding the similarity between Centroid values and test documents. k*N operations are to be done. Where k, is category number and N is the number of test documents. These results obtained are given in table4. The largest value in each line among these similarity values gives us the class that test document will be assigned to. This step is the test sub-phase of the language identification system.

Detection accurateness of centroid based language identification method is given in Table 4.Success rate of proposed method with letter feature set is shown in Table 4

Our study has acceptable detection rate, this situation has seen in Table 4. Main advantage of our method is its speed. Using of letter feature set has been increased the speed of language identification system. As a result, we can increase the speed of the language identification using smaller feature sets like letter features sets. Thus, it can be claimed that when centroid based document classification supported with letter feature set gives better performance and lower operation time.

5   Conclusion and Further Study

Data mining is a partially new technique of finding meaningful information and useful patterns from large amount of data. It has been applied generally to structural data stored at databases. Therefore, data mining is considered as one of knowledge discovery steps for databases. After realizing that concepts of data mining could be applied also to data, which are not structural, text mining was born as a new field.

Text categorization plays important role at text mining. By this technique, text documents can be assigned to previously defined classes automatically. In text categorization operation, documents are represented according to frequency information on words that are concerned in these documents and in that way documents enter into the classification process.

In this study, we proposed that documents would be represented by letter frequencies instead of word frequencies. To prove this we have tried our approach in language identification. The results of the experiments appeared to be agreeable. Thus, it has been revealed that letter feature set can be used for language based recognition types. As a result, it is shown that the letter feature sets can be successfully used for language identification of text documents.

References

1. Y. Ogawa and M. Iwasaki, A new character-based indexing method using frequency data for Japanese documents, Proceedings of the 13th Annual International ACM SIGIR Conference on Research and Development in Information Retrieval, pp. 1995
2. Gregory Grefenstette, Comparing two language identification schemes, JADT 1995, 3rd International conference on Statistical Analysis of Textual data, Rome, Dec 11–13, 1995
3. P. H. A. Sneath and R. R. Sokal., Numerical Taxonomy. W. H. Freeman, San Francisco, 1973
4. Cavnar, W and Trenkle, J., N-gram-based text categorization. In Proceedings of SDAIR-94, 3rd Annual Symposium on Document Analysis and Information Retrieval, pp.161–175, 1994.
5. D. Benedetto, E. Caglioti, and V. Loreto, Language trees and zipping. Physical Review Letters, 88:4(2002).
6. G. Salton, Automatic Text Processing: The Transformation, Analysis, and Retrieval of Information by Computer. Addison-Wesley, 1989
7. E.-H. Han and G. Karypis, Centroid-based document classification: Analysis and experimental results. In Principles of Data Mining and Knowledge Discovery, pages 424–431, 2000.
8. Ari Visa, Technology of Text Mining, P. Perner (Ed.): MLDM 2001, LNAI 2123, pp. 1–11, 2001.
9. Stephen Johnson, Solving the problem of language recognition Technical report, School of Computer Studies, University of Leeds, 1993
10. Gavin Churcher, Distinctive character sequences, 1994, personal communication
11. Judith Hayes, Language Recognition using two and three letter clusters. Technical report, School of Computer Studies, University of Leeds, 1993
12. Lee-Feng Chien and Hsiao-Tieh Pu, Important Issues on Chinese Information Retrieval, Computational Linguistics and Chinese Language Processing. Vol. 1, No. 1, August 1996, pp. 205–221.

Author Index

Lecture Notes in Computer Science

For information about Vols. 1–2858
please contact your bookseller or Springer-Verlag

Vol. 2893: J.-B. Stefani, I. Demeure, D. Hagimont (Eds.), Distributed Applications and Interoperable Systems. Proceedings, 2003. XIII, 311 pages. 2003.

Vol. 2894: C.S. Laih (Ed.), Advances in Cryptology - ASIACRYPT 2003. Proceedings, 2003. XIII, 543 pages. 2003.

Vol. 2895: A. Ohori (Ed.), Programming Languages and Systems. Proceedings, 2003. XIII, 427 pages. 2003.

Vol. 2896: V.A. Saraswat (Ed.), Advances in Computing Science – ASIAN 2003. Proceedings, 2003. VIII, 305 pages. 2003.

Vol. 2897: O. Balet, G. Subsol, P. Torguet (Eds.), Virtual Storytelling. Proceedings, 2003. XI, 240 pages. 2003.

Vol. 2898: K.G. Paterson (Ed.), Cryptography and Coding. Proceedings, 2003. IX, 385 pages. 2003.

Vol. 2899: G. Ventre, R. Canonico (Eds.), Interactive Multimedia on Next Generation Networks. Proceedings, 2003. XIV, 420 pages. 2003.

Vol. 2900: M. Bidoit, P.D. Mosses, CASL User Manual. XIII, 240 pages. 2004.

Vol. 2901: F. Bry, N. Henze, J. Maluszyński (Eds.), Principles and Practice of Semantic Web Reasoning. Proceedings, 2003. X, 209 pages. 2003.

Vol. 2902: F. Moura Pires, S. Abreu (Eds.), Progress in Artificial Intelligence. Proceedings, 2003. XV, 504 pages. 2003. (Subseries LNAI).

Vol. 2903: T.D. Gedeon, L.C.C. Fung (Eds.), AI 2003: Advances in Artificial Intelligence. Proceedings, 2003. XVI, 1075 pages. 2003. (Subseries LNAI).

Vol. 2904: T. Johansson, S. Maitra (Eds.), Progress in Cryptology – INDOCRYPT 2003. Proceedings, 2003. XI, 431 pages. 2003.

Vol. 2905: A. Sanfeliu, J. Ruiz-Shulcloper (Eds.), Progress in Pattern Recognition, Speech and Image Analysis. Proceedings, 2003. XVII, 693 pages. 2003.

Vol. 2906: T. Ibaraki, N. Katoh, H. Ono (Eds.), Algorithms and Computation. Proceedings, 2003. XVII, 748 pages. 2003.

Vol. 2908: K. Chae, M. Yung (Eds.), Information Security Applications. Proceedings, 2003. XII, 506 pages. 2004.

Vol. 2910: M.E. Orlowska, S. Weerawarana, M.P. Papazoglou, J. Yang (Eds.), Service-Oriented Computing – ICSOC 2003. Proceedings, 2003. XIV, 576 pages. 2003.

Vol. 2911: T.M.T. Sembok, H.B. Zaman, H. Chen, S.R. Urs, S.H.Myaeng (Eds.), Digital Libraries: Technology and Management of Indigenous Knowledge for Global Access. Proceedings, 2003. XX, 703 pages. 2003.

Vol. 2912: G. Liotta (Ed.), Graph Drawing. Proceedings, 2003. XV, 542 pages. 2004.

Vol. 2913: T.M. Pinkston, V.K. Prasanna (Eds.), High Performance Computing – HiPC 2003. Proceedings, 2003. XX, 512 pages. 2003.

Vol. 2914: P.K. Pandya, J. Radhakrishnan (Eds.), FST TCS 2003: Foundations of Software Technology and Theoretical Computer Science. Proceedings, 2003. XIII, 446 pages. 2003.

Vol. 2916: C. Palamidessi (Ed.), Logic Programming. Proceedings, 2003. XII, 520 pages. 2003.

Vol. 2918: S.R. Das, S.K. Das (Eds.), Distributed Computing – IWDC 2003. Proceedings, 2003. XIV, 394 pages. 2003.

Vol. 2919: E. Giunchiglia, A. Tacchella (Eds.), Theory a Applications of Satisfiability Testing. Proceedings, 20 XI, 530 pages. 2004.

Vol. 2920: H. Karl, A. Willig, A. Wolisz (Eds.), Wi less Sensor Networks. Proceedings, 2004. XIV, 365 pag 2004.

Vol. 2921: G. Lausen, D. Suciu (Eds.), Database Progra ming Languages. Proceedings, 2003. X, 279 pages. 20

Vol. 2922: F. Dignum (Ed.), Advances in Agent Commu cation. Proceedings, 2003. X, 403 pages. 2004. (Subser LNAI).

Vol. 2923: V. Lifschitz, I. Niemelä (Eds.), Logic Progra ming and Nonmonotonic Reasoning. Proceedings, 20 IX, 365 pages. 2004. (Subseries LNAI).

Vol. 2924: J. Callan, F. Crestani, M. Sanderson (Eds.), D tributed Multimedia Information Retrieval. Proceedin 2003. XII, 173 pages. 2004.

Vol. 2926: L. van Elst, V. Dignum, A. Abecker (Eds Agent-Mediated Knowledge Management. Proceedin 2003. XI, 428 pages. 2004. (Subseries LNAI).

Vol. 2927: D. Hales, B. Edmonds, E. Norling, J. Rouch (Eds.), Multi-Agent-Based Simulation III. Proceedin 2003. X, 209 pages. 2003. (Subseries LNAI).

Vol. 2928: R. Battiti, M. Conti, R. Lo Cigno (Eds.), Wi less On-Demand Network Systems. Proceedings, 20 XIV, 402 pages. 2004.

Vol. 2929: H. de Swart, E. Orlowska, G. Schmidt, Roubens (Eds.), Theory and Applications of Relatior Structures as Knowledge Instruments. Proceedings. V 273 pages. 2003.

Vol. 2931: A. Petrenko, A. Ulrich (Eds.), Formal A proaches to Software Testing. Proceedings, 2003. VI 267 pages. 2004.

Vol. 2932: P. Van Emde Boas, J. Pokorný, M. Bielikov J. Štuller (Eds.), SOFSEM 2004: Theory and Practice Computer Science. Proceedings, 2004. XIII, 385 page 2004.

Vol. 2933: C. Martín-Vide, G. Mauri, G. Păun, G. Roze berg, A. Salomaa (Eds.), Membrane Computing. Procee ings, 2003. VIII, 383 pages. 2004.

Vol. 2935: P. Giorgini, J.P. Müller, J. Odell (Eds.), Ager Oriented Software Engineering IV. Proceedings, 2003. 247 pages. 2004.

Vol. 2937: B. Steffen, G. Levi (Eds.), Verification, Mod Checking, and Abstract Interpretation. Proceedings, 200 XI, 325 pages. 2004.

Vol. 2938: Z. Zhang, C. Zhang, Agent-Based Hybrid Inte ligent Systems. XV, 196 pages. 2004. (Subseries LNAI

Vol. 2942: D. Seipel, J.M. Turull-Torres (Eds.), Found tions of Information and Knowledge Systems. Procee ings, 2004. X, 321 pages. 2004.

Vol. 2944: K. Aberer, M. Koubarakis, V. Kalogeraki (Eds Databases, Information Systems, and Peer-to-Peer Con puting. Proceedings, 2003. X, 249 pages. 2004.

Vol. 2945: A. Gelbukh (Ed.), Computational Lingui tics and Intelligent Text Processing. Proceedings, 200 XVIII, 651 pages. 2004.

Vol. 2946: R. Focardi, R. Gorrieri (Eds.), Foundations Security Analysis and Design II. VII, 267 pages. 2004.

Vol. 2950: N. Jonoska, G. Păun, G. Rozenberg (Eds.), A pects of Molecular Computing. XI, 391 pages. 2004.